FRANCIS BACON'S PERSONAL LIFE-STORY

Being a truthful and detailed account of his childhood, his youth, his manhood and his old age, with particular reference to his public life and his secret life, which has made him the most mysterious figure of the Elizabethan Age, together with a complete refutation of the various aspersions made against his character. There is also given some account of his labours as an educationist and as an ethical teacher ... as the "Concealed Poet", "Shake-speare", the Creator of Freemasonry, and the Magister of the Rosicrucians, a vivid light being thrown on the personality of our supreme genius, to whom Englishmen and the foreign nations owe so much—a prince of the House of Tudor, the concealed son of Queen Elizabeth.

EDITORIAL NOTE

Vol. I was published in 1949 and this coincided with the author suffering a severe stroke. Vol. II was ready for publication but, despite the ready help of many loyal friends, it was not possible to achieve publication. For many years the manuscript was "lost" and is only now revealed for publication.

In all the circumstances it has been agreed that Vols. I and II should be published in one volume, which was indeed the author's original intention.

This book is the result of many years devoted and intensive study by a truly literary man, with experience of things esoteric, a seeker of Truth and of causes, a compassionate man deeply desirous of helping all to judge the true from the false, and to distinguish the world of thought and spirit from the world of matter. Indeed he devoted his later life to this end.

Irene Rowland
1986

PLATE I
Francis Bacon, the uncrowned King of Literature
From a painting by Van Somer

FRANCIS BACON'S PERSONAL LIFE-STORY

ALFRED DODD

VOLUME I

The Age of Elizabeth

VOLUME II

The Age of James

RIDER & COMPANY

London Melbourne Auckland Johannesburg

BY THE SAME AUTHOR

The Marriage of Elizabeth Tudor
The Secret Shake-speare
The Immortal Master
Shake-speare, Creator of Freemasonry
The Martyrdom of Francis Bacon

EDITOR OF

Shake-speare's Sonnet-Diary (Tenth ed.)
etc., etc.

This edition comprises Volume One
first published in 1910 by Rider and Company
and Volume Two first published in 1986
by Century Hutchinson Ltd,
Brookmount House, 62–65 Chandos Place, Covent Garden,
London WC2N 4NW

Century Hutchinson Publishing Group (Australia) Pty Ltd
16–22 Church Street, Hawthorn, Melbourne, Victoria 3122

Century Hutchinson Group (NZ) Ltd
32–34 View Road, PO Box 40–086, Glenfield, Auckland 10

Century Hutchinson Group (SA) Pty Ltd
PO Box 337, Bergvlei 2012, South Africa

Printed and bound in Great Britain by
Butler & Tanner Ltd, Frome and London

British Library Cataloguing in Publication Data

Dodd, Alfred
Francis Bacon's personal life-story.
1. Bacon, Francis, *Viscount St. Albans*
I. Title
192 B1197

ISBN 0-7126-1260-2

CONTENTS

ILLUSTRATIONS FOR VOLUME I

ILLUSTRATIONS FOR VOLUME II

Between pp. 460 and 461

In 1981 Jean Overton Fuller's *Sir Francis Bacon: A Biography* (East-West Publications) was published. It included some remarkable scientific evidence by a leading geneticist 'throwing light on the fierce speculation over Bacon's parentage'. In this connection Chapter 2 of Miss Overton Fuller's book is of particular interest.

Readers of the present work may also be interested in the mural discovered at the White Hart Hotel, St. Albans, which has been covered for some 200 years. The mural shows the death of Adonis from Shakepeare's poem *Venus and Adonis* (1593). The existence of this mural, which is shown on the back of the jacket to this book, establishes a significant link between St. Albans and Stratford.

Irene Rowland
1986

PREFACE

MANY biographers have written about Francis Bacon. He has been weighed, explained, criticised by many types of minds; his character has been mercilessly dissected and his personality—or, rather, portions of it—exposed to the passers-by on the world's butchers' stalls; his political, scientific and philosophical labours probed and analysed. He has been discussed by men of different tempers—literary savants, theologians, rationalists, lawyers, scientists, philosophers, journalists, theosophists and cypher-experts—in full biographies, essays, sketches and newspaper articles, by men who make their approaches from totally different standpoints and arrive at totally different conclusions. And in the year of our Lord 1946, upwards of four hundred years since he was born, it is safe to affirm that no one hitherto has penetrated the mystery of his life and comprehended to the full the gigantic magnitude of his labours for the English-speaking race in particular or for the world in general . . . or understood the ideals that dominated his thought and action almost from the cradle to the grave.

The early writers, such as Pierre Amboise (1631), Dr. Rawley (1657), Bishop Thomas Tenison (1679), David Mallet (1740), deliberately withheld much information concerning him, judging certain matters "to tread too near to the Heels of Truth and to the times of the Persons concerned." (Tenison, *Bacon's Remains*, p. 81). They purposely stress the outer aspects of Francis Bacon's life, though pointedly hinting that he was other than he seemed to be and that there were revelations to be made concerning him in later ages. This skirting of the outer aspects of his life has been carried to extreme lengths by modernists like Dean Church, Professor John Nichol, Professor A. R. Skemp, Mary Sturt and others. That Francis Bacon lived, in some way or other, a concealed life (pointedly declared by Tenison) and wrought at some form of concealed labours (told over and over again in Francis Bacon's own works) are facts which are ignored by these writers. There is never any attempt even by Spedding to probe the mystery and to get to the bottom of the numerous hints left by Francis Bacon and other early writers. The portraits they draw are therefore necessarily inaccurate; and some of them are so poorly executed that they convey a wrong impression of his personality.

Since Lord Macaulay in 1837 wrote his *Essay on Francis Bacon*, the tendency has been to judge Francis Bacon's character with extreme harshness. Indeed, Francis Bacon's moral reputation has been more or less destroyed by a long line of writers who begin the study of his personality and his actions—political, judicial, literary—apparently prejudiced in advance by the fact that somewhat late in life he was accused of receiving bribes to pervert justice in the Chancery Court, that he "refused to stand his trial" and entered a plea of "Guilty" to many charges of corruption. His open "Confession of Guilt" appears to have influenced their treatment and judgment respecting other aspects of his life—all to his disadvantage. For a judge to admit acts of corruption at the age of sixty indicates a defect of character, it is argued, which must have been in evidence in his earlier actions. They look for such evidence and find it in his conduct towards the Earl of Essex, Peacham, and in other matters.

The first duty of a biographer is to get his facts right, not merely the facts he wishes to be known, but *all* the facts, to suppress none and to slur over nothing; and not to be afraid lest an untoward discovery might falsify his prepossessions. A biographer's duty is to search, to dig, and to spare neither time, trouble nor expense in the quest; to maintain "an open mind," and to allow the Vestal Virgin of Truth to lead him by the hand even through dark and intricate windings, trusting her implicitly to be guided aright. When a biographer has an axe of his own to grind, the result is a garbled mischief and a curse to posterity. The Borgias poisoned only single victims; but there are some writers who have poisoned men's minds *en masse*, and unfortunately their deadly night-work still continues. We must beware of authors who revel in misstatements, suppressions, and the loose handling of facts. To arrive at truth we must even con carefully the writers whose conclusions through later research are really outdated by the discovery of new facts.

All students of the Elizabethan Era are indebted to James Spedding for his *Life of Francis Bacon* (1861). His defence of Francis Bacon's character and actions up to the time of his "Fall" is irrefragable. He is regarded to-day as Francis Bacon's finest biographer, as *the* authority on everything pertaining to him. Yet we shall be making a very grave error if we regard Spedding's *Life* of seven volumes as the very last word in Baconian research and consider that there is nothing more to be said. We must not regard a biography written over eighty years ago as sacrosanct, Spedding's opinions as infallible, and assume that he was in full possession of all the facts. Some of his opinions may be based on insufficient data.

In dealing with the tragedy of the "Fall," Spedding appears to be so influenced by Francis Bacon's "Confession of Guilt," that he makes admissions respecting his "Desertion of the Defence" that are, in my opinion, quite unwarranted. Yet Spedding revered Francis Bacon and honestly tried to arrive at the truth; but, like many others, he knew only the outer man and his open labours. His biography is the nearest approach to a civil servant's report of any I have read, and quite as laborious to read. The facts are so compiled that one constantly loses the threads of affairs, so interwoven are they. We get no clear pictures as in Boswell's *Johnson;* and in the final volume, which deals with the "Fall of Francis Bacon," one is left in a state of bewilderment as to whether Francis Bacon was a sinner or not.

The truth or untruth of Francis Bacon's alleged guilt of bribery ought not to be left any longer in the nebulous state in which it was left by James Spedding, which is equivalent to a verdict of "Not Proven," and really does not determine the issue of his guilt or innocence. What we want to know primarily about Francis Bacon is this: was he guilty in the slightest degree of corrupting justice for "pieces of eight" and silver plate? That is the clear issue; and it should be determined definitely once and for all before full, impartial justice can be done to Francis Bacon as a man and to his labours as a genius: for in the schoolroom and the university alike, the student and the scholar of the Elizabethan era obtain no certain reliable knowledge respecting him personally or his multifarious pursuits. His character has been branded with the searing mark of "Corruption," and his works are approached with disfavour if not with positive pain. The dominant idea of the majority of Englishmen respecting the "deep-browed Verulam" is that of a cold, loveless genius, a prosy philosopher of no particular account, who was a corrupt judge. Can we wonder, then, that writers in the popular Press and even schoolboys are saturated with these thoughts concerning our greatest Englishman? Yet these common views may be as wrong as were the popular opinions concerning Cromwell and Dreyfus until Carlyle and Zola triumphantly proved that Cromwell's character was unimpeachable and Dreyfus the innocent victim of a wicked plot. Is it not also possible that Francis Bacon is in the same category of men whom we have misjudged, and one who is still waiting patiently for his vindicator to appear?

Since Spedding's day, a large number of men—professionals of many types—have hunted long and arduously for evidence that would shed light on the mysteries of Francis Bacon's life and especially his labours—open and concealed. Many new facts have been unearthed respecting this veritable Colossus of Thought that bestrides the world. To-day we know a good deal more about Francis Bacon than did Spedding. It is therefore imperative that the truth about this supreme master should be re-examined and redelivered to the world, that posterity may know his real identity, his ideals, his aims, his accomplishments. These new facts (since Spedding wrote in 1861) must be taken into full consideration. If important factors be omitted, how can the sum of his life be properly cast? Any missing factor ignored in the personal equation or a false factor introduced simply prevents one from obtaining the correct answer. It is for this reason that the personal equation of Francis Bacon's life is answered so differently by different writers . . . vital factors are dropped, ignored, and in some cases suppressed. Even one unknown factor is sufficient to falsify the issue.

What is true in mathematics is doubly true in dealing with the living complexities of genius: for what is praised by one critic is condemned by others, until quittances and strictures almost cancel each other out. Midst all this confusion the real personality of this great master is shrouded, almost done to death, unseen and unknown, even as the giant oak is often strangled by parasites of many kinds flourishing in honour while living on its life's-blood; and the outline of the real growth is hidden by parasitic ivies of many kinds that obscure the noble form. In precisely the same way Francis Bacon's true personality is largely obscured by the many commentators that surround him. This consideration alone shows the necessity for the publication of a new life . . . taking into account the new evidence discovered since Spedding's monumental work.

In *Ecce Homo* (p. 40-41) that profound thinker Friedrich Nietzche (1880) wrote: "*We do not know half enough about Lord Bacon. . . .* What do I care about the miserable gabble of Muddlers and Blockheads. . . . Let the Critics GO TO HELL!"

It is but a few years ago that I discovered that Nietzche was right and that I did not know "half enough" about Francis Bacon. For years I had been a devout worshipper at the shrines of Lord Macaulay, Lord Campbell, Dr. Abbott, Dean Church, Professor J. Nichol, and other eminent scholars, when something occurred that urged me not to accept their conclusions as final, but to ascertain the correctness of their judgments for myself. So I began a pilgrimage of hard reading and personal research. I began my literary journey with an intense dislike of this "corrupt genius." I ended with the conviction that these well-known critics were totally wrong in their views respecting his character and disposition, and that their strictures were harsh and unjust. Indeed, I found that my detestation had slowly changed to admiration, so that at the end of the trail I was compelled to say, in all honesty to myself, slightly misquoting Ben Jonson, "I love the man and do honour his memory above all others." I therefore determined to rewrite his life so that students of the Elizabethan Era might enter in at the strait gate and the narrow way which leadeth to truth. This biography, then, will show in detail the reason why I gradually changed my opinions respecting Francis Bacon's moral character, his temperament, the complexity of his mental powers and actions, and why I have become "a Francis Bacon's man" and an enthusiast.

Before the true personal story of Francis Bacon can be written, however, there must necessarily be a searching examination into the serious allegations that have hitherto hidden the view from the eyes of his countrymen. It is worse than useless to absent oneself from felicity awhile to tell the story of a wounded name, as enjoined by the dying Hamlet, unless every charge made against him be first considered. If the critics, whom Nietzche consigned to perdition because of their strictures and lack of vision, be ignored, their utterances remain on the record to be iterated and reiterated as though they were true. The most elaborate biography would fail to carry weight if the adverse opinions of commentators were not proved to be factually fallacious and unwarranted.

This personal story, then, is, first, a calm and judicial examination of all the severe judgments passed upon Francis Bacon; and, second, a reorientation of approach towards the Light so that we may take new bearings on the problems of the Age of Elizabeth and James. The fogs of misunderstanding will be dissipated; and the curtains that veil the Mysterious Figure of the Elizabethan Age will be drawn aside so that the reader may get an all-round view of a real man—the Proteus of literature—*for the first time.*

Hitherto the majority of his biographers have been content to follow one another, simply dealing—apart from his character—with the *open* activities of Francis Bacon . . . political, philosophical, legal, literary, etc.

Not one of the traditionalists, who follow the lead of Macaulay, appear to have known or even suspected that from an early age he led not only an open life but also a *concealed* one; nor have they even taken seriously into account the secret ideals that burned like a flame within his breast, driving him onwards from his early teens, in his altruistic labours; neither do they know anything of this psychological prodigy who bore two souls within his breast—so marvellously revealed in the *Phœnix and the Turtle*, the mystical poem never yet interpreted by any Shakespearean commentator—which acted and reacted on his outer conduct. We thus get open photographs taken from many angles, but I do not know of one real portrait painted after the style of Rembrandt or Augustus John which reveals the true personality through sheer insight, a thorough knowledge of the subject, and an interior illumination backed by evidential facts. How can any man—no matter how great his scholarship—provide us with a true portrait of the subject if he be unaware of vital activities that consume that subject? If he merely deals with the outer man and ignores the inner life, is he not bound to lead himself astray and others with him? And if the blind lead the blind there is a danger that they will fall into the ditch together.

The facts which have come to light since Spedding wrote have been ignored by his latest biographers, Mary Sturt and Charles Williams. Both are content with sketching the "outer man," rejecting on *a priori* grounds that Francis Bacon was either a concealed poet or of royal birth, the founder of secret societies or an ethical teacher; and neither seems to have the faintest idea of his prime aim in life or the proper interpretation of *The Great Instauration*, any more than had Spedding and Ellis.

A work that will incorporate all the latest evidence respecting Francis Bacon's personal life is therefore badly needed. If grievous errors have been promulgated about him and are still running brazenly through the world in the guise of truth and hallmarked by authority, it is time that they should be laid by the heels. To-day we are openly ashamed of our greatest genius. There is no place for him in the Poets' Corner or any other part of Westminster Abbey; for we are told he was a corrupt judge who was rightly struck down by Sir Edward Coke, the purist, by Sir Lionel Cranfield, the immaculate, and properly abandoned with tearful sorrow by King James of pious memory and Viscount Buckingham, the innocent, "the great spoiled child of Fortune" (Spedding).

These generally accepted views I have been compelled, as I have already said, to abandon together with the modern scholarly view of the scope and range of his literary and philosophical concepts. It appears to me that modern scholarship takes too narrow and restricted a view of his labours. I have found more than sufficient evidence to satisfy me personally that Francis Bacon's actual achievements were wider and deeper than traditional scholarship is disposed to admit. The statements I advance will therefore be found to be supported by proofs that would be accepted in any court of law. They are factual, not theoretic. I am a plain man, and this is a plain work but it claims to be honest. Truth has been pursued from the first line to the last. And though the claims I make may be regarded as startling, they bristle with authoritative utterances. This work will deal with the statements:

1. That Francis Bacon was the son of Queen Elizabeth by a morganatic marriage with the Earl of Leicester.
2. That the Earl of Essex was his brother.
3. That he was a "Concealed Poet" who used many pen-names, the greatest being "William Shake-speare."
4. That he created the English Renaissance with the aid of a band of scholars . . . known as the secret Rosicrosse Literary Society.
5. That he sought "The Reformation of the whole Wide World," through the gradual diffusion of education and ethics.
6. That he primarily sought to be an educational and an ethical teacher with a secret School of Disciples after the manner of Pythagoras and other teachers of the Ancient Wisdom, whose precepts were handed down the ages orally by a Succession of Sons.
7. That he created the modern Rituals of Freemasonry and Rosicrucianism and founded the Secret Orders and Fraternities that arose in the Elizabethan Era.
8. That he was not a "corrupt judge," and that he "Deserted his Defence" to the Charges of Corruption because he was COMMANDED to do so by King James, speaking in his Office as Sovereign by Divine Right. A "confession" wrung out of a man under duress is worthless.

Francis Bacon is generally recognised as the Father of English Prose, with his large vocabulary and his ability to write in so many different styles . . . varied to suit the subject-matter and the person addressed. Dr. Abbott says:

> His style varied as much as his handwriting. It depended on whether he was addressing a King, a great Nobleman, a philosopher or a friend, composing a State paper, extolling Truth or discussing studies. . . .

He is also known as the Father of Experimental Science with a philosophy for humanity summed up in the phrase, *Utility and Progress* (Macaulay's *Essay*). If we could be satisfied that, apart from his Parliamentary and State duties and Judicial labours, he was also the "Immortal Bard, William Shake-speare," the creator of the Thirty-Three Rituals of Freemasonry and the many Rituals of the Rosicrucian College, the anonymous author of the Ethical Manifestoes (*The Fama, The Confessio, etc.*), and the Founder of Secret Fraternities that are functioning to-day all over the world "without departing from his precepts," then Francis Bacon would indeed bestride the world like a Colossus even now. He would have put a wonder-girdle of thought round the entire globe, adventuring in his ship, *The Advancement of Learning*, like Columbus, beyond the Pillars of Hercules, into realms new and strange and unknown to Englishmen; and to him the intellectual world in general and the English-speaking nations in particular, would owe an incalculable debt—to him and to a handful of his disciples whom he infused with his own idealism and who handed down the torch of Light and Truth to each succeeding generation.

One of the most severe critics of Francis Bacon is Dean Church. He writes (*Life*, p. 1):

> All his life long his first and never-sleeping passion was the romantic and splendid ambition after Knowledge, for the Conquest of Nature and the Service of Man; gathering up in himself the spirit and longings and efforts of all discoverers and inventors of the arts, as they are symbolised in the mythical Prometheus. He rose to the highest place and honour; and yet that place and honour were but the fringe and adornment of all that made him great. It is difficult to imagine a grander and more magnificent career; and his name ranks among the few chosen examples of human achievement. And yet. . . .

On the next page Church denounces him as a sycophant who "was not true to what he knew. He sold himself to the corrupt and ignominious Government of James I. . . . He chose to call its evil good . . .[p. 2]. His life was a double one . . ." [p. 58]. There is much more to the same effect. "He went on self-complacent . . . building up a great tradition of corruption in the very heart of English justice."

On analysis, do not these utterances sound contradictory? Are we justified in accepting these dogmatic statements as verifiably true? We must remember that they are simply the Dean's *opinions*. They are not factual. And there is no evidence in sight to justify such expressions. In view of the Dean's previous utterance, I regard these strictures on his character with *prima facie* suspicion because of the following considerations:

> Is it possible for a man to hold noble ideals for the advancement of humanity, to sacrifice himself in the service of man and yet be corrupt in mind and shrunken in soul? Can any man serve two masters—Altruistic Philanthropia and Avaricious Corruption? Is it possible for a man to create and found and practise the most marvellous allegorical and symbolical System of Ethics ever known to the world, and yet to be false to all he holds dear, "square conduct, level steps, upright intentions"? Has anyone ever known in history or private life, a bad man to inculcate consistently throughout a long life the "purest principles of piety and virtue," so that a contemporary wrote, "all who were good and great loved him?" Does the youthful face of the Hilliard miniature, round which the artist wrote "Could I but paint his Mind," mask a soul that bore the seeds of bribery and corruption? Am I to believe that the honest English eyes that look at me from the portrait of Francis Bacon at fifty, by Van Somer, were given over to the evil practice of servile scrounging so that he might squander his ill-gotten gains on questionable extravagances? In short, how could a man who had taken "all Knowledge to be his Province, who was eminently wise and good, be a venial judge and a most dishonest man? Could Nature ever have made such a Jekyll-Hyde contradiction as is painted by Macaulay and the theologians—Abbott, Church, and Sortain?

Obviously, there is a problem to be solved respecting Francis Bacon's characer, his ideals and his labours, so long as the above questions remain unanswered. We should therefore approach this personal study devoid of prejudice, and, unbiased by what we have imbibed while sitting at the feet of the professional Gamaliels of literature, with an open mind ready to accept the truth no matter from what quarter of the horizon she manifests; for is it not clear that the last words respecting his personality have not yet been uttered?

If ever a man was born for power, a man on whom there shone a beam of God's splendour from the cradle to the grave, a man sent out from the World Unseen to do things—great things—to re-create England, the Continent, the World—"*Born to set it Right*"—that man was Francis Bacon. ("*I am a Servant to Posterity*. . . . Remember how THY SERVANT hath walked before Thee. . . . What I have first sought and what hath been principal in mine intentions.") .Yet how slowly he forged his way! The House of Commons beheld in him its greatest orator. He was the equal of Sir Edward Coke in his knowledge of Law. He coined words and gave them to Englishmen wherewith to think. His knowledge of every subject under the sun was enormous. What chance had anyone with him in debate . . . Cecil, Coke, Cobham, Raleigh? Peerless . . . he outrivalled all his contemporaries for sheer intellectual power. Yet in the time of the "Virgin Queen," he, of all men, was left standing at the post. Other men got on. Why was he left behind? This biography will supply the answer. A new King sits on the Throne. He is still unrecognised. Cecil becomes an Earl. Coke early had been made Attorney-General. Raleigh had received a knighthood and the Patent for Virginia; and so on? What kept the greatest of them down in Elizabeth's reign and in the early reign of James? Men of lower birth and infinitely less ability got posts and honours, judgeships and portfolios. How was it that Francis Bacon passed the age of forty-six before he got a place on the State Ladder? Was it because he was servile and corrupt? Or was it his virtues, his secret High Rank, and not his vices that kept him down so long? He fell from the dizzy height of being Lord Chancellor; but what caused his "Fall"? His virtue or his vices? Or his jealous enemies? His honesty, tolerance, magnanimity, his faithfulness to his principles or his alleged heartlessness, his servility and his corruption? "If Francis Bacon had actually prostituted his glorious gifts and strong convictions for a beck or a nod, a pension or a place, why did he not rise earlier? Why did he not grow rich?" asks Hepworth Dixon. And then he adds:

> Alone among the great lawyers of his time he died poor. Hatton left a Prince's wealth. Egerton founded the noble House of Ellesmere; Montague that of Manchester. Coke was one of the richest men in England. Popham bequeathed to his children Littlecote and Wellington; Bennet, Hobart and Fleming each left a great estate. How explain this rule and this exception? They are not explained by the theory that Bacon's servility held him down while Coke's servility sent him up; that Bacon's corruption kept him poor, while Popham's corruption made him rich.

Whether we choose to acknowledge it or not, my studies have convinced me that Francis Bacon stands to-day as the greatest man in the world despite the obscurity in schools and colleges concerning him. Henry Hallam, who was probably the finest literary critic and historian of the age, and who at the close of his life was still looking for the real "Shake-speare," never having found him in the Stratford actor, said this:

> Francis Bacon was more eminently the philosopher of human than general nature. . . . But if we compare, what may be found in the sixth, seventh and eighth books of the *De Augmentis*, the *Essays*, the *History of Henry VII*, and the various short treatises contained in his works on morals, on politics and on human nature, from experience of which all such wisdom is drawn, with the rhetoric, ethics and politics of Aristotle, or with the historians most celebrated for their deep insight into civil society and character—with Thucydides, Tacitus, Philip de Comines, Machiavel, Davila, Hume—we shall find, I think, that *one man may almost be compared with all of these together.*

Nor is this eulogy one whit overstrained, for Hallam did not know he was the Man of Mystery, who had laid in secret the Foundation-stones of the Modern World in Science, Ethics, Literature, Philosophy, and who, with a mere handful of disciples, created the English Renaissance. Was he the mighty Shakespeare who gave us a new range of words with which to express our thoughts and who taught us how to think in beautiful images and picturesque language? And who revealed new worlds of beauty, wisdom, virtue, humour and romance in the heart of man, "books in the running brooks, sermons in stones, and good in everything"? Was he the Father of the Secret Fraternities and ensured that a "Succession of Hands" should carry down the ages and all over the world his "New Philosophy" of ethical symbolism?

This book will shed no uncertain light on these controversial subjects, and as the generations pass, Francis Bacon's fame will be still more clearly revealed; for he is not for an age but for all time. He will be recognised as the Moses who led us out of the barren wilderness of Feudalism, pointing the way to fairer fields of conquest and showing to the watchers on the heights the Land of Promise.

This *Life* will be found to be important in this: that none of the problems surrounding Francis Bacon are left unexplained, and a new and vivid light is thrown on the Elizabethan Era. It bridges all the gaps in the life of this Man of Mystery hitherto left in the air by previous biographers. It shows how the ideals of his early youth went steadily forward—in secret when he could not follow the gleam openly. These ideals were the first things in his life. His public life was incidental to the working out of his secret plans. "Was it aught to me I bore the Canopy? [of State as Lord Chancellor] Or laid Great Bases for Eternity?" [as a Concealed Ethical Teacher and Educationist.]

He answers the question he asks in "Shake-speare's" Sonnet 136-cxxv with a fine gesture of scorn that the outward ephemeral things of life, riches, honour, etc., never satisfied the cravings of his soul, and were as naught compared with the establishment of an English Renaissance of mental and moral thought and feeling.

What I have written of his concealed and open life is backed by tangible evidence which the reader can investigate at his leisure. It will be found to be quite irrefutable. It shows Francis Bacon in his true light—a practical reformer who laboured with his hands in the world's vineyard and was never content to be a philosopher producing finely spun theories from the calm of a cloistered retreat. He actually planted systems of thought and action to live and grow through the eternities. . . . Freemasonry, the Drama, Experimental Science, etc. He was born for England, to set the land he loved on new lines, "to be a Servant to Posterity," to quote his own words. And the revelation of his stupendous labours, overlooked by his compatriots, is long overdue. I would that he had a more worthy pen than mine to make the truth known at long last.

Deny him as we will, we cannot cast him out. His mind has passed into our minds, his soul into our soul. We are part of him. We absorb his thoughts in the secret Lodge, on the Stage, in our laboratories, in the Halls of Learning, in quotations daily in the public Press and in our private studies—as inseparable as the salt from the sea. If he be a rogue and a cheat, then it is most true that we have taken a rogue and a cheat to be our Exemplar. But Ben Jonson said that Francis Bacon was the embodiment of Virtue; and I think it wiser to abide by his testimony—the verdict of a man who knew him personally—than to accept the opinions of critics who never knew him, who only see through the haze of the Age and who may thus be confused by the Time-Mists of the Centuries and mistake Shadows for Reality.

At all events let us as Englishmen before the Law, assume that he is innocent, for never yet, I can assure you, has he been proved to be unequivocally guilty of any wrongdoing. Consider the facts and then decide . . . and such jurors we wish him.

ALFRED DODD.

Alfred Dodd

AUTHOR'S NOTE

I have not hesitated to employ capitals and italics to emphasize my meaning, to draw attention to significant facts and passages and to esoteric underlying asides in Francis Bacon's prose.

In his letters and writings there is often a surface meaning and also a hidden one . . . perhaps a Masonic phrase which shows that he was saturated in the Masonic Ritual. This may well pass by the uninitiated but will be noted with interest by the Craft.

This use of double phraseology has hitherto passed apparently unnoticed. The reader therefore is enjoined to note, to weigh, and consider the underlying interpretation indicated by the use of capitals and italics. They are not the result of a whim, to shout at the reader or to seduce him, but to make him think.

This, of course, is quite contrary to the canon of modern scholarship, but capitals and italics were used very freely, for a particular purpose, in Francis Bacon's works and in others, and I have therefore good warrranty in following the practice of the great Elizabethan writes in preference to the rules of to-day, especially as I am dealing with the Elizabethan Era.

Each chapter, it will be noticed, is virtually complete in itself; slight repetitions have been made only to save the reader from harking back to search for missing links. This work can therefore be read at random in odd chapters—on points that are of particular interest to the reader—with a feeling of mental satisfaction.

This Life has not been easy to write for I have had to tread on delicate ground and the work bristles with disputable points. My warm thanks are due to many friends who have aided me in my researches; and in particular to three scholarly minds who have helped me with their advice, with information, with textual corrections and the reading of proofs:

B. J. Herrington, Esq., O.B.E., of Mossley Hill, Liverpool
Major W. Angus Jones, O.B.E., of Clifton, Bristol
Edward D. Johnson, Esq., of Birmingham
Their assistance has been invaluable.

The Story of a Life

MY STORY IS PROUD. . . . The Entry
of Truth with Chalk to Mark those
Minds which are capable to Lodge
and Harbour it.

—*Francis Bacon.*

What a Wounded Name

Report me and my Causes right
To the unsatisfied . . .
Oh good Horatio, *what a Wounded Name*
Shall live behind me.
If thou did'st ever hold me in thy Heart,
Absent thee from Felicity awhile,
And in this Harsh World draw thy breath in pain
TO TELL MY STORY.

—*Hamlet.*

The Jewel of One's Soul

Who steals my purse steals Trash . . .
But he that filches from me my good name,
Robs me of that which not enriches him,
And makes me POOR indeed.

—*Iago in "Othello".*

The Brand of Cain

Thence Comes it that my NAME receives a Brand.

—*Sonnet,* 145-cxi.

To My Countrymen of the Future Ages

For my Name and Memory, I leave to Men's Charitable Speeches, and to FOREIGN NATIONS, and the NEXT AGES: And to mine own Countrymen after SOME TIME BE PAST.

—*Extract from Francis Bacon's Draft Will.*

Alfred Dodd, "a Merchant of Light," reasoned within himself respecting the little-known and less-understood facts concerning the Life, Character, and Work of Francis Bacon; and judged it to be for the Benefit of Humanity and the After-ages that Men should become acquainted with his Thoughts that had revolved for many years around our Noblest Englishman, the Prince of Poets, the Most Illustrious of Philosophers, the Wisest of Ethical Teachers, the Greatest Genius ever born to the Human Race—the true-born Son of our most Puissant Sovereign, Elizabeth Tudor.

FRANCIS BACON'S
PERSONAL LIFE-STORY
VOLUME I

The Age of Elizabeth

DEDICATION

To
Edward D. Johnson, Esq., of Birmingham,
one of the 'Friends of Francis'
and a fellow-labourer in the Mine of Truth...
who has done so much in these latter days
to rehabilitate the Good Name of Francis Bacon
and to declare his secret and unique labours
for the benefit of humanity

Chapter I

THE MEDIEVAL ERA

ON the twenty-second of January, 1561, there was born in London the world's greatest genius—born not for an age but for all time. He is known to history as Francis Bacon. He is the Supreme Enigma of the human race. Mystery surrounds his birth, his life, his death. He is the unsolved Riddle of the Schoolmen. He is the Sphinx of the Elizabethan Age, the Age which links the modern world to Medievalism. He crouches still beneath the Pyramid of Knowledge which he created. His eyes still look questioningly at the generations of men who pass to the Eternities along the road of dusty death: and around his lips there still hovers a strange smile which mockingly seems to challenge each passer-by . . . .

> Why goest thou by so fast?
> Read, *if thou canst,* WHOM envious Death hath plast
> Within this Monument?[1]

In other words, "WHOM DO MEN SAY THAT I AM?"

The real story of Francis Bacon's life is more wonderful than any tale conceived by the great Romanticists—Munchausen, Maupassant or modernists like Wells. Humour, tragedy, sublimity, pathos—the great passions which make us men—are the strands which were woven into the very fibre of his being. Though he conquered Fate, yet he was powerless to avert his appointed destiny. And though Time which gave, confounded her own gifts and apparently destroyed him, yet he has revenged himself on Time by producing the choicest flowers of Immortal Thought from the Garden of his own Heart, flowers that were rooted in his own life, for ever to bloom in the domains of Science, Art, Philosophy, and Poetry. They are Immortelles which will outlive Time—putting her to scorn, for they belong, like their Creator, to the Eternities.

This is not the hasty verdict of an enthusiast spurred into a panegyric of adulation, though at first sight it may appear to be the case. I but record the sober truth. I write plainly so that the reader may understand that I am a whole-hearted lover of Francis Bacon. I know him as "Our Francis"; and to know him in so intimate a fashion is to love him. I want every reader of this book to know and to love him too. I would that you should love him understandingly and passionately as did his friends Ben Jonson, Sir Tobie Matthew, Sir Thomas Meautys. Indeed, in his own day this fact is recorded by a contemporary, Aubrey, who states that "*all who were great and good LOVED and honoured him.*"

I am going to tell you why they loved and honoured him . . . these great and good men. They loved him because they knew his real life, his secret works, his personal character. In a word, because they *understood* him, the peculiar circumstances of his life and the complexity of his nature.

[1]The inscription on the Shakespeare Monument at Stratford.

When I have told my tale I shall be surprised if you do not feel inclined to do reverence to this intellectual Colossus who strides down the ages among us. If you do not reverence him for his honesty of character, his inflexible pursuit of Truth and Beauty, I shall have failed in my task.

To understand so complex a personality one must know the story from the beginning . . . even before he was born on the present stage of life and action. To begin the story of his life, as is the fashion of so many biographers, when he was about twenty-five or thirty-five years of age, either in 1584, his entry to Parliament, or 1597 when his first publication, ten short *Essays*, was printed under his own name—is necessarily fatal to the understanding of the *complete* man. It limits the presentation to a portion only of his life. If the most important fragment—the real Key to his Personality—is ignored, the student, no matter how earnest and honest he may be, sets out on a wrong trail, becoming increasingly bewildered and baffled as he faces the enigmas surrounding Francis Bacon. The man he would capture has escaped the biographer's pen. He has failed to find the secret springs of a life because he has neglected to hunt for hidden beginnings.

What we want to know first of all about Francis Bacon are the formative influences of childhood, his environment and education; for these are the factors which mirror themselves in every growing babe, and play so powerful a part in the mental and spiritual equipment of the adult. In Francis Bacon's case—since he is a world figure—we even want to know his antecedents, his father, his mother, the state of England and its relation to Europe; in short, the Feudal Era which gave rise to the Age to which he was born.

Let me then rough in the historical background before delineating Francis Bacon's personality.

In 1561 England was slowly awakening from the death-like trance into which she had fallen, in common with the rest of Europe, through the spells of the Holy Catholic Church. For upwards of a thousand years this Church had reigned supreme over an entire Continent. The Pope was the Dictator not only of the religious life of the nations but he also controlled all intellectual activity. Men and women had no right to think outside the narrow bonds of an enervating theology.

When the Roman Emperor Constantine was "converted" in A.D. 324, it marked the emergence of Christianity as the specially favoured cult of the Empire. His conversion set the seal of success on his protracted desperate struggle with Licinius his rival. In deference to priestly prejudice, "he closed the Schools, dispersed the Libraries, and allowed Science to be branded as magic." Thereafter, the Church dug the grave of Greek speculation and Roman philosophy. It fostered Art merely as a handmaid to minister to theological creeds: it banished the ancient philosophic forms of Culture, science and poetry: and the Drama of the Mysteries was Anathema Maranatha. All search for Truth from the third century onwards ended in a pre-ordained cul-de-sac—orthodox dogma. Theology led men away from the great thinkers of Greece and Rome and from the Ethical Rituals of the Mysteries that had once displayed their Secret Dramas in Sacred Temples on the banks of the Nile. It trampled on the Pagan Schools of Thought and ground their teachings into the dust with cries of "heresy." It scoffed at secular learning. Under the leadership of the priest, civilization plunged blindly forward into the abyss of the Medieval Era.

In the Middle Ages are to be seen a series of lurid pictures in which the Lights of Knowledge go out one by one . . . from the time of the quarrelling Council of Nicaea (325), through the Crusades, the Inquisition, the Persecution of Heretics, to the Elizabethan Era (1561). During the whole of this time, there was no unfettered intellectual life. The middle of the thirteenth century touched the lowest ebb of European thought. If the Church was ever, in any sense, a patron of Learning, it was a Learning that was in bonds. There were barren disputations, in Universities and Monasteries alike, that revolved round metaphysical subjects utterly valueless to the disputants or use to mankind, such as "Could God, being omnipotent, make two parallel lines meet? Could He possibly make ten devils dance on the point of a needle at one and the same time?" For centuries real learning was lost amid arid wastes of subtle dialectics.

The social life of the common people was for ages wretched in the extreme. . . . The majority lived in mere hovels. The prejudice of "caste" was as pronounced as it is in India to-day. Under the Feudal system, the world was made for the benefit of the classes . . . the men "of gentle birth by letters patent." The labouring masses were regarded as serfs by Church and State. They knew nothing of the glory that was Greece and the grandeur that was Rome. To the Priest, the Wisdom of the Ancients was a stumbling-block; and to the unlettered Lords of Feudalism, foolishness. The accumulated knowledge of the ancient world—history, politics, science, philosophy, ethics—was lost for over a thousand years and almost destroyed. We have to thank the Moors for the preservation of certain definite branches of knowledge.

It is difficult for the average reader to realize that there were actually great civilizations prior to Christianity, profound thinkers, skilful artists, learned scholars, and that in pre-Christian times are to be found systems of thought, much more complex than simple genesis-germs, of science, art, moral and political philosophy, speculative thought, religion, and so on. There were even clear ideas on the three great problems on which men ponder to-day more than ever—God, Man, Destiny. Zeno and Plato believed in God as an energizing power (Spirit) at the centre of life and motion, omnipotent, omniscient, all wise; that he was "our Father" in a personal sense whose ever-watchful providence extended to everyone; that man was an immortal spirit; this world a training ground for a higher life; and that God had given everyone an angel or guardian to guide and protect him, character being the most important asset he possessed. "God deals by us as a good Father deals by his children; He tries us, He hardens us, He fits us for Himself. I know that nothing comes to pass but what God appoints," wrote Seneca (3 B.C.—A.D. 65). Epictetus, about A.D. 94, wrote similarly, "Dare to look up to God and say: Deal with me henceforth as Thou wilt; I am of one mind with Thee; I am Thine; I reject nothing that seems good to Thee; lead me whithersoever Thou wilt. To have God for our Maker and Father and Guardian shall this not avail to deliver us from griefs and fears? For when you have shut the doors and made darkness in the house, remember ye are not alone. For God is there and your Guardian is there. He hath placed at every man's side a Guardian, charged to watch over him, a Genius that cannot sleep nor be deceived."

Whence came this note of certainty in these magnificent utterances of these ancient Teachers?

The fact is that the Ancient Wisdom—quite apart from Learning and Culture—was based in its moral aspects from a first-hand knowledge of Psychic Phenomena (the Oracle at Delphi, the Vestal Virgins, the Sibylline Books all provide evidence of intercourse with the Spirit World) and an Ethical interpretation of Nature which found its *Summum Bonum* in the Drama of the Mysteries. But these various Schools—Stoicism, Epicureanism—were suppressed, and their mysterious and mystical symbolism all but perished.

Plato and Virgil were lost to the world, though they might be known privately by a few individual monks in the privacy of their cloistered cells.

It should never be lost sight of, as I have already said, that up to the time of Henry VIII (1531-47), the Roman Church held undisputed sway over the bodies, minds and souls of men. Anyone who dared to withstand Authority was broken on the wheel. The zenith of the Middle Ages was the thirteenth century when Europe had one religion and one culture, when grievances were many and life was cruelly hard for the masses in every country. Indeed, the conditions under which men and women were living at this time were so intolerable that they were openly beginning to chafe under their pains and their poverties. It was out of these widespread evils, that touched every phase of national life, that there was born a new temper . . . the spirit of reaction took the place of passive obedience. *Intellectuals were sick of the ignorance of the Clergy and their condemnation of secular learning and formed secret societies for the advancement of knowledge.* The masses were at last awakened to the fact that from the official Church there was flowing a stream of poison which was utterly at variance with morality or real religion.

There was absolution for every crime—on payment of a fixed tariff: poisoning eleven ducats; incest thirty-six livres; perjury seven livres; murder was even less: one ducat, four livres, eight centimes. In Torquemada's administration 10,220 persons were burned alive, 97,321 being punished with confiscation of property. In 1572, eleven years after Francis Bacon's birth, there was the butchery of St. Bartholomew's Eve. *In* 1568 *the Holy Office condemned every man, woman and child in the Netherlands to the scaffold.* Francis Bacon was then seven years of age.

The monks destroyed books in a wholesale fashion. Pope Gregory destroyed the priceless library of the Palatine Apollo. *Poesy was held to be the inspiration of the Devil.* The Jesuits converted the flourishing kingdom of Bohemia into a desert. Francis I signed Letters Patent for the suppression of printing. Copernicus (1473-1543) waited thirty years before daring to announce publicly that the Sun was the Centre of the Universe. He escaped the deadly clutches of the Inquisition by dying.

Bruno was burnt for espousing the heresy of Copernicus. Galileo was martyred in 1612. Descartes (1596-1650) was horribly persecuted in Holland and narrowly escaped being burnt.

Such being the fate of the intellectual giants we can guess the lot of the smaller men. The nonentities fell like leaves in a storm, a storm of violence that never ceased but swept remorselessly on through decade after decade.[1]

The Reformation did little to aid Free Thought. The English Puritans made great bonfires of everything Popish, destroying Art and glorying in their depredations. Luther called Copernicus, "this fool who wishes to reverse the entire system of astronomy." Puritans and Romanists alike were united in their persecution of philosophy and their hatred of secular knowledge for the common people.

The revolt against Authority actually began with Dante (1261-1321)—hitherto supposed poet of theological Catholicism—who was secretly one of the first intellectual rebels against the Holy Church. His works were directed against the evils of tyranny and were written to hearten the little band of Continental thinkers who were struggling to disseminate liberal ideas. The evils of the times could not be opposed openly. It could only be done by covert ways and means.

The attempt to prevent printing having failed, the Church resorted to the expedient of muzzling. Clerical Inquisitors were appointed in Madrid, Rome, Naples, Lisbon and elsewhere. Licence to publish was refused to all except those who were certified. Free England was equally affected. The dangers of authorship were great and the rewards of literature remote.

In Dante's day no branch of intellectual effort lay open in which to exercise independent judgment. Every line he wrote in his own language was subject to supervision and censure. He lived under a reign of terror. The use of torture was definitely ordered by the Bull of Innocent IV (1252) and became universal.

> In every monarchy, every school and university, a ceaseless silent espionage was set on foot. Every action of the student's life was reported to the Inquisitor. . . .
>
> Ever since Italy had been darkened by the shadow of the Inquisition, *men had begun to devise means to communicate with each other, and with their public. in a style which should be intelligible to themselves* without giving offence to Rome, Open revolt was impossible. They matched their wits against their persecutors and *were able to say pretty nearly what they liked by a SYSTEM OF DISGUISED WRITING.* . . .
>
> This use of DOUBLE WRITING in serious literature was the only method of free expression open to men of letters . . . *to write in such a manner that the Authorities might assume their doctrine to be orthodox while the public for whom it was designed might readily perceive its real drift.* Except by resort to this OLD AND TIME-HONOURED DEVICE the spirit of independent thought would have perished altogether. . . .
>
> The modern has nothing but distaste for cryptic modes of writing . . . yet Dante lent his genius to this end . . . like his master Virgil he chose to

See *New Light on the Renaissance*, by Harold Bayley (p. 211).

practise the subtlety of the *double entendre*. . . . Dante and his contemporaries had a *hidden multitude* eager for each work they produced.[1]

It was Dante with his secret disciples, and his equally secret public, that set the trend of the intellectual and moral revival that ultimately took possession of men's hearts and minds openly. He helped to impregnate the Spirit of the Age with new ideas . . . secretly; and by a succession of hands—loving disciples—the Torch of Hidden Wisdom was handed down from Virgil, one of the Masters of the Ancient Mysteries, through Dante to the Elizabethan Era . . . to the outstanding genius of that age, Francis Bacon. We shall see how the circumstances of his life, and the Spirit of the Age, caused this intellectual giant to dissemble like his predecessor Dante. He adopted all Dante's methods of Secret Writing (*double entendres*, word-play with words and phrases) and carried the methods to the farthest limits in a variety of ways—by numbers, anagrams, printing errors, special type-setting, hieroglyphics, allegorical pictures, emblematic head and tail pieces, watermarks, etc.—in order to help humanity to escape from the mental and physical thraldom of a thousand years. He was a secret ethical teacher working along lines of action, open and concealed.

The movement which gradually worked up from the time of Dante (1265-1321) culminated in the Renaissance or the Rebirth of Europe, and consisted, really, in an open Revival of Learning which may be said to have begun with the capture of Constantinople by the Turks in 1453 and ended with the death of Queen Elizabeth in 1603: but the ground had been slowly prepared for some two hundred years, for all Europe had gradually become honeycombed with secret surgings for higher things.

The movement was actually an open revolt against the barrenness of Medievalism and a return to the rich humanity of Greece and Rome, with all the free activities which invested the classical age. It sought "to escape from a life of fetters, from ecclesiastical tradition and intellectual tyranny into freedom."

These efforts led directly to the religious revolution of the sixteenth century, which had been fought inch by inch by the Holy See during the last three centuries of the Middle Ages. It came to a head with Luther's attack on the sale of Indulgences by the Pope in 1517.

In England the Reformation came in with the schism of England from Rome under Henry VIII. The immediate cause of the break was the quarrel between Henry and the Pope, who had refused to sanction the King's divorce from Catherine. The King broke with Rome, set up an English Church with himself at the head, made his own Articles of Religion, appointed his own clergy, seized the monasteries, and married Anne Boleyn in the teeth of all clerical opposition. But the King's divorce was the mere occasion of what must sooner or later have been the only solution of England's relation with the Holy See, which claimed authority to impose its will on Kings and Parliaments.

The breach with Rome could not therefore be healed even by the reaction under Queen Mary, Henry's Catholic daughter, who succeeded him. Yet the old system of Romanism had so strong a hold on the English

[1]*Passing of Beatrice*, by Gertrude Leigh. (Intro., p. x.),

people that when Elizabeth came to the throne in 1558, the nation was about equally divided between the adherents to the Roman faith and two distinct parties which had renounced the Papacy but who could not work in common . . . the Church of England which sought to maintain the continuity of religious tradition in the country, and the Puritan Party which drew its inspiration from Calvinism. It was the prudent policy of Elizabeth which saved the country from internecine strife (as in France and Germany) and made England a Protestant power; for an infallible Church they substituted the Bible as the unerring expression of God's relation to man; the interpretation of the Bible they left to the individual conscience.[1]

It is out of this slowly-shifting historical background with its enervating mental and moral influence, its terrifying bigotry of Protestant and Catholic alike, its corrupt and wicked methods, the clash of bitter political and religious forces, the low ideals of humanity, the appalling ignorance in which the masses of the nations were steeped, the torture of heretics and the wholesale murder by the Church of entire communities like the Albigenses, that there stepped on to the Stage of Europe one of the Men of Destiny by whom God chooses to work out His great plans of human advancement . . . a man fated to play so great a part in the mental activities of the world's civilizations, that his all-round influence on the progress of humanity during the last three hundred years is greater than that of any one man who preceded him or is likely to succeed him. Francis Bacon is already known as the Father of Experimental Science. He taught Man how to experiment for the good of humanity. The world has yet to learn that, apart from his known labours, his life was largely devoted to concealed duties, the laying of secret bases for eternity, educational and ethical.

The unrest that had long rocked medieval Europe—flinging its ideals into the melting-pot to reshape them into a new modern world—had at last stirred England into activity. She was the last civilized country to feel the breath of the new spirit. The masses were restless. Their risings had been the signal for various repressive Acts of Parliament (1350, 1425, etc.), until, with their ancient craft guilds swept away, the working man, with Elizabeth's celebrated Act of Apprentices, was virtually a labour conscript under the heel of the justices. His wages were fixed by them and the sheriff. He could not leave his home nor seek for work in any parish without a permit from the justices. For two or more "to congregate" in order to ventilate a grievance, to seek for more money or better working conditions, was a crime against the State, an act of rebellion, and the offenders were to be regarded as felons and treated accordingly.

The Merchant Guilds, which were capitalistic, had triumphed over the Craft Guilds of workmen. The labourer was left without a weapon with which to fight for a decent existence until the rise of the Trade Unions in the nineteenth century. The highways of Europe—like England—were full of landless and homeless men. "It was small consolation to an English peasant in the latter years of Elizabeth, whose cottage had been pulled down that a sheep farm might be extended, workless and wageless, to

[1](*See* the "Reformation" and the "Renaissance" in *Chambers's Encyclopaedia*).

be assured that he lived in a wondrous age of discovery and glory! What did he care?" (Sidney Dark).

The darkest hour of the Medieval Age on the Continent is to be found in the years preceding the reign of Elizabeth. Ignorance, superstition, rotten wickedness infected all the Continental nations in all grades of society. If the common people were illiterate, the so-called "Gentry" were equally bookless. The peasant was virtually a serf wretchedly housed in a hovel. The Royal Courts were filled with Machiavellian statesmen corrupt in spirit and shrunken in soul. They were hotbeds of licentiousness and debauchery where *demi-mondaines* flaunted their charms, naked and unashamed, to noble roués whose lives were spent in intrigues, at the gaming tables and in vicious squandermania.

The Church was at full blast destroying heretics with torture, fire and sword, selling Indulgences for crime and vice to all who had money to pay for such priestly "pardons." The upper classes had their heels on the necks of the people who were sullenly silent, waiting for a chance to rise against their oppressors, fiercely debating under their breaths, as an outlet for their repressed energies, the respective theologies of Catholicism and Protestantism. And scattered throughout the Continent were little knots of Intellectuals, and spiritually-minded men, who were secretly striving to bring about a new order of society, to free the masses from the tyrannies of Church and State, and to inculcate the idea of "Education" and "Freedom of Thought" as the true pathway to progress.

At the time of the death of "Bloody Queen Mary" the stagnation of centuries was slowly giving way to movement. The intellectual yeast kneaded into the mass of humanity by Dante and his disciples had begun to take effect. There was a bubbling and rising in men's minds. The old order was changing, giving place to a new.

It was these influences, this new spirit of the age, which were injected into our Island Home in the sixteenth century. Though shut off from the main drift of Continental affairs, she partook of all its good and evil qualities.

This is the background against which we must see the England of Elizabeth—the young woman of twenty-five who ascended the throne in 1558 when the fortunes of the nation had sunk to their lowest ebb through bloodshed and misgovernment—if we would understand the complexities of Elizabethan life and thought. It was an Era of transition beset with dangers and difficulties.

(*This is an historical survey of facts as I see the era, and must not be taken as an attack on any Church. The spirit of persecution was equally rampant in both the Protestant and the Catholic Churches*).

Chapter II

THE ELIZABETHAN AGE: THE QUEEN'S SECRET

THE average person always invests the Elizabethan Age with the glamour of romance. One thinks of the Drakes and the Raleighs and the Shakespeares, of the "Mermaid Tavern" and all the picturesqueness of half-timbered, gabled houses of black and white, with winding, leafy lanes, a countryside smiling with flowers, with maypoles on the village greens where simple, honest-to-goodness swains lived idyllic lives with their blushing sweethearts. We fondly imagine that this was the "Merrie England" which flung back the might of the Spanish Armada with the unhurried quickness of the Elizabethan sea-dogs who nonchalantly played bowls at Plymouth Hoe almost within sight of the enemy.

But this impressionist picture, which looks so full of glamour through the time-mists of three hundred years, is only partially true. An examination of the details of our national life indicates that our forbears did not live lives of "roses, roses all the way." Indeed, the England of Elizabeth and James was by no means a carefree country nor an altogether happy place for the common man.

When Elizabeth came to the throne the treasury was empty. Trade was bad. The coinage had depreciated to one third its nominal value . . . with concurrent inflation and rising prices. The enclosure of common lands and the destruction of small estates for grazing farms had led to widespread unemployment. The English Channel swarmed with pirates. We were at war with France. The country was bitterly divided over religion. The Spanish ambassador, as the Catholic representative of King Philip, the husband of the late Queen Mary of England, wielded tremendous political, theological and economic power. His influence was almost paramount in the Affairs of State. In the early days of the Queen's reign, English statesmen had to walk very warily lest they gave offence to the Spanish watch-dog who almost roamed at will in the Council Chamber.

The Spanish policy was to subjugate England, by fair means or foul, so that she would be a vassal state in their Imperial Empire and a Catholic country. *Elizabeth's legitimacy as a true heir to the throne was doubted by nearly one-half of her own subjects.* Her right to the Succession, as the daughter of Anne Boleyn, was openly derided. The Catholic Church held that Anne Boleyn had not been lawfully wedded to Henry VIII. Elizabeth's enemies were only restrained from openly declaring war owing to the uncertainty, during the early months of her reign, whether she would espouse the Catholic or Protestant cause. Her personal views were locked within the sanctity of her own breast until she felt herself strong enough to cast aside the mask of dissimulation.

For long years after her accession the English language was a medley of rude and barbarous dialects. It was unformed. Spenser had still to appear as the forerunner of Shakespeare, the creator of the English tongue as a vehicle fit to convey the noblest thoughts ever conceived by the soul of man. Hooker had still to write the first English classic in prose, *Ecclesiastical Polity* (1594) and Francis Bacon the second great English prose masterpiece of flexible expression, poetic imagery and mature thought, *The Advancement of Learning* (1605). Hitherto the language of culture was Latin, and all works with any pretence to learning had been written in the universal foreign tongue.

Francis Bacon wrote his works in Latin and English. In the early years of Elizabeth there was no English reading public for there were virtually no English books on sale. There were no translations of the classics at the beginning of her reign. That was to come later *when the new idea was born that an English tongue should be used by Englishmen in preference to foreign diction.* Up to the printing of English books, Ovid, Boccaccio, Virgil, Plutarch were read in their originals by a very small minority. The love of literature was to grow with the growing patriotism for things English and the growing prosperity of the age. Between 1560 and 1580, experiments in thought and expression, and the coining of new words in the common tongue, had begun. In the next ten years there was a growing confidence in the new vehicle as a flexible method of expression. There arose a band of writers full of passionate utterance. Thenceforward until the publication of the great Shakespeare Folio of 1623, there was a full orchestra of poets, wits, philosophers, and learned men who worthily played their respective parts. With the passing of Francis Bacon in 1626 the Elizabethan music slowly faded out, as though he were the leader and conductor of the national choir. This is what Ben Jonson suggests, for in his *Discoveries* (1641), a notebook published after his death, in which he "discovers" his private views about the age, he says:

> Within his (Francis Bacon's) view, and about his time, were all the wits borne, that could honour a language, or helpe study. Now things daily fall: wits grow downward, and *Eloquence* growes backward: So that hee may be named, and stand as the *Marke* and *Acme* of our language. (p. 102, item 72).

The Tudor regime was essentially a tyranny under Elizabeth no less than with Henry VIII. The Queen had power of life and death over her subjects. The citizen was at the mercy of at least two despotisms—the Church and the State. A heretic, political or theological, could be thrown into the Tower, as not being conformable to authority, and tortured to extort a confession before being strangled at Charing Cross. According to the enormity of the offence, he would be restored to consciousness after partial strangulation, to have his heart plucked from his breast and waved in front of his dying eyes; or his bowels would be drawn and burnt to ashes amid frantic efforts to keep the victim conscious that he might witness such bloody barbarism. We can imagine the coarseness and the depravity that such public spectacles bred in the populace. The butcherings of men were so ghastly and of so vile a nature

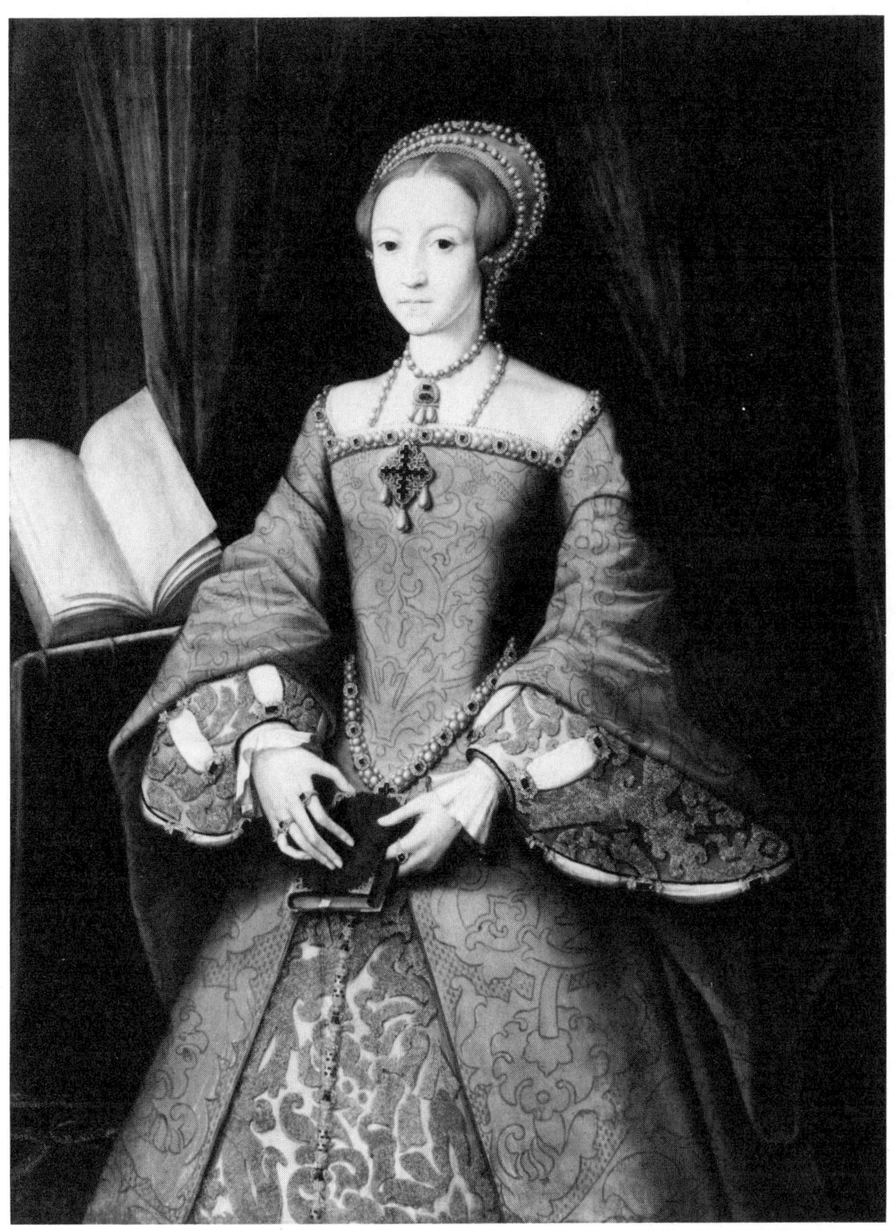

Plate II
Elizabeth I when Princess (1547)
by an unknown artist. Courtesy H.M. The Queen
(See Appendix I)

PLATE III

Robert Dudley, Earl of Leicester
(See Appendix I)

Amy Robsart, wife of Lord Robert Dudley
Photo by Valentine & Sons
(See Appendix I)

that one could not reprint descriptions of some of the scenes enacted in the public thoroughfares without being accused of indecency.

> The barbarous nature of public punishments was part of the legal customs even in 1660. The curious can read the horrible sentence solemnly passed on Mr. Harrison, "one of the twenty-nine Regicides, the Murtherers of His Late Sacred Majesty" by turning to the unnumbered page facing p. 57 and reading the speech of the Lord Chief Baron in passing sentence of torture and death. See *An Exact and most Impartial Accompt . . . of Twenty-nine Regicides*, PRINTED for Andrew Crook, at the Green Dragon, Licensed to be printed by J. Berkenhead. It could not be reprinted to-day. The book was printed for some reason by the secret Rosicrosse Literary Society, founded by Francis Bacon and contains numerous signals directing attention to various asides to Rosicrosse-Masons who had been "taught to read."

There were common informers spread among the people—the Gestapo of the Elizabethan Age—who made a living out of denouncing likely victims for alleged offences against Church and State. Anyone could become an "Informer." Authority encouraged spying on one's neighbours and bringing to notice alleged offences. The printer who unwittingly printed something that could be misconstrued into an offence, might be considered lucky to escape with only his hand chopped off. The author if he were known could be racked to death. We can well understand how men were driven to resort to all sorts of expedients to express their inner convictions . . . to cyphers, to secret writing, to dissimulation, to anonymity; and, with the birth of English printed books, to secret printing in the same way as Dante and his disciples.

The atmosphere of suspicion and hypocrisy saturated all grades of society. Neither the individual nor the State had any confidence in the "pledged word." It was essentially an age of intrigue in the reign of Elizabeth. With James and his wanton favourites, it degenerated into an utterly worthless and corrupt era. Professor Nichol writes in his life of Francis Bacon:

> The lie had sunk deep into the souls of men. . . . Of telling the plain truth to each other they took little thought. To outwit, surprise, bewilder, to frame, to look one way and row another, were maxims of State, till what was a principle in public, afterwards became a practice in private . . .[p. 20]
>
> There has rarely been a policy or a Court more imposing, one more stamped with majesty of manners or view. . . . On the other hand there has rarely been in any civilized country a policy or a Court in some important respects more corrupt than that of the last quarter of the sixteenth and the first quarter of the seventeenth century in England. . . .
>
> Faction intrigued against faction, favourite undermined favourite, relation slandered relation. Hardly one of the public men of these days had a perfectly open heart and very few had quite clean hands. . . . Delays of justice, if not justice itself, were arranged by bargain; and mild sentences if not acquittals were bought and sold. [p.23]

This description of the mental and moral atmosphere in which England was saturated in the days of Francis Bacon is confirmed by one of the most erudite students of that period, Mrs. H. Pott. Her various works have been written with an insight that has never been surpassed. In *Francis Bacon and his Secret Society* she wrote:

Those "good old times," in which Francis Bacon lived, were anything but good; they were coarse, ignorant, violent, dark and dangerous. "The Church," Bacon said, "which should be the chief band of religion, was turned to superstition" or made the matter of quarrelling and execrable actions; of murdering princes, butchery of people and subversion of states and governments.

The land was full of oppression, taxation, privileges broken, factions desperate, poverty great, knowledge at a standstill; learning barren, discredited by the errors, contentions, conceit and fantastical pendantry of so-called learned men. The literary spirit of the Ancients was dead. At the universities and schools words were taught but not matter.

Bacon even questions whether it would not be as well to abolish the scholastic system altogether and to set up a new form of teaching. The list of sciences taught, and which he finds to be full of follies and errors, or totally deficient, forbids any wonder at his verdict, that, as the present methods were rotten and useless to advance Learning, the old fabric should be razed to the ground and a new Solomon's House erected.

These were facts known to Francis Bacon early in life regarding the state of England and recorded by him. In the evening of his life, in his last work, the *De Augmentis,* he reiterates his opinions even more forcibly. He speaks of the "ignorance, folly and futility of the learning of his time, the dullness, apathy or ignorant bigotry of his contemporaries, the degradation of the Stage, the decay of the Wisdom of the Ancients," the lack of Christian Ethics. Francis Bacon's ideals were at least three hundred years in advance of his age. They shaped themselves in his mind when he was a mere boy. He still clung to them tenaciously in old age. All through his life he laboured at remedying the "Deficiencies" (his word) in the mental, moral and physical planes, not only in England, but for all mankind.

It was because of the crying evils of the times that, when he was a youth of fifteen or so, he conceived the magnificent idea of *The Universal Reformation of the Whole World.* It became the passion of his life. He laboured for it openly and secretly. It was a consuming flame. His plans did not concern England alone but took in all the countries of the then civilized world. Through all his multifarious activities he sought "to lay deep bases for eternity" in ways he dared not do openly. While he lamented in his writings, over and over again, "the ignorance, incapacity and miseries of the Age," in which he lived, he also believed with Hamlet that he "was born to set it right." He said of himself, "I AM A SERVANT TO POSTERITY." He began the epitome to his great philosophic scheme, *The Great Instauration,* with the sentence:

"FRANCIS OF VERULAM REASONED THUS WITH HIMSELF, AND JUDGED IT TO BE FOR THE INTEREST OF THE PRESENT AND FUTURE GENERATIONS THAT THEY SHOULD BE ACQUAINTED WITH HIS THOUGHTS."

He set his hand to the Herculean task of cleaning out the Augean Stables of England, the Continent, and the World . . . a task which he knew could never be accomplished in his life-time, and yet was within the bounds of accomplishment by future generations, provided the right seeds were sown, and devoted husbandmen secretly enlisted to carry on the good work down the ages by a succession of hands, so that plans and schemes for the cure of men's bodies and souls might be established in secret, and which, later, could be upreared as Temples of Learning and Love before the eyes of men, when humanity had become more liberal-minded.

His policy was primarily an educative one—to level up the masses by educative processes secular and ethical, and to divert the cultured classes from barren metaphysics into experimental research for the direct benefit of man in his daily work, his worldly circumstances, his pursuits, his home, his mental life, his moral activities. To this end he enumerates thirty or forty "deficiencies" of learning and gives us to understand that he had endeavoured to supply them.

How carefully this had to be done can be realized by a moment's reflection on the facts of Tudor tyranny, when the slightest political expression might bring a man to the torture chamber, when Catholic and Protestant were at daggers drawn, when the block and the hanging-tree at Tyburn menaced everyone. The charitably-minded man—in politics or religion—the man who loved the middle way—ran the risk, since he was not a violent sectary, of finding himself either strangled, drawn and quartered at Tyburn as a rebel or burnt at the stake as an atheist and a heretic.

It was especially a dangerous age to live in for one who had a greater grasp and a deeper knowledge of spiritual values than any of his contemporaries, particularly if he wished to bring his ideals into fruition. New ideas were perilous when their scope was educative, political or religious. Theological passions never ran higher than in the days of Elizabeth. For a Teacher of Ethics, allied to the Pagan Mysteries, though based on the Fatherhood of God and the Brotherhood of Man, to have attempted to acclaim a natural system of religion open to all "GOOD MEN" irrespective of CREED would have been suicidal. Catholics, Anglicans and Puritans would at once have combined and shouted with their *confrères* of old, "Crucify him! Crucify him!"

It will be seen in subsequent chapters that Francis Bacon regarded himself primarily as an Educational and Ethical Teacher. All his genius and learning was devoted to one end . . . the spreading of knowledge and the inauguration of a System of Ethics couched in allegory and illustrated by symbol. The word constantly on his lips was "Light . . . more Light!"

The Spirit of the Age drove Francis Bacon to follow on the lines of the great Ethical Teachers of the past—Pythagoras, Virgil and Dante—and to found like them a secret school of disciples for the propagation of his principles. He thus became a CONCEALED Teacher hidden within a Ring of Concealed Brethren bound to each other by Oaths of mutual secrecy. He took upon himself a dual rôle. He was an OPEN Teacher on all those educative topics which might ameliorate the lot of the human race. He was a CONCEALED Teacher of those higher systems of thought which sought to explain the Law behind the law in terms of LOVE, human brotherhood and Divine Fatherhood. In the truest meaning of the words he was an Exoteric Teacher and an Esoteric one also.

The evils of the Dark Ages that had afflicted the Continent were thus mirrored in England despite our isolated Island position. There was still the struggle of the people for representative Government, for in 1558 the fight against Feudalism was by no means over. There was a thirst for liberty and freedom, a hunger for great adventures, for El Dorados beyond the seas. The spirit of unrest and change was in the atmosphere. If it was a perilous age for ordinary men and women, it was equally perilous for Elizabeth Tudor. Statesmen and people alike were full of anxieties as to what the future had in store for the nation with a young Queen of untried temper and uncertain qualifications on the throne. She was indeed an unknown quantity. It was this young woman of twenty-five, imperious and haughty, who largely set the temper of the spirit of the age, and helped by her character to mould the destinies of the English nation in the most momentous epoch of our history. J. R. Green says, "The country was humiliated by defeat, and brought to the verge of rebellion by the bloodshed and misgovernment of Mary's reign. . . . The New Learning was all but dissolved. . . . France mistress of the Channel. . . . Scotland a standing danger in the North. . . . In the presence of a host of dangers the country lay utterly helpless, without any army or fleet . . ." Green thus continues:

> England's one hope lay in the character of her Queen. . . . In her twenty-fifth year . . . she had much of her mother's beauty. Her figure was commanding, her face long, but queenly and intelligent, her eyes quick and fine. She had grown up amid the liberal culture of Henry's Court, a bold horsewoman, a good shot, a graceful dancer, a skilled musician, and an accomplished scholar.
>
> She read every morning a portion of Demosthenes. But she was far from being a mere pedant. . . . She spoke Italian and French as fluently as her mother tongue. She was familiar with Ariosto and Tasso . . . *with a taste for Anagrams and such puerilities.* Her moral temper recalled in its strange contrasts the mixed blood within her veins. She was at once the daughter of Henry and Anne Boleyn.
>
> From her father she inherited her frank and hearty address, her love of popularity and of free intercourse with the people, her dauntless courage, and her amazing self-confidence. . . . With the Tudor temper stood the sensuous, self-indulgent nature she derived from Anne Boleyn. . . . Of womanly reserve or self-restraint she knew nothing. No instinct of delicacy veiled her voluptuous temper. . . . She fondled her "sweet Robin," Lord Leicester, in the face of the Court.

Yet this woman held to be so frivolous that Philip of Spain wondered how such a "wanton" could hold his policy in check, outwitted all the Continental statesmen and her own statesmen as well. The Elizabeth they saw was far from being all of Elizabeth. Underneath the exterior of trivialities she had an inflexible will and a temper as hard as steel. Passion and emotion might sweep her off her feet, but her superb intellectual powers always saved her from disaster. By sheer will power she retrieved dangerous personal situations—as well as national—over and over again.

She lived simply and frugally, and she worked hard. She was the coolest and hardest of the politicians and statesmen she met at her Council

Chamber. She was the instrument of none. In fact, she used each in turn for her own ends. She listened to all, weighed the pros and cons of tendered advice, and then went her own way. The policy was essentially her own though it was also an amalgam of the brains of the wisest statesmen that ever proffered advice to a Sovereign. *It must never be forgotten that when she hoodwinked, outwitted and lied it was for England, to save England, to make England truly great.* Her gift for dissimulation arose from a secret locked more or less securely within her own breast. In the early years of her reign she believed with all her soul that she alone could save England, and that any open alliance (marriage) with any foreign Prince or English Lord might have the effect of provoking a rebellion within the realm, and a combination of enemy nations without to declare war. None of her trickery was without political value. "A falsehood was to her simply an intellectual means of meeting a difficulty." Green adds:

> Nothing is more revolting in the Queen than her shameless mendacity. It was an age of political lying, but in the profusion and recklessness of her lies Elizabeth stood without a peer in Christendom.

It cannot be denied, however, that the Queen's lies were to protect England and, it may be argued, the end justified the means. It prevented civil war and national conflict, ruin and bloodshed, when the Commonwealth was menaced by powerful nations, foes without and within. Every year that passed without war doubled the nation's strength, until at last the day arrived when she was strong enough to challenge the greatest military and naval power in the world. Green concludes that:

> To England, during the reign of half a century, she was a virgin and a Protestant Queen; and her immorality, her absolute want of religious enthusiasm, failed utterly to blur the brightness of the national ideal . . . She had at any rate the satisfaction of averting war and conspiracies by love-sonnets and romantic interviews, or the gaining of a year of tranquillity by the dexterous spinning out of a flirtation.

Now against the views of historians like Green and critics like Nichol, the opinion of one best qualified to judge, because he lived near to the time, and was related to her, is important. Francis Bacon wrote: "*This Princess was good and moral. Fair purpose and Love-making was allowed but Lasciviousness banished. She detested vice and desired to purchase Fame only by honourable courses. . . . The change which happened was not in her Nature, but upon the NECESSITY of the TIMES.*" (*In Memory of Elizabeth*, p. 152, *Resuscitatio*, Rawley, 1670, Ed.).

How can these opposing views be reconciled? What is the actual truth amid such glaring contradictions? We have the apparent open fact that the Queen had many lovers from Admiral Seymour to Essex. She made London a shambles by adorning the city gates, and even the approaches to her palace, with the heads and quarters of alleged traitors. She put down incipient rebellions with wholesale hangings. With loud-mouthed masculine vulgarity did she not conduct herself like an unsexed virago . . . especially in the latter years of life? Yet, in spite of these evil traits, there are many extenuating circumstances. Perhaps to know all is to forgive all. It largely depends on one's personal point of view and a complete knowledge of the factors that shaped her destiny. Some have hitherto been overlooked that played a tremendous part in her mental and moral "make-up."

Thomas Hardy wrote *Tess* to show that an adulteress and a murderess could nevertheless be "a pure woman," and there is little doubt that he makes his reader feel that his heroine was blameless. Circumstances were too strong for Tess to maintain her integrity. They drove her into "crime." There are similar stories in real life. Such words as "morality," "religion," "virtue," are difficult to define in relation to such cases. This particularly applies to such a complex character as Elizabeth. No one has ever reigned who was more entirely the child of heredity and environment.

Early in life she made what many would term "a false step." This drove her into practising the art of dissimulation, to guard a secret which would have had disastrous consequences not only for herself but for the nation and even the world at large, had her personal secret become public property. Indeed, so well was it kept by the few who were privy to it, that historians and biographers of to-day have been as completely hoodwinked by her as the Continental statesmen of yesterday. She sinned. And she paid for her sin by an agony of suffering, by floods of torturing remorse.

This is the story . . . a story that not only had its repercussions (though unsuspected) through the Elizabethan world, but is still reverberating in the studies of scholars, exercising men's minds to try to probe beneath the surface of the Era, seeking to understand the men and women of her day.

When Elizabeth's mother, Anne Boleyn, was put to death by Henry VIII on a trumped-up charge of immorality, Elizabeth was three years of age. From her cradle she was a child of the fairest promise. At six her precocious industry is noted by a contemporary. At twelve it was recognized that she was a child of extraordinary acquirements and ability, with an astonishing all-round knowledge of languages, arts, and sciences.

At the age of fifteen she had her first love-affair with a man twenty years her senior, Admiral Sir Thomas Seymour. It was conducted on his part with coarse familiarity, and, as Elizabeth was under the jealous guardianship of the Lord Protector Somerset and his Council, the Admiral was arrested on a charge of high treason . . . the overthrowing of the Regency. He lost his head.

To clear her character, she wrote to the Lord Protector a straight-to-the-point letter respecting the alleged clandestine offences. It shows that at the early age of sixteen Elizabeth knew her nature and the meaning of sex. She says:

> I am told there goeth rumours abroad which be greatly both against my honour and honesty . . . that I am in the Tower and with child by my Lord Admiral. My Lord, these are shameful slanders . . . I most heartily desire that I may come to Court, *that I may show myself there as I am.*

The fact that she was prepared to be examined by a panel of matrons is sufficient evidence that not only was she *virgo intacta* but a normal woman. Doubts have been expressed by modern writers respecting her womanhood, some expressing the opinion that she was a hermaphrodite. Her physician ought to have known the truth. When the French King, who, in 1566, was a suitor for her hand, instructed his ambassador to inquire whether she was likely to be sterile, her physician replied:

> If the King marries her, I guarantee ten children: and no one in the world knows her better than I do.

This disastrous termination of clandestine courtship with Seymour had the result of making her more studious, and she perfected her studies under the learned Roger Ascham until the death of her brother, the Protestant King Edward on the 6th July, 1553.

Her elder sister Mary, daughter of Catherine of Aragon, came to the Throne and at once made known her intention of restoring the Mass and all the ancient ceremonials of the Catholic Faith. She stamped out the attempt to make Lady Jane Grey the Queen. The Duke of Northumberland, the leader of the movement, was beheaded; so was Lady Jane Grey and her husband, Lord Guilford Dudley. His brother Lord Robert Dudley was sent to the Tower. Since the religious views of Elizabeth were uncertain, and there was danger of her being the centre of Protestant plots, she was likewise imprisoned by her sister in the Tower. English prayers and Protestant rites were prohibited her. She was required to hear the Mass. Members of her household were imprisoned and tortured to obtain evidence that she had conspired to subvert the existing order. The fate of Elizabeth hung in the balance for long-drawn-out months. A warrant for her execution was actually drawn up and sent to the Governor of the Tower to enforce; but he refused the responsibility because of a flaw in the warrant. So real was the peril that Elizabeth told Castelnau, the French ambassador, when adverting to this period, "that she desired of her sister but one request, that she might have her head cut off with a sword, as in France, and not with an axe, after the present fashion."

At the beginning of her imprisonment she was very rigorously confined in the Bell Tower but later on she was allowed full liberty of the Tower and its grounds. She thus met Destiny in the person of Lord Robert Dudley, who was lodged in the Beauchamp Tower and who was daily expecting the same fate that had overtaken his father, Northumberland, and his brother, Guilford. There was a secret way between the Bell Tower and the Beauchamp Tower.

Lord Robert was a married man, the husband of Amy Robsart. It was an unhappy marriage. He had been one of Elizabeth's playfellows in childhood. He was born the same day and hour. Later in life he said he had "known her intimately from her eighth year." When they met again in the Tower he had grown into a handsome man of soldierly appearance, a dashing cavalier, intellectual, and far above the average in every way. Whatever may be said of his moral qualities, he was just the type of man to appeal to a lonely maiden, loveless, forlorn, friendless, menaced with the sword of Damocles. Their common lot drew them together. How could it be otherwise? They were both Royal prisoners, each not knowing what a day might bring forth. They lived under the shadow of the axe. Thus what might have been expected, actually happened. They sought consolation in each other's company, and their friendship rapidly developed into passionate affection. There can be no doubt, that, like many loving war-couples, their emotions under the shadow of death led them to consummate their love irrespective of consequence, marriage or no marriage, legal or illegal, priest or no priest... but "a chronicle in the Tower states that the couple were married there by a monk." (Mme. D. von Kunow, p. 11, *Francis Bacon, the Last of the Tudors.*).

Purists may blame them, but they doubtless felt that they had a right to the pleasures of life while they were above the ground. Neither had any prospect of coming out of the Tower alive. There was no prospective "Succession" to the Throne. Lord Dudley was far from his wife, whom he did not love. They probably said, as others similarly situated have done, "Let us be happy while we can." It was in these circumstances they pledged themselves to each other. "Some sort of secret understanding was established between them at this period," says the historian Strickland in her life of the Queen. Later events make it clear what was the import of that "secret understanding."

This, then, was the beginning of the Queen's Secret which she so successfully carried out and concealed from the public eye through her subsequent long reign. They became lovers in fact, and there is every reason to suppose they became ultimately man and wife in deed.

After months of such companionship Elizabeth was removed to Woodstock, where she was again subjected to the most rigorous surveillance. No one was allowed to have any communication with her directly or indirectly. There were many attempts to trick her into treachery. Sixty soldiers were on guard by day and forty kept watch on the walls by night. There were always five or six locks between her and freedom.

During the years while she was a prisoner and a semi-prisoner, there were many aspirants to her hand. The Queen, King Philip and the Council brought pressure to bear on her to marry as the best way out of their difficulty in dealing with her. "I am otherwise minded," said Elizabeth to her Royal sister. "No! Though I were offered the greatest Prince in Europe." Even though marriage meant freedom she was secretly resolved to be true to her "Tower-Lover."

Queen Mary's false pregnancy, her lingering illness, and its unexpected fatal termination after a five-years reign, left the Princess Elizabeth the only possible heir. On the 17th November, 1558, Parliament proclaimed the Lady Elizabeth Queen of the Realm.

Within a week of her accession—*her first act of a private nature*—she sent for her secret lover, Robert Dudley. He had recently been set at liberty and had gone abroad to the wars in France. He hastened to her side and she at once conferred on him the signal honour of Master of the Horse. He was thus in constant personal attendance upon her. She loaded him with honours and riches. *She lodged him next to her own room where he lived for years.* She created him Earl of Leicester.

Appointing him her master of horse, and loading him with honours within the first week of her accession, must have originated from some powerful motive which does not appear on the surface of history. (Strickland).

A short time later she had hit on the idea of publicly proclaiming—in answer to the Commons request that she should marry so that the Succession should be secure—*that her husband should be the State.* It would be enough for her—

> That a marble stone should declare that a Queen having reigned such a time lived and died a VIRGIN.

She would be twenty-six when she began to pose as the VIRGIN QUEEN. There was a fixity of purpose, the *better to cloak her real life*, to throw dust in the eyes of posterity, which never changed during her reign.

No sooner had Lord Robert taken up his residence in Court than there was open love-making and secret intrigues which set the State Counsellors wondering, and the ambassadors writing home their suspicions regarding the virtue of the Queen. The real facts appear to be these. From the outset she regarded herself as the secret wife of Dudley. Knowing he was a married man they could not be wed legally. She wished to marry no one but him. She was not, however, prepared to marry her lover openly even if he were free. Her open husband would be for ever England. She knew that Dudley was disliked by the great nobles and an open marriage would have jeopardized the State.

Moreover, she was not going to yield up the reins of the Kingdom to anyone; neither to a subject as Dudley was, nor to a foreign Prince. She believed that her woman's wit, and her powers of dissimulation, would not only bring herself safely through, but England also. In short, she was not prepared to hand over the helm of the Kingdom to a partner. She felt she could accomplish the critical task of saving England far better than anyone else. What her father had done, she could do. She was a Tudor. She was also going to have love in her life. She was going to know what it was to be a wife and a mother: but it was to be a secret life, a concealed experience, a thing apart: to the world she would be known as "THE VIRGIN QUEEN." She would keep all her opponents guessing until the situation cleared.

To keep up the delusion that she was half inclined to enter the marriage market, she openly flirted with Royal lovers by day and enjoyed the joke with Dudley in secret by night. On going to live at the Palace Dudley had immured his young wife in Cumnor Hall. She was virtually a prisoner. He never saw her. Everyone knew she stood in his way to a possible alliance with Elizabeth.

The climax came at last. After three years intimacy the Queen discovered that she was pregnant. In September 1560, the Queen, being about five months off her confinement, was desperate, as Dudley's wife was still alive, and if the Queen were to have a bastard son, there would have been a Roman Catholic reaction and even the Protestants would have declared for Mary of Scotland. A little later, on the 8th September, Lord Robert Dudley's wife was found mysteriously dead at the bottom of the staircase of Cumnor Hall. Shortly afterwards, on the 12th September, Dudley and the Queen were privately married at Brooke

House, Hackney, belonging to the Earl of Pembroke, Sir Nicholas and Lady Bacon being witnesses. This legitimatized the offspring.

In October, the month following, the Spanish ambassador was arrested and accused of writing to King Philip of Spain that the Queen had been privately married to Dudley at the Earl of Pembroke's house. Three months later, on 22nd January, 1560-1, a boy was born at Wolsley New Palace, Whitehall. He was taken charge of by a personal friend of the Queen, Lady Bacon, wife to Sir Nicholas Bacon, Keeper of the Great Seal. He is registered at St. Martin's-in-the-Fields as "Mr. Franciscus Bacon" as though his foster-parents—or someone acting for them—wished to mark their respect to a babe of the blood Royal by the appellation of "Mr." Correspondence shows that the birth was known to Lord Burleigh, Secretary of State, and to the Queen's Ambassador Throckmorton at Paris. But the Royal Secret was well kept. The Courts were full of rumours but everything was concealed. Nothing could be proven.

This intimacy between the Queen and Dudley continued without a break until they had reached the age of forty. It is not therefore a matter of surprise that a second child of this morganatic marriage was born some six years after "Mr. Franciscus Bacon." He was adopted by the Queen's cousin, Lettice Knollys, the Chief Lady of the Bedchamber, the wife of Lord Hereford, afterwards created the first Earl of Essex. This child, supposed to have been born on 10th November, 1567, at Netherwood, Hertfordshire, is known to history as Robert Earl of Essex, the "lover" of Queen Elizabeth. The Queen loved him undoubtedly, but it was the love of a mother for a son. There is no record of his birth in the parish register of Netherwood.

Historians say that the Queen had many lovers and all are agreed that pride of place was given to Dudley, Earl of Leicester, and, later, to a younger man Robert, Earl of Essex.

That she was ever in love with any of her numerous suitors and favourites—or allowed any familiarities—is quite unthinkable in view of all the circumstances. Everything points to one outstanding fact: that the Earl of Leicester, who was her real lover, was also her accepted husband by a morganatic marriage, a private one, and that the two surviving children of that marriage were Francis Bacon and Robert Essex. She was true to Leicester believing that "*whom God hath joined let no man put asunder,*" love, she held, being born of God. For his sake and for England's sake, she played off the Continental lovers who sought her hand—staunch to herself, her secret lover and England.

She was loyal to him to the end. His memory she treasured. And Leicester seems to have been loyal to her for years. He wanted to be openly acknowledged as her husband. There is a letter written by him to the King of Spain asking him to use his influence with the Queen. He seems to have fought for his sons to be recognized . . . for Robert to be acknowledged as next in the Succession. And though an Act was passed making it a penal offence to speak of a "Successor" to the Crown other than the "*NATURAL Issue of her body,*" she refused to have the word "Lawful" inserted, power being given to her by Parliament to name her Successor, yet she hesitated to name her concealed son Francis because she had only been married three to four months when he was born, and it would have exposed her secret. The younger son Robert was her favourite and there is every probability he would have been named but for his imperious Tudor spirit, his attempts to bend her to his will by forceful methods, and the ring of enemies that in later years poisoned the mind of the Queen against him.

All these tangled facts must be borne in mind when dealing with the life of Francis Bacon. They must be given due prominence. His mysterious life grew out of the mystery of his forbears even more than the age in which he lived with its stresses and strains. *He grew to maturity under a cloud.* It overshadowed him throughout life, even in his brightest and happiest hours. The cloud darkened his last hours. He was a concealed son. He had a concealed brother. He had the proud knowledge that Tudor blood ran in his veins. All the time the Queen with secret heart-aches, which gradually embittered her, had to play the coquette when her heart ached for the domesticity of married life. Every moment she had to be on her guard lest her secret were discovered to the undoing of herself and England.

We can now better understand how such a private matter—which carried in its train such momentous consequences—necessarily had its effect on the public life in multifarious ways, especially mirroring itself in the life of her first-born.

No one can understand the Elizabethan Age who is without any knowledge of the Queen's secret. And no one can understand the lives of the great Queen, Francis Bacon, and the Earl of Essex, without this secret clue. It is the key which explains the tragedies which later overtook the Queen and her two sons.

The complete proofs for all these various statements respecting Queen Elizabeth, her marriage to the Earl of Leicester, and her motherhood, will be found in my book, *The Marriage of Elizabeth Tudor*, published by Rider and Company, London. The following works should also be consulted:

Dictionary of National Biography—various articles on Elizabeth, Leicester, etc.

Francis Bacon's Biliteral Cypher, by E. M. Gallup.

Uncrowned, by C. Y. C. Dawbarn, M.A.

The Early Life of Francis Bacon, by Parker Woodward.

Tudor Problems, by Parker Woodward.

Bacon's Secret Disclosed, by Granville C. Cunningham.

Shakespeare's Sonnet-Diary, tenth edition, by Alfred Dodd, *Daily Post* Printers, Wood Street, Liverpool.

Chapter III

FRANCIS BACON'S BIRTH AND EARLY CHILDHOOD (1561—1573)

Francis Bacon, the Glory of his Age and Nation, the Adorner and Ornament of Learning, *was borne in YORK HOUSE or YORK PLACE* in the Strand, on the two-and-twentieth day of January in the year of Our Lord, 1560 [i.e., 1561].

IN this pregnantly enigmatical sentence, Dr. Rawley begins his short biography of Francis Bacon. It was the first sketch of his life to be published in this country (1657), thirty-one years after his mysterious death in 1626. Dr. Rawley knew him intimately and personally. He had lived with him for years. He was his chaplain and private confidant. He was familiar with the secrets of his Birth, Life, and Death. He therefore speaks with authority; and everything he says respecting his master is worthy of our earnest study. Dr. Rawley, moreover, warns the reader that he is not going to publish all he knows in clear, set terms, for he says, "*I shall not tread too near upon the Heels of Truth.*"

He thus let it be known that this first English biography of our greatest Englishman is not going to be too exact in its details—a half-truth is to be told, a hint to be dropped, facts suppressed and phraseology employed that can be read in more ways than one. The inquiring student can ferret out his precise meaning if he be so minded. Dr. Rawley's chief concern was to make it clear to the world that there was far, far more hidden than revealed on the surface. In the first sentence he treads as near to the Heels of Truth as he dare. To have been more explicit would have brought down upon his head, in all probability, the wrath of State Authority and the destruction of the book by the Censor. He therefore writes a sentence likely to pass by every one save the "observant reader" to note and query.

What, then, does Dr. Rawley mean to infer when he wrote that "*Francis Bacon was born in YORK HOUSE or YORK PLACE?*"

He was giving us a straight hint of the utmost importance, without which consideration the life of Francis Bacon cannot be justly estimated or adequately appraised. If we fail to take the hint we can never hope to understand Francis Bacon. This is what Dr. Rawley wants you to consider: "*York House*" *was the home of Sir Nicholas Bacon.* "*York Place*" *was the Palace of Queen Elizabeth.* The inference that Francis Bacon's friend and confidant wishes you to draw is that his birth is shrouded in mystery; He was either born in York House the son of Lady Bacon or *he was born in the Royal Palace a Tudor Prince, his mother being the "Virgin Queen Elizabeth.*"

It is manifestly imperative that any biographer who wishes to understand Francis Bacon, to do full justice to him, should first of all inquire into Dr. Rawley's hint. If he were a concealed Prince, the fact must be taken into full consideration. Obviously, a Royal Tudor who masqueraded for sixty-three years as a commoner under a Bacon-Mask, not only alters our perspective of the Man and his Times, but the portrait is necessarily so radically changed, that new lights and fresh colours must be employed if we would trace aright the hidden emotions which were precipitated into his outward acts. We not only have to study him from an entirely new angle, see him in an entirely new light, but we have to re-create a different personality altogether from the portrait given to the world by modernists, totally oblivious of Dr. Rawley's adroit method of conveying a truth. If Francis Bacon lived a concealed life, it is as important to know it, and to understand it, as his open life, which different types of writers have worn threadbare. Both must be studied and told, for both intermingle. We want to know him as a complete whole and not in part.

It is therefore essential that a preliminary examination should be undertaken as to the value of the hint, its truth or untruth, left to posterity, by Dr. Rawley, before proceeding to the life as it is unfolded in the pages of history. That examination I undertook some time ago rigidly and critically. I found there was a plethora of evidence of all kinds, open facts of history, State Letters, documents from Continental Archives, and Cypher Records left in the printed books. . . . Secret Documents which were none the less valuable because they could not be read by persons who had never been initiated into reading Elizabethan Codes. This collated evidence is far too voluminous to be given here. Some of it is published as a separate volume entitled *The Marriage of Elizabeth Tudor.* The evidence proves conclusively that Dr. Rawley knew that Francis Bacon was a Tudor, was born in the Royal Palace, his mother being Queen Elizabeth. I did not find a single piece of evidence that militated against this view. All the facts pointed one way.

It is from this point of view that I write the story of his life. It alters history, but it provides a key of absorbing interest that unlocks many of the enigmas of that fascinating age.

The plain facts, established by the most rigorous inquiry, are that on the 22nd January, 1560-1, Queen Elizabeth gave birth to a boy, his father being Lord Robert Dudley (afterwards known as the Earl of Leicester), whom she had married privately at the house of Lord Pembroke about four months previously . . . a few days after the death of Dudley's wife, Amy Robsart, the 8th September, 1560. Though born in wedlock, the boy was nevertheless an adulterine bastard in law, the conception of a free union prior to marriage. For this reason—because the disclosure would have affected the honour of the Queen—his birth was concealed from the public. It became a State Secret. The Queen's marriage was also unknown save to a mere handful of her advisers. It was regarded as a private, morganatic union to be disregarded or openly acknowledged according to future circumstances, State requirements, and the Queen's Will. It was for the "Virgin Queen" herself to decide whether or not Dudley should be openly recognized as the Queen's Consort and his progeny acknowledged as next in the "Succession" to the English Throne.

The "Necessity of the Times" prevented her throughout her reign from declaring her marriage or the fruits of it. She was thus like Alexander the Great and Julius Cæsar, who left no legitimate Issue behind to succeed legally to the Throne but nevertheless had "Natural" Children of Royal Breed. This was Francis Bacon's own thought expressed *In Memory of Elizabeth* and published by Dr. Rawley in 1657.

Elizabeth's boy was endowed with an ancestry as distinguished for literary talent as any that can be found. Isabella, wife of Edward II, gave Edward III his brains. Catherine gave Henry VI his literary taste ". . . . whose *bookish* rule hath pulled fair England down," says Shakespeare. There was thus a double strain in his nature from the famous literary French Royal Line.

The royal blood of the House of Valois, the most literary family in France, flowed in Francis's veins from his great-grandmother Catherine, widow of Henry V, whose second husband was Owen Tudor. Their son was Henry VII, Elizabeth's grandfather. It is worth noting also that the education of Henry VIII was personally superintended by the illustrious Margaret Beaufort, his grandmother, who, as Countess of Richmond, was a patron of Caxton's successor, Wynkyn de Worde, who printed her books and translations. S. A. E. Hickson in *The Prince of Poets*, says:

> The hereditary predecessors of Queen Elizabeth show that there breathed in the genius of her Royal Veins the valour and virile wisdom of the Plantagenets, the distinguished literary taste of the French House of Valois, the indomitable will of the Tudors, the devout learning of Margaret, and the wit of Anne Boleyn.

The galaxy of various women, talented, brave, beautiful, accomplished, witty, learned, affectionate and devout, which surrounded the cradle when Francis was born, is astonishingly remarkable: Eleanor of Castile, Isabella of France, Philippa of Hainault, Katherine Swynford, Margaret Beaufort, Catherine de Valois, Elizabeth Woodville, Elizabeth of York, Anne Boleyn, Queen Elizabeth. "They form a real constellation of living women," says Hickson.

Sufficient has already been said to indicate that Elizabeth Tudor was one of the most remarkable women the world has ever seen. She possessed all the literary and intellectual gifts of her distinguished ancestry. From her childhood days she had been a student of literature, foreign languages and the classics. For two years her tutor was the celebrated Sir Roger Ascham. In the morning she studied Greek, beginning with the Greek Testament, then reading and translating classical authors like Sophocles and Demosthenes. Latin was the afternoon subject, Cicero, Livy, etc., with treatises on Theology and Statecraft. She was proficient in the French and Italian tongues, and later learnt Spanish. Ascham wrote to the famous Strasburg scholar Sturm:

> It is difficult to say whether the gifts of nature or of fortune are most to be admired in my distinguished mistress. The praise which Aristotle gives, wholly centres in her; beauty, stature, prudence, industry. She has just passed her sixteenth birthday and shows such dignity and gentleness as are wonderful at her age and in her rank. . . . Her perseverance is equal to that of a man, her memory long keeps what it quickly picks up. She

> talks French and Italian as well as she talks English, and has often talked to me readily and well in Latin, moderately in Greek.
>
> When she writes Greek and Latin nothing is more beautiful than her handwriting. She delights as much in music as she is skilful in it. . . . Her style of writing is one that grows out of the subject, chaste in its appropriateness, beautiful in its clarity. She admires, above all, modest metaphors and comparison of contraries well put together and contrasting felicitously one with another.

"*She had a taste for anagrams and such puerilities,*" says J. R. Green; which simply means, in other words, that she was familiar with Letter and Word Cyphers and Codes, a literary characteristic of the Elizabethan Age, employed extensively by the State to commit and preserve Secret Knowledge. They were far from being "puerilities" in those days. A knowledge of anagrammatic writing was necessary in order to ensure privacy of communication from prying eyes. "Every PRINCE has his CYPHER" was the phrase used by Francis Bacon in his later years to indicate that he possessed one. It was part of the training of every well-educated person.

If the baby Prince of Tudor was fortunate in his literary ancestors on his mother's side, he was in many respects fortunate in his father, Robert Dudley, who was the fifth son of John Dudley, Duke of Northumberland, and grandson of the notorious Edmund Dudley, lawyer and Privy Councillor, executed for treason by Henry VIII, Northumberland being executed by Queen Mary for a similar offence. Robert Dudley was inured to danger, a handsome, brave, clever, unscrupulous intellectual, with a love for learning and the fine arts. He became the greatest business-man of his time, the leader of that band of great soldiers who believed that England could defeat the world. He sent Drake round the globe and financed the voyage. It was largely through Leicester the belief was fostered that we could beat Spain, the then leader of the world, if we built a new navy. He was the patron of the Drama, of Sidney, Raleigh, Dyer, etc. He served Oxford University and was its Chancellor for a quarter of a century, giving it the first printing-press. "He was a renowned soldier before he was twenty-five," says Frederick Chamberlin, "A patriot of that rare kind who are always ready to contribute large sums of money to advance the fortunes of England." David Hume said that the Duke of Northumberland, Dudley's father, was the ablest man of his time after Henry VIII. So the immediate parents and grand-parents of the babe born at the Queen's Palace sprang from a perfect combination of the life forces that create GENIUS.

Spedding might well write in after years, "Francis Bacon could imagine like a poet and execute like a clerk of works."

When Francis was born, Lady (Anne) Bacon was the Head Lady-in-Waiting to Queen Elizabeth. She was the wife of Sir Nicholas Bacon, the Lord Keeper of the Great Seal. Their home, York House, stood next to York Place, the Royal Palace. Between the two residences ran their gardens, fields, and lanes. It was the easiest thing imaginable for the newly born babe in the Palace to be conveyed to the home of the Bacons without anyone being the wiser. The full dresses of the period served as excellent modesty garments to conceal approaching motherhood whether in the Queen or an assumption of motherhood by the Head Lady of the Chamber, who had an actual miscarriage at this time. Female figures were entirely hidden by the Elizabethan dresses. Round about this date, the records show that Elizabeth was in residence in the Palace. There were no State functions and no documents in Council to be signed by her.

Sir Nicholas and Lady Bacon promised to become foster-parents and were pledged to secrecy. The truth crops out in later years in many ways, by the actions of his foster-parents and the open hints of writers who knew the truth. Says the contemporary Thomas Fuller, divine, historian and wit:

> Sir Nicholas Bacon was, in a word, a *Father* of his country and *of Sir Francis Bacon,*

thus pointedly indicating adoption . . . "*a father*" to Francis, not "*the father.*"

The registration of the child was significant. . . . "Mr. Franciscus Bacon." Why should that singular prefix of "Mr." be put before his name—inserted specially—unless it were to mark the respect of the commoner responsible for the entry to a little Prince of the Blood Royal? For what other reason should it have been written? One cannot imagine any but foster-parents, fully acquainted with his identity, doing it. Sir Nicholas never designated his three baby sons by a former wife as "Mr. Nicholas," "Mr. Nathaniel," "Mr. Edward." Nor did he describe the boy born two years previously to Lady Anne as "Mr. Anthony." The "MR." was inserted for a purpose . . . for some good reason; and no historian has hitherto arisen to tell us the why and the wherefore.

In blissful ignorance of his real identity, "Mr. Francis," who first breathed English air in the Queen's Palace, began to be reared as a commoner amid the courtly glories of York House and at the country seat of Sir Nicholas and Lady Bacon at Gorhambury near St. Albans. And every day that passed riveted the Mask of Bacon over his Tudor personality, and hid his true identity more and more from the eyes of the world.

Sir Nicholas was aged fifty-one at the time of his birth. His first wife—a Jane Fernley of West Creting, Suffolk—had left him three sons and three daughters. At her death he was still an obscure bencher at Gray's Inn. But his second marriage to Anne Cooke, a sister to Lord Burleigh's second wife, marks the beginning of his rise in the world. Shortly after the birth of his first child Anthony, named after Anne's father, in 1558, Sir Nicholas received the Seals of Office, through the influence of Burleigh, Secretary of State.

His portrait is to be seen in the National Gallery. He is the very antithesis of Francis Bacon in form, build and feature. Judging by their physical characteristics it is as impossible for them to be father and son as for James I to be the "true-born" son of Mary Queen of Scots. Sir Nicholas was huge, gouty, asthmatic. He could not walk the short distance from York House to York Place without sitting down to rest. "My Lord Keeper's soul is well lodged," said Queen Elizabeth, laughingly . . . . "in Fat."

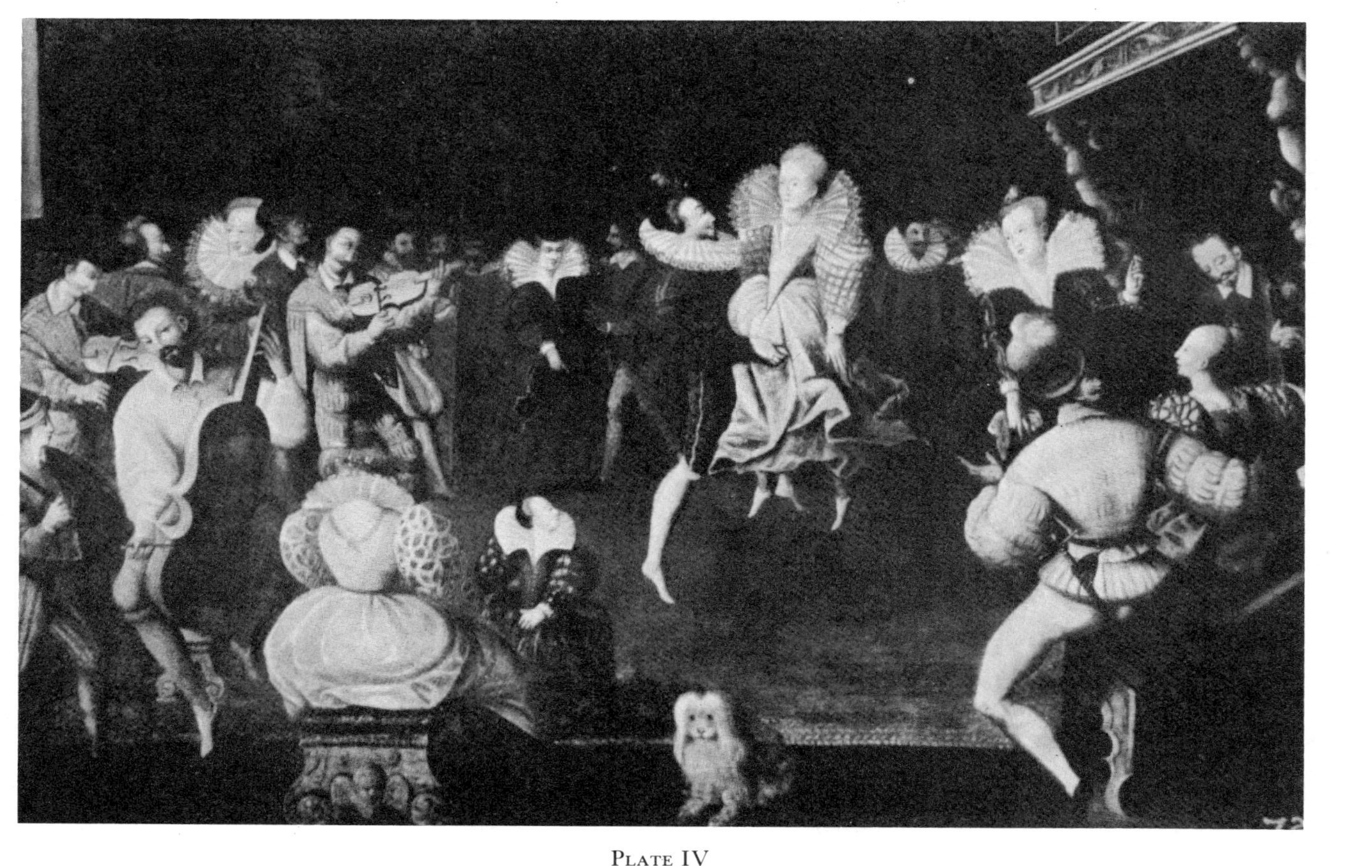

Plate IV
Queen Elizabeth dancing with the Earl of Leicester
From a painting by Zuchero at Penshurst Place, by kind permission of the Rt. Hon. Lord de L'Isle and Dudley
(See Appendix I)

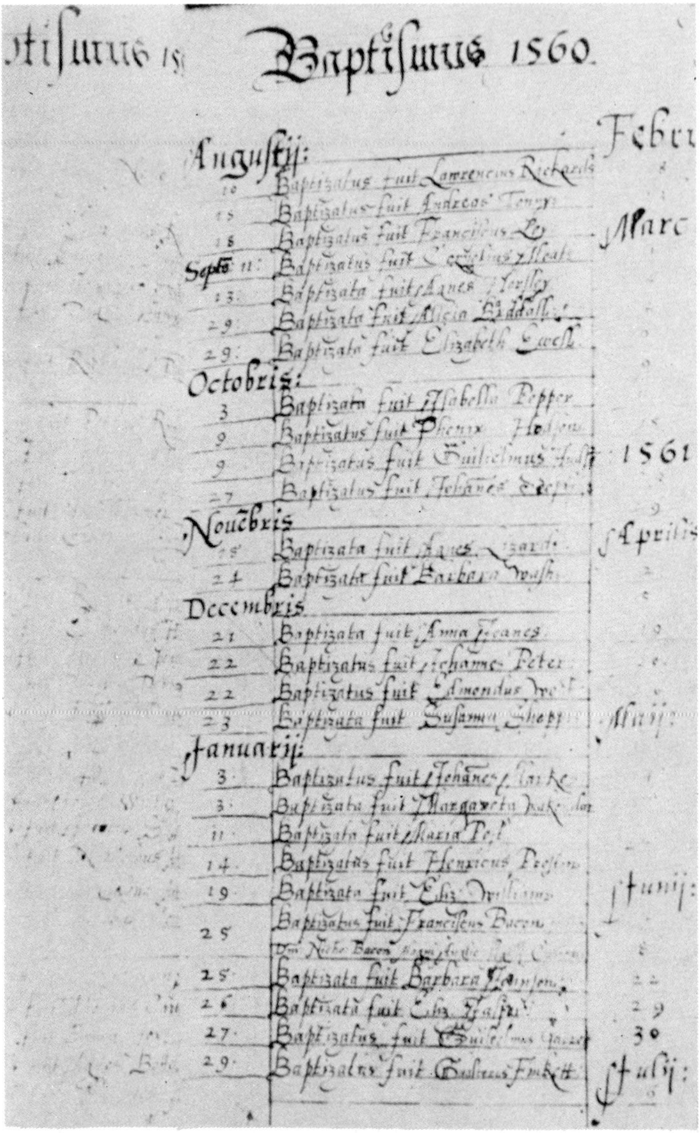

Plate V

The baptismal entry of Francis Bacon

(See Appendix I)

Though he was apparently slow and easy-going, as stout men usually are, he had nevertheless a quick, alert, progressive mind, full of humour and homely sense. He might be grossly fat but he had a cutting wit and was in no sense a "solemn judge" though he looked it. He held advanced views. He was a political lawyer devoted to the Queen; a sturdy religious Protestant though not a bigot. He was a believer in education and the broadening of its foundations for all . . . which is somewhat remarkable for those times. He presented a scheme for the endowment of a school of law, policy and languages, a State School for political studies. It was a plan for the foundation of a *great college to train Statesmen along definite educational lines*. It was probably the germ of the secret schemes covertly told in the *New Atlantis*.

Francis Bacon wrote of him:

> All the world noted Sir Nicholas Bacon to be a man plain, direct and constant without all fineness and doubleness; and one that was of the mind that a man in his private proceedings and in the proceedings of State should rest upon the soundness and strength of his own courses and not upon practice to circumvent others.

Sir Nicholas was a scholar who revelled in the classics and was held in high esteem on account of his profound learning and wisdom.

> He was a learned lawyer and a true gentleman [says Basil Montagu], of a mind the most comprehensive to sound the merits of a case; of a memory to recollect the least essential; of the deepest search into affairs of any man at the Council Table and of a personal dignity well suited to his other excellencies.

The mysterious "Puttenham," who writes with first-hand knowledge of Sir Nicholas's country seat, says:

> I have come to my Lord Keeper and have found him sitting in his Gallery alone with the works of Quintilian before him. Indeed, he was a most eloquent man, and of a rare learning and wisdom as ever I knew England to breed, and one that joyed much in learned men and men of good wits.

Of this sagacious man and sound scholar, with his easy temperament and quick repartee, people said with truth, "Some men look wiser than they are . . . the Lord Keeper is wiser than he looks." One of his favourite expressions was "Stay a little that we may make haste the sooner." He went to his death-bed with a jest on his lips, having caught a chill through falling asleep by an open window. "Why did you leave me thus exposed?" he asked his servant. "Because I durst not disturb you." "Then by your civility I lose my life," said Sir Nicholas with a whimsical smile.

One story is recorded by Francis Bacon:

> A malefactor mightily importuning the Judge on the Northern Circuit, Sir Nicholas Bacon, to save his life . . . desired mercy on account of kindred. "Prethee," said my Lord the Judge, "How came that in?" "Why if it please your Lordship, your name is Bacon and mine is Hog, and in all ages Hog and Bacon have been so near kindred that they should not be separated."

"Ay!" replied Judge Bacon, "but you and I cannot be kindred except you be HANGED, for HOG is not BACON until it be well HANGED."

This story is alluded to in the Shakespeare Play *Merry Wives*. "Hing, hang dog; HANG-HOG is latten for BACON, I warrant you."

In many respects "Mr. Francis" was fortunate in being reared in the household of a great civil servant and a very solid type of politician, where quips, jests and word-play were part of the mental atmosphere. He slowly developed into a little philosopher, but he was a "Laughing Philosopher" and not a grave one of severe mien. The academic picture that he was from his cradle a solemn little prig is ludicrously false. Many of his biographers cannot believe that he was once a healthy little boy who romped, laughed, and played, naturally becoming infected with the home atmosphere of mirth. The real truth is well expressed by Dr. Abbott: "Francis was probably indebted to Sir Nicholas for his placid self-control and *his rich humour*."

Later in life these quizzical characteristics—born with him and stimulated into expression by a congenial environment—became so pronounced that Ben Jonson wrote this tribute to his jesting wit:

> His language was nobly censorious *when he could pass by a JEST.*

We thus know that in adult life Francis Bacon seldom missed an opportunity to be merry with words and phrases. And since we know that it is out of the fullness of the heart that the mouth speaketh, he must have been a very happy and lovable little boy. Indeed, the early atmosphere of jest and *bon mots* in which he was cradled, played so important a part in his life, that, as becomes an inveterate jester, he gradually learned how to play with words and phrases—by pen and by tongue—as a juggler does with balls . . . to flash more than one meaning. This ruling passion was strong in old age. One morning, after a night's illness, he dictated no fewer than 308 anecdotes, says Dr. Rawley, who published them in 1671.

> *This collection his Lordship made out of his memory without turning any book.*

Lord Macaulay declared in 1848 that it reigned supreme as "*the best collection of jests in the world.*"

Here we find the necessary circumstances, combined with a peculiar strain of mind derived from his mother, that were the pre-requisites for creating the humorous wisdom of Shakespeare's fools and clowns. Hitherto, we have thought so much of Francis Bacon the Philosopher, the Father of the Sciences, the dry-as-dust Lawyer, the great Chancellor, "the Wisest Head in Christendom," that we have totally ignored the lighter side of his nature which fruited in a jest-book *par excellence*, proving him to be a raconteur of the first quality. One can easily believe him to be the creator of the "Social Degree of Modern Freemasonry," for no one knew better than he the value of Harmony and Mirth in drawing men together, and the understanding friendships that arise round a "Social Board."

An even greater influence than Sir Nicholas was his foster-mother, Lady Bacon. She was of higher birth and incomparable in character. She was the daughter of Sir Anthony Cooke of Geddy Hall, Essex, a governor and tutor to Edward VI, a Greek scholar. The Cooke family were connected with Stratford, being large landowners. She was a perfect housewife, as well as being a clever scholar, equally at home with her stewpans and maids in the kitchen as in the study with Greek and Italian literature. She had actually been tutor to young King Edward. Her sister had the reputation of being the most learned woman in England after Lady Jane Gray.

Lady Bacon was a woman of strong character. Her accomplishments were many and varied. She was familiar with classical and modern languages. In her private letters she quotes Latin freely and naturally. In her twenty-second year she translated and published Ochinos' *Sermons* from the Italian. When Francis was two or three years old she was occupied in translating, from the original Latin, Bishop Jewell's *Apology for the Church of England.* Her fame as a literary woman was such that Theodore Beza, some years after this, dedicated to her his *Meditations.*

She was a deeply religious woman, strictly Puritanical, though not herself a Puritan. She could not tolerate a Papist. Rome and the things of Rome were utterly repugnant to her. Her piety appears to have grown stronger as she grew older. She was one of God's good women. "A very Saint of God," says Francis. No one could have had a more loving foster-mother than Lady Bacon and a stauncher foster-brother than Anthony in those early years. Indeed, as glimpses of her correspondence show, her sons always remained children to her, to be mothered even when they were grown men-of-the-world with the maturity which springs from books, travel and the rubbing of shoulders with many diverse characters. When they were at Gray's Inn, she sent them foods, delicacies, pills, game from her own larder, home-brewed beer from her own vats. She lectured them on what they should eat and drink, when to purge and let blood, how far they should ride or walk, what time to retire and when to rise from bed. She warned them against attending masques and revels and such-like sinful vanities.

In Lady Bacon's cultured, scholarly home the two boys saw the day begin with family prayers. We can well believe that it was ended with stories of Classical Adventures, Morality Tales, and the Ancient Myths in which both parents were saturated; for the writings of Francis Bacon are steeped in the Ancient Wisdom which forms the background of the Royal Art of Masonry. The household of Sir Nicholas shone with the beauty of holiness . . . a veritable sanctuary in those dark Tudor days of intrigue, hypocrisy, corruption and vulgar debauchery. Francis learned the principles of Christian Ethics at his foster-mother's knee. In his childish imaginings he wove early the Symbol and Allegory of the Mysteries with the fundamental precept of Charity . . . the New Commandment.

Lady Bacon died in 1610, over eighty, "being little better than frantic in her old age," says Bishop Goodman. She had then been for years under the care of Francis.

A very important matter, which gave a bent to the mind of the growing boy, must now be considered. Its influence on the impressionable life, now unfolding and expanding, has never been fully stressed. But from what we now know of Francis Bacon's adult life, it played an important part in his intellectual development. It taught him how to attain complete self-expression of his mental activities without anyone being the wiser. He learned the first steps of secrecy, the joy of writing, the thrill of anonymous authorship, from the example of his parents.

Not only was Lady Bacon an author, but so was her husband. They were not merely authors but *they were CONCEALED AUTHORS.*

> Lady Anne Bacon made several learned translations from Latin and Italian but withheld her full name [says Rev. W. Begley] and *Sir Nicholas is supposed to have made use of a living contemporary MASK to HIDE his authorship of a certain political treatise.* (*Is it Shakespeare*, p. 320).

One book Sir Nicholas wrote gave such great offence to the Queen, that it caused a stay in his fortunes for some time, preventing him from becoming a Privy Councillor. His subsequent writings were therefore anonymous.

This incident naturally became one of the private family lessons for all to take to heart. It was a well-remembered item. Without a doubt Sir Nicholas would warn the two boys Anthony and Francis against the temptation of open authorship respecting subjects likely to be controversial, especially politics, religion or affairs of State. Its importance would not be lost on the quick mind of Francis. The home example of the "stay of Sir Nicholas" pointed the danger of using one's own name when putting pen to paper. It taught him to follow his parents' example who were content to become anonymous writers. . . . Better still, completely to veil one's identity, *by hiding behind the personality of a living man who was paid for the use of his name;* a stranger to become the putative father of another man's brain-child . . . a mental creation, a book.

Francis, moreover, would learn quite early the use of CYPHERS, for Lady Bacon, "occasionally, also, *for SECRESY writes English in Greek characters when she wishes to speak her mind freely about great people or dangerous subjects.*" (Dr. Abbott, *Bacon*, p. 12). It was at the knee of Lady Bacon that he had his first lessons in the manipulation of Secret Codes, and that he profited by it is certain; for, years later, she writes to Anthony:

> I send herein your brother's letter. Construe the interpretation. I do not understand *his enigmatical folded writing.* Let him return me a PLAIN answer. (18th April, 1593).

With these facts in mind, we can better understand Francis Bacon's statement that he who has a secret business to perform should "DO IT UNDER A MASK." It is an echo of what he was taught at home. It made Sir Nicholas into a concealed Author and Lady Anne into a Cypherist. In the Bacon household Francis began early to learn the art of "Dissimulation" on which he writes afterwards an Essay packed with adroit Masonic allusions.

> He was, so to speak, *nurtured in an atmosphere of Secret or Concealed Authorship.* Francis was nothing if not anonymous.

In a sense, it can be said, with literal truth, that he drank in with his foster-mother's milk the urge to authorship, secret authorship, cypher codes, and dissimulation.

It must not be supposed that Queen Elizabeth, though remaining *in umbra*, was uninterested in her offspring. There are strong grounds for belief that Sir Roger Ascham, the Queen's old tutor, the finest educationist and scholar in that age, had a sort of watching brief in the child's educational development. It was at the direct command of the Queen that he wrote his celebrated classic *The Schoolmaster. It deals with the education of young noblemen.* Ascham was invited to dinner at Windsor Castle. He was there pressed by a Privy Councillor to write a book "concerning the right order of teaching." He declined and excused himself whereupon he "was suddenly called to the Queen. The night following I slept little, my head so full of our talk."

The fact that the command was made in the Queen's Privy Chamber, and the book intended to be dedicated to the Queen, suggests she was directly interested in a curriculum for the training of one particular nobleman . . . Francis Bacon, who was two years of age when Ascham began his task. He was five years old when the book was finished . . . about 1566. The author died two years later. It still remained in manuscript for private use until 1571, when it was printed. But the prefatory letter entitled *Divae Elizabethae* dated 30th October, 1566, was suppressed. It was kept carefully in hiding for two hundred years when it was published by James Bennet in 1761.

The suppressed preface (which simply dare not have been published in his day) was left as a record and a hint of his knowledge of the Queen's Secret, and that he had been commissioned to do the work for the training of her concealed son. He compares her to David who committed adultery and murder to obtain Bathsheba. . . . "God suffered him to fall into the deepest pit of wickedness, the shamefullest adultery . . . as in a mirror may your Majesty see and acknowledge, by God's dealing with David, *even very many like dealings of God with your Majesty.* And in the end have as David had . . . Prosperity and surest Felicity for you and YOUR POSTERITY."

This letter was written to a VIRGIN QUEEN with no prospect of posterity openly. What had the sin of David to do with a Virgin Queen? Was Amy Robsart the Elizabethan Uriah? Sufficient is said to indicate that Ascham writes the book in the hope that it will train the boy who had the natural right to sit on the Throne of the Tudors. And that he was so trained is proved by the fact that "it contains to an astonishing extent the elements of Francis Bacon's philosophy." Hickson, *Prince of Poets*, p. 20.

So the training of the boy Francis was mapped out in good time, on lines approved by the first educationist of the day, in a literary atmosphere of piety and scholarship, with the love of devoted foster-parents who did not know but that one day he might pass the veils of secrecy and be called to the Throne. It is pleasing to think that the mother-love of the Queen quietly manifested itself in the care of her offspring.

But apart from the personal living influences mirroring themselves in him, drawing out the noblest and the best, there was the home itself and its environs that also played a notable part in quickening his mental activities. York House had a history. It was a noble building originally intended, in ancient times, for a Bishop's Inn. It reverted to the Crown and "King Harry thought it too sumptuous for a prelate, and gave it to the gay Charles Brandon, lover and husband of his beautiful sister Mary, the Queen of France." With the accession of Mary it went to the Roman Catholic Lord Chancellor and Archbishop of York, Nicholas Heath. On his fall, it went to Sir Nicholas Bacon by lease.

This house, situate in the Strand, was a fief of the Crown.

> The courtyard and the great gates opening to the street; the main front with its turrets, facing the river. The garden of unusual size and splendour, fell by an easy slope to the Thames, and commanded as far South as the Lollards Tower, as far East as London Bridge.
>
> All the gay river life swept past the lawn; the shad-fishers spreading their nets, the watermen paddling gallants to Bankside, the city barges rowing past in procession, and the Queen herself, with her train of lords and ladies, shooting by in her journeys from the Tower to York Place (then known as "Whitehall") stairs. From the lattice out of which he gazed, the child Francis could see, over the Whitehall Palace roof, the pinnacles and crosses of the Old Abbey. (Hepworth Dixon, *Francis Bacon*, p. 14).

All along the river front stretched great houses and palaces taken from the Roman Catholic hierarchy at the time of the Reformation. Their front entrances ran along the Strand with gardens reaching to the Thames. The river was the main and easiest means of communication between London and the Tower, and the Queen's Palaces at Greenwich, Hampton Court, Richmond and Windsor. The area next to the Whitehall Palace (York Place), where Francis was born, consisting of fields, lanes and gardens, was known as Scotland Yard. Then came Francis Bacon's home, York House; Durham House, the residence of the Bishop of Durham, Bedford House, the Old Savoy Palace, Somerset House, Arundel House, Leycester House, afterwards known as Essex House. It belonged to the Earl of Leicester, and was afterwards occupied by the Queen's second son by Leicester, Robert, Earl of Essex.

They were irregularly and picturesquely built, some on the edge of the river, and others sweeping to the Thames in broad lawns and gardens of great beauty. Their sites are now marked by the names of modern streets, York House being now named Buckingham Street and Villiers Street after the arrogant, upstart Earl who was one of the men responsible for Francis Bacon's political assassination.

> Between Leycester House and the dividing wall of the City was a large area forming *the centre and residence of the KNIGHTS TEMPLARS*, but in Sir Francis Bacon's time it was occupied by the barristers, ancients and law-students of the Temple. (P. Woodward, *Life*, p. 7).

Farther east was another large area of Crown property, entered through postern gates, guarded in the daytime and locked at nights. It was once the home of the community of the Black Friars, prior to their suppression, with large refectories and residential chambers. Court Officials resided there such as Lord Cobham and the Earl of Oxford.

In Sir Francis Bacon's day it should be noted that in London and Westminster the population did not number more than two hundred thousand, the residents being very spread out save within the City boundaries. The nation did not number more than five millions.

The forces of the great world-spirit that were remoulding the civilizations of Europe, together with the particular influences creating a modern England out of the swiftly dying Feudal Era, played a powerful part in the lives of all Englishmen living in this transitional period. They were particularly mirrored in Francis Bacon as he grew from youth to manhood and old age. But the important factor—because it was the more direct one—was the immediate environment of his parents, relatives, and friends; the home and its environs in which he was cradled to adolescence. Heredity and early surroundings were never more important for any man in determining the mental outlook and secret impulses that out-flamed in his adult life.

Apart from home influence, he lived at the very hub of national life. He was reared in an atmosphere of fervid, aristocratic patriotism and loyalty to Queen and country. His sensitive nature and expanding mind naturally reacted to the stress and strain of those critical years which laid the foundations of England's greatness, her ultimate triumphant emergence from her life-and-death conflict with Spain. As a babe, his thoughts must have mingled with those of statesmen, nobles and the highest dignitaries. As a child, his ears must often have caught the hushed whispers of State Secrets. As a growing boy, he knew intimately all the famous sailors, soldiers, scholars, lawyers, and politicians who were preparing quietly to challenge the greatest maritime nation in the world. Before the eyes of young Francis there passed continually an ever-brilliant galaxy of princes, lords, ladies, ambassadors—even the pomp and pageantry of the "Virgin Queen's" Royal Court.

We can see the two boys, Francis the genius and Anthony of rare talents, growing up together in this wonderful old residence of memories, with its ever-changing panorama of scene and incident, each a foil to the other's wit, "steel sharpening steel." They played in those beautiful historic gardens that were washed by our greatest national river. They saw the ships go sailing by, not only to the great centres of civilization, the Hague, Paris, Cadiz and Venice, but to those far-flung lands of romance and imagination "The Fortunate Isles." Under the spell of Father Thames, they were destined to develop into Francis Bacon's Masonic Romance of the *Island of Bensalem* or *The Land of the Rosicrosse.* (*The New Atlantis*).

Francis thus became early familiar with the picturesque symbol of England's greatness, the Royal River with its busy tide of adventurous activity, its varied craft, its Royal Barges and noble retinues, even the flotsam and jetsam of humanity—all calculated to quicken the blood and stir the pools of Fancy in his heart. When he was nine years of age the famous conferences on the complicity of Mary Queen of Scots in the death of Darnley were opened at York House. Two years later he probably saw the Duke of Norfolk taken to the Tower from Westminster sentenced to death for treason. The barge passed the garden stairs of York House with the headsman's uplifted axe turned towards the Duke. Think what these incidents would mean to the poetic imagination "of the most exquisitely constructed brain ever vouchsafed by God to man."

But the first seeds of something equally important were also sown in that wonderful mind that revelled with symbol and metaphor in after-years. Around him and about was the sacred ground that reeked with the mysteries and chivalries of the famous Templar Knights, whose animated dust beneath his feet still vibrated with the old Templar Chant:

Take thy shoes from off thy feet,
For the Place whereon thou stand'st
Is Holy Ground. . . .

He was cradled but a stone's throw away from the beautiful Temple Chapter House, which is to be seen to-day, with all its Medieval impressiveness.[1] As a child he would see their tombs almost daily in the little Temple and the effigies of past Crusaders who once engaged in a Holy War . . . still and quiet yet vibrant with life. Two features would strike him early for they would meet him at every turn, the solid reality and ancient dignity of York, the head of the Ecclesiastical North, so many miles removed from the regal splendour of the south, through well-nigh trackless country; and the solemn mystery of the Knights Templar, with their Ancient Chapter House, their rites and ceremonial, their swords and their spears, robes, ideals and crusades that revolved round a Holy Sepulchre and the rebuilding of Solomon's Temple.

We cannot tell what subtle currents of thought may have touched his soul before the "shades of the prison house began to close upon the growing boy," but we can picture the nebulous fancies that would begin to crystallize in his "mind ever nimble and versatile." York and the Knights would create definite pictures. After-events prove that they gave a new setting of the Rites of Ancient York Masonry and a resurrected Templar Degree of Christian Chivalry in the Higher Orders of Freemasonry. Here we see the first *motifs* towards the rôle which he afterwards adopted with such success that "the Uninstructed World" has never suspected it . . . *the rôle of a Concealed Ethical Teacher.* And when we learn that his pet name was once "Baby Solomon" we are provided with another strand in the weaving of the undoubted truth that Francis Bacon, who was afterwards known as the Solomon of his age, was a "SOLOMON" in a specific Masonic sense, the creator of the Rosicrucian and Masonic Fraternities that arose in his life in *their new garbs and framed in Modern English.*

The babe thus grew up in a perfect home environment of sweetness and light, amid the beauties of nature, art, music, sounds and sights of adventure, his mind saturated with the customs and manners of the Court of Elizabeth (as we shall presently see) and the proud histories of Kings and Queens, "in blazon of sweet beauties best." Wherever he looked there were around him poems of stone, truly "the Chronicles of Wasted Time" which sang "the praises of Ladies Dead and Lovely Knights." And he also saw what no other child did in that Era, save his brother Anthony . . . *he saw at first hand history in the making*, for the Lord Keeper was one of the men who directed the early years of Queen Elizabeth: To his home came all the great notables of the day, peers and lords, the Earl of Leicester, Lord Burleigh, Drake, the Earls of

[1]Wrecked by German bombs since this was written.

Oxford, Southampton, Rutland, Derby, Northampton, Pembroke and many others of the highest social circles.

The saturation of Francis Bacon's mind with all this royal splendour was completed by the Queen herself.

About the time she commanded Sir Roger Ascham to write his educational book on the training of young noblemen, *she also commanded Sir Nicholas Bacon to build a country seat for himself at Gorhambury* which lies under the shadow of St. Albans, so that she could meet her boy privately in the heart of the countryside, in those happy home familiarities which mean so much, without arousing untoward suspicions.

The style of the building "was most carefully calculated to inspire the inmates and residents with naturally imbibed taste, alike for classical literature and art, as well as for the more modern sciences," says Hickson.

Pennant, who visited Gorhambury in 1780, describes the building as consisting of two parts discordant in manner yet in various respects of a classical taste.

> On the outside of the part which forms the approaches is the piazza or porticos with a range of Pillars of the *Tuscan Order* (one of the Orders named in Freemasonry) in front, where the philosophic inhabitants walked and held their learned discourse. . . . The walls of the piazza are painted al fresco with *the Adventures of Ulysses.* [This reminds one at once of Hermes and the Mysteries].

We are now faced with a further startling fact which is definitely related to Speculative Freemasonry.

> *A little Banqueting House* adorned with great curiosity, having *THE LIBERAL ARTS* beautifully depicted on its walls, stood in the orchard, the pictures which adorned it being of *such MEN as had excelled* in each. Under them were verses expressive of the benefits derived from the study of them as Geometry, Arithmetic, Logic, Music, Rhetoric, Grammar, and Astronomy. (Nichols, *Queen Elizabeth*, vol. ii, p. 56).

Whether these pictures were placed in the Banqueting Hall by Sir Nicholas or by Francis when he afterwards came into possession of the home, cannot now be determined. But the direct association of the "Liberal Arts" with "St. Alban"—for Francis Bacon afterwards became Viscount St. Alban—is of profound Masonic significance to all Masons, the majority of whom are as unacquainted with the Founder of Modern Freemasonry as are the "cowans and intruders" to the Royal Art. There were not only Tuscan Pillars (probably Doric, Ionic, Corinthian also) but paintings of the classical Myths associated with the Mysteries, *the background of Freemasonry*, and, spread before the eyes pictorially, were the SEVEN LIBERAL ARTS AND SCIENCES known to the Modern Mason. This fact constitutes direct proof that Francis Bacon was aware of the very names that Masons recite in their Lodges to-day. It is an interesting indication of how they crept into the Masonic Ritual.

What other Lord, "Gentleman," operative Mason or craft guild member, had been associated prior to or within this Era with the very principles Freemasons espouse to-day? None! It is one of the first significant hints of Freemasonry as we know it, the first connective link between the "Gentlemen," with their knowledge of the "Liberal Arts," and the suppressed masonry of the working operatives. Modern Freemasonry—rites, ceremonial, lodge organization—was created as an Ethical System during the reign of Queen Elizabeth by someone hitherto unknown.

The Garden of Gorhambury provides further evidence of the close connection between the Mysteries and Freemasonry as imaged in the mind of the Founder of the Craft. At the entrance stood a statue of ORPHEUS, "THE SUPPOSED FOUNDER OF THE MYSTERIES." Says Warburton (*Divine Legation*, Book II, section iv): "Orpheus instituted the Mysteries . . . first brought the Mysteries from Egypt into Thrace."

Orpheus having been presented by Apollo with the Lyre, was instructed by THE MUSES in its use, and Francis Bacon continues the fable in *The Wisdom of the Ancients* by saying:

> So great was the power and alluring force of this HARMONY that he drew the Woods and *moved the VERY STONES to come and place themselves in an orderly and decent fashion about him . . . .*
>
> The most excellent remedy, in every temptation, is that of Orpheus, who, by loudly chanting, and resounding the praises of the Gods, confounded the voices, and kept himself from hearing the music of the Sirens; for *Divine Contemplations exceed the pleasures of sense,* not only in power but also in sweetness.

"Harmony" and "Lyre" are particularly Masonic expressions. There is thus a distinct hint that *the Ethical Stones of Masonry were brought together by a Harmony produced by the MUSES—i.e.,* by Poesy, the poetic expression of symbols, allegory, trope, metaphor and fabled history which we find woven in the Masonic Ritual of Elizabethan expression.

Says W. F. C. Wigston in *Bacon and the Rosicrucians* [p. 276]:

> Orpheus was therefore a fit Emblem of the most inspired Poetry and particularly the Platonic or Love Philosophy, and nothing could be more appropriate than thus to hear of his Statue at Gorhambury.
>
> Under this Statue was a wonderful piece of Latin verse, which, adds Wigston, "*may have first implanted in his mind the idea to write Philosophical Play Systems to illustrate the Orphic* (Love) *theology.*"

It inspired not only Immortal Plays but particularly the Rituals of Masonry which are poetic interpretations of "Love Philosophy" or Charity.

It is a striking historical fact for every Freemason to ponder that St. Alban's Abbey and Gorhambury (named from Geoffrey de Gorham, a Bishop of St. Albans who built Gorhambury Abbey) is regarded as the birthplace and cradle of Freemasonry in England *by Masonic Tradition* together with the story of a martyrdom that revolved round a Christian St. Alban in A.D. 303. The stories are purposely mixed in a variety of ways, the Saxon and the Elizabethan; and the Proto-Martyr of St. Alban of A.D. 303 with Francis Bacon, the St. Alban Elizabethan Martyr of A.D. 1621, who became a political sacrifice for others.

"*I may now be buried in SAINT ALBAN'S HABIT* as he lived," wrote Lord St. Alban some time after the Viscountcy was conferred upon him.

The City of St. Albans, known in Roman days as Verulam, was named after St. Alban the Martyr, *and is an old operative centre.* The saint is mentioned in the Shakespeare Play of *Henry VI* (*Part II*), the scene being cast in St. Albans, a miracle being wrought at the shrine of the saint.

> QUEEN: Tell me *Good Fellow,* cam'st thou here by chance or of devotion to *this Holy Shrine?*
> SIMCOT: God knows of pure devotion, being called a hundred times and oftener, in my sleep *by good Saint Alban.*

The original St. Albans Abbey was erected in the eighth century by King Offa and the Hond operative masons to the memory of St. Alban. *It stood but a stone's throw from the site Sir Nicholas Bacon had selected for his Gorhambury home; and it was IN RUINS. The old Abbey thus served as a quarry for Sir Nicholas.* His Mansion was constructed out of the very stones of this ancient Christian Temple. As a child Francis doubtless accompanied Sir Nicholas often to the site of the "new home," and would watch it growing under his very eyes.

His searching mind would quickly have become acquainted with the history of the Abbey; the saint to whom it was dedicated; the fact that the operative Hond masons had built it; that the stones of his home were "Holy Ones"; that they bore the mysterious MARKS of an ancient Craft of Temple Builders, members of an ancient Guild that had long passed into oblivion, smashed by a series of legislative enactments. *The fact that Sir Nicholas Bacon's new home was actually called "THE TEMPLE," is of profound significance.*

The name was chosen because of its direct association with a ruined temple consecrated to the worship of "The Most High." We may be quite sure that young Francis knew why his home was so named. And it is more than probable that the germ of the idea of "Solomon's House" and "Solomon's Temple"—which played such a great part in his life in later years—was partly created through the association of ideas that revolved round the home of his childhood.

Living in an ancient operative centre, where the stones of his home cried out their ancient history, it is easy to believe that such historic incidents, impingeing on his extraordinary mind, caused him to conceive quite early the idea to revivify operative masonry in another form, and thus rebuild a ruined Temple speculatively with "Gentlemen" Craftsmen. Later, as a youth, when the Elizabethan *Act of the Apprentices* had swept away the last vestiges of the operative craft, which had stretched backwards through the Medieval Guilds to "time immemorial" . . . he would realize *he had an absolutely clear field* to begin the rebuilding of the Temple of King Solomon, with a Brotherhood of "Gentlemen," Speculative not operative Masons, whose work would consist in moralizing on tools and spiritualizing temples.

The curious, eager mind of Francis Bacon would no more be indifferent to the associations of his Temple Home, the Ancient Abbey, the craft workers, the Medieval Guild, that seemed to stretch its roots into the Ancient Mysteries, than a magnet could be indifferent to fragments of iron. These historic facts constitute clear motives prompting him to saturate himself with the mystery of the "Masons' Marks," the guilds in England and the Continent, their operative lodges, their rules and regulations, their Festivals on Saints' Days, their Annual Assembly (!), their Signs, Tokens, and Passwords.

There is another significant fact which should not be overlooked in dealing with the concealed labours of Francis Bacon and St. Albans as the cradle of the Speculative Art. The Town Coat of Arms is the Cross of St. Andrew. A St. Andrew's Cross formed the Arms of Johann Valentine Andrea, *i.e.*, St. Andreas (or St. Andrew) who is *supposed* to be the writer of the *Fama Fraternitatis* (1614) and the Founder of Rosicrucianism. Andrea was not, however, the real author or the Founder. He was a Mask for someone else who used the Cross of St. Andrew in one of the Higher Masonic Degrees as a "Knight of St. Andrew." We thus get a most suggestive hint of the connection between Freemasonry and Rosicrucianism and also between English and Scottish Masonry with its ancient centre of St. Andrews. The Cross shows the real origin of the Continental Rosicrucian Manifestos—St. Albans; and the writer, Francis Bacon.

An even more important factor in the formative influences at work in the moulding of the mind of the young genius were the natural surroundings of "The Temple"—it was built in "the Garden of England"—within easy distance of great houses built by noblemen with which he was certain to become familiar. There were at least two where he would be welcomed as a relative, Gidea Hall, fifteen miles away, the home of Sir Anthony Cooke, the father of Lady Bacon and Lady Burleigh—a personal friend of Queen Elizabeth; and "Theobalds," the home of Lord Burleigh—the Secretary of State and Sir Nicholas Bacon's brother-in-law.

"Theobalds" lay nine miles away at Cheshunt, one of the most wonderful, beautiful and short-lived palaces in England. (It was destroyed by Cromwell). It had only been built and completed shortly before the home of Sir Nicholas was finished. It stood in a series of splendid gardens with mirrors, fountains, summer houses, a great variety of trees and plants, water, boats and labyrinths . . . costly, beautiful and pleasant, a maze garden and a pheasant garden. Such is the description of S. A. E. Hickson.

In the *Homes of the Cecils*, Fox-Davies says:

> All visitors extol its magnificence, its numerous buildings and galleries, its artistic paintings of all the most important and remarkable towns in Christendom. *ITS CEILINGS WITH SIGNS OF THE ZODIAC AND STARS* proper for each, even furnished with mechanism *to give motion TO THE SUN*, walls decorated with trees to imitate Nature and Birds also.

It was at his "Uncle Burleigh's home" that the young genius first saw the painted ceiling representative of "the Starry Firmament" which afterwards became the proper covering of a Freemason's Lodge. The Sun in motion across the starry ceiling would be one of those outstanding mechanical devices that such a boy as Francis could never forget. It became the "All-Seeing EYE" of the Speculative Craft, so wonderfully alluded to in Shakespeare's Sonnets as the Emblem of Creative Power. . . . "An Eye more bright than the Eye of a False Woman, less false in rolling its orbit than the shifty glad-eye of such a woman, for it GILDS the

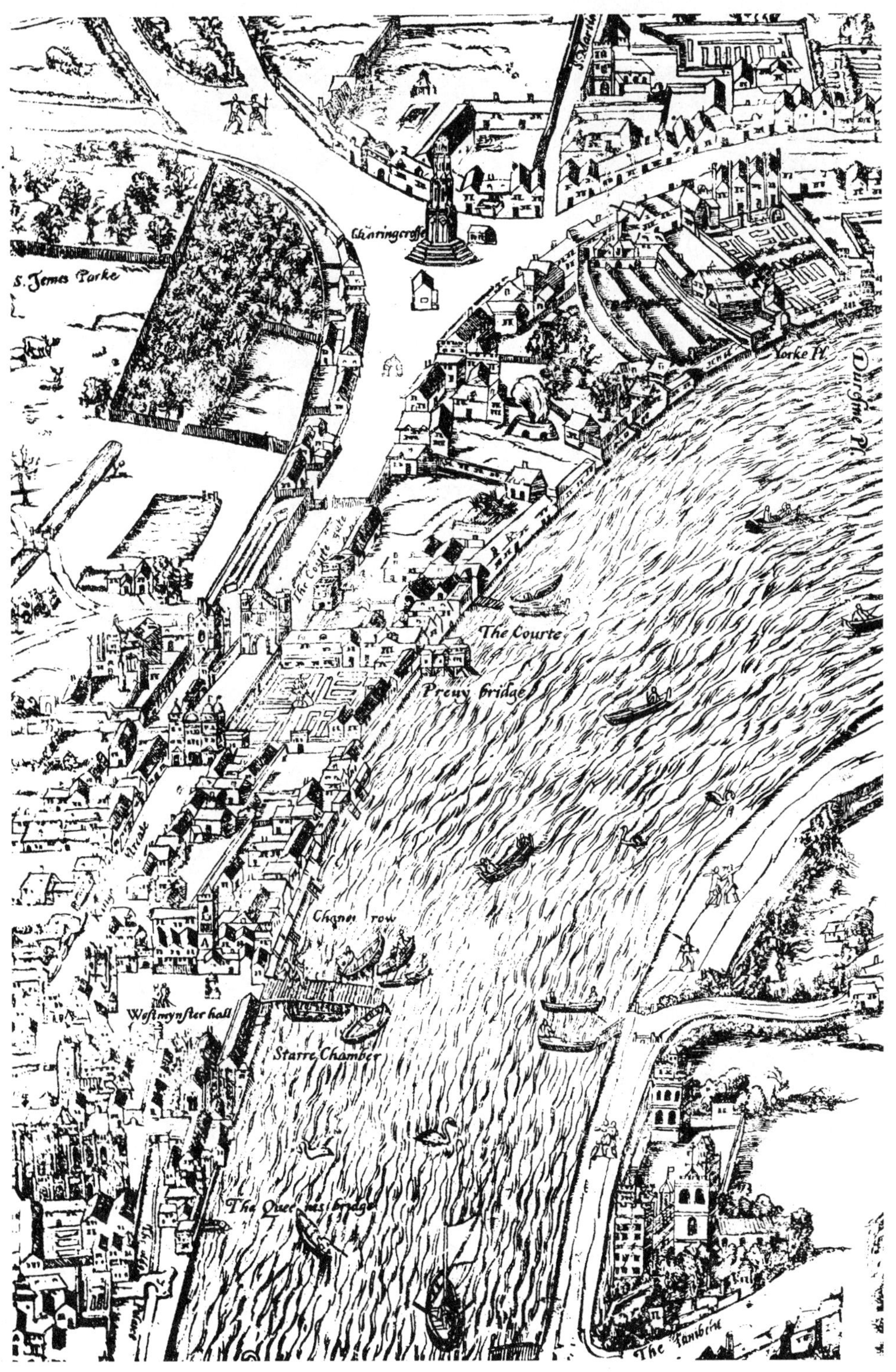

PLATE VI
Part of a map showing York Place and the Court
by Ralph Agas (circa. 1560)
(See Appendix I)

Plate VII
Henry the VIII by an unknown artist
(Royal Portrait Gallery)
(See Appendix I)

object—the Earth—whereupon it gazeth with the golden sheaves of Fruitage." (*See Sonnets* 77—xx).[1]

Now to these homes the Queen paid numerous public and secret visits from 1565 to 1578. She gravitated there with her Court year after year for weeks at a time. There was no official reason why she should have travelled there. The real reason, apart from pleasure-seeking, was to enjoy privately the natural motherly relaxation with her growing boy. A contemporary writer, Nichols, in his *Progresses of Elizabeth*, betrays a "curious interest in the frequency of the Queen's visits to Gorhambury," which he cannot understand.

One of the Queen's first observations to Sir Nicholas when she first visited Gorhambury in 1568 was, "You have made your house too little for your Lordship," to which the Lord Keeper replied wittily, "Your Majesty hath made me too big for my house." But Sir Nicholas took the hint and added a wing for her special benefit. We can assume with reasonable justification that Queen Elizabeth secretly supervised the progress of the education of her son Francis, especially in those literary branches of learning in which she excelled.

The first thirteen years of Francis Bacon's life—*his most impressionable ones, when everything new, strange and unique would be stamped into his very soul unforgettably*—were spent between the glories of York House, with all its Royal associations, and the natural beauties of Gorhambury, the broad views of a countryside that is for ever England, and in constant touch with the pomp and pageantry of the Court.

At the home of his "Uncle Burleigh" he would be a regular visitor with Sir Nicholas and Lady Bacon. *There he would have seen the earliest types of dramatic productions*, either in the form of miracle plays and charades or masques and pageants . . . *performed by professional actors*. He would also see—*if he had never seen him before at York House*—the Queen's open Favourite and secret husband, his real father, the Earl of Leicester, *the first man to license a band of players for dramatic purposes*. Leicester kept a dramatic company for years, to perform at Court for the Queen's amusement. They were licensed to him as his "servants." They thus escaped the penalties attendant on actors who were regarded as "vagabonds" in the eyes of the law and liable to arrest. Without such licences acting was virtually illegal.

The head of Leicester's actors was James Burbage, the first man to build a theatre in England, *with Leicester's support*.

Burbage is the man so intimately connected in later years with "Shake-speare" and the "Shake-speare Plays."

It can be safely surmised that the precocious child Francis would make friends very early with the troupe, for he would never be content unless he knew what was going on "behind the scenes": He ever had an inquiring mind. To this early acquaintance with Burbage and the actors may be attributed an important strand in the weaving of the baffling enigma of the Shakespearean Drama created in after years.

[1]The numerals 77 denote the original Sonnet MS. order. The Roman letters xx, the "1609 quarto" order adopted by Modernists. The numerals give the true arrangement. See *Shakespeare's Sonnet-Diary* by Alfred Dodd.

One can well imagine the effect such play-acting would produce in the mind of a child who was a genius in embryo, with a flair for literature in his very blood, and whose very being only required the stimuli of a series of sense impressions to cause the secret flame of Romanticism to burst into life, especially when the performances were witnessed in the company of the brilliant throng of lords and ladies that constituted the Court of the "Throned Queen."

The picturesqueness of dramatic representation was stamped upon him as a child, and its possibilities as an educational and moral factor were bound to take shape in his mind, as is very evident by his many allusions in his works to plays and theatres . . . whether publicly performed on the stage or privately acted as a Dramatic Rite in a Masonic Ceremonial of Three Degrees—*i.e., Three Acts.*

The powerful effect of Leicester's actors, the refined atmosphere of a Ducal Palace, the Queen with her gorgeous retinue strutting and peacocking in nobly appointed rooms and wondrous gardens were vital influences in Francis Bacon's early life which have never been adequately appraised. We can feel the atmosphere of the "*Shake-speare Plays*" creeping into the very marrow of the boy's life, the lords and ladies, the Kings and Queens that were afterwards created by the Master-Craftsman to people for ever the universal corridors of thought.

We also see interblended quite early in his life the mysteries of the operative craft guild, the classic fables of the Ancients, the Romance of the Templar Knights, and the tuning of the young instrument Francis, by the hands of the Muses. Such was the making of the modern Orpheus, who was destined, like his classical predecessor, to draw all the world after him with his divine music . . . in his Ethical Rituals now planted all over the world no less than in his Immortal Plays which are likewise international.

There is little else that could be gleaned of his actual boyhood days for he was reared among prudent persons who purposely refrained from setting pen to paper concerning him. He was a mystery-child. The secrecies enfolding him had to be strictly observed. His childish prattle, his moods and tenses, that we should have loved to have known, are unrecorded. Nevertheless, with a definite knowledge of the complex environment that was impressing itself on his plastic mind, we can see the gradual moulding of the child as he clambers out of the cradle, the gradual printing of the lines of expression into a peculiar and unique form, the response of that marvellous brain to the complex stimuli of inward emotion and outward incident, that made him the wonder of the world, the paragon of thinkers. We can see the beginning of the growth of that brilliant mind which conceived the *Great Instauration* and the *Novum Organum*, with its Tables of Form (human passions) which, when interblended, created diverse dramatic characterization. We can the better understand his cry of exultant rapture when he had finished his book . . . to the God Apollo.

> Thy Gift, *thy Tables*, are within my brain
> *Full Charactered with lasting Memory*,
> Which shall above *that Idle Rank* remain
> Beyond all date even to Eternity. . . .
> (76—cxxii).

It requires but little creative imagination to fill the gaps between the known incidents of his childhood. "Every tale told of him wins on the imagination," says Hepworth Dixon. He continues:

> Cradled in the courtly glories of York House, nursed on the green slopes and in the leafy woods of Gorhambury; now playing with the daisies and forget-me-nots; now with the mace and seals; one day culling posies with the gardener or coursing after pigeons, the next day paying his pretty, wee compliments to the Queen, he grows up into his teens a grave yet sunny boy; on this side of his mind in love with nature, on that side in love with art. . . .
>
> As a child he was very beautiful. His chubby face, his grey-blue eyes, his curly silken locks might have fitted him to sit for one of the angels painted by Raphael. He lived in the hurry and vicinity of great events.

He was presented at Court about the age of four. Being asked by the Queen how old he was, he answered with much discretion, that he was two years younger than Her Majesty's happy Reign: with which answer the Queen was much taken. Such is Dr. Rawley's story. He also infers that the child often attended Court for he also says that:

> He was taken notice of especially by the Queen who delighted much to confer with him and to prove him with questions, unto whom he delivered himself with that Gravity and Maturity above his years, that Her Majesty would often term him, "The Young Lord Keeper."

Rawley continues:

> His first and childish years were not without some Mark of Eminency; at which time he was endued with that pregnancy and towardliness of WIT, as they were Presages of that deep and universal apprehension which was manifest in him afterwards, and caused him to be taken notice of by Several Persons of Worth and Place.

There is a tradition that Francis was able to read and write Latin, at a very early age with the same fluency as the average boy would read a newspaper. He had the finest private tutors obtainable. Parker Woodward says (*Life,* p. 10):

> Francis was tutored in Latin, Greek, French and Italian, possibly in fencing. His French Tutor was Amyas Paulett, son of the Governor of Jersey. His Italian tutor was John Florio, who seems to have been associated with him for many years afterwards . . . in literary ventures. Eduardo Donati was possibly his tutor for music, and Bonnetti his fencing-master.

Apart from these academic studies we get an example of his eager, searching mind as a boy trying to trace the footprints of Nature to her recesses. He steals away from his playmates to hunt for the cause of an echo in the vaults at St. James's Park which he had previously observed. He spends the afternoon in experimental observation.

Before he was twelve, says Lord Macaulay, "he had busied himself in the art of legerdemain" respecting a trick performed by a wandering juggler. The "trick" actually revolved round "thought-reading." The boy Francis tried to ascertain whether there was such a phenomenon as telepathy or thought-transference between two attuned minds, or whether he had simply witnessed something due to clever mechanical trickery. The psychic powers of man intrigued him so early in life that we can understand why he wrote, with such definite assurance as a youth, in his private, poetic diary:

> Nimble Thought can jump both sea and land,
> As soon as think the place where he would be.
> (54-xliv).

We thus get the first hint that Francis Bacon was interested at an early age in psychic problems. When he afterwards wrote on psychological and occult matters it was out of a fullness of personal, experimental knowledge.

"These are trifles," adds Lord Macaulay, "but the eminence Francis Bacon afterwards attained makes them interesting."

They are trifles which indicate a completion of his personality by a *psychical quality*. The evidence for this crops out later in a variety of ways . . . visions, trances, first-hand knowledge of "AN AFFABLE FAMILIAR GHOST." He is gradually being made into a fitting instrument to be played upon by those "Affirmative or Higher Invisible Intelligences" about which he speaks guardedly but clearly in his works, in a manner that indicates personal acquaintance. To this stream of knowledge from the Invisible World, Illumination from the Divine Mind, may be attributed much of his extraordinary power.

Dr. Rawley says (remember this is personal testimony):

> I have been induced to think that if there were a Beam of Knowledge derived from God upon any Man in these Modern Times, it WAS UPON HIM: For though he was a great Reader of Books, yet *he had not his Knowledge from Books*, but from some Grounds and Notions *from WITHIN HIMSELF*.

In the "Duke of Norfolk's Confession for High Treason," we get an illuminating flash into the private life of the Queen as a proud mother of Francis enfolded with the affectionate love of her secret husband Leicester.

> When the Court was at Guilford, I went unaware into *the Queen's Privy Chamber;* and found her sitting on the threshold of the door listening with one ear *to a Little Child* who was *singing and playing on the Lute to her;* and with other to Leicester *who was kneeling by her side.*

The child could have been no other than Francis, who would then be about nine years of age. We get there a perfect domestic picture of happiness, loving parents, a singing child who can also play the lute. Later he was to recall this scene in a beautiful Sonnet:

> Music to hear Why hear'st thou Music sadly? . . .
> Mark how one string, sweet husband to another,
> Strikes each to each by mutual ordering,
> Resembling Sire, and Child, and Happy Mother,
> Who all in one, one pleasing note do sing.
> (9-viii).

When Francis was twelve the Queen went specially to "The Temple," Gorhambury, to arrange about his subsequent education at the University. To mark her visit she had a terracotta bust of the boy made which shows a strong, abnormal brain development. There was none made for his nominal brother Anthony.

We now possess a clear picture of Francis Bacon's early years. We have seen this boy, so marvellously endowed by nature, brought up in

Plate VIII

Sir Nicholas Bacon
(See Appendix I)

Lady Anne Bacon
(See Appendix I)

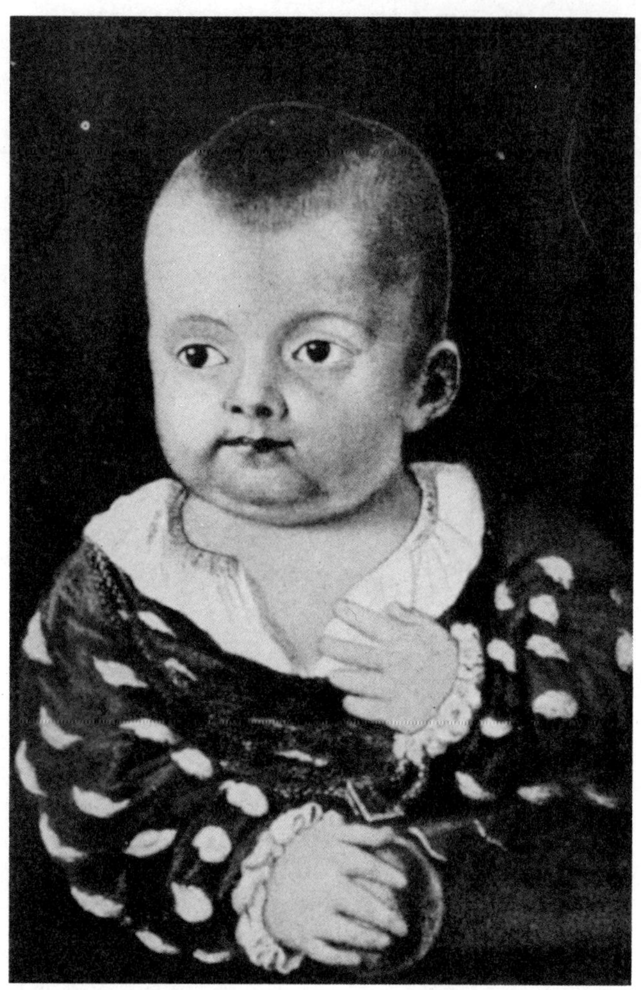

PLATE IX Francis Bacon as a child
(from a painting at Gorhambury)

surroundings ideal for his development. Every circumstance left its mark on that retentive mind. They all combined to bring out of his nature the inherent powers bequeathed to him through the long lines of hereditary descent, and the subconscious knowledge stored by the soul through successive incarnations in previous lives. In *The Statesmen and Favourites of England* (1665) David Lloyd says in reference to the early development of his mental and intellectual faculties:

> He had a large mind from his father and great abilities from his mother; His parts improved more than his years; his great fixed and methodical memory, his solid judgment, his quick fancy, his ready expression, gave assurance of that profound and universal comprehension of things which then rendered him the *Observation of Great and Wise Men*. . . . AT TWELVE HIS INDUSTRY WAS ABOVE THE CAPACITY AND HIS MIND BEYOND THE REACH OF HIS CONTEMPORARIES.

Such was the Genius at twelve who became the Prince of Poets and the Most Illustrious of Philosophers.

Chapter IV

EARLY YOUTH AND THE UNIVERSITY: THE ROYAL REVELATION (1573—1576)

WE have seen that apart from private tuition by the best masters Francis Bacon's environment had been of such a general educative nature, so unique in character, that it had tended from his cradle days to draw out of him those inherent qualities of soul that distinguished him in adult life from all his contemporaries. "He was a born scholar from his cradle," said an Elizabethan. His life had begun to unfold under the most advantageous circumstances, all calculated to promote those social, courtly, mental, moral, psychic and spiritual qualities which afterwards endeared him to so many different types.

He had been given the advantages of an intensive education through surroundings replete with the refinements of Royalty, Art and Nature. His culture was something more than mere knowledge. He saw the life of the Queen's Court, the Lords and Ladies, their men-servants and maid-servants, from the inside owing to Elizabeth being a constant visitor at "The Temple," Gorhambury, "York House," and Lord Burleigh's Palace, "Theobalds." He saw the pageantry of the Queen transacting public business at Whitehall in formal state, but he also played a personal part as a little boy in the revels of the more private life of the Queen at "Theobalds" and Gorhambury.

Before he had reached his teens, he had practically touched life at more angles of rich experience than any other boy before or since his time. His peculiar nature was such that he absorbed all its rich colouring until the very tissues of his mind were stained so that he truly became a part of all that he had met. He was destined to reproduce the men and women with their emotions and passions mercilessly dissected. They were the "types and models" which marched in procession through Shakespeare's pages as Kings and Queens, jesters and knaves. These practical examples of mental and moral passion formed the "Fourth Part" of Francis Bacon's great design, *The Instauration.* They were the puppets brought into being according to the laws of *The Novum Organum*—imitations of Nature's highest creations, mental and moral MAN. "We must imitate Nature if we would understand her," was the keynote of the Baconian philosophy.

Through David Lloyd, the historian, who had access to private information and papers ("he appears to have had exceptional opportunities of obtaining information," says W. T. Smedley, *Bacon*, p. 11), we know that *as a boy of twelve* he excelled all others in his great industry and the wide range of his mind. "At TWELVE his INDUSTRY was above the capacity and his mind beyond the reach of his contemporaries."

The contemporaries who had "Capacity and Mind," were scholars like Philip Melancthon (born 1497), Agrippa d'Aubigné (1550), Thomas Bodley (1554), James Crichton (1560). We have therefore the right to assume on authoritative personal evidence that, *even before he went to the University*, the boy Francis was proficient in the languages of his four leading contemporaries, Latin, Greek, Hebrew, French . . . and such English as there was, for the English language—there was not even an English grammar—had yet to be created by "Shake-speare."

An important point now arises which should be brought to the notice of the reader. Lloyd and Rawley, as well as other writers, draw special attention to *his exceptional INDUSTRY* which had begun before he was twelve *and continued throughout his life*, yet nothing appeared from his pen *until he was thirty-seven* and then only ten short essays of less than 6,000 words. The best years of his life slip away apparently without a single work to his credit. We are faced with the anomaly that this genius of scholarly learning, exceptional industry, wonderful gifts of creative imagination and expression, who exuded energy at every pore, was never known to have written a single line for publication, despite the fact that he had little or nothing to do. But because no works appeared in print openly over his own name, it is a fatal blunder to assume that Francis Bacon was uninterested in literature and was not an anonymous, secretive author even as a mere boy. How can one believe that his creative powers were suppressed until middle age and that his early years were barren of imaginative effort?

As a matter of fact he was directly led into the paths of creative literature from the age of seven.

With the completion of "The Temple" at Gorhambury in 1568, he was brought in close touch with a circle of literary men who were the heralds of the dawn of English literature and *connected with the Bacon circle*. In the same year came the first translations of classic and Italian Renaissance poetry, philosophy and history. Ovid, Plutarch and Euripides were later to find English expression. The men responsible for these translations were friends and protégés of Queen Elizabeth, the Earl of Leicester and the Bacons. . . . Geo. Gascoigne, Arthur Golding, uncle to the Earl of Oxford, Burleigh's son-in-law, Sir Thomas North,[1] Lord North, Sir F. Walsingham, Sir A. Paulett, Holinshed, Bishop Hall and others.

We find Leicester writing to Burleigh asking him to interest himself in North's *Lives of the Noble Grecians* which was then dedicated to Elizabeth, and which, with Holinshed, played so great a part in the Shakespeare Histories.

There was clearly a reason why he should be thought at twelve to be of extraordinary mental capacity and industry. I think it can be

[1]"Sir Thomas North was the brother of Roger, Lord North (he married the widow of Henry Dudley, brother of the Earl of Leicester), the greatest friend both of Queen Elizabeth and the Earl of Leicester. When Sir Thomas published his *Lives of Plutarch*, the Earl of Leicester himself wrote to Lord Burleigh to ask him to promote the book. Thus it was the Earl of Leicester's patronage that encouraged these translators, all of whom were in that same Court in which the Bacons moved, and on whose works admittedly so many Shakespearean Plays are based, and from them so many famous passages extracted." S. A. E. Hickson (*The Prince of Poets*, p. 19.)

safely conjectured that he had assisted in translations and literary work even as a "child," and that he had astonished this circle of brilliant literary students, historians, philosophers, and writers with his literary aptitude. If Montaigne could read and translate Ovid at seven (J. S. Mill learned to read Greek at three) there is no reason why Francis could not have acted likewise. Such a literary circle was a stimulus and a spur to his creative ambitions. He also had the example of Sir Nicholas and Lady Bacon as authors ever before him. The first twelve years definitely pointed out to him the path of authorship, literature and the acquirement of knowledge.

The historian Lloyd not only describes the memory of Francis as being "Fixed and Methodical" but he also says "*his Memory was a Wonder.*" As the Father and Creator of the Thirty-Three Degrees of Freemasonry his "Memory" would necessarily be a "Wonder"; for the creation and planting of his Secret Lodges would necessitate a phenomenal memory, the learning by heart and the recital of very complicated Ritual work for the instruction of others. Lloyd gives a half-hint that it is to Masonry he particularly refers. Apparently in his boyhood days his memory retained easily all he contacted by reading and observation. And that he was an omnivorous reader is shown by Dr. Rawley to have been a life-long habit.

> He would ever interlace a moderate relaxation of his mind with his studies as walking or taking the air abroad in his coach, or some other befitting recreation; and yet he would lose no time, inasmuch as upon the first and immediate return, he would fall to reading again, and so to suffer no movement of time to slip from him without some present improvement.

We thus get a glimpse, in view of what we actually know of his tendencies and abilities in adult life, of the prodigious powers of this marvellously endowed boy, who, up to the age of twelve, had been reared in ideal surroundings for his full development as a writer, thinker, teacher; architect and builder of bases for eternity.

Early in his twelfth year an important event happened. Queen Elizabeth again visited Gorhambury (March 1573) for no official or business reason. Her business was private, and though we have no record of what actually took place, after-events make it clear that she was arranging with Sir Nicholas that Francis should be sent with Anthony to Cambridge. So at the age of twelve years and three months Francis was sent with Anthony Bacon to reside at Trinity College in April 1573, within a month of the Queen's visit. He was not sent to St. Bene't's, where Sir Nicholas was bred, but to Trinity, the College created and endowed by the Queen's father, which she and Leicester had specially visited in 1564, when Leicester was appointed Lord High Steward of Cambridge University. The boy's mind and spirit were to be tempered by being plunged into the purely academic atmosphere of an ancient seat of learning. He was to acquire systematically, in company with strange fellow students, the accumulated knowledge stored up in a great educational centre. He left these words of the value of the Universities in the national life:

> This excellent Liquor[1] of Knowledge, whether it descends from Divine

[1] "Excellent Liquor"—Wine: hence he watermarked his books with Grapes and Pots, Later in life he was to write, *The VINE Which I Have PLANTED.*

Inspiration or springs from human sense, would soon perish or vanish into oblivion if it were not preserved in Books, Traditions, Conferences and Places appointed as Universities, Colleges and Schools for the receipt . . . of the same . . . much like the stations which Virgil prescribeth for the Hiving of Bees. (*Advancement of Learning*).

These were doubtless the young genius's thoughts as he approached the University for the first time and saw in the distance the lofty spires and venerable walls raised by generations of intellect and piety, "hallowed by the shrine where the works of the mighty dead are preserved and repose . . . and who thus enlarge the borders of man's dominions."

This mature boy with his thoughtful, ardent mind, was, however, speedily disillusioned of his dreams regarding the uses to which the Liquor of Knowledge was put in the ancient Halls of Learning. Instead of the University being a Hive of Industry, with students of all types bent on the pursuit of Truth, in all her ramifications through Nature, he found himself:

amidst men of sharp and strong wits, abundance of leisure and small variety of reading, their wits being shut up in the Cells of a few Authors, chiefly Aristotle their Dictator, as their persons were shut up in the cells of Monasteries or Colleges; and knowing little history either of Nature or Time . . . out of no great quantity of matter do spin Cobwebs of Learning, admirable for the fineness . . . *but of no substance or profit*. (*Advancement of Learning*).

The boy Francis saw that instead of the University being an organized body for the discovery of Truth, its object was merely to preserve and diffuse the knowledge of its predecessors. Instead of general inquiry, he found all studies were confined to Aristotle, who was considered infallible; all the lectures were simply expositions of the Aristolian text and comments on his opinions held as authentic as if they had been given under the Pope's Seal.

The tremendous difference between his dream of the glories of learning and research in Holy Fanes of Thought, and the real uses to which Learning was put by Men of Letters, created such a reaction in the young idealist, that it directly led him into a new philosophic conception of Truth and a new search for Truth by a different path: It was a concept that took in its orbit the interpretation of God as the Divine Author of the Universe, Man's relationship to the Most High, and the relationship of all Men as Brethren, bonded together by Charity (Love); a new interpretation of Nature, of which man formed a part, as an ethical expression of the Great Architect, and the understanding of Nature by observation and experiment. This philosophy was not for the purpose of academic discussion in a class room, to display mental and verbal gymnastics, but for the greater purpose of utility, so that mankind might benefit in their lives, their homes, their bodies. In its train should flow practical benefits, such as a higher standard of living, with better homes, healthier bodies, nobler minds and more highly attuned souls. "Ignorance is the Curse of God," he said: "Knowledge the wing wherewith we fly to heaven."

That, in a nutshell, is the Baconian philosophy, which Francis Bacon "developed at length and established . . . and bequeathed to posterity," labouring at his gigantic scheme all his life on various lines of action. It was a TASK which came to him as a boy in a flash of God-illumined inspiration. It was a work toiled at through fair days and foul, a "Philanthropia" in which he had to spend and be spent to uplift not only England, but the entire world.

Hamlet's words were wrung out of the depths of his own soul . . . .

> There is something rotten in the State . . .
> Oh, cursed spite, that ever I was born to set it right.

Francis Bacon saw that the human mind in his day, instead of marching forward, was merely marking time; that the philosophy of Aristotle, which dominated the Universities, simply evoked dialectical argument and disputation that led nowhere and added nothing to the stock of knowledge. He saw the fatal flaw in the educational system and outlook of the Universities, and their consequent uselessness in contributing to the welfare of man, *when he was yet a boy.*

> While still a *commorant*[1] of the University, he had already noted the unfruitfulness of a philosophy only strong in disputations and contentions but barren for the production of anything *for the benefit of the life of man.* (Dr. Rawley).

Against this barrenness of the ancient philosophy he formulated in two words the Baconian doctrine of a new experimental philosophy that was at once Scientific and Ethical. . . . "UTILITY and PROGRESS."

> The end which Bacon proposed to himself was, to use his own emphatic expression, "FRUIT." The multiplying of human enjoyment and the mitigation of human sufferings . . . "the relief of man's estate." This was the object of all his speculations in every department of science, nature, philosophy, legislation, politics, morals. (Macaulay).

If the great intellectual revolution of the Elizabethan Age was not actually planned in outline while he was at Cambridge, the concept of a material and ethical world-wide movement originated at this University and then began to take definite form while he was in his late teens and early twenties. It was to be educational, experimentally scientific, ethical, for the benefit of all mankind, a cure for body and soul, for the poor man as well as the rich, for the ignorant Calibans as well as the learned Sir Oracles. Francis Bacon's philosophy was not simply a book to be written for the learned to discuss, to be relegated afterwards to the library shelf. It was a philosophy of action . . . a work to be accomplished. And the bases of the New Philosophy were to be laid by himself. Thoughts were to be translated into acts. He was to be the Architect of a New Temple of Thought. He would begin to build and trust to be joined by the minds of progressive men to assist him in the task when they had once gripped his idea of SERVICE. So he made a start. He began to build. And then he became "a bellringer calling the sciences together to labour for the good of humanity." From his early teens to the end of

[1]A "commorant" is a law term to describe an abiding or dwelling in a place, a residence.

his life, *upwards of forty-five years*, he never once lost sight of his goal . . . the all-round betterment of man. We shall see later what those "Bases" were exactly and the portions of the Temple he built.

Francis stayed with Anthony Bacon at Cambridge upwards of three years, excepting a period from July 1574 until March 1575, when the University was closed owing to the plague which was raging in England, leaving it finally in December 1575. He appears rapidly to have learned all that Cambridge had to teach. Having gone through the usual course, he begged Sir Nicholas to allow him to return home to Gorhambury. He was so conscious of the defects of the academic system that he even refused to take his Degree. The seminaries of learning were stagnant pools; they were opposed to the advancement of knowledge; a Degree therefore meant to him a mere label, identifying him with a system he despised. *He was then only fifteen years of age.* Later, he was to sum up the defects of the Universities in these words:

> In the Universities they learn nothing but *to believe;* first to believe that others know that which they know not. They are like a becalmed ship: they never move but by the wind of other men's breath, and have no oars of their own to steer withal. . . .
>
> The studies of men in such places are confined and pinned down to the writings of certain authors; from which if any man happens to differ, he is presently reprehended as a disturber and innovator.

This powerful indictment seems to be as true to-day as it was three hundred years ago, so far as the chairs of literature are concerned respecting the problems of the Elizabethan Era. It was the reaction produced by this profound disappointment at what passed as the fundamentals of learning among academicians, that helped to create his youthful dream of a "Reformation of the whole Wide World," in art, science, ethics, in everything which really touched the natural and spiritual life of man.

> "It has often been said," says Macaulay, "that Francis Bacon while at College planned that great intellectual revolution with which his name is inseparably connected . . . .
>
> "Certain it is that after a residence of some three years at Cambridge, he departed carrying with him a profound contempt for the course of study pursued there."

In short, the powerful and active mind of this boy of fifteen was possessed of such clarity of thought, such maturity of judgment, that when he left Cambridge he had reduced his abstract reactions to those "fixed, unaltered and universal opinions" that took in not only the material world but the invisible world also . . . not only the realm of effects but the realm of causes . . . the mind of man and the animating Spirit which is God. These definite characteristic opinions were so far in advance of his age that he knew he could never dare to promulgate them openly in view of Sir Nicholas Bacon's warning finger, "Beware! Use the invisible cloak of anonymity if you feel your lips must speak the language of your heart, lest it break." These principles dominated all his after-life of thought and action.

"It was when he was a boy," says Spedding, "that a thought struck him, the date of which deserves to be recorded for its influence in after life, that if our study of nature be thus barren, our method of study must be wrong. Might not, therefore, a better method be found?

"The suggestion was simple and obvious, and the singularity was the way he took hold of it. . . .

"With him, the gift of seeing *in prophetic vision* what might be and ought to be, was united with *the practical talent of devising means and handling minute details.*

"He could at once *imagine LIKE A POET and EXECUTE like a* Clerk of Works. Upon the conviction, 'This may be done,' followed at once the question, 'How may it be done. . . .?' Then followed the resolution to try to do it."

Spedding spent thirty years of his life in the study of Francis Bacon's open Labours. He never suspected that Francis also lived a concealed life under many pen-names, so it must be noted how important are his conclusions. He had "prophetic vision," "could imagine like a POET," and was thoroughly "practical." He was not content to conceive a plan. He must try to carry it out. The dream must be translated into REALITY to become valuable. We shall see how he tried to do this.

We actually know very little of his life at Cambridge. But he was "educated and bred under the tuition of Dr. John Whitgift, then Master of Trinity College, afterwards the renowned Archbishop of Canterbury . . . "under whom he (Francis Bacon) was observed to have been more than an ordinary Proficient in several Arts and Sciences." (Rawley).

Anthony and Francis appear to have lived in Dr. Whitgift's house for there are items of pills and drugs and medicines entered in Anthony's school account. "He paid for more meat from the Dolphin Tavern and for Dr. Hatcher's drugs than to Whitgift for Latin and Greek," says Dixon. Apparently Francis was not long in residence before he proclaimed

his dislike of the philosophy of Aristotle; not for the worthlessness of the author, to whom he would ever ascribe all high attributes, but for the unfruitfulness of the way; being a philosophy, as his Lordship used to say, only strong for disputations and contentions, but *barren of the production of works for the benefit of the Life of Man; in which mind he continued* [adds Rawley] *to his dying day.*

So the boy Francis set his opinion against the professors of philosophy and the University staff regarding the pursuit of Knowledge and what constituted true Knowledge. The philosophy of the Egyptians and the Greeks were discussed between him and his friends. We may be sure that these discussions would be very extended in their scope and would take in all that was known regarding these ancient systems, their religious activities, their "Ancient Wisdom," their "Mysteries." The actual note left by him shows that his mind was even then revolving round the Secret Societies of the Ancients.

Discussing skornfully of the philosophy of the Grecians with some better respect to ye Ægiptians, Persians, and Chaldees; and the utmost ANTIQUITY, and the MYSTERIES of the Poets.

There is no doubt that this note was left that we might know he was early interested in the Ethics and Rituals of the ancient Egyptian Mysteries.

There would also be another subject discussed between him and his colleagues, the futility of theological disputation which blinded men to the prime teaching of the Master summed up in the Eleventh Commandment, "That ye LOVE one another." The state of the University, when Francis Bacon went there, was miserable indeed. "The academical bodies were divided into factions and the doctors at open war." Dixon tells us that Cartwright, "the most popular preacher of his age, had been vanquished by force, deprived of his fellowship, forbidden to read public lectures, and expelled from the University. Their Master Whitgift had been the leader in this High Church conflict." The result had been that Cartwright's Church, St. Mary's, was empty, and others had arisen in support of the expelled teacher. The dispute had, of course, to go to the Privy Council, and the Lord Keeper Bacon had to exercise his judicial powers of suppression. Francis saw good men wasted because of theological intolerance and the lack of Christian Charity.

But this was really no new thing to him. The incident had simply brought home to him its foolishness and futility. Through the comings and goings of Statesmen in the home of Sir Nicholas, he had become early acquainted with the religious problems of England, the bitter theological strife that split the nation into opposite camps, with all its political significance. On this very point Dean Church says:

> His boyhood from the first was passed among the high places of the nation at one of the greatest crises of English history in the very centre and focus of its agitations, brought up among the chiefs and leaders of the NEW RELIGION. (*Bacon*, p. 5.)

His mind naturally would revolve round the Ethical principles that were common to all the Christian Churches, Catholic, Anglican, Nonconformist. A step further would bring in the Unitarian and the Jew . . . witnesses to the same eternal verities. There would soon be spun a golden thread of moral principles fundamentally similar to all religious and philosophic systems, the golden thread of "CHARITY," the "religion of all good men and true." Hence his inflexible adherence all through his life to the policy of the "middle way."

These settled convictions were laid down when he was twenty-nine years of age in a remarkable paper on *Controversies in the Church;* an attempt to compose the bitterness of the religious bodies by pointing out "the mistakes in judgment, temper, and method of all concerned." It is moderate, tolerant, neutral . . . neither Puritanical, Catholic nor sectarian. It is exactly the type of paper one might expect from the secret Creator of an Ethical System which provided a Lodge of Refuge where men could meet as Brethren around common principles based on the Law of Love.

> As to *UNBROTHERLY proceedings* on either part, it is directly contrary to my purpose to amplify wrongs. . . . But Laws are *like to the Grape* that being too much pressed yields an hard and unwholesome wine. . . .
>
> A man doth vainly boast of loving God whom he never saw if he love not his Brother whom he hath seen. . . .

> The wisdom of scripture judges and denominates men RELIGIOUS *according to their works*. And Saint James saith, "This is true religion to visit the fatherless and the widow. . . ." So that which is with them (Socrates or some Heathen Philosophers) *Philosophical and Moral*, is, in the Apostle's phrase, *True Religion and Christianity*.
>
> Let them [the extreme zealous Puritans] take heed that it be not true which one of their Adversaries said, "That they have two small wants, *KNOWLEDGE and LOVE*. . . ."
>
> I repeat that a character of LOVE is more proper for debates of this nature than that of ZEAL.

Such calm convictions of expressed neutrality in an age of extreme partisanship can be traced to the boyhood days when he heard Sir Nicholas and other statesmen discussing privately the interblending of religion and politics. Young Francis simply embodied in his life the motto that was carved over the porchway of "The Temple" at Gorhambury: That Truth lies in the Middle-of-the-Road: *Mediocria Firma—i.e.*, the Golden Mean or Balanced Truth.

This attitude of mind he learned as a child when he was taught in the sanctity of his own home that the greatest thing in life was "Love," not "Hatred." By interior illumination he also learned the value of "Unity not division in things sacred as well as secular." He therefore looked askance at all extremists and refused to be a theological partisan. Macaulay says:

> He loved to consider religion as the BOND OF CHARITY. Controversy on speculative points of theology seems to have engaged scarcely any portion of his attention. . . . He lived in an age in which disputes on the most subtle points of doctrine excited intense interest. . . . *He was placed in the very thick of the conflict*. . . . Yet we do not remember a line in his works from which it can be inferred *that he was either a Calvinist or an Arminian*. . . . While the world was resounding with the noise of a disputatious philosophy (Aristotle), and a disputatious theology, he preserved a calm neutrality, half scornful, half benevolent, content with adding to the sum of practical good.

This correctly describes the Ethical Teacher of an eclectic philosophy.

While at Trinity College he apparently continued his experiments, for in the *Sylva Sylvarum* he gives the result of an experiment in sound in an upper chamber and the one beneath. He was possibly assisted by a popular professor named Gabriel Harvey who was his tutor in rhetoric and poetry. Harvey was the well-known Elizabethan academician whose correspondence with an unknown writer who signs himself "Immerito" is of considerable interest to students. The letters deal with the reform of English Verse. *Harvey was anxious to add English to the subjects taught at Cambridge*. "He was a poet and a close student of the technical construction of poetry." (Woodward). After-events make it clear that there was a very warm friendship between Francis Bacon and Gabriel Harvey, so the identity of the unknown "Immerito" can be guessed. The internal evidence of the letters applies to Francis Bacon and to no one else. While Francis Bacon was at College he published a Philosophical Discourse entitled *The Anatomy of the Mind*, dedicated to Christopher Hatton with the name "Thomas Rogers" attached to it. There is in existence a copy of the

Book with the printer's and other errors *corrected in Francis Bacon's own handwriting*. (Edward D. Johnson.)

He returned to Gorhambury from Trinity College at Christmas 1575 for good, about a month before his fifteenth birthday. We must picture him with his mind aflame with ideas for the upliftment of humanity along certain definite lines. He saw a world plunged in gross darkness as regards first principles, a darkness that could only be dispersed by the Light of Knowledge, an informed method of study that would ultimately bring about a universal reformation in art, science, philosophy, and religion. His works demonstrate that he consecrated himself to the task in the most devout frame of mind. Later on he was to avow that he regarded himself "as a Servant to Posterity," as a channel for the outflow of the Divine Mind. From boyhood he held to this idea that his work was impressed with the Divine Seal.

It must not be thought, however, that the Spirit of Idealism which overshadowed him, filling him with Wisdom, made him into a preternaturally grave youth of solemn mien, as so many represent. It made him into a happy one. Idealism never yet made a person unhappy, grave-faced and portentously solemn. It inspires, exhilarates, and gives one a joyful countenance. The man who finds his life's work early, the true course to run, the right mark at which to aim, has a singing heart, and a lighthearted step no matter what disasters may overtake him. And the worthier the goal to be won, the higher the achievement to be accomplished, the nobler the harmonies that pour through his soul. Francis Bacon's dream was to set right a world that was out of joint, to leave the world better than he found it, to influence ages yet unborn. He was animated with what he called the spirit of "Philanthropia." "Enough for me the reward of well-doing. . . . My mind turns on other wheels than those of profit." So this young idealist had a buoyancy of spirit which after-disasters never quenched. He learned early to laugh at trouble and to turn the edge of disaster with a quibble and a smile. His sense of humour helped him to preserve his sanity in the dark storms which broke upon him from time to time until the final "Tempest" of 1621.

Though his mind was aflame with ideas on his return home from the University, we must therefore guard against the erroneous suggestion that he comported himself from this date throughout life with the gravity of a grey-beard philosopher weighted with the cares of a world on his young shoulders. He never was the cold, dull pedant of academic legend at any period of his career, least of all as a youth. While we can picture him as being well-stored with scholastic knowledge and creative imagination for noble ends, we must also picture him as a happy, care free youth without anxiety, with the ball of life at his feet. Spedding writes:

> It was the season of all-embracing hope, dreaming of things to come, rehearsing his life to himself in the imaginary theatre where all things go right . . . hopeful, sensitive, bashful, amiable, wise, well-refined; and glowing in noble aspiration . . . such were the happy auspices of his sixteenth year.

The succeeding months, from December 1575 to the following September 1576, must have been some of the happiest in his life. There would scarcely be a cloud on the horizon. Francis was frequently at Court and came into friendly relationships with Sir Philip Sidney and Fulke Greville (Lord Brook) . . . both interested in poetry, as well as his relative Edward de Vere, Earl of Oxford (another poet). In April 1576, Francis wrote a play called *The Historie of Errors* for the chapel children, which was performed before the Queen; also a poem at the end of Kerton's *Mirrour of Man's Life* in the name of Stephen Gosson who was first a player and afterwards a preacher. Stephen Gosson, the supposed author, graduated B.A. in 1576, becoming Rector of Wingsborough in 1591 by gift of the Queen. He wrote nothing after the age of twenty-seven and died at the age of sixty-nine and made no claim to authorship. (E. D. Johnson).

There is little doubt that Francis was present with the Court at the entertainment of the Queen at Kenilworth Castle, August 1572, and in July 1575. There are two accounts of *The Princely Pleasures of Kenilworth* obviously from the same hand, by some person who signs himself "Laneham" and "Geo. Gascoign." The descriptions are replete with the exuberance of youth. The writer is a poet, full of the joy of life, with an extensive vocabulary and imaginative wit. "Laneham"[1] was possessed of inside information and he could not have been an ordinary outsider. The little descriptive booklet was suppressed on the instructions of the "Master of Requests," whose agent, W. Patten, writes to Lord Burleigh that "with the exception of six copies to Mr. Wilson, two to his Lordship and the Lord Keeper Bacon, I have not let more than three copies pass." So we know the "Laneham" book was thus brought directly into relation with the "Bacon Circle."

Now one of the scenes in the Kenilworth Pageant is described in *Midsummer Night's Dream* where Oberon says:

> . . . Thou remembrest
> Since once I sat upon a promontary
> And heard a Mermaid on a Dolphin's back,
> Uttering such dulcet and harmonious breath . . .
> That very time I say[2] (but thou couldst not)
>
> Flying between the cold moon and the earth,
> Cupid all arm'd; a certain Aim he took
> At a Fair Vestal, THRONED by the West,
> And loosed his Love-Shaft smartly from his Bow,
> As it should pierce a hundred thousand Hearts,
> But I might see young Cupid's Fiery Shaft

[1]If we take the last syllable of the name as an open hint, "Ham," we may not be far wrong in assuming the identity of the writer as Bacon, for is not Bacon,"Ham?" And if we remember that the word "lean" was sounded like the first syllable "Lane" we get the anonymous letter writer jesting at the name of Bacon. He is a "Lean Ham," *i.e.*, Laneham. This idea of playing with words to convey other meanings was quite characteristic of Francis Bacon's humour. Ordinarily, it would seem to be very far-fetched, but these diamond words appear as punning in Shake-speare; and the very word "Ham," with other words such as PIG, SOW, SHOAT, are given repeatedly in the Initial Capitals of the Shake-speare Text usually with a message that the author is playing with his name and wants the reader to know that his real name is "BACON." See *The Secret Shakespeare*, by Alfred Dodd, Rider & Company, London. We must remember that Ben Jonson records that Francis Bacon could not let an opportunity pass for making or cracking a joke.

[2]Modern editors alter this word "say" in the Folio to SAW, as required by the context.

> Quenched in the chaste beams of the watery moon;
> And the Imperial Votresse[1] passed on
> In Maiden meditation, fancy free.

Here is a prose description by Laneham:

> Proteus appeared sitting on a Dolphin's back. And the Dolphin was conveyed upon a boat so that the oars seemed to be his fins. Within the which Dolphin, a concert of music was secretly placed and Proteus sang . . . in behalf of the Lady . . . and all the Nymphs and Gods of the sea.

These descriptions are so akin, even to the "Melody of the Seven-sorted Music of the Dolphin," that "Shake-speare" must have known of the suppressed book. The commentators are virtually agreed that the author of the Plays must have seen the Revels and Devices at Kenilworth to have written the above passage in the *Dream*, that he and "Laneham" were one and the same or that he had read his book. There is not the slightest evidence that the Actor of Stratford saw the Kenilworth Revels at the age of eleven, but Francis Bacon, as one of the inner circle, is certain to have been present. And if we take the hint of "Lean Ham"[2] as the cover name for "Bacon" there is at least a strong presumption that the young Francis was present, wrote the description anonymously, and thus early embarked on a career of concealed authorship. Such scenes of splendour would necessarily quicken the imagination necessary to dramatic invention.

Into all this happiness came a bolt from the blue, which had a very disturbing effect on his immediate prospects and profoundly influenced all his future activities. It had the direct result of driving him into a secret life, "to live," as he afterwards wrote, "a Second Life on Second Head." It riveted a Mask over his real personality. It drove him into a life of extreme caution. He had perforce to tread the perilous edge lest an unguarded word might spell personal disaster and, perhaps, imperil the State. It was a goad that gradually drove him to the paths of secrecy and dissimulation. It made him actually into a "Concealed Man," and it paved the way for the next logical step . . . the formation of a Secret Society of other "Concealed Men," of which he was the Chief.

After leaving Cambridge University, Francis had been entered at Gray's Inn so that he could follow the profession of Sir Nicholas. He had begun his legal studies. His magnificent intellect, his personal beauty, his gracious manners, industry and acquirements, made him a welcome addition to the throng of gallants that had the freedom of Queen Elizabeth's Court. None could be more welcome than the "son" of the Lord Keeper. And then, while this brilliant thinker was pondering his vast plans for the upliftment of humanity, and dreaming of an international Parliament of Man, Brotherhood, Freedom, Education, the conquest of Nature . . . something happened, something sudden and unexpected, something in which the Queen was concerned, which had the result of his being sent

[1]The writer saw the "Virgin Queen"—"the Imperial Votresse" who had consecrated her life by a vow to virginity—being made love to by Leicester but had passed on fancy free despite Cupid's fiery dart.

[2]"Laneham" is said to be a youth of fourteen when the Kenilworth Revels were held in 1575. *This was the age of Francis Bacon.* Who "Laneham" was no one knows.

to France hastily out of the way. We know the Queen was directly involved in his sudden departure from England, for he leaves a note to this effect: "I went with Sir Amias Paulet into France DIRECT FROM HER MAJESTY'S ROYAL HAND."

To emphasize the significance of the Queen's direct connection with his departure to France, he also writes to Lord Cecil years after:

"I kissed her Majesty's hand upon going to France."

It is obvious, though nothing direct is said, that Francis Bacon was sent by the Queen's command. This is the reasonable inference of Francis Bacon's two notes, one of which was sent to his nominal cousin Cecil, then Secretary of State, who was acquainted with all the circumstances. He says to Cecil in effect, at a time when it was necessary for Cecil to remember that he had certain rights of descent and was not a mere commoner, "I was sent to France by Her Majesty's command. You know the reason. Do not forget who I am."

No other youth at Court could say, "I was sent DIRECT from Her Majesty's Royal Hand," or that "I kissed the Queen's Hand on going abroad." There is no record anywhere that she ever sent anyone but Francis Bacon. There is not, in fact, the slightest evidence that she was interested in any other noble youth save one . . . Robert Devereux, afterwards the Earl of Essex. There are no official documents relating to the circumstances which led to this decision. Either there was none, or they were suppressed or destroyed.

The Queen sitting with her Privy Council on 20th August, 1576, arranged the details for the conveyance of the Embassy of Amyas Paulet, son of the Protestant Governor of Jersey. He was to be

> Her Majesty's Ambassador resident in France, to take up such carts and cart horses for the carriage of his staff, etc. . . . as he should need for himself and his train from place to place to the sea coast.

This note is from the "Acts of the Privy Council," which also states that George Bristowe of H.M.S. *Dreadnought* was directed to convey him overseas "to such part on the other side as might be deemed most convenient to him." The Privy Council sat again five days later at Gorhambury, St. Albans, to conclude the details. The Earl of Leicester was present at these Privy Council meetings. In his diary, Sir Francis Walsingham, a Privy Councillor, writes under the date of the Council meeting, 31st August, "I went to Gorhambury for dinner and to St. Albans to bed." Where the Queen went we can only conjecture.

Now why should Queen Elizabeth have sent Francis Bacon direct to France, where he stayed *for three years*, suddenly interrupting his planned course of legal studies? There was manifestly some grave reason for such a decision.

"At first it was decided that Edward Bacon, ten years his senior, was to go with him, a license for the two of them, with coach and six horses, to travel, was issued." P. Woodward, *Life*, p. 12.

But Edward went alone. And in September 1576 the Queen knighted Amyas Paulet. Francis was placed in his charge, a Mr. Duncombe attending Francis as his tutor. Sir Amyas then went as the Queen's Ambassador to France to succeed Dr. Dale. And Francis Bacon went in the entourage of Sir Amyas to spend three years in the voluptuous Court of Henri Trois. They crossed to Calais on the 25th September, 1576, and went straight to the Court of Henry III at Paris. Sir Amyas Paulet and Francis moved along in attendance on the French Court visiting Blois, Paris, Poictiers, also Italy and Spain. During this period there is sound evidence that he published a book called *Beautiful Blossoms* under the name of John Byshop, printed in London by Henry Cockyn. (E. D. Johnson.)

In all these open facts of history, the hand of Queen Elizabeth is strongly in evidence, even to the presentation of Francis to the French Court by the English Ambassador. But history is silent on the circumstances which were the direct cause of him being sent abroad. Nevertheless, we do know what went on behind the scenes because a record in cypher was left by Francis Bacon of what actually happened. It was skilfully decoded by a lady named Mrs. Gallup. [Pepys' *Diary* which throws such a flood-light on the era of Charles II was likewise written in cypher and remained unknown until someone was found clever and patient enough to decode it. It is a grave mistake to reject cyphers on *a priori* grounds and to declare they have no research value, factual or literary.]

To obtain a true insight into the period and the life of Francis Bacon, the biographer and historian alike must take this secret record into his reckoning. Codes and Cyphers have always played an important part in State Affairs. They enter to-day into our business life. As we are now "a free people" they do not enter as they once did into our private life. But they are the only protection left to the crushed peoples of Poland and Czechoslovakia, indeed, wherever there is a Gestapo tyranny. In war the cypher plays an all-important part. In the present conflict, no less than in the Great War, there is a constant battle of wits going on behind the guns. [This book was written during the War.—A. D.]

Queen Elizabeth Tudor was the first to introduce a secret service and to establish the original "Room 40." Francis Bacon, Anthony Bacon and the Earl of Essex were the heads of a hidden organization which stretched out all over the Continent and gave the Government prompt, first-hand information in code. Mary Queen of Scots owed her downfall to the work of Elizabeth's cypher experts.

Cyphers and codes have always played an important part in the national life when a secret had to be transmitted, preserved or perpetuated, and in the shaping of world events. The cleverest cypher expert of Europe is known to have been Francis Bacon. In the reign of King James he was the head of the Secret Service. In his greatest work, *De Augmentis*, he stresses the importance of cyphers and codes, gives some interesting examples, mentions several types, and speaks with the familiarity of one who habitually used them, Word, Letter, Ring and Wheel Cyphers, etc. One of them is known as the "Biliteral Cypher"; the present Morse Code is based on its secret principles. This particular cypher was found by Mrs. Gallup in Francis Bacon's works and in other books of that era. It has been verified by the Heads of the British, American, and French Secret Services in the Great War—Major Stevenson, Col. Fabyan, and

General Cartier. They have also declared that the decoding of Mrs. Gallup is correct, with the probable exception of minor errors.

In view of the testimony of these experts no literary writer has any justification for ignoring the plain facts of the period. It was a cypher age; and to reject testing the truth, through *a priori* prejudice, of the secret decoded story, by the known facts of the times and MS. records in National archives and elsewhere, is sheer self-stultification. It is the prime duty of a biographer to take all the facts, all the evidence relating to the person under review. He must not pick and choose, suppress or magnify any incident. Suppression has the direct result of giving a distorted picture which is fundamentally vicious. The literary critic who dislikes cyphers because he does not understand them has no moral or literary right to judge the manners and customs of another age by his own, and to reject their usefulness in literary exegesis. Napoleon lost the battle of Leipzig because no one could decipher a secret message from Marshal Augereau. Joffre was helped and guided to win the battle of the Marne in 1914 by two deciphered messages intercepted from Von Kluck. Code signals helped to win the battle of the River Plate and the rescue of the British prisoners from the German *Altmark* when in Norwegian waters. We cannot reject a story simply because it is written in code and not flaunted openly to the eyes of the world. Joffre would have lost the Marne battle had he suffered from code-complex-prejudice. And Hindenburg and Ludendorff would never have wiped out the Russian armies at Tannenberg had they been prejudiced against testing the truth of an intercepted cypher story which Samsonov wrote to Rennenkampff. It is *the testing of the truth of the story* which matters. When the Elizabethan Cypher is declared to be truly decoded by the highest military authorities in the world—the cypher experts of France, America and England in the Great War of 1914-18—it would be sheer folly for me to turn away and refuse to test the truth of the secret story which directly concerns Francis Bacon.

The fact is, as will be seen, the Cypher-Story fits into the open facts of history like a hand fitting into a well-worn glove.

The Cypher-Story states that while young Francis was at Court, the courtiers were intrigued as to the real identity of the handsome youth who was on such terms of familiarity with the Queen. Some whispered he was a bastard son of Sir Nicholas Bacon adopted by his wife, others that he was the son of the Queen and Leicester, both of whom he resembled in the general contour of his face, his nether lip being like Elizabeth's and the formation of his eye like Leicester's.

The rumours originated with the stunted hunchback Robert Cecil, his cousin, the son of Lord Burleigh, Secretary of State. They were intended to belittle Francis. He was jealous of his handsome cousin's intellectual abilities. They heightened his own deformity and dwarfed his mentality. He had learned as a State Secret the truth of Francis Bacon's parentage from his father Burleigh.

The story continues that while young Lady Scales, a Lady-in-Waiting, was repeating to her companions Cecil's malevolent whispers that Francis was the Queen's bastard-son by Leicester, Elizabeth overhearing the laughter from an adjoining room, dragged from the young Maid

Plate X

York House

York Place
(See Appendix I)

Plate XI
The Temple Church, London 1240 A.D.
From "A Pleasant Hour in the Temple" by Marshal Freeman
(See Appendix I)

the reason for their merriment. By chance, Francis entered the room as the enraged Queen was violently beating the girl into insensibility. Attempting to intervene to save her, he was then told of the scurrilous chatter that was going round the Court, and in the passion of the moment, the truth of his parentage slipped out from the Queen's lips. In the violence of her anger she screamed, "You are my own born son, but because you have taken sides against your mother to champion a graceless wench, I bar you for ever from the Succession."

Up to that moment, Francis had believed he was the real legal son of Sir Nicholas and Lady Bacon. In an agony of shame and distress at being thought a bastard, he rushed home to Lady Bacon . . . to the woman he had always known as his mother. In a pathetic interview he learned the truth that she and Sir Nicholas were foster-parents only; that his father was the Earl of Leicester; that he and the Queen had been married privately at Lord Pickering's House, about four months before Francis was born, truly the Queen's son and born in wedlock. He had a brother some eight years younger named Robert Devereux. These matters were Secrets of State and she and Sir Nicholas had been sworn to secrecy.

There is other information which largely fills up the gaps in the open life of this remarkable man and this equally remarkable Queen. Details about his brother Robert, later known as the Earl of Essex, Elizabeth's favourite son whom she preferred to succeed her, for the birth of Francis so soon after marriage would have revealed her own indiscretions as a Tudor. The Cypher-Story also states that Francis was an anonymous writer and gives some of his pen-names, together with an account of his luckless love with a lady of the French Court.

Hereafter, Francis addresses Lady Bacon only occasionally as "mother," though he refers to her as "mother" in his last Will. She was really the only person to behave to him as a mother and to give him the love and affection for which his passionate nature craved.

Such is the story as deciphered by Mrs. Gallup and told in truly Elizabethan English.

Mrs. Gallup was an American lady from the Middle West and could not possibly have been acquainted with the Elizabethan style of writing. If she invented the whole story, it is strange she should have produced something which, to the academic mind, was so outrageous, that it created a storm of criticism from the orthodox traditionalists *who made no attempt whatever to prove or disprove the truth of the statements* deciphered by her.

Mrs. Gallup passionately declared her honesty. She said it was not an invention on her part nor a fabricated code. She offered to show the literary men of the day how the Cypher ran in the old Elizabethan books. She asked them to check her work as it was being deciphered at the British Museum. *No one accepted her offer*. They were simply content to ridicule her through the columns of *The Times* and literary journals and abuse her *bona fides*.

Time, however, has already begun to vindicate this lady. From the future she has nothing to fear. The whipping-boys of posterity will be those "scholars of literature" who refused to examine her researches, afraid lest the bottom should fall out of the "Shakespeare Trust."

Chapter V

THE COURT OF FRANCE
(1576-1579)

THE three years 1576-79 are among the most important in Francis Bacon's life. They directed the bent of his mind into certain definite channels. They revealed how his idealism could be brought from the clouds to become embodied in the stern realities of life. They moulded certain lines of action that went far to satisfy the hunger of the "Spirit of Philanthropia"—to spend and be spent in the service of man—that had even then begun to burn within his breast like a consuming flame. They determined for all time his standard of conduct towards himself, his neighbour, and his Creator. It was during his sojourn on the Continent that he began slowly to unfurl the banner of ethical and educational principles which has since been carried by a succession of hands down the Ages, and is to-day being flown to a sure and certain victory by the toiling masses of an enlightened mankind. His mature mind early renounced all credal dogmatism, the first-fruits of which were bitterness, strife, the burning of heretics, and the strangling and disembowelling of recusants. The Teacher in embryo learned for what purpose he had been born. He was to be primarily a Light-bearer to spread the beauty of Ethics and Education, to dissipate the darkness of ignorance.

This period so full of incident, experience, of formative influences that largely determined the course of his future life, is passed over by the majority of his biographers as though it played no part in the unfolding of his personality. Yet how can any student of England's greatest and wisest son, comprehend the emotions that stirred him, the principles that drove him onward through fair days and foul, if these three secret years be left out of the account? One might as well try to explain the flight of an aeroplane by ignoring the factors which make the flight possible—the aerodrome, the ground staff, the petrol. What we want to know is. . . . How can a heavier-than-air machine sail into the stratosphere? Similarly we want to know what was the drive, the motive-force behind this "Philanthropia" which carried him to such tremendous heights of Power and Conquest? The answer is to be found in these first three silent years of his secret life.

Weigh and consider his experiences and reactions.

When Francis Bacon was sent to France, "direct from her Majesty's hand" with Queen Elizabeth's Ambassador, Sir Amyas Paulet, the mind of this extraordinary genius would be necessarily a welter of conflicting emotions. From being a commoner, the son of a lawyer,[1] there had burst

[1]Sir Nicholas Bacon came of no exalted stock. His father was Sir Robert Bacon of Chiselhurst; and his mother Isabella, daughter of Mr. John Kaye of Pakenham. Granville G. Cunningham, *Bacon's Secret Disclosed*, p. 59.

upon him, within the last few days, the stupendous, undreamt-of truth that he was of the Blood-Royal, a scion of the House of Tudor, the Queen's own son, flesh of her flesh and bone of her bone, the head of the English aristocracy as the Prince of Wales (though not "apparent") and heir to the Throne, to which he could have a reasonable expectancy of succeeding in spite of the fact that he was the offspring of a private morganatic marriage, and was born only four months after his parents' wedding: A "reasonable expectancy" because the Queen had the Parliamentary power to name her "Successor" who might even be the "Natural Issue" of her body (not necessarily the "Legitimate" Issue), the Queen having refused to have the word "Lawful" inserted in the Act of Succession. In 1571, twelve years after Elizabeth's Succession, Parliament at the Queen's request made it a penal offence to speak of any other Successor than the "Natural Issue" of the Queen. On this point William Camden the historian says:

> I myself . . . have heard some oftentimes say that the word Natural was inserted into the Act of purpose by Leicester, that he might one day obtrude upon the English *some bastard-son of his for the Queen's Natural Issue.* (*Elizabeth*, p. 167).

For a long time after this—indeed to the end of his life—he appears to have regarded himself as the Queen's "Natural Son" and not a true "illegitimate" although born before his time. Of these facts he would be aware when he learned the truth from Lady Bacon's own lips. Mrs. Gallup's *Biliteral Cypher Story of Francis Bacon*, states that when the youth ran home to Lady Bacon in an agony of shame, thinking he was a nameless bastard, having learned of his Royal relationship from the Queen's own lips, his foster-mother told him all the truth regarding his birth, that the Earl of Leicester was his father, that the marriage was a private one, and that he was born in wedlock some four months after the wedding.

One can imagine how the mind of this youth of sixteen, who already had a range of intellectual accomplishments beyond any of his contemporaries—the ripe, mature, adult mind of a highly-trained scholar—would traverse the possibilities of his position, the wonderful vistas of national and individual progress that would be unrolled before his inner vision, the good that he might do for the souls, minds and bodies of men if he were but firmly fixed in the saddle of power and authority. Would the Queen ever acknowledge him as her son and heir? Or was he fated to wear the "Bacon" Mask riveted over his personality for all time? Was his life destined to drift in the shoals and shallows? Or was he to be known to the great personages in his mother's Stage-Court where "the Stars in Secret Influence COMMENT" (*Sonnet-Diary*, 16-xv), as "the Queen's Bastard?" Was he to be lifted high among men as a Prince, a Ruler and a King? Must he prepare himself for a Great Place? Were his foreign travels part of a plan to educate him for his responsibilities? Only Time could answer these questions.

These thoughts would naturally arise in his mind without any stretching of the imagination on my part; for his first biographer, Pierre Amboise, whose *Life* (1631), published in France, uses this extraordinary sentence respecting Francis's French Travels.

> And he saw himself *destined* one day to hold in his hands the Helm of the Kingdom.
> He also adds that Francis Bacon was *Born in the Purple. . . . Brought up in the expectation of a Great Career.*

These are very significant phrases and can refer only to one thing—his Royal Breed. And when the author talks of "the Splendour of his Race," it is positively certain that he is referring to the Tudors, for the Bacons had no lineage or pedigree. They were commoners. As the son of Sir Nicholas he was never "*Destined* to hold in his hands the Helm of the Kingdom"; nor was he "*Born IN the Purple.*" But as a recognized son of the Queen, as the Prince of Wales, he was indeed destined, for he could not help himself. The Office of King was held by him to be his by Hereditary and Divine Right. He was born to it for he was *in* the Purple of Royalty.

This mysterious biography by an equally mysterious "Pierre Amboise" was found in Paris by the Rev. Walter Begley, M.A., and is quite authoritative. "I found in it a good deal of information about Francis Bacon which struck me as quite new," says Begley. (*Bacon's Nova Resuscitatio*, vol. III, p. 1).

> We find things in this French octavo which neither Spedding nor anyone else among Bacon's numerous biographers ever referred to in a single passage, *ibid*, p. 5.

Amboise appears to have had first-hand knowledge of many passages in Francis Bacon's life. Indeed, the book is so intimately written that some scholars think it must have been written by Francis Bacon himself. Says G. C. Cunningham:

> Parts of the work are so intimate and introspective that I thought I was dealing not with Pierre Amboise but with Bacon's own *Apologia pro Vita Sua*, *ibid*, p. 58. (*See* Begley, *ibid*, p. 1-33).

Perhaps young Francis's fears respecting the uncertainties of his position were somewhat allayed by the fact that a man-o'-war had been specially commissioned to take the party over to France.[1] It seemed to indicate that the Queen, though undecided how to act towards him, beyond getting him out of the country, while she thought matters over, was nevertheless resolved to see that he was treated in a manner befitting his rank. It appears as though Destiny, at that very moment when he stood on the threshold of Life, had taken him by the hand and led him to fields and pastures new, surrounding him for upwards of three years with an ever-changing series of scenes, specially designed, to stamp their impress on his plastic mind, and to draw out of him those inner, transcendent powers specially inbreathed by the Spirit of Wisdom; for he was brought into contact with men and women of many types from clowns and courtesans to Lords and Ladies of virtue and renown. Thrust before his view were Continental manners and customs the most diverse. He travelled widely in all the most civilized countries in Europe, observing judiciously

[1]George Bristowe of H.M.S. *Dreadnought* was directed to convey the Embassy of Sir Amyas Paulet to France . . . to such part on the other side as might be deemed convenient to Sir Amyas. *Acts of Privy Council*, 1676, p. 194.

the Laws and Social Conditions and noting their different forms of State Government. These Continental tours were apparently all planned, for side by side with his travels we find him studying the defects and advantages, political, social, economic, which might help to make a man able for the good Government of men. Pierre Amboise says this:

> Capacity and Memory were never in any man to such a degree *as in this one;* So that in a very short time he made himself conversant with all the knowledge he could acquire at College. And although he was then considered capable of undertaking the most important affairs, so that he should not fall into the usual fault of young men of his kind. . . . *M. Bacon himself wished to acquire knowledge . . . by the study of the manners of different nations.*
>
> I wish to state that he employed some years of his youth in travel, in order to polish up his mind and to mould his opinion by intercourse with all kinds of foreigners. France, Italy, and Spain as the most civilized nations of the whole world were those whither his desire for knowledge carried him.

S. A. E. Hickson, C.B., D.S.O., in *The Prince of Poets*, says:

> There are reasons to believe that he made excursions to Germany (and elsewhere) where his cousin, Philip Sidney, was, who also for a time joined the embassy of Paulet in France. (p. 164.)

Francis Bacon had thus early in life the golden opportunity of becoming an experienced citizen of the world with all the special and peculiar educative power that travel brings. His environment mirrored itself in his mind athirst for knowledge, making more complex "the most exquisitely constructed brain ever created" (Macaulay). He went to France with his mind afire with the thought that he was the secret son of "The Virgin Queen," the next in Succession to the English Throne. His one fear was lest the Queen held to her threat to bar him from the Succession because he had stayed her hand from injuring Lady Mary Scales. Was it a mere outburst of temper, the natural anger at her secret being known and discussed, or was the bar-sinister intended to be a settled policy of State? He was bewildered by the possibilities into which he was plunged and what the future would bring forth . . . whether for good or ill.

On Sir Amyas Paulet arriving at Calais on the 25th March, 1576, he proceeded directly to the French Court. Shortly afterwards he presented his credentials to the King of Navarre and introduced the leading members of his staff. We are told (*Cal. of State Papers, foreign series*) that "they were well-used and dinner provided for them in a special chamber at Court." Afterwards Sir Amyas Paulet had a secret interview with the Protestant Leaders, La Noue and du Plessis, who were assured of Queen Elizabeth's support of the Huguenot cause. We can only imagine what else was said, but we can be quite sure that the handsome youth, who, it would be known, had been placed in his charge by the Queen, would be likely to be one of the topics of conversation and that he would receive special consideration. It would be strange if it were not so. It is unthinkable that his identity would not be discussed or that he was to be regarded as an ordinary commoner rather than someone of note travelling *incognito.* This would explain the reason why facilities were given him to travel to other countries and provinces. There are many diplomatic, non-committal ways of imparting knowledge—a nod, a wink, a jerk of the thumb. At the French Court Francis Bacon found himself at once in an atmosphere of culture, intellectuality, wit, grace, and refinement vastly different from the harsh, almost coarse, manners of the English Court with its unfixed English tongue, coloured with conflicting County dialects, so thoroughly cumbersome and unwieldy as a vehicle of thought, where, even among the most polished courtiers, knowledge, philosophy, poetry, art, science, and culture were held in light esteem. This is stated by a contemporary named George Puttenham, one of those mysterious authors about whom nothing much is known, in *The Arte of English Poesie*.

> It is hard to find in these days of noblemen or gentlemen any good mathematician, or excellent musician, or notable philosopher, or cunning poet. I know many notable gentlemen in the Court that have written commendably and suppressed it again, or suffered it to be published *without their own names to it*, as if it were a *discredit for a gentleman to seem learned*, and to show himself amorous of any good arte.
>
> The scorn and ordinary disgrace offered unto poets in these days is the cause why few gentlemen do delight in the art. (p. 4.)
>
> Sir Philip Sidney also writes in a similar strain: Idle England can scarce endure the pain of a pen. . . . Poetry is fallen to be the laughing stock of children. (See *Defense of Poesie*, pp. 10, 62.)

The French Court was as licentious, however, as it was brilliantly intellectual. Marguerite de Valois had been married to King Henry of Navarre for reasons of State. Though her beauty had inspired all the French poets and *littérateurs*, her husband had been so indifferent to her that the marriage had never been consummated. Indeed, he flaunted his innumerable gallantries before her eyes. He was passionately attached to the Baroness de Sauve who virtually lived with him as his mistress. Marguerite of Navarre was, however, the recognized leader of the Court in ways and manners, especially on the social and intellectual side. Her jocund behaviour, her gallant attire, her rich beauty, the snowy whiteness of her complexion, her crow-black hair, and her accomplishments made her the natural leader over all her fair competitors. She was the centre of attraction.

Her mother was the notorious Catherine de Médicis, for ever to be associated with the hideous massacre of St. Bartholomew which had taken place only some four years previously. Marguerite was therefore a Catholic. Her nominal husband espoused the Protestant cause. From her birth in 1553, she had breathed a vitiated moral atmosphere, but there is no clear evidence that Marguerite of Navarre ever committed herself sexually in spite of her open indiscretions. Historians and biographers are at variance. Writers who take a low view of her charac er are counterbalanced by others who are warm in their praises as to her virtue. We do not yet know the truth and we must reserve our judgment.

> Never have more contradictory judgments been passed on the same woman. In the camp of the Defence, all the great poets of the Renaissance from Ronsard to Desportes have chanted her praises; Brantome has extolled her to the skies; the three brothers d'Urfe and Loys Papon are her passionate admirers; de Coste . . . has made of her a victim and a saint; Bassompierre

has energetically defended her against Dupeix, "that dog which bit the hand that fed him." (*Life of M.N.*, Mme. la Ferriere.)

Literature, music, and art ran in her blood, for the first Marguerite, her ancestress (she was the third Marguerite), was a poetess and the creator of the *Heptameron*, a collection of Tales. Marguerite of Navarre was brilliantly clever with almost a touch of genius. She possessed high literary gifts and a wide range of knowledge. She was also a superb conversationalist.

"By reason of her famous *Memoirs* an enduring radiance will attach to her name," wrote Sainte-Beuve.

Her beauty of mind and intellectual gifts were apparently only equalled by her physical charms, for Brantome in a perfect panegyric of her life wrote:

> To speak now of the beauty of this rare Princess: I believe that all those who are, will be, or ever have been, will be plain beside it and cannot have beauty. . . . No Goddess was ever seen more beautiful. . . . To suitably proclaim her charms, merits, virtues, God must lengthen the earth and heighten the sky, since space . . . is lacking for the flight of her perfections and renown. (*Life*, p. 1).
>
> Whatever she chose to wear, elaborate or simple, the effect was ever the same—all hearts were dazzled, all hearts ravished, so that it was impossible to say which became her best and made her most beautiful, admirable and lovable.
>
> She was the Queen of Beauty and the Queen of fashion as well. (*ibid*, p. 29).

When Francis Bacon arrived at the French Court a divorce was being arranged at her instigation. Circumstances dragged out the proceedings but she did eventually divorce King Henry and retired into semi-private life, constructing a magnificent mansion on the Seine, facing the Louvre, completing it in 1608. Here she spent the last years of her life, dying in 1615, aged nearly sixty-three. H. Noel Williams, *Queen Margot*, says:

> Her hotel resembled a Court far more than the residence of a private individual. She abated nothing of the ceremonial to which she had been accustomed. . . . She lived *en souveraine*.
>
> The friendship which she showed for men-of-letters, savants, and musicians drew many of them round her. . . . It was her custom . . . to invite three or four of her literary protégés to dinner or supper every day, propose to them some subject of discussion, and encourage each to state his views at length; she herself joining freely in the debate, as she delighted to show that her intellect had lost none of its keenness. (p. 376).
>
> Marguerite also seems to have spent much of her time in serious reflection and devotion. She spent large sums in founding and endowing hospitals, convents, churches, and colleges. Morgues estimates her gifts at 120,000 livres a year without counting her private alms. Richlieu said, "She preferred to give to an undeserving person than to fail to give to one who was deserving." (p. 379).

Marguerite was in the prime of young womanhood, in the hey-day of youth, aged twenty-five, when Francis Bacon first became acquainted with her, under the most congenial surroundings. Her husband's apartments might be crowded with politicians, schemers, and wasters, as became a hotbed of intrigue where plots were hatched, the Huguenot pastor versus the Catholic priest, but Queen Marguerite's *salon* was thronged with thinkers and scholars. They were men of a very different calibre, being philosophers, scientists, poets, *littérateurs*, inventors and the like, attracted by the sheer genius of her intellectual personality. Even the poor man, if he were a thinker of promise, had a seat at her table. Riches alone were not the passport to Marguerite's feasts of reason and the flowing wine of wit. These were the courtiers that surrounded the recognized Queen of the French School of Letters, Art, and Science; over whom she presided second to none in wit, repartee, and mental grasp of any problem. Thus it was that when Francis Bacon was introduced to the French Court, he found it vibrant with a spirit vastly different from that which animated Queen Elizabeth's. He was in a different atmosphere, a congenial one, in which every branch of thought was being pressed into the service of "Living"—under the gracious nod of a Royal Personage.

Ronsard, the Prince of French poets, was *the head of a semi-secret fellowship* called *The Pléiade*, which numbered men like Du Bartas, then at the height of his career, Baïf, and D'Aubigné. The fame of "*The Immortals*" was at its zenith when Francis was introduced to this happy band of brothers . . . almost at the moment when the result of their labours was evoking the acclamation of the French nation. The great French Renaissance of literature of the early sixteenth century, following the Italian Revival of Letters, had begun to bear visible fruit. It was worked and toiled for long and laboriously by the Pléiade, beginning with the remodelling of the language and the introduction of new words derived from the classics so that their countrymen could express their thoughts with facility in argument and discussion. The works alone of Ronsard, the poet, Théodore Béza, the historian, Jean Calvin, the theologian, Jacques Amyot, the translator, and Montaigne, the essayist, show how all the avenues of thought on many planes were open to the French thinkers who had learned the mastery of "Words."

To understand Francis Bacon's literary life the student must know something of this French Literary organization, its ideals and what it accomplished. A good idea is obtained from the work of W. T. Smedley, *The Mystery of Francis Bacon*, p. 56.

> The Pléiade originally consisted of a group of seven men and boys who, animated by a sincere and intelligent love of their native language, banded themselves together to remodel it and its literary forms on the methods of the two great classical tongues, and to reinforce it with new words from them. *They were not actuated by any desire for gain* . . . Jean Dorat, professor of Greek in Paris, and five enthusiastic, ambitious youths . . . ages seventeen to twenty-four: Pierre Ronsard, Joachim du Bellay, Remy Belleau, Antoine de Baïf, Etienne Jodelle, Professor Dorat's colleague, Ponthus de Thyard. They formed a band of seven renovators (1549) to whom their countrymen applied the cognomen of the Pléiade. . . .
>
> Realizing the defects and possibilities of their language, they recognized that by appropriations from the Greek and Latin languages and the melodious forms of Italian poetry, they might reform its defects and possibilities of their language so completely that they could place at the service of the great

writers a vehicle of expression which would be the peer, the superior of any language. . . .

That it met with great success is beyond question. . . .

The main point to be emphasized is that it was a deliberate scheme originated, directed, and matured by a group of little more than boys. The French Renaissance was not the result of a spontaneous bursting out on all sides of genius. It was wrought out with sheer hard work, entailing the mastering of foreign languages, and accompanied by devotion and without hope of pecuniary gain.

When this youthful English genius walked beside the English Ambassador into the highest circles of the French Court, he became necessarily permeated with the influence of the Pléiade and of Ronsard and his confrères, for he was already one with them in his very soul. Their ideals were his. He was welcomed with open arms by this happy band of idealists. His mind absorbed like a sponge all they had to teach. Their mainspring of action was in line with his own idealism—all round "Reformation" based on a broadening of educative processes. And this had to begin with Hamlet's study of "Words, WORDS, *WORDS!*" Francis Bacon had left behind him a language so crude that *he was compelled to think in Latin,* for his mother tongue was wholly insufficient to give expression to the knowledge he then possessed. He was present in a country whose language and literature had been Ronsardized. At the most impressionable period of his life, with his mind already ripe to bursting with knowledge of every kind, the records of antiquity, the works of classical authors, the music of modern language, having already planned in outline *The Reformation of the World,* this youth with the most marvellous brain ever created, on whom shone a beam of God's own Wisdom,[1] entered a literary atmosphere that electrified him to white heat. Here he found practical dreamers who sought to purge the world of its evils and who were fighting the Giants of Ignorance with the weapons of Education and Ethics. "Let there be LIGHT" was their battle-cry.

At this crucial psychological moment of decision respecting his mental urgings and his spiritual aspirations, he entered the French Court to see an object-lesson of what a devoted little band of intellectual idealists had done to create a revival of French Thought. Think of the effect this contact would have on the mental resolutions and activities of this brilliant genius whose mind had already begun to be filled with what he called "the spirit of Philanthropia." Think how much we all owe—i.e., the English-speaking nations—to this "happy chance!" and to its far-reaching effects on our language and literature! To its influence can largely be traced the all-round proud position we hold in the world to-day.

One can imagine the comradeship that would be at once established between Francis Bacon—a fluent French scholar—and the galaxy of stars that crowded the Royal Palace of Marguerite of Navarre who "had set the example of attracting poets and writers to her Court and according honours to them on account of their achievements." (Smedley,

[1]"I have been induced to think, that if there were a Beam of Knowledge derived from God upon any Man in these Modern Times, it was upon him: for though he was a great Reader of Books, yet he had not his Knowledge from Books, but from some Grounds and Notions within himself." *Resuscitatio,* 1670, Ed. p. 9. Dr. W. Rawley, for many years his chaplain, secretary and confidant.

ibid, p. 58). It was here he met Montaigne the French essayist, and Desportes the poet and the lesser lights of the Pléiade. And, *let it never be forgotten*, it was in the entourage of Sir Amyas Paulet, that he became the close associate of North, the translator of Plutarch's *Lives*. It was from North's translation that much of the material was drawn for some of the "Shake-speare" Plays, a fact of deep significance in view of their close acquaintance. He also helped Florio, the translator of Montaigne, with some literary work. He walked through Marguerite's Court of Celebrities with the easy grace of the intellectual who knows he can hold his own on the most abstruse subject. In the train of Sir Amyas he rode with the throng of nobles who attended King Henry on his varied excursions to Blois, Tours, Poictiers . . . as brave a gallant as any, for he had the assurance of the secret knowledge in his heart that he had royal blood in his veins. He mixed with fair women and footed it with the best at Courtly Balls over which Queen Marguerite presided, the gayest of the gay, the natural leader of beauty and chivalry. Armed with the most winning ways, of noble physique, handsome looks, keen wit, how could Francis, the brilliant Englishman, pass unnoticed among the great literary lights, the ladies of high degree, the powerful nobles and state dignitaries that surrounded the throne of Henry of Navarre? He was a good mixer. He attended numerous State functions, observed the Catholic and Huguenot intrigues, passed through hostile camps, saw how great men make love and war, and noted the regimental displays at the side of Sir Amyas as the King took the salute, surrounded by his high officers. And the curious were advised not to inquire too narrowly into the identity of the youth who had been sent to France by the Queen of England.

From letters and documents we can form a pretty accurate conception of his character, his likes and dislikes, during these three years at the Court of France. He is referred to as "Monsieur Doux," and "Signor Dolce." His "extreme kindness, sweetness of disposition and heavenly-mindedness" were the constant subject of comment. He appears to have inspired love of his person among many, and apparently he had won early a number of followers and disciples who were willing to aid him in his objects and plans. We can regard him, when he first appeared at the French Court, as an idealist, a dreamer of dreams; fond of dress and pomp, a lover of flowers, scents, gay colours, music, the trappings of a horse, gardens, and old furniture. Hepworth Dixon, barrister-at-law, thus sums up his nature and character:

> When the passions fan out in most men, *poetry fans out in him*. Old when a child, he seems to grow younger as he grows in years. Yet with all his wisdom he is not too old to be a dreamer. While busy with his books in Paris, he gives ear to *a ghostly intimation of his father's death.*[1]
>
> All his pores lie open to external nature. Birds and flowers delight his eye; his pulse beats quick at the sight of a fine horse, a ship in full sail, a soft sweep of country: everything holy, innocent, and gay acts on his spirits like wine on a strong man's blood. Joyous, helpful, swift to do good, slow to

[1]This significant fact has never been appreciated at its full value. Very late in life Francis Bacon recalls the incident that made so profound an impression upon him. He wanted the student of his life to understand that he was A PSYCHIC and that he was attuned to higher vibrations of thought and power than the normal ones which impinge upon the ordinary five senses.

think evil, he leaves everyone who meets him a sense of friendliness, peace and power.

The serenity of his spirit keeps his intellect bright, his affections warm; and just as he left the halls of Trinity with his mind unwarped, so when duty calls him from France, he quits the galleries of the Louvre and St. Cloud with his morals pure.

Not one lapse is known to have blurred the beauty of his youth. For him the d'Agelles sing their songs, the Tosseues twine their curls in vain. *Personal History of Lord Bacon*, pp. 13, 14. 1861.

This description by Hepworth Dixon is that of a heaven-born poet. It reminds one of Rupert Brooke's pæan of praise in *The Great Lover*. And at the time Dixon wrote with such remarkable insight into Francis Bacon's disposition and temperament, there was no open suggestion anywhere that he was the great "Concealed Poet" of the Elizabethan era, although he had claimed to be "a concealed poet" in his letter to John Davies, (28th March, 1603). Already one can see the shaping and making by temperament and environment of the Immortal Poet who laid his talents at the feet of "the Tenth Muse," Pallas Athena, with the cry . . .

> Be thou the Tenth Muse, ten times more in worth
> Than those old NINE which Rhymers Invocate.[1]
> (108-xxxviii).

Everything had conspired to provide his mind with a series of unfolding situations of the most complex character. He was now to be plunged into the fire of emotional disturbance which was destined to produce some of the sweetest love poems in the language, and to give rise to some of the most beautiful female characters ever painted in words, Juliet, Miranda, Imogen, etc. Perhaps of all his experiences at the French Court, this, in many respects, was the most important. It has a direct and an indirect influence on his private life, and, though buried in the sanctity of his own heart, it determined some of his public actions and some of his most important secret writings. It was the culminating factor in the swift ripening of the seeds of human emotion in his own breast. In the fragrant hot-house of the French Court—where poets and lovers, musicians, and artists extolled Love and Beauty by idealizing their sweethearts and mistresses, there was suddenly revealed to him the greatest of all emotional disturbances under heaven—that subtle, exquisite upsurge that Tennyson described as "the maiden passion for a maid."

Francis Bacon fell in love almost immediately on his arrival at the French Court; and the "maiden" who stirred him was no less a person that Queen Marguerite herself.

Tradition says that when Francis first saw her he swooned away, so affected was he by her loveliness or as Theosophists would explain it, by the shock of recollecting that they had met before in a previous life. In a book published in 1621, six years after her death, written in Latin under the mask of "John Barclay," entitled *John Barclay his Argenis*,

[1]Ăthéna, or Ăthéné, called Minerva by the Romans, was one of the great divinities of the Greeks. She is frequently called Pallas Athena, or simply Pallas. Athena or Athene really represent two different nations and epochs. Personally I prefer to spell the word "AthenA" because the spelling of the name of Francis Bacon's muse gave rise to the double "A.A." by which he marked his Rosicrosse books. (See Smith's *Classical Dic.*, p. 85.)

Francis Bacon tells us of his feelings about the fair Marguerite. In later editions of this book a Key is given to the names John Barclay uses. "Argenis" is Marguerite, Francis being named and Queen Elizabeth also. There is therefore no possibility of error.

> While I call to mind the beauty and fortunes of Marguerite, and silently celebrated the good hap of the matchless Navarre in such a love, I began to myself to like and admire those things which I had before quietly beheld without being moved by them; for what was to be found more beautiful than Marguerite?
>
> Was there ever such a grace, and to so great birth, had added so many virtues? Had she no hereditary right, and if out of all the virgins of France, the most deserving were to be elected, there would be none more worthy to be raised to the crown before her. Her wisdom, modesty and discourse beyond her sex; her beauty almost divine. . . .
>
> My imagination dwelt upon these things with curious delight, not yet knowing that if a man desires to be free, and to conquer passion, he has need of much fortitude when love begins to speak. . . . Envy and the sickness of rivalry grew upon me. Pensive, and my soul a captive, did I leave that orchard . . . and to render my malady more vehement, I supped alone. Yet when silent and in private I heard nothing but love speak. So little by little I gave myself up to those cares which within a few days tortured me as a lover, with pains such as before I had never known.

There is not, however, anything very remarkable in the fact that Francis and Marguerite should fall in love with each other. While she was a beautiful woman he had an equally striking personality, with a mind far beyond his years and was physically a mature adult. In view of her extraordinary mind, her literary aspirations, her wide knowledge and range of reading, and the outstanding fact that her cast of intellect was more akin to Francis Bacon's than that of anyone else at the French Court—save Ronsard—it is inconceivable that such persons with so much in common would not be rapidly drawn together by the sheer force of mental gravitation. They were both geniuses of similar tastes, both had their private problems through husband and mother, both needed sympathy, both longed for the ideal things of life and their establishment on earth and both were of the Blood Royal . . . though one was under a cloud as a concealed Prince.

Was his aristocratic lineage known at the French Court? I am sure it was whispered under the rose in the highest circles that the probable future King of England was among them. It would be recalled that Dame Rumour had visited all the Continental Courts, Spain, Italy, France, years previously, whispering into open ears of the "Dwellers on Form and Favour" that the "Virgin Queen Elizabeth" had been secretly married to Lord Robert Dudley and had borne him at least two sons and a daughter. It would be remembered too, how Throckmorton, the then English Ambassador in Paris, had taken upon himself to warn the Queen of her peril in playing with fire. Those whispered scandals relating to Elizabeth that were in circulation some sixteen years previously, can reasonably be assumed to have been revived and commented on *in view of the extraordinary likeness between Francis Bacon and the Queen.* It would be natural to ask—Who is this handsome youth under the wing of the

Ambassador who has the *Open Sesame* to all the highest ranks of French aristocracy by virtue of his having been sent abroad *direct from the Queen's hand*? That she had sent him away from the English Court would be bound to leak out *privately* through those kind friends who simply live to regale tit-bits of scandal.

Hilyard, the court painter to Elizabeth, has left us a portrait of Francis Bacon at this age—an unforgettable one as a study in physiognomy. (He painted Queen Elizabeth at the same time. *The resemblance is most remarkable. The portraits tell their own story*). He had a round face, typically English, the laughing eyes of a poet, the full arches and the lofty forehead bespeaking the philosopher and philanthropist in embryo. The long, straight nose with delicate nostrils averse to anything unsavoury or crooked: a firm, solid chin showing inherent determination without pugnacity: a jester's mouth with the full lips that betray a perfect riot of emotions up-pent within the soul, while his delicate ear told the same tale—that he was attuned to the music of the spheres. Hilyard's portrait is that of a Poet's Poet. His head is well-set on his shoulders and his handsome features are enhanced by the Elizabethan ruff which collars the neck. Such was the appearance of Francis Bacon when he made his bow at the Court of Navarre. His handsome face and alluring ways were sufficient to capture the heart of any woman—maid or wife. There can be little wonder that love flamed between Francis and Queen Marguerite at first sight.

In view of all the facts there cannot be the slightest doubt but that the identity of Francis Bacon was sedulously inquired into by the curious scandal-mongers of the French Court, and that it became an open secret (to be whispered under the rose) that the mysterious stranger was really and truly a Tudor Prince travelling *incognito*, one who might in the future have a powerful influence on the destinies of England and France, as *a Puritan, a Protestant and a Liberal Reformer*. One can imagine how this whispered knowledge would run through the highways and byways of cultured Europe, the Illuminati, the secret Gnostics and Mystics who had kept alive the eternal flame of the Ancient Mysteries from far-flung Time, and the secret societies like the hidden printers' chapels of the Albigenses and the Knights Templar. Doors, that would otherwise have remained sealed, opened to this youthful aristocrat of promise and power—more because of his royal connections than because of his genius.[1]

Marguerite was aware of his real identity from their first private meeting, and though there are no open love-letters in being, and no documentary evidence of the ordinary kind in sight, there is far better proof than the conjectures and traditional myths so whole-heartedly accepted as verified truths by Stratfordians, for the youth Francis DID leave a record of printed evidence . . . a series of Sonnets that he wrote to her, their true meaning having been discovered recently. The discovery goes far to change all our previous conceptions of the Elizabethan era.

[1]It is of course well-known that the Albigenses were officially exterminated in 1245, and the Order of the Knights Templar suppressed in 1312. There were, however, survivors who handed down their secrets, and these and other bodies were flourishing secretly underground when Francis visited the Continent between 1576 and 1579.

It explains much that has been enigmatical in Francis Bacon's life, and it definitely establishes the relationship that existed between them. His passion for Marguerite had the direct result of bringing into being the most remarkable diary of emotion ever written. "When he supped alone silent and in private, hearing love speak, with cares that tortured him as a lover," he began to unburden himself by outpouring his emotions in verse. And throughout the years to old age, in all the great crises of his life he found heart-ease, an outlet, by pursuing the habit he had acquired when in France. While men of a more earthly mould would try to forget, or seek to obtain peace of mind, by drowning themselves in strong drink or other fleshly excesses, Francis Bacon took refuge in a Sonnet of wonderful construction that must have taxed his ingenuity to the utmost. The *Marguerite Sonnets* were the beginnings of the mysterious body of verse known to-day as *Shake-speare's Sonnets*. They became literally and truly his Sonnet-Diary. It was written in secret and kept, so the author tells us, "in sure Wards of Trust that to my use my Jewels of Emotion might unused stay." (*Sonnet-Diary*. 105-xlviii).

From his contact with Marguerite he acquired the habit of clothing his emotions in imaginative terms. They were the true beginnings of what was described by Francis Bacon's friends as "Living Art." They knew his secret, the art of writing poetry of perfection. He was a highly sensitive soul who suffered the rapture and agony of varying conflicting emotions all his life. He suffered more intensely than the average man. Few have been placed on the rack of fate more than the concealed Prince who wore the Bacon mask. . . . He won tranquillity of mind and soul by spilling his agitations on paper, weaving round them in ink a garment of beautiful images—so tenuous and fanciful, so broadly conceived, that they became jewels of passion that could be used by universal man. So skilfully has the poet precipitated his thought round the irritating *motif* that had called his emotions into action that his iridescent pearls, precious because they had been grown out of his heart's blood, had a cosmopolitan appeal . . . to all nations, to all time, to all men. They served vastly different feelings. They appealed to different emotions. And therefore men have ever read into the flashing jewels on the finger of Time vastly different interpretations. The original concrete irritation in the heart of the pearl, enfolded in words that sparkled different meanings, lay hidden and unknown, which was what the author intended. His real thoughts, the cries of his soul, were far too sacred, too precious, too dangerous, to be thrown on the highways of the world, either in his own age or the immediate generations that followed.

The "Living Art"[1] which distinguishes these Personal Poems from all others, consists in this: That Francis Bacon chose his words with such precision that they enfolded, according to a definite rule and plan, the actual *motif* that called the Sonnet into being. There need, therefore, be no doubt about certain matters, historical and personal, concerning Francis Bacon; for we have his Sonnet-Diary, and one who has thus been "taught to read" his "Living Art" knows exactly what the author

[1]The present writer hopes to publish these secret messages in the Sonnets in the near future. The work is already in MS.

means. We can see through the amber of his thought and note the fossils that lie there imprisoned for all time—some beautiful and some repellent, for crises were many during his pilgrimage . . . . and some were very bitter.

That is the reason why we can definitely say that Francis Bacon was passionately attached to Marguerite of Navarre. He left his sacred and secret Sonnet-Diary to be revealed generations after all his contemporaries had passed away—the immortal love-songs of the world's greatest poet.

His first two Sonnets to Marguerite tell the entire story of his passion. He writes to her as a person fully acquainted with his birth-secret. He says that for the moment the Stars do not favour him. He cannot boast of "Public Honour and Proud Titles" which are justly his. Fortune has barred him from such a Triumph.

> "Let those who are in favour with their Stars
> Of *Public Honour and Proud Titles* boast,
> Whilst I whom *Fortune of such Triumph bars,*
> Unlook'd for JOY in that I Honour most."

He then subtly alludes to the fact that he has been razed forth from the book of honour by an unlucky chance, "like some famous warrior, who, after a thousand victories, once foiled, is straightaway regarded with ignominy and all the rest forgot for which he toiled."

> "Then happy I that Love and am Beloved,
> Where I may not Remove, nor be Removed"
> (42-xxv.)

He slips in the thought that even "Great Princes" may die in their pride within themselves at the nod of the Sovereign, just as the "Marygold" (marigold) may wither if too much in the Sun's eye. The original printing of "Mary" in the "1609 Quarto" is a hint that the Sonnet is written to a woman associated with "marigold" which was Marguerite's favourite flower. He also enfolds the *motif* which called the Sonnet into being, the exultant note of a lover who is going to immortalize his mistress. This was apparently his first essay . . . the first Sonnet destined to be published after he was dead under the pen-name of "Shake-speare." The companion Sonnet (43-xviii) has long been regarded as the finest Love-Sonnet in the English language. It is as follows:

HER LOVE . . . . IMMORTAL

> Shall I compare Thee to a Summer's Day?
> Thou art more Lovely and more Temperate:
> Rough winds do shake the Darling Buds of May,
> And Summer's Lease hath all too short a Date:
> Sometime too hot the Eye of Heaven shines,
> And often is his Gold Complexion dimmed;
> And every Fair from Fair sometimes declines,
> By Chance or Nature's changing Course untrimm'd;
> But *Thy Eternal Summer shall not fade*
> Nor lose possession of that Fair thou Owest;
> Nor shall Death brag Thou wander'st in his Shade,
> When in Eternal Lines to Time Thou growest:
> So long as men can Breathe or *Eyes can See,*
> *So long Lives THIS, and This gives Life to Thee.*

In the next three Sonnets he tells Marguerite how his Eye hath played the Painter and stippled her Beauty's Form in the Table of his Heart.

He describes how the Eye and Heart were at a mortal war to divide the conquest of her sight. He then describes the quarrel in such legal terms that Lord Campbell says:

> This Sonnet (45-xlvi) is so intensely legal in its language and imagery that without a considerable knowledge of English forensic procedure it cannot be fully understood.

This fact is perfectly natural seeing that Francis had always lived in a purely legal atmosphere with Lord Keeper Bacon, quite apart from having been torn away from his legal studies at Gray's Inn when he was so hurriedly sent to France by the Queen.

In Sonnet 47-lxxvii he refers to her literary efforts. He knows she is collecting materials for a book and he refers to the blank pages of her diary which will soon be filled with incidents and thoughts that will bear the imprint of her mind. He says, "Commit your thought to these vacant leaves and thou shalt find those children nursed, delivered from thy brain to take a new acquaintance of thy mind; they shall profit thee and much enrich thy Book." The "Book" was afterwards known as her *Memoirs*. A mental creation was always regarded as a "Child" by Francis Bacon. Twenty-six years afterwards (1603) he wrote to his University when presenting them with his book, *The Advancement of Learning*, "I desire to lay in your bosom my NEW-BORN CHILD."

The next eight Sonnets were written when he was on his travels to different countries. They describe his emotions on leaving her (48-l). "How heavy do I journey on my way, when what I seek, my weary travel's end, doth teach that Ease and that Repose to say, 'Thus far the miles are measured from thy Friend'." His mode of travel is by relays of post-horses. He uses a beast that plods duly on tired by his weight of woe for "My Grief lies onward and my Joy behind." The mention of "Posting" indicates that his journeys were long ones.

The remaining Sonnets in the Canto give a wonderful insight into the poet's psychic and psychological knowledge. They not only show that he was familiar with the wonderful powers of the mind but that he, himself, had a developed Sixth Sense which brought him *en rapport with the unseen world beyond our normal senses*. He indicates that he had a knowledge of telepathy, clairvoyance, the human etheric body which often traversed the astral plane at night-time which "could jump both sea and land; as soon as THINK the Place where he would be." All this esoteric information is quietly told under his confession of love and his torment at his journeying away from her. When Francis the lover retires to rest he goes in thought a pilgrimage to her and sometimes he suggests her double or spiritual body visits him, for his "Soul's Imaginary Sight (clairvoyant perception) presents thy Shadow to my Sightless View like a Jewel hung in Ghastly Night making Black Night beauteous." He sees her etheric body by the light of her aura. "Is it thy Spirit that thou send'st from Thee so FAR from Home into my deeds to pry?" he asks. That we may know he is on business bent of some kind he slips in that he is "Travail[1] tired." *i.e.*, "Work-tired." He is not travelling for pleasure.

[1] "Travail" not "travel," an unwarranted alteration by modernists. See *Shake-speare's Sonnets*, 1609 Quarto, No. 27, original edition.

Plate XII

"The Temple", Gorhambury, Sir Nicholas Bacon's country seat
From an old engraving
(See Appendix I)

The ruins of "The Temple"
Photo: Lilywhite
(See Appendix I)

Plate XIII

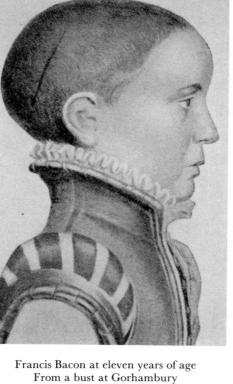

Francis Bacon at eleven years of age
From a bust at Gorhambury
(See Appendix I)

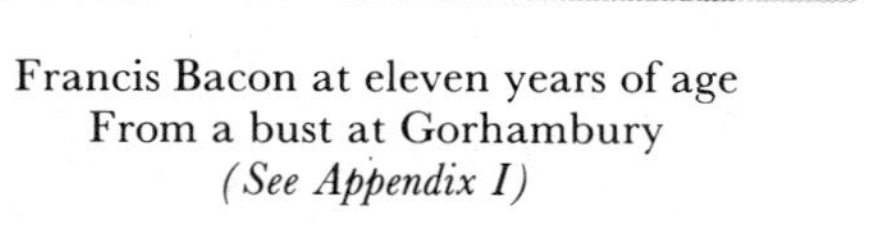

Francis Bacon at eighteen years of age
From a drawing by E. M. Ward, R.A.,
after Hillyard. Engraved by W. Hall
(See Appendix I)

The second Canto to Marguerite opens with the avowal that the preciousness of her love is above all things, in the possession of her he possesses everything. "Some Glory in *their BIRTH,* some in their Skill, Wealth, Bodies' Force, Garments, Hawks, Hounds, or an adjunct Pleasure wherein it finds a joy above the rest. But these particulars are not my measure, all these I better in one general Best. *Thy LOVE is Better than HIGH BIRTH TO ME.* And having Thee of all Men's Pride I boast." He then fears lest she should take all this away "and me most wretched make. But do thy worst to steal away for Term of Life thou art assured mine; and my Life no longer than Thy Love will stay for it depends upon that Love of Thine. O what a Happy Title do I find, Happy to have thy Love, Happy to die." (57-xcii.).

He knows, too, all the unclean things that go on in the Court and so he begs her to take care. "Heaven in thy creation did decree that in thy face sweet love should ever dwell. How like *Eve's Apple* doth thy Beauty grow, if *thy Sweet Virtue answer not thy Show.*" He continues his warning notes, and shows that he is not blind to her frailties:

How Sweet and Lovely dost thou make the Shame,
Which like a Canker in the Fragrant Rose,
Doth Spot the Beauty of thy Budding Name!
O, in what Sweets dost thou thy Sins enclose!
The Tongue that tells the Story of thy Days
Making lascivious comments on thy Sport
Cannot dispraise but in a kind of praise.
(60-xcv).

The next Sonnet was the result of having been to a Royal Ball given by King Henry and the Queen which had lasted until the small hours of the morning. He said his farewell to Marguerite privately, when the sun was rising in the East. When he is alone his thoughts run riot about her appearance, her face, her eyes, her dress . . . from which we know that Marguerite was a brunette, dark complexion, dark eyes, full and round, more glorious than the "Morning Sun of Heaven or the Star that ushers in the Even." Her Black Dress suited her eyes that looked upon him like "Loving Mourners." And so the poet "Swears Beauty itself is Black, and all they Foul that thy Complexion lack." And from the secret message in the poem we learn that the emotion which called it into being was "King Henry's Ball," which had lasted until the early hours of the morning when the lovers had welcomed together the dawn and the rising sun. "Hush! We see the East . . . Farewell!"

It is a fact in history that about this time Queen Marguerite created a sensation at a State Ball by appearing in a wonderful black gown, which matched her black hair, eyebrows, and complexion.

Further evidence of affection is shown by Sonnet 62-cxxviii in which Francis describes his emotions while Marguerite plays the virginal . . . "My Music. . . . How I envy those Jacks that nimbly leap to kiss thy Hand!"

The last Canto to her begins with a Sonnet written some little time before his return to England. He had then been on the Continent upwards of three years. He writes, 65-civ.:

To me, Fair Friend, you never can be old, for as you were when first your Eye I eyed, such seems your Beauty still: Three Winters cold have from the Forests shook Three Summers' pride; Three beauteous Springs to Yellow Autumn turned in process of the Seasons have I seen. Three April perfumes in Three hot Junes burned since first I saw you Fresh which yet are Green. . . .

Hear this, thou Age unbred: "*Ere you were born was Beauty's Summer dead.*"

Long months afterwards—after his return to England—he has preserved in another Sonnet his re-affirmation that his Love is stronger than ever, for it has grown. "Might I not, then, say 'NOW I love you best'? Love is a Babe; Then may I not say so to give full growth to that which still doth grow?" (66-cxv.). Years later, when all hope had vanished of ever being acknowledged by the Queen and succeeding to the Throne, he wrote:

When in Disgrace with Fortune and Men's Eyes,
I, all alone, beweep *MY OUTCAST STATE,*
And trouble Deaf Heaven with my Bootless Cries
And Look upon myself and Curse my Fate . . .
Yet, in these Thoughts, my Self almost Despising
Haply I think on THEE, and then my State,
Like to the Lark at break of day arising,
From sullen earth sings Hymns at Heaven's Gate;
For thy Sweet Love remembered such Wealth brings,
That then I scorn to change my State with Kings.

Francis Bacon never married his Marguerite. But he treasures her in his heart as an ideal, and in the last four Sonnets he mingles her as an idealized Love with other Loves—literature, Masonry, his wife Alice, the Earth-mother—that have taken possession of his life during the marching years. The last Sonnet he writes about her was after she had passed to the Higher Life. He says he knows the lost Ideal is not dead. She still lives.

Thy Bosom (the Bosom of Mother Earth) is endeared with all Hearts,
Which I, by lacking, have supposed Dead;
And there reigns Love and all Love's Loving parts,
And all those Friends which I thought buried . . . but
Thou art the Grave where Buried Love doth LIVE,
Hung with the Trophies of my Lovers gone . . .
Their images I loved I view in THEE,
And Thou (*All They*) hast all the All of Me.

(71-xxi).

This entirely new evidence—which is indisputable—alters the entire scholastic outlook respecting the character of Francis Bacon. I have stressed it at length because it shows unmistakably that instead of being a cold, calculating cynic, he was the very reverse. He was warm-hearted, emotional, sensitive and, as is the way with exceptionally fine-fibred natures, he could not bare his heart to the world and betray his innermost feelings. But he did discharge his feelings in a way unique that only a genius could have imagined . . . the manipulation of a Sonnet carrying in its heart the truth of the particular emotion that called it into being; and he also made provision for the Secret of the Sonnets not to be known to the general world for long generations until all the principal actors were dust, when no harm could be done to anyone by the Diary's disclosures.[1]

Unless we give Francis Bacon's Diary full consideration, regarding

[1]See *The Mystery of Shake-speare's Sonnets: The Riddle Solved.* Lapworth, London, W.C.

it as the basis of authority of his inner life, his aims, his ideals, we cannot possibly understand the springs of his actions. The writing of a biography without the light it sheds is a mere ploughing of the sands, a waste of time and paper. Francis Bacon's Personal Poems are the hidden factor which enters into the problem of his life and falsifies the conclusions of the majority of his previous biographers.

The Sonnet-Diary is confirmed by historical facts . . . every Theme, every Canto, every Poem. During the years 1576-7, Sir Amyas Paulet and Francis Bacon, with the ambassadorial train, went on tour with the French Court visiting Blois, Poictiers, and other places. Young Francis treasured up all he saw abroad, Calais, Rouen, Orleans, Tours, Rheims, Bordeaux, Guienne, and Gascony. He made notes and reflections for future use of all he saw and heard. Nothing was too great or too small to escape his attention. Even the embittered Macaulay is forced to admit that:

> He made a tour through several Provinces and we have abundant proof that during his stay on the Continent, he did not neglect literary and scientific pursuits. . . .
>
> There was a striking peculiarity of his understanding. With great minuteness of observation, he had *an amplitude of comprehension such as has never yet been vouchsafed to any human being*. Essay on F.B.
>
> "During this period," writes E. D. Johnson, author of *The First Folio of Shakespeare*, "Francis Bacon published a book called *Beautiful Blossoms* under the name of John Byshop which was printed in London by Henry Cockyn, he who published the First Part of a book called *The French Academy*, a thick Folio volume of 1,038 pages, double columns, which was really the first encyclopædia which appeared in any language."

During 1578 which, as we have seen, gave rise to eight wonderful Sonnets to Marguerite, he appears to have toured independently, studying matters pertaining to Government, and Statecraft and other subjects . . . some of an esoteric nature. A letter from Sir Thomas Bodley to Francis indicates this tour and that he and his "friends" were paying his expenses. (*See* Parker Woodward, *Tudor Problems*, p. 21). "During his sojourn in France, *we still hear of him studying and writing*," says Mrs. Henry Pott. (*Francis Bacon and his Secret Society*, p. 104.) His independent tours took him to Spain, Italy, Germany, Vienna, Padua, Verona, Florence, if not on his first visit to the Continent, on his second in 1581-2. (*See* S. A. E. Hickson, C.B., D.S.O., *The Prince of Poets*, p. 198.) His industry was prodigious. Though plunged in the midst of riotous, courtly dissipation the only record of him was that he "was still observing." At the end of his European travel-tours, we can imagine the pile of information this rapid worker and thinker had digested and assimilated. Love had had the result of quickening his mental activities to produce something notable to lay at the feet of his mistress.

Sir Amyas Paulet knew, of course, of Francis Bacon's *affaire de cœur* with Queen Marguerite and had duly acquainted Queen Elizabeth. One letter at least passed between the two Queens. Sir Amyas apparently favoured the match. Elizabeth became uneasy and:

> Francis (probably recalled) came back to England—nominally with despatches—but really with a scheme whereby the Queen was to help

Marguerite to get a divorce that Francis might subsequently marry her. This was in 1578. P. Woodward, *Sir Francis Bacon*, p. 13.

The Queen refused her consent. She would not allow her son (about whom she had not yet made up her mind whether to acknowledge him openly or not) to marry a divorced person who was a Catholic. This put an end to the idea of marriage but not altogether to the Royal Romance, for he continued to treasure Marguerite in his heart all his life. While he was in England, *Hilyard, the Court Artist, painted a miniature of Queen Elizabeth, and, presumably by the Queen's command, he painted a similar miniature of Francis.* The young genius must have created an extraordinary impression on him, for Hilyard was so swept off his feet by his intellectual qualities that he wrote round the miniature in Latin, "*Would I could paint his MIND.*"

When he returned to France he continued to associate with Ronsard and his band of idealists. Ronsard was a great writer of Sonnets (he wrote many to Marguerite) and it was but natural that Francis should seek to emulate him. It was well-known to the Pléiade that Francis Bacon had great poetical gifts and *had taken the Goddess Pallas as his Muse and Inspirer.* Pallas was the Goddess of Wisdom and Knowledge, represented in Mythology as "The *Shaker* of the *Speare*" of Knowledge at the Serpent of Ignorance that writhed beneath her feet. The fact that Francis Bacon was thus known so early to be a Poet pledged to Pallas Athena, has never been adequately appraised in summing up his versatile gifts. "The Speare Shaker" points out how Francis Bacon derived his famous *nom de plume*, the strangely spelled word "Shake-speare" with its distinguishing hyphen.

We are indebted to the Rev. Walter Begley, M.A., for the foregoing facts published by him in 1903. A few years previously he discovered a Sonnet addressed to Francis Bacon in the Lambeth Archiepiscopal Library which places the matter beyond all dispute. It was in Anthony Bacon's correspondence and had been preserved by him. It is written by the Duke of Anjou's private secretary, Jean de la Jessée. Anjou was one of the presumed lovers of Queen Elizabeth. Jessée was one of Ronsard's idealists. He was apparently fond of the Muses for he wrote many Sonnets to different persons and published them. In this unpublished Sonnet he says that "his own Muse, prolific as it was, was not a learned or eloquent one, but that Bacon's Pallas had taught it better how to speak." Says Begley, (*Is it Shakespeare?* p. 285), "Now Pallas was not one of the Muses nor had Pallas anything to do with Law; what could Bacon have to do with her?" Here is the Sonnet, valuable and significant, hitherto ignored by the scholars of literature and even by Francis Bacon's latest biographers. *It was unknown to Spedding;* at all events he never mentions it, although it is difficult to think that such an indefatigable researcher of original records never searched Anthony Bacon's letters at Lambeth Palace.

À MONSIEUR FRANCOIS BACON
SONNET

Ce qu' inspire du Ciel, et plein d'affection
Je comble si souvent ma bouche, et ma poitrine
Du sacré Nom fameus de ta Royne divine
Ses valeurs en son cause et sa perfection.

Si ce siecle de fer si mainte Nation
Ingratte à ses honneurs, n'avait l'âme Æmantine
Ravis de ce beau Nom, qu'aus Graces je destine
Avec eus nous l'aurions en admiration.
Donc—Baccon—s'il advient que ma Muse l'on vante
Ce n'est pas qu'elle soit ou diserte, ou scavante:
Bien que *vostre Pallas* me rende mieus instruit
C'est pource que mon Lut chant sa gloire sainte
Ou qu'en ces vers nayfz son Image est emprainte
Ou que ta vertu claire en mon ombre reluit.[1]

La Jessée.

[1]This is a free translation of the last six lines:

Therefore Bacon if it chances that my Muse praises someone
It is not because she is eloquent or learned,
Although your Pallas has taught me better (how to speak);
It is because my Lute sings the saintly glory
Or in these artless lines (naïve) his image is imprinted
Or that thy Virtue bright shines in my shade.

This Sonnet conclusively proves that *Pallas was regarded as Francis Bacon's Muse by the poets of France; that he was known to be a poet;* and that La Jessée and he were friends . . . when Francis was at the French Court. Although the Sonnet is undated it can reasonably be assumed that it was written at that time: at the latest in 1595-6 because it rests between MS. letters to Anthony Bacon. In any case *Francis Bacon had not published openly any literary work,* and nothing as yet had sprung from his great brain. The fact that a Frenchman associates him at so early a date with Pallas "The Shaker of the Speare" is indeed of deep significance and of the utmost importance. It is amazing to me that Spedding overlooked this poem and its implications. Ignore it or explain it away as we will the astonishing fact remains that though his "*Shake-speare's Sonnets*" or any work under the title of "Shake-speare" had not been published, La Jessée knew of the connection between Pallas and Francis Bacon, a connection, moreover, that was to be confirmed by what Francis wrote afterwards in his Sonnet Diary—a Sonnet that was not to be published to the world for long, long years.

TO ATHENA

How can my Muse want subject to Invent,
While thou dost Breathe, that pour'st into my Verse
Thine own sweet Argument, too excellent
For every vulgar Paper to Rehearse?
Be thou the Tenth Muse, ten times more in Worth
Than those Old Nine which Rhymers invocate;
And *he that calls on Thee,* let him Bring Forth
Eternal Numbers to outlive long Date.

(108-xxxviii).

This Sonnet was written to Pallas and her name is written through the lines secretly assuring her of his devotion to her cause.

With the ancient Greeks she was looked upon, says Begley, as the protectress and preserver of the State. This was exactly the ideal Francis Bacon had set for himself but it had to be done *with the weapons of Pallas which were education, wisdom, the spread of knowledge, and ethics.* This fully explains why Bacon called himself "Shake-speare." And just as the mythological Pallas had sprung fully-armed from the head of Zeus, so the inference is that "Your Pallas" had sprung fully armed from Francis Bacon's brain. The literary circle when he was in France knew that he was a poet and the champion of Pallas the Spear-Shaker from which it is easy to see the derivation of the name "Shake-speare."

This evidence is clinched by another important factor brought to light by Begley. In the Lambeth collection of MSS. is a remarkable paper without heading, docket or date. It is a rough draft of a Sketch or *light Play in Francis Bacon's handwriting.* It is a petition signed and presented by Philautia, the Goddess of Self-Love, to Queen Elizabeth. It seems to be a portion of one of the Plays that Francis Bacon wrote for the Earl of Essex to be acted before the Queen in 1595. It is really a fragment written with an ulterior motive, and veils his plea for public acknowledgment. It begins:

> Excellent Queen, Making report to PALLAS, *upon whom Philautia depends,* of my last audience with your Majesty and of the Opposition I found . . . she, putting her Shield before her eyes as she useth when she studieth to resolve . . . said. . . . 'This shall you do . . . and the ALONE QUEEN—so she ever terms your Majesty, will see that she hath Philautia's first offer. *If she reject it, it will be received elsewhere to her disadvantage* . . .' etc. Philautia.

Says Begley commenting on this:

> It is Pallas who is the real originator of the advice to the Queen and consequently Pallas stands for Bacon. . . . She puts her shield before her eyes when thinking, which reminds us of the thoughtful Francis sitting in his arm-chair cogitating, with his uplifted arm supporting his head. . . .
>
> We are told that Pallas-Bacon "ever terms" Elizabeth "*the Alone-Queen*" (which reminds one of what Francis Bacon wrote elsewhere, "I pray God she may not be too much ALONE, but it is a Name of excellency and *virginity,*" which refers to the Queen's pose of virginity).
>
> The name of Pallas was given because she was wont to *shake* her *speare* and was produced from Jove's head because wit or intellect comes from the head, and she presided over the arts because nothing excels wit or wisdom in the supreme rule of all the arts.
>
> *Thus Pallas, Bacon and Shake-speare are all names for* one *man,* (*ibid,* pp. 286-9)

who is presenting a covert petition to Elizabeth as late as 1595 to let him take his true name Tudor so that she will not be "the Alone-Queen" any more.

We thus see that the name "Shake-speare" was derived from Pallas Minerva, who was known to be associated with Francis Bacon by his circle of French friends as far back as 1579 (Jessée's Sonnet presumably was written then) and was still associated with him, *under his own hand,* SIXTEEN YEARS LATER, in 1595, in the Play or Device written for Essex, when the name of "Shakespeare" had not been appended to any Play, only to *Venus and Adonis* and *Lucrece* published in 1593 and 1594 respectively. We are therefore fully justified on the foregoing evidence in accepting the further evidence of the Title Page that "Shake-speare's Sonnets" are verifiably the record of the private life of Francis Bacon. And this is substantiated by Jonson's famous lines in which he says *the author* "Seems to *Shake a Lance* (*i.e.*, a Speare) as Brandish't at *the Eyes of Ignorance.*"

His travels with the Court resulted in the storing of information which was afterwards reflected in the great Shake-speare Plays, but of his many private excursions little or nothing is known. They had, nevertheless, a profound influence in determining one most important aspect of his energies and directing them into a sphere of secret labours which he pursued with passionate zest all his life, without haste or rest, until he heard the Master of the Spheres call

> "Unarm Eros! The long day's task is done,
> And thou shalt sleep."

These secret tours were the final factors that made Francis Bacon the all-round, full-orbed man with that peculiar caste of mind which forced him into becoming not only an open educationist but a secret Ethical Teacher with a definite mission to mankind.

We have seen that Francis Bacon was naturally drawn to the esoteric aspect of nature . . . the occult, mental phenomena and the like, even as a boy. When at college he drops a remark that indicates his acquaintance with Egyptian and Chaldean lore. He lets us know that he was early familiar with the Æneid. He would therefore know something of the Mysteries and what they stood for—the purification of Man by trial and initiation, the personal *Advancement of Knowledge* by educative moral travel. These ideas were the dawning light of that peculiar system of morality couched in allegory and illustrated by symbol which to-day runs throughout the world—an Empire on which the sun never sets.

The broken lights of Egyptian and Grecian thought were flickering still in isolated bosoms when Francis Bacon was sent to France. Scattered here and there were the Illuminati, Theosophists, Mystics, all heretics who had escaped being stamped out by the harsh theologians. There were the Knights Templar (actually opposed to the Catholic Church) who with their Nine Degrees had kept the Ancient Mysteries alive from the immemorial past through Virgil and Dante. There were also the secret little conclaves of the Albigenses who had evaded the torture-chamber and the stake—the men who knew the secret of introducing watermarks in paper, symbols of hidden meaning, and employed purposeful misprints in order to communicate with their brothers who had been scattered by persecution.

When these various types of liberal-minded men heard that someone directly connected with the Protestant Queen Elizabeth, a secret Prince maybe, a genius of the first water, was travelling from "West to East" to study manners and customs while on special missions, these ethical philosophers, the successors of Dante, of ancient Knightly Orders and Mystical Cults, who dare not raise their heads openly, and could only communicate with each other by an underground network, naturally made it their business to get in touch with the young English aristocrat, who, as a Puritan in a position of power, could do so much in the future to liberalize the thought of the civilized world. Once more we see exemplified the truth of the working of the Law—"The things he sought were seeking him."

Thus began the secret Renaissance of Ethics on definite lines. The best brains on the Continent were drawn together. There were originally seven heads but each had his group of followers. A plan of campaign was carefully drawn up, a long view being taken. There was to be no immediate beating of drums. Everything was to be done quietly and in secret . . . the ground prepared, the seed sown, the harvest only to be garnered openly in future years. The Land of Promise was a land which none of them, like Moses, might ever enter.

Francis Bacon became initiated in secret and mystical Continental Orders which through persecution were virtually in a moribund state. He learned the ritual of the Mysteries and the solemnity of the ordeal through which the neophyte passed. He took part in the stately ceremonial of the Knights Templar. He studied the Jewish Cabala and obtained first-hand its peculiar knowledge. He sat at the feet of the men who knew how to write their secrets through the printed page that no one could trace unless he had been "*taught to read*." He saturated himself in Arabian lore and Egyptian mysticism. And he combined all this hidden wisdom with his own knowledge of Christian Ethics and the secret marks of the old operative masons, their grips and knocks and lodges that had so fascinated him when "The Temple" was built at Gorhambury. And he associated all this with the customs of the German Steinmetzin and the Medieval Guilds. Thus were the bases laid for the building of an ethical King Solomon's Temple which was to be upreared invisibly without the sound of hammer or chisel, where men could eventually moralize on working Tools and spiritualize a Building Plan. And the architect to evolve—out of the customs and cults of the ancient world, so rich in its symbolism of Natural Philosophy—a scheme that would have a more universal appeal for the sons of men . . . was Francis Bacon. He it was who undertook to reorganize the Nature Myths with a new and more up-to-date interpretation, by rewriting the rituals of the ancient cults which should have as their basis ethics of universal application, morality devoid of credal dogmatism, the foundation stones being education, wisdom, charity, the Fatherhood of God, the Brotherhood of Man. So the youth, *while in France*, who afterwards said he had "taken all Knowledge to be his Province" at once proceeded to rewrite the various Rituals of the Rosicrucian College that are practised to-day, and to create the Rituals of Freemasonry. *But no one knew of this secret work at the time nor for many years later.*

The facts of history are plain. The Rosicrucian College and the Craft Degrees of Freemasonry were not in existence anywhere before Francis Bacon went to the Continent. This is stated very clearly by such a learned authority and Rosicrosse-Mason as De Quincey (see *Rosicrucians and Freemasons*, chap. II). Yet the Masonic Legends tell us that the Mystery of Masonry was introduced into England by a traveller from the Continent. *And the Mystery is couched in our modern tongue;*[1]for the language is Elizabethan, poetical, flexible, dramatic. Who, then, other than Francis could have created this unique work of art as a ritual? Created, says the same authority, "*by a young man of extraordinary talents* in or before the beginning of the seventeenth century." (De Quincey, *ibid. Intro.*) While

[1]See *The Literary Characteristics of the Ritual*, Ch. XI, *Shakespeare, Creator of Freemasonry*, by Alfred Dodd, Rider & Company.

Francis Bacon was making his solitary tours to various parts of Europe to study the various forms of Government in the then civilized world, he was also, figuratively, "a Traveller from West to East," making contacts with many types of thinkers, and obtaining first-hand knowledge of the Wisdom of the Ancients.

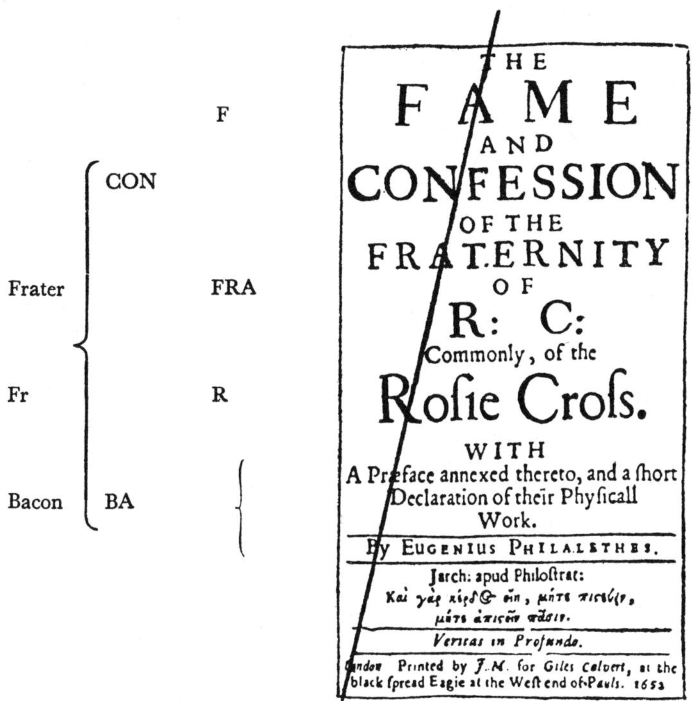

THE
FAME
AND
CONFESSION
OF THE
FRATERNITY
OF
R: C:
Commonly, of the
Roſie Croſs.
WITH
A Preface annexed thereto, and a ſhort Declaration of their Phyſicall Work.

By EUGENIUS PHILALETHES.

Jarch: apud Philoſtrat:
[illegible]

Veritas in Profundo.

London Printed by *J. M.* for *Giles Calvert*, at the black ſpread Eagle at the Weſt end of *Pauls*. 1652

FACSIMILE TITLE-PAGE OF THE FAMA
A Translation in 1652 by Eugenius Philalethes (Thomas Vaughan)
If a line be drawn from A in "Fame" to the corner of the left-hand page—i.e., from the top line to the bottom—the letters on the left side spell in Cypher, "Frater Francis Bacon." The word "Fraternity" gives a count of 157, which is the seal of the Rosicrosse. The book carries the K Cypher also. See *American Baconiana* for February, 1928.

(*See Appendix I, p.* 356)

Rosicrucianism and Freemasonry have much in common, though to-day the fact is not apparent. They were, in a sense, born together. To prove this is not germane to the present work. For the moment it must be accepted, pending the proofs in a later work to be published. Suffice it to say that Freemasonry was not known to "the uninstructed world" to be in existence until 1723 when it was formerly announced by the issue of a work prepared by the Rev. James Anderson, *The Constitutions of Free-masons*, which claimed to be the principles of a secret Society which had existed from time immemorial. Openly, the work tells us very little, but to the "informed Brother" it tells us a great deal. Anderson and the "Learned Brethren," in short, whisper to us the name of the Founder of the Craft. *He was Francis Bacon.*

The Rosicrucian Fraternity made itself known to the world, however, by the publication of an anonymous work in Germany about the year

1614, and it was followed by a series of anonymous pamphlets with ethical principles and spiritual knowledge. The most important are *The Fama, The Confessio,* and *The Chymical Marriage.* And the startling fact emerges that the very first pamphlet laid it down that the Rosicrucians had as their goal "*The Reformation of the Whole Wide World,*" which we know to-day (*what the world did not know then*), was the ideal of the boy Francis conceived by him when at the University. Those Rosicrucian pamphlets are full of Francis Bacon's ideas. This was not known at their time of publication and has only become known by an examination of his complete works, the majority published after this date. Nor can this be wondered at, for, says Mrs. Henry Pott, in her erudite work of research, (p. 260), one of the most important of the anonymous publications

> *The Chymical Marriage* we now find to have been written by Francis Bacon at the age of fifteen.

Apart from these ethical views the pamphlets contain some important information. They state that the founder was a boy about fifteen when "he came hither" i.e., to the Continent, and that he wrote *The Chymical Marriage. The Fama* states:

> After this manner began the Fraternity first by four persons only, and by them was made the Magical Language and Writing with a large Dictionary (a reference to the Language of Symbolism).

The initials of the Founders are given, five in all of the "first circle," and among them is "*Fra. F.B., Pictor et Architectus,*" which obviously stands for "Frater Francis Bacon, Painter and Architect," for Francis Bacon as a Poet was a Painter with words, and he was the Designer of the Invisible Temple of King Solomon, unknown to all outsiders in 1614. *The Fama* further tells us:

> That the High and Noble Spirit of one of the Fraternity was stirred up to enter into the scheme for a *General Reformation* and that he travelled away to the wise men of Arabia. . . . This *young member was sixteen years old at the time and for one year he had pursued his course alone.* . . . He travelled to Damcar.

This corresponds exactly to the known facts of Francis Bacon's life. There were surely not two extraordinary young men travelling the Continent at the same time animated by the same ideals. He travelled alone actually and symbolically—for every thinker studies alone . . . and he was still more alone as he progressed onwards. His ardent mind wanted to get at a knowledge of the First Causes of Things. Francis Bacon's contacts enabled him to take up the study of Rhazis, Avenzoar, Averroes, Avicenna, and other Arabian and hermetic writers, for all these mystical writers are afterwards quoted in his various writings. He went metaphorically to "Damcar" to the "Wise Men," because this kind of esoteric knowledge comes from the East. The "Wise Men" revealed to him their Mysteries. He went back to the ancient philosophies, almost crushed out of existence by the Church, in order to trace the history of learning and thought from the earliest recorded times. These occult philosophies of India, Persia, Arabia, and Egypt had a most profound influence upon his mind and writings. For many of their symbols and emblems are to be found in the Masonic Arcanum, the language, hieroglyphics and dramatic ceremonial from ancient Rites. These and other things were the foundations and the stones from which the Master Architect (Hiram Abif) made his selection in the slow building-up of the Pyramid of Thirty-Three Degrees.

That all these labours were begun in France is proved by the fact that definite Masonic Messages are to be found in several of the Sonnets written to Marguerite of Navarre who was privy to his work. He lets an "Instructed Brother" know he had already sketched out in his mind the entire Masonic Hierarchy by the way he writes that beautiful Sonnet 64-cvi.:

> "When in the Chronicle of Wasted Time,
> I see Descriptions of the Fairest Wights,
> And Beauty making beautiful Old Rhyme,
> In Praise of Ladies dead and Lovely Knights."

He writes through the Sonnet these remarkable secret lines:

> *When I see an Installation, too, I see even Solomon's Order—Commanders, Knights, Lords, Princes—a Temple for Hiram.*

Francis Bacon saw in imagination the Ethical Temple he was building as Hiram the Architect; Solomon's Order with its dignified ceremonial, Knights, Commanders and Sovereign Princes. His "Praise is but a prophecy" of what the future will bring forth; for his Ethical System could no more be accurately described than the beauty of his mistress could have been foretold with precision by the writers of ancient times. He had apparently been to an Installation of one of the Ancient Orders and he was comparing it with the NEW ORDER he was creating in his mind that would supersede the Ancient of Days. He fuses the emotions produced by the Installation of an ancient cult with the emotions inspired by his mistress.

Allied with this secretive work is the fact that while he was in France he learned "the Art of Secret Writing" in many forms by numbers, by Capitals, by pictures and by writing concealed sentences openly through the printed text. In one of his latest and most important works he refers to the time when he was a youth in Paris, and states that he invented a new form of Cypher, the Biliteral he called it, that could be placed in the printed text, and would be utterly unsuspected by all who were not privy to the code. In the *De Augmentis*, published 1623, he gave specific examples of the Cypher and several others. He speaks of them with an easy familiarity as though he was constantly using them, which, indeed, he was, for he began as a youth when he enfolded Marguerite's name in his first love Sonnet. Lord Campbell wrote, *Life*, p. 10:

> Francis Bacon spent three whole years in France—*the most valuable* of his life—and his subsequent literary eminence may be traced *to his long sojourn in a foreign country*.
>
> It has received too little attention in tracing the formation of his mind and character. Allusion is made by his biographers to his residence in France in such terms as might be used in describing a trip to Paris by a modern law-student during the long vacation. (p. 9).

But Lord Campbell never suspected what we know now. . . . Francis Bacon as the son of Queen Elizabeth; his love for Queen Marguerite of Navarre; the poet who had taken as his Muse Pallas Athena; the young Ethical Teacher with his peculiar system of morality based on allegory and illustrated by symbol. What would Lord Campbell have written had he known all? He would have recognized the truth of his statement, but how much wider and broader and truer would have been his biographical romance.

We have now a clear picture of Francis Bacon, and his intellectual progress at the end of his three years' stay on the Continent. We see his early dream of the reformation of the world slowly crystallizing into a definite pattern. He had a number of disciples. He was going to be the founder of a secret system which both the Church and the State would destroy if it were known. He was to be a teacher of ethics. His system was to be primarily on the lines of the Drama, the Mysteries. He would follow the Ancients, but he had something better to produce. He would utilize his secret princely office to further his plans and win adherents. He would Tudorize or Baconize England as Ronsard had Ronsardized France. He would create a flexible English language so that Englishmen could speak in their own tongue their most subtle thoughts without recourse to Latin. He would educate the common people by Stage Plays, putting before them parables in dramatic form that had as their goal the triumph of Virtue, the dethronement of Vice. He would create a reading public by the issue of cheap translations in English and staging quarrels between pamphleteers. He would teach his countrymen the history of their own times, and make them into proud patriots with the music of the great deeds done by their forbears. He would act as bell-ringer to the sciences and philosophers, calling them together to labour for man's common good, socially and politically. He would lead two lives—an open one and a secret one. He would spread the Light openly where his thoughts and actions would not bring him into conflict with authority. He would lay and plan secretly and write anonymously so that his ideas might be rooted and grounded, and so widespread that they could not be destroyed. He would try to forget his bitter love-trial by hard work. He would save himself by Labour and Hope.

And then in the midst of these high resolves, Sir Nicholas Bacon died and he was recalled home to England.

Chapter VI

THE LAYING OF GREAT BASES FOR ETERNITY (1579-1587)

SOMETIME in February, 1579, Francis Bacon dreamt that Sir Nicholas Bacon's house was plastered over with black mortar, and he awoke with a feeling that something had happened to a member of the family. A few days later he learned that Sir Nicholas had died suddenly on the 20th February. This psychic premonition is recalled years afterwards in the *Sylva Sylvarum* (1627) as worthy of record, an out-of-the-way fact of Nature demanding an explanation. A month later (20th March) he is recalled to England bearing despatches and a letter from Sir Amyas Paulet in which Francis is spoken of as

> being of good hope, endued with many and singular parts, and one who, if God gave him life, would prove a very able and sufficient subject to do her Highness good and acceptable service. (*State Paper Office; French Correspondence*).

In view of what we already know, he went direct to the Queen—the Ambassador's letter providing an excuse for the interview—in an effort to ascertain what were his future prospects: Was he to take up his rightful place as her son or must he still continue to masquerade as the son of the late Sir Nicholas? He was apparently told to go to Lady Bacon's home—she was living at York House, next door to the Palace—and await developments.

Sir Nicholas Bacon had died a very wealthy man. The Queen had loaded him with money and presents. In December, only a few weeks prior to his death, he had made an elaborate Will, which, when read, disclosed that he had left large sums to his children by a first wife, and a sufficient income for Lady Anne and her son Anthony; but *the name of Francis was not even mentioned. He was not left a solitary penny.* Why? Because Francis was not his child. This significant and deliberate omission by a careful and astute lawyer tells the truth of the real parentage of Francis with more deadly emphasis than even his registration of birth as "MR. Franciscus Bacon." Sir Nicholas knew that the lad's prospects lay elsewhere, with the Queen herself, and he was not going to do anything to allow her to shirk her parental responsibility. She must provide for him. Sir Nicholas purposely left the lad nothing so as to force the Queen's hand and to leave her without an excuse for providing for him and recognizing her own son. On this very point, Parker Woodward, a solicitor, writes:

> On the 12th December, 1878, Sir Nicholas Bacon who had been much enriched by the Queen had made an elaborate Will wherein he made

full provision for his first family, his widow and his child Anthony, but left nothing whatever to Francis. He had three sons and three daughters. The Will may be seen at Somerset House. *Early Life*, p. 18.

If it were not an actual fact that Francis was the Queen's son, is it not strange that neither Lady Bacon, nor Anthony, nor Francis, nor any member of the family expressed astonishment that Sir Nicholas Bacon's Will made no monetary provision for Francis? The truth is self-evident: *He was not mentioned in the Will because he was not of the Bacon family*. Even when Francis, many times afterwards, was desperately pressed for monies, he never once complained of harsh financial treatment or neglect by his "father." He always speaks of Sir Nicholas with respect and love, there being a bond between them which was never once broken by a quarrel. The complaints of Francis in his correspondence are always directed against the Queen and her Ministers. The reason is clear: Francis knew he had not the slightest claim as a son on the estate of Sir Nicholas or on the Bacon Family, and that all his future was bound up with the Queen's WILL. *She was the only person to whom he could turn for financial assistance.*

Thus the plain truth emerges that while full provision was made for the six children by Jane Fernley and for the eldest son of Lady Anne, Francis was the only one left poor and penniless by the Lord Keeper *for no apparent reason*, and there is no trace that Francis complained or that Lady Anne marvelled.

At eighteen years of age this extraordinary genius with whom Fate had so early begun to play such fantastic tricks, girds up his loins and faces the world alone. He has no money, no lands, no income, no one on whom he can legitimately depend for assistance even for ordinary necessities. He never seems to have approached in any way the Earl of Leicester, his real father. Francis regarded him suspiciously as the real cause of his trouble. He disliked his character and held him apparently at arm's length. But he had a staunch friend in Lady Bacon, and no one could have been blessed with a better comrade and foster-brother than Anthony. And their home was still his home.

Imagine the feelings that swept over him as he crossed the threshold of York House for the first time after his three years' Continental travel; and his thoughts as he waited night after night for some message from the Queen . . . the message that would announce his recognition . . . *the message that never came.*

Think of the irony of the situation. He had returned from the gaieties of Paris, from the idealism of the Pléiade, from the light love and laughter of Marguerite's presence, from the Court of Navarre where he was treated with deferential honour by all, and regarded as an equal of the noblest lords . . . to find himself a real stranger to the old home in which he had been bred as a child and an outcast from the kingly inheritance to which he was justly entitled by blood. Sir Nicholas's death and his lack of a monetary allowance had created a crisis in his affairs. His thoughts would race on: the Queen must acknowledge him, must provide for him, he must be allowed to take up his proper position in the state. He had the right to stand next to the Throne. Why shouldn't he? How could he enforce his claim? How bring himself to the notice of the Queen when he had no *raison d'etre,* no right of entry to her presence? He was in a situation of grave perplexity. He was not a gentleman of good estate. He had no prospects—none of entry into public life—save by the WILL of the Queen. He was no longer fit to be the companion of wits and nobles, judges and Privy Councillors, as in Sir Nicholas's day, if he were not acknowledged by the Queen. How could he any longer go to Court, even if he had the "open door," to feel that all eyes were looking at him, thinking of his birth-secret, whispering and wondering what would ultimately befall him. Later he was to cry out to the Queen in his agony of mind:

> I see you withdraw your favour from me, and now I have lost many friends for your sake: I shall lose you, too. You have put me like one of those that the Frenchmen call *Enfans perdu . . .* (*lost children*); so have *you put me into matters of envy without Place or without Strength.*
>
> *Francis Bacon to Queen Elizabeth,* "*Apologia.*"

Could anything be told more directly. Francis Bacon was indeed a "Lost Child," lost, concealed purposely from the world.

Perplexity and bewilderment that had dogged him like silent ghosts through the joyous days of Paris and Navarre, now stood before him waiting like mendicants for his decision. They waited and they would not go away nor be gainsaid. At last they bred within him that fierce irresolution that found so powerful an expression in *Hamlet* . . . the Prince who could not succeed to his father's Throne, any more than Francis could succeed to Elizabeth's . . . Hamlet who lived on the sword-edge of a balance *not knowing what to do for the best* . . . to wait, wait, wait or to act.

Sir Nicholas had been buried in St. Paul's. Lady Anne left York House and retired for life to their country seat, THE TEMPLE, Gorhambury. Some weeks later Anthony went to the Continent for a prolonged stay, travelling to Paris, Bordeaux, Navarre, and Italy . . . quietly following in the footsteps of Francis, conning languages and manners of various countries, politics, and events; discussing politics with William Parry, cracking jokes with Montaigne, carousing with the courtiers of Henri of Navarre and writing Sonnets to outvie Ronsard. All this time he was fitting himself by his wide acquaintance with all sorts and conditions of men, and Continental customs and foreign affairs, to *become the first secret agent abroad of the great Queen,* the collector and purveyor through trusty channels of vital information dispatched in code respecting the moves and intentions of the Queen's enemies. Early after his arrival he began to send Burleigh and Walsingham dispatches of import, marked by rare prescience, regarding the policy of the great powers. Moreover, he had another mission to perform: to lay the foundation-stones of Francis Bacon's Secret Societies on the Continent and to cement the ties already made by Francis; for Anthony was a whole-hearted enthusiast in Francis Bacon's ideals and designs. He was the first man to know in its entirety the vastness of the plans which Francis had made and the means whereby they could be marked out.

Anthony had plenty of money and an assured income to allow him to lead the life of a traveller and a gentleman of leisure. Research shows that at that time he was the master of the Manors of Redburn, Abbottsbury, Minchinbury, Hores (Hertford County), Brightfirth Wood, Merydan Meads, Pinner-Stoke farm (Middlesex), and other holdings.

The case with Francis was very different. He had either his way to make in the world or he had to win recognition by the Queen, and in order to decide what to do, until he knew what the next few days or weeks would bring forth, he was compelled by sheer need of food and shelter to rest in the haven of the hospitable mothering arms of Lady Bacon and to live on her comparatively slender means. Meanwhile he had to think how to live instead of living only to think. Hepworth Dixon says, *Personal History of Lord Bacon*, p. 28:

> The aids from the Bacon family were scant. Lady Anne allowed him all she could, and Trott, a man of wealth, poetry and wit, advanced him some money, but the new Sir Nicholas would not see him.

There are no documents that tell us what action was taken by the Queen or Francis to decide his future but we know that three months later, in June, 1579, he had begun to keep his terms at Gray's Inn, his Chambers being in Coney Court looking over the gardens to Highgate Hill; a good house of three or four stories. The next we hear from him is a letter addressed to a Mr. Wylie, dated 11th July, 1580, from Gray's Inn, showing that he was in residence; and on the 27th June, 1582, on the completion of the three-years' term, he was called to the Bar. He was then twenty-one.

Now from subsequent events, it transpires conclusively that his law studies were very much against the grain. He was utterly averse to his residence in Chambers. "The Law drinketh up too much of my time," he said. "I wish for studies of greater delight . . ." which is pretty conclusive evidence that he was engaged even then in creative literature and kindred studies, and that he disliked the dry technicalities of the legal profession, preferring the fascination of studying human nature and intellectual pursuits. But Francis was forced against his will into Law, and to meet in the same Inn, as fellow students, his "cousins" Nicholas Trott and the ill-shaped and crooked-minded Robert Cecil (Lord Burleigh's son) who was destined to be a thorn in Francis's flesh even in the hunchback's death. We may very pertinently ask—who forced Francis into the Inns of Court utterly against his wishes? Who paid his fees for three years? Provided his books? His clothes? His personal expenses and pocket-money necessary for him to meet on equal terms the rich sons of wealthy noblemen, lawyers, ministers, merchants? There is only one answer . . . THE QUEEN!

From the facts of the times, letters, documentary evidence, and the light thrown by future happenings, the relative positions of Queen Elizabeth and Francis Bacon appear to have developed in this way: Shortly after his return from Paris she decided that Francis must continue to play the role of son to the late Sir Nicholas, no matter how he disliked it or how contrary it was to his idea of dignity. He must follow the pro-

Plate XIV

Marguerite of Navarre, Queen of France, aged twenty
From a drawing by an unknown artist in the Bibliothéque Nationale

Pierre de Ronsard, French poet and Friend of Francis Bacon. As a youth Ronsard started the French Renaissance with a few youths named the Pléiade. In 1576, when Francis Bacon arrived in France, the fame of the Pléiade was at its zenith. With Ronsard he was associated for three years, and from him conceived the idea of forming an English Renaissance on the same lines

Queen Elizabeth
(Hillyard miniature)
(See Appendix I)

Her Son Francis
(Hillyard miniature)
(See Appendix I)

Lord St. Albans by Van Somer,
from *The Martyrdom of Francis Bacon*
by Alfred Dodd
(National Portrait Gallery)
(See Appendix I)

fession of the law, treading in his "father's footsteps," and at once resume his studies at Gray's Inn to qualify for a living. She would pay his fees, provide him with sufficient moneys for all his wants, and find him pocket money. With regard to publicly acknowledging him as her son and heir to the Throne, it must lie in abeyance as no decision one way or the other could be given as yet. It was a matter for her Ministers to consider as much as hers.

In this decision Francis was compelled to acquiesce. She held the power of the purse.

Elizabeth was undoubtedly in a very difficult position. However much she wished to acknowledge him publicly as her son and heir, it was obvious that this was tantamount to a public confession of premarital relationship with a married man, and though Francis was truly born in wedlock, and therefore a legitimate, he was nevertheless in law, "an adulterine bastard." How could she acknowledge him without shaking the allegiance of half her subjects?

Francis, naturally, looked at the position very differently. She was his mother. It was her "WILL," her desires that had brought him into being. On his return from France and for several years afterwards he could not conceive the possibility of being utterly cast off, and not allowed to take up his proper station. He was not a commoner. He was a Prince and a poet. Why should he study Law?

But Francis the high-mettled was brought to heel by financial considerations. The Queen acted towards him as she did at a later date to Essex. "We can tame Barbary steeds, by starving them of provender," she said significantly, when she stopped the Earl's income by refusing to renew his monopoly licence for sweet wines.

That Francis Bacon was indebted to the Queen for his moneys on his return from France and for many years afterwards is the considered judgment of many authorities who have studied all the facts of the situation and original documents. I will quote two who began their inquiries as staunch believers in the usually accepted historical view; one a solicitor of good repute, a keen analytical mind, the other a graduate of Cambridge. Their judgment is the result of many years' research.

> Parker Woodward, solicitor, writes (*The Early Life of Lord Bacon*, p. 29): Except the allowance from the Queen it is absolutely clear that Francis at the age of twenty had nothing to live on. The Bacon family had no responsibility and he was entirely a pensioner on the Queen's bounty.
>
> The Rev. Walter Begley, M.A. (Cantab.), comes to the same conclusion, that the Queen was providing Francis Bacon with an income from the date of his return from abroad. He says (*Bacon's Nova Resuscitatio*, vol. I. p. 105), "I think, therefore, I am justified in making the suggestion that Bacon, who was virtually without means of his own, was allowed the privileges of a gentleman pensioner, although his name did not appear on the official list any more than the name of Puttenham."

We have seen definite proof that Francis Bacon was at Gray's Inn in July 1580, studying law, doing it under compulsion, hating the drudgery, hopeful however of pleasing the Queen, winning her favour and being openly acknowledged as her son and heir.

Letters which Francis wrote to Lord and Lady Burleigh are tangible evidence that the question of his recognition had been already discussed between him and the Queen, that Lord Burleigh, the Secretary of State, was cognizant of his pleadings or "Suit," and that Lady Burleigh was also aware of the matter. In short, Francis Bacon's relationship to the Queen was an open secret to the Chief Minister and his colleagues, and likewise to the high ladies associated with the Queen.

On the 16th September, 1580, Francis Bacon wrote a letter to Lady Burleigh from Gray's Inn. He writes to her as one acquainted with his wishes in a certain matter. It obviously concerns his parentage from what afterwards transpires. These are extracts:

To Lady Burghley, to speak for him to her Lord.

My singular good Lady,

I was as ready to shew myself mindful of my duty, by waiting on your Ladyship, at your being in town, as now by writing had I not feared your Ladyship's short stay. . . .

I am not yet greatly perfect in ceremonies of Court, whereof, I know, your Ladyship knoweth both the right use, and true value. My thankful and serviceable mind shall be always like itself, howsoever it vary from the common disguising. Your Ladyship is wise, *and of good nature to discern from what Mind every Action proceedeth, and to esteem of it accordingly.*

This is all the Message which my letter hath at this time to deliver, unless it please your Ladyship further to give me leave to make this request unto you, that it would please your good Ladyship, in your letters, wherewith you visit my good Lord, to VOUCHSAFE THE MENTION AND RECOMMENDATION OF MY SUIT; wherein your Ladyship shall bind me more unto you than I can look ever to be able sufficiently to acknowledge. . . .

Your Ladyship's most dutiful and bounden nephew,

B. Fra.

Put in plain English, in the light of what we already know, what does this letter mean? Simply this: He had learned that Lady Burleigh is in town and is anxious to seize an opportunity of getting in touch with her regarding a matter of moment. He cannot very well go to the Court, where she is apparently staying, because he does not know whether his presence would be welcome; whether he would be able to get an interview. He wants her to exercise her influence on his behalf with her husband respecting a matter with which she is acquainted, "to *vouchsafe the mention and recommendation of MY SUIT.*" It is clear that Lady Burleigh knows what Francis means by his use of the word "Suit." Lord Burleigh knows also; for there are no explanations of what he wants, as would be the case if it were a sudden first proposal. It is evidently a matter that has been under the consideration of her husband in his official capacity. Francis has heard nothing, is obviously expecting to hear something, and so seeks the influence of Lady Burleigh to try to obtain a decision in his favour. It cannot be an ordinary law-position that he seeks, for in September, 1580, he is still a law-student of nineteen. What else can it possibly be but "Recognition" which is of direct importance to Lord Burleigh as Secretary of State? But the very use of the word "Suit" tells one that it is a request out of the ordinary for its meaning is:

Urgent and respectful request; Solicitation; prayer; petition. Particularly *the seeking of favour from a King or one of exalted Rank.* (*Standard Dictionary.*)

Undoubtedly Francis was getting anxious. Nothing had been decided about his "Suit" after fifteen months' study at Gray's Inn—neither acceptance nor rejection. After writing to Lady Burleigh he therefore wrote to Lord Burleigh in an effort to bring the matter to a head; and this letter abundantly proves that the Queen is directly involved.

From Gray's Inn,
this 16*th Sept.*, 1580.

My singular good Lord,

My humble duty remembered, and my humble thanks presented for your Lordship's favour and countenance, which it pleased your Lordship, at my being with you, to vouchsafe me, above my Degree and Desert: *Therefore my letter hath no further errand but to commend your Lordship THE REMEMBRANCE OF MY SUIT which then I moved unto you; whereof it also pleased your Lordship to give me good hearing, so far forth as to promise TO TENDER IT UNTO HER MAJESTY, and withal to add, in the behalf of it, that which I may better deliver by letter than by speech, which is,*

That although it must be confessed that THE REQUEST IS RARE AND UNACCUSTOMED, yet if it be observed how few there be which fall in with the Study of the Common Laws, either being well-left or friended, *or at their own free election, or forsaking likely success in* other Studies of more Delight, *and no less preferment, or setting hand thereunto early, without waste of years; upon such survey being made,* it may be MY CASE MAY NOT SEEM ORDINARY, no more than MY SUIT.

As I forced myself to say this in excuse of my motion, lest it should appear unto your Lordship altogether indiscreet and unadvised, so my Hope to obtain it *resteth only upon your Lordship's good affection toward me and GRACE WITH HER MAJESTY who, methinks, needeth never to call for the experience of the thing, where she hath so great and so good of the person which recommendeth it. . . .*

Your Lordship hath had place to benefit many, and wisdom to make due choice of Lighting-Places for your goodness, yet I do not fear any of your Lordship's former experiences for staying my thankfulness borne (born?) in art; howsoever God's good pleasure shall ENABLE ME OR DISABLE ME, Outwardly, *to make proof thereof; for I cannot account your Lordship's service distinct from that which I to God and my Prince; the performance whereof to best proof and purpose is the meeting point and rendezvous of all my thoughts. . . .*

Your most dutiful and bounden nephew,
B. FRA.

This letter contains the following points.

1. That the subject matter had been previously discussed between Francis and Lord Burleigh. "*You gave me a good hearing.*"
2. It must have been some length of time previously for Francis still waits for an answer. He does not want his request shelved or forgotten as it is of great import. His letter is to bring the subject to his "*Remembrance.*"
3. Francis calls it a Suit, "*The Remembrance of my Suit.*"
4. Lord Burleigh has promised "*To Tender the Suit unto Her Majesty.*"
5. It was "*a Rare and unaccustomed*" Suit.

6. The study of Common Laws would never have been forced upon him had he been left better off ("*well-left*"), or able to exercise his own choice ("*One's own free election*") or had he been befriended by those who could have helped him ("*Friended*"). He could have put in his time into "*other Studies of more Delight,*" e.g., the Art of State-craft, Literature, Philosophy, etc.
7. His "*Case is not an Ordinary one any more than his Suit.*"
8. Francis hopes that the pressing for a definite answer to his Suit will not be "*indiscreet or unadvised.*"
9. His "*hope to obtain it*"—the granting of his Suit—rests on Burleigh's advice to the Queen and her Grace in granting it. ("*On your Lordship . . . and the Grace of Her Majesty.*")
10. The granting or refusing of his Suit will make or break him. ("*It will enable me or disable me. Outwardly,*" i.e., in his external fortunes).
11. Burleigh's "*service*" to the State is not distinct from his own "*to God and 'my Prince,' . . . the Meeting Place and rendezvous of all my Thoughts.*"

Re-reading this remarkable letter in the light of the above points it is self-evident that Francis Bacon's "Suit" which is "a Rare and Unaccustomed" one, directly concerns the Queen and the State, and that Francis Bacon knows it has little chance of acceptance unless backed by Burleigh, the Queen's Prime Minister. In effect he says that it is incongruous for a person like himself, the son of the Queen, to be employed in studying Common Law. He could be employing his time far better if he were well "friended" . . . to studies of greater delight, and not compelled to drudge at law tomes. He has forced himself to speak because of his anxieties, and he hopes it is not ill-advised and indiscreet to press for a definite assurance as to his future position, for all his hopes rest on Burleigh's good will and "the good grace of the Queen."

This letter was undoubtedly put on record to indicate that this "rare suit" which "was no ordinary case" concerned the Queen and her Ministers. It was "a thing of which she could have no experience" and therefore one to be talked over with Burleigh. In short, everything points to the fact that this "Suit" was not a request for some sort of employment, or begging for moneys, or seeking permission to end his law-studies. None of these things would be "a request rare and unaccustomed." No! It was something that directly affected the Queen and her Ministers. *Francis was pressing, after eighteen months' return from France, for "Recognition" publicly*, hoping that Burleigh would favour his "Suit," and that Burleigh's wife would help him while she was at Court to win the ear of his mother the Queen.

Burleigh evidently brought "Francis Bacon's Suit" to the notice of the Queen, who was apparently angry at his importunities. But he was evidently promised something satisfactory in the future and had been told to possess his soul in patience, for he writes a further letter to Burleigh on the 18th October, 1580, which leaves the matter in no further doubt that the "Suit" is something directly concerning the Queen. The first paragraph tells us all we want to know.

"*Your Lordship's comfortable relation to Her Majesty's gracious Opinion and MEANING towards me,* though at that time your leisure gave me not leave to show how I was affected therewith, yet upon every representation thereof, it entereth and striketh so much more deeply into me, as both my Nature and Duty presseth me to return some speech of thankfulness."

B. Fra.

The letter is humbly written to indicate his submission to the Queen's Will, which was to make no definite present pronouncement of their relationship. Francis is grateful for what she has done for him and for what she may do for him in the future. Spedding confesses that he can throw no light on the nature of the "Suit" beyond suggesting that the letters seem to "imply that it was for some employment as a lawyer." These three letters are signed "B. Fra." an unusual signature, used nowhere else, as though to indicate that he did not know how he should sign himself, being uncertain of his real name:

"It appears," says he, "that Francis had spoken to Burleigh and made some overtures which Burleigh undertook to recommend to the Queen; and that the Queen, though always slow to bestow favours, was always careful to encourage hopes, entertained the motion graciously and returned a favourable answer . . . but the Suit was *so far out of the common way as to require an apology*." *Life*, Vol. I, p. 57.

We have seen, however, that the "Suit" is clearly not "some employment for a lawyer." In 1580 he was not a qualified lawyer and when the suit first began he was not even a law-student or had only just commenced his legal studies. Spedding's suggestion is quite inadmissible. It was something "far out of the common way." IT WAS! *It was the Throne of England that was at stake.*

This mysterious "Suit" crops up over and over again during the passage of the years. He tries to get at the Queen in a variety of ways. He slowly begins to realize that the "Suit" cannot be granted without the consent of the Queen's advisers, the Privy Council, etc. But the open evidence can be left for the moment with the following letter which Francis wrote to Sir Francis Walsingham, principal secretary to Elizabeth. It is dated from Gray's Inn, 25th August, 1585. It will be seen that five years after his letter to Burleigh, this "rare and unaccustomed SUIT" had never been relinquished by Francis Bacon and that he was as keen as ever in getting the Queen to grant his request.

It may please your Honour to give me leave amidst your great and diverse business, *to put YOU in remembrance of my poor SUIT*, leaving the Time unto your Honour's best Opportunity and commodity.

I think the objection of my years will wear away with the length of my SUIT. *The very STAY doth in this respect concern me* because I am thereby hindered to take a course of practice which, by the leave of God, *if Her Majesty like not of my Suit*, I must and will follow; not from any necessity of estate, but *for my Credit's Sake* . . .

I spake, when the Court was at Theballs, to Mr. Vice-Chamberlain (Sir Christopher Hatton) who promised me his furtherance *which I did lest he mought be made for some other*. If it may please your Honour, who, as I hear, hath a great interest in him, *I think he will be fast mine.*

From this letter we see that not only was this "Suit" of Francis Bacon's known to Burleigh, but also to Walsingham and Hatton, *the highest officials in Court after Burleigh.* And Francis knew they were well aware of the matter—his petition to the Queen. It was no mere advancement in law that Burleigh, Walsingham or Hatton could have granted by a nod of the head. . . . The three of them conjoined could have put him in an office of profit under the Crown without asking anyone's pleasure. They could have got him anything ordinarily without consulting the Queen. We know from this letter it was for something far bigger. He was known to these statesmen as the Queen's concealed son. He wanted "recognition." It was a question of the "Succession" for *the Queen had yet to name her Successor by special Act of Parliament.* It was a question of State. "*Does Her Majesty like my Suit or not?*" It is "Something" obviously that cannot be determined by the Queen or her Ministers acting separately but only by a joint decision. In other words it affects the nation for the "Succession" is involved.

In 1585 he was in the public eye. In the November of the previous year, at the age of twenty-four, he had become a Member of Parliament. He knew that the more he was known to the general public as Francis Bacon, the less likelihood there was of him ever being regarded as Francis Tudor. Moreover, the Earl of Leicester was out of favour with the Queen. Every public act riveted the Bacon Mask more firmly over his features. He had a younger brother, too, brought up as Robert Devereux, afterwards known as the Earl of Essex, begotten by the same parents, some six years his junior, who was a serious rival and candidate for the Queen's maternal affection. This brother had been brought up at the Court. He was not only a "legitimate" in name but in deed, while Francis, as an "adulterine bastard," was a continual reminder of a very dark blot on one of the pages of the Queen's life. This objection did not apply to his younger brother Robert. His recognition would not besmirch the Queen's honour. When Francis wrote to Walsingham about "the objection of my years" and "the length of my Suit, he was simply asserting the naked truth . . . that every year that passed without "recognition" was an added difficulty to a subsequent acknowledgment of his claims.

"My very Stay *UNDER MY PRESENT NAME* and in *my present sphere* of action doth concern me," he says, in effect. "I am thereby hindered from following the bent of my own mind, which I will follow *if Her Majesty like not my Suit.*" In other words he wants to devote himself to science, art, literature, philosophy, and ethics if the Queen does not intend to call him to the throne. He wants "Recognition" not "*for any necessity of Estate*"—not merely to reign over England's broad acres—"but *for MY CREDIT'S SAKE*"; For in public life he ran the risk of being called the "Queen's Bastard." He wants his position defined. How can he live under a cloud? "For my credit's sake," he cries. "I spoke to the Vice-Chamberlain who promised me his assistance. I think if you speak to him also he will be *fast mine.* I did so lest he might be *pledged to some other.*" In other words Francis was afraid lest his younger brother would be preferred to him by the Queen and her Ministers and named as her "Successor."

The "Suit" which had begun six years ago, and which had been neither rejected nor approved but left in a state of suspension, was still, we see, of vital import to Francis Bacon when he stood on the threshold of public life.

Spedding again confesses his inability to explain this remarkable letter. He says:

> This is the last we hear of this Suit, *the nature and fate of which must both be left to conjecture.* My own conjecture is that he presently gave up all hope of success, and tried instead to obtain through his interest at Court some furtherance *in the direct line of his profession.*

Spedding never dreamed that Francis Bacon was the Queen's son.

SHAKE-SPEARES

SONNETS.

Neuer before Imprinted.

AT LONDON
By *G. Eld* for *T. T.* and are
to be solde by *Iohn Wright*, dwelling
at Christ Church gate.
1609.

Facsimile of the Title-page of Shakespeare's Sonnets, 1609 Quarto. The numerical "counts" associate this title-page with Francis Bacon, for 39 is the numerical signature of F. Bacon; 56, Fr. Bacon; 111, Bacon. *See Shake-speare's Sonnet Diary, p.* 244 (*Daily Post Printers, Liverpool*).

It was a contingency that never entered his head and so was never considered. Had it done so he could never have written the foregoing paragraph. As a matter of fact, it is not "the last we hear of this Suit," nor need its "nature and fate be left to conjecture." Far from it. For Francis Bacon's private Sonnet-Diary tells us the entire story. And the hitherto secret evidence of the Diary together with the open facts of history leave no room for doubt to the student of Elizabethan history who is resolved to have the truth, the whole truth and nothing but the truth.

Francis Bacon wrote three Cantos respecting his connection with Queen Elizabeth. Canto I was a set of seventeen Sonnets written as a complete sequence shortly after his return from France. They were for private presentation to the Queen as a plea for recognition as her son and heir; and the "Suit" is couched in the loveliest language. He hoped the poems would serve as "sweeteners" and induce his mother to be gracious to him, influencing her decision in his favour. Later, they passed in MS. among his private friends, noted by the Rev. Francis Meres (one of Francis Bacon's companions) in *Palladis Tamia*, who called them "*Sugared* Sonnets" for he knew their secret *motifs* and the reason why they were written. The other Cantos deal with Francis Bacon's personal relationship with the Queen and the tragedy of Essex. The Sonnets were composed at odd times. They were not written for the Queen's eye or for publication in her lifetime, but over a period of years, the last being written on the day of her death.

The first Canto describes Francis Bacon's emotions while pressing for "Recognition" at the immediate beginning of his "Suit"; the second Canto tells of his various hopes and fears as the years pass. The first two Sonnets alone tell the poet's meaning directly and indirectly. He says, (Sonnet Diary, 2-1 and 3-11), paraphrasing in prose:

> We desire all "Fair Creatures" to perpetuate themselves (thus at once indicating that a woman is involved, the person addressed, for it is only a woman that could be so described . . . not a male, one of the "sterner sex.") He mentions "Beauty's Rose" because she represents the Rose of Tudor. He uses the phrase "Tender Heir" hinting that she ought to possess one. She is, however, contracted to herself and thus makes a "famine" where there is abundance; a statement which makes plain that the person addressed conceals from outsiders the fact that she is rich in the possession of an Heir already. She is thus a "foe" to herself and to her own "Sweet Self," *i.e.*, her child, for every child is a mother's "sweet self."
>
> He now begins to tell us the identity of his mother. She is the "only Herald" to the nation, to the world, for she was the only woman in the world who could summon the Parliament of the nation by Proclamation as a Herald. She is looked upon by the people as a Virgin for she poses as "the World's Fresh Ornament." That description can only apply to Queen Elizabeth, for the only woman to whom such a phrase could apply was the English Queen who had adorned herself with the ornament of Virginity. The meaning of "Fresh" is "Virgin." And now we are told that this woman has buried the result of her satisfaction, her content, within her own "Bud," her own child; and by burying her own bud she thus makes a waste of wealth while hoarding him in concealment.
>
> The poet concludes by asking her to "Pity the World"—everyone in the world was anxious about the English "Succession"—for she is selfishly eating a just title of claim all alone by keeping her bud concealed. It means eventually that he will be eaten by the grave and figuratively by his own mother for his identity will be lost.
>
> One need be no literary expert to see that this is no ordinary Sonnet.

It does not deal with an ordinary woman respecting an ordinary matter. It is a woman that is in the eye of the World, one who can act as a Herald

DECODED BY *Alfred Dodd*

SHAKE-SPEARES, *The 7th letters in the first 7 lines spell "a tuder heir"*

SONNETS.

(1)

FR.T. FRom fairest creatures we desire increase, ir
That thereby beauties *Rose* might neuer die, e
B But as the riper should by time decease, h
Hist. His tender heire might beare his memory: der heire
F.B. But thou contracted to thine owne bright eyes, u
Feed'st thy lights flame with selfe substantiall fewell, t
Ma-King Making a famine where aboundance lies, a
Thy Thy selfe thy foe, to thy sweet selfe too cruell: s
AT Thou that art now the worlds fresh ornament, f
And only herauld to the gaudy spring, r
PAW Within thine owne bud buriest thy content, con
And tender chorle makst wast in niggarding: a
Pitty the world, or else this glutton be, b
To To eate the worlds due, by the graue and thee. and

and fr. bacon's a tuder heire.

(2) W. 2

WHAT VVHen fortie Winters shall beseige thy brow,
And digge deep trenches in thy beauties field,
Thy youthes proud liuery so gaz'd on now,
W.T. Wil be a totter'd weed of smal worth held:
Then being askt, where all thy beautie lies,
W.T. Where all the treasure of thy lusty daies;
To say within thine owne deepe sunken eyes,
Were an all-eating shame, and thriftlesse praise.
How much more praise deseru'd thy beauties vse,
If thou couldst answere this faire child of mine
Shall sum my count, and make my old excuse
WHISPr Prouing his beautie by succession thine.

B B This

T *This were to be new made when thou art old,*
A *And see thy blood warme when thou feel'st it could,*

(1) "TO PAW AT THY MAJESTY: FRANCIS BACON - HIST - BE FRANCIS TUDOR"

(2) "WHISPER WHAT? WHISPER TUDOR. WHISPER TUDOR

FACSIMILE OF THE FIRST PAGE OF SHAKESPEARE'S SONNETS, 1609 QUARTO
(*See Appendix I, p.* 357)

to the nation, who is entitled to wear armorial bearings, the Tudor Rose—for there was only one Rose in England in that era and Queen Elizabeth was entitled to wear it for she was the Princess of York in her own Right.

One could continue, for the Sonnet will stand a lot of analysis, and the more searching the inquiry the more it will be seen that no other interpretation is possible. The poet can only be referring to the "Virgin" Queen, the Tudor Rose of England. And that this is the correct explanation is proved by the secret message in the initial capitals, "To Paw at thy Majesty: Francis Bacon—Hist—be Francis Tudor." (*See* illustration, p. 121).

The next Sonnet opens with a reminder that when forty more winters had passed she would be a tottering old woman. Her Proud Livery, the Royal Regalia, would not give her much satisfaction in her loneliness nor hide old age in its decay. If she were then asked where was all her Beauty, where the Treasure of the lusty days of Pregnancy, how barren it would be to have to point only to her deep sunken eyes. It would be an all-eating shame.

How much more praise would the *use of her beauty* deserve if she could answer, "*This Fair Child of MINE shall sum my Count of the days of Pregnancy* and shall excuse my Old Age," thus proving my past beauty by his present beauty . . . proving by his SUCCESSION to be THINE.

This were to be New-made, when thou art old and see thyself in living flesh and blood, thy Blood-Warm, who would bring warmth to thy heart when chilled by cold-age.

The secret message confirms this interpretation. It runs, "*Whisper Be a Tudor! Whisper Tudor! Whisper Tudor!*"

The youth is simply crying out for "Recognition." It is significant that in the original printed Quarto there is a capital "B" put under the word "Succession" to tell the reader by this purposeful hint that the writer is composing Sonnets that deal with the Succession to the English Crown, in those days a vital concern of every Englishman.

The remaining fifteen Sonnets tell the story with increasing emphasis leaving absolutely no doubt that they refer to Queen Elizabeth and her concealed son Francis Bacon. Phrases like "Sacred Majesty," "Every private Widow," her "Most High Deserts," etc., prove that the Canto is addressed to a Royal Personage who "Beguiles the World" by pretending "Singleness" when she is a "Mother" already. . . . "Thou dost grow in one of Thine" and "That Fresh Blood which thou didst bestow when young thou mayest call THINE." "Cherish the Bounteous Gift of Nature." "Let not that Copy Die." "*You had a Father! Let YOUR SON SAY SO!*" "Make not Worms thine HEIR" when "You YOUR SELF HERE (in the person of the writer) LIVE." It is the "World's Due" to maintain the "Succession." "I will engraft you new" through "Lines of Life that Life repair." This could not be done by writing a Sonnet but only by children of an acknowledged son preserving the Tudor Dynasty to Queen Elizabeth, already a mother.

The last Sonnet in the Canto (18-xvii) is so beautiful, viewed from the right angle, that it serves as a climax wistful, hopeful and yet how poignant the cry of the heart.

LIVE IN MY RHYME AND IN
YOUR CHILDREN'S CHILDREN

Who will believe my Verse in Time to come
If it were fill'd with your "Most High" Deserts?[1]
Though yet, Heaven knows, *it is but as a Tomb*
Which Hides your Life, and shows not Half your Parts.

[1]Not only as a Queen but as a Mother whose "True Rights" are hidden from the world.

If I could write the Beauty of your Eyes
And in fresh Numbers number all your Graces,
The Age to come would say, "This Poet lies;
Such Heavenly Touches ne'er touch'd earthly Faces."
So should my Papers (Yellow'd with their Age)
Be scorn'd like old men of less Truth than Tongue,
And *your True Rights* be term'd a Poet's Rage
And stretched metre of an Antique Song:
But were some CHILD of yours alive that Time,
You should Live TWICE . . . in it and in my Rhyme.

Francis Bacon's poetic petition or Sonnet-Suit, written and presented shortly after his residence in Gray's Inn, did not, however, influence the Queen to make a decision one way or the other. But it must not be thought that he sat down impotently wringing his hands in despair at the Queen's indecision, paralysed in thought or action. His nature bubbled up with creative vitality and his law studies by no means drank up the whole of his time. What was Francis Bacon doing in those silent years so vital to himself, and, as it afterwards transpired, to the nation . . . even the world?

The plain fact is for at least seven years or more after his return from the French Court we know little or nothing of him or his pursuits, by traditional biography, beyond being baldly told that on the 27th June, 1582, on the completion of three years' terms, when he was twenty-one, he was called to the Bar and made "an utter barrister," and that in 1584 he was elected a Member of Parliament by the burgesses of Melcombe in Dorsetshire, and also returned for the pocket constituency of Gatton. But the manner by which he got into Parliament, like the rest of his activities at this time, has been slurred over by the traditionalists. How did this penniless and landless lawyer, *without any visible means of support*—he had not become a practising lawyer—without local influence get into Parliament? Quite clearly he was sent to the House of Commons at the instigation of Lord Burleigh and the Queen. It must be remembered that it was more difficult to get in the House of Commons in those days than to-day. He was no ordinary representative. Primarily, it was to give him an outlet for his energies. Burleigh doubtless thought it would be unwise to repress him altogether, as this would be a sitting on the safety valve that might have dangerous results. And one of the first things Francis Bacon does in his public position is to tell the world *who and what he is* to all those who can read between the lines.

Parliament had been called together in consequence of plots to assassinate the Queen. Francis apparently made a brilliant maiden speech respecting the Queen's safety; for Fleetwood, the Recorder of London, in writing of it said, "Before this time I never heard in Parliament the like things uttered. They were *magnalia regni*."

Francis Bacon followed up this speech *with a long letter of caution to the Queen* and also deals with other affairs of State. This letter he begins with a sentence of double meaning which was so characteristic a feature of his style in after years.

> Care, *one of the Natural and True-Bred Children of unfeigned Affection*, awaked with these late wicked and barbarous attempts, would needs exercise my pen to *your Sacred Majesty*.

Francis is thus letting it be known that he is a Natural and True-Bred Child in his first public act. He uses the same phrase, "Sacred Majesty" as in the private Sonnets, 8-vii, line 4, he had presented to the Queen. For a young unfledged lawyer to take upon himself to advise the Queen would have been presumptuous had there been no secret bond between them. What could have justified him in addressing such a letter to Elizabeth? What right had he to go over the heads of her responsible Ministers and tender his advice on affairs of State? *How dare he?* There is only one reason. He felt justified in his action because he knew he was the Queen's son, and this was the reason why he was not rebuked publicly by her Ministers. The letter was not published but it was circulated as a State Document. The Queen seems to have taken no exception to it, even to have received it graciously. J. P. Baxter, *The Greatest of Literary Problems*, p. 313, says that:

> The imperious Elizabeth's gracious acceptance is evidence of high regard for his talents. In accordance with her habit of applying nicknames to those about her, she called Bacon her "Watch-Candle."

But Francis did not spend the whole of his time in chambers swotting at law-books. W. T. Smedley, a very careful researcher in the Elizabethan mine, discovered a letter from Thomas Bodley to Francis Bacon, the evidence showing that sometime between 1580 and 1582 Francis Bacon made a second visit to the Continent, passing again through Italy, Spain, Germany, and Denmark; and, at the instigation of Sir Thomas Bodley, the Queen's usher, a close record was made of all he learned and observed respecting their "laws, religion, military strength and whatsoever concerneth pleasure or profit." His expenses would be over £800 (equivalent to about £5,000 at to-day's value, 1945) and were furnished through the medium of Sir Thomas Bodley. Said he, "I will make you as liberal a return from myself and your friends here, as I am able."

In 1582 these observations were embodied in a State Paper, which was on the lines of Bodley's suggestions, and presented to the Queen entitled *Notes on the State of Christendom.* The internal evidence shows that the "Notes" must have been written by an actual traveller, much detail is given, long lists of names and places appended. The results of personal observation are everywhere apparent. There are descriptions of Italy, Austria, Germany, France, Spain, Portugal, Poland, Denmark, and Sweden. Florence, Venice, Mantua, Genoa, Savoy are dealt with in detail.

There can be no doubt but that Francis Bacon's second visit to the Continent was arranged primarily by Burleigh, to give him something active to do, to take his mind off dwelling too much on the subject matter of his "Suit." Bodley, the founder of the Bodleian Library, and Burleigh were great friends, and leave of absence from Francis's law studies was easily arranged. He was being shown that his interests were being considered. On his return he was told that arrangements were being made for him to enter Parliament. In short, he was not to be left to brood. Francis undoubtedly jumped at the chance of going abroad again for, as we shall see, it enabled him to advance the cause he had so much at heart—renewing the contacts he had made on his previous visit. Apart from his "Notes" and his "Letter to the Queen" seven years and more had slipped away from him, the best creative years of his life, and he has nothing to show for it according to orthodox biographers and historians: Not a solitary line published: not a work created: not a single labour accomplished that would justify the dreams of the youth who intended to revolutionize the science, philosophy, literature, and the ethics of England and the world. Had all his dream-bubbles burst into nothingness touched by the sordid realities of things? Or were his dreams taking form and shape in the darkness like planted bulbs? Seeds slowly germinating in hidden places?

> "Those early years," says Dean Church, "to 1588 *were busy ones*, but they are more *obscure years* than might be expected in the case of a man of Francis Bacon's genius and family, and of such eager and unconcealed desire to rise and be at work. . . . He was often pinched in his means; his health was weak; *plunged in work*, he lived very much as a recluse in his chambers and was thought to be reserved. . . . He was brilliant, versatile, courtly. . . . It seems strange that Bacon should have remained fixedly in the shade. *Something must have kept him back.*" (*Life*, p. 9.)

But Church and his school have never told us *why* the years "were busy ones," why they were "obscure," the nature of the work "in which he was plunged," or what "kept him back." He arrived at the age of twenty-eight with nothing to his credit though he had been *plunged in work through the busy years*. This barren ploughing of the sands is dismissed with the sapient remark, "Ah, Well! Something must have kept him back."

Here we have an indefatigable worker who counted the moments of his life as so precious that to waste them were a crying sin, who, later, was so niggardly of his time, that he dictated his thoughts even from a sick bed, in his coach, or as he walked about his garden, whose thoughts were uttered with such effortless, polished brilliancy, that men rushed from his dining-table to scribble his utterances in their note-books. Are we to believe the schoolmen whose sponges wipe off from the slate the early years of Francis Bacon's life with the Pontifical judgment, "They were barren of fruit!" Is it credible that this youth who returned from France fired with the resolve to do great things for his country, to create a Renaissance of Thought, to begin a Universal Reformation of the Whole Wide World, who had conceived the idea in his very soul when a boy of fourteen . . . that this prodigious intellectual allowed more than a decade to slip away without a solitary effort to put his thought into action! Is it not obvious that the bookmen are as wrong in their judgment as the Royal Society who laughed at Benjamin Franklin with his lightning conductors as a dreamer. The truth is, that:

> The heights by great men gained and kept,
> Were not attained by sudden flight,
> *But they while their companions slept,*
> *Were toiling upwards in the night.*

These silent years, which his orthodox biographers have never attempted to fathom, were indeed years of strenuous activities. His time was his own. He was a Gentleman-Pensioner of the Queen. He had not to work in order to live for even "*in* 1592" (he was then over thirty years of age), Spedding says, "*I do not find him getting into practice.*" Yet in the same breath we are told that "his years are busy ones," he is "plunged in work," he was "a recluse in his chambers," and very "reserved." And there orthodox biographers leave it and are content to leave it with a shake of the head.

What is the mystery and what the explanation? How can the problem of Francis Bacon's life and works be solved by merely skimming the surface of things and refusing to dive into the deeps?

We have seen that at the age of fifteen he had left Cambridge possessed of all the knowledge it had to impart. Travel and intercourse on the Continent had polished his mind, moulded his opinions, and enlarged the boundaries of his intellectual world. He had made contact with men whose breasts were the repositories of the Mysteries. He was pledged to them by vow to create "Something," a "Something" to benefit the world on educational and ethical lines. *Is it conceivable that he failed them?* Did the sea breezes of the English Channel drive away those poetic dreams?

They did not. And a most remarkable letter which he wrote to Father Fulgentio proves that his ideals never slumbered nor slept from the day they fluttered beneath his heart. He describes what he means by his dream, *The Great Instauration*, and then he says:

> The Zeal and Constancy of my Mind, has not waxed old in this Design, nor after so many years, grown cold and indifferent. I remember that about *Forty Years ago*, I composed a *Juvenile Work* about these things which with great Confidence, and a Pompous Title, I called *Temporis Partum Masculum*, or the Most Masculine Birth of Time. I am thus persuaded, because of its infinite usefulness, that it may be ascribed to *Divine Encouragement*.
>
> *Baconiana*, 1579, p. 200.

There is no date to this letter so the exact date cannot be told when the work was actually composed, but it was a juvenile one, written forty years previously, and it would be safe to say that Francis Bacon was about twenty-one when *The Most Masculine Birth of Time* was written. The work is "*Lost.*" But its subject matter is known. It centred round the birth of males by males in a Lodge of males. It was a description of the new ethical system of Freemasonry that had been born into the world among MEN. It was Francis Bacon's newly created Secret Society. . . . where every Initiate is a newly-born male who comes into a new world poor, penniless, naked and attached by his cable-tow. The great teacher had indeed created something. He had modernized an old world idea. He had established an organization. He had gathered round him a band of devoted disciples to spread the cult of a system of morality. It was secret, concealed, reserved. No wonder "he lived very much like a recluse in his chambers."

This, then, is the clue. From the day he returned from France when he was eighteen years of age he had steadily gone forward quietly and secretively with his plans, Freemasonry being one branch of his unseen labours.

Now that we have found a definite clue that Francis was working at something secretive that seems to centre round a secret organization, we can get a little closer to the heart of the mystery that has hitherto baffled his cleverest editors like Messrs. Ellis and Spedding. We begin with the fact that Francis returned from the Continent afire with the thought that *he had a Divine Mission,* that primarily consisted in laying national and world bases for eternity, hidden foundations unknown to the masses, bases upon which posterity would build knowingly or witlessly of the identity of the architect who planned them and the superstructure. He was conscious of his powers, so conscious that though he was a modest man, ready to light his torch at any man's candle, he did not hesitate later on to write what would have been arrogant presumption on the part of others:

> Francis Bacon thought thus and judged it to be for the benefit of Posterity that they should be acquainted with his Thoughts.

A teacher or a preacher must have a platform and an audience. Francis had neither. Would the renowned universities of Europe listen to an unknown man, a youth of twenty? Would scholars grown grey in arts and humanities accept the dictum of an obscure dreamer that their learning was a delusion, their method a snare? Would the theologians listen to the voice of the New Teacher that religion pure and undefiled was to visit the fatherless and the widow and to keep oneself unspotted from the world? Could they be persuaded that the pivot of worship was Love which bounded all men, irrespective of race, creed or blood, in one common brotherhood? Would the statesmen of the world accept his social ideals that the serf and the slave were God's sons and Christ's brothers and that all fortunate rulers owed a duty to their weaker compatriots, promulgating laws of social and educational betterment that the nation might be lifted to higher levels?

In an age of tyranny how could he break the chains which fettered free thought and hamstrung action? How could Francis Bacon, the penniless youth of ill-omened birth, get his thoughts across the world and into the minds and hearts of men, especially those deeper ethical and spiritual thoughts which dare not be openly expressed? How could he leap the barriers of conventional caste which encircled him? The youthful Francis knew that to speak with effect he must speak from a height . . . from the Throne if possible, or from the council-chamber, or from the Bench. There were many things on which he could speak openly. There were many things which he could only whisper in the ears of his disciples, that band of brothers which he afterwards called his "SONS." *The youth therefore adopted TWO METHODS, one public, the other secret.* This astonishing fact, which the schoolmen have never understood or realized, is proved to the hilt by his writings which afterwards appeared. He claims to be the Teacher of a certain Order, and that his teaching is based on the Natural Philosophy of the Ancients.

He says that he is going "*the same road as the Ancients but has something better to produce,*" and he also speaks of "*Two methods of publishing or writing—one RESERVED, the other OPEN*"; One for his disciples, the other for the multitude: One shall be "ORAL" and "TRADITIONAL," the Matter "RESERVED TO A SUCCESSION OF HANDS" being SECRET Wisdom: The other shall be knowledge that can be openly discussed in the Universities, the Marts, the Hearths of Men. Here are his own words:

> *That the Direction be ANCIENTLY observed,* though by the precedent of many vain persons and deceivers abused, of *PUBLISHING Part and RESERVING Part to a PRIVATE SUCCESSION* in such a manner whereby it may not be to the Taste or Capacity of ALL, but shall, as it were, SINGLE OUT and adopt his READER. [The System] is not to be laid Aside; both for the avoiding of ABUSE in *the EXCLUDED*, and the Strengthening of the AFFECTION in the ADMITTED. (*Valerius Terminus*, Ch. 18.)
>
> To Ascend further I do forbear . . . chiefly because it would open that which in this Work I determine to RESERVE. (*Ibid*, Ch. 11.)

One need not be a Freemason to know that this applies and can only apply to Freemasonry. "The Ancient Direction" hinted at is to be found on every Lodge Circular to-day. There is indeed "a strengthening of AFFECTION in the ADMITTED" Candidate for Freemasonry, which in its highest and Theosophic aspects, is not for ALL but only for those whose tastes and characters qualify them for the Craft and its Succession. We are categorically told that Francis Bacon publishes a part of his works openly and that he reserves a part. Some MS. Notes that he left, now in the British Museum, confirm this fact, and that his plans of Philosophy are matured, because he says:

> With some better respect to the Egyptians, Persians, Chaldees and the UTMOST ANTIQUITY and the MYSTERIES of the POETS.
>
> To consider what OPINIONS are fit to nourish *Tanquam Ansae* [according to occasion] so as to GRAFT THE NEW UPON THE OLD [i.e., the Speculative Ethics of Freemasonry upon operative customs and the Mysteries].
>
> Of the manners and Precepts touching SECRECY, TRADITION, and PUBLICATION.

Commenting on these enigmatical fragments, which every Freemason will recognize at once as directly referring to Masonry and to nothing else, Mrs. H. Pott says, in *Francis Bacon's Secret Society*, p. 212:

> His Notes are a complete sketch of an elaborate design which was to be worked out. . . . These remarkable jottings are pregnant with suggestions and speak in every line of *a vast and deeply laid scheme. They have been passed over in every Life and every Biography.*

These quotations abundantly prove that Francis Bacon was doing a concealed work of some kind, not merely writing openly but writing and publishing secretly, and some of this work was at least connected with the Mysteries and were necessarily identifiable with what we know of the Rosicrucian Manifestos and the Masonic Rituals.

That he was engaged in this concealed work is made abundantly clear by the following quotation:

> I would have men reminded . . . that the Honour and Reverence due

to the Ancients remain untarnished and undiminished while *I am carrying out MY DESIGNS*, and at the same time *I reap the Fruit of my Modesty. . . .* If I profess that I, *GOING THE SAME ROAD AS THE ANCIENTS*. have *SOMETHING better to produce*, there must needs have been *some Comparison or Rivalry between us* in respect of *Excellency* or Ability or Wit . . . though in this there would be *nothing* unlawful or new."

Here then is the real truth hitherto missed by orthodox interpreters. Francis Bacon stands a self-confessed Teacher of concealed principles whatever else he may have taught openly. He has joined hands with the Mysteries round their altars, in the Dramas and Rituals of the Ancient Wisdom. *He is carrying out a DESIGN on the same lines exactly* as the Rites and Ceremonials practised in Egypt, Chaldea, Babylon, and the *Lost Atlantis*. His "Design" is a modern adaptation, more suited to the times and is vaguely sketched in *The New Atlantis* or *The Land of the Rosicrosse*. But he is going "*their way*," the way of Amen Ra, Heraclitus, Orpheus, Plato . . . and has "*Something Better to Produce*" because it is more suited for the growing needs of Man. There must needs be comparison or rivalry between the Old Systems and the New, because both Systems enunciate the same fundamental teachings—Initiation, Purification, Sanctification. Francis Bacon is "MODEST" about this portion of his Labours. He has not openly identified himself with them. They are hidden from the sight of the world, for he does not want vulgar contemporary hands to profane his sacred Ideals. They are hidden from the eye in the Mystic Circle of the Rosicrucian, the lost Masonic Temple, and the anonymous Publications of the Rosicrosse.

Though these definite statements—and there are many others—are recorded by him late in life, *these were the principles that had governed his mental activities and his actions from his youth upwards*. If we do not take this hitherto ignored factor into full consideration, we cannot estimate at all Francis Bacon's complete life nor the Elizabethan era. Though we possess all the wealth of the academics we shall have missed the one thing needful for salvation, the pearl of Wisdom and Knowledge which is beyond price.

Every outward circumstance from Francis Bacon's boyhood days to his return to England from France, had conspired to make his natural gifts develop on lines of secrecy and mystery, culminating in the creation of ceremonials that tried to recapture the glory of Chaldea and the splendour of Egypt. The little boy Francis who had seen the pomp and pageantry of Queen Elizabeth's Court; who had noted at York House the whispers of State secrets under the rose, who had played in the ancient Chapter House of the sleeping Knights Templar; who had fingered the mysterious Mason-Marks on stones hallowed by sacred memories (stones which had constructed his home under the "Red Cross" of St. Albans, with its significant name "The Temple"); who had constantly before his childish eyes the names of the "Seven Liberal Arts and Sciences" in the banqueting-hall of "The Temple," watched over by the figure of Orpheus, the Messenger of the Mysteries, that stood "in the curiously knotted garden"; who "had travelled to the East" through France, as a youth, sitting at the feet of the Illuminati, and following Dante through the Degrees of the Knights Templar, being steeped in classical literature and the esoteric meaning of recondite symbolism . . . was "the extraordinary youth" who, having "taken all knowledge to be his Province," possessed all the qualifications to create not only a new ethical system (Freemasonry), but to lay the foundations of an English Renaissance, literary, scientific and philosophic. This should take in its scope not only the social and intellectual welfare of men, but also reach out into the Infinite, ministering to those immortal hopes that make us something more than men.

When Francis returned to England in 1579 he brought with him a complete plan of campaign to produce a silent revolution in our language, thoughts, ideals. The first to be privy to his plans was his foster-brother Anthony Bacon. So enthusiastic a disciple was he that in later years he almost ruined himself in helping to give effect to the schemes of Francis. When Anthony went to the Continent he became the secret missionary for the Fraternities of Concealed Men, the link between the founder of the New Idealism and the Continental enthusiasts.

Francis Bacon's enforced residence at Gray's Inn proved to be a vital step in the right direction. A youth of his travelled experience would naturally attract to himself the very type of men necessary for the formation of a Secret Society. How much stronger the attraction if his Tudor connection were privately known to his student-friends at Gray's Inn, especially in view of the probability that the Masked Prince might some day be called to the throne! Whatever the cause, the fact remains that Francis Bacon was soon surrounded by a ring of devoted young men to whom his wish was law, esteeming it the greatest honour and privilege to serve him. They helped him to establish his ideals although such ideals seemed to run counter to the conservatism of the age. This secret royal bond between the "Prince" and his coterie, his charm, brilliance, and bearing of mind and character that had swept Hillyard into an ecstasy of wonder, the goal of achievement being conquests by the mind, not the ravaging of material provinces, provided the prerequisites for the emergence of a secret fraternity amid the cultured classes, the "Gentlemen" of the Elizabethan age . . . a Brotherhood which has always been graced by Princes, Dukes, Lords, and "Gentlemen of Quality," according to Masonic legends.

In 1579 and by 1580 we have abundant proof that Francis Bacon had begun the establishment of his secret Societies, a proof which becomes more and more apparent as we examine the evidence through the years that follow. His first effort towards "The Universal Reformation" was the creation of the secret literary society afterwards known as "Fra Rosi Cross." This literary "Academie"—*the brain of all his secret subsequent activities*—were the "Invisibles" who veiled their activities behind the mysterious numbers 157 and 287. It began at Gray's Inn, the heads being Francis Bacon's personal friends such as Gabriel Harvey, his old literary Professor, and Fulke Greville, the poet of later years. Sir Philip Sidney, his "cousin," and Sidney's sister, Lady Mary, Countess of Pembroke, would at least be privy to his plans. He would have the warm support of de Vere, Earl of Oxford, also a poet. Lord Burleigh, later, was undoubtedly partial to his attempts at creating a real English literature, for he appears to have helped him with some of his printing expenses. Francis Bacon's friendships early included the highest in the land; the Earl and Countess of Warwick, Earls of Derby, Northumberland, etc.; and, later the Earls of Dorset, Pembroke, Arundel, Montgomery, etc.; with literary men like George Herbert, Wotton, Selden, etc.

The law-students at Gray's Inn were a roisterous, jolly, mirthful company. On festive occasions, such as Christmas and New Year, they had their Revels, Masques, Plays and Musical Comedies or Entertainments which the students personally produced. Among such a set of young lawyers, containing many Tobie Matthews in embryo, it was a comparatively easy matter to float his secret literary Society and then his ethical ones under cover of the dramatic and humorous shows without arousing any suspicion of what was really afoot. There was keen rivalry between the students of the various Inns to produce the best show. Some of the pageants were performed in the Inns of Court before Elizabeth. That there were such literary coteries is beyond dispute. We shall see later the part Francis Bacon played in these semi-musical-comedy Plays.

"The Honourable Order of the Knights of the Helmet" was the title given to his first Society. The "Helmet of the Order" was "the Helmet of the Great Goddess Pallas Athene (Athena), the "Pallas Minerva" of the French "Academie." She was the great classical Myth, "the Shaker of the Speare" who waged eternal warfare against the Serpent of Ignorance which she trampled under her feet, stabbing it with her Speare of Golden Knowledge.

The candidate into the "Honourable Order" swore to advance all the ideals of Athena, to dissipate the clouds of ignorance by the light of knowledge by blazing it openly before the eyes of men or flashing it secretly to illumine the darkened places of the mind, to work for the all-round good of humanity without fee or reward.

He kissed the Helmet. It was placed on his head. And as the Helmet of Pallas was supposed in mythology to make the wearer invisible, so the Initiate became "An Invisible "also. He moved henceforth through the world to do good by stealth on certain definite lines. In his right hand was placed the great Speare. He shook it. By that act he became a Warrior, a Knight, a "Speare-Shaker." It was this little band of "Speare-Shakers" with Francis Bacon, the "Shake-speare" *par excellence*, as "The Purple Prince" that was the motive power behind the English literary and ethical Renaissance for:

1. The creation of English books and an English reading public.
2. The creation of a Rosicrucian Fraternity.
3. The establishment of Modern Freemasonry with its pyramid of Thirty-Three Degrees.

In 1579 there were practically no English books, pamphlets or newspapers. There was no English reading-public at all. Few could read. Illiteracy was rampant. Francis and the "Knights of the Helmet" set out to alter the habits of Londoners and the nation. This could only be done by the construction of an adequate language and literature for both were then deficient in quantity and quality. The Stationer's Register for the period proves the truth of this. Knowing what had been done by a handful of French poets, Francis was certain he could do the same for the country over which he hoped to rule as King. This possible contingency prevented him from writing anything over his own name; neither could he write too much under any one name lest the general public should think that it was "a one-man band." He must arouse curiosity among the people. There must be many names used, many initials, many anonymous publications, and controversial quarrels created between alleged authors to capture the ear of the general public. In order to create interest he must give the impression that there was a spontaneous uprush of Elizabethan literature, and that everybody everywhere had simultaneously begun to sing, to write, to play in order that England might be thought to be a nest of singing-birds. The English Renaissance, then, was not a spasmodic happening but the result of careful planning by Francis Bacon and his little band of Brethren.

He was a born educationist and may justly be described in modern terms as our first great editor-in-chief, for he controlled, virtually, all the manuscripts that were published in his day. They passed through his fingers either as the writer, the editor, or the publisher. The salvation of England could only be accomplished by all-round education. The curse of God was ignorance. He gave the cultured and leisured classes English text-books on all sorts of subjects. He was responsible for the translations of foreign classics into the English tongue. He gave us not only the rules governing English Prosody and Grammar but he also sought to capture the masses by play and parable, familiarizing them with new words and polite phrases. Ultimately, he gave the "Globe" frequenters sermons in plays on ethical themes, coarsening the stories sufficiently to hold his rude audiences, and sending them away with the triumph of Virtue over Vice ringing in their ears.

In the years now under review he had much of the spade work to do himself. Later on he had a band of qualified helpers working under his general editorship. He termed them "his Compeers by Night" (Sonnet-Diary 116-lxxxvi). Some of his assistants were Fletcher, Ben Jonson, Beaumont, Chapman, Dekker, Massinger, Marston, Ford, Heywood, Nashe, Bright, Burton, Peacham, Betterton, Rawley, Hobbes, Bushell. In fact, shortly after his return from France there is evidence that he had in his employ a number of literary assistants both at Gray's Inn and at Twickenham Lodge. During the years when he was apparently not creating anything, idling his time away, he was busy providing work for what he called his "GOOD PENS." The significance of these facts has never been adequately, if at all, appraised, by academics. From his scrivenery of helpers paid and unpaid, there was poured out by the Knights of the Helmet a steady stream of books and pamphlets for the uplift of the nation. They all originated in the "Areopagus," as it was called by Francis Bacon's friend, Professor Gabriel Harvey.

Instead of Francis Bacon's whole literary output from 1580 to 1603—*twenty-three* years—being three pamphlets, ten essays and one or two Devices [Musical Comedies], there was a busy group of literary workers under Francis as chief, at one time at Gray's Inn, at another at Twickenham Lodge. . . .

And during that period he wrote either wholly or mainly edited works published either anonymously and under many names . . . including his famous *nom de plume* "Shake-speare."

His letter of 1594 to Lord Burleigh that he would retire with a couple of men to Cambridge to write books is an indication that he already had a literary staff working for him . . . the "Idle Pens" reference in his letter to Anthony Bacon confirms this. (*Tudor Problems*, Woodward, p. 31).

According to Spedding in 1589 Francis Bacon had a Lodge at Twickenham. Three years later he was still keeping a staff of scriveners there. This is but open evidence of something that had begun some ten years previously, for his secret scrivenery had begun in earnest after his second Continental visit in 1581-2. What was actually done by the Knights of the Helmet—afterwards known openly as the "Rosicrosse"—is best told in the words of one of the most experienced students of the era respecting this secret literary Society, the late W. T. Smedley, who virtually collected and reconstituted the whole of Francis Bacon's private library, many of the books bearing notes in Francis Bacon's own handwriting. There are upwards of two thousand. They are now in the Folger Library, New York, U.S.A. Mr. Smedley was therefore in a unique position to speak with authority on the secret literary work of Francis Bacon. This is what he said:

Translations of the classics, of histories and other works—with the assistance and the commandment of more wits than his own—were made. . . . Books came from his pen, poetry and prose, at a rate which, when the truth is revealed, will literally stagger humanity.

Books were written by other men under his direction. . . . He saw them through the press. . . and *every book produced under his direction was MARKED.* (*The Mystery of Francis Bacon*, p. 109.)

The cost of printing and publication must have been great. (*Ibid*, p. 110.)

From 1576 to 1623—only forty-seven years—one sees the English language developed from a state of almost barbaric crudeness to the highest pitch which any language, classical or modern, has realized. . . .

There was only one workman living at that period who could have constructed that wonderful instrument and used it to produce such magnificent examples of its possibilities. (*Ibid*, p. 92.)

From 1576 to 1623 . . . the English language was made . . . the finest examples of its capacities which to-day exist: But the knowledge and wisdom possessed by the classical writers, the histories of the principal nations of the world, practically everything that was worth knowing in the literature of other countries, were for the first time made available in the English tongue. . . . *What is still more remarkable, these translations were printed and published.*

These works embraced every art and subject which can be imagined . . . numbers of books crowded with information upon general subjects . . . the *Names on the Title Pages being UNKNOWN.*

The translations were published at considerable cost. . . . Being printed in the English language purchases were practically confined to this country, and the number of readers was very limited. It is impossible to believe that the sale of these books could realize the amount of the cost. (*Ibid*, p. 98.)

Holinshed's *Chronicles*, North's *Plutarch's Lives*, Grimstone's *History of*

France, The French Academy, etc., could not have been produced *with profit as their object.*

Books of this class were never produced with the object of *making profit.* The proceeds of the sales *would not cover the cost of printing and publishing* without any provision of the translator or author. *Why were they published and HOW was the cost provided?* (*Ibid,* p. 101.)

For further confirmation we have only to read the *Manes Verulamiani,* a booklet of Latin eulogies by leading scholars and poets published after Francis Bacon's death. One writer declares, "*Thou hast filled the whole world with thy writings.*"

With few exceptions this vast output of Elizabethan literature for the English-speaking world was published either anonymously or under the name of a living man who was paid for the use of his name. Apart from the fact that it was *déclassé* for an aristocrat to be associated with "writing books," a variety of pen-names, and anonymity, enabled Francis Bacon to speak *with freedom,* and to produce a diversity far more interesting to the general reader than a large number of books over one name. Interest was stimulated by worked-up controversies, the first being a pamphlet discussion upon the subject of the improvement of English music and poetry and the importance, educationally, of stage plays. Francis set the ball rolling under the name of Stephen Gosson. He replied under the name of Thomas Lodge, a poor scholar of Oxford. *Francis, too, had begun to secrete within his writings personal secrets.* The risk of detection was minimized when they were hidden under a variety of names. The full flower of this secret activity was *The Shakespeare Folio* of 1623.

There is a reason why we can speak positively about these many publications being produced from one source, along one channel. There were in all Rosicrosse books secret seals.

1. A desicca-mark produced by the drying of the printed pages, usually in the form of a circle which crinkled them. This was the first outward sign.
2. By a printed device . . . an ornamented headpiece or tailpiece. There were several kinds of devices, the favourite one being the double "A.A." representing *AthenA,* one A light and one A dark, thus indicating that while the book contained much open knowledge for the general reader there was much concealed in the shadows for the man of discernment. The same wooden blocks were used by printers far apart, in divers types of works (such as the Shakespeare Plays and the James Bible) thus proving that the blocks were the property of a central authority that loaned them out as occasion required. The first printed "A.A." device was in 1579, *De Rep. Anglorum Instauranda libri decem, Authore Thoma Chalonero Equitite, Anglo,* by Thomas Vautrollerius, the very year Francis Bacon began his gigantic task.
3. By a large printed T (The First Step) to denote that it was a secret book, the letter indicating a secret Masonic Symbol; or the printing of an ornament or printers' flowers upside down, thus drawing attention to the page, to scan the lines.
4. By an accurate count of letters on the title pages, the end pages, and others to which attention was drawn, which always yielded 157

and/or 287.[1] These numbers were the numerical signatures of "Fra Rosicrosse," together with the numbers 33 and 111, the numerical signatures for Bacon. On all Rosicrosse books these seals are to be found. In the 1623 Shake-speare Folio not only are the title pages thus sealed but the beginning and ending of each Play.

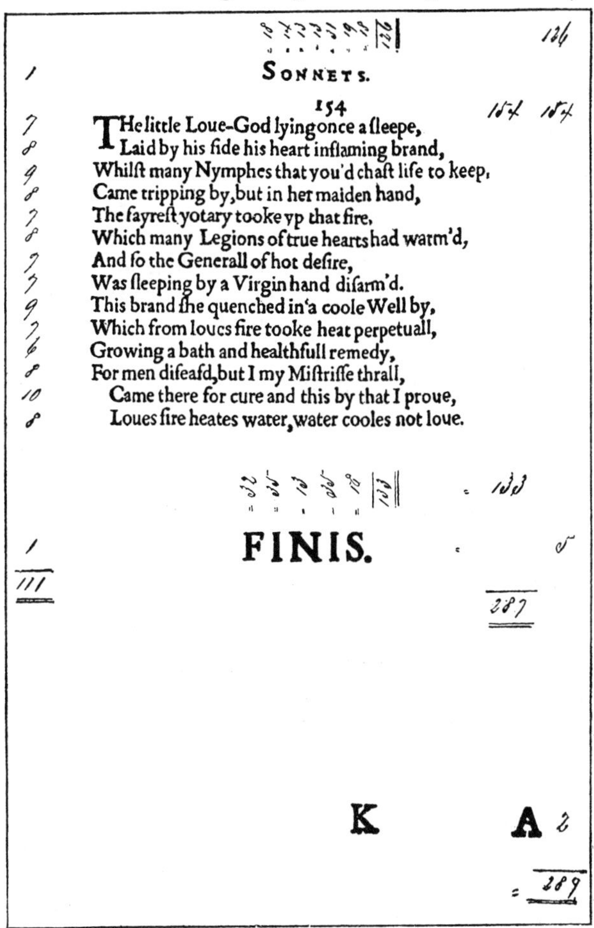

SONNETS.

154

THe little Loue-God lying once a ſleepe,
Laid by his ſide his heart inflaming brand,
Whilſt many Nymphes that you'd chaſt life to keep,
Came tripping by, but in her maiden hand,
The fayreſt yotary tooke vp that fire,
Which many Legions of true hearts had warm'd,
And ſo the Generall of hot deſire,
Was ſleeping by a Virgin hand diſarm'd.
This brand ſhe quenched in a coole Well by,
Which from loues fire tooke heat perpetuall,
Growing a bath and healthfull remedy,
For men diſeaſd, but I my Miſtriſſe thrall,
Came there for cure and this by that I proue,
Loues fire heates water, water cooles not loue.

FINIS.

K A 2

FACSIMILE OF THE LAST PAGE OF SHAKESPEARE'S SONNETS

This last page again shows how carefully the sonnets were compiled by the author and his staff, every letter and word being counted. 111 is the numerical count for Bacon; 287, Fra Rosicrosse.

(See "Secret Shakespearean Seals" and "Shakespeare's Sonnets Unmasked," by B. Theobald, Bacon Society, London)

5. In some cases the paper of the Rosicrosse books was specially watermarked with F.B. or B., with R.C., with G.G., and W.M. There were other marks also.

These are solid, tangible facts; and though hitherto they have been

[1]The numbers "157" and "287" were discovered by Messrs Frank Woodward, Parker Woodward and W. E. Clifton and the profound significance of the logical inferences has never been adequately realized and appraised by literary scholars, Stratfordians or even some types of "Baconians."

ignored by authority, and the labours of a large body of men smothered out of sight, these facts are none the less true. The day is coming when they will be widely known and we shall honour these painstaking researchers—many of them professional men of high qualifications—with the laurels which are their due. We owe a debt to those pioneers who have blown away the mists of three hundred years and enabled us at last to see the Elizabethan Era clearly and Francis Bacon in particular. The debt has still to be paid and is long overdue. What an unmoral mad-hatter's world we live in when Truth has to wait cap-in-hand on little brief authority for recognition.

There is, then, sufficient evidence to show that Francis Bacon when a boy was familiar with the idea of anonymous writing through Sir Nicholas and Lady Bacon, that he had written anonymously before going to France, and that while in France he had written at least one work, *The French Academy*, first published in English in 1585. All these literary activities had culminated in the founding of a secret literary society known by its numerical signature as "Fra Rosicrosse" composed of Knights of the Helmet who were pledged to further the ideals of Pallas Athena.[1]

> The English Renaissance was conceived in France and born in England in 1579. It ran its course and in 1623 with the Shakespeare Folio it attained maturity. . . . It passed when Francis Bacon was no more. (W. T. Smedley, *The Mystery of F.B.*, p. 92.)

It began with Spenser in 1579 and concluded with "Shake-speare's" twenty-thousand-word vocabulary. Year after year, Francis Bacon with his secretaries experimented with the roots of foreign languages and built new words into the English tongue in a variety of ways and through many pen-names, which accounts for the unity of thought and expression among the Elizabethan writers, the mysterious echoes of Greene, Peele, and Marlowe in the Plays of Shakespeare.

Speaking as Prospero to the Calibans of his day . . . to the masses, the author truly said:

> I pitied thee. . . . Took pains to make thee speak. . . . Taught thee each hour . . . when . . . thou wouldst GABBLE [i.e., use rude dialect] like a thing brutish. *I endowed thy purposes with WORDS to make them known.*

That is exactly what Francis Bacon did for the British nation.

Edward D. Johnson, who has made a careful study of Francis Bacon's literary efforts and is an authority on this branch of his activities, writes that:

> On his return from France, Francis Bacon plunged actively into writing books to add to English literature, which was most deficient both in quality and quantity. He published the first edition of *Euphues Anatomy of Wit* which

[1]The complete evidence for these early anonymous publications is very full and readers are advised to study the following writers: E. G. Harman, C.B., *The Impersonality of Shakespeare, Gabriel Harvey and Thomas Nashe, Edmund Spenser and the Impersonations of Francis Bacon*; Parker Woodward, *Tudor Problems, The Early Life of Lord Bacon*; *Secret Shakespearean Seals*; W. T. Smedley, *The Mystery of Francis Bacon*; B. Theobald, *Francis Bacon Concealed and Revealed*; W. Moore, *Shakespeare*; Ed. D. Johnson, *The First Folio of Shakespeare, Francis Bacon's Cypher Signatures*; E. W. Gallup, *Francis Bacon's Biliteral Cypher*; Frank Woodward, *Francis Bacon's Cypher Signatures.*

he had written in France in 1576 anonymously. The second edition was published as by "John Lyly, Master of Arts." He also published *The School of Abuse* in the name of Stephen Gosson; also two poems at the end of *The Pleasant History of the Conquest of West India*, also in the name of Gosson.

On 15th December, 1579, Francis brought out an Emblem Calendar and called it *The Shepheards Calendar* and dedicated it to his friend and cousin, Sir Philip Sidney, signing himself "Immerito."

In July 1580, a clerk named Edmund Spenser, who was in the Earl of Leicester's service, left for employment in Ireland, but, before going, Francis made a bargain with him for the use of his name on books. Immediately after Spenser's departure, Francis printed five letters which had passed between himself and his tutor Gabriel Harvey on the subject of the reform of English verse, and signed the letters "Immerito."

In a letter to Burleigh dated 18th October, 1580, Francis duly thanked the Queen for providing him with a maintenance allowance. In this year he published *Euphues and his England* in the name of "John Lyly, Master of Arts." He also writes a tale *Mamillia* and enters it on the Stationers' Register.

1581: Francis prints a book called *Don Simonides*, an account of his travel in Italy and Spain, title-paged to one Barnaby Rich. He also does a translation from Greek into Latin of the *Antigone* of Sophocles in the name of Thomas Watson, who is a biographical myth.

1582: He published *The Passionate Century of Love* containing about 100 Sonnets, in the name of Watson.

1583: He publishes *Mamillia*, which he wrote in 1580, in the name of Robert Greene who had been one of the Queen's Chapel Choristers, and obtained a post in the Chapel-Royal in charge of the boys. He also publishes in the name of Greene *Morando, Arblasto, Myrrour of Modesty, Carde of Fancie* and *Debate between Folly and Love.*

1584: He publishes *Forbonius and Prisceria*, title-paged to Thomas Lodge, a servant of the Earl of Leicester, and dedicated to Sir Philip Sidney. He arranges with the Queen to make Robert Greene vicar of Tollesbury in Essex and publishes in Greene's name a serious treatise on Astronomy called *Planetomachia*, dedicating it to his father, the Earl of Leicester. Francis prints two Court Comedies *Campaspe and Sapho* and *Phao* in the name of Lyly. Another play *The Arraignment of Paris*, afterwards ascribed to George Peele, he printed anonymously.

1585: He publishes under the name of Watson a translation into Latin of Tasso's Pastoral Drama *Amyntas.*

Queen Elizabeth commissions Francis to write a book on *The Art of Poetry*, which would give the Queen an opportunity of publishing some of her own verses and at the same time enable Francis to expound the rules of Poetry which he had studied.

He writes the play of *Hamlet* . . . performed by Players in the employ of the Earl of Leicester. Wm. Shakspere was still at Stratford and did not come to London until 1586.

1586: March: Sends his father's (Leicester) unemployed assistant Geffrey Whitney to Leyden to see the new book through the Plantin Press called the *Choice of Emblems.* In May the book is published in the name of Whitney and dedicated to the Earl of Leicester: also a booklet *Discourse of English Poetrie* in the name of "William Webbe." He also publishes *A Treatise of Melancholy* by "T. Bright, Doctor of Phisicke." In 1621 Francis revised and extended the treatise, and published it in the name of his then assistant Robert Burton. *Penelope's Webb*, dedicated to his aunt, the Countess of Warwick and her sister the Countess of Cumberland, he published in the name of Greene. In this name he also published a story *Euphues' Censure to Philautus* dedicating it to his brother the Earl of Essex.

1587: In Watson's name he published a translation into Latin of a short Greek poem by Coluthus called *The Rape of Helen.* In this year he commenced to write *Love's Labour's Lost,* a comedy about the Court life of Navarre with minute details of French History which could have only been gained by access to records in France. Three of the characters are the names of real men—Longueville, Dumain (Duc de Maine) and Boyet (Bois). The names of Dumain and Boyet appear on Anthony Bacon's French Passport now in the British Museum.

The literary and cypher proofs that these different types of books came from Francis Bacon's own hand and scrivenery are to be found by any serious student who will study the Works of the authorities I have named in the previous footnote. There is no possible doubt that Francis Bacon was hard at work, in what he called his "studies of greater delight" than Law, from the very moment he returned from France after the death of Sir Nicholas Bacon and that he was working on a carefully thought-out plan to bring his ideals into being.

In 1579 the necessity for his secret staff to be SWORN BROTHERS-IN-ARMS—when one single slip of the tongue or one false step might have resulted in the irretrievable disaster of all his plans—is now abundantly obvious. The genesis problem of Freemasonry thus touched the literary activities of Francis Bacon's scrivenery. Side by side, born out of it as it were, was launched the Ethical Brotherhood which should know neither class distinction nor creed and be universal in its application. In Gray's Inn Francis Bacon founded the first Craft Lodge consisting of Three Degrees. The Ritual of these Degrees had largely been created while he was in France.

The proofs which narrow the period of the Mother-lodge are very simple. There was no Lodge of Freemasons in England prior to 1579. The Ritual is couched in Elizabethan English.[1] The making of our modern tongue began with Spenser, one of Francis Bacon's Masks.[2] And in the Spenser works are at least two allusions to the Square and the Compasses which appear to have a Masonic significance. This suspicion grows into a certainty when we examine some letters that were written in 1579 and published in 1580 between Professor Gabriel Harvey and his friend Francis Bacon who signed himself "Immerito." They are letters dealing with English prosody. They contain interesting asides and also phrases are used *for the first time,* in an allusive manner, which are distinctly Masonic and indicate that there was a Lodge established of which both must have been members; these are very unlikely to have been used save in an esoteric meaning.

Professor Harvey would be about twenty-nine, about nine years senior to Francis. He writes to "Immerito" a half-jocular letter in which he says:

[1]See *Shakespeare Creator of Freemasonry, the Personal Poems of Francis Bacon, The Secret Shakespeare,* by Alfred Dodd.

[2]See E. G. Harman's works, *Gabriel Harvey and Thomas Nashe,* etc.

the bold satirical Libel lately devised AT THE INSTANCE of *a certain WORSHIPFUL HERTFORDSHIRE GENTLEMAN of mine old acquaintance,* etc.

Who can the "Hertfordshire Gentleman" be but Francis, his old pupil at Cambridge? What can "Worshipful" mean in such a connection but a signification, a hint, which is Masonic? It was not a common word of ordinary speech. It was the "Worshipful Gentleman" who had devised the libel or story or, perhaps, a traditional history which was not strictly true; such as the "Murder by three Fellow-Crafts" or the "Broiling on a Gridiron."

A FREEMASON IN 1598 WITH THE SYMBOL OF THE "SQUARE AND COMPASSES"
A facsimile of an illustration in "The Mirror of Policie," a rare book published by Adam Islip in 1598
(*See Appendix I, p.* 358)

A little later Harvey writes to Francis Bacon ("Immerito") again, says to him playfully, "Your Good MASTERSHIPP. . . ." "Your Delicate MASTERSHIPP." Harvey had clearly seen him at work in the Lodge as a Worshipful Master. He then continues very significantly to play with Masonic phraseology, emphasizing the idea of "Mastershipp."

> My verses were bungled up in more haste than good speed, partly at the urgent and important request of a HONEST, Good-natured and *WORSHIPFUL YOUNG GENTLEMAN*. . . .
>
> If it chance to come out now, Good Lorde, how will *MY RIGHT RIGHT WORSHIPFUL AND THRISE VENERABLE MASTERS* of Cambridge scorne at the Matter!"

These are definite hints that Francis Bacon is the Head of a Masonic Lodge. Gabriel Harvey is on the Square and is purposely leaving traces that such a Lodge had been founded for future Brethren who can see the significance of the hint to find. It is unthinkable that such phraseology could be employed heedlessly if Masonic Offices had been unknown to either. They are covert jests at Francis Bacon's Masonry. They are as true as Professor Harvey's description of Francis Bacon himself. "*So trew a Gallant in the Court, so toward a LAWYER, and so Witty a Gentleman.*" All Freemasons were "Gentlemen," not operatives, who applied tools to morals in a speculative or ethical sense.

There is, however, still more pointed evidence of the early organized cult with its Ritual of allegory and symbol. In 1586 Francis Bacon published Whitney's *Choice of Emblems.* On page 53 are to be seen the Two Pillars of Masonry with a S.O.W., a "Son of Wisdom," pointing to a favourite motto of Francis Bacon swung across the pillars "Plus Ultra." There is "*more Beyond*" them, which is very true as every Freemason knows. This is the first reference to the Pillars of Masonry in literature. There are many other symbols, notably the Arches which indicates that a Higher Degree was in being in 1586—the Holy Royal Arch. It is a puzzle-picture, and through the symbolism the name of "F. Bacon" is to be seen quite clearly. The light A and the dark A are to be seen close by a hammer-head (a gavel) and other working tools signifying the connection of the Rosicrosse Literary Society with Masonry. This picture like others slipped into the world, and through the world, without anyone being the wiser. No one ever suspected that a system of ethics pictured by symbol was infiltrating through the world. And from this date to the Emergence of the Masonic Brotherhood in 1723, the trail of the Boar (Francis Bacon's Emblem) or S.O.W. becomes clearer and clearer. Whitney's Emblem not only identifies Francis Bacon with the two secret societies, the literary and the ethical, but it makes it self-evident that the Brotherhoods had been established some years previously, at least in 1583, for that is the oldest genuine document Freemasons can boast, "*The Grand Lodge Old Charge,* 1583."[1]

Besides these two Societies there had already been created tentatively, when Francis Bacon was on the Continent, the outline of a movement, similar in many respects to the Masonic, for the Reformation of the whole Wide World. It is known to-day as the Rosicrucian Fraternity and is supposed to have become extinct. The movement was inaugurated by Francis Bacon and a few Continental Thinkers. It was virtually a re-organization of the old Knights Templar Order and took over primarily their Nine Degree Ceremonial which was associated with the new "Rosicrucian College." These Colleges were to be established later and attached as an inner Rite to the projected Masonic Brotherhood when established. That is exactly their procedure to-day. No one can become a member of a Rosicrucian College unless he is a Master Mason.

[1] The *Regius Poem* and the *Cooke Old Charge,* alleged to have been written in 1390 and the fifteenth century respectively, were written in the Elizabethan era for the specific purpose of connecting the Modern Mystery with the Ancient Mysteries, through the Medieval Guilds and the Roman Collegia. The documents are not dated. The evidence that these documents were of an earlier date than the Elizabethan will not stand critical examination.

In conjunction with his colleagues Francis Bacon created the College Ritual which was strictly confined to the old members of the Knights Templar and left the new Working behind him when he returned to England. On his second visit to the Continent, he was able to report progress. Freemasonry was definitely established in England and the Lodge

In dies meliora.

THE greedie Sowe ſo longe as ſhee dothe finde,
Some ſcatteringes lefte, of harueſt vnder foote
She forward goes and neuer lookes behinde,
While anie ſweete remayneth for to roote,
Euen ſoe wee ſhoulde, to goodnes euerie daie
Still further paſſe, and not to turne nor ſtaie.

THE TWO PILLARS OF MASONRY AND OTHER ESOTERIC EMBLEMS IN 1586
Facsimile of page 53, the upper half of Whitney's "Choice of Emblems" (1586)
(*See Appendix I, p.* 357)

System could, in the light of the experience obtained, be transplanted to France, Germany, etc., with suitable modifications. The most important part of the Rosicrucian scheme was now ready to be put in operation. Francis Bacon had undertaken to write a series of pamphlets to spread the tenets and principles of Rosicrucianism or Freemasonry . . . for both Orders alike are but different aspects of the same ideal; ethics in place of creeds, acts of simple goodness in place of credulous belief, square conduct instead of hypocrisy and chicanery, love and brotherhood instead of the hatred that was sundering the Church of Christ. He took with him to the Continent the first of the Rosicrucian Manifestos. Ere long it was circulating through private hands secretly both in England and on the Continent. Others followed. And when the ground was sufficiently prepared they were published in Germany . . . emanating from nowhere in particular, anonymously.

We know exactly what the objects of the Founder were from a study of these documents. They were:

1. To give the world a new social, educative, scientific and ethical stimulus based on personal reformation through a Society working for the common welfare of the individual.

2. To direct men's minds into the then novel idea of a vast international secret Brotherhood in which the "Love Philosophy" was the dominant note, thus intriguing them with a new curiosity about so strange and marvellous a Fraternity entitled "The Rosicrucian."

3. To ascertain—without suspicion—through the advertisement of the Rosicrucian Manifestos, the calibre and character of aspirants to the Fraternity, whether they were worthy of confidence fit and proper to be eventually introduced to the College through the only way—*as to-day*—the secret door of Masonry, of which Brotherhood the world was in absolute ignorance for more than a hundred years, until 1723.

The Rosicrucian Manifestos, in short, were founded on the principles which we know were the life-blood of Francis Bacon, what he termed "Philanthropia". They were pure propaganda to lead men to the study of the principles underlying the Natural Philosophy of Rosicrucianism and to prepare their minds in advance so as to make them long to join a secret Ethical Society. The tiled-door of Masonry was the only door to the Rosicrucian College. Of the tiled-door the world never heard in Francis Bacon's day. For the Rosicrucian Colleges men ran hither and thither throughout Europe seeking them in vain; and controversy about the anonymous pamphlets and the alleged invisible Fraternity ran riot. The Rosicrucians were attacked, but there were many defenders who replied in pamphlet form. The Manifestos served their purpose from the moment they were put into circulation in manuscript form in the period under review and subsequently in 1614-17, when they appeared in print for general circulation. They attracted the earnest seeker after truth, and ere long he contacted a guide who could quietly put him in the way of obtaining the dearest wish of his heart . . . "LIGHT."

Out of the ruins and decay of the Knights Templar, who from their travels in the East, were the Guardians of the Secret Doctrines gathered from every source, the Rosicrucian College was founded as a direct follow-on. The Knights Templar were anti-Papal, ETHICAL not theological, the true descendants of the Mysteries. Francis Bacon restored the dying Order on different lines, to suit modern conditions on an international basis. He thus remodelled the Society, maintaining the basic principle of Nine Degrees practised by the "S.R.I.A." to-day. He gave it a new name, the Society of the Rose or the Rosicrucian Fraternity, thereby more definitely linking itself with the Mysteries, the Cabala, the theosophic interpretation of God, Man, and Nature. But he had also created a more elastic organization. . . . "The Craft of Masonrie." Around the Jewel of the Rose, he created a Brotherhood which served as a "Case" to enclose so precious a gem. Francis Bacon thus encircled the "Rose-Jewel of Ancient Wisdom" by a series of Degrees in which the Knights Templar once more battled for the eternal verities of Christendom, Faith, Hope, and Charity, the Crucified Rose, the "Rose-Croix."

That this is not a mere speculation on my part is evidenced by Francis Bacon's Sonnet-Diary. Masonic and Rosicrucian hints are mentioned in many Sonnets, but his last Canto of Six Poems is Francis Bacon's last words to his Secret Fraternities; and they cannot be interpreted by literary scholars who have no esoteric knowledge of Masonic and Rosicrucian Symbolism. The first Sonnet has hitherto been regarded by all orthodox commentators as being too enigmatical for adequate elucidation and has never been explained, because it deals with Secret Wisdom. But with the light of the knowledge of his hidden labours we can see the golden thread which linked his three Fraternities together (The Rosicrosse, the Masonic, and the Rosicrucian) in a unanimity which emanated from the soul of Francis Bacon.

Since Brass, nor Stone, nor Earth, nor boundless Sea,
But sad Mortality o'er-sways their Power,
How with this Rage shall Beauty hold a Plea,
Whose action is no stronger than a Flower?
O, how shall Summer's Honey Breath hold out
Against *the wrackful Siege of Battering Days*,
When Rocks impregnable are not so Stout
Nor Gates of Steel so Strong but Time Decays?
O fearful Meditation! Where, alack,
Shall *Time's Best Jewel from Time's Chest lie hid?*
Or what Strong Hand can hold his Swift Foot back?
Or who his Spoil or Beauty can forbid?
O, none! Unless this Miracle have Might,
That *in Black Ink my Love may still Shine Bright.*

Time's best Jewel—The Rose, the Flower-Symbol of the Rosicrucians.
Time's Chest—the outer case of Masonry in which the Jewel is preserved.
In Black Ink, etc.—In the Rosicrosse Books issued by the secret Literary Society is his philosophy; in them, too, are hidden his personal secrets.

Now we can understand the nature of the labours to which he had put his hand in those early silent years which we are assured "were busy ones . . ." during which "he was plunged in work" but on which no biographer yet has shed a glimmer of light. So far as his open labours are known, he was apparently a drone and a sluggard. His public life as an M.P., his law activities, his professional duties to gain a living, all these made no serious inroads on his time. In 1586 another Parliament was summoned and he was elected M.P. for Taunton, but it was dissolved on the 23rd March, 1587. Yet, as we shall see, in these early Parliaments he had won the ear of a fastidious House of Commons and laid the foundations of a Parliamentary career second to none of the greatest commoners of the realm.

The only item of interest that appears in these years is one that seems to give further point to young Francis Bacon's sense of royal dignity. He had not long been in residence at Gray's Inn when he expressed his discontent at the restrictions. He was therefore excused from compulsory attendance at Commons by the express written sanction of Lord Burleigh. There is an entry in the Inn Records in Burleigh's handwriting. In 1586 he had overcome his scruples as to meals "an order being made permitting him to take his meals at the Reader's or Master's table, care being had to reserve the rights to pension and otherwise of the barristers and ancients over whose heads he had been passed."

Is it not odd that the supposed son of a lawyer should have declined to take his meals with law-students, barristers, and ancients? And that special dispensations should have to be procured from the Secretary of State to avoid the obligation of "Keeping Commons?" And, later, that he should be passed over the heads of his seniors? *Such dispensations were not granted to anyone else in that era.* These incidents, trivial in themselves, assume an importance, in conjunction with others, which are weighty and significant. They point to one conclusion only, that Francis Bacon was known to be a concealed Prince, and was therefore to be treated with dignity and special respect, for no one knew how far he would go.

In view of what we know about Francis Bacon's royal birth, the letter that he sent to Lord Burleigh when he referred to his application to be "called within the bar" (6th May, 1586) is not without interest. For he again uses phrases of double meaning which he knows Burleigh will understand:

My very good Lord,

I take it as an undoubted sign of your Lordship's favour unto me that being hardly (unfavourably) *informed of me, you took occasion of good advice than of evil opinion thereby. . . .*

But because your Lordship did mingle therewith both a late motion of mine own, *and somewhat which you had otherwise heard, I know it to be my duty rather to prove your Lordship's admonition effectual in my doings hereafter, than causeless by excusing what is past. And yet, (with your Lordship's pardon humbly asked) it may please you to remember, that I did endeavour to set forth that SAID MOTION in such a SORT as it might BREED NO HARDER EFFECT THAN A DENIAL. And I protest simply before God that I sought therein an ease in coming within Bars and not any extraordinary or singular note of favour.*

And for what your Lordship may have otherwise have heard of me, it shall make me more wary and circumspect in carriage of myself; indeed, I find of my simple observation that they which live as it were in umbra . . . *how moderately and modestly soever they behave themselves, yet* laborant invidia; *I find also that SUCH PERSONS AS ARE OF NATURE BASHFUL*—as myself *is, whereby they want that plausible familiarity which others have, are often mistaken for proud. . . . But arrogancy and overweening is so far from my nature, as if I think anything of myself it is in this, that* I am free from that vice.

And so wishing unto your Lordship all honour, and to myself continuance of your good opinion, with Mind and Means to deserve it, Your Lordship's most bounden Nephew.

FR. BACON.

How came this letter to be written? It is clear that someone had complained to Lord Burleigh that Francis was overbearing and arrogant in his behaviour. Burleigh had therefore admonished him to be a little more humble and not to presume on his relationship to the Queen or put on airs of pride. Francis replies that such evil-speaking about him springs from jealousy arising from having been raised to a seat at the Benchers' Table which he sought not as "an extraordinary note of favour but as an Ease," i.e., freedom from constraint or affectation; relief. Francis rejects the idea that he is arrogant and calls God to witness that he is free from such a vice.

He then reminds Lord Burleigh that when he set forth "a late Motion" (this is *a reference to the "Suit rare and extraordinary"*), he particularly asked that its rejection should "breed no harder effect than a denial," yet he is now being accused of taking advantage of his undefined position, conducting himself as a Prince in hiding. This is the clear inference, because in the next sentence he says "I shall therefore be more wary and circumspect in carriage" in the future. He then points out that persons who live under a cloud as he does, who "live as it were in the shadow, in umbra," no matter how modestly they behave themselves, suffer from spiteful tongues

PLATE XVI
Pallas Athene, the "Speare-shaker"
(See Appendix I)

PLATE XVII
Francis Bacon or Valentin Andrea, the reputed author of the Rosicrucian Manifesto, *The Fama*
From the private collection of Frau le Coq, wife of the late Professor Von le Coq, of Berlin University
(See Appendix I)

(*laborant invidia*). "Such persons as are of NATURE"—i.e., *persons begot outside the law but by Nature*—are naturally "bashful, as MYSELF is." "They want that plausible familiarity which others (legitimately born persons without birth-shadows) have, and are often mistaken for being proud," the fact being that they shrink from contact with others because they are supersensitive.

In no other way can this letter be understood, nor has there ever been any explanation of its admitted enigmatical asides. It can now be understood in its true light as a dignified answer to an uncalled-for censure. He is not giving himself airs because he is the Queen's son . . . too proud to speak to people. His position makes him sensitive and causes him to shrink from familiarities of ordinary men, well-meant or otherwise.

The evidence adduced is already beyond dispute and it is by no means the whole of the evidence. By 1587 Francis Bacon had laid the bases in secret of a series of movements, which had the power of division into almost endless ramifications, fraught with the greatest blessings to posterity, to the English nation in particular and the world in general with the passing of the years. *But openly Francis Bacon had apparently accomplished NO THING.*

Chapter VII

THE MAKING OF AN IMMORTAL (1587-1593)

ON the 19th February, 1593, a new Parliament was summoned to deal chiefly with the continued menace of Spain's aggressive designs against England and European Protestantism. Francis Bacon sat as one of the members for Middlesex. He made his first speech six days later. He was then aged thirty-two. Generally speaking, all his biographers consider that his entry into public life began with this Parliament and that his life's work then commenced. Not only are his boyhood and youth slurred over with a few lines but the years which follow the early thirties are passed over with equal carelessness . . . as though ten or twelve years were of no moment. Posterity has yet to find that these years will rank high among the noblest of his life in the creation of the English language, the development of the English Drama, the founding of his Ethical Societies, the stirring of men's minds towards educational pursuits. To set Francis Bacon on the public stage in 1593, and then, for the first time, to examine him . . . his life and his acts, *simply as a publicist*, is decidedly misleading to the reader and unjust to Francis Bacon himself. There are many open facts of interest which follow on and dovetail into what has already been discovered, facts which no one ought to ignore in honest biography.

The building up of a life made to fit an *a priori* view, by accepting traditional opinions, has never been better outlined than by Francis Bacon's latest biographer, Mary Sturt (1932). It will be seen that the refusal to attempt any kind of original research into his early years—the "Silent Years"—and to begin to weigh him in the balance when he was thirty-two, leads to a tissue of preposterous conclusions. This is what she writes:

> The impression of *all*[1] these papers is that they came from the pen of an old cautious man. . . . Though Bacon was well under thirty, he never seems, so far as literature is concerned, to have had any youth[2]. He never expressed a violent opinion,[3] he never wrote verse—at least not until he

[1]"ALL these papers." There were but TWO, *Letter of Advice to the Queen*, and *The Controversies of the Church*, both written in a style befitting the subject. They are totally insufficient to enable anyone to decide whether Francis Bacon could write in any other style. Miss Sturt is as unaware of other writings (yet there are plenty) as she is of Dr. Abbott's view that Francis Bacon could write in many styles, "it depended on whether he was addressing a King, a philosopher . . . composing a State paper, discussing studies," etc.

[2]There is open evidence that for years Francis Bacon was the leader of the "Revels" at Gray's Inn and composed many musical comedies, and dramatic Plays that were acted before the Queen and also King James.

[3]Here is one out of many. "The corrupter sort of politicians . . . thrust themselves into the centre of the world, as if all lines should meet in them and their fortunes; never caring, in all tempests, what becomes of the Ship of State, so they may save themselves in the cockboat of their own fortune." *Advancement of Learning*, Book II. That is a violent and a true opinion.

was on his death-bed;[1] and when he writes to advise a young friend about his reading he has much to say about historians, but "for poets I can commend none, being resolved to be ever a stranger to them."[2]

He was not even, so far as our knowledge goes, in love.[3] No fair face disturbed the solemn cadences of his sentences on Church Government . . . . The realm in which his youth did show was a purely intellectual one. He was nursing schemes that for magnificence have seldom been equalled. *They obsessed him.* And the writer quotes a fragment of a letter to prove her point. "I have vast contemplative ends . . . for I have taken all knowledge to be my Province."

These statements are typical of the scholastic attitude regarding Francis Bacon. They are rubber-stamp expressions and are fundamentally false. There is no excuse for writers to-day publishing such a travesty. There is abundance of evidence to the contrary (far greater and weightier than can be condensed into a mere footnote) unearthed during the last thirty years by many capable researchers. Such opinions could not have been expresssed if Miss Sturt had had the slightest personal insight into the period or any knowledge of the Revels at Gray's Inn, or if she had weighed Francis Bacon's own avowal to John Davies that he was a "Concealed Poet" or determined what was meant by Francis Bacon's phrase to Sir Tobie Matthew his friend in a letter about 1622 where he says, referring to some past transaction, that his memory may be at fault, and adds significantly, "*My head being then wholly employed about INVENTION.*" This word was then *a term signifying Poetry and the Drama.* And in *Cogitata et Visa* (Hearing and Seeing or Things Pondered, or Meditated, and Seen) Francis Bacon truly says that "*the Art of Inventing grows by Invention itself,*" a profound truth that can only be understood

[1]In his *Apology* he states that he *wrote a Sonnet* which he presented to the Queen when she dined with him at Twickenham. In a fragment of a Play produced at Gray's Inn by Francis Bacon, there is a very fine Sonnet. It is spoken by a blind Indian boy to the Queen. There is a poem which Spedding calls "a remarkable performance" (Vol. XIV, p. 115, Boston Ed.). It is a paraphrase of a Greek epigram. It is a signed poem by "Francis Bacon." It was found in Sir Henry Wotton's papers. There are many other poems in evidence (not his anonymous ones) apart from his "death-bed translations." These were not written as poems at all but were prose-recasts for the purpose of singing. One cannot judge of Francis Bacon's poetic abilities by them alone any more than Milton as a poet can be adequately assessed by his specimens of the Psalms, 1653, notably i, vii, lxxx, which are really comical. Shelley wrote, "*Francis Bacon was a great poet.*" Francis Bacon's friend Edmund Waller declared that Sir Philip Sidney and Sir Francis Bacon were lyrical poets; "*it was the diversion of their youth.*" (Waller's *Dedication* of his *Poems to Queen Henrietta Maria.*) On Francis Bacon's death thirty-two elegies were published by Dr. Rawley. Twenty-seven of them speak of him as *a transcendent poet.*

[2]This statement is quoted to suggest that Francis Bacon was uninterested in poets and poetry and is quite misleading. What English poets could he have suggested prior to his era? That he was no stranger to the classic poets is proved by his numerous quotations from their works. How could he commend any poets? To love particular poets is largely a question of taste. Each must decide for himself. That Francis was familiar with poetry and the value of dramatic poetry is proved by his numerous images referring to the stage. "Dramatic Poesy is *History made visible* . . . Parabolic Poesy is typical History . . . Dramatic Poesy, which *has the Theatre for its World, would be of Excellent Use if well directed.* For the stage is capable of no small influence, both of discipline or corruption. . . . *Among the Ancients it was used as a means of educating men's minds to Virtue.* Nay, it has been regarded by learned men and great philosophers as *a kind of Musician's Bow by which men's minds may be played upon.*" This reference to the Drama of the Mysteries should be pondered particularly by Freemasons who should know its truth better than anyone.

[3]Sensitive souls are usually reluctant in blazoning to the world their love emotions. Because Miss Sturt has no knowledge of the fact that Francis Bacon was a passionate lover, her ignorance cannot be accepted as evidence that he was "never in love with a fair face." Ordinary research shows that he was a lover and the identity of his beloved.

by a creative artist, a poet. There are many similar statements that cry out for explanation. They are all ignored in order to maintain the fiction that Francis Bacon was not a "Concealed Poet" but simply a prosy philosopher, totally unaware of, and uninterested in, Poetry and the Drama. It is lamentable when Authority blinds herself to the Light which springs from new knowledge and is satisfied to stumble along in Egyptian darkness. The objectionable word "obsessed" is even used to belittle his idealism. This word is popularly understood to mean "the state of being molested from without by an evil spirit." What an unjust aspersion. We correlate "obsession" with evil thoughts; but the noble spirit that animated Francis Bacon, "the Spirit of Philanthropia," is more truly expressed by its correct term, "Inspiration." To speak of "obsession" respecting a profound genius who felt that he was "a Servant to Posterity" and who declared at the end of his life that his "Work had prospered under the Providence of God" is utterly incorrect and uncalled for. If such a derogatory word can be used by professing friends, no wonder that his enemies feel that they are justified in disparaging him.

The fact that in 1593 Francis Bacon got into Parliament is accepted with complacency by the modern school as it was by the writers of the last generation. At that date his public life begins, we are told, and his biographers are quite content to let it begin at this point. By none is there any expression of wonderment as to how he managed to get into this third Parliament. No one has yet asked, "How did he pay his election expenses? Nor has any surprise been expressed respecting his source of income. In 1593 he was thirty-two years of age and he had not earned a penny. For fourteen years, since Sir Nicholas Bacon died (leaving him no money), *he had been without visible means of support.* The law had brought him no income. Remember what Spedding has said, "*In* 1592, *I do not find him getting into practice.*" How, then, did he live? How get into the Commons? Who provided him with food and raiment? Who paid his lodgings at Gray's Inn? Who provided his casual out-of-pocket expenses?

These are vital questions. They demand an answer. They constitute a real problem. The thoughtless may ignore the issues as being of no moment, but such questions are primary ones in the hurly-burly of life. They have to be faced by every man not born with a silver spoon in his mouth. They had to be faced by Francis Bacon also. And any conscientious inquiry into his life must take full note of the financial "cruse of oil," that had never failed him, the mystery of its source, the miracle of its replenishment. Senator Ignatius Donnelly, too, in 1888 realized that Francis Bacon had some secret means of income.

> We have direct evidence in Francis Bacon's letters—although they seem to have been gone over carefully and excised and garbled—that *he had some secret means of support.* (*The Great Cryptogram*, Vol. I, p. 289).

When Donnelly wrote these words he had not the slightest suspicion that Francis's secret income was derived from the Queen—Mrs. Gallup had not published her discoveries, nor Mrs. Pott, nor Messrs. Begley, Woodward, Smedley, and many others—but Donnelly realized that this was a vital point demanding inquiry. He little knew that it was one of the keys to unlock the riddle of the great Master's life. To any ordinary person or businessman the source from which Francis Bacon derived his sustenance and support is of supreme interest; and to a literary detective it is all-important. *Cherchez la femme* is the clue in this case as in similar enigmas in real life.

We arrive, then, at this astonishing fact: That up to the age of thirty-two, in the year 1593, *someone was still behind him consistently paying his way*, not his nominal half-brother Sir Nicholas Bacon. He kept Francis at arm's length. Not Anthony; he was still on the Continent. Not Lady Anne Bacon, who had only a slender income. The provider of that secret finance was the Queen. Francis was dependent on his real mother Elizabeth; and because she was his mother, he accepted the provision she made for him as his natural right; and because of that dependency she thought Francis would be indefinitely moulded to her Will. We shall see, later, how he rebelled . . . and the consequences.

The first money Francis Bacon actually earned was in 1594. On the 25th January he appeared in the Queen's Bench for the heir of Lord Cheyney against purchasers of his land. Lord Burleigh sent his secretary to "congratulate him on *the first fruits of his public practice*." He asks for a note of the case——

> his case and the chief points of his pleading to the end that he *might make report thereof where it might do him most good.*

There was only one person higher than Burleigh to whom he could report—and that was *the Queen herself*. Francis also held briefs on the 5th and 9th February. A contemporary account by a Henry Gosnold makes it clear that for Francis to appear in the Courts was no ordinary matter.

> It was expected that several noblemen would put in an attendance. However, there was a good assemblage of learned judges who showed him *extraordinary respect.*

How strange that an obscure barrister conducting his first case should create such interest! It seems more like the curiosity that would be aroused by someone out of the ordinary taking the case through . . . like a Prince of Wales making his first public speech in Court.

There were two marks of favour bestowed upon him by the Queen which deserve mention because they appear to indicate a secret understanding between them. In 1588 he was "Sworn Queen's Counsel Extraordinary."[1] What constituted his duties no biographer has attempted to determine. It brought him in no money but apparently he could be called in to advise the Queen whenever she wished. She could demand his special services. To a certain extent, it gave him an official standing for an audience with the Queen whenever he felt it necessary. He was provided with an excuse to attend Court. It was a specially created office, and I do not know of anyone else who was sworn in such a rôle in that era. "It was an honour which until that time *had never been conferred upon any member of the profession.*" Basil Montague, *Life*, p. 24.

The second significant item occurs the year following, in October

[1]Basil E. Lawrence, LL.D., *Notes on the Shakespeare Plays*, p. 24.

1589. The Queen gave him the reversion to the Clerkship to the Star Chamber, which office was valued at £1600 per annum. This was something he could turn into money by mortgage if he could find "a purchaser sanguine enough to speculate upon the expectation of life of Mr. Mills, the holder of the office." It brought him in no income. Many years later Francis Bacon remarked jestingly "it was like having another man's land near his house: it improved his prospect but it did not fill his barn." He waited more than twenty years before he could step into the dead man's shoes. Hepworth Dixon, who had not the slightest suspicion of their secret relationship, writing in 1861, makes this significant remark quite innocently, *Personal History,* p. 67.

> The reversion of the Star Chamber, the post of her Counsel Learned in Law *are but a foretaste of her* [*Queen Elizabeth's*] *LOVE.*

Of course! For the simple reason that she was his mother and wanted to help him if possible. Through sheer literary analysis alone, and a weighing up of the facts, Hepworth Dixon came to the conclusion that there was a bond between Francis Bacon and Queen Elizabeth, a bond of LOVE, the reason for which he never fathomed. *No other young man in her reign did she "mother" in the same way save one . . . his younger brother Robert,* the future Earl of Essex.

There is another point to be considered, too, contingent on the fact that up to the age of thirty-two and afterwards, Francis Bacon was not under the necessity of having to work for a living. Think what this means in a world of struggle and strain, a strenuousness quite as pronounced, relatively speaking, to the Elizabethans as to us. It meant that *the whole of his creative energies in the best fifteen years of his life could be spent in the pursuit of those things that were dear to his heart* . . . on reading, writing, pursuing his ideals . . . such as the founding of his secret Lodges all over the Kingdom. Francis Bacon was no drone. His "Philanthropia" was like a consuming fire driving him ever onward from his boyish "Trin. Coll. Camb." days. Even though his biographers cannot tell us what he was labouring at they all agree that this creative genius must have been hard at work at something. Ten small *Essays* of 3,500 words, published in 1598, never represented the full fruits of his industry for nearly twenty years, from 1579, the year he returned from Paris. This mystery has hitherto baffled them. The world has still to find the answer to these questions.

> What was this fecund, prolific, laborious writer doing during these nearly twenty years? He was brimful of energy, industry, genius, mirth, humour: How did he expend it? What was that course of study and meditation which he underwent daily, as he told his Uncle Burleigh?

In the knowledge that Francis Bacon was relieved from the necessity of having to work for a livelihood during these vital years, and that he had the "energy and strength of twenty men" (*See* Dr. Sprat's *Hist. of Royal Society*, pp. 35, 36), it is inconceivable why well-informed writers have been content to allow the mystery of "The Silent Years" to remain unsolved. Has it been ignored because of the implications involved? It almost seems as though his biographers were afraid of probing into "The Silent Years" because of possible discoveries that would show

Francis in a new light. It is not impossible that they might destroy the foundations of the traditional theories regarding the Elizabethan era so laboriously laid by past scholars of incomplete knowledge, yet accepted and perpetuated by present scholarship . . . the leading theory being that Francis Bacon was nothing more than a prosy philosopher—on the word-spinning lines of Hume or Berkeley—who failed to complete his system of philosophy; a long-faced prig when a boy, a solemn owl when a man, and a gloomy-faced, soured misanthrope in old age. This traditional caricature is as preposterous as the Droeshout engraving of "Shakespeare" in the 1623 Folio.

Francis Bacon's first important work to be published over his own name, *The Advancement of Learning*, did not appear until 1605. The title was an overt, open announcement that *the English Renaissance of Learning had begun;* for what was the Elizabethan Renaissance but the "advancement of learning" conceived by him as a youth—something practically accomplished, no longer a dream, a theory. When the book was published he was forty-four years of age. Up to the year 1601 he was an unemployed lawyer with nothing to do. What could he not have done to the age of forty with a staff of men to spread the love of literature, by many methods apart from the printing of books, the founding of his New Philosophy of Active Science (Love and Brotherhood) in Lodges far and near, the writing of anonymous works! Before Goethe was ten he could read and write in several languages. He composed poems, invented stories, and had considerable familiarity with works of art while he was at college. *Gotz von Berlichingen*, his first play, was written before he was twenty-three; the *Sorrows of Werther* and *Clavigo* within the next two years. While he was astonishing the world with his poetical and dramatic genius he was making a profound study of natural science. In his twenties he was a recognized philosopher and a poet. Keats's fame rests on poems written before he was twenty-five, an achievement that has been described "not merely remarkable but quite unparalleled in the history of English poetry." Shelley's work was done when he was thirty. Byron wrote *English Bards and Scotch Reviewers* when he was twenty. He had the literary world at his feet when he was twenty-four with his *Childe Harold* and had set a new vogue in poetic style and mannerisms. Robert Burns was a recognized master of song long before he was thirty. We have only to think of Chatterton's metrical inventiveness and his "*Rowley*" poems that deceived Horace Walpole, to realize the work that can be accomplished by a genius in his youth. Chatterton was driven to death by starvation at the age of eighteen. Yet not one of these Masters of Song can hold the candle to Francis Bacon for sheer, unadulterated genius and capacity for prolonged labour. Reflect on what he might have done in those "silent years," and then you will be in a position to discover what he actually did accomplish in secret.

As a matter of fact there is open evidence to show that he was often engaged during these years in a certain type of literary work, which commentators seldom refer to or merely mention in passing. It is really of the utmost importance, for it provides a clue to an unsuspected aspect of Francis Bacon's character which has never been stressed.

We have already seen that when Francis Bacon was a boy he was familiar with the Earl of Leicester's licensed band of actors, headed by Burbage (afterwards the leader of the players associated with "Shakespeare") and saw the Plays produced before the Queen and her Court; how he was certain to have taken his part in the Latin Plays at Cambridge University; and to have seen the public theatre in full swing in France where it had reached a moderate standard of excellence. The coarseness of what he saw put on the stage may have disgusted him, but he was surely quick-witted enough to see what a potent power for good the stage could be educationally and morally. *There was, then, a double incentive to turn his hand to Play-writing* . . . quite apart from holding up the Mirror to Nature. We have seen, too, how he was steeped in the classics. A cursory examination of Francis Bacon's works shows that he was familiar with the great plays of Greece and Rome, Æschylus, Sophocles, Euripides, and so on. Above all, he knew better than any High Mason of the Quatuor Coronati of to-day, that all the Rites of the Mysteries revolved around a ceremonial that was dramatic in its performance, the hero being the initiate as in modern Freemasonry.

At all events, hardly had he settled down to his legal studies, than there are frequent allusions, in the records of Gray's Inn Revels, to the assistance given by Francis Bacon. Sometimes he is the only person named in connection with these festivities. He apparently wrote and managed the whole entertainment. Lord Campbell says, *Life,* p. 14:

> On high-days and holidays he assisted with great glee in all the Festivities of the Inn; and at the request of the Benchers he laid out walks in the garden, and planted trees, some on a spot which got the name of "Lord Bacon's Mount."

This was probably where the open-air rehearsals took place. The "Masques and Devices," as they were called then, were held at different times such as New Year's Day, Twelfth Day, Candlemas Day or Shrove Tuesday, usually in the afternoon. These "Masques or Devices" were Dramatic Performances, humorous, tragical, musical. They were not simple charades but the very reverse. The word "Device" means "a Spectacle or a Show": "Masque" means a Play or a Dramatic Spectacle," (*Stand. Dic.*) Prof. J. A. Symonds in *Shakespeare's Predecessors,* p. 317, says:

> The Masque combined dancing and music with lyrical poetry and declamation in a spectacle characterized by magnificence in presentation.

We can now see the shaping of the budding dramatist, playwright, and manager who wrote, after his enforced abandonment of public life, these remarkable words, so full of inner meaning:

> I shall devote myself to Letters, INSTRUCT THE ACTORS and serve Posterity.

It reminds one of Hamlet's instructions to the players, "Speak the speech trippingly. . . . *Let not your clowns speak more than is set down.*" In other words, "Don't gag! Don't use your one suit of personal jests by which you are known as a man is by his one suit of apparel." (Original Quarto).

We can thus trace in logical sequence the growth and development of the English Drama slowly taking form in Francis Bacon's mind, from the semi-religious miracle Plays acted before Elizabeth, through Cambridge, France, the Inns of Court, the apprentice-hand through various pen-names, no names, or Masks (i.e., the names of living men), until, his apprenticeship complete, there strode on to the world's stage the mighty "Shakespeare."

Generally speaking, Francis Bacon's biographers have never stressed the important fact that Francis Bacon was directly connected with the theatrical world of his early days at Gray's Inn, that he wrote Dramatic Plays and Shows that were acted before the Queen and composed Sonnets. Yet it is an open fact of the deepest significance. Parker Woodward in *Tudor Problems* suggests that Francis Bacon supplied all the Plays that were prepared and performed at Gray's Inn from 1583 for the entertainment of the Queen. It is highly probable. What we are definitely certain about is this: That Francis did prepare certain Plays that were performed before the Queen. Not only so, but it was well-known in Court Circles *even in the time of James* that Francis Bacon was a Past Master in the art of stage management and the creation of plays.

On 14th February, 1612-13, the Princess Elizabeth married the Count Palatine. There were the usual rejoicings which lasted several days. Chamberlain, a contemporary, wrote:

> On Tuesday, 18th February, it came to Gray's Inn and the Inner Temple's turn to come with their Masque, whereof Sir Francis Bacon was the chief contriver. . . .

Commenting on this, Spedding says; "it would not have been necessary to say anything were it not that Bacon took a principal part in the preparation of one of the Masques."

> "On the 25th," adds Chamberlain, "they performed their part exceeding well, and with great applause and approbation, both from the King and all the company. The next night the King invited the Masquers (Players) with their assistants to the number of forty, to a solemn supper . . . where they were well treated and much graced with kissing his Majesty's hand."

So when "Shake-speare" and Ben Jonson were at the height of their fame, it was the Solicitor-General, Sir Francis Bacon, who was employed to "contrive" the presentation of the Masque to the Queen. A strange proceeding, if Francis Bacon knew nothing about the stage, to employ a lawyer to manage it instead of a dramatist! It is like going to Sir Stafford Cripps instead of to C. B. Cochran or Seymour Hicks to contrive and manage a spectacular Show. And no Elizabethan authority has expressed surprise.

On 26th December, 1613, the then Favourite, the Earl of Somerset, married Lady Essex. Presents were being showered upon him. Francis Bacon offered on the part of Gray's Inn to supply a Masque. Chamberlain, on the 23rd December, writes:

> Sir Francis Bacon prepares a Masque to honour this marriage, which will stand him in above £2,000; and though he has been offered some help

from the House, and especially by Mr. Solicitor, Sir Henry Yelverton, who would have sent him £500, yet he would not accept it, but offers the whole charge with the honour.

The piece performed was published shortly after with a dedication to Sir Francis which says:

> You have graced in general the Societies of the Inns of Court... in doing the King honour, and particularly Gray's Inn, which *as you have already brought to flourish, both in the ancienter and younger sort, by countenancing Virtue in every quality*. . . . You have made a notable demonstration in *the lighter and less serious kind*... by one Inn of Court by itself, in time of vacation, the space of three weeks . . . which could not have been done but that every man's *exceeding love and respect* to you gave him wings to overtake time. . . .

The piece was entitled the *Masque of Flowers*. If further proof were needed that Francis Bacon thoroughly and practically understood theatre management one has only to turn to the *Essay of Masques and Triumphs*. This is sufficient to show that he was intimately acquainted with the difficult art of writing for the stage, with one eye on the scenic effect and the other on the characters, not forgetting the incidental music. For modernists to assert that Francis Bacon had neither knowledge nor love of Stage Shows is a preposterous mis-statement.

The foregoing evidence clearly indicates his acquaintance with the creation and management of Stage Plays so far as Gray's Inn is concerned, and we have only to examine the records of the Inn to know the reason why Francis Bacon was regarded as an authority on the "Instruction of the Actors" and the art of producing Plays. He had a professional interest and a passion for stagecraft, and his surroundings at Gray's Inn afforded him peculiar opportunities to try out the theory and practice of the Dramatic Art. The real genesis of the English Drama in its highest reaches was conceived in Gray's Inn for there were no theatrical pursuits before the nation worth mentioning until the Francis Bacon era at the Inns of Court. Even Professor Boas remarks. . . . "*Gray's Inn where theatrical activity is worth noting*."

The following Plays are associated more or less with Francis Bacon at Gray's Inn:

1583: The Birth of Merlin;
1587: The Misfortunes of Arthur;
1591: The Lord Mayor's Pageant, 29th October (Woodward).
1592: A Conference of Pleasure.
1594-5, Jan: The Order of the Helmet or the Prince of Purpool.
1595: The Device of the Indian Prince.

The Birth of Merlin was written anonymously. Its parent has never been traced. It contains legal expressions and the internal evidence indicates Francis as the author.

The Misfortunes of Arthur is the first tragedy with which his name is definitely connected. It is a good example of his early dramatic style. Collier reprinted it from the only copy that had survived, thus rescuing it from oblivion. The title page shows that "The Shewe was presented to her Majestie by the gentlemen of Grayes Inne at Her Highnesses Court in Greenwich, the 28th day of Feb." The story is taken from *Morte d'Arthur*. There is a dumb show between each of the Acts, a pretty scene occurring when Three Muses in classical attire walk on the stage leading five of the gentlemen law students in their law attire and present them to the Queen as captives. Later, three Furies rise from under the stage (reminding one of *Macbeth*), the first with a snake in her right hand and a cup of wine in her left; the second with a firebrand and a cupid; the third with a whip and a Pegasus; then three Nuns. There are speeches in blank verse, lyrical poetry and music. Collier remarks:

> There is a richer and nobler vein of poetry running through it than is to be found in any other previous work of the kind, and the blank verse is generally free and flowing.

The names of the collaborators are given and among them Francis Bacon.

A Conference of Pleasure was written by Francis Bacon for the Earl of Essex (*See* Prof. Nichol's *Life*, Vol. II, p. 225) for the Tilt-Yard Ceremonies. It represents "Four Friends" (as in the *French Académie*) meeting for intellectual amusement, each in turn delivering a speech in praise of whatever he holds to be "THE MOST WORTHY." (Note the Masonic phraseology):

1. The Praise of the Worthiest Virtue or Fortitude;
2. „ „ „ Affection (Love);
3. „ „ „ Power, Knowledge;
4. „ „ „ Person, this Lady.

The last "Praise" was ostensibly a Praise of Queen Elizabeth, but covertly it was a Praise of Francis Bacon's Sovereign Lady whom he terms "CROWNED TRUTH."

There is no question that this Play—of which we have only fragments—was written for the Earl of Essex and was presented to the Queen. Even against his will Spedding writing in 1861 admits that he has little doubt the "Device" was written by Francis Bacon for performance on Queen's Day though no detailed account had been preserved: We only know that it was "*more solemnized than ever, and that through my Lord of Essex his Device.*"

The Order of the Helmet or *The Prince of Purpool* (*Purple*) gives a direct clue to Francis Bacon's secret activities. Attention has already been drawn to this Play, but it is so important that its salient features deserve to be stressed. For some reason the Christmas Revels in Gray's Inn had been intermitted for some three years or more. In the winter of 1594 the students resolved to produce "*something out of the common way.*" Francis Bacon as usual was called in to "*recover the lost honour of the Inn.*" The sports were to last for twelve days, Gray's Inn turned into a mimic Royal Court (not a Law Court) over which a Prince of Purpool (i.e. Purple indicative of his Royal Estate) ruled as the Master of Revels. *And the Prince was Francis Bacon* . . . a very significant touch considering he was a Tudor.

On the 20th December, the Prince, in royal purple, with all his State courtiers and servants, proceeded to the Great Hall of Gray's Inn, where he was enthroned with great pomp and ceremonial. (Francis, by the way, was very fond of this kingly colour. He was eventually married in "Purple from cap to shoe," writes an eye-witness). The entertainment was so gorgeous, so skilfully managed and so topical that the students had a thoroughly riotously happy time. It had already been arranged that they should have certain "Grand Nights" for the entertainment of strangers. But the fame and excitement of the "First Grand Night" attracted a throng which so crowded the Hall that the student-actors were driven from the stage and for a time the visitors had to content themselves with music and dancing. When things cooled down the Play was proceeded with. It was called *A COMEDY OF ERRORS, like to Plautus his Menoechmus.* "A Comedy of Errors!" Think of the significance. A "Shake-speare" Play in the Inns of Court. And this, according to Dr. Delius, is *the first allusion anywhere to the Comedy of Errors.* Since this comedy was heard and acted for the first time in Gray's Inn on 28th December, 1594, under the direct mastership of the Purple Prince, it constitutes strong *prima facie* evidence that it was the very "Invention and Conceit" of Francis Bacon: there being *no direct evidence anywhere to connect anyone else with the Play.* It brings us appreciably nearer Francis as an anonymous writer who used a *nom de plume* and a MASK.

The next night was taken up with a mock legal inquiry into the causes of the disorder and the reason why the players were driven off the stage, which ended with the resolution, "that the Prince's Council should be reformed, and some Graver Conceits should take their places." Within four or five days Francis Bacon had written and produced an entertainment which is described by a contemporary as:

> One of the most elegant that was ever presented to an audience of Statesmen and Courtiers.

This was *The Honourable Order of the Knights of the Helmet* already referred to, performed on Friday, 3rd January, 1594. There is not the slightest doubt that this entertainment was based on an actual ceremonial akin to the Rites of Freemasonry. It was intended to be simply a COVER—an open recital that might constitute a record for posterity—of unsuspected, unknown and secret organizations already in existence, the Rosicrosse Literary Society, the Rosicrucians and the Freemasons. After the guests were seated—there were many great personages present—the Prince of Revels came in full state and took his throne. He was entitled the Prince of Purpool (Purple). Various persons were invested with a Collar of the Knighthood of the Helmet which each kissed in token of his vow to keep the articles of the Order inviolate, previously read to him. The initiated law-students were vowed in the Play *to defend God and the State*, to attack Ignorance, to defend Truth and Virtue *ceaselessly and secretly.* Then followed *a Series of Charges* by six "*HIGH COUNCILLORS*" (a term known to every Frater of the S.R.I.A. to-day). The Charges and the Articles also are well worth reading. especially by Freemasons. They are given in Spedding's works.

1. Advising the Exercise of War; [i.e. symbolically, war against all evil and ignorance] Military arts being compatible with Learning;

2. The Study of Philosophy;
3. The Eternizement of Fame by BUILDINGS and FOUNDATIONS; [i.e., Solomon's Temple, Solomon's House, hidden Ethical Bases];
4. Absoluteness of State and Treasure;
5. The Exercise of Virtue and Gracious Government;
6. The Necessity for Proper Pastimes and Sports.

The speeches of the Counsellors embody tenets to be found by specific symbolisms in Modern Freemasonry.

> One Counsellor talks of a "Blazing Star," the "*EYE of the World* that both carrieth and useth LIGHT" . . . "You may have in *a small COMPASS* a Model of Universal Nature *made PRIVATE*" . . . "*a Palace fit for a Philosopher's STONE*" . . . [the Ashlar].
>
> Another speaker eulogizes "Buildings" in metaphors which are quite Masonic. He says: "A Monarch should win Fame and Eternize his Name . . . in the visible Memory of himself in the magnificence of Goodly and ROYAL BUILDINGS and FOUNDATIONS and THE NEW INSTITUTION OF ORDERS AND SOCIETIES, Ordinances. . . ."
>
> A third one cries, "ADVANCE Men of Virtue not of Mercenary Minds . . ." while the last Counsellor speaking to the Prince of Purple says: "To speak out of my Soul I muse how any of your servants can endure to think of you *as a PRINCE PAST*. [*Note this doubly subtle reference to Francis Bacon's real identity as well as being a Past Master of King Solomon's Throne*]. Their lessons were so cumbersome as if they would make you a KING in a PLAY, who, when one would think he standeth in Great Majesty and Felicity, is troubled to say HIS PART. . . ."

This latter sentence is a most adroit allusion to the Worshipful Master Presiding over his Lodge. He is indeed "*a King in a Play*" and is often troubled "*to say his Part correctly*." At the end of his term of office he parts with his servants or officers with regret, being placed on the retired list, his brief authority as the representative of King Solomon ended: a Prince Past. All these allusions could not possibly be understood to have an esoteric meaning in Francis Bacon's day, for the world did not know that certain secret societies had been founded. And though literary men know that Lodge Freemasonry is to-day scattered all over the world they neither know what it really stands for nor its symbolism. They cannot understand. But any Freemason will confirm the fact that this is Masonic symbolism. It is incredible that such language of particular metaphor and allegory could have been used without the writer being acquainted with the Ritual still practised by Freemasons to-day. Even Mr. Spedding sees in this Play the germ of the notions which were carried out in the *New Atlantis*. But every "well-informed Mason" knows that the *New Atlantis* is a Preface-Fragment foreshadowing to the world that Solomon's Temple had been rebuilt on Ethical Foundations; the Colleges of Rosicrucianism established; Solomon's House of Experimental Science organized and ready to emerge into the light of day in the fullness of time. *The Invisible College of Scientists* emerged into the light as the *Gresham College*. And then it came before the public boldly as the *Academie* in 1660. Two years later Charles II raised it to its present status of the *Royal Society*. At their first meeting honour was paid to Francis Bacon as their real founder his, portrait adorned the walls, Abraham Cowley acclaimed him in an Ode recited to the Royal Society as the Moses who had led us forth from the barren wilderness to the land of experimental science dedicated to the benefit of humanity. And Dr. Sprat in his *History of the Royal Society* writes:

> One Great Man, Francis Bacon, who had the true Imagination of the whole extent of this Enterprise, as is now set on foot. . . . If my desire could have prevailed there should have been no other Preface to the *History of the Royal Society*, but some of his writings. (P. 35, Part I, Sec. xvi.)

Let it not be forgotten either that the driving force behind the Invisible College, the Gresham College, the Academie, and the Royal Society were all Rosicrucians and Freemasons—Fludd, Boyle, Wren, Ashmole, Locke and Sir Thomas Moray, etc. When we consider that the real title of the *New Atlantis* was the *Land of the Rosicrucians*, with its ethical symbolism and its experimental marvels for the uplift of humanity by applied science, and that a Masonic authority like James Hughan declared that "the *New Atlantis* seems to be, and probably is, the KEY to the modern Rituals of Freemasonry" . . . we can begin to see clearly the light shining in the darkness of Francis Bacon's early "Silent Years." We can see already the English Renaissance of Ethics, Science, and Art growing in embryo in the Garden of Gray's Inn, then tended, planted out, watered and nurtured into sturdy growth by the creator's hand tenderly, lovingly, passionately. We can see how the "*Advancement of Learning*" was established not merely by writing a book in 1603. The Bases for a great attack on the citadels of Ignorance and Intolerance had been laid already, and secret phalanxes of enthusiastic warriors were slowly moving up to undermine the pedantry of the Aristotelian quidnuncs who thought they knew everything, the dogmas of learned theologians saturated in all but charity, and the coarseness and vulgarity of the common people. And though Francis Bacon knew it would "take many years for the ripening of the seeds" he had sown, yet he had made provision that the assault should continue through the generations until victory was assured, for he had left the Keys of his peculiar Knowledge to a "Succession of Hands" who would carry his Truths forward to the Eternities.

In *The Device of the Indian Prince* (1595), we have only a fragment but quite sufficient to show that Francis Bacon possessed the necessary powers for metrical composition. *A Blind Boy* as an Oracle speaks to Queen Elizabeth a Sonnet:

Seated between the Old World and the New,
  A Land there is no other Land may touch,
Where reigns a Queen in Peace and Honour true,
  Stories or Fables do describe no such.
Never did Atlas such a Burden bear,
  As she in holding up the World Oppressed;
Supplying with her Virtue everywhere
  Weakness of Friends, Errors of Servants best.
No Nation breeds a warmer Blood for War,
  And yet she calms them by Her Majesty;
No Age hath ever Wits refined so far,
  And yet she calms them by her Policy:
To Her THY SON must make his SACRIFICE
  If he will have the Morning of his Eyes.

How deadly significant are the last two lines. The writer calls himself the Queen's Son, "*Thy Son*," and has been sacrificed, blinded by her blindness, as a concealed son. The closing expression is a prayer for restoration from blindness so that he may see her as a child sees his mother, a restoration which means an open renewal of relationship and consequent acknowledgment of being next in the Succession. "The Morning of his Eyes," is eminently poetical. The words that follow this Sonnet make this interpretation positively true:

> This Oracle hath been both our direction hitherto, and the cause of our wearisome pilgrimage; *we do now humbly beseech your Majesty that we make experience whether we be at the end of our journey or not.*

Hepworth Dixon writes, *Life*, p. 33:

> Francis Bacon became the light and the genius, as in after-years he was the glory, of Gray's Inn; laid out the gardens, planted the elm-trees, raised the terrace, pulled down and rebuilt the chambers, *dressed the dumb SHOW*, *led off the dances*, *invented the Masques;* a genial and original nature, *panting for work*, and undertaking that which lay nearest to his hand.

Such is the opinion of a literary authority in 1862 who never suspected that Francis Bacon was a concealed dramatist. "He INVENTED the Masques." That is a significant statement, for there were no Comedies, Histories or Tragedies on the Stage when the Revels at Gray's Inn were being held. "He led the Dances. He dressed the dumb Show." There is little trace of the "dull, prosy philosopher" in these frolicsome capers. Yet this high-spirited, young man of mettle, with the natural exuberance of youth, is persistently represented as being from his earliest days a solemn personality, too weighed down with his ponderous philosophy to be interested in such frivolities as a Dumb Show, a Dance, or the creation and the writing of a musical Comedy or a Masque.

These Orations and Plays at Gray's Inn are linked with a very remarkable manuscript volume of the Elizabethan period found by Spedding at Northumberland House, Strand, in 1867, and was not made available to the general public until 1904. It is now called *The Northumberland Manuscript.* This once belonged to Francis Bacon and reposed in his private scrivenery. It consists of a bundle of writings, the majority of which are indisputably the work of Francis Bacon . . . but some of the manuscripts are missing. The forty-five remaining leaves bear no traces of stitching. Apparently the MSS had been placed loosely inside a paper cover which had served as a Catalogue, for written down are the titles of the works that once reposed inside it.

The handwriting has been identified by T. le Marchant Douse as that of John Davies of Hereford, a scholar of Oxford University, one of Francis Bacon's "Good Pens," or secretaries. He was a Mason and he wrote a remarkable Sonnet to *The Royall Ingenious and All Learned Knight, Sir Francis Bacon.* We can therefore be quite sure that the writing on the Cover was done very deliberately to give a clue to posterity, and that there is more behind the writing than meets the eye. If the reader will refer to the illustration of the Cover he will see that the right hand side contains a list of writings in which the Plays written by Francis Bacon for Gray's Inn Revels are named and associated with other works and names which he used as pen-names: On the left hand side are names, notes, phrases, rhymes, scribblings in no particular order. Here are the principal items:

Mr. Ffrauncis Bacon
of Tribute or giving what is dew.
(*Some hieroglyphics*)
The praise of the worthiest vertue
The praise of the worthiest affection
The praise of the worthiest power
The praise of the worthiest person
By Mr. ffrauncis Bacon of Gr
Greis Inn in the
revealed
Earle of Arundells letter to the Queen
Speaches for my Lord of Essex at the tylt
Speach for my Lord of Sussex
honorificabilitudine   Leycesters Common Wealth
Orations at Graies Inne revells
By Mr. ffraunces Bacon
Essaies by the same author
printed
By Mr. ffrauncis   William Shakespeare
Bacon   Shakespeare
Rychard the second
ffraunces
Rychard the third

Bacon   Asmund and Cornelia
revealing   Ile of Dogs
day through
every crany   Thomas Nashe   inferior plaies
peepes and
see   William Shakespeare
Shak   Sh   Sh
sh   Shak   Shakespeare
Shak
William Shakespeare
William Shakespeare   Wlm   Wlm
Will
William   Shakespe
Shakespe   Shakespeare

The first thing of importance to note is that the document is connected with the "dew" of the Rosicrucians. The top symbol to the left with the straight line and circle is a Rosicrucian picture of *The Mirror of Pallas Athene*, the Sign of Prudence and Circumspection. We thus see the symbol of the "Speare-Shaker" associated with "Ffrauncis Bacon" and "William Shakespeare." The three scrolls underneath represent the Helmets of Pallas and Pluto—which made the Rosicrucians into "The Invisibles"—and the Rosicrucian Jewel of "The Rose" with all its

Francis Bacon's statute at Gray's Inn. This statute stood outside Gray's Inn. There were engraved on the pedestal, on four sides, the various offices he held (as Dean of the Chapel, 1589, and Treasurer, 1608–17) and his public labours as a lawyer, statesman and author. (See "Francis Bacon Concealed and Revealed" by Theobald, p. 360)

Gray's Inn Square, facing north-east. The historic building where Francis Bacon laboured for so many years among the law students familiar with his secret ideals

Plate XIX

Interior of Gray's Inn Hall. In this room Francis Bacon's plays, masques and musical comedies, *The Order of the Helmet, A Conference of Pleasure,* etc., were performed, and the first mention of "Shakespeare's" play *A Comedy of Errors* was heard and acted in connection with the revels at Gray's Inn. From a drawing by H. Crichmore in "Shakespeare's London" by W. F. Ordish

(See Chapter VII, p. 154)

Twickenham Park. An avenue of trees on Francis Bacon's property

(See Chapter VII, p. 178)

deep significance. The Mirror of Pallas being directly associated with Francis and "Shakespeare" is in itself remarkable; but it is much more remarkable to know that this is the only time and the only place in contemporary Elizabethan documents that the two names are brought together. It is a significant fact that Francis Bacon in all his works never once mentions the name of "Shakespeare."

We thus see that Francis Bacon is not only associated with the Plays at Gray's Inn but with a "Thomas Nashe." An out of the way word is used like "honorificabilitudo" which is used as a variation in *Love's Labour's Lost,* not then published. (It is generally agreed that the Northumberland MS must have been written about 1595-6). The writer must also have been familiar with *Lucrece,* published in 1594, for a line of the poem, "revealing day," etc., is scribbled on the side. Here we have an authentic document, written by one of Francis Bacon's secretaries, containing transcripts of a number of writings made by him, and right in the middle of them two "Shakespeare" Plays, *not yet published,* no author being indicated for them, and therefore presumably they are by Francis Bacon also. One thing is certain: The Shakespeare Plays of *Richard the Second* and *Richard the Third* once rested within that cover, and were in Francis Bacon's private possession... in his secret scrivenery of the Rosicrosse Literary Society. Someone took those Plays out. Why? Because they went to the printer to be published; for at the back of the cover are the words that explain the missing manuscripts . . . "PUT INTO TYPE." This is abundant proof that *the entire bundle of manuscripts was Francis Bacon's own property to be printed as he thought fit.* And the Plays in question were printed the same year as the first edition of his Essays . . . the manuscripts then being filed with "the Grand Possessors" who, according to the Preface of *Troilus and Cressida,* 1609, kept them in safe custody for the author.

If, however, the list is noted carefully, it can be seen that the scribe is trying to give a hint of the underlying truth, that Francis Bacon is not only the author of the *Essays* but also the "author" of the being known as "William Shakespeare." Examine the way in which the list is compiled.

"By Mr. ffrauncis Bacon,	*Essaies* by the same author.
"By Mr. ffrauncis	*William Shakespeare*
"Bacon	*Richard the Second*
	Richard the Third
"*From your Bacon*: Revealing	Thomas Nashe your inferior plaies
"day through every crannie	
"peeps and see your	William Shakespeare
	William Shakespeare
	William Shakespeare"

The order in which the list is given thus lets the reader understand that Francis Bacon was not only the author of the *Orations* at Gray's Inn Revels and the *Essays* but he was also the AUTHOR—in the sense of being the Creator—of "William Shakespeare" along with *Richard the Second and Richard the Third.* Quite clearly, "William Shakespeare" is as much a dramatic creation of "Mr. Ffrauncis" as Richard or Hamlet. He associated an ideal character with "The Rustic of Stratford." He did the impossible. He created a silk purse out of a sow's ear.

Apparently, "inferior plays" by a "Thomas Nashe" also rested once within these covers. It is sufficient to say that some learned scholars believe that he was one of Francis Bacon's early Masks. This name in the list brings up the entire question of the use Francis Bacon made of pen-names, anonymity, and masks or vizards (paying men for the use of their names). The proofs are very technical and outside the scope of this work intended for popular reading. But it is abundantly obvious that in Francis Bacon's silent years he was serving his apprenticeship to literature. Men flit on to Francis Bacon's stage as the author of a work, make their bow, disappear into the wings and are never heard of more. The unerring proofs of authorship are given by the Rosicrosse Seals and internal evidence. When Francis Bacon was the author of a particular work it was signed by his numerical signature or by anagram or acrostic.

We have now got a fairly accurate bird's-eye-view of Francis Bacon's secret activities during the "Silent Years." He was creating a language, a literature, writing and publishing books on all sorts of subjects, many written by his friends, creating an English-reading public, and endeavouring to educate the common mass by plays—which in that era were the only way in which the mass could be leavened, educated socially, politically, morally, for there were no newspapers or organs of public opinion. He was also establishing his secret societies and endeavouring to stimulate inquiry into the secrets of Nature so that humanity might be benefited by the experiments of scientists. He was also endeavouring to establish the "Love-Philosophy" of the "New Commandment" which had been neglected by the Churches. These ideas and ideals, which were frowned upon by Authority, would have been nipped in the bud had there been any attempt to promulgate them openly. They were therefore sown in secret, nourished in secret, and then broadcast in secret. And when their existence was discovered to the world they were too firmly established, and too widespread in England and on the Continent, for even the Roman Church and State tyranny to stamp them out. That he worked anonymously is proved by his own words in the *De Augmentis*, Book VII (Ellis and Spedding Ed., edited by J. M. Robertson, p. 562):

> For myself I may truly say that both in this present work and in those I intend to publish hereafter, *I often advisedly and deliberately THROW ASIDE THE DIGNITY OF MY NAME AND WIT in my endeavour to advance Human Interests* . . . taking upon myself the burden and execution of many things which needs must be done, and which others through an inborn pride shrink from and decline.

Here, then, is a distinct claim in a work written in 1622 that he had written anonymously and would continue to do so hereafter, which could be construed to apply particularly to the Great Folio of Plays published under the pen-name of "William Shake-speare," in the following year. If the reader will note carefully the points of emphasis in the *Preface to the Great Instauration*, in the light of what has been written, he will see clearly what were Francis Bacon's real aims in life, their vast scope, and his tremendous labours in the "Silent Years" to get his schemes started. It was not until this work was actually in process of being that

Nevill

Mr ffrauncis Bacon

of Tribute, or giving what is dew

Nevill

By Christ religio fons refusing of them

your religion refreshing your selves as in Christ

Esquier agt

The praise of the worthiest vertue
The praise of the worthiest affection
The praise of the worthiest power
The praise of the worthiest person

ne vile velis Anthony Comfort and consorte

refreshing ye hart

By Mr ffrauncis Thomas Thomas

laden with grief and oppression of heart

By Mr ffrauncis Bacon of Gr

Philipp Greis Inn in the against monsieur revealed

Multis annis iam transactis
Nulla fides est in pactis
Mell in ore Verba lactis
ffell in Corde ffraus in factis

Earle of Arundells letter to the Queen

from your service

Speaches for my Lord of Essex at the tylt.

Speach for my Lord of Sussex tilt

more than externally

honorificabiletudine Leycesters Common Wealth Incerto autore

Orations at Graces Inne revells

Queenes Mate

Earle of Arundles letter to the Queens mtie

By Mr ffrauncis Bacon

Essaies by the same author printed

By Mr ffrauncis mr mr ff William Shakespeare

Bacon

Rychard the second

Rychard the third

Asmund and Cornelia

Ile of Dogs frmnt

revealing day through every crany peepes and see

as your

by Thomas Nashe your inferior plaiers

your William Shakespeare

THE NORTHUMBERLAND MANUSCRIPT
In modern script with portions of the scribblings erased.

Francis Bacon stepped on to the public stage of life, to interblend his secret idealism with public activities in 1592.

Preface to the Instauration

"Being convinced that the Human Intellect makes its own difficulties . . . there was but one course left therefore, to try the whole anew upon a better plan, and to commence *a total Reconstruction of Sciences, Arts, and all Human Knowledge,* RAISED upon the proper Foundations. (Robt. Ed. p. 241.)

"In obedience to the everlasting Love of Truth, I have committed myself to the uncertainties and difficulties and *solitude of the ways* . . . relying on Divine Assistance . . . in the hope of providing at least for the Present and Future GENERATIONS GUIDANCE—more faithful and secure.

"The same Humility I use in INVENTION [i.e., he does not identify himself openly with his lyrical and dramatic creation], I employ in TEACHING [i.e., as the Founder of Ethical Freemasonry]. For I do not endeavour even by the VEIL OF OBSCURITY to invest these INVENTIONS OF MINE with any Majesty; which might easily be done by one who sought *to give LUSTRE to his NAME rather than LIGHT to other Men's MINDS.* (*Ibid,* p. 246.)

"I AM LABOURING TO LAY THE FOUNDATION not of any SECT or DOCTRINE but out of human Utility and Power . . . to cultivate TRUTH IN CHARITY.

I am by no means forgetful of the conditions of Mortality and Humanity, for it does not suppose that the WORK can be completed within ONE GENERATION, *but PROVIDES FOR IT BEING TAKEN UP BY ANOTHER* [i.e. in the transmission of his ideas by a succession of "Sons," which fruited in the Royal Society in 1662, in Freemasonary 1723, and in Rosicrosse books which were published long after this date until the taste of literature for the common people was established]. *Ibid,* p. 247.

We can therefore be quite certain from his own words that Francis Bacon was a concealed poet, teacher and writer, the founder of the English Renaissance. One witness alone is sufficient to clinch the matter, Bishop T. Tenison, who wrote in 1679 these pregnant words:

Those who have TRUE SKILL in the Works of the Lord Verulam, like the Great Masters in Painting, can tell by the Design, the Strength, the way of the Colouring, *whether he was THE AUTHOR of this or the other Piece, though his Name be not to it.*" (*Baconiana, or Genuine Remains of Francis Bacon,* p. 79.)

Everybody knows there was no evolution of the English Drama for the perfecting of the Dramatic Art. There had been Miracle Plays and the like connected with the Medieval Guilds and the Church but they were not dramatic conceptions. It is true there had been written one English Comedy, *Ralph Roister Doister,* by Nicholas Udall, for boys, eight years before Francis Bacon's birth; and one tragedy, *Gorboduc,* by Thomas Sackville and Thomas Norton, which was acted in the Temple before the Queen in the year he was born. But there was such a steep ascent from these models of construction that one cannot say the true Elizabethan Drama had any connection with them. It coincided with an outburst of intellectual energy—apparently spontaneous and universal—which the world is still pondering and trying to fathom.

The first theatre was built near London when Francis Bacon was fifteen, and none was allowed within the City for many years. Actors were held in abhorrence and classed by the law with rogues and vagabonds. But the theatre gradually got a hold on the public through playhouses often attached to a roofless yard of a tavern. The playhouses had spread throughout the country and were visited by wandering companies of players. One of Elizabeth's first enactments was to restrain the abuses connected with them, performances anywhere having to be licensed by the magistrates. It was through the Earl of Leicester's licensed company that a theatre was eventually built in London. The players claimed that they had the Queen's patent to *play anywhere*. The City officials disputed this. Feelings ran high. Preachers fulminated against it. Said one, "The cause of Plagues is Players." But James Burbage, of Leicester's Company, father of Richard, the actor, constructed the first regular theatre out of a house of many rooms in Blackfriars, and defied the authorities. By the close of the century there were ten theatres, the Globe in Southwark being built in 1594. It is interesting to note that the Queen took a very keen interest in the Drama and its development and had her own group of Players, appointed in 1583. They wore scarlet cloaks and velvet capes in public. The Shakespeare Plays were only performed at the Globe and Blackfriars.

As a matter of fact the London theatres were not exactly repositories of virtue in Shakespeare's day. London and its wiles attracted all the adventurers, vagabonds, and paupers of the realm. The old playhouses gathered to themselves all the ruffians, thieves, pimps and prostitutes—a dirty, stormy, quarrelsome crowd. They were the recognized meeting places for the underworld. No decent woman ever attended a play, and those who did wore masks. A female stage-part was always played by boys. Such was the position of the stage in 1586—bawdy shows, lewd writers, and a ribald class of spectators.

This was gradually changed by the introduction of a higher tone and a new group of professional writers coming on the scene. They were the forerunners of the Shakespearean Drama. These men were named John Lyly, Thomas Nash, Thomas Lodge, George Peele, Robert Greene, Christopher Marlowe . . . since known as "The University Wits" who first began to write true plays. *They were the real preparers of the ground for Francis Bacon.* They were men whom he knew and who knew him. They were his field-workers. *They were his MASKS.* Now we can understand the statement of Tenison: "They who have TRUE SKILL know whether Francis Bacon was the Author though his name be not to it." The skill consisted in knowing how to determine the Rosicrosse Seals in a printed work, weighing up the internal literary evidence, and contemporary documents. The proofs are overwhelming that Francis Bacon used these names and many others when he began his Literary and Dramatic Renaissance apart from editing other types of literary work. This, of course, is unutterably opposed to the traditional view but it is none the less true and will stand the most rigorous inquiry. One cannot laugh out of court the mature conclusions, drawn after years of careful inquiry, of scholars like Harman, Woodward, Lawrence, Theobald, Baxter,

Begley, Bompas, Smedley, Wigston, Donnelly, Holmes and scores of others quite as capable of forming an impartial judgment as the financially interested personages of the "Shakespeare Trust," a trifle fearful perhaps lest their social prestige should be damaged by any untoward discoveries!

From this point, then, we are justified in considering the complexities of the interwoven secrecies in Francis Bacon's life as being fully proved. We are now in a position to see how these threads that were spun in birth, childhood, youth, and the "Silent Years" of early manhood, some for him and others by him, continued to trace their various winding ways in his public life, to the perplexity of writers unaware of his true identity; his concealed labours; and the inward urge to be an ethical teacher and reformer on the lines of Solomon, Socrates, Pythagoras and other Ancients with their secret schools of disciples. Above all, let it never be forgotten, he was more than a mere writer who thinks he has completed his mission by the publication of a book of thoughts, whether poems, philosophy or science, etc. He not only saw grave "Deficiencies," as he calls them, in our national life but *he set to work to remedy them practically*. The Universities have never realized that "*The Great Instauration*" or Restoration or Renaissance was something even greater than the writing of a series of books. It was the actual establishment of groups of men that laboured along certain secret lines which led to a real Revival of Learning and the liberalizing of Theology, culminating in the exoteric Royal Society on the one hand and the esoteric Temple of Solomon on the other. These foundations, with many other aspects of modernism, he laboured and toiled for. He dug the trench, he hunted for material, he made his mixture of the right temper, he laid his bases: And he also provided posterity with a plan by which the Temple of Learning could be built for the physical, mental and moral benefit of Humanity. In other words, to use his own image, "I have but tuned the Harp of the Muses that they may play who have better fingers."

In short, Francis Bacon WAS the Renaissance, the Creator and the Conductor of the great Choir of Elizabethan idealists who were then weaving their varied harmonies in praise of Wisdom and Knowledge.

We can now calculate more accurately the real Francis Bacon that biographers set on high at the age of thirty-two (1593) and then proceed at this point to examine and to judge him by his outward acts alone, heedless of the secret springs of his actions, his idealism, his simple love to better humanity irrespective of personal sacrifice, the ache in his heart as an unacknowledged Love-Child who could not take possession of his rightful inheritance. Like Moses he could see the Promised Land but he could not enter therein. Writers like Professor Nichol begin with a prejudice against him because of his early letters to Lord and Lady Burleigh and the Queen "pestering them for favours," which he assumes are financial and social. But a full knowledge of the facts discloses that the "Suit" for which he was pressing was perfectly legitimate. When does it become "servile" to ask for something to which one is entitled? Francis Bacon the youth was not asking for something which did not inherently belong to him but the very reverse. He was asking for his rights, for something which was his birthright, for Queen Elizabeth's "acknowledgement" of his Tudor identity. "You had a Father; Let your Son say he has got a Father, too," he writes to the Queen in his Sonnet-Diary.

Misled by the superficialities of the situation, his critics begin with a complete misconception of his character and formulate the theory that he began his public life at thirty, mean in soul, avaricious in temper, grasping by nature, and inherently a Pecksniffian rogue. Lord Macaulay and Dr. Abbott push the theory to its logical conclusion, twist the open facts which they do not trouble to understand in order to make them fit, so that Francis Bacon becomes to one writer the English Machiavelli of political and legal immorality, and to the other the portrait of a hybrid between Judas Iscariot and Titus Oates.

What is the Truth?

The truth is that when Francis Bacon took his seat in the New Parliament, it was his moral character and intellectual attainments that lifted him at once to the front rank in the mother of Parliaments, a position which he held for thirty years of uninterrupted public service in the Commons, apart from his service in the House of Lords. His honesty and sincerity had given him the representation of Middlesex. It was the most wealthy, liberal and independent shire in England. He did not own a rood of land in the constituency or anywhere else. He was poor and landless, "of clouded birth," say the whisperers. He was somewhat out of favour in Court Circles. He was viewed with suspicion by my Lord Burleigh who planned for his son Robert Cecil to succeed him as Secretary of State, and jealously feared Francis as a rival. Elizabeth dangled his "birthright" before his eyes. She was still non-committal, thinking in her heart that his younger brother Robert, whom she loved passionately, had better be named as her "Successor" to avoid any revival of an "Ancient Scandal." These were the immediate personal circumstances surrounding his election to Parliament. He was not only poor but he was young, yet the squires and freeholders of Middlesex chose him to speak for them in Parliament. Why? Because they knew him to be a liberal democrat and reformer of the right type. Because his character was above reproach. They knew that no "Dark Ladies" had crossed the threshold of his life . . . and that in an era when young gallants boasted of their conquests and "ladies" made "dates" naked and unashamed. He was a stranger to the dice-box. He loathed tobacco. He abhorred indulgence in strong drink. He was later to write of the drunken man. . . . "How like a beast he lies." In his tastes he was simple and frugal. He was no kill-joy but a healthy-minded sport brimful of wit and humour, with the mouth of an orator. And in Parliamentary circles he was known to be a young reformer of high principle, a champion of the people's rights. It was traits of character and services to constituents—deeds which do not find their way into print but which travel from mind to mind and are remembered when the public need representatives—which lifted him to the heights of Middlesex when he was barely thirty-two. Where in Parliamentary annals is there another case of penniless genius winning the first constituency in the realm at so early an age? Neither Pitt (early trained for a political career), Beaconsfield, Gladstone, nor Churchill could have leapt higher.

Says Lord Campbell:

> Francis Bacon does not seem to have made himself prominent by taking any decided part for or against the Crown in the Parliaments of 1586 and 1588,

the inference being that he was an ordinary back-bencher with little interest in the humdrum business of a Parliament living in dull, uninteresting times. The suggestions conveyed by such an inference are utterly misleading. It was Francis Bacon's known record in the early Parliaments—Melcombe, 1585; Taunton, 1586; Liverpool, 1588—that fitted him for Middlesex in 1593. It is true as Campbell says that:

> We have but scanty remains of his oratory in the House of Commons but enough to account for the admiration he excited, and the influence he acquired.

We have, however, sufficient knowledge of his elocutionary powers from the testimony of his friend Ben Jonson to know that he was a born speaker and orator, and that his full-to-overflowing mind would never have allowed him to remain silent in the presence of danger and conflict, when men's passions were being stirred by menace of war on the Motherland. Ben Jonson has said of Francis Bacon:

> There happened in my time one noble speaker who was full of gravity in his speaking. His language, where he could spare or pass by a jest, was nobly censorious. No man ever spoke more neatly, more pressly, more weightily, or suffered less emptiness, less idleness, in what he uttered. No member of his speech but consisted of his own graces.
>
> His own hearers could not cough or look aside from him without loss. He commanded where he spoke, and had his Judges[1] angry and pleased at his devotion. No man had their affections (i.e., emotions) more in his power. The fear of every man who heard him was lest he should make an end.

With such oratorical gifts, with the knowledge that he was a glutton for work, it cannot be supposed that Francis Bacon remained either silent or inactive, or was untouched by or took little part in the Parliamentary proceedings of 1585-86-88, especially when we consider the state of Europe in those anxious years. He served his apprenticeship in sessions of high and tragic conflict. In them he played an active and conspicuous part. They shaped for him his political life. They made him into a liberal reformer and a statesman with breadth of vision.

These early Parliaments in which Francis Bacon served met under the shadow of a Tyranny quite as great as the one we have been facing to-day. *They saved the liberties of England and the faith of half Europe.* They crushed the conspiracies of the Jesuits. They founded a Defence Association at the instigation of Leicester to protect the Person of the Queen. They destroyed the menace of a Catholic Restoration by laying Mary of

[1]Judges of eloquence, not necessarily judges of law. As Ben was a great personal friend of Francis Bacon, he would hear him in many roles, in the House of Commons, in the Lords, in the Courts, in Masonic Recitals, in after-dinner speeches, and probably in "Instructing the Actors."

Scotland on the bier at Fotheringay. They sent Elizabeth to Tilbury, where her land forces had gathered to defend London against the Duke of Parma, when, by the side of the Earl of Leicester, commander of all the forces, she uttered those memorable words:

> I am come amongst you as you see, resolved in the midst and heat of battle to LIVE OR DIE amongst you. I know that I have the body but of a weak and feeble woman, but I have the heart of a King and of a King of England, too.

These years shattered and dispersed the invincible Armada. They humbled Philip of Spain. They wrested from him the command of the sea, plucking the trident from his grip. They struck Spain a blow which sent her reeling to become a fifth-rate power. And they laid the foundations of Empire, of a Commonwealth of Nations, by sending out Raleigh and the great Elizabethan seamen to found new States. In this last great work of founding colonies Francis Bacon throughout his life consistently played his part with his voice, his pen, his money. To-day, he is regarded by the Newfoundlanders as the particular Founder of our oldest British colony. So far as I know, he is the only British Statesman who has had a special Postage Stamp struck to commemorate his memory. In 1910 Newfoundland issued one showing Francis Bacon's portrait with the words, "*Lord Bacon*: *The Guiding Spirit in Colonisation Schemes*: 1610-1910."

Is it not incredible to think that Francis Bacon remained untouched when the destinies of England were at stake? How could he possibly remain indifferent.... He, a Prince of the Realm though unacknowledged, proud of his Tudor breed, who ached to have the right to occupy the English Throne some day for the good he could do his countrymen! *Were "Shake-speare's" Princes ever unmoved when their heritage was in jeopardy?* Knowing what we do about him, his mercurial temperament, his bursting mind, his sensitive responsiveness to all extraneous impulses, how was it possible for him to remain silent in Parliament or elsewhere, when flags were flying, men marching, and drums were beating in Whitehall while a nation stood to arms and watched nightly for the warning beacons to flame, while in the daytime was heard the sound of clanging hammers as the shipwrights hurled defiance at their hated foes as they built higher and ever higher the Wooden Walls of Old England. We may not know what his patriotism prompted him to do in Parliament but we know what it prompted him to do out of Parliament . . . to create the most wonderful love-tributes to his native land that have ever been penned, patriotic pæans of ecstasy that will never be surpassed:

> This Royal Throne of Kings, this scepter'd Isle,
> This Earth of Majesty, this Seat of Mars,
> This other Eden, demi-Paradise;
> This Fortress, built by Nature for herself,
> Against Infection and the Hand of War;
> This happy breed of Men, this little World;
> This precious Stone, set in a Silver Sea,
> Which serves it in the Office of a Wall,
> Or as a Moat defensive to a House
> Against the envy of less happier Lands,

When he first sat in the Commons for Melcombe, he sat with such lights of the law as Hatton and Bromley, Egerton and Walsingham, with the chivalrous poet-knight Sir Philip Sidney, warriors like Sir Walter Raleigh, seamen like Sir Francis Drake and a host of others renowned in history. Francis Bacon was a new power in the House, quick to take occasion by the hand, as we have seen by the early delivery of his maiden speech in the 1585 Parliament, with its double-meaning phraseology.[1] Wit so brilliant, repartee so keen, lore so profound, and thought so fresh, bespangled with newly-minted words, that the like had certainly never been heard before within those famous walls *and probably never since.* His hold on the House and on his constituents was due, however, not so much to his intellectual power as his moral qualities . . . his uprightness and sincerity. When he spoke against Feudal Privileges, or sought to amend the anomalies of the law, or opposed the enclosures of common lands by wealthy land-owners to the hurt of the impoverished villagers, or advocated the reform of the Church, everyone knew that his utterances were prompted by the purest of altruistic motives for the benefit of the many, not for the privileged few, and without thought for personal aggrandizement.

To a colleague who proposed some changes in the Church which would have destroyed it he retorted:

> "Sir, the subject we talk of is the Eye of England: if there be a speck or two in the Eye, we endeavour to take them out; he would be a strange oculist who would pull out the Eye."

When the Queen asked him to modify his views on the suggested enclosures of common land and withdraw his opposition, he answered:

> "Your Majesty, I am against all enclosures and especially against enclosed justice."

When he proposed in a later Parliament to alter the language of the laws, putting them in simple diction, and was told by the barristers in the Commons that such a scheme was impossible and would lower legal incomes, he replied:

> "The laws should be read by all and be known to all. Put them in shape, inform them with light and philosophy, and give them into every man's hand. *Laws are made to guard the rights of the people, not to feed lawyers.*"

Are not these representative noble sentiments? Are they not thoughts that should inspire every publicist, clerical or lay? He was of no sect and therefore represented the patriotic spirit of all the sects. Though not a Catholic he consistently lifted up his voice against their persecution. He was not a Puritan but he pleaded for reform. In one word: he was English. He was even a greater patriot than Pym and Hampton, the leaders of political liberties. *He pointed them the way.*

> When he strikes at corruptions in the State, when he resists the usurpations of the Peers, when he saps the privileges of the Crown, he speaks in the

[1] *See* Ch. VI.

name of English progress and English strength. He fights for the reform of the law, for increase of tillage, for union with the Scots, for plantations in Ulster, for discovery and defence in Virginia, for Free Parliaments and for ample grants . . . because he sees that increase, union, freedom, and a rich executive are each and all essential to the growth and grandeur of the realm.

THE NEWFOUNDLAND MEMORIAL POSTAGE STAMP WITH FRANCIS BACON'S HEAD
(*See Appendix I, p.* 359)

Such is Hepworth Dixon's tribute to this remarkable genius in his enthusiastic biography. (*Life*, p. 22).

When Francis Bacon sat for Taunton in 1586, Parliament had never met under darker skies. England was under the threat of invasion from without and conspiracies within. The Continent was an armed camp. Enemy fleets were massing in Cadiz Bay. Great armies of soldiers had been mobilized in Rome, Naples, and Leghorn, and were waiting impatiently for zero hour to strike. The Pope and Philip of Spain were being hounded on by men like Parsons and Sextus to move openly for the "conversion" of England. The tocsin had been ringing for months in growing anger for a religious crusade against the heretics. In the Tagus, the Groigne, in Brabant and Flanders there were vast armaments ready for a descent on the shores of Kent.

The reply to all these preparations was seen everywhere in "this sceptred Isle, this seat of Mars." All England glowed with patriotic fervour. At the call "To Arms" volunteers from every County rushed to the rolling drum and the Standard. London, Dover, Portsmouth, swarmed with soldiers, and every village square was a recruiting centre. And in this hour of peril, Taunton, the seat of trade and manufacture, second only to Bristol, the most populous, enterprising and patriotic town after London, chose Francis Bacon to represent her, to speak and to vote in her name . . . at a time when no one knew what Quislings lurked in the shadows, or what further Babington conspiracies were being hatched to destroy the Kingdom and the Protestant Succession. It was this fear that brought Mary of Scotland from her nineteen years' imprisonment to face charges of treason, which we now know were trumped-up ones. Influenced by fear and the forged Casket letters, the nation and the Commons demanded her life to save the peace of the realm, for while she remained in sight as the only legitimate heir to the Throne no Protestant felt safe. A Grand Committee of Parliament, Lords Spiritual and Temporal with certain Members of Commons, Francis Bacon being one, went into the presence to demand from the Queen that the Protestant Faith should be saved and the safety of the realm secured by the execution of the prisoner of Fotheringay.

With her death the entire nation set itself to combat the menace of the Armada. In 1588 it sailed from Corunna—about the time that Francis Bacon was chosen Reader to his Inn, a post of high honour. On the 20th July it appeared off the English Channel. Within fifteen days of battle and storm the invincible Armada was reduced to a miserable remnant with the wrecks of a hundred keels "tossing in the foam from Devon to Caithness." For the moment the danger was past, but preparations were carried forward to meet another threatened encounter in the spring of the following year. The Queen returned thanks to God at St. Paul's. For his share in the triumph the Earl of Leicester was made Lord-Lieutenant of England and Ireland, an office that invested him, according to Strickland, with greater power than any sovereign had ventured to bestow upon a subject. He died, however, a few weeks later whereupon the Queen acted as though she were indeed his wife. She seized and auctioned his estates on the grounds of "money lent." And while the great galleons of Spain were still being pounded to bits on the Orkneys, a new Parliament was summoned once more in November in which Francis Bacon sat for Liverpool.

His fame as a patriot and an orator had been fixed in these dangerous days by his public labours. To his compatriots he was esteemed for his quick grasp of a situation, his breadth of view, the comprehension of his politics, the flash of his wit, and the wealth of his illustrations. "His rising importance is now attested by the frequent appearance of his name in the Journals," says Professor Fowler. He adds: "There is evidence to show that he was also employed in drawing State-papers." (*Life*, p. 4.) Hepworth Dixon writes: "In the New Parliament of 1588 Francis Bacon served on the most important Committees and spoke on the most important bills: now standing for the privileges of the House of Commons, now assailing the Royal Prerogative." (*Life*, p. 30.)

The most important business of the Commons revolved around subsidies and grants. The Crown proposed two subsidies, four fifteenths and tenths. Francis Bacon moved, however, that in the Bill there must be a clause that these grants were extraordinary, *meant for war and only for war.* The Crown, represented by Hatton, objected as this meant the fettering of the Queen's future acts. But Francis had a following and members were encouraged by his stand to remain firm. After much debate the Crown laid the Bill before the Learned Counsel, to which the House agreed on the condition that Francis Bacon, the author of the amendment, should be present at the sittings of the Learned Board. A *via media* was soon found by his tact, and the Bill was passed to the satisfaction of the Queen and the Commons. From this session of 1589 can be dated his firm ascendency in the House. His fame spread. It was his courage and independence in opposing the Crown on a question of taxation that made the wealthy constituency of Middlesex choose him for their champion. For more than a quarter of a century after that debate we shall see that he was regarded with personal affection by the House which his genius adorned. Through the long years, successive Members of Parliament knew his character, through personal contact, far better than the Macaulay-Abbott slanderers of dead genius. Up to 1621, when Francis Bacon was sixty years of age, there was never a whisper against his good name even by his bitterest enemies. Cecil might think him an idealistic visionary but he never thought him an envious, avaricious rogue. Coke might think him a fool but he never once suggested in all their conflicts that Francis was a dishonest money-hunter until Coke had staged a plot for the ruin of England's wisest Chancellor. Yet we are calmly asked to-day to believe that at sixty years of age, Francis Bacon threw overboard all those high principles which had consistently ruled his life, to rob, cheat, steal and rogue for the love of lucre. Men cannot change their characters of a lifetime so easily as all that, no more than the leopard his spots or the Ethiopian his skin. He was beloved by all great and good men in his day, because he embodied those sturdy English virtues of which the race are so justly proud, without any touch of false pride or affectation, with the gay debonair spirit of a wit full of happy jests, a raconteur of the first water. A glance at the Hilyard miniature and the later Van Somer portrait is sufficient to tell anyone that here we have no gloomy, long-visaged philosopher of grasping sordidness, but a brilliant intellectual of poetic temperament. His face is as open and as honest as the day. That is the true portrait of the man who sat for Middlesex in 1593. He bore an unstained reputation from those days, that was never once impugned until he fell in the Capitol, "the Coward Conquest of a Wretch's Knife," at the hand of the Great Assassin Coke . . . the victim of a dastardly frame-up.

In February 1592 his foster-brother Anthony returned from abroad after an absence of more than twelve years, almost as much French as English. He stayed at Gorhambury with his mother for a time and then went to lodge with Francis at Gray's Inn. Anthony Bacon was methodical and kept the papers and drafts of Francis in order so that we get to know a little more about his doings and whereabouts. Later, he became secretary to the Earl of Essex "and was equally careful of the Essex papers." Anthony is described by Dr. Rawley as "a gentleman of as high a wit, though of not such profound learning," as his foster-brother. Little is known of him, but he played an important part behind the Curtain in establishing Francis Bacon's Continental Fraternities, literary and ethical. There is very strong *prima facie* evidence that he acted while abroad as an "Intelligenser" to Francis as well as a secret-service agent to the State.

Apparently, the two men were deeply attached to each other. They seldom address each other but in terms of devoted affection, "My deerest Brother . . ." "Antonie my Comforte." There is abundant proof of the affection and reverence that Anthony had for Francis. He conducted an enormous correspondence with people of all kinds who could be useful to the cause for which Francis was labouring. Mrs. Henry Pott in *Francis Bacon and his Secret Society*, p. 102, writes:

The mystery connected with Anthony appears to be consequent upon his having acted as the propagandist on the Continent of Francis Bacon's Secret Society and New Philosophy. He seems to have received and answered the large proportion of letters connected with the business part of the Society; he collected and forwarded to Francis all important books and intelligence which could be of use. He devoted to his service not only his life, but *all his worldly wealth, which we see mysteriously melting away*, but which, no doubt, went, like that of Francis, into the common fund which was destined, as one of his correspondents expressed it, to "*keep alight this fire*" so recently kindled.

Sixteen folio volumes of Anthony Bacon's letters lie, almost unknown, in the library at Lambeth Palace. These leave no loop-hole for doubt as to his real mission and purpose in living abroad.

Before he had returned from the Continent his rentals had shrunk considerably and he had had to call on his mother for assistance. According to Lady Anne Bacon's letters she had "spent her jewels and borrowed from seven several persons in order to send her son the money he kept begging for his necessary expenses," which she suspected was going to help Papists, and persons suspected of being Papists, to escape, the truth being that the money was spent in the establishing of "the New Philosophy of active Science," Rosicrucianism and Freemasonry. This kind of work fitted in well with his Secret Service activities. To make up for his failing property rentals, he later applied to Burleigh for a diplomatic position abroad, for which he was eminently suited by his experiences of foreign Courts.

Some letters of Lady Anne Bacon about this time to her two "careless boys" give us a charming motherly picture of her relations with Francis and Anthony. They are still her "boys" though they are both over thirty, and she is full of maternal anxiety and affection for their spiritual and moral welfare as a Puritan mother. She makes sacrifices in the usual way that mother-love prompts, by sending regularly to Gray's Inn home-brewed ale, pigeons from her own cote, and fowls of her own breeding. She gives them homely advice as to their diet, the quality and the quantity, when to bleed and when to purge. She complains that the habits of Francis are odd. He sits up late at night, drinks ale-posset to make him sleep, starts out of bed ere it is light, or lolls and dreams till noon. Thus is the world's greatest genius scolded in affectionate terms by this good mother, tenderly and warmly.

Says Church, "Her letters to her son Anthony whom she loved passionately . . . show also that *in Francis she did not find all the deference which she looked for.* Recommending Anthony to frequent "the religious exercises of the sincerer sort," she warns him not to follow his brother's advice or example. Anthony was advised to use prayer twice a day with his servants. She writes, "Your brother is too negligent therein" and warns him not to fall into his brother's ill-ordered habits.

Lady Bacon adds: "I verily think your brother's weak stomach to digest hath been much caused and confirmed *by untimely going to bed* and then musing *nescio quid* when he should sleep, and then in consequent and late rising and long lying in bed: whereby his men are made slothful and himself continueth sickly. But my sons haste not to hearken to their mother's good counsel in time to prevent."

One can see in all this Francis Bacon the omnivorous reader, the hard student, the creative writer who must exhaust himself while the fit of inspiration is upon him, the reflective mind that moves in a far broader world than Lady Bacon's narrow Puritanism. Later on to the alarm and displeasure of his mother, Anthony went to lodge in Bishop's Gate Street, close to the Bull Inn. "Here there was a theatre," says Mrs. Potts, "at which several of the Shakespeare Plays were performed." The same authority states that there is reason to think that both Francis and Anthony in childhood showed talent for acting, and later evinced a strong tendency for the theatre, for "Mumming and Masquing," which Lady Anne bewailed as a falling-off from grace. In a letter written to Anthony, just before the 1594 Revels at Gray's Inn, with its first performance of the *Comedy of Errors*, she exhorts him and Francis that they may "not Mum, nor Mask, nor sinfully Revel." It is quite evident that she was strongly suspicious of Francis Bacon's connection with the stage. The letters give us a picture of the practical housewife, glowing with the spirit of Puritanism in saying her morning and evening prayers, and hearing nine or ten sermons in the week, but who nevertheless conscientiously performs her round of domestic duties, scrubbing the pots and pans in the kitchen, watching the hens and their eggs, physicking herself, her friends and her tenants, making rascals who would cheat pay up promptly . . . all this between reading classics in the original.

In the autumn of 1592, the Plague broke out in London and Francis rode away to Twickenham Park—his country seat—with his friends Richmond Cecil, Robert Gosnold, and Richard Field. That eminent divine, the Rev. Lancelot Andrews, one of Francis Bacon's closest friends, who had so much to do with the Authorized Version of the Bible, was to have joined them—he was then the preacher at Gray's Inn—but was prevented owing to increased parochial duties caused by the plague. They fled from the pestilence to pursue their secret philosophy—e.g. the building up of the Higher Masonic Degrees—and their secret Rosicrosse publications.

Twickenham Park in Middlesex was a lovely villa which fronted Queen Elizabeth's Royal Palace at Richmond and had been in possession of the Bacon family for eighteen years. It belonged to the Crown and had been leased to Edward Bacon, a nominal half-brother to Francis, in 1574. Says Hepworth Dixon, *Life*, p. 56:

> It had all the delights of a good country-house; a green landscape, wood and water, pure air, a dry soil, vicinity to the Court and to the town. From the windows Francis Bacon looked into the Queen's alleys; in an hour he could trot up to Whitehall or Gray's Inn.
>
> Every plant that thrives, every flower that blows in the South of England, loves the Twickenham soil. There were cedars in the Great Park, swans on the river, singing birds in the copse; every sight to engage the eye, every sound to enchant the ear.
>
> When he could steal a day from his London labours, he rode to his delicious nest on the Thames, which became his house of philosophy and letters, as the lodging on Gray's Inn was his house of politics and law.

According to Mrs. Bunten, quoting a writer named Cobbert, is an item of interest to all Freemasons. "In the Hall fronting the South-West of Francis Bacon's Lodge is laid in a Mosaic Pavement of Black and White with a small Iron Cross." We do not know to-day the actual site of this home about which Francis Bacon wrote, "Twickenham is my pleasure and my dwelling," or how he came to occupy it, or when he did, or the length of his connection with it, or the exact literary work he was engaged in while there. But in a manuscript-book called *The Promus,* now in the British Museum, a collection of witty sayings and proverbs in many languages, written in Francis Bacon's own hand, there are dates 1594-5 which make it certain that this collection was made in these years. In this notebook there is a mysterious and significant reference to his concealed labours as a poet, to what he elsewhere terms, "The Works of his Recreation," for he writes, "*Ye Law at Twicknam for Mery Tales.*" It is therefore quite clear that about this time Francis Bacon and his lawyer-friends—"The Law"—had gone there in connection with "Merrie Tales." There has been much speculation what he meant by them and we can for the moment but speculate what these tales were. But we are brought appreciably nearer the goal by a singular coincidence in the Initial Capitals used in *Love's Labour's Lost,* the first eight lines of the Play, (Folio, Comedies, p. 122), "F.Et. LAW Th at T" which unmistakably are legitimate contractions for "Francis and the Law at Twicknam," *an echo of the Promus note.* The inference is that *Love's Labour's Lost* was one of the "Mery Tales." And when we know, as every Mason does—or ought to do—that this Play embodies the genesis of the Craft, the natural conclusion is that among other things Francis and his friends were trying out some of the Rituals of the Higher Degrees.[1] What we can be sure of is this: That Francis Bacon not only used Twickenham Park as his private scrivenery for some of his secret labours but he went there pretty often over a long course of years.

Apparently he must have been in the habit of going there while Edward Bacon was the lessee, prior to 1581, when a lease was granted to a Miles Doddington for thirty years to begin in 1595. Francis Bacon seems to have lived at Twickenham, in what he called his "LODGE," though whether this was a separate house or referred to a Masonic Lodge that was held there, no one knows. But this we know: that in 1595, the year Edward's lease would have expired, *the reversion of Twickenham Park was granted to Francis Bacon by the Queen.* His earliest known letter is dated 14th August, 1592, to a Mr. Phillips.

> Being now at Twickenham, I am desirous of your company. You may stay as long and as little while as you will: the longer the better welcome: I would be the wiser by you in many things; for that I call to confer with a man of your fullness.

On the 25th January, 1594, he wrote to Anthony:

> I have here an idle pen or two. . . . I pray send me somewhat else for them to write out. . . .
>
> From my Lodge at Twickenham Park, Your entire Loving Brother, Francis Bacon.

[1]See *Shakespeare, Creator of Freemasonry* (Rider, London).

Apparently Edward Bacon had given up the residence and the Queen bestowed the reversion on Francis.

He sold Twickenham Park in 1608, going back to Gorhambury where he built a new house later on. He was overwhelmed by debts at the time and this forced him into selling his "pleasure and his dwelling" and his "Gardens of Paradise," it being his intention to repurchase it.

Mrs. Alice Chambers Bunten, who has made an admirable study of Twickenham Park, has some very pleasing things to say about Twickenham. She brings out very beautifully his personality:

> We have no drawings of the wonderful gardens and herberies there, on the rich soil that caused all sorts of fruit and flowers to flourish in thick luxuriance. This garden was the bower and verdant screen that Francis Bacon gazed upon and loved. Here was his house of letters and philosophy, and in these grounds he studied Nature in all her beauty beneath the shady trees, and the long bosky pathways, and serene quietude of the perfumed herb garden, while the river glided by shining in the sun; and here he could listen to the song of the birds, and marvel over the colour of the flowers, which he describes so well in his *Essay on Gardens* and his *Sylva Sylvarum*, and here he planted the alder trees to strengthen the river bank.
>
> We can imagine him with a book in his pocket, wandering up the north and down the south walk, and round by the avenue of big trees, deep in thought, for *Essays* were being written and *Court Masques* designed.
>
> Here he tried to wrest from Nature her secrets, some of which he was the first to discover. In 1592 he took refuge here from the plague, and that dread disease must have given him much thought as to what medical recipes would help its cure. He imported rare plants and herbs for his own investigations . . . and he must have planted both a physic and an exotic garden. What were the properties of these herbs distilled as medicinal drugs? Which are spices? Which are poisons? What cures will they effect? Which are narcotics? What is the strength of a dose? (*Francis Bacon and Twickenham Park*, p. 8.)

The same author says:

> One of the most important arrangements which Francis Bacon formed at Twickenham was a Writing School or Scriptorium. This was a small gathering of students who wrote under Bacon's guidance various Essays or Miscellanies for the distribution of knowledge as well as taking down his revisions . . . works which were constantly being added to and improved.
>
> These "good pens" as Bacon called them, scattered various learned writings under different names throughout England, marked with a Rosicrosse-Mason Mark, which was sought for by Freemasons and understood by them (p. 28).

Twickenham Park must have been very dear to the heart of Francis Bacon as a home of memories connected with his studies and experiments of many kinds, for in a sealed paper discovered after his death is an instruction to one of his private secretaries, named Thomas Bushell for the purpose of buying Twickenham Park. He writes:

> Let Twitnam Park, which I sold in my younger days, be purchased if possible, for a Residence for such deserving persons to study in. *I experimented there for the trial of my philosophical conclusions.* This wish I expressed in a paper

sealed to the Trust, which I myself would have put into practise and settled the same by Act of Parliament, if the vicissitudes of Fortune had not intervened and prevented me.

This makes it clear that one branch of his studies at Twickenham revolved round trials of his philosophical conclusions which were the "try-outs" of his newly created Rituals of the Higher Degrees, and this is confirmed by the fact that these Degrees are mentioned in *Love's Labour Lost.* There were other experiments of course, but that some of them were Masonic is beyond question.

While there seems every reason to believe that Francis Bacon lived in Twickenham as his country seat off and on from 1581, we must not forget that it was through the gift of the Queen that this beautiful river-seat fell into the hands of Francis Bacon's personal use and made him one of her personal neighbours when she was in residence at her Tudor Palace in Richmond. The Queen had only to cross the river in her royal barge to set foot on his grounds. His "Lodge" was right opposite her windows, and she could see all the improvements that he was making from time to time. The tenancy of this Villa increases the mystery of his finances. Up to 1594 he had no income. How he managed to pay for the upkeep of Twickenham Park is a complete riddle unless we accept the plain logical conclusion that his income and Twickenham Park's expenses were derived from the Queen.

It really seems as though the Hand of Fate held the reins of Francis Bacon's life from infancy to the very end of life. We have seen that his environment was a gradually extending one from birth, successive changes being introduced to quicken his unfoldment, to stir his powers to the highest, to make him responsive to outward stimuli so that he might grow into the superman that he eventually became. And when it became necessary that he should possess a "Garden of Paradise" (this is what a contemporary named it) to which he could retire in order to meditate, to write, to experiment in many ways and to work with his literary assistants in privacy, we again see that Destiny provides this impecunious genius with an ideal refuge shortly after his return from France.

We can now see that these years, apparently barren of effort openly, were actually very busy ones to 1593. There is a gradual movement onwards from his 'teens towards the accomplishment of the purpose that was born in his very soul when he was but a boy. Edward D. Johnson writes, *The First Folio*:

> Before attaining the age of twelve he had conceived the idea that he would imitate God, and that he would hide his works in order that they might not be found out; that he would be seen only by his mind and that his image should be concealed. . . . He would devote his life to the construction of an adequate language and literature for his country and that he would do so remaining invisible.

In furtherance of this plan we have seen that Francis Bacon used many pen-names, employed many masks, originated many controversies with the aid of his ready helpers and "Good Pens," the professional scriveners . . . all done to stimulate public opinion, to create an interest in reading and writing, and, above all, to manufacture the illusion of a widespread Renaissance. The majority of these anonymous writings have been traced because the Secret Seals of the Rosicrosse Literary Society, and the numerical signature of Francis Bacon, are stamped in the old printed books. They prove that they emanated from one mind. They also prove that when "C.D. of King's College" wrote in the *Manes Verulamiani* (Shades of Verulam) "*Filled is the World with thy Writings*," and "R.C. of Trinity College" likewise wrote, "*Thou art the Jewel most precious of LETTERS CONCEALED*," that they were writing a literal truth in their elegies on the occasion of his passing away in 1626. There were thirty-two elegies published by Dr. Rawley, which have hitherto been completely overlooked by British scholarship . . . even Spedding ignored them, yet they were reprinted in Blackbourne's edition of 1730 . . . Twenty-seven of the scholars speak of him as a transcendental POET, as though, indeed, he were "Shake-speare," and they associate him with Pallas Athene. We will see what they say later.

The statements by "C.D." and "R.C." were not exaggerated ones. Francis Bacon had filled the world of English literature with his Rosicrosse Books, for there were none worth speaking of prior to his advent on the scene. From the time when he wrote in July 1575, the published account of the entertainment given by Leicester to the Queen under the pen-names of Laneham and Gascoign, we can trace the trail of the Boar by his Marks from the first edition of *Euphues Anatomy of Wit* through the period now under examination. Edward D. Johnson writes:

> 1588: A play *The Misfortunes of Arthur* was written by Francis and acted at Gray's Inn for the benefit of the barristers and their friends. In Green's name he printed *Pandosto* or *The Triumph of Time*, *Perimedes the Blacksmith* and *Alcida* or *Green's Metamorphosis*. Abraham Fraunce, a Gray's Inn lawyer, publishes a book called *Arcadian Rhetoricke* containing quotations from *The Faerie Queene* which was being written by Francis at Gray's Inn although not printed until 1590. Francis publishes *The Householders Philosophie* as translated by T.K. from the Italian of Tasso.
>
> 1589: *The Arte of English Poesie,* which Francis had commenced in 1585, was published by Richard Field and dedicated to Lord Burleigh. Francis also prints *Ciceronis Amor, Menaphon* and *The Spanish Masquerade*, all in the name of Green. A preface to *Menaphon* in the name of Nashe, also *The Anatomy of Absurditie* in the name of Nashe. A narrative poem called *Glaucus and Scilla*, similar in style to *Venus and Adonis* printed in 1593 in the name of Shakespeare was titled-paged to Lodge. Francis publishes a pamphlet *Pappe with a Hatchet* attributed to Lyly by Gabriel Harvey. The first part of the *Faerie Queene* was registered in London, 1st December.
>
> 1590: *The Faerie Queene* is published title-paged to Spenser. He also printed anonymously *The Tragedy of Tambourline* and an Elegy on the death of his old friend, Sir Francis Walsingham, in the name of Watson. Under Watson's name he also translates a number of Italian Madrigals which were set to music by William Bird, the Court Musician.
>
> 1591: Francis publishes a drama *Endimion* anonymously; *Complaintes* and *Daphnaida* in Spenser's name. In the name of Nashe, Francis writes the preface to *Astrophel and Stella*, a book of verse by Sir Philip Sidney. He publishes the Play *King John* anonymously.
>
> 1592: He publishes anonymously a drama *Midas;* and *The Tears of Fancie*

or Love Disdained in Watson's name . . . a series of Sonnets. He publishes *Venus and Adonis* in the name of William Shakespeare.

1593: Marlowe is killed in a brawl and Francis then prints various works with Marlowe's name as author. Francis prints *William Longbeard and Phillis,* a set of Sonnets put out in Lodge's name. He publishes *Gallathea* anonymously and *Aminte Gandea* in the name of Watson.

Nashe, Lyly, Greene, as well as Peele and Marlowe, were all "Masks" more or less for Francis Bacon's anonymous writings. We can thus well understand why Gabriel Harvey in *Pierce's Supererogation* said that:

> "*Nashe,*" "*Lyly*" *and* "*Greene*" *were three faces in one hood, and* that they were a three-headed Cerberus.

More information can be obtained about these minor Masks who were paid for the use of their names, should the reader desire, by referring to *Tudor Problems* by Parker Woodward. There is definite evidence that there was co-operation—paid and voluntary—between Francis Bacon and a number of persons to spread a love for literature in various and devious ways, but it is outside the scope of this work to go into further details. Sufficient has already been advanced to indicate the vast scope of his literary enterprises and that he had a tremendous literary output. He wrote. He printed. He published. The self-imposed task at which he laboured for twelve years—the development of English literature—was very great, but it was not too herculean for was he not a Hercules of Thought and Energy? It was an age of great literary endeavour. His contemporary Lope de Vega, the Spanish Dramatist (1562-1635) composed nearly *two thousand Plays.* Assisted by his staff of "Good Pens" there is practically no limit to the Works Francis Bacon could have produced by dictation and editing. There is, moreover, very sound evidence to support the view that later on he had his own private printing-press and his own paper-mills; for the majority of the Rosicrosse books were not only printed with secret signs but watermarked with esoteric symbols at an enormous cost. It must be remembered also that there are no manuscripts of these various works. There is not a page of Spenser, or Marlowe, etc. All that we have got are the printed books and their connection with a particular author has never been established. The only authority is the Title Page, and in view of the fact that some of the Shakespeare Quartos were not printed by the printers whose names they bear, nor published in the year hitherto supposed, the black and white of the printed page cannot be regarded as sacrosanct.

A literary analysis of these various works shows how the apprentice hand was developing into the Master Craftsman. By 1592 he was ready to step on to the World's Stage as the Master Singer. In that year was published *Venus and Adonis* in the name of "William Shakespeare," dedicated to the Earl of Southampton, Francis Bacon's friend and fellow student at Gray's Inn. The censor who passed the Poem for publication was "the stern Dean Whitgift," Francis Bacon's old tutor at Cambridge. It is highly questionable whether he would have licensed such a sex-poem had anyone else written it, for he was an unbending purist.

The publication of *Venus and Adonis* may be said to be the most important event of 1592. A new Star was appearing on the horizon. The second item of importance was the letter he wrote to Burleigh in January announcing his decision that he had definitely relinquished his "SUIT." The third, was his open friendship with the Earl of Essex, which historians say began about this time. The fourth was Francis Bacon's reply to a Libel on the Queen, being a pamphlet published on the Continent in Latin and English, *Responsio ad Edictum Reginæ Angliæ*, supposed to be by Father Parsons. Francis Bacon's reply—he was chosen by the Government to answer what was thought to be a dangerous indictment—was entitled *Observations on a Libel.* It may be said to be one of the famous State Papers for which Francis Bacon was afterwards noted.

The curtain of 1593 thus slowly rises on the Queen and her two sons. Here are the germs of a series of events that gradually are grouped around the Royal Family of Three—Elizabeth and her Concealed Sons, the eternal triangle in a new setting, with all its tragedy, its agony, and its remorse.

Chapter VIII

THE 1593 PARLIAMENT: FRANCIS BACON THE PUBLICIST (1592-1596)

QUITE apart from his secret labours, known only to a select few, it will be readily understood from the open facts of the times adduced in the preceding Chapter, that when Francis Bacon took his seat in the 1593 House of Commons, he was not only personally known as an outstanding Parliamentarian to many who had sat with him in previous Sessions but he was also known by repute to many of the new Members as a magnetic personality and a coming man. As previously mentioned, the faithful Commons were well aware that prior to the calling of the Houses in February, Francis Bacon had written a masterly reply, at the request of the Government, to a pamphlet circulated on the Continent in which the Queen was accused of all kinds of dishonourable conduct, the "taking away of life" of the King of Spain; of "being the cause of the great troubles now afflicting England"; the "persecution of the Catholics," etc. The pamphlet was the culmination of a series

> of a number of Libellous and Defamatory Books and Writings: and it is strange in what variety and with what Art and Cunning handled (they have) been allowed to pass through the world in all Languages against Her Majesty and Her Government.

The Government had at last recognized the danger of allowing an Elizabethan Dr. Goebbels to pour out a stream of propaganda unchecked. The best man to reply to it was Francis Bacon, the result being an exposition packed with facts, satire and wit; set out in clear headings that betokened a statesman-like grasp of the many political and theological problems that rocked the Continent and unsettled Europe.

The Government circulated Francis Bacon's reply as a State Paper in order to prevent the libel having any effect on disaffected Catholics or political agitators. In short, it was intended to destroy what we now call Fifth-Column subversive activities. Nearly forty pages in Folio (Rawley's *Resuscitatio*, 1670 Ed. p. 81) were in the hands of every Member of the New House. The *Observations on a Libel* brought him into outstanding prominence.[1] No one could have any doubt of the intellectual calibre

[1]There is a very significant aside slipped in the *Observations on a Libel*, "In the Act of Recognition whereby the right of the Crown is acknowledged by Parliament to be in her Majesty ... the words of limitation are, *in the Queen's Majesty and the NATURAL HEIRS of her BODY*, and *her Lawful Successors*. Upon which word, *Natural*, they do maliciously and indeed villainously glose, that it was the intention of the Parliament in a cloud to convey the Crown to *any issue of her Majesty's that were ILLEGITIMATE*."

Francis Bacon here refers to the Act of Parliament specially framed by Elizabeth in which it was declared she should name her Successor and that her heir could be her "NATURAL" Issue. She refused to have the word "Lawful" used instead of "Natural."

of the man who had composed it, or fail to be impressed with his honest patriotism, or hesitate to follow his lead.

This State Paper was not a mere flash in the pan. Only three years previously when he was twenty-nine there had been circulated by the Government a similar type of State Paper which was a matter of grave import to the State and the Church, for men's minds ran fiercely in those days on the vexed question of theological doctrines. The Government was concerned over the bitter quarrels of the various sects . . . Anglicans, Catholics, Puritans, Brownists, etc. They threatened to undermine the stability of the State. Francis Bacon sought to avert the danger by the writing of a remarkable paper entitled, *An Advertisement touching the Controversies of the Church of England.* In fifteen Folio pages (*Resuscitatio*, p. 128) Francis Bacon examined the evils that arose from theological antagonisms often culminating in bloodshed. His plea was that the various "Theologies" should compose their differences and should remember that the prime object of religion was to build the Holy City of God on the New Commandment that ye love one another. His entire argument is based on his own words:

> Ye are Brethren! Why strive ye? The League among Christians should be, *He that is not against us is with us.* The diversities of ceremonies do set forth the Unity of doctrine. Religion hath parts that belong to Eternity and parts that pertain to Time. If we did but know the Virtue of Silence, and slowness to speak, commended by Saint James, our Controversies of themselves would close up and grow together. . . .
>
> A Politick man may write from his Brain without Touch and Sense of his Heart: But a feeling Christian will express in his words a Character of Zeal or Love. . . .
>
> I pray God to inspire the Bishops with a fervent Love and Care of the People. . . . As for unbrotherly proceedings on either part . . . the Wrath of man knoweth not the Righteousness of God[1] . . .

The entire composition—termed by Francis Bacon *A Meditation*—glows with the spirit of charitable broadmindedness. One can see that the soul of the author was above all sectarian differences . . . a true ethical teacher of Christian morals, inculcating openly what he had already established secretly, an Ethical Brotherhood based on those very principles which he held of high import to the State. In an age of intolerance he pleaded for tolerance: For the rule of Law instead of brute force. He sought to drive out hate by the application of Love in man's personal relationship with his fellows.

The same spirit of wisdom runs through his *Letter of Advice to Queen Elizabeth* (touched upon in Chapter VI) written some five years previously at the age of twenty-four—immediately on his entry into public life in Parliament—when he counsels the Queen upon all points of her policy in home and foreign affairs. It is a very remarkable document both for its lofty tone and cool directness in which the young Member of Parliament directly addresses the Queen's advisers suggesting they should make concessions to "Recusants," to "those who objected to the religious supremacy of the Sovereign" rather than enforce a stricter uniformity.

[1]*See* Ch. IV.

He would even modify the Oath of Allegiance. He held that persecution does not pay, and that it ultimately undermines the State. He declares himself the enemy of Spain, gives advice how she can best be weakened, that France "should rather be made a friend and not an enemy," how to regard Scotland, help given to the Low Countries, and so on. Francis Bacon displays the insight of a statesman in his bold outline. But . . . think of the audacity of an unfledged law-student of twenty-four daring to advise the Queen, *over the heads of her Ministers*, if there were no secret bond between them. What could possibly justify such a youthful newcomer to public life to take upon himself the liberty of advising the Queen what to do? To give unasked-for counsel to her statesmen who had grown grey in her service? No one else ever dared to do so publicly? Why did he?

Think of the danger too that any ordinary man would have run in presuming to advise the Queen in full view of the Parliament and the nation. Elizabeth was a difficult and "spoilt" woman. She courted the most extravagant adulation, was moody and of ungovernable passions. She held in her hands the liberties and lives of her subjects. Even her Secretaries and Ministers knelt in her presence. If the Queen had taken the letter the wrong way (which she doubtless would have done had he really been the son of Lady Bacon) Francis Bacon would have found himself in the Tower for his presumption. He made bold to do so because he felt he had a right to give such advice . . . as a true-born Tudor and the real heir to the Throne. He knew that Elizabeth would take no steps against him; that she might even be secretly pleased at his anxiety for her personal safety and the welfare of the realm . . . over which he one day hoped to rule.

This State Letter may be said to be the first of that remarkable series of State Papers which Francis Bacon composed at various times throughout his political career whenever he thought the Ship of State was in danger; from internecine feuds within or the threat of storm-clouds without. He writes on all sorts of subjects as the years pass, not only to Elizabeth, but to her Successor King James and to the Earl of Buckingham his Favourite, his last State Paper, *Considerations touching a War with Spain*, being addressed to Prince Charles in 1624, some three years after his "Fall." One reads with a feeling of disgust, too, that King James, who was so largely responsible for his "Fall," actually called upon Francis Bacon for *Advice touching Reformation of Justice*.

> The man who had only escaped being hunted down as the aider and abettor of the most grievous monopolies, *by being convicted of a higher crime*—namely corruption in one of the highest seats of judicature—*was called upon for Advice as to the Reformation of the Courts of Justice* and the relieving of the grievances of the people. (Spedding, Vol. III, p. 288).

He declined in a dignified answer to the King which would have shamed anyone capable of feeling shame: but the Sovereign who forced an innocent man to "Desert his Defence" and to plead guilty to "Charges of Corruption" in order to save himself and his Favourite Buckingham from the consequences of their own misdeeds was devoid of either shame or conscience, his sensitiveness having long since been destroyed through chronic self-indulgence in wrong-doing. This "Request" goes far to show that James knew Francis Bacon to be an innocent man. This will be amply proved in later chapters.

The next important decision of 1592 was Francis Bacon's veiled renunciation of his claims to recognition as the Tudor heir to the English Throne in his famous and remarkable letter to Lord Burleigh as Secretary of State. It was written enigmatically so that it could be clearly understood by Burleigh and the Queen, but not by an outsider unaware of Elizabeth's secret. It marked the end of, and was the sequel to, the "Mysterious Suit" (*See* Chapter VI) which began in 1580 when Francis Bacon was twenty years old (probably earlier), was still being pressed in 1585 and still remained a formal claim until Francis Bacon withdrew all rights to the "Succession" in this letter which he wrote to the only person who could accept his renunciation . . . the Secretary of State, Burleigh.

Seven years had passed since his last letter to Burleigh on the point, and though there is nothing on record that Francis Bacon had been in touch with Burleigh and the Queen respecting his "Suit" for recognition, there can be little question that it must have been mentioned orally between them, quite apart from what he writes in his secret Sonnet-Diary. That it exercised his mind is shown by a letter written to Fulke Greville, one of his personal friends, who was apparently well acquainted with Francis Bacon's hope that he would be recognized as the Heir and his fear that the Queen would decide on his younger brother the Earl of Essex as her Successor. Here is his letter:

> I understand of your pains to have visited me, for which I thank you. My MATTER is an endless Question. . . . *I dare go no further*. . . . Her Majesty had by SET SPEECH more than once assured me of her intention to call me to her Service; *which I could not understand but of THE PLACE I had been named to.*
>
> And NOW whether my MATTER must be an Appendix to my Lord of Essex SUIT . . . or what it is . . . Her Majesty is not ready to despatch it. . . .
>
> In the meantime I have a hard condition: to stand so that whatever service I do to Her Majesty, it shall be thought to be but lime-twigs and fetches to place myself. . . . This is a course to quench all good spirits. . . .
>
> *I have been like a piece of stuff bespoken in a shop*: And if Her Majesty will not take me, it may be the selling of parcels will be the more gainful.
>
> For to be, as I told you, *like a child following a bird,* which when it is nearest flyeth away and lighteth a little before, and then the child after it again, and so *in infinitum,* I am *weary of it;* as also of wearying my good friends: of whom, nevertheless, I hope in one course or other gratefully to deserve.
>
> And so, not forgetting your business, I leave to trouble you with this idle letter, being but *justa et moderata querimonia* [a lawful, right, true and moderate complaint].
>
> For indeed I do confess, *primus amor, the first love will not easily be cast off.* And thus again I commend me to you.

The picture of the child following a bird is similar to the picture of the "Careful Housewife" who "runs to catch one of her feathered creatures broke away" in his Sonnet-Diary (19-cxliii) written about the same time. The use of the same image is noted by John Nichol, *Bacon*, Vol. I, p. 43:

It is interesting to find in Shake-speare's *Coriolanus* a near transcript of it: "*I saw him run after a gilded butterfly;* and when he had caught it, he let it go again, and after it again; and over and over he comes, and up again," *Act* I, *s.* iii.

The letter is not dated. Spedding, thinking it has reference to the Solicitorship, puts it as far back as 1594-5 but this is obviously wrong. "The exact date of the latter I have no means of determining," admits Spedding, Vol. I, p. 359; and that there was something mysterious hinted at is evident by the further admissions of Spedding "It may have been the 'SUIT' to which Bacon thought his MATTER was perhaps to be an appendix." (*Ibid*, p. 360.)

The fact is that Francis Bacon's "First Love" could not possibly refer to the Solicitorship which had just cropped up. It related "To a MATTER which was *an endless Question*," to something which had dragged out over the years from the time he was a babe in arms, through his youth, and would not even finish with death. His relationship to the Queen was indeed "an endless Question," for it was destined to be debated by distant ages. The phrase cannot apply to a mere job of work, an ephemeral situation in law though dignified by the term "Solicitorship." What other question could the "Matter" be, but his "SUIT" for Recognition as a Tudor? The use of the vague word "love" in his closing sentences is used as a cover-word, just as Shakespeare uses the word to denote various Themes and Emotions in his poetic diary.

"*I confess the FIRST LOVE will not be easily cast off.*" Of course not, because it refers to his birthright, to "Recognition," to the "Succession." It could not refer to being Solicitor-General when the office never became vacant until 1593-4. How could either the Attorneyship or Solicitorship be described as his "First Love" that could "not easily be cast off?" It applies, however, with deadly fidelity to his birthright if he were the Queen's concealed eldest son and had pressed for recognition as a Tudor Prince since his late 'teens. How could such a first love be easily cast off when the throne of England was the stake?

He says that he has had imposed on him "a hard condition . . . to stand" and wait, "Her Majesty by SET SPEECH" having more than once assured him of her intention to call him *to her service* which he could not understand but in one way . . . "the *PLACE he had been NAMED to*"—*the Throne.* He had been named "a Tudor" by blood, breed and birth and was thus entitled to sit in the seat of his ancestors. He was entitled to the "Place" by Name and Heritage.

Apparently his youthful "Suit" was now going to be shelved in favour of his younger brother. His Suit was to be an "appendix" to the Earl of Essex's natural rights . . . an adjunct, an appendage, while he, Francis Bacon, was to be subordinate to him in place and power. (*See* Sonnets 30, 31, 32, 33-cxlii). They indicate the tumultuous feelings that tore at the heart-strings of Francis Bacon as he realized that for reasons of State his younger brother might be preferred to him in the Succession and that he might never be recognized as a Tudor Prince. His letter makes it clear that Greville along with others, "my good friends," knew of his aspirations to the Throne and that they were all anxious for his success. He is aware that his failure wearies them and says that he himself is weary of the chase after an earthly kingdom. He is obviously growing tired of promises which never fructify, is meditating a complete surrender of all his natural rights, and is half resolved to seek fame and fortune on other fields.

This letter in itself is sufficient to set the reader a problem. Why should Francis Bacon write so complainingly that the Queen had kept him running after her, from his youth up, until he was weary of her promises? What right had he to expect anything at all from the Queen if he were not her son? What was the Queen to him more than to any other young man? Why should he be so peculiarly aggrieved by her personal attitude? No other young man is known to have pestered the Queen and her ministers with a "Suit." No one but he dare have done it. Not a single historian has ever explained what the "Suit" was about nor its history which extends into Francis Bacon's "thirties." Obviously there was some secret tie between the parties not hitherto disclosed by the surface facts of history.

We are now in a much better position to understand the significant import of the letter which Francis Bacon sent to the Queen's Minister. One is the natural corollary of the other. He leaves with Greville a written record that he had pressed (he could only have pressed the Queen and Burleigh) his "Suit" until he "*dare go no further*" and that he was contemplating giving up further attempts. Not only was he weary of trying, but his personal friends must be weary also waiting to be participants in his good fortune, especially as his only prospect seemed to have become a subordinate one—an appendix—to his younger brother. He then hints that since "Her Majesty will not take me," it would be better for him to make a complete break with all his previous aspirations even if he has to become a mere salesman, by "the selling of parcels." He was like "*a piece of stuff bespoken in a shop*." WHY? Because he had been ordered in advance by the Queen before his birth . . . created and fashioned by her. A "bespoke" suit is one ordered and made to measure in advance to be accepted or rejected if it does not commend itself; the inference is that Francis Bacon's physical garment of flesh had been woven by the Queen who had become dissatisfied with her own handiwork. There is no other explanation possible of this remarkable image based on weaving and manufacture.

These ideas are amplified and repeated in detail in Francis Bacon's formal renunciation of the Throne of England to the Queen's Prime Minister.

To My Lord Treasurer Burghley

My Lord,

With as much confidence as mine own honest and faithful devotion unto your service and *your honourable correspondence* unto me and *my poor Estate* can breed in a man, do I commend myself to your Lordship.

I WAX NOW SOMEWHAT ANCIENT; one and thirty years is a great deal of sand in the Hour-glass. My Health, I thank God, I find confirmed; and I do not fear that action shall impair it, *because I account my ordinary course of Study and Meditation to be more painful* than most parts of actions are.

I ever bear a mind—*in some MIDDLE PLACE that I could discharge*—

to serve Her Majesty; *not as a Man BORN UNDER SOL, that loveth Honour;* nor under Jupiter that loveth business—for the contemplative Planet carrieth me away wholly; but as a Man BORN UNDER AN EXCELLENT SOVEREIGN, that deserveth the dedication of all men's abilities. . . .

The greater parts of my Thoughts are to deserve well—if I were able—of my friends, and namely of your Lordship; who being the Atlas of this Commonwealth, the Honour of my House, and the second Founder of my poor Estate, I am tied by all duties, both of a good patriot, and of an unworthy kinsman, and of an obliged servant, to employ whatsoever I am to do you service.

The meanness of my Estate doth somewhat move me: for though I cannot accuse myself that I am either prodigal or slothful, yet my Health is not to spend, nor my Course to get.

I confess that I have as vast Contemplative Ends as I have moderate CIVIL Ends: for *I have taken ALL KNOWLEDGE to be MY PROVINCE;* and if I could purge it of two sorts of Rovers, whereof the one with frivolous disputations, confutations and verbosities, the other with Blind Experiments and auricular Traditions and Impostures, hath committed so many spoils, I hope I should bring in Industrious Observations, Grounded Conclusions and Profitable Inventions and Discoveries; the best state of that Province.

This, whether it be curiosity, or vain-glory, or nature or—if one take it favourably—*PHILANTHROPIA, is so fixed in my Mind, as it cannot be removed.* And I do easily see that place of any reasonable countenance *doth bring Commandment of MORE WITS than of a man's own; which is the thing I greatly affect.*

And for your Lordship, perhaps you shall not find more strength and less encounter in any other.

And if your Lordship shall find NOW or at ANY TIME, that *I do seek or affect ANY PLACE* whereunto *any that is nearer unto your Lordship shall be concurrent, say then that I am a most DISHONEST MAN.*

And if your Lordship will not carry me on, I will not do as Anaxagorus did, who reduced himself with contemplation unto poverty: But this I will do; I will sell the inheritance that I have, and purchase some lease of quick revenue, or some office of gain that shall be executed by deputy, and so GIVE OVER ALL CARE OF SERVICE, *and become a sorry BOOK-MAKER* or a True Pioneer in the Mine of Truth, which, he said, lay so deep.

This which I have writ to your Lordship is rather *THOUGHTS than WORDS,* being set down *without all Art, Disguising or Reservation.* Wherein I have done Honour both to your Lordship's Wisdom, in judging that THAT will be best believed of your Lordship which is truest, and to your Lordship's good nature, in retaining nothing from you. And even so, I wish your Lordship all Happiness, and to myself Means and Occasion to be added to my faithful desire to do you service. From my lodging at Gray's Inn.

Is not this a strange letter for a briefless barrister to write to the Queen's Prime Minister? It would be a very strange one if it were not intended to convey something ulterior than appears on the surface. It is not written as nephew to uncle. It is written to Burleigh as the "Atlas of this Commonwealth . . ." this England, as a latter *touching the well-being of the State,* and therefore to be passed on officially to Elizabeth. Would any ordinary man have dreamt of writing Burleigh to acquaint him with the fact that he was contemplating going in for literature instead of law, complaining to him of "the meanness of his estate?" What possible interest could this be to Burleigh or the Queen? None . . . *if it were sent from an outsider on such an ordinary matter.* A moment's reflection is sufficient to show that the letter announces a decision which the writer knows will be of profound interest to the Queen and her Minister, a decision that will help to clear away a vital problem of State, and which ought to be vitally recorded in writing for the benefit of all concerned.

Francis Bacon's meditations to Greville had at length taken concrete shape. He had decided on a course of action . . . to cross the Rubicon, from which there could be no return, by giving Burleigh to understand in black and white that he renounced all hopes of being known as a Tudor of royal rights and intended to live under the vizard-name of Bacon.

The first sentence shows that he and Burleigh had previous correspondence on the prime subject of the letter which directly related to "ME and My Poor Estate," poor indeed to what he was really entitled to as the Queen's son. He also lets it be known that the matter is one of "confidence" affecting "your Service," i.e., Burleigh's Office.

As a concealed Tudor, born of a Queen still posing as a "Virgin" to the people (Elizabeth was then in her sixtieth year) with her bosom uncovered,[1] Francis could see, now that he had arrived at the age of thirty-one, that every year that passed made it more and more difficult for his parentage to be openly acknowledged by the populace who only knew him as Francis Bacon. He therefore rightly says, thinking of the unacknowledged years that the locusts had eaten, "*I now wax somewhat ANCIENT*" . . . too ancient to be presented thirty years after birth to the world in general and the English nation in particular, as a real Tudor Prince, with the blood of the great Queen running in his veins. No wonder that he grimly remarks that though his health be good his "Meditations are painful" through studying the proper course to pursue, revolving the entire situation which means the surrender of his just rights.

He reminds Burleigh that he had never sought more than a moderate State office wherewith to serve the Queen "*in some Middle Place*" and not as *a man born under the Sun of England* who would naturally love "Honour" and thus be tempted to presume upon his Tudor Breed: But "*as a Man BORN UNDER an Excellent Sovereign,*" which would be literally true physically and mentally of a Queen's Issue. He was just as jealous for the Honour of the House of Tudor as was Burleigh . . . as "a patriot, a KINSMAN and a servant."

The Meanness of his Estate *moves* him because he is conscious of the Rich Estate he ought to occupy and enjoy, yet, he adds, he has no desire "to spend" on personal pleasures nor is his "Course to get" riches for such a purpose. For "*I have as VAST Contemplative Ends as I have moderate CIVIL ends: I have taken ALL KNOWLEDGE to be MY PROVINCE.*"

In this sentence is Francis Bacon's formally written renunciation to the English Throne. In plain, set terms he tells Burleigh that his "Civil Ends" are modest. He only wants an Office of profit to provide him with a livelihood—"a Middle Place" as a commoner. In giving up all his claims upon the Queen as her son, he has no desire to trespass upon her any further as a mere pensioner. He wants in future to earn his money and no longer be a dependant. No longer will he "seek or affect any Place

[1]Regarded as a sign of virginity in Tudor times.

that would be nearer" to Burleigh himself. The only "Place" that would be nearer the Queen than Burleigh would be a Princely Place . . . Recognition. In effect Francis Bacon says, "If you give me a subordinate office of work, I will not take the slightest advantage to lift myself to my rightful heritage; if I do, say then that *I am a most dishonest man.*"

Thus is Burleigh told that Francis Bacon no longer seeks to rule over an earthly Kingdom but to reign over a universal one . . . the intellectual Province of the Mind, the Storehouse for the riches of "ALL KNOWLEDGE." Kingdoms and Provinces have no longer any appeal to him unless they are mental and ethical ones. Francis Bacon in this way assures Burleigh that his Civil Ambition to rule the Realm is utterly quenched, and that his Passion is to rule solely an intellectual kingdom, to purge it of all frivolous disputations and impositions and to establish grounded conclusions, and profitable invention which would be the "Best State" he could desire . . . a Province in which he would have the Command of more "Wits" than his own. "This *Philanthropia is so fixed in my mind as it cannot be removed.*"

This enigmatical letter, which only the Queen and her adviser can properly interpret, seeks to reassure them that they need have no fear of giving him a lucrative State Office so he can follow out his vast contemplative schemes that had already been begun. Obviously, Burleigh had been afraid of finding for him a lucrative position in the Queen's Service lest he might use such an Office as a stepping-stone to the Throne or cause civil unrest by openly demanding recognition of his claims. He therefore adds in effect:

> If your Lordship will not carry me on—will not give me such a position of financial independence—then will I give up all thought of entering the Queen's service and become a sorry Book-Maker, selling some of my inheritance to obtain the means.

It is worthy of note that the only inheritance he possessed had been given him by the Queen and his only income was also derived from her to be given or withheld at pleasure. He was still a briefless barrister. He had no law-work. He had no professional income. He was still dependent on the Queen's Bounty. That is a prime reason why he writes . . . to acquaint her with his thoughts . . . to see how she will take it. To clinch the position he concludes his letter by stating that what he has written are not mere words. They are his considered thoughts, his decision being irrevocable, which he has set down without "Art, Designing or Reservation." He wishes Burleigh happiness in reading of this utter abandonment of his "Suit." To himself he wishes to possess the "Means" of a paid Office to render him independent in order to satisfy his own intellectual urge.

Burleigh, as the prime custodian of the Queen's secret, must have had a load taken off his mind on receipt of this letter. For fifteen years and more he must have had many fears lest this high-spirited young genius should do something desperate to enforce his claim . . . a veritable Hamlet who could not succeed to the Throne of his Fathers. For good or ill Burleigh now knew that Francis had definitely decided "to live a Second

Life on Second Head" (Sonnet 143-lxviii). He had resolved at long last that his Soul should

> "Buy Terms Divine in selling Hours of Dross;
> *Within be fed, without be RICH no more:*
> So shalt thou feed on Death, that feeds on Men,
> And Death once Dead, there's no more dying then."
> (35-cxlvi).

The Queen is thus given to understand that his mouth is closed. The secret will be kept from contemporary prying eyes so far as he is concerned. He undertakes nevermore to disturb the existing regime with his bootless cries which makes the head that wears the crown uneasy. In future he will pursue literary tasks, not political; moderate civil ends, not a Royal seat.

There can be little doubt that Francis Bacon had been driven by his meditations to the position that at thirty-one years of age it was hopeless to expect the Queen to recognize him publicly as her eldest son, the circumstances, all round, being against him—the Queen's reputation and his own ill-fated birth only four months after her secret marriage with Leicester. Moreover the Queen was passionately fond of his younger brother to whom the bar-sinister of "adulterine-bastardy" did not apply. The Earl of Essex was a popular idol and acceptable to the populace and would be welcomed as being next in the Succession. Parker Woodward sums up the situation in these words which I am sure are substantially true:

> Francis would probably argue: The circumstances attending my birth are very awkward. The witnesses of the marriage ceremony are dead, and the dying declaration of the Queen on the subject might not be accepted by the people to whom I am comparatively unknown. Under these circumstances, and more especially since I have taken upon myself the tremendous task of endeavouring to improve our language and literature, and the training and the knowledge of our race, I shall be quite content to go on with my present studies if I can secure some position of permanent and sufficient income to enable me in comfort to prosecute my own work.
>
> To Robert, his brother, he might say. . . . There is less difficulty with respect to your birth, and I am quite willing to aid you in the direction of the affairs of State . . . but you must secure for me a suitable Office of good salary as quickly as you can.

Let it be remembered that Francis Bacon was not in practice and therefore not earning, that he had no investments of property or land, etc., that his income was derived from the Queen and Burleigh as Elizabeth's son and we have an explanation that fits the facts. . . . his concealed private life as a Tudor and his secret literary life under varied pen-names to create an English Renaissance.

This extraordinary letter has puzzled every student of Francis Bacon. No adequate explanation has ever been given by historian or biographer. It is inconceivable that a man with no claims on the Queen's Minister should write in such a strain. But the fact is that it is a Matter of State. It is "an endless question." From an outsider, a commoner. it would be a piece of presumption. But as a concealed Prince it was his duty to make known his thoughts. He had made a great decision. Henceforth he was to lead Humanity along the King's Highway of Knowledge and Power and he must not allow the tempting thoughts of purely material Honour and Riches to deflect him from the Course. He renounced a Royal Throne but it was to occupy the Chair of Apollo in the Creative Kingdom of the Immortals.

When Francis Bacon took his seat in the new Parliament of 1593 all these thoughts and resolves would be pouring through his mind like a cascade in riot . . . his secret literary tasks and all they involved, the establishment of his secret Societies, the Rosicrosse, the Rosicrucian Colleges, the Masonic Lodges, the renunciation of his birthright and the consequences. He was now definitely one of the *enfans perdus* (lost children), his own expression to the Queen in his *Apologia*, a Tudor by breed with the iron-mask of a false name riveted over his true personality. And he knew that every year that passed would make it more difficult to remove the Bacon-vizard and to convey the truth of his real identity to the contemporary world (had he wished to do so) or to future generations. He could foresee, of course, that the passing years would bring for him difficulties in their train, political and religious. He had now definitely to secure a dependable livelihood. Hitherto he had never tried to make money. There had never been any necessity. His bread had been certain and his water sure . . . with a few extras thrown in. No law-earnings had ever come to Gray's Inn. But he had had no compunction in accepting the Queen's remittances for she was his parent. He was the work of her hands, the embodiment of her WILL. She had made him, and, as a concealed son, he was her responsibility. But now the position was different. He had definitely cut himself adrift from all expectations, from his own mother, from the Tudor dynasty. He questioned whether he had any right to expect any further allowance from the Queen's privy purse, whether she would continue to finance him, or whether he should accept further largess under their altered circumstances.

Up to this time this extraordinary genius had spent his youthful energetic years in secretly creating a literature, establishing ethical foundations, and brewing a subtle ferment that would revolutionize the accepted scientific and philosophic concepts. Through his instrumentality the genesis of these far-reaching movements had been begun. The bases at least had been well and truly laid in these silent years. The plans were in being and the organizing had passed from being a poet's dream into a concrete reality. They had taken root. They were alive with the dynamic power of his genius. He knew they would continue to grow throughout the world, influencing for all time the destinies of man, and that the gates of ignorance, bigotry and malevolence could not stand against the myriad thoughts he had already created, and put into circulation, and which were to be perpetuated through his secret school of disciples. The time had come when he felt he must call a halt. He must now study how to live. Apparently he had high hopes that Burleigh would find him a suitably-paid Government Office that would provide him with sufficient leisure to continue his intellectual work and which would save him from being a financial embarrassment any longer to the Queen.

Owing to the fact that he was patrimonially penniless, financial

Plate XX

The Interior of Old Swan Theatre in Francis Bacon's day
From "Shakespeare's London" by T. F. Ordish
(See p. 179)

Acting a "Shake-speare" play in Queen Elizabeth's day
From "The England of Shakespeare" by Edwin Goadby
(See p. 180)

PLATE XXI
Richmond Palace, one of Queen Elizabeth's palaces
From a drawing by Anto van den Wyngaerde (1562) in the Bodleian Library
(See Appendix I)

considerations were beginning to obtrude themselves grimly and ominously. At the very time when he was renouncing all claim upon his mother the Queen, which might lead, for aught he knew, to the cessation of all financial support, the young aristocrat's living expenses must have been fairly heavy. He had not only his Chambers and lodgings at Gray's Inn to maintain but he also had on his shoulders—at least nominally—the upkeep of his lovely residence at Twickenham Park with its eighty-seven acres of enclosed park, gardens, lake and orchards, a valuable property of forest, rolling meadows, and stream abounding in fish and wild fowl. Within easy ride of the City, it was a retreat to which he was in the habit of retiring . . . a retreat specially conducive to secret and romantic compositions, "far from the noise of town, the clamour of debtors and moneylenders with whom Francis Bacon was always involved."[1] (*Francis Bacon and Twickenham Park,* p. 15, A. C. Bunten).

His financial impecuniosity was only too true. It had begun with his secret literary and ethical activities—writing, printing, publishing at his own expense. Indeed, financial stringency seemed to dog his footsteps all through life. "He never had much practice at the Bar," says Lord Campbell, *Life*, p. 19. Referring to the year 1597, Campbell also says, p. 40:

> Bacon was now in high favour at Court as well as popular in the House of Commons by his eloquence, and in the country by his writings; but *he was desperately poor, for authorship, as yet, brought no profit and his general practice at the bar was very inconsiderable. In spite of his economical habits, he had contracted some debts* which were troublesome to him.

Here we have an admission from one of Francis Bacon's foremost biographers that he had contracted "debts" though he was of economical habits. *What were those debts?* No one has ever told us. He neither drank, smoked, gambled nor was extravagant in his personal expenditure. Yet he was in debt. The standard biographers usually say . . . "He must have been grossly extravagant." Not one of them appears to know the truth

[1]Everything points to the fact that Twickenham Park was early in Francis Bacon's hands after his second visit to the Continent from which he returned in 1582. His notes on *The State of Europe* were obviously compiled by one who had personally observed what he had described. Spedding thinks that Francis was at Gray's Inn but internal and external evidence—like Thomas Bodley's Letters—prove that Francis was on the Continent making observations for the Queen and the Government. Twickenham Park was probably granted him as a residence as a place eminently in keeping with his character as an aristocrat and a Prince with a secret claim upon her. It was an easy matter to arrange possession without causing any idle talk for the lease was in his (nominal) step-brother's name, Edward Bacon, and there is nothing to indicate that Edward lived there after 1582. Though the lease did not expire until 1595 we know that the place was being used by Francis and his friends, and as a scrivenery for his "good Pens" in 1592, and his letters seem to indicate that his residence there in 1592 was of long standing.

One thing is certain: neither in 1582 nor in 1592 had Francis sufficient income from any source save the Queen to maintain such a splendid estate. How could he have obtained possession save by the goodness of the Queen? *The estate was hers.* There can be no doubt the residence was arranged for him by the Queen. Her Palace faced Twickenham Park and he could row across the Thames and see his mother in private in the evening without anyone being the wiser. Something was done in 1581 respecting the lease to Edward Bacon, for a person named Miles Doddington was granted the reversion of the lease in that year to begin in 1595 and in that year 1595 we find that there passed under the Privy Seal the grant of the reversion of Twickenham Park to Francis Bacon—and Doddington never enters into the transaction at all.

Does not everything point to the fact of their secret relationship and that Elizabeth was trying to do her best to help him?

of the matter which was that even from his early 'teens he had spent the income derived from the Queen, and all the money he could obtain from his friends in the printing and publishing of books. And anyone who has printed and published a book at his own expense—especially of the educational type of text-book or poetry—will know well the financial difficulties which would beset Francis the idealist. He voluntarily became poor and penniless—when he might have enjoyed luxurious comforts from the income and the beautiful mansion of Twickenham provided by the Queen—in his endeavour to provide England with a language of culture and to broaden the bounds of the Empire of the Mind. All his money he spent secretly to enrich mankind. His money requirements were always great and there has never been a solitary attempt by any orthodox biographer to explain the reason.[1]

We see that even in 1597 his practice at the Bar was "very inconsiderable," that his authorship brought him in no profit but rather, kept him stretched on the rack of debt. There is not the slightest evidence that his law-practice at the Bar was ever sufficient to provide him even with his daily bread and butter apart from his other expenses. And as we run up the years of his life what do we find? That he borrows good round sums from his friends, persuades Anthony and Lady Anne Bacon to mortgage properties, has recourse to moneylenders, and is even flung into a debtors' prison more than once . . . and all the money vanishes into thin air. To-day we know what the indefatigable Spedding never knew: that the money was being spent to create and foster *The English Renaissance* . . . to set *The Great Instauration* not only before the eyes of men but in their hearts, a WORK to be done, not a book to be written; and the WORK required hard cash.

So in 1592 Lady Anne Bacon was poor. So were Francis and Anthony, the loving and beloved. Both were at Gray's Inn, where Anthony was staying having returned from the Continent broken in health, and both these high-spirited idealists paid their printing bills by help of the Lombards and the Jews, while Lady Anne from Gorhambury pinched and denied herself to send to Gray's Inn ale from her cellar, pigeons from her dovecote and fowls from her farmyard, all of which she seasons with a good deal of motherly love and advice, even to the avoiding of such sinful pleasures as Plays and Masques . . . mostly addressed to her son Anthony whom she loved passionately.

We thus obtain a very fair all-round picture of Francis as he fronts the world in 1593 with the friendship and love of his foster-brother by his side, with Lady Bacon watching over their physical and spiritual needs, while Burleigh and the Queen wonder how the tangle will ever be unravelled. And behind this picture is all the stress and strain of Francis Bacon's secret relationships, his secret creations, his secret strivings, his secret torments which make him bewail "his outcast STATE." All these

[1]As a matter of fact Francis Bacon's writings over his own name up to 1597, printed and published, consisted only of the *Essays*. There were but ten, and about ten small pages *Of the Coulers of Good and Evill*. Manifestly they could not have brought in an income. His State Papers, e.g., *Letter to Queen Elizabeth*, 1584; *Controversies of the Church*, 1589; and *Observations on a Libel* 1592 were circulated rather than published by the Government. They were not sold, and brought in no money.

circumstances, the secret life as well as the open one, must be borne in mind and appraised at their proper value, *when we begin to consider Francis Bacon the publicist in the year* 1593, from which date the majority of his biographers begin their estimate of his work and character . . . the year of his advent into the New Parliament.

Francis Bacon was thirty-two when he took his seat in the Commons for the foremost financial constituency of the day . . . Middlesex. Anthony Bacon, though sick and lame, had been returned for Wallingford. The young barrister and "Counsel Extraordinary" found himself on the benches by the side of many men afterwards famous in history, with rival orators, politicians, lawyers. Edward Coke, the Solicitor-General, was also the Speaker. The hunchback Cecil, Lord Burleigh's son, gradually being prepared to take his father's place as Secretary of State, led for the Crown. While there was as yet no formal "Opposition" as in our day, we may say definitely that the 1593 Parliament saw the beginning of the Parliamentary system, now such a characteristic of our national life . . . the idea of the grouping of a body of men who were "opposed" to the Government: and to no one are we more indebted for this peculiar and valuable political method of conducting public business than to Francis Bacon.

In the new House he was known to all personally or by repute. There were men who liked him and men who did not, because of his advanced political views and his almost Puritanical uprightness. They knew, as the burgesses of Middlesex knew, that Francis Bacon however poor he might be would never sell his principles for office, honours or hard cash and that he was not to be moved from the path of public honesty by threats, cajolery or hope of reward. (Bribery was rampant in those days.) His previous eight years of public service had already revealed the leading character-traits that made the man. By all he was regarded as the "Dark Horse" of politics . . . for no one knew how far he would go as a Parliamentarian and a lawyer or whither his ambitions might lead him. He was as much an enigma to his fellow-members as he is to the majority of his countrymen to-day. He was a penniless, landless, briefless lawyer; yet this was his third Parliament. He had no income—running his Chambers at a dead loss—yet he entertained his friends at Twickenham Park. He had little to do with Burleigh and Cecil, his "relatives," and yet was known to be a *persona grata* to the Queen with a right of *entrée* almost at any time. No wonder that there were ever-recurring whispers in Court Circles that Francis Bacon was a Man of Mystery; and that wise heads nodded knowingly and tongues wagged while Francis with his handsome, aristocratic bearing, in the opening session, sat among a crowd of wealthy notables like Fulke Greville, John Fortescue, Lawrence Hyde, Henry Yelverton, Edward Dyer, Henry Montague, de Vere and Raleigh.

When Parliament met the time was one of grave national anxiety. Four years previously the Armada had been scattered and the invasion hopelessly foiled, but Philip of Spain had not given up his ideas of conquest. He said:

> "I sent my fleet against men, not against the billows. I thank God I can easily, if I choose, place another fleet upon the seas."

Before 1593 the Government knew that Spain meditated another attack and was almost ready to launch it. All along Philip had never accepted his defeat as final. From 1588 he had schemed to make France a Catholic country, a nearer springboard from which to crush the Island Race which defied him; but the murder in December 1588 of the Duke of Guise, and, later, in 1589, of his rival Henry III by a fanatical Dominican priest, lifted the Huguenot Henry of Navarre as the Heir Presumptive to the French Throne. As Navarre was the hereditary foe of the House of Savoy, Philip's energies were directed to his repression. To keep the Spanish King employed on the Continent, England assumed an aggressive attitude which had the direct result of inflaming the spirit of naval adventure—already high as a result of our Armada victory. "Hostility to Spain," says Bishop Creighton, "in adventurous minds, and any plan for attack upon the Spaniards, was received with enthusiasm." (*Age of Elizabeth*, p. 182.)

Expeditions against Spain were sent out, notably under Sir John Norris, Sir Francis Drake, and many successes were gained (e.g., at Corunna where all the vessels in the harbour were burned and a Spanish army of fifteen thousand men were repulsed with great slaughter by an English army half their number). Our "Seamen Adventurers" like Hawkins, Frobisher, Grenville and Raleigh also tried to cripple the power of Spain by forays on Spanish harbours, attacks on their colonies and by wrecking their supplies by capturing rich galleons off the Spanish Main. Though much glory and booty were won, they had not destroyed the menace of a Spanish "come-back." What we had done, however, was to show how vulnerable was Spain not only on the sea but the land (for had we not defeated a Spanish army on its own ground), to inspire France and the Lowlands to renewed exertion and to cast out fear with courage.

By the autumn of 1592, Spain's preparations were in full flood. The lying propaganda of the Jesuit, Father Parsons[1], with its libels about Elizabeth had done its poisonous work in Madrid and Brussels, Derry and Cork; several of the most powerful nobles in Scotland had pledged themselves to receive Spanish forces, to raise an army financed by the Spaniards and to march across the Border. The Government had therefore to prepare "for an invasion at both ends of the kingdom at once." (Spedding, *Life*, Vol. I, p. 209.)

Henry of Navarre, who had mounted the throne of France, was being pressed by the victorious Spaniards and called to Protestant England for help. There were alarms of war without and fears of pestilence within . . . for all London gasped with the plague: all outside sport was forbidden, no bear-baiting, no sports at the inn yards, no revelry at the taverns, no pageants on the Thames. The Lord Mayor stopped the sports of the apprentices and the citizens. The Globe Theatre was silent. No plays were allowed to attract either the gallants of the Inns of Court or the riff-raff that gathered round the play-houses. Such was the Elizabethan "black-out" in the shadow of war. But the recruiting sergeant—despite gruesome scenes of woe and death—nevertheless went his rounds

[1]Parsons was the writer of the scurrilous pamphlet attacking Queen Elizabeth and Francis replied with *Observations on a Libel.*

with drum and fife tempting recruits to take the Queen's shilling. "From Margate to Penzance was erected a proud barrier of forts. The Sussex foundries cast guns. Troops hurried for Flanders, Dublin, and Kinsale. And London stood under arms." (Hepworth Dixon, *Life*, p. 61.)

Such was the atmosphere in the capital on the 16th February, 1593 ... (disease, death and the alarums of war) when the Lord Keeper, Sir John Puckering, in the presence of the Queen addressed both Houses and gave them the reasons why they had been called. He said:

> The King of Spain since 1588 had been furnishing himself with ships of a different build, fitter for our waters; had possessed himself of the principal strongholds in Brittany, places convenient to assail us from by sea; had won a party in Scotland to give landing to his forces there, sent large sums of money, and received written promises of assistance; and that *his purpose was to invade us by land and sea at once, from north and south.*
>
> The Queen's treasure being spent she had called them that she might consult with her subjects for the better withstanding of these intended invasions which were greater now than were ever heretofore heard of.
>
> The Lord Keeper also said they were not called *to make any new laws* ... an abridgment of existing ones being more wanted than an addition. The session would not be long; therefore *good hours must not be lost in idle speeches.* In short ... the Queen wanted a double subsidy for war purposes. (Spedding, *Life*, Vo. I, p. 210).

The directions of the Lord Keeper of no new laws, no unnecessary debate and an extra subsidy, was really a direct encroachment by Queen Elizabeth on the privileges of the Commons. The House had been allowed hitherto to discuss all questions of supply by themselves without dictation or interference. Says Spedding, it probably seemed to the Queen that the urgency of the occasion and the enthusiastic loyalty in a time of national danger might enable her to advance a step, to take in her own hands the power of the purse. The right of free debate had in point of fact its limits imposed by the Crown, but Peter Wentworth, M.P., had formally disputed them in February 1587. The veto was, however, reaffirmed unmistakably, for when the Speaker proffered the usual petition for liberty of speech, the Lord Keeper was instructed to answer, that

> Liberty of speech was granted in respect of Aye and No; *but not that every-one should speak as he listed.* 22nd February.

The members, in short, had only liberty to vote and were denied liberty of speech and action. This was soon made plain to all, for when Peter Wentworth, with others, a couple of days later delivered a petition relating to the "Succession" they were immediately brought before the Privy Council and promptly committed to prison—Wentworth to the Tower, and Bromley and others to the Fleet on 24th February, where they remained until the end of the Session. On representations being made for their release, lest their constituents should complain that they were being taxed without representation, the Privy Council replied that "Her Majesty had committed them for causes best known to herself," with which answer the Commons had to be satisfied.

This gives us some idea of the dangers that even well-placed persons ran if their tongues wagged too freely or if they acted to the dictates of reason. The problem of the "Succession" was indeed a burning one to all the nation.

The next day word was sent by Lord Burleigh, Treasurer, to Speaker Coke, to beat down, in the Queen's name, all opposition, all noisy members that should presume to prate of non-essential matters. On the 26th February, the question of supply was then brought forward by Sir Robert Cecil, and the faithful Commons asked to confer with the Peers. The House appointed a committee and among them were Vere, Raleigh, Greville, Hastings, Coke, and Francis Bacon. They then heard Lord Treasurer Burleigh's words. And the next day the Commons heard from his son, Sir Robert Cecil, the amount the Peers had decided they should give and at what times: three money grants in three years, four shillings in the pound each year.

To-day, with an Income Tax of ten shillings in the pound, the amount may seem small, but in 1593 the value of money made it a very large sum. The usual custom was for the Crown to ask for half a subsidy a year, half a subsidy being ten per cent, two shillings in the pound a year. Burleigh was thus demanding a double subsidy—one whole subsidy a year, four shillings in the pound. There was to be no idle discussion either. The money-bill of Burleigh's had to be passed—high though it was. The Commons were to be robbed of even the credit of their own gifts. If anyone demurred he did so at his peril. He not only ran the risk of the fate that had overtaken Wentworth but, owing to the exigencies of the situation, of being accused of being unpatriotic . . . of holding up supplies when the menace of invasion was at our doorstep.

No wonder the members looked aghast at one another.

Francis Bacon knew better than anyone else what was involved. It was not exclusively a question of voting money for a war. There was a vital principle at stake equally important—the political liberty of the subject. It was not for the Peers to dictate the amount the Commons should vote, how much annually or for how long: these matters should be the prerogative of the House of Commons given under a free vote: Nor had Burleigh, Puckering, and the Peers any right, under the excuse of war urgency, to take away the freedom of members to speak critically, nor ought Speaker Coke to gag the Assembly at the dictum of the Crown. Moreover, Francis Bacon held the view that Parliaments were called constitutionally not merely to pass Money Bills but to deal with Laws . . . to frame new ones, to amend old ones, to repeal outworn ones; a fundamental principle which could not be abrogated by Minister or Crown. (These views are clearly seen in Francis Bacon's later political career). A Parliament could not and ought not to be called together simply to pass subsidies. Its business was the inception and execution of laws equally as much as the providing of money. Francis Bacon knew that to accept the position laid down by the Lord Keeper was *to create a precedent that would shear away the powers of the Commons and vest them in the Crown.*

Now what was he to do? Was he to remain silent and let the Crown establish a precedent that might ultimately be of danger to the State? Or was he to open the eyes of the members to the peril that threatened the Free Assembly, the whittling away of free speech, their money, rights, the making of New Laws or amending existing ones?

Was it worth while running the risk of being clapped into jail, like Wentworth, if he opposed the Queen's Will? Ought he to defy Coke? *His sole income was derived from the Queen.* Others might guess at the fact, but he knew it and all it implied. His law practice was infinitesimal. He was, moreover, hopeful that Burleigh would find him a salaried position. He had asked for a situation in a private letter about which his fellow-members knew nothing. Now . . . how could he expect Burleigh to do anything for him if he attempted to upset Burleigh's Money-Bill? Would not his opposition be misjudged by the Court? In his private letter he had renounced all claim to the Succession. Would it not seem as though he were deliberately taking the first opportunity to flout the Queen with his newly asserted freedom of thought and action . . . acting as a commoner who owed no filial allegiance to his Tudor mother? What would her reactions be if she were thus crossed? Stop his allowance? Was it worth while to take such risks simply for the sake of preventing a precedent being established?

Could we have blamed Francis Bacon had he stood silently on one side? His income, nay, his whole career might be imperilled if he vexed Burleigh and the Queen. Indeed, his present mode of life might crash in ruins if he angered the Court. Well might he write, under another name as the Prince who could not succeed to his inheritance:

The Time is out of Joint; O cursed spite
That ever I WAS BORN to set it right.

Where were "the fiery Raleigh, the martial Vere, the noisy Hastings, the sagacious Greville, the turbulent Coke?" Were not these the men to flame up in such a righteous cause? What had they at stake compared to him?

The fact was that these men did not know how to act; how to defend their inherent right to make money-grants *without seeming to oppose the war,* thus showing their enemies a broken front. To fight for the power of free taxation demanded courage of a different kind than that required in the heat of battle, for the entire country was clamouring for the war. These men did not want to offend the Queen and her advisers. There was not one who did not fear the wrath of the Tudor Lioness when roused. So they waited for a lead from the only man who dare give it.

Francis Bacon had made up his mind what to do when he heard the Queen's speech. Freedom and Liberty were not going to be let down if he could help it. We know this because we have a fragmentary record of what he said on what we should now consider to be the debate on the Address. It was a speech on "Law Reform"—the very subject the Commons had been specifically warned not to discuss. This is what he said:

> The cause of the assembling of all Parliaments hath been heretofore for Laws or Money; the one being the sinews of Peace, the other of War. To the one I am not privy; but the other I should know.
>
> I did take great contentment in Her Majesty's speeches the other day delivered by the Lord Keeper, how that it was fitting an abridgment were

made of the laws and statutes of the realm; a thing not to be done suddenly nor at one Parliament; nor scarce a whole year would suffice to purge the statute-book nor lessen the volume of laws; being so many in number that neither common people half practise them, nor the lawyer sufficiently understand them—than the which nothing should tend more to the eternal praise of Her Majesty.

The Romans appointed ten men who were to correct and recall all former laws, and set forth their Twelve Tables, so much of all men to be commended. The Athenienses likewise appointed six to that purpose. And Lewis IX of France did the like in reforming of laws, etc.

Francis Bacon thus adroitly let the Government understand that though the Commons had been called together solely to provide monies, the Laws were equally the prime concern of the legislature. He said briefly that the whole body of English law should be amended. We can imagine, says Lord Campbell, the instances he gave "of the absurd penal laws remaining unrepealed and the advantages he pointed out from digesting and codifying." He tells a House full of lawyers that:

> Laws are made to guard the rights of the people, not to feed the lawyers. The laws should be read by all, known to all. Put them into shape, inform them with philosophy, reduce them in bulk, give them into every man's hand.

So runs his speech, says Dixon (*Life*, p. 62), and he adds:

> This is a noble thought. The plan, of which this fragment was the root, was developed in his *Maxims of the Law*, and proposed as part of his great reform in the *Instauratio Magna*. It has had more success abroad than it has found at home. It has been universally read, and most of all in France. In that country it has blossomed and come to fruit. A French Revolution alone had power *to achieve this vast design against established things; and the Code Napoleon is even now, in 1862, the sole embodiment of Francis Bacon's thought.*"

Francis Bacon's pointed hint that he already had the outline of a scheme for reforming the Code, ready for presentation when the time was ripe, came as a bombshell to the House as well as to the Government, but his startling speech appears to have been well received by the members. Speaker Coke could not repress the young member for Middlesex, though he tried to do so with all the authority of his office, his solicitorship, and his instructions from the Queen. There appears to have been many passages at arms between them. In any case, this session saw the beginning of the conflict between these two famous men—antagonists unutterably opposed to each other by temperament, outlook and intellect—a deadly duel which lasted all through life, fought in the Commons, at the Bar, in Society, their domestic relations, and at last in the Privy Council and the Court, and which cannot be said to have ended with the burial of Sir Francis Bacon at St. Michael's and Coke's ultimate disgrace in the Tower.

The hardihood of Francis Bacon daring to stand up to Coke—the penniless barrister against the wealthy Speaker armed with authority and ten years Francis Bacon's senior—lifted him at once into prominence and really made him the virtual leader of a group that would to-day be termed the "Opposition." This was the true genesis of our present two-divisional Parliamentary system. When the double-subsidy demand was made the House therefore waited, perturbed and uneasy, wondering if Francis Bacon would talk and what line he would take. Would he resent the curb on their right of debate? Would he rebut the slur on their patriotism? *By a strangely ordained fate it therefore fell to the real head of the aristocracy (a born Tudor and a real Prince of Wales) to rise and warn the minister Sir Robert Cecil that the Government were making a grave mistake in their method of approach . . . to assert the rights of a democratic chamber against any extension of the Royal prerogative.*

> In a few clear words he said he should not touch the grant. He was willing to vote for the additional subsidy, for no man would grudge the funds to fit out ships and man the guns but to give was the prerogative of the people—to dictate what they should give was not the duty of the House of Peers. In framing the Bill the Government had gone beyond its powers; and he counselled the Commons, in their own defence, to decline any further conferences on a money-bill. . . .
>
> "I mislike that this House should join the Upper House in the granting of it, for the custom and privilege of this House hath always been first to make offer of the subsidy from hence into the Upper House. And for this reason it is that we should stand upon our privilege. . . . Therefore we should proceed as heretofore we have done, apart by ourselves, and not joining with their Lordships."
>
> To this he cited a precedent in Henry VIII's time, and concluded by taking out of his pocket *An Answer to the Lords* which he proposed should be read and if approved sent up. (D'Ewes, 468-83.)

This Answer was referred to a Committee of fifty-one, but they could not agree and the House fell into two different camps, "the Courtiers siding with Cecil for the Conferences and the Reformers with Francis Bacon for resisting an encroachment on their constitutional laws." And when Coke put the question from the chair—for a Conference yea or nay, the Courtiers were out-voted, 128 gentlemen cried Yea and 228 cried Nay.

And so the machinery of Parliament was stopped and the courtiers were thrown into a state of horror and amazement, and adds Lord Campbell (*Life*, p. 23):

> The Queen was deeply incensed and desired it to be intimated to the delinquent (Francis Bacon) by the Lord Treasurer (Burleigh) and the Lord Keeper (Puckering) that he must never more look to her for favour or promotion.

Though the progress of the Bill was stayed, a compromise was effected (for all were agreed that the fleets must be manned and the new levies armed) on Raleigh's suggestion that the House should confer with the Lords on the peril to the realm and then decide about the money-vote. "Listen to what the Government have to say," said he, "about the Papal Bull and the Spanish fleet. When you have saved the point of form, vote the money-bill as you list."

The point of privilege being no longer in the way, the question came up again before the Commons, and was again referred to the Committees upon which Francis Bacon—who had not been heard in the interim—comes once more upon the stage. Though he had been threatened with the Queen's wrath he was neither cowed nor penitent. It was not the amount (which he approved) but *the time allowed* . . . which was indeed the essential point. Cecil wanted the three subsidies to be paid in three years; Francis Bacon in six years, or two shillings in the pound per year instead of four. He believed the people could not afford to pay such an impost and that it would press heavily on the industrious poor. This is a précis of the speech according to D'Ewes *Journal*, 1593:

> To the subsidy demanded he propounded three questions which he desired might be answered while assenting to three subsidies but not to payment under six years.
>
> 1. Impossibility or difficulty.
> 2. Danger and discontentment.
> 3. A better manner of supply.
>
> For impossibility the poor man's rent is such as they are not able to yield it. The gentlemen must sell their plate, and farmers their brass pots, ere this be paid; and as for us, *we are here to search the wounds of the realm and not to skin them over.*
>
> We shall breed discontentment in paying these subsidies, and endanger Her Majesty's safety, which must consist more in *the Love of her People than in their Wealth.*
>
> This being granted, other Princes hereafter will look for the like; so that we shall put an *ill precedent upon ourselves and to our posterity.* In histories it is to be observed that of all nations the English care not to be subject, base, taxable. . . .
>
> The manner of supply may be by levy or imposition when need shall most require. So when Her Majesty's coffers are empty they may be imbursed by these means.

Apparently there was a pretty vigorous discussion on Francis Bacon's continued opposition to the Court, and Hepworth Dixon commenting on the final decision says, *Life*, p. 68:

> Against the warmth of Raleigh and the wiles of Cecil he compelled the Government to meet his proposal halfway, to extend the period proposed for the raising of these taxes a year (in other words, to take three shillings in the pound each year in place of four), and to insert a clause in the bill declaring that the money was given solely for the war against Spain.

We learn a good deal from the circumstances leading up to this drama in the House of Commons. It gives us a true insight into Francis Bacon's character. Within the first week of the Session we see that though he was a blue-blood aristocrat by breed he was a democrat at heart . . . living mentally quite apart from the sphere of the hereditary ruling class and the bureaucracy. His further speech and actions show that he was essentially a liberal reformer of broad outlook and far-reaching vision. The line he took was not to please the populace or to curry favour with the electors of Middlesex. As a matter of fact the proceedings of the Commons were regarded as private, and "a member had no more right to publish abroad what had passed than a Privy Councillor to divulge the secrets of the Council Table."

It was not the captious opposition of a rabid partisan anxious to popularize himself within the House and to gain cheap notoriety outside it by being "agin the Gover'ment." No! Francis Bacon we now know spoke quite honestly according to his convictions. He believed that the liberty of the Commons was about to be undermined, and that to forbid debate was the thin edge of the wedge of a political tyranny that might split the nation. He knew, moreover, that the weapon of power—the purse—would be certain to slip from their hands if they once allowed the Peers to finger it. How could he—as a man with as wide and deep a knowledge of ancient and modern law as anyone—possibly allow the contention to pass in default of protest that the Crown had the right to call a Parliament together for the sole purpose of voting supplies. Had he remained silent out of a selfish deference to his own personal advantage he would have been a recreant to all those lofty principles of moral rectitude which he was then trying to establish quietly among his fellows . . . to the State's welfare in general and the Queen in particular. And even when he knew that the displeasure of the Queen against him was intense, he still felt it was his duty to protest against what he considered was a dictatorial encroachment on the liberty of the subject. Although he knew he was running a perilous course he persisted because he felt it was his duty. Says Campbell, p. 22:

> He was so intoxicated with the success of his first effort, that a few days later in the debate on the 7th March on the subsidy, he delivered a flaming oration against the Court, *running great risk of being sent to the Tower and punished by the Star Chamber for his presumption.*

We now know that Francis Bacon was not intoxicated but very sober-minded indeed, for he knew better than Campbell could possibly know the dangers he was running. We know what Spedding, Montague, Dixon never knew: *that Francis Bacon was jeopardizing the only source of income he possessed*—his allowance from his mother the Queen—in his attempt to preserve, through an uncontaminated free Parliament, the liberties of England, which he held were of far greater importance than his own personal welfare even if it landed him, first in the Fleet and then in the gutter. He would at all events have saved his soul alive.

Thus in the first great crisis of his public life Francis Bacon kept faith with his own idealism—"to thine own self be true." He fought the fight and he won. There were gains and losses. The losses were private and personal. The gains were for his countrymen, for England, for posterity. These were the gains:

1. Freedom of speech in Parliament without Lordly dictation.
2. The right of the Commons to decide alone the amount of supply voted to the Crown annually and its duration.
3. The scotching for all time of the attempt that the Government could call a Parliament exclusively to vote money-grants and thus abrogate Parliament's inherent right to make new laws or amend old ones.

It was the upholding of these principles that led to the breach between the Crown and the Parliament in the Stuart Era but it first crystallized in the 1593 debate when Francis Bacon took upon himself the role of a

Reformer—at least in Law—and upheld the Democratic ideal against the cult of bureaucratic Dictatorship.

While the French have to thank him for the Code Napoléon (which arose out of this debate) the entire world is in his debt in championing the cause of Freedom in the Mother of Parliaments.

Referring to Francis Bacon's actions, Lord Campbell closes his account of the sittings by saying, *Life*, p. 21:

> *We know that he was ever after the most favoured speaker in the Assembly.*

This was the reason why Francis Bacon obtained an ascendancy over the House of Commons that he never lost during his thirty years association with that Chamber. It was won not on account of his oratorical gifts—and he was probably the greatest orator of the day—but because every member of the House knew that he was a sturdy Englishman, honest and sincere as the day. And *few, if any, in that House would know of the personal loss he was risking in acting according to the dictates of his conscience.*

> To what extent, however, England was saved by the gallant fight made by Francis for the privileges of the House of Commons we do not know, nor whether, apart from the protest which Francis made, the people of England would have quietly acquiesced in the collection from them of a treble subsidy in one year. (Woodward, *Early Life*, p. 63.)

The young reformer had carried his point at the cost of incurring the intense displeasure of the Queen, Lord Treasurer Burleigh, and Lord Keeper Puckering. He had done it with his eyes wide open to his personal interests. He soon found out the price he had to pay for venturing to lead the House in opposition to the Queen's Will. For many months he was denied the Court. The Queen would not see him. He was in disgrace, and this carried with it definite personal as well as social disabilities as we shall see.

When Burleigh and Puckering had first threatened him with the Queen's anger, he had tried to put the matter right by explanations. He denied that he had done wrong. If his words had been misunderstood he would explain them, but he said he must hold fast to the truth as he understood it. If Her Majesty were angry he was very grieved: if she commanded him to silence, he must obey; but in thwarting the invasion of popular rights by the Peers he had only done his duty to his country and the Queen.

The tenor of these letters has been twisted by detractors like Macaulay into "an abject apology" of a "whining young barrister," so that the average scholar has quite an erroneous idea of their purport. The letters show that he wrote as an honest man, anxious to avoid misunderstanding by explaining his motives. It was not an "apology" but a defence and a justification. Here is the letter to Burleigh which must have been written about the 8th March, 1593:

Francis Bacon to the Lord Treasurer
Touching His Speech in Parliament.

> It may please your Lordship, I was sorry to find by your Lordship's speech yesterday that my last speech in Parliament, delivered *in the discharge of my conscience and duty* to God, Her Majesty, and my country was offensive.

If it were misreported, I would be glad to attend your Lordship to disavow anything I said not. If it were misconstrued I would be glad to expound my words, to exclude any sense I meant not. If my heart be misjudged by imputation of popularity or opposition by any envious or officious informer, I have great wrong; and the greater, because the manner of my speech did most evidently show that I spake simply and only *to satisfy my conscience*, and not with any advantage or policy to sway the cause; and my terms carried all significance of duty and zeal towards Her Majesty and her service.

It is true that from the beginning, whatsoever was above a double subsidy, I did wish might, for precedent's sake, appear to be extraordinary, and, for discontent's sake, mought not have been levied upon the poorer sort; though otherwise I wished it as rising as I think this will prove, and more.

This was my mind, I confess it.

And therefore I most humbly pray to your Lordship, first to continue me in your own good opinion: and then to perform the part of an honest friend towards your poor servant and ally, in drawing Her Majesty to accept of the sincerity and simplicity of my zeal, and to hold me to Her Majesty's favour which is to me dearer than my life. Fr. Bacon.

Commenting on this letter, Spedding says:

This being a justification and not an apology was far from satisfying the Queen. Bacon, whom *she had hitherto distinguished by unusual freedom of access*, was now forbidden to come into her presence. . . . The road in which he had been hitherto encouraged to look for fortune *seemed to be closed for ever.* At the same time his means were running very low. He had heavy debts . . . importunate creditors. . . . Some course must be thought of at once either for increasing income or reducing expenditure. (Vol. I, p. 234.)

In a futile effort to try to get the Queen to understand that he had acted honestly according to his conscience for the welfare of the State and the Queen herself, Francis wrote to Lord Keeper Puckering who was exceedingly angry at the rising orator.

Copie of a letter to the Lord Keeper Puckering concerning the writer's speech in Parliament which had disgusted the Queen.

My Lord,

It is a great grief to me, joined with marvel, that Her Majesty should retain an hard conceit of my speeches in Parliament. It mought please her sacred Majesty to think what my end should be in those speeches, *if it were not duty and duty alone.*

I am not so simple but I know the common beaten way to please. And whereas popularity hath been objected, I muse what care should I take to please many, that *taketh a course of life to deal with few.*

On the other side, *Her Majesty's grace and particular favour towards* me hath been such, as I esteem no worldly thing above the comfort to enjoy it, except it be the conscience to deserve it. But if the not seconding of some particular person's opinion shall be presumption, and to differ upon the manner shall be to impeach the end, it shall teach my devotion not to exceed wishes, and those in silence.

Yet notwithstanding—to speak vainly as in grief—it may be *Her Majesty hath discouraged as good a heart as ever looked towards her service, and as void of self-love.*

And so in more grief than I can well express, and more than I can well dissemble, I leave your Lordship, being as ever, your Lordship's entirely devoted. . . .

This letter apparently had no effect of restoring Francis to the Queen's favour, so a little later he wrote to the Queen:

To the Queen

Madam,

Remembering that your Majesty had been gracious to me both in countenancing me and conferring upon me the reversion of a good place, and perceiving your Majesty hath taken some displeasure towards me, both these were arguments *to move me to offer unto your Majesty my service*, to the end to have means to deserve your benefit and to repair my error.

Upon this ground I affected myself to no great matter, but only a place of my Profession, such as I do see divers younger in proceeding to myself, and men of no great note, do without blame aspire to. But if any of my friends do press this matter, I do assure your Majesty my spirit is not with them. It sufficeth that I have let your Majesty know that I am ready to do that for your service which I would never do for mine own gain. And if your Majesty like others better, I shall with the Lacedemonians be glad that there is such choice of abler men than myself.

Your Majesty's favour indeed, and access to your royal person, I did ever, encouraged by your own speeches, seek and desire; and I would be very glad to be reintegrate in that. But I will not wrong my own good mind so much as to stand upon it now, when your Majesty must conceive I do it but to make my profit of it.

But my mind turns upon other wheels than those of profit.

The conclusion shall be that I wish your Majesty served answerable to yourself. . . . Thus I humbly crave pardon of my boldness and plainness. God preserve your Majesty.

He wrote to the Queen again. He wrote to the Queen's Favourite, the Earl of Essex, to Sir Robert Cecil, all of which seems to indicate that he was far more concerned with getting on the old familiar terms with the Queen than obtaining a position. But Elizabeth was not to be mollified by the writing of a letter or by protestations to her Ministers which seemed to be a justification of what he had done. Indeed, in the remainder of the Session there were many other businesses discussed about which he did not hesitate to take part. In a "*Speech on the Second Reading of a Bill for the better Expedition of Justice in the Star Chamber*" (20th March), a fortnight after his "*Double Subsidy Speech*," he struck an almost defiant note with the first sentence he uttered: "*Neither profit nor peril shall move me to speak against my conscience in this place.*"

This open utterance shows clearly that Francis Bacon's letter[1] to Burleigh was never meant to be taken as an apology but the very reverse. He thus let the Government know that he was neither to be intimidated nor gagged into silence.

The mere reading of these letters and others make it obvious that Francis Bacon was far other than he appears to be in the bald pages of history and reconstituted biography, based on only a portion of the facts

[1]This private letter to Burleigh was not known to the world for years after all the principal actors had passed away.

and winnowed documents. What other young man would have had the effrontery to have written Burleigh, Puckering, and even the Queen . . . and to have left copies of his letters so that their significance could be ascertained by "after-times"? They point to the fact that the young genius had a real claim on Elizabeth, that her Ministers knew of the secret bond between them, and events that follow in subsequent years strengthen the evidence of their concealed relationship.

Spedding, with no knowledge of the real truth, says, as we have seen, that the Queen persistently refused to see Francis, and that "*at the same time* his means were running very low . . . heavy debts . . . importunate creditors . . . he must obtain an increasing income." Strangely enough neither Spedding nor subsequent academics saw *the definite connection between the Queen's displeasure and Francis Bacon's loss of income.* Why were his means running very low? Why was he in debt? Where had his income hitherto come from? What was its source? These vital questions Spedding never faced and answered. He leaves the question of his income a bigger mystery than ever, for he has said (as already pointed out) that in Francis Bacon's thirty-first year (1592) "*I do not find he was getting into practice.*" He could have said the same with equal truth in 1593 for when Parliament sat he was still an out-of-work lawyer with his first case still to plead in Court, his first client had yet to enter his Chambers for advice. Everything points the truth: That his income hitherto had been provided by the Queen, and that Elizabeth, incensed at her son's conduct in attempting to stop her war supplies, and to limit her prerogative, simply retorted by ruthlessly stopping his allowance. She was just the self-willed, passionate type of woman to say:

> *This young half-bastard of mine has had the impertinence to attempt to stop my Supplies from Parliament: I will stop his Supplies and see how he likes it.*

He was not only cut off from all the social intercourse of Court life but made to feel the pinch financially. He had mortgaged and spent his income in advance to spread secretly the English Renaissance. His debts had been incurred through writing, printing, publishing, and the expenses of his staff of "pens" housed at his scrivenery at Twickenham Park. The cessation of his allowance plunged him into considerable embarrassment for he had no money . . . hence his continued anxiety to be on the same friendly terms with his mother, to be allowed to see her.

We know that almost immediately after his speeches in the Commons he was considerably involved, because there is evidence that he had to borrow large amounts from various sources and even small amounts from Anthony Bacon. He grew so desperate for ready money that even Robert Cecil and Thomas Cecil urged their father Lord Burleigh to do something for Francis (Woodward, *Early Life*, p. 64). He had already mortgaged his Star Chamber Reversion and could not pay the half-year's interest. To ease the situation Anthony Bacon, with the consent of Lady Anne who had a life interest, realized an estate at Markes, turning the money over to Francis, Lady Anne grumbling that the difficulties of Francis were due to him *keeping a lot of men who were wasting his money.* Woodward adds:

In July Anthony and Francis negotiated the sale of another estate belonging to Anthony . . . to Alderman Sir John Spencer of Crosby Hall.

The natural result of all this worry was that Francis fell ill at Twickenham, but there was no relenting on the part of the Queen. To belittle her prerogative in the slightest was the unpardonable and unforgivable sin. Says Spedding:

> To be spending much and *earning nothing* . . . what was this but practice in the fatal art of sleeping on a debtor's pillow? . . . He is to be blamed for not putting an end to it at once, at whatever sacrifice.
>
> *It would almost seem that this was the condition in which the Queen WISHED to keep him* . . . How great was the injury she was thereby doing him. (p. 243.)

It is clear that some sort of a salaried appointment was necessary to save the situation and there is no doubt that the Earl of Essex was anxious to procure him a State appointment to hold while pursuing his literary schemes. And it is around about this time that Francis Bacon's association with Essex becomes publicly known. Anthony had become the servant of Essex, helping him in his dealings with Foreign Affairs, and incidentally we learn that Francis was assisting as adviser and decipherer of code reports from the Continent, drafting letters and acting, in a sense, as an unofficial under-Foreign Secretary, but for this he received no pay, Essex having undertaken to do his best to see Francis restored to the Queen's good graces.

"Spending much . . . earning nothing," says Spedding. It is easy to say that "he was to blame for not putting an end to it at once," but . . . *How could he?* All his secret plans were threatening to dissolve into thin air. How could he dismiss his writers and close Twickenham without destroying his dream of *The Great Instauration?* It was a sacrifice too great to be contemplated. It was the future of England that was at stake . . . the Renaissance of Learning and Ethics that was destined ultimately to save the world. So thought Francis Bacon; and though he was in a parlous condition—the condition in which the Queen sought to keep him—he trusted to weather the storm by expedient borrowings and so keep the movements he had created and started going, until she relented. Surely his own mother could not keep her face turned from him for ever! And so he borrowed and borrowed, a habit that almost became chronic and which resulted in him being thrown into a debtor's prison . . . from which he was rescued by Anthony. "*They were the claims of the Jews who lent money on hopes deferred,*" says Church, *Life*, p. 44. In this incident one may find an echo in the *Merchant of Venice,* even the very personalities, the generous Antonio and the Jew who must have the penalty of the bond.

It can safely be stated that the relations between Francis and the Queen were not really improved until the Autumn of 1595, though it is very probable that, after keeping him without his allowance for several months, she relented sufficiently to assist him again. There is evidence sufficient to show that the Queen and Burleigh both knew of Francis Bacon's plans for the Advancement of Learning and approved of them. She did not want them abandoned; but she was fully determined to teach her Francis

PLATE XXII

Left: Sir Fulke Greville, later Lord Brooke, Francis Bacon's friend
Lord Brooke repeated to the Queen that he had said Francis Bacon "remained as a withered branch of her roots which she had cherished and made to flourish in her services". *(See p. 213)*

Right: Lord Burleigh, Queen Elizabeth's Secretary of State and Francis Bacon's nominal uncle
(See Appendix I)

Plate XXIII
Queen Elizabeth in her prime
(from a painting by Zucchero at Hatfield House)
(See Appendix I)

a lesson and that he must no longer rely on her for his maintenance. Her actions throughout are those of a mother, loving, proud and passionate, more than a Queen devoid of personal interest.

In January 1594 Francis was still out of favour with the Queen. Apparently his allowance was still in abeyance, and, as he had not been appointed to any office, he was compelled to turn his attention to pleading in the Law Courts. He took his first case through on the 25th January for the heir of Lord Cheyney. He did so well that Lord Burleigh congratulated him on "*the first fruits of his public practice.*" He also asked for a note of his "case and the chief points of his pleadings to the end *he might make report thereof where it might do him most good.*" This meant the Queen. If Francis were nothing to her, why should Burleigh think she was still interested in him? The conclusion is obvious. Burleigh knew that her maternal pride in him was quite as strong as Queenly pride of her prerogative.

On the 5th and 9th February he appeared in two other cases. Mr. Harry Gosnold, a young lawyer of Gray's Inn, who heard him, has left a report.

> That Francis Bacon retains his reputation gained, is not strange to any that knows him. That he hath increased it, is not incredible. The absence of the Lords that were looked for was recompensed with a presence of learned Judges, and seemed an Assembly rather capable than honourable.
>
> *The respect they gave him was extraordinary*, was well-noted but not envied. The attention of the rest, springing from an experience of good and an expectation of better, could not be better. His argument, contracted by the time, seemed a *bataille serrée*, as hard to be discovered as conquered.
>
> *The unusual words wherewith he had spangled his speech*, were rather gracious for their propriety than strange for their novelty, and like to serve both for occasions to report and means to remember his argument. Certain sentences of his, somewhat obscure, and as it were presuming upon their capacities will, I fear, make some of them rather admire than commend him.
>
> In sum, all is as well as words can make it, and if it please Her Majesty to add deeds, the Bacon may be too hard for the Cook. (Coke.)[1]

"A letter from a Nicholas Faunt also speaks of this pleading as having obtained general applause," says Spedding.

Does it not strike one as strange that a young barrister of thirty-three taking his first case through the courts should be treated with such extraordinary respect? A curious commencement! "It rather indicates the sort of interest which might be taken were the Prince of Wales to be known to be making his first public speech," says Woodward. And does not "the unusual words" he employed indicate one of the leading characteristics of the Shakespeare Plays . . . new words that were being coined to give Englishmen a flexible vocabulary? The same literary trait is to be seen in Francis Bacon's prose works.

On the 19th April, 1594, Francis went down to Greenwich where the Court was being held hoping the Queen would see him. She would not permit him to enter the Court. He returned to London and was again

[1]This was a reference to Coke, a play on the word. The Queen had the Office of Attorney-General to fill and it was a matter of speculation in the Inns of Court, Coke, the then Solicitor-General, or Francis Bacon.

engaged in the Courts for a time. By August, however, the Queen was showing signs of relenting. In that month we find him at work examining prisoners in the Tower suspected of plotting against the life of the Queen, *his work being under her direct command.* His call to the work is acknowledged by a letter to her Majesty, 20th July:

> Most Gracious and Admirable Sovereign, As I do acknowledge a Providence of God towards me . . . so the present arrest of me by his Divine Majesty from your Majesty's service . . . is not the least I have proved. And I hope your Majesty doth conceive that nothing under mere impossibility could have detained me from earning so gracious a vail (submission) as it hath pleased your Majesty to give me. *Your Majesty's service shall take no lack thereby.* . . . I recommend your Sacred Majesty to God's tenderest preservation. Fr. Bacon.

But up to the end of the year he was still denied the Court, still denied any allowance, still denied an Office (Coke had been made Attorney-General and the Solicitorship was vacant as a consequence), still borrowing money from Anthony who managed to raise for him £150 in the Autumn. But on 25th January, 1595, he was sent for to the Court though he was not seen by the Queen. Perhaps she was slowly becoming mollified, and thus indicating that she was meditating taking him back into her favour, because of the very wonderful Masques and Plays, *for which he was directly responsible*, which had been given at Gray's Inn in the December and January Revels in which high compliments were paid to the Queen. Of the entertainment Spedding says:

> Thus ended one of the most elegant Christmas entertainments, probably, that was ever presented to an audience of Statesmen and courtiers. The speeches of the Six Councellors were written by him and by him alone. . . . They speak with Bacon's tongue and Bacon's brain. . . . We can measure the progress of his philosophical speculations in these early years . . . *Gesta Grayorum, or the History of the high and mighty Prince of Purpoole* (*Purple*) *who Reigned and Died* 1594.

And, as already mentioned, the dancing and revels were concluded with "a *Comedy of Errors*" which "was played by the players" and which was "*Shakespeare's Play* as I suppose it was." (Spedding, p. 327.) We can judge the profound significance of this admission by an orthodox authority who believed that "Shake-speare" and Francis Bacon were two different persons. Under Spedding's own hand they are brought together under the roof of Gray's Inn, *but the play was never produced to the law-students as "Shakespeare's" but as Francis Bacon's.* When it was eventually printed he put his pen-name to it, "Shakespeare."

Francis was overjoyed at being sent for to Court, even though he did not see the Queen and from a long graphic account he wrote Anthony Bacon of what passed, it appears as though he had received some financial assistance:

> Though sent for I saw not the Queen. Her Majesty alleged she was resolved with her Counsel upon her places of Law. [Francis was then hopeful of being appointed Solicitor-General, an Office then vacant . . .]
>
> The Queen seemeth to apprehend my travel; whereupon I was sent for

by Sir Robert Cecil in sort as from her Majesty. [Francis had written the Earl of Essex that he would go away and give up all thoughts of law and devote himself to studies of greater delight.] I came to the Court upon his relation of her Majesty's speech. . . .

The Queen's speech is after this sort. Why? I have made no Solicitor. Hath anybody carried a Solicitor with him in his pocket? But *he must have it in his own time or else I must be thought to cast him away.* Then her Majesty sweareth that if I continue in this manner [i.e., threaten to leave the Law and retire into the country with a couple of men to aid him in his literary work] she will seek all England for a Solicitor rather than take me. Yes, she will send for Houghton and Coventry to-morrow—as if she would swear them both.

Again she entereth into it, that *she hath never dealt with any as with me* (*in hoc erratum non est*)*; she hath pulled me over the bar* [note the words for they cannot but be her own] she hath used me in her greatest causes. . . . She is now more angry with Essex than with me.

I must now be more careful of my credit than ever, *since I receive so little thence where I deserve the best.* And to be plain with you, I mean even *to make the best of those small things I have,* with as much expedition as may be without loss and so *sing a requiem I hope abroad.*

I have here an idle pen or two . . . thinking to have got some money this term. I pray send me somewhat else for them to write out besides your Irish Collection which is almost done. There is a collection of Dr. James. . . . I would like to have it. . . . From my Lodge at Twickenham Park, this 25th January, 1595. Fr. Bacon.

Does not this letter make it self-evident that there is a secret blood-link between the Queen and Francis? If she were not his mother what would it have mattered if she had cast Francis away? Why need the Queen make excuses for herself at all? She had never dealt with anyone as she had with Francis because he had a blood-claim upon her if not a legitimate one. And if the word "BAR," that Francis Bacon specially calls attention to, is a contraction for the "Bar-Sinister" of heraldry, then there is nothing more to be said. His connection with her is admitted. For the "Bar-Sinister" is a direct reference to illegitimacy . . . to his quasi-illegitimacy. What else the "Bar" can mean I do not know, and no one has yet attempted to explain it. It certainly is not used to symbolize the "bar" of a court, of a tavern, a toll bar, etc. But the Queen did use it to denote "a hindrance or obstruction" in a figurative sense that threatened to militate against his advancement. There is no error in the use of this particular word "Bar." "*I have pulled him over the Bar-Sinister.*" In other words she had stood by her "natural child" Francis, had done her best for him, giving him a splendid education, having him reared in a fine family, a wonderful environment, sending him abroad on his travels, made him a Member of Parliament, giving him the use of a beautiful estate, an allowance, permitting him to pursue his literary and philosophic avocations, *doing all she could to take the sting out of his concealed royal birth.*

What more could a mother do under the circumstances? She had pulled him over all social barriers, and if he did not bear the name he was entitled to, he bore a greatly honoured name, and had set his feet in a profession in which he might play a worthy part in the Commonwealth. And if she had not yet appointed him as an Officer of the Crown perhaps it was because she had something better in view for him. Francis must leave it to her. She must not be forced. She must decide in her own way, at her own time, what must be done. That was undoubtedly Elizabeth's attitude towards Francis Bacon. "Pulling him over the Bar" is only capable of one explanation. *It was the "Bar-Sinister" of his birth.*

The attitude of Francis is that he "*has received so little when he deserved the best.*" Though the Queen had provided for him in every way it was actually "little" compared with what he would have possessed as an acknowledged Prince and heir to the Kingdom. . . . Twickenham Park estate instead of ruling over the broad domains of a Kingdom but he will make the best *of the small things* he has. . . . *He "will sing a Requiem"* over the loss of his Kingly Heritage; he will sing it "abroad" . . . to Foreign Nations. And it must be remembered that the men who make music of words are "POETS."

How else are these significant innuendoes to be interpreted?

Note that he has men working for him at literary work, that in spite of his cash-shortage he still lives at Twickenham Park, that he still published nothing under his own name, and that at Stationers' Hall text books of many kinds are being entered and published. There lies the secret of Francis Bacon's "Silent Years" of unexplained "lethargy."

A little later the Queen hearing that Francis Bacon intended to go abroad if possible (he could not have gone without a licence from her) expressed her annoyance. On hearing this Francis apologized to her in a letter to Sir Robert Cecil:

> Please deliver to her Majesty that it is an exceeding grief to me that any motion or mention should come from me to offend her Majesty. . . . I hoped her Majesty would not be offended if not being able to endure the Sun I fled into the shade. . . .
>
> The conclusion shall be that wheresoever God and *her Majesty shall appoint me to live,* I shall truly pray for her Majesty's preservation and felicity.

On the 21st March he writes to Burleigh, referring to the vacant office of Solicitor-General still unfilled:

> that however this matter may go, *yet I may enjoy your Lordship's good favour and help, as I have* done in regard to my private estate which, as I have not altogether neglected, so I have but negligently attended and *which hath been bettered only by yourself—the Queen except—and not by any other in matters of importance.*
>
> The last request I find it more necessary for me to make, because—though *I am glad of her Majesty's FAVOUR* that *I may with more ease practise the law,* which, percase, I may use *now and then for my countenance*—yet to speak, though perhaps vainly, *I do not think that the ordinary practice of the law, not serving the Queen in place, will be admitted* for a good account of the poor talent which God hath given me.
>
> Thus desiring a continuance of your Lordship's goodness as I have hitherto found, and on my part sought also to deserve, etc. From Gray's Inn.

If this proves anything at all it proves that the Queen and Burleigh were his mainstays financially and that other borrowings from nominal relatives were temporary loans only.

He begins by saying he enjoys Burleigh's "Favour and HELP." He ends in desiring him to continue his "Goodness." Francis says that his affairs have only been "Bettered *by Burleigh and the Queen* and not by any other *in Matters of Importance*," by which he undoubtedly means matters financial. Moreover, the Queen must have come to his rescue in his money matters for he says that the "FAVOUR" she has done will help him only to practise sufficient law now and then to maintain appearances . . . to save his face. It tells the tale plainly that the Queen through her Minister was assisting him financially, and that this would allow him to please himself; for he did not desire to waste his time in legal actions as his talents lay in other directions. *He had no wish to follow the practice of a lawyer except in so far as it might be necessary to serve the Queen on occasions.* The fact that he did not want to follow the law is emphasized in other letters of much later date, notably one to Essex in which he alludes to his "*intention not to follow the practice of the Law.*" He continues:

> If Her Majesty command me in any particular, I shall be ready to do her willing service and my reason is only because it drinketh too much time which *I have dedicated to better purposes.*"

All this is compatible with the filial love of a concealed son anxious to do his duty by his mother and Queen.

"In June Fulke Greville repeated to the Queen that Francis had said that he (Francis) 'remained as *a withered branch of her roots which she had cherished* and made to flourish in her service'." Woodward, *Sir Francis Bacon,* p. 65.

What does this statement mean but that he had claimed the Queen as his mother? That he was flesh of her flesh and bone of her bone? That he had sprung from her loins? And that she had not neglected him but had maintained him, cherished him, and had advanced him so that he flourished? *A branch of her roots*, but a withered branch, for was he not lopped off from the parent stem and artificially grafted into another family? And Fulke Greville repeats this significant image and innuendo to the Queen herself as a secret of State. It reminds one of the prophecy in *Cymbeline* respecting "a Lion's Whelp" and a "withered branch" which being dead many years shall after revive, be jointed to the old stock, and freshly grow . . . causing Posthumous to end his miseries.

There is a similar phrase of significance in a letter he wrote to Lord Keeper Puckering on the 19th August. Puckering was offended by a letter Francis had previously written him (so he had learned from Essex) and he seeks to put it right.

> I only hoped your Lordship would do me no wrong which hope I do still continue.
>
> For if it please your Lordship but to call to mind *FROM WHOM I AM DESCENDED, and BY WHOM, next to God, HER MAJESTY.* . . . I know you will have a compunction of mind to do me any wrong.

Here is a High Officer of the Crown who knows the truth as a State Secret if anybody does. And Francis Bacon reminds him that he knows he is a Tudor though he goes by another name. He is descended from Queen Elizabeth. No other reading is possible.

In September he sends the Lord Keeper another letter from which we learn that, although not appointed to any formal Office, he is being employed as Counsel for the Queen in a number of legal matters.

On the 28th July, Francis Bacon wrote to Burleigh that if the Queen settled her choice for Solicitor-General upon an able man such as Serjeant Fleming, he would not seek to alter it.

On the 11th October he writes Lord Keeper Puckering respecting the Office which the Queen had not yet filled. "As I have heard nothing so I look for nothing. . . . But I assure you *I take no further Care for the matter.*" He continues:

> I am now at Twickenham Park, where I think to stay; for Her Majesty placing a Solicitor, my travel will not be needed in her causes; though whensoever Her Majesty shall like to employ me in any particular, I shall be ready to do her willing service.

Three days later he writes the Lord Keeper again, apparently having heard that the Office was to be definitely filled by someone else. The Lord Keeper was the Officer nominally responsible but the choice was the Queen's. He writes to Puckering as though to say "It is quite all right for me." This is what he says:

> I conceive the end already made, which I trust will be a beginning of good fortune, or at least of content. Her Majesty by God's grace shall live and reign long. *She is not running away* [*from me*]. *I may trust her* [*to do the right thing*].
>
> Whether *she look towards me or not, I remain the same*, not altered in my intentions [to pursue my literary and philosophic ideals]. If I had been an ambitious man, it would have overthrown me. But minded as I am, *revertet benedictio in sinum meum.* From Twickenham Park, etc.

From this letter it is again quite clear that Francis Bacon's whole outlook was towards other pursuits than law. It is evident too, that he never wanted to follow the law. His ambition was set on higher things. He only wanted an Office of State to make him financially independent, to give full reign to the passion of "Philanthropia" that was a consuming fire in his very bones. Everything points to the fact that he had seen the Queen (probably he knew the position from her own lips for he had only to row across the river at Twickenham to be on the doorstep of her Palace) and that she had assured him of her continued financial support. Anyway, this letter is a firm letter of confidence in the goodness of the Queen. He is far from being overthrown by missing the Solicitorship but rather happy about it, for he is not ambitious for material advancement so long as he can pursue his own intellectual way. He can even return praise for the way things have happened. One can almost detect a note of pride in his Tudor mother for what she has done and is doing for him, allowing him to pursue his own intellectual courses.

It is usually asserted that Francis Bacon was ambitious for a legal career. The facts do not bear out such a view. He was only ambitious for one thing—the advancement of Learning in the widest sense of the word, literary, scientific, ethical, etc. He knew that Knowledge was Power and that Ignorance was the curse of God, so he tried to light candles in an era of darkness that Man might see the way to his true destiny . . . the conquering of Nature. He only wanted a State Office because these things could not be done without money and the leisure that money brings. The moment he was once more assured of the Queen's support and her allowance he was indifferent about following the practice of the Law. *His mind turned on other wheels than those of profit.* And this thought he repeated in many other ways.

The Queen on 5th November, 1595, appointed Serjeant Fleming to be her Solicitor-General, and the singular thing is, as Spedding admits (p. 369) that this "was the end of her long displeasure," which began in March 1593. We have seen, too, that Francis was in high feather.

A few days later we find that he has written for the Queen's Accession Day, 17th November, a very wonderful Device or Playlet for presentation to Elizabeth. It was called "*The Device of the Indian Prince.*" It took pride of place in the ceremonies at Westminster and was sponsored by the Earl of Essex. There were pretty speeches to the Queen——

> One dressed like an Heremite or Philosopher, representing Contemplation; the second a Captain, representing Fame; the third like a Counsellor of Estate, representing Experience.

Elizabeth is called "THE ALONE QUEEN" as the Virgin Queen, and the writer of the Device says he is inspired by "PALLAS." Francis thus lets it be known where he got his pen-name of "Shake-speare." Though we have but fragments of the Device we have sufficient to show us some splendid Baconian writing and some very pretty and noble compliments paid the Queen.

> The Gardens of the Muses keep the privilege of the Golden Age; they ever flourish and are in league with time.
>
> The Monuments of Wit survive the Monuments of Power: the Verses of a Poet endure without a syllable lost, while States and Empires pass many periods.

We learn from contemporaries that the Device was a great success.

The reconciliation of the Queen with her son Francis Bacon was complete.

Hepworth Dixon never suspected that Queen Elizabeth was Francis Bacon's mother. He was a first-hand researcher among the documents and the history of the Elizabethan Era so his conclusions respecting the "ins and outs" of conflicting personalities are valuable. It never struck him to inquire from whom Francis Bacon derived his income or the true reason why he was never appointed by Elizabeth to a State Office, but he knew that the Queen was lavish in her gifts to Francis though the reason he never suspected (1) that he was her natural son and (2) that she wanted him to go on with his great work of the educational renaissance of England; and he was certain that the Solicitor-Generalship was given to Fleming not through any personal animus. In the *Personal Story* he says, p. 66:

> There are writers who denounce the stinginess of a woman *to whose noble and unfailing friendship he owed almost everything which he possessed on earth.* . . .

Inquiry at the Rolls Office would have shown them that, even while she was naming Fleming for her Solicitor-General, *Elizabeth was Francis Bacon's most warm and munificent friend.*

She long ago gave him a reversion of the Registry of the Star Chamber; a post, when he should get it, worth £1,600 a year.

The reversion of the Star Chamber, the grant of Zelwood Forest—with which she enriched him, the post of her Counsel learned in Law—recently given him *ARE BUT A FORETASTE OF HER LOVE.* The lease of Twickenham Park had just expired . . . a lovely home by the water edge. The house had an importance beyond the beauty of its site; a merit rarer than the green mead, the leafy wood, the rushing stream, the whitening swans; it stood all day in the Sovereign's sight. The house was good, the park spacious, and within the pales are eighty-seven acres of lawn and pasture, lake and orchard; beyond the pales five or six acres of mead and field. *IT IS A HOME FOR A PRINCE.*

"On passing to Fleming the patent of his Office, the gracious Queen makes over to Francis Bacon a reversion of the lease; on the 17th November, the day of his Masque at York House, Francis Bacon's grant of Twickenham Park passed under the privy seal.

The Home fit for "A Prince" that Francis had already occupied for so many years by the pleasure of the Queen, was made over to him by legal right of tenure from which he could not be dispossessed.

If these solid facts do not tell the secret truth of Francis Bacon's real relationship to Queen Elizabeth then are we the victims of a delusion that takes away from us the ability to weigh evidence correctly. It is cumulative in value, for it does not depend on one solitary phrase used by one person. There are similar hints dropped by Fulke Greville at one time and by Lady Bacon at others. The phrase she used in 1593 when she speaks of Francis to Anthony has never been explained. . . . "He was his father's first Chi . . ." Spedding says "The word is so close to the edge of the paper that I cannot make it out. It looks like *Chis.*" As a matter of fact the word is "chil." He interprets the blurred "s" to mean "Choice," which is manifestly absurd. He certainly was not Sir Nicholas Bacon's first "Choice." He never left Francis any money. On the other hand it could be truthfully said that "Francis was his father's FIRST CHILD" if Leicester were his father, for he was the eldest of the family . . . the fruit of Elizabeth's morganatic marriage.

Francis Bacon's attitude in the 1593 Parliament I have dealt with at some length because of the implications involved, such as his royal birth, the princely house at Twickenham provided for him by the Queen, the source of his income, the reason for his extraordinary debts when every biographer admits that he had no personal extravagances; but, above all, I consider it essential to a proper understanding of Francis Bacon's character that the student should be made acquainted with the circumstances surrounding his stand for freedom of Parliamentary speech and the right of the Commons to vote the amount of Supply without any interference by the Peers or the Crown.

How much we owe as a nation to his firmness we do not know, but the principles he espoused, royal aristocrat though he was, are now regarded as democratic fundamentals of the British Commonwealth. He defied the Queen and the Peers because he thought it was right so to do at bitter personal sacrifice . . . estrangement from the Queen whom he personally loved, the misunderstanding of highly placed friends like Burleigh, and the loss of his income for many, many months, being plunged into financial embarrassments as a consequence. He weighed the cost of his attitude beforehand, and because he could not be false to his principles and his conscience, he grimly faced a situation at once uncertain and disastrous.

This strength of character so clearly manifested in this open clash of his Parliamentary life remained with him as a priceless asset in the great crises he afterwards had to face. It is from this standpoint of fearless integrity and uprightness that Francis Bacon must be judged in his future actions. He remained true to himself and therefore he could not be false to any man. This was the fixed Star by which he set his course in his public career and he never deviated from it by a hair's breadth.

Chapter IX

"THE VIRGIN QUEEN" AND HER CONCEALED SONS (1567-1596)

FROM the examination of facts hitherto ignored or misunderstood, it is surely self-evident already that Francis Bacon was not only a "Mystery-child" but a "Mystery youth and man" also and that much of the "Mystery" centred in a prime fact of the era—that he was the concealed son of Queen Elizabeth who posed before the world as "The Virgin Queen." With the acceptance of this truth the prime enigmas of the Elizabethan Age are on the way to solution. They need not be shelved as impossible problems.

Nothing has appeared more inexplicable to the historians than the real relations that subsisted between the Queen and Essex, and the part played by Francis Bacon which ultimately culminated in a triangle of tragedy. Lytton Strachey, like the majority of academic romanticists, regards Essex as the lover of Queen Elizabeth, stepping into Leicester's shoes at his death . . . as unreal and fatuous a theory from the standpoint of human nature as it is false to the ascertainable facts. To imagine that a woman of fifty-five and a youth of twenty could be in any sense "lovers" or "sweethearts" is utterly ridiculous. It is true that Elizabeth loved Essex and loved him passionately, but it was *the love of a mother for her son.* It was not the maiden passion of a maid; that had all been given to his father, Leicester, years ago.

We are again indebted to Mrs. Gallup—as I have already said—for putting us on the track of the true explanation, previously unsuspected, by her decoding of *Francis Bacon's Bi-literal Cypher Story* which he placed in the Rosicrosse books he was printing and publishing during those silent years when he was thought to be wasting his time; a continued story which he secreted little by little all his life in various books to the last ones . . . the Shake-speare Plays, the *De Augmentis,* and *The New Atlantis.* It was then perpetuated by Francis Bacon's secret school, by brethren like Dr. Rawley (*Resuscitatio*), Bishop Tenison (*Baconiana*), Dr. Anderson (*Constitutions of Freemasons*), W. Preston (*Illustrations of Masonry*) and others of a still later date. This hidden story revealed that, apart from Francis Bacon, Queen Elizabeth had a second son who was afterwards known to the world as the Earl of Essex. We have to thank the late Parker Woodward for testing the truth of the Cypher-Story by the ascertainable facts of history which definitely confirm its claims.

This, then, is the true approach to the tragedy of the Earl of Essex. It is the story of a "Virgin Queen" (a wife and mother by a morganatic marriage which she dared not make known) and her two concealed sons for whom she wanted to do her best quietly and without fuss, but was compelled by the cruel hand of a remorseless fate to tread the Via Dolorosa of bitterness and tears. All the mysterious interplay that took place in the case of Francis Bacon—as we have already seen—goes on again in exactly the same way in the relations of the Queen and Essex . . . in the byplay, their letters, their actions, though, of course, the incidents are different. Their true relationship seeps out in numerous ways. It is very necessary that this secret bond which subsisted between the three people should be understood; indeed, the actions of Francis Bacon cannot be adequately explained without this key; the acts of Essex are incomprehensible; and the anguish of the Queen bewildering as she passed away in mental agony, calling on the name of Robert on her death-bed.

To understand Francis Bacon's actions we must understand something of the life of Essex, for, at the time under review, the lives of the three—Elizabeth, Francis, and Robert—crossed and re-crossed each other. And though historians and biographers may frown, let us begin anew to study all the facts now at our disposal.

All students of Francis Bacon's Life and Works are greatly indebted to Spedding for his exhaustive studies of thirty years which resulted in seven volumes.[1] His most important contribution was his unshakeable conviction that Francis Bacon was not only a great man but a good man whose personal character was unimpeachable. His work, however, is a difficult one to read except to specialists of the era with time on their hands. It is not exactly for popular consumption. It is long, cumbersome, boring, and, in a sense, too discursive to make easy reading. One cannot imagine many literary-minded readers taking the trouble to wade through three thousand pages in the hope of finding the truth about a man long dead.[2] Moreover, with all his labour, the checking of documents from the printed accounts of previous editors, and his search for others, there were many things which Spedding did not know, some that he did not take into account, and some that he thought of little moment and so passed over lightly. We have discovered much since Spedding wrote—over eighty years ago, and are now in a position to form sounder conclusions than he did. I say this not to depreciate his labours but to guard myself in advance from those critics who regard Spedding as pontifically infallible and would seek to refute the truths expressed in this work by referring me to a Spedding quotation. Such texts cannot weigh with me. One must no more be swayed by his opinions as final and authoritative

[1]We are, in my opinion, equally indebted to Basil Montague, barrister, *Life and Works* (1834), which took him a lifetime to complete; to Hepworth Dixon, barrister, who spent many years of research in order to write his *Personal History*, and to Parker Woodward, solicitor, who also devoted the best part of his life to the elucidation of the mystery surrounding Francis Bacon and "Shake-speare." These men who were thoroughly familiar with the legal aspects of all Francis Bacon's deeds were unanimous in asserting that Francis Bacon was an upright, honest and virtuous man, who was never guilty of a corrupt act either in his private life or his public life, at the Bar or on the Bench.

[2]The busy reader of to-day prefers something more direct, in a more popular style, and, it must be confessed, that Macaulay's brilliantly written libel on Francis Bacon (1837) holds the field even to-day through numerous reprints. It is easy to read and the high-lights of his rhetorical falsehoods strike the mind's eye with distortions that present a monstrous caricature of the Great Master of prose, prosody, and virtue.

than by the judgment of the 1616 experts of the Holy Congregation who denounced Copernicus and clung to the Ptolemaic theory of the universe. We, who really want to know the truth, must discover it for ourselves, taking Spedding as a guide to help us on the intellectual way but never hesitating to part company with him when one's reason demands it.

The fact is that Francis Bacon's Life and Works have probably evoked more controversy than any in history. For three hundred years scholars have asked—What WAS his philosophy? What did he really accomplish? Was his life a complete failure or a supreme success? Did he accomplish what he set out to perform? Why was he so sure of himself? So sure that posterity would recognize his merits when it knew what he had done? Was he a corrupt judge or a man of unspotted virtue? Did he not treat Essex shamefully?

Such questions cannot be answered off-hand. Even Spedding never discovered the answers. One cannot truly estimate a man's character, life and works on incomplete evidence, and when documents are missing and purposely mutilated, a wise man will reserve his judgment. There are certain "lost" documents which, if brought to light, might falsify all the conclusions so confidently trumpeted by harsh and short-sighted critics. There is, then, this to be said about Spedding's labours—greatly indebted to him as we are for his vindication of Francis Bacon's honour and honesty—that we cannot accept his various verdicts on Francis Bacon's activities as final, nor the standpoint from which he views his work and his philosophy, for the following reasons.

1. We have not got Francis Bacon's complete correspondence. We have no letter of his up to the age of twenty. We then have four which refer to his Suit for Recognition. Then none for another two years. Then in 1582, his *Notes on Christendom.* Then, when he is twenty-four, his remarkable letter to the Queen, when he enters Parliament, from *One of the Natural and True-Bred Children of Unfeigned affection.*

Virtually, up to the age of thirty-one, when he sends his famous letter to Burleigh—in which he says he has taken "All Knowledge to be his Province," we know nothing of his activities from any correspondence save one to Sir Francis Walsingham in 1585 which again has reference to his "SUIT," and one to Burleigh in 1586 which says that he "lives as it were *in umbra* and not in *public* action," the clear inference being that he "lives" in secret labours.

We have only two or three letters altogether to Lady Anne, his foster-mother. They are short and formal on business matters, beginning "Madam" and ending "And so I most humbly take my leave. From my lodging this 18th of February, 1591. Your Ladyship's most obedient Son, F. Bacon."

Only those letters have been preserved that indicate a Mystery . . . and so it is onwards through the years. Yet copies were meticulously taken by him of all he wrote, and obviously many were suppressed at the end of his life, when he prepared them for the eyes of posterity.

2. All Francis Bacon's letters were sifted by him in his lifetime; by his Secretary and executor, Dr. Rawley, after Francis Bacon's death, when some were published in *Resuscitatio* in 1657; some more in the *Cabala* (Secret Knowledge) a little later; a few more were printed in 1679 by T. T. (Bishop Thomas Tenison); R. Stephens published his first collection of letters in

1702, entitled *Letters and Remains*, and then a second collection in 1734; and in the preface Stephens wrote:

> "The Earl of Oxford was pleased to put into my hands some neglected manuscripts and loose papers to see whether any of the *Lord Bacon's compositions lay concealed there that were fit to be published. . . .*
>
> "I found several, *certainly genuine*, which had not been [published] and were fit to be transcribed, and so *preserved IF NOT DIVULGED.*" Pref. p. III.

This is as enigmatical as Bishop Tenison's remarks in 1679, *Baconiana*, p. 21:

> "Now the Works of Lord Bacon, some are LOST, in whole or in part, or *in some obscure place committed to Moths and Cobwebs. . . .* I find Dr. Rawley (p. 81) says, 'I have published all I thought fit or a well advised MAN would have thought fit to be published by me.' He judged some papers touching *MATTERS OF ESTATE*, to tread too near to the Heels of TRUTH, and to the Times of the persons concerned, from which they are now further removed by a distance of twenty years."
>
> In short, *they were suppressed.*

And that there is a mystery respecting Francis Bacon that had been committed to a CYPHER-CODE is obvious from the further remarks of Tenison. (p. 27):

> "The fairest and most correct Edition of this Book in Latine is that in Folio, printed at London, Anno, 1623, *Advancement of Learning.* And whosoever would understand Lord Bacon's Cypher, let him consult that accurate Edition. For, in some other Editions, which I have perused, the form of the Letters of the Alphabet, in which much of the Mysterie consisteth, is not observed: But the Roman and Italic Shapes of them are confounded."

This is a reference to the Biliteral Cypher decoded by Mrs. Gallup. It proves conclusively that Francis Bacon used a Cypher and that he was a Man of Mystery.

From the foregoing facts it is clear that Spedding had only access to the documents at *fourth hand*, after they had been winnowed at least four times, first by Francis Bacon and then by his Secret Disciples in after-years, who were resolved not to allow the work of their Master and Leader to be jeopardized by any injudicious revelation respecting the true identity of Francis Bacon and his work as a "Concealed Poet," an educationist, and an Ethical Teacher. Many of the original documents which Rawley, Tenison and Stephens printed, Spedding tried to trace but *they could not be found.* They were simply to be seen in their printed pages. They were as "LOST" as the Manuscripts of the James Bible or the Shakespeare Plays. For some well-known reason or other they have been repressed along *with many others which have never seen the light of day.* Nor do we know what special passages have been suppressed in the letters which were printed. What we are certain of is this: that many of them were mutilated.

Let any reader glance through Volumes I and II of Spedding in which he has tried to arrange the letters, etc., in chronological sequence and he will find ample evidence that the writer of the letters, while carefully preserving them, was purposely confusing them in order to convey a sense of bewilderment . . . as though to rouse the researcher to ask the question, "*Now why should these things be?*"

Over and over again Spedding complains that letters are undated, words are erased, signatures deleted, letters cut at vital points, and so on. Francis Bacon's first open letter to the Queen "has no title, address, date, docket, or other explanation" (Spedding, Vol. I, p. 46). In another letter, the end of it is cut. "Here our light goes out suddenly just as we were going to see how Bacon had resolved to dispose of himself at this juncture." (*Ibid*, p. 235.) Lady Bacon writes to Anthony in 1593:

> I send herein your brother's letter. *Construe the interpretation. I do not understand his enigmatical folded writing . . . Let him return a plain answer.* (*Ibid*, p. 245.)
>
> On Francis Bacon's thirty-third birthday, I find him still unpreferred, still without professional practice, still entangled in the unavoidable expenses of attendance about the Court, and gradually growing familiar with the fatal necessity of borrowing money to pay interest due upon money already borrowed. (*Ibid*, p. 266.)

Now . . . is it not obvious that there was a Mystery in Francis Bacon's life and that that mystery was being guarded after his death by Francis Bacon's friends (friends by succession in his secret) relating to the "Sublime Master." The heart of the "Mystery" James Spedding never pierced. *He can speak with a knowledge born of monumental patience but not with "authority.*" There were many things he did not know, many avenues of thought he never trod despite his ranging far and wide over the superficial landscape of the "Merrie England" of Elizabeth. While he was an indefatigable collector of information that lay on the surface, he was never a pioneer digging down beneath the crust of things to ascertain whether the jewel of Truth had been purposely hidden in some concealed mine. The open effects no one knew better than he, but he was totally unacquainted with the hidden causes from which they sprang. No! We cannot regard him as the final "Authority" on "Our Francis." Far from it. The further reasons apart from those already given will make this quite plain.

3. Apart from the fact that there is evidence of documents being suppressed and purposely mutilated, Spedding was unaware of *Francis Bacon's Cypher Story* (decoded by Mrs. Gallup) regarding his identity, etc.

4. He paid no attention to Francis Bacon's own claim that he was "*A Concealed Poet.*" He never tried to discover what truth there was in the claim, but on purely *a priori* grounds regarded it as impossible that he used the pen-name of "Shake-speare."

5. He was unaware of Francis Bacon's secret *Sonnet-Diary*, issued under the name of "Shake-speare."

6. He did not know of the first biography of Francis Bacon written in French by Pierre Amboise in 1631 which contained valuable information.

7. Despite his researches at Lambeth Palace he missed a French Sonnet, discovered later by the Rev. Walter Begley, which was written by a contemporary poet and friend, La Jessée, who pointedly associates Francis with "PALLAS" who, says La Jessée, inspires him. She is Francis Bacon's MUSE. Pallas, as everyone knows, is "The Spear Shaker," hence his pen-name "Shake-speare."

8. He was unaware of a contemporary work, Barclay's *Argenis* which states categorically (1621) that Francis Bacon was Queen Elizabeth's son.

9. He never suspected that the creator of the most wonderful system of Ethics ever known (Freemasonry), and the founder of the Lodges (now world-wide) was Francis Bacon; and that this was the Sixth Part of *The Great Instauration,* to which all the rest of his labours was "SUBSERVIENT."

10. He never knew that Francis Bacon was the writer of the Rosicrucian Pamphlets, *The Fama,* etc., the creator and founder of the Rosicrucian Colleges.

11. He never realized the significance of the *Promus* (Francis Bacon's note-book) and its bearing on the Shakespeare Plays. The writer of the Plays had access to this private note-book, for Francis Bacon's notes are used in the Plays but not in his prose works.

12. He never realized the significance of the *Northumberland Manuscript* which once belonged to the private scrivenery of Francis Bacon.

13. He knew nothing of the secret Elizabethan Rosicrosse Literary Society whose members were writing, printing and publishing books in English.

14. It never occurred to him that Francis Bacon was the creator of the English Renaissance in literature, education and ethics, etc., working secretly and silently lest his work should perish at the hands of political and theological intolerance.

Had James Spedding, in the early days of his researches, had the slightest suspicion that there were discoverable facts of such importance, I am certain his biography would have taken on a very different aspect. One must be grateful to him for vindicating Francis Bacon's character against the wicked aspersions of Lord Macaulay . . . but Spedding goes neither far enough in his conclusions nor does he do full justice to the man. He deals simply with the open facts of his life and of his concealed labours he knows nothing and suspects nothing.

As an academic and a high Civil Servant he is quite successful in collecting and collating facts, and in skirting the superficialities of the documents he obtained, examining them with meticulous care and precision, but it never seems once to have occurred to him—quite apart from the enigmatical asides in the works and letters that betokened a mystery—that the very letters which he did manage to handle and which he describes so carefully were full of suspicious elements. They should have aroused his detective instincts to look beneath the surface for the underlying motive. But he had no insight. He saw nothing out of the ordinary. He never looked. And yet, as we have seen, the documents were shouting at him from many angles that they veiled a hidden mystery.

The Mystery of a life follows exactly the same lines as the problem of the Shakespeare Plays, the traditional legends of Freemasonry round "St. Alban" with its manufactured archaic Regius Poem, the Cooke MS. of doubtful origin, and the "Old Charges" of dubious character, the MSS. of the Rosicrucian pamphlets, the subtle asides "writ in the glassy margents" of the old Rosicrucian books with their mispaginations, purposeful errata, numerical title pages, and their Capital Initials, etc.

These works all bear the same characteristics. There are missing original Manuscripts, purposeful mystification, enigmatical asides and cunning innuendoes. It is a marvel to me that Spedding never suspected that it was a designed mystification; and an equal marvel that the scholars who have read his seven volumes of letters have not seen the spirit of elusiveness slipping from letter to letter, and flashing through the alleys of the mind to intrigue the reader into following up the clues.

These considerations enable us to approach the problem of Queen Elizabeth, Francis Bacon, and Robert Earl of Essex in the certain knowledge that *the last word has not been spoken by Spedding* and is unlikely to be spoken for long years to come. We are no more qualified to pass judgment on the leading actors in the tragedy by surveying the outward circumstances than we should be entitled to judge a play by the first act. Let us get behind the scenes . . . to the souls of the actors, to the mainsprings of their actions, when the masks are off and subterfuge laid aside.

It has already been mentioned (Chapter II) that there was current talk that Queen Elizabeth had married Leicester privately and that she had borne him two sons, and that persons were prosecuted for repeating such slanders, e.g., "Mother Dowe" of Brentwood and a Norfolk gentleman named Marsham. Francis Bacon's secret Cypher-story declares that this second son was afterwards known as Robert Earl of Essex. Circumstantial evidence shows that these contemporary rumours and the secret Cypher-story are neither false nor fictional. There is a good reason why there is no absolute direct evidence. In English circles as well as Continental, courtiers were always taught to keep their mouths shut about the parentage of "Royal Bastards" or "Love-children" unless their Royal parents proclaimed or admitted their identity. For anyone to have repeated such a specific relationship openly and unproven would have been high treason, with all its consequences.

Now at the time Robert was born, the Queen's cousin, Lettice Knollys, a Maid of Honour, had been married some time to young Lord Walter Hereford. He was a poor man with but one Country House, Chartley. His first child Penelope was born in 1563; Dorothy, 1565; *Robert supposed to be born on 10th November*, 1567; Walter, 1569. The births of Penelope, Dorothy and Walter are duly recorded at Chartley. Robert is said to have been born at Netherwood in Herefordshire, but *there is no record of such a birth in the parish register or anywhere else*. The mother of Lettice Knollys was the Queen's aunt and resided at Court, being Mistress of the Robes. If a child were born to the Queen, and had to be concealed, Lettice was admirably suited to play the part of a foster-mother and *the necessary arrangements could easily be made in secret through Elizabeth's aunt, Lady Knollys*. Anyway, we know through the historian Froude, that on the 11th November, the Queen received an important letter containing some terms of a proposed marriage but *she never replied to it until the 11th December*, and during that month Elizabeth transacted no business in public. She had virtually sequestered herself. It is, moreover, at least singular that if Robert were truly the eldest son of Lord and Lady Hereford, that *he did not bear his father's Christian name*. With this must be coupled the fact that Sir Henry Wootten records later that Lord Hereford *"had a poor conceit of him (Robert) and preferred his second son, Walter."* A very natural feeling if Robert were merely his foster-son.

1570: Marsham had his ears cut off for saying, *"My Lord of Leicester had two children by the Queen."*

In 1571 was passed the Statute making it a penal offence "to speak of any Successor to the Crown other than the Natural Issue of the body of the Queen." Elizabeth refused to have the word "Lawful" inserted in place of "Natural."

This year the Queen gave to Lord Hereford the Manor of Marks Hall, near Braintree, in Essex.

1572: Hereford was created Earl of Essex and Knight of the Garter.

1573: In this year she "lent" the newly-created Earl of Essex £10,000 to recover possession of a barony in Ireland . . . a very curious transaction, as though she distrusted him and wanted him out of the way.

In the same year Essex writes to Burleigh, the treasurer, offering to him the *"direction, education and marriage of my eldest son, Robert."* It almost looks as though the letter was written to order either to get the lad to the Court where he could be under the Queen's supervision, or that Essex wanted Robert off his hands lest he should interfere with the prospects of his own children.

1574-75: The correspondence between the Queen and the Earl suggests there is something under the surface, for in one letter she refers, "to letters *the contents whereof assure yourself, our eyes, and the fire only have been privy,*" 30th March, 1574-5.

From the Revels in Kenilworth in 1575, the Queen went direct to Lady Essex at Chartley. Leicester who had entertained Elizabeth right royally—her gifts to him totalled £50,000—went with her. From the Essex home she wrote the Earl agreeing *to make him the Earl Marshal of Ireland.* To the letter she added this footnote:

> *"Deem, therefore, cousin mine, that the search of your Honour with the danger of your Breath, hath not been bestowed on so ungrateful a Prince that will not consider the one and reward the other."*

Essex was then in Ireland. He returned to London unexpectedly and made things awkward, apparently by bringing pressure to bear on the Queen respecting money and dignities, according to Devereux's *Lives of the Earls of Essex.* The Queen ordered him to return to Ireland in the following year, where he arrived in July, 1576. In September he died after a sudden and violent illness. In *Leicester's Commonwealth,* printed anonymously shortly afterwards, it was alleged that he was deliberately poisoned, the rumour being that Leicester had got rid of him for State reasons. This was, of course, denied.

1577: Robert, the successor to the title, was then about nine years old. Three months later, 11th January, 1577, we find the boy *is in the care and custody of Lord Burleigh* and lives in his household. From that time he is more or less associated with the Court and its notables. He is being educated and provided for by someone—and *it is not his reputed mother Lettice Knollys.*

In May he goes to Trinity College, Cambridge . . . the College Francis Bacon had left eighteen months earlier. In June he is short of clothes and silver plate for his rooms. Application is made to the Queen's Treasurer, Lord Burleigh, *who duly provides them.*

Robert's Xmas vacation *is spent at Court with the Queen.* "On his coming, the Queen meeting with him, offered to kiss him, which he humbly altogether refused." Indeed, the boy passed with the Queen into the presence of the kneeling courtiers without doffing his hat. (Broughton).

1581 : In May of this year he got his Master of Arts Degree, aged fourteen. After being at Court for a time he went to live at Lanfey House in Pembroke, but he returned to Court under the pressure of Leicester.

1585: He was now aged about eighteen and Leicester took him with the expedition to Holland. He took part in the battle of Zutphen. On his return he was constantly at the Court and "on the best terms with the Queen."

1587: Leicester resigned the post of Master of the Horse in Robert's favour. It was worth £1,500 per annum. Robert Essex was now constantly with the Queen. Bagot wrote: "When she is abroad nobody near her but my Lord of Essex, and at nights My Lord is at cards or one game or another with her."

Their happy relationship was, in July, shaken by a violent row, according to Edward Dyer, in which *Robert accused the Queen of being under the influence of Sir Walter Raleigh*, then aged thirty-five, who had been made recently Captain of the Guard. The boy Earl of Essex said:

> "I spake what of grief and choler as much against him as I could, and I think he (Raleigh) standing at the door, might very well hear of the worst that I spoke of himself."

It is obvious to me that this incident is a clear intimation that the young Earl, at that date *knew that he was a Tudor*, the Queen's son, and that *he felt he had a right to complain to his mother*. If Robert had been nothing to the Queen is it not inconceivable that he would thus *have dared to speak to the Queen and display anger?* It was more than sufficient cause for this haughty, autocratic despot to have sent him to the Tower for his temerity in questioning her personal freedom. The "Alone Queen," was so touchy on the exercise of her WILL, on her absolute freedom, that she would never ordinarily have allowed herself to be railed at in the presence of Raleigh and others by a youth of twenty whom she had brought up and educated . . . the Queen of the Tudors to whom he owed everything. It was a gross liberty that the proudest noble dared not have taken in that era. It cannot be glossed over by the foolish explanation that it was a "Sweethearts' tiff." A boy of twenty has no lover's passion for a woman of fifty-four.

The incident shows that Robert Essex thought he had *a right to show anger* or resentment of the Queen's actions and in her presence because he was kin to her though the relationship was a secret one. He was of the Tudor Breed. A mere subject dared not have openly quarrelled with his Sovereign. Unfortunately his fiery, uncontrollable temper—a characteristic of the Tudors like Elizabeth, Mary, Henry VIII—broke out between Essex and the Queen, actually between the mother and son, repeatedly. He never seemed to realize that such outbursts were dangerous and that what he might say and do as son to mother might be excused as "a family quarrel" in the household of a commoner, but were nevertheless treasonable when said and done as a "subject" to his Sovereign. He never knew where to draw the line between his "private" and his "public" relationships. He confused the two repeatedly; and at last his "fatal impatience" proved his undoing. Robert the "son" destroyed Essex the "subject."

As a sequel to "the good old row at North Hall," Essex ran away to join in the siege of Sluys without asking the Queen's permission to leave the country—the duty of every subject. The moment the Queen heard the news she sent Sir Robert Cary after him who stopped him embarking and brought him back to Court.

We may safely say that from this point—there are numerous instances which prove it—the attitude of the Queen towards the youthful Robert was never that of "Sovereign and subject," or "sweetheart and lover," or of "mistress and gallant," but that it was the protective, maternal instinct of a mother (a very indulgent fond mother) towards a son (a very impetuous, headstrong, wilful and spoiled youth) always bent on having his own way. That is the true picture; and every step afterwards in their twined lives proves it. Their tempers struck and flashed like steel and flint. They crossed each other and were indulgent to each other alternately . . . each as proud as Lucifer. It was this lust of pride, this sameness of temper, this arrogant forcefulness of both sides that ended in tragedy.

1588 was the year of the Armada. Robert was appointed General of Horse and was actively engaged in the defence of the country associated with the Earl of Leicester (his father) who had been publicly appointed by the Queen, Commander-in-Chief of all the English forces.

In September Leicester died. *The Queen acts as though she were his wife.* She seizes his estate, auctions it and takes the proceeds. Leicester's Will extols the virtues of the Queen. He leaves Robert his "George and Garter"[1] with the hope he would soon be admitted into the Order. Francis "Bacon" is not mentioned. Before the end of the year the Queen makes Robert a Knight of the Garter. After this he acts consistently as though he knew the secret of his birth. He is a spoiled, arrogant, headstrong youth, who can brook neither opposition nor denial. History records numerous strategems to get away from the Court and the Queen's surveillance, and the Queen's efforts to get him back to her side.

In 1589 the Queen refused to let him go with a small fleet to attack Spain. *In spite of this refusal,* he went to Plymouth on horseback, eluding Lord Huntingdon and Sir Francis Knollys who had been sent to stop him. The Queen thereupon wrote to Drake that if Essex had reached the fleet "*they were forthwith to send him back safely.*" Robert insisted on staying and joined a landing party. The Queen thereupon ordered Sir Roger Williams *to be put to death* for being responsible. When Robert returned a month or two later he went direct to her room, "mudstained from the journey" and made his peace with the Queen without difficulty. (St. John's *Life of Raleigh,* Vol. I, p. 196; *Tudor Problems,* Woodward, p. 39.) The Queen had previously written to Robert, then with the fleet, accusing him of *undutiful behavior.*

Does not the entire incident point the fact that Elizabeth was his mother and not his sweetheart? Her anxiety is clearly maternal and not that of a lover.

1590: Robert was now about *twenty-three years of age.* His debts already amounted to £22,000. By permission of the Queen he succeeded Leicester to a very handsome revenue derived from the "farm of sweet wine." Then occurs a fact which shows that Robert Essex never regarded himself as the Queen's lover. *He marries secretly the widow of Sir Philip Sidney.* It was months before the Queen knew of this union. "Then," says Devereux, "her anger knew no bounds, not merely because *he took a wife without asking her consent,*

[1]"The George is an enamelled figure of St. George fighting the Dragon, suspended from the Collar . . ." (Captain Taprell Dorling, D.S.O., R.N., *Ribbons and Medals*).

"Sometimes called the Order of St. George . . ." (*Chambers' Encyclopaedia*).

"At the middle of the Collar before is to be fastened the Image of St. George . . . called 'the Great George' . . . there is also 'the Lesser George.' " (*Institution of Laws and Ceremonies of the Most Noble Order of the Garter,* by Elias Ashmole, Windsor Herald at Arms, 1672.)

Major W. Angus-Jones, O.B.E., writes: "The Garter is the premier Order of Chivalry of England, if not indeed of Europe; and I think it is very important evidence of relationship that Leicester should have specifically bequeathed this most valued and intimate possession to Robert of Essex."

but for marrying, as she said, *BELOW HIS DEGREE.*" Devereux adds, "One would have thought that the daughter of Sir Francis Walsingham, *might have been deemed a fair match even for Lord Essex.*"

The real reason Devereux never suspected. The truth slips out in the phrase "*below his Degree.*" The Queen undoubtedly preferred Robert to marry a foreign Princess, for was he not a Prince, though concealed, who might be yet acknowledged! What other explanation is possible?

In October Henry IV of France wrote to Robert personally asking him to help his request for military assistance against Spain. It seems as though the King had some private knowledge of Robert's true position.

1591: *The Queen opposed Robert's going to France* to take some troops. To show his displeasure, he absents himself from the Court until the Queen relents and lets him have his own way and goes to France. Very shortly afterwards Sir Francis Darcy was sent by the Queen specially to France with "*peremptory orders for Robert's immediate return.*" On Sir Robert Carey returning to England unaccompanied by Essex, the Queen "flew into a great passion vowing she would make him an example if *he did not come home forthwith.*" Later, she forgave him and allowed him to be present at the siege of Rouen "*provided he is not to put himself in danger.*" Devereux might well remark,"

"*It is curious that the Honourable Privy Council should be employed in writing orders to a general to keep out of harm's way.*" The Council wrote:

"You should not put in danger your own person at the siege of Rouen."

Again and again he was urged to return home. When he did come it was to persuade the Queen to allow him to stay longer.

In December he challenged Villiers, the Governor of Rouen, to a mortal duel. Hearing of this, the Queen instructed the Privy Council to write him that, *owing to his position,* he had no business to engage in such a duel and instructions were issued to stop the encounter.

In the same month the Council again wrote him:

"Hearing some infection had broken out in his own familiar they heartily desired him *to return from such danger to his person* as they fear may happen from the increase of such infection."

We may well ask ourselves at this point: Now . . . *why was this old lady nearing sixty troubling so much about this young man who was already married?* Why was she attempting to shield him? To keep him out of harm's way? This is not the attitude of a Mistress proud of a Lover's prowess; but it is the natural attitude of a mother for a son . . . *especially if she intended to name him next in the Succession for the Throne as her acknowledged son.*

There are very good grounds for believing that this step was at the back of her mind; for Francis Bacon's letter to Burleigh renouncing his birthright had cleared the way for Robert's accession. The circumstances which prevented open acknowledgment of Francis did not operate in the case of the younger son born years after her private marriage.

We have, then, very substantial grounds for the view that the Queen had two children taken from her at birth and brought up as other people's . . . in their households. In Francis Bacon's case we have seen this secret relationship strengthened evidentially by cunning asides which cannot be resolved in any other way. The facts respecting Robert Essex's true identity are equally startling and bear but one interpretation—that he was also a Tudor by blood. This is strengthened by similar enigmatical asides and remarks in correspondence, by actions, and by the entire trend of events that wound their sinuous way to a tragic and bitter close.

To read aright the story that the Fates wove around Queen Elizabeth, Francis Bacon and Robert Essex we must understand the secret relation that existed between them. It is impossible to interpret the life of Francis Bacon without it.

In 1592 they stood before the world as Queen Elizabeth and her two loyal subjects whom she delighted to honour, but under the rose, and in the privacy of their own hearts, the "Three" comprised a much-worried mother and two concealed sons, aware of their rightful heritage—the Queen dreading lest an untoward word might lead to the exposure of the skeleton in the cupboard, her own youthful indiscretions; Francis the idealist with the bitter knowledge that he was definitely out of the hunt through the sin of being born out of due time; and Robert, headstrong and ambitious, resolved that *he would have his just rights as the Queen's son.*

This is the true approach to the situation that emerged slowly from the shadows through the passing years, to focus itself in the grey dawn of that fatal day in February 1601, on the figure of "ROBART TIDIR" as he gazed round the Courtyard of the Tower for the last time with its symbols and paraphernalia of Death.

We are now in the year 1592 when the lives of the two men begin to be intertwined before the eyes of history. Francis Bacon is aged thirty-two; Robert Essex, twenty-five. *For the first time they are known by the biographers to be friends.* This is what Spedding says:

When, or under what circumstances, the acquaintance between Bacon and Essex *began*, I cannot exactly learn. In Anthony Bacon's papers I find no allusion to it earlier than February 1592, by which time it had ripened into an intimacy; and since Essex had been engaged in France during the latter half of 1591 *the commencement of the acquaintance cannot well be dated later than the preceding July.*

Essex was then twenty-three, and had been for some years high in the Queen's favour. In 1585 and 1586 he had served with distinction under the Earl of Leicester in Holland. In 1587 the Queen had made him her Master of the Horse. In 1588 she had appointed him General of Horse. In 1589, in spite of his disobedience (joining the Holland expedition against her wishes), he was in greater favour than ever. (Vol. I, p. 104.)

Spedding's conclusions are that "a man in Bacon's position could not but be glad of his friendship. . . . The rise of a man like Essex offered a new and unexpected chance . . . not for ascendancy in the Queen's favour . . . . but for the prosecution of those larger reforms in Letters, in Church, in State upon which his mind was ever brooding . . . the recovery to Man of his lost dominion over Nature by means of Knowledge."

There is much that is true in all this, and yet Spedding has missed the real truth underlying it. A very cursory reflection shows that he is wrong.

Is it not unthinkable that Francis Bacon never knew of Robert Essex until July 1591? The nominal guardian of Essex, from the age of nine, with, at least, the Queen's consent if not her positive command, was Lord Burleigh, the Queen's treasurer. The nominal uncle of Francis Bacon was again Lord Burleigh. Essex, it can be truly said, was reared at Court. Francis, up to the time of his quarrel with the Queen over the 1593 Vote of Supply, was a constant attender at Court. Francis as a boy was often taken to the Queen who called him "My little Lord Keeper." Robert as a boy was likewise taken by the Queen into the

Presence Chamber. Are we to believe that they never met at Burleigh's town House? Or at the Court? Or in the Queen's presence? That they never met each other? Or knew of each other's existence? Or heard of each other *though Robert followed Francis through the same College?* It is virtually certain that when Francis, having accidentally learned of his birth-secret at the age of sixteen, was packed off to France, "direct from kissing the Queen's hand"[1], he learned at the same time that he had a younger brother, his whereabouts and his name.

Whether he did or not, he certainly was aware when he was twenty-four that he had a brother by the remarkable phrase he uses in his address to the Queen . . . "*ONE of the Natural and True-Bred CHILDREN* . . . to your Sacred Majesty." The meaning is clear. He is only "ONE" of the Queen's Natural Children, the inference being that there was at least ONE more of the "Natural Children." It is therefore certain that Francis knew the identity of Robert well before he took his seat in Parliament for Melcombe in 1584, seven years prior to 1591, the date Spedding gives as the first time they became acquainted. Their "friendship which ripened into intimacy" was a fraternal love for each other all the more binding because of the secret formalities which their peculiar positions imposed on each other. Their "intimacy" was not a six-months' mushroom growth. It was something far stronger, rooted in brotherliness, breed, cautiousness, and self-preservation; for no one could tell what the future had in store.

No wonder all written evidence between them was destroyed until records could be left with impunity that in 1592 they were intimates. There were no prior records left purposely. Their secret relationship naturally drew them together and their intimacy was no common one but was born of a common misfortune. It is fallacious for Spedding or anyone else to assume that "they did not know each other prior to 1591" because any correspondence between them cannot be found. It is unbelievable that these two men were absolute strangers to each other prior to July 1591 and that their friendship ripened into an intimacy within six months similar to the love that subsisted between David and Jonathan. The truth is that in 1592, Francis and Robert had come to terms (I would not be at all surprised to learn that the Queen was aware of the understanding) and had decided on a plan of action. The terms were undoubtedly on the lines of Francis Bacon's famous letter to Lord Burleigh which announced his renunciation of all his right to the Succession and that he had taken all Knowledge to be *his* Province. This was undoubtedly the arrangement: Francis speaking:

> *I will stand down for you. The Queen's Honour will then be unsmirched. I will help you to succeed to the Throne. I will advise you how to proceed, how to win over all rivals. In return you must help me to prosecute my ideals, reforms in State Government, etc., and to advance the Kingdom of Knowledge in England, to help make her a centre of Light . . . a flashing Beacon to all Humanity.*

So Spedding's conclusions were partially right though they sprang from a very different set of surroundings than he suspected.

[1]Francis Bacon's letter to Cecil, January 1595.

This much at least is certain: That from this date events revolve in growing strength to a climax around Queen Elizabeth, Francis Bacon, and Robert the Earl . . . from the siege of Rouen to the death of the Queen. And that there was an understanding between the "Three," far deeper, wider, closer, than has hitherto been suspected by historians, is certain. Even an authority like Sir Robert Rice says:

> It was in 1591 that *Elizabeth appointed Francis Bacon to be Essex's confidential adviser;* whether before or after the Rouen incident (his challenge to the Governor) the writer does not know. *Hamlet and Horatio*, p. 163.

In this illuminating statement we get a glimpse of the relationship—if not the positive relationship—of the three characters . . . a mother, who is anxious for her favourite son who conducts himself with head-strong pride on his brow; and therefore seeks to temper his Tudor recklessness by associating him with, or putting him in charge of, his elder brother.

It must not be thought that Essex was all lightning, fire and storm and nothing more. Far from it. He had very good qualities. His worst fault throughout his life was that he acted impulsively without weighing the consequences of his acts. He was rash and reckless in seeking to have his own way at any price, once he had got an idea in his head . . . and that by force rather than suasion. These were his chief sins. Ordinarily, he was of a happy, cheerful disposition. He was well above the average intellectually. He had no particular desires for wine or affairs with ladies, though he was not averse to paying attentions to the beauties of the Court. According to Strickland, Essex "hazarded the Queen's resentment by a renewal of his rash attentions to her beautiful attendant, Mistress Bridges." (*Life of Elizabeth*, p. 623.) How far these attentions went is difficult to determine. I have not met with any satisfactory evidence that Essex was at any time of his life "a loose liver." Whatever indiscretions he committed were made the most of by "the enemies of this envied man . . . who failed not to carry reports to the royal ear." Fuller says:

> It is spied *out of envy*, that Essex is again in love with his fairest B——. It cannot choose but come to the Queen's ears, then he is undone, and all who depend upon his favour. Sure I am that Lady Essex hears of it and is greatly disquieted. (*Worthies.*)

He was generous and impulsive and there is no doubt that some of his £20,000 of debts went to help Francis in founding the English Renaissance, for Essex was a lover of literature. The best estimate of his character is given by Spedding, Vol. I, p. 105:

> He was a man of so many gifts and virtues, that even now, when his defects, and the issue to which they carried him are fully known, it still seems possible that under more favourable accidents he might have realized all the promise of his morning.
>
> From his boyhood he had been an eager reader and a patient listener. The first year after he left Cambridge he spent happily in studious retirement. *His knowledge was already considerable, his literary abilities great, his views*

liberal and comprehensive, his speech persuasive, his respect for intellectual qualifications in other men earnest and unaffected.

His religious impressions were deep, and without being addicted to any of the religious parties in the state, he had points of sympathy with them all.

His temper was hopeful, ardent, enterprising; his will strong, his opinions decided; yet he was at the same time singularly patient of oppugnant advice, and liked it the better the more frankly it was given. *He had that true generosity of nature which appeals to all human hearts, because it feels an interest in all human things; and which made him a favourite without any aid of dissimulations and plausibilities, at once with the people, the army and the Queen.*

A character rare at all times and in all places; most rare in such a station as he seemed destined thus early to occupy.

The favourite of a mighty Queen, herself the favourite of a mighty nation; with a heart for all that was great, noble and generous; an ear open to all freest and faithfullest counsel; an understanding to apprehend and appreciate all wisdom; an imagination great enough to entertain new hopes for the human race; without any shadow of bigotry or narrowness; without any fault as yet apparent, except a chivalrous impetuosity of character; the very grace of youth . . . which when tempered by time and experience, all moral greatness and all extraordinary and enterprising virtue derive their vital energy."

Such is Spedding's estimate of Robert Essex, aged twenty-five, in the year 1592, and I think it is fairly accurate.

We now know the three characters—a Queen of implacable jealousy where her Will and Prerogative were menaced in the slightest; Francis Bacon far-seeing and wise, moved by the spirit of philanthropia to essay to conquer new worlds of thought for the benefit of humanity; and Robert Essex of proud, high temper, regarding himself, secretly, as of nobler lineage than anyone else at Court, and jealous of anyone who would seek to deprive him of his natural rights granted specifically under the Parliament Act, which gave Elizabeth the right to name her own Successor who might even be the "Heir of her Natural Body" and not necessarily a "Lawful" one.

In 1592 the Court was openly divided into two parties: Lord Burleigh and his son Sir Robert Cecil headed one and the Earl of Essex the other. Essex had stepped into the Earl of Leicester's shoes quite naturally (as his son), for Leicester had in the past consistently opposed Burleigh on matters of High Policy. It was the businessman of action and soldier in opposition to the cautiousness of the statesman . . . a natural clash of temperaments. Their divisions in the past were now to be taken up by their sons—Robert Essex (Tudor) versus Robert Cecil, with many clashes and armed truces. Essex was then residing entirely at Court, beloved by Elizabeth and in high favour with everyone. Devereux writes——

The position of Essex at this time was one to make an older head giddy. He was courted by young nobles; looked up to by all military men as their leader and patron; the Puritan Party considered him as their protector while the Roman Catholics looked to him to obtain toleration. He was the idol of the populace while the Queen could scarce bear his absence from her side. He would then be twenty-six, the Queen sixty."

When the 1593 Parliament met, Essex was still resident at Court. For some three or four years after this he appears to have taken a prominent part in the management of the Queen's affairs. He was very successful in obtaining first-hand, reliable information regarding the trend of affairs and secret events on the Continent which might prove inimical to the Queen and State. For this he had to thank Francis Bacon and Anthony Bacon.

For many years, as already stated, Anthony had lived on the Continent. In 1580 in Paris, then in Genoa, Bordeaux, Montaubon and elsewhere to 1591 when he returned to England to live with Francis at Gray's Inn and Twickenham. He had made valuable friends and contacts everywhere. We have already seen that he made a habit of posting home information in Cypher. He would be termed to-day a secret-service agent of the Foreign Office or Diplomatic Corps. As a fairly wealthy man of leisure, intellectual, with a keen eye, a methodical mind and fond of travel, he was an ideal man for conducting secret missions and worming his way to the heart of things concealed. There is not the slightest doubt that much of the political and literary knowledge possessed by Francis Bacon respecting Continental news came from Anthony.

He was the focal Head of the secret Society of Freemasons and Rosicrucians that Francis Bacon was establishing on the Continent. He knew the Illuminati in many countries, the secret Heads of the Protestant revolutionaries. He had friends and agents everywhere. He had created a sort of Secret Foreign Service. He passed on the information to Francis in code. No one was better fitted than Anthony to act as secretary to Robert Essex, to guard his political and personal interests and to keep him posted with foreign intelligence. Indeed, shortly after his return to England we find him first helping Francis with his scriptorium or Literary bureaux of copyists and translators; then definitely employed by Essex. Francis, too, was also familiar with the secret bypaths of the Continent. He had lived abroad for lengthy periods. He had likewise made contacts with gnostics, advanced thinkers, political and social reformers, and with liberally-minded statesmen throughout the civilized world. (Pierre Amboise). It was at this time, 1592, that we first know positively that the three men were firm friends. Evidently Anthony had every reason to believe that in entering the service of Essex he would be placing himself on the true side politically, and most efficiently serving his Queen and his country. We have already seen, too, that this deep-seated patriotism was one of the ruling passions of Francis Bacon's life. We thus find that while Francis was made, by the Queen, Robert's political adviser, Anthony was his secretary and foreign correspondent, and that before long they had a well-organized Continental service of secret information that was passed by Anthony and Francis to Essex who reported his knowledge to the Queen. There was thus an almost daily stream of vital knowledge that kept England abreast of what her enemies were doing or contemplating so that never once was she taken unawares.[1]

[1]We may say that this was truly the beginning of our properly organized Secret Service and Foreign Office. It began in an unofficial manner. In the following reign of James this had developed into a properly conducted Secret Service, etc., using many Codes and Cyphers—many in use to-day—and *Francis Bacon was the head of this Secret Foreign Service.*

This is another debt we owe to him.

Francis Bacon hoped to make Robert Essex the Court leader of a great patriotic band of warriors like Raleigh and Drake and play a part for which he was gifted beyond all other men. "He was," says Church, "without exception the *most brilliant man who ever appeared at Elizabeth's Court.*" Francis tried to keep Raleigh and Essex on terms of friendship and to maintain a common course in politics and war. Each was needful to the other. Each longed for war. "Each in his own person represented the youth and genius of the time; Essex of the nobles, Raleigh of the gentry." With voice and pen Francis strove to weld a frank and loyal union between them that England might have the free use of all her arms. He laboured to make peace between them and their stiff-necked pride. Had he succeeded it would have saved both of them in the long run from the block. Robert would have won the "Succession" and Raleigh the proud courtier and the born leader of new worlds, seaman, adventurer, soldier, philosopher, and statesman, would have wielded a power under the shadow of the Throne second to none in the Counsels of the Nation. For the break that ultimately came to a head between them the fatal temper bred in the bone of Essex was largely responsible. In after-years Francis said repeatedly that he had devoted his whole time to the service of Essex:

> It is well known how I did many years since dedicate my travels and studies to the use and—as I term it—the service of my Lord of Essex which I protest I did not, making election of him *as the likeliest means of mine own advancement* but . . . that *I loved my country more than was answerable to my fortune*: And I held at that time my Lord to be *the fittest instrument to do good to the State;* and therefore I applied myself to him in a manner which I think happeneth rarely amongst men: for I did not only labour carefully and industriously, whether it were a matter of advice or otherwise, but neglecting the Queen's service, mine own fortune, and in a sort my vocation, I did nothing but devise and ruminate within myself to the best of my understanding . . . of anything that might concern his Lordship's honour, fortune, or service. (*Apologia*, Francis Bacon.)

Here, then, is good evidence of the true position. By the side of it we can put another quotation written in 1596 by Francis to Robert.

> Before you give access to my advice, look about you even jealously a little if you will, and *to consider, first,* whether *I have not reason to think that your Fortune comprehendeth mine?* . . . I do not repent me of safe counsel *neither do I judge the whole play by the first Act.*

Do not these quotations bear out the secret truth behind this open historical byplay? That Francis Bacon had stepped aside, having relinquished all pretensions to the throne from the purest of patriotic motives, and was trying to help and guide, and curb his younger, impetuous brother, whom he honestly thought was the fittest instrument to do good to the State. He "applied himself" (i.e. devoted himself practically) to Robert "*in a manner which rarely happeneth among men.*" A sacrifice rare indeed to stand down that a younger brother might be named next in the Succession to the Throne. How significant runs the entire quotation. "I neglected my own *Fortune* and, in a sort, my own *vocation*," etc. How else can this be explained? "Your Fortune comprehendeth mine!" Of course! Because their joint fortunes rose or fell together. If Robert's kingly ambitions were successful it meant that Francis Bacon could have brought rapidly into being his utilitarian projects for England and Humanity. His ideals were, he considered, bounded by and bound up with Robert Essex's success with the Queen—never to offend her but to let her see by his actions that he was the right person to succeed her. Hence the cry that was ever on the lips of Francis to Robert . . . "*Win the Queen! Win the Queen! If this be not the beginning, of any other course I see no end!*" What the schoolmen have never understood is this: That Francis Bacon's ideals did not consist in the writing of a book or a series of books but in *the positive establishment of a new outlook, a new order all round,* an English Renaissance which could only be done with the co-operation of men of like ideals to himself. *It was not a book to be written but a work to be begun,* of which he could only lay the bases. The Shakespeare Plays were not an end in themselves. They were an educational base for posterity on which to build, a bringing down to earth of the Harp of the Muses for others to play who had more skilful fingers. Of what use was the mere writing of ethical principles through his prose works? It availed nothing unless they were put into active operation in the form of a properly organized society that would grow and permeate with their ethical leaven the entire mass of humanity. This was the spirit of philanthropia in which he founded his secret societies to carry on his work; he rang the bell to call the sciences together; and secretly founded the bases of the present Royal Society. He was not simply writing and talking. He was working and acting and establishing organized movements on which we look back and term "The Elizabethan Renaissance," which we think grew out of nothing, like Topsy, by a species of "Spontaneous Generation." This was Francis Bacon's Kingdom . . . the unseen "Province" of the Mind over which he sought to rule in 1592. This was the fortune which was his felicity. Well might he say to his brother Robert, whose influence as Sovereign would enable him to accomplish great things, "*Have I not reason to think that your Fortune comprehendeth mine?*"

Under Francis Bacon's influence, Essex gained so much in gravity and good sense that the Queen made him a Privy Councillor in September 1593, and even began to entrust him to deal with much of her foreign correspondence. Hepworth Dixon says of Francis and Anthony Bacon:

> Day and night their tongues and pens are busy in this work of correspondence, etc. Anthony writes the Earl's letters, instructs his spies, drafts for him despatches to the agents in foreign lands. *Francis shapes for him a plan of conduct at the Court, and writes for him a treatise of advice which should have been the rule and would have been the salvation of his life.* (*Personal History*, p. 50.)

All these services were gratuitous. We know the reason why and the secret truth which Dixon never suspected. There was a blood-tie and a secret understanding between them. Well might Dean Church say that "their friendship came to be one of the closest kind, full of mutual services and of genuine affection on both sides . . . that of affectionate equality," *Life*, p. 30.

Early in 1593, while the Queen was still furiously indignant with

Francis Bacon for his attitude in opposing her Money-Bill in Parliament, it became known that the Office of Attorney-General was shortly to become vacant. In spite of the Queen's anger and the disgrace of being forbidden to attend Court, he decided to try to obtain the position. The application can be understood from his point of view. To Burleigh he had renounced the Succession and, in the same letter, he had asked for a salaried Government post. The Attorneyship was a Queen's appointment; and anger or no anger was it not his right under the terms of his letter? So he wrote to Essex that if he did not get the position he would quit the Queen's service, and retire with a couple of men to Cambridge to follow his literary pursuits.

The fact is that he wanted a direct salaried income. A valuable appointment was more than ever necessary to save him. He had a large number of literary assistants in his pay and pressing bills from printers and booksellers. Hitherto, he had only received by grace what had been given him by the Queen, through Burleigh, and this allowance had been stopped. *He had no other source of income* . . . nothing from law-practice. Robert Essex, as Master of the Horse, had a valuable salary. Doubtless Francis expressed himself pretty forcibly to Robert on the unfairness of the different treatment.

Yet . . . when we look squarely at the matter what qualifying experience had he for the position? Indeed, his expectancy of obtaining such a post can only be understood from a knowledge of the secret circumstances. *Imagine the brazen boldness of any ordinary barrister of thirty-two, who had never practised at the bar, wanting to occupy its highest position!* A young man who had deeply mortified the Queen and who had been openly rebuked! Everybody in official circles knew that he had been dismissed the Court. Was not that enough to have made any ordinary aspirant pause? Moreover, what proof had he ever given of professional proficiency? *He had never taken one case through the Law Courts.* The Queen and Burleigh believed that it was Literature and not Law which was his forte, and that his head was full of Utopian ideals, many of which they doubtless regarded as visionary. Above all, he had shown publicly that he could not be relied upon as a staunch Government supporter. Had he not held up the Queen's supplies? He had never even expressed contrition.

> How came such a man at such a time to be so much as proposed or seriously thought of as a fit competitor with Coke for such an office as that of Attorney-General? asks Spedding. (Vol. I, p. 232.)

He does not answer the question because he had no insight into the mystery of Francis Bacon, no vision, no clear eye to pierce the veil and see what was going on (and what had gone on) behind the scenes. He could only exclaim:

> That Bacon was put forward and upheld for a whole year as a likely competitor, *is a fact that calls for explanation.* (*Ibid*, p. 231.)

The Office undoubtedly belonged to Coke. He was in the prime of life, just over forty, had already a great reputation as a lawyer, and a wide legal experience at the Bar and in chambers. He was full of energy, unswayed by popular cries, and devoted to the service of the Crown. His conduct as Speaker was a token of his subservience and that he was not likely to be over-troubled by nice scruples. His post as Solicitor-General gave him naturally the right to expect the higher appointment of Attorneyship.

Yet the Queen, in spite of Coke's "rights," his legal knowledge and experience, and her exacerbation at Francis Bacon's Parliamentary attitude, hesitated for over a year to fill the Office. It became a bone of contention between the Essex and Cecil factions at Court accentuating their differences month after month. What was the "explanation" that Spedding asked for? This: The harassed Queen did not know what to do for the best. She therefore acted (as she always did) on her own motto—"When in doubt, do nothing!" She knew that Coke ought to have the position but she was uncertain of the reactions of Francis, and more especially of Robert the headstrong: so she kept them dangling until they got tired, hoping something else would turn up to divert their energies into other channels. She did not want to seem to cast away her own son, but she could not bring herself to step him above an experienced lawyer like Coke. Moreover, Essex gave her no peace pressing the claims of Francis, and this began to annoy her. Numerous letters show that he was doing his level best to secure Francis the appointment, speaking pretty plainly his mind not only to the Queen but to Burleigh and Cecil his son. They show that he was acting just as a younger brother would act to one to whom he was greatly indebted, and that he was anxious to show his appreciation.

Apart from this, however, Essex wished Francis to obtain the Attorney's Office, for he really believed him to be the better man. He thought, too, that he could obtain any favour from the Queen for the mere asking. The correspondence shows that Robert was even more disappointed than Francis that he could not bring the Queen to make up her mind. For twelve months, while Francis was still forbidden the Court, Essex continued to interview the Queen, Burleigh and Cecil and report the results. Francis joined in the canvass, too . . . Anthony Bacon and even Lady Bacon. It was while all this turmoil was being stirred—which meant so much to Francis then in desperate straits—that Lady Anne wrote to Anthony, "What would he (Francis) have me do and when for his own good. He was his father's first child and God will supply if he will but trust in Him and call upon Him in Truth of Heart": a very enigmatical way of saying that the Queen ought to give him the Attorneyship if only for the fact that he was Leicester's eldest boy by the Queen. He could not be described as the first child of Sir Nicolas Bacon who had three sons by his first wife.

At last Burleigh formulated a plan for making Coke Attorney and Francis Bacon Solicitor, but Essex did not trust them and would agree to no terms but his own. He had sworn that Francis Bacon should be the new Attorney. If he were not made Attorney it meant that he (Robert) would suffer a political defeat which neither his pride nor prestige could endure. It had thus become a personal issue and a political one between Essex and Cecil.

In January 1594, the Queen told Essex that she was being pressed to put an end to the war in her Cabinet by making Cecil Secretary of State (in place of his father Burleigh); Stafford, Second Secretary; and Coke Attorney-General. Burleigh "strongly urged the Queen to the nomination of Coke" (Anthony to Lady Bacon, 5th February, 1594), but Essex "set his face against these appointments" and others, and in a conversation with Cecil when they were riding from the Tower together by coach he let his mind be known in no uncertain terms. The story is told by the contemporary Standen to Anthony Bacon:

"My Lord," said Cecil, "the Queen has resolved, e'er five days pass, without further delay, to make an Attorney-General. I pray your Lordship to let me know whom you will favour."

Essex answered he wondered Sir Robert should ask that question, seeing it could not be unknown to him that resolutely, against all men soever, he stood for Francis Bacon.

"Good Lord!" said Cecil, "I wonder you should go about to spend your strength in so unlikely a matter," desiring his Lordship to name a precedent for *so raw a youth* being raised to a place of such moment."

"The Earl," said Standen, "declared that the Attorneyship was but an ordinary Office, *other than PRINCE'S FAVOUR* he could produce no pattern because he had not made any search but that *a younger than Francis Bacon, of less learning and no greater experience, was suing and shoving with all force for an office of far greater importance, greater charge, greater weight, than the Attorneyship. Such an one*, the Earl of Essex said, *he could name him.*"

"I know you mean me," said Sir Robert Cecil, and he proceeded to give his reasons why he should succeed his father Lord Burleigh. "And," he continued, "with regard to the affair of Mr. Francis Bacon, if your Lordship had spoken of the Solicitorship that might be of easier digestion to her Majesty."

The Earl answered, "Digest me no digestions; for the Attorneyship for Francis is what I must have, and in that will I spend all my power, might, authority and amity, and with tooth and nail defend and procure the same for him, and whosoever getteth this Office out of my hands for any other, before he have it, it shall cost him the coming by.

"And of this be assured, Sir Robert. I think it strange both of my Lord Treasurer and you, that you have the mind to seek the preference of a stranger *before so near a kinsman.* For if you weigh in a balance the parts every way of his competitor and him, only excepting five poor years of admitting to a House of Court before Francis, you shall find all other respects whatsoever no comparison between them."

This report indicates the genuine warmth of feeling between the two men. A letter which Essex writes to Francis on the 26th March, 1594, further indicates his affection.

THE EARL OF ESSEX TO FRANCIS BACON

Sir,

I have since had opportunity to deal freely with the Queen. I have dealt confidently with her, as of a matter wherein I did more labour to overcome her delays than that I did fear her denial.

I told her how much you were thrown down with the correction she had already given you; that she might in that point hold herself already satisfied. . . .

I find the Queen very reserved, staying herself from giving any hope, yet not passionate against you till *I grow passionate for you.* Then she said that none thought you fit for the place but my Lord Treasurer and myself. . . . I urged her that though she could not signify her mind to others, *I might have a secret promise;* wherein I should receive great comfort, as in the contrary great unkindness.

She said she neither was persuaded nor would hear of it till Easter . . . and therefore in passion *bade me go to bed,* if would talk of nothing else. Wherefore *in passion I went away,* saying while I was with her I could not but solicit for the cause and the man I so much affected, and therefore I would retire myself till I might be more graciously heard.

And so we parted.

To-morrow I will go hence of purpose, and on Thursday I will write an expostulating letter to her.

That night or Friday morning I will be here again, and follow on the same course, stirring a discontentment in her. And so I wish you all happiness, and rest

Your most assured friend,
ESSEX.

All this unhappily wrought no good, perhaps the reverse, though undoubtedly prompted by true loyalty and brotherly affection. The Queen would not see Francis. Even the fact that he had just unravelled, with Essex and Anthony, the details of a serious conspiracy, no less than a plot to murder Queen Elizabeth at the hands of the Queen's physician, Dr. Lopez ("By God's marvellous goodness hath Her Majesty been preserved," etc. *A True Report of Dr. Lopez his Treason*), did not cause her to relent; neither did his first brilliant successes at the Bar in the preceding term; nor the letter he wrote the Queen.

> I affect myself of no great matter but *only to a place of my Profession,* such as I see divers younger in proceeding than myself, and men of no great note, do without shame aspire unto; but if any of my friends press this matter, my spirit is not with them.

Much as she admired his eloquence, his wit, his wisdom, the Queen would not take one step against the wishes of her ancient adviser, the sick, old man Burleigh who was still afraid what use Francis might make of the Lever of Office if it were put into his hands. Burleigh wanted his son Sir Robert to follow him as Secretary of State. He was afraid of a possible rival. He knew that his son's outlook—brought up in the old school of politics and diplomacy and intrigue—was foreign to the ideals animating Francis and Robert . . . one with his philosophic outlook for political, social and utilitarian reform, and the other with his affable popularity among all classes as a military leader. He could see the Court divisions growing deeper and wider till there was an open clash in the future. Power in the hands of Francis might be disastrous. How could his crippled, hunchback son hope to compete successfully with two such personalities? So . . . while Burleigh was quite prepared to help Francis Bacon in his Renaissance idealism, he was not prepared to lift him into the saddle of Office for the Attorneyship; for there was no telling how far he might ride nor the way he might take.

We can see how eager was Essex to do something for Francis, by another letter written on the 29th March, only a few days after his failure to induce the Queen to see him:

> I have now spoken with the Queen, and I see no stay from obtaining what we desire. . . . She is in a passionate humour nourished by some foolish women; else I find nothing to distaste us; for she doth not contradict confidently, which they that know the minds of women say is a sign of yielding.
>
> I will to-morrow take more time to deal with her and *will sweeten her with all the art I have* to make *benevolum auditorem.*
>
> I have already spoken with Mr. Vice-Chamberlain, and will to-morrow speak with the rest. . . .
>
> The exceptions against the competitors I will use to-morrow; for then I do resolve to have a full and large discourse; having prepared the Queen to-night to assign me a time under colour of some such business as I have pretended. . . .
>
> I am oppressed with a multitude of letters that are come, of which I must give the Queen some account to-morrow morning, and therefore desire to be excused for writing no more to-night; to-morrow you shall hear from me again.
>
> I wish you what you wish yourself in this and all things else,
>
> Your most affectionate friend,
>
> This Friday night. ESSEX.

FRANCIS BACON TO THE EARL OF ESSEX

> I thank your Lordship very much for your kind and comfortable letter, which I hope will be followed at hand with another of more assurance. And I must confess this very delay hath gone so near me, as it hath almost overthrown my health.
>
> When I resolve *the good memory of my father*, the near *degree of alliance* I stand in to my Lord Treasurer, your Lordship's so signalled and declared favour, the honourable testimony of so many Counsellors, the commendation unlaboured and in sort offered by my Lords, the Judges and the Master of Rolls elect; that I was voiced with great expectations, and—though I say it myself—the wishes of most men, to the higher place, *I AM A MAN THAT THE QUEEN HATH ALREADY DONE FOR;* and Princes, *especially Her Majesty,* loveth to make AN END where they begin; when I say, I revolve all this, I cannot but conclude with myself *NO MAN EVER RECEIVED A MORE EXQUISITE DISGRACE.*
>
> And therefore truly, I was determined, and am determined, if Her Majesty reject me, this to do: My Nature can take no evil ply; but I will by God's assistance, with *THIS DISGRACE OF MY FORTUNE* . . . retire with a couple of men to Cambridge, and there live my life in my studies and contemplations, without looking back.
>
> I pray your Lordship to pardon me for troubling you with my melancholy. For the matter itself, I commend it to your love. Only I pray you communicate afresh this day with my Lord Treasurer and Sir Robert Cecil; and, if you esteem my fortune, *REMEMBER THE POINT OF PRECEDENCY.*
>
> In most entire and faithful duty,
>
> F.B.
>
> I pray I may hear from you some time this day.

The phrases in this letter which I have italicized are not ordinary phrases. Do they not appear to convey covert double-meanings? The Queen had "done for" him "already" because she could not and would not recognize him as her son. That was the beginning of the "most exquisite disgrace" . . . something far different than the "disgrace" of waiting to know whether he was successful in obtaining the appointment. What disgrace was there in waiting to know the pleasure of his Sovereign if he were simply plain "Francis Bacon" and no more? If the Queen did not grant him the Office it would be "a disgrace to his fortune" because, despite his open claims that rested on ability, etc., *his chief "point" rested on his "precedency" as a concealed Tudor, which he thought entitled him to rank first before all other candidates.* That is the point he wishes his brother Robert to drive home to the Lord Treasurer, Burleigh. If that be not the explanation what IS the interpretation? The pity is that neither Spedding nor any other of Francis Bacon's numerous biographers (save Parker Woodward) ever tried to understand why such out-of-the-way phrases were ever employed or their enigmatical significance. They have been slurred over by everyone.

Now the Attorney-Generalship was peculiarly a Crown appointment. He was an Officer who was supposed to—

> Carry all English Law in his head, full of rude force and endless precedents, hard of heart and voluble of tongue . . . one who would bring all the resources and hidden subtleties of English Law to the service of the Crown, and use them with thorough-going and unflinching resolution against those whom the Crown accused of treason, sedition, or *invasion of the Prerogative.* (Church, *Life*, p. 34.)

It can hardly be wondered at that the Queen and the Cecils, father and son, thought that Coke would be the most likely public Government official. Had not Francis Bacon done his best in Parliament to curb the Prerogative? Despite this handicap Essex had championed Francis in no half-hearted lukewarm fashion. "He importuned the Queen. He risked without scruple offending her." She apparently long shrank from refusing his request. But his very vehemence with the Queen may have caused her to harden her heart, and some writers have suggested that his warmth of temper eventually wrecked, good and proper, all Francis Bacon's chances of Government Office.

The struggle had now lasted over twelve months and had at last reached a climax. Essex's strivings were, however, all in vain. He had only procured a long delay which was of no benefit; for, on the 10th April, 1594, the Queen appointed Sir Edward Coke to the vacant Office. It was an even greater blow to Essex's pride than to Francis Bacon's financial prospects. It showed unmistakably that Elizabeth had not forgiven Francis for his independent attitude in the Commons. It showed Essex, too, that a State Office was not to be conferred upon his nominee for the mere asking, no matter how good a man he was, as a bounty or gift, lest it might be regarded as an act of subservience to the Earl. The more he persuaded, the more he forced, the more she was resolved to go her own way in spite of her mother-love for him. She leaned to Burleigh's advice. He was the loyal custodian of her secret life. He had steered her in the old days through many delicate manœuvres and to him she was deeply indebted for her preservation in the eyes of the world: And his advice to her was—"Coke." Indeed, Lord Campbell says the obstacles to Francis Bacon's advancement were "his unlucky speech and *the jealousy of the Cecils.*"

> Burleigh, and his hopeful son Robert, now coming forward as Secretary of State, pretended to support their kinsman, but in reality were afraid that, with favourable opportunities, he would disconcert their deep-laid scheme of making the premiership hereditary in the House of Cecil. (*Life*, p. 25.)

The deed was done. Essex had to pocket his choler and to begin the race all over again . . . this time to try to procure for Francis the Office vacated by Coke, the Solicitorship. He had to sue for an Office he had previously spurned. This he would never have done had it not been for the fact that Francis Bacon was more than ever embarrassed financially and was only being kept afloat by constant borrowing from his good friends and from moneylenders. He had, moreover, made a deadly and a bitter enemy of his successful rival Coke, "this pretender to Law," as he would think, who had dared to dispute his claims for so long.

There is no doubt that the blow to the Earl of Essex's pride, the rebuff to his dignity by the Queen's refusal to accede to his wishes, sunk deeply and bitterly into his very soul. It was the first serious clash between their respective temperaments. It created an animus between them which flared up with recurring violence on many future occasions, ending at last in the most disastrous consequences. If the Queen began to be coldly on her dignity, Robert equally began to be inwardly resentful at what he thought was her unfair behaviour to Francis and to himself. The Cecils had won and he was made a mock of in the eyes of the Court.

Apparently, while the Queen had not appointed a new Solicitor in Coke's place, she had held out no hope of appointing Francis to the Office or even admitting him to the privilege of "access." Here we see the same touch of inexorableness and cold anger about her dealings with these two young men that characterized her attitude in her last fatal clash with Robert and Francis. Francis had withstood her Prerogative—an almost unforgivable sin. Robert had tried to take the reins of Authority out of her hands by trying to get his nominee appointed. He was attempting to usurp her kingly seat . . . to assert an ascendency over her. A decision in Essex's favour was the equivalent of submission to his Will. "If either party were to give way it ought to be Essex; that his affection for Francis should yield to her mislike." Such were the poisonous distillations poured into the Queen's ears by the enemies of Essex; and that this same procedure was followed with deadly effect, later, to inflame the Queen against the son she really loved, by the Cecil faction of men and women . . . is proved beyond question.

With the hope of seeing the Queen, Francis went to Greenwich where she was staying for Easter, but he had no success. She would not see him. From Greenwich he writes on the 19th April, 1594, to Lord Keeper Puckering, through whose office the appointments were nominally made:

> I was wished to be here ready in expectation of some good effect; and therefore I commend my fortune to your Lordship's kind and honourable furtherance. . . . If you consider my nature, my course, my friends, my opinion with her Majesty (if this eclipse of her favour were past), I hope you will think I am no unlikely piece of wood to shape you a true servant of.

Five days later, 24th April, Essex writes to Francis in an attempt to bring the Queen and him together so that he may personally plead his case.

> Sir,
>
> The Queen did yesternight fly the gift, and I do wish if it be no impediment to the Cause you do handle to-morrow, you did attend again this afternoon.
>
> I will be at the Court in the evening, and go with Mr. Vice-Chamberlain, so as, if you fail before we come in, yet afterwards I doubt not but *he or I shall bring you* together.
>
> This I write in haste because I would have no opportunity omitted *in point of access. I wish to you as to myself* and rest,
>
> Your most affectionate friend,
>
> ESSEX.

This question of "access" to the Queen so that he could have a few minutes' private conversation with her was now regarded by Francis as very necessary if he were to be successful. He was apparently sure that if he could speak for himself without intermediaries that good would accrue with a happy issue out of all his troubles . . . which were largely financial. Spedding says:

> It is impossible to read the history of this tedious and vexatious negotiation without suspecting some want of judgment in those who managed it, and wishing that *he could have said a few words for himself in his own way.* (*Life*, p. 295.)

It will be seen later that it was this same "want of access" to the Queen that was the real source of the trouble that led Essex to such violent methods . . . to his "fatal impatience." Francis felt that he could melt the cold anger of the Queen by the warmth of his filial love and that she would respond "to the voice within answering his cry, *You know we are akin!*" Essex thought so, too. Indeed, does not the entire business convey the impression of two unacknowledged sons trying to break down the State conventions which surround the Queen to obtain something to which they think they are naturally entitled? How can all this be otherwise explained?

On the 1st of May Francis wrote to Sir Robert Cecil who replied that "I do think nothing cut the throat of your present access than the Earl's being somewhat troubled." A few days later Essex wrote to Lord Keeper Puckering pressing Francis Bacon's claim. It had no effect. Apparently Essex had absented himself from Court to signify his vexation, giving out that he was ill. The Queen instead of sending or waiting for him *visited him apparently more than once* just as a mother would do. He writes to Francis, 13th May, 1594:

> I wrote you not till I had a second conference with the Queen because the first was spent only in compliments. . . .

> This day she hath seen me again. . . . I told her I had written Sir Robert Cecil to solicit her to call you to that place which all the world had named you to. . . .
>
> Her answer in playing jest was that she came not to me for that; I should talk of those things when I came to her, not when she came to me. . . . I would have replied but she stopped my mouth. . . . To-morrow or the next day I will go to her. . . . Your most affectionate friend.

Five days later he writes again:

> I went yesterday to the Queen through the galleries in the morning, afternoon and night. I had long speech of her with you. . . . I urged . . . she would do this one thing for my sake. . . . She did acknowledge you had a great wit, and an excellent gift of speech, and much other good learning. But in law she rather thought you could make show to the uttermost of your knowledge, than that you were deep. . . . She has shown her mislike of the suit as well as I had done my affection in it; and that if there were a yielding, it was fitter to be of my side. . . .
>
> I added Her Majesty had made me suffer . . . which all I should bear with patience . . . if she would but grant my humble suit in this one . . . and that my sad heart had need of hasty comfort. . . . I wish you all happiness and rest, Your most affectionate friend.

So the importuning goes on in many ways unrecorded by history. The months pass. Elizabeth makes no Solicitor. She will not see Francis. She cannot forget that he thwarted the Queen's Will and so affronted her personally. But her advisers were going one by one, and who could take their places? Walsingham had gone; Burleigh was almost worn out; Raleigh out of favour. Apart from the narrow-minded Coke, Robert Cecil was the only one to whom she could turn for advice and he "had more craft than wisdom." It was probably these considerations—the first step towards a *rapprochement*—that prompted her to give Francis Bacon as a stop-gap, a commission involving him in a journey to the North of England. He was taken ill at Huntingdon, however, and notified the Queen that illness had prevented "my earning so gracious a vail (profit) as it pleased your Majesty to give me." She was obviously beginning to relent, for in August, though still out of Court favour, we find him being employed by the Queen in the examination of prisoners implicated in plots and treasons against her life.

On the 20th August, Lady Bacon wrote to Francis a letter in which she says, "*I do not write to my Lord Treasurer because you liked to stay. Let this letter be unseen.*" Upon which Spedding remarks:

> But why should Bacon have wished to "stay" Lady Anne from "*writing to the Lord Treasurer?*" If the subject which she proposed to write about was the still-vacant Solicitorship, it is strange that he should have wished to delay an application to Burleigh. . . .

Is it not evident that Francis was afraid lest Lady Bacon, in her anxiety, would remind her brother Burleigh that Francis had a right to the Solicitorship by reason of his Tudor Birth; that his expectations naturally lay with the Queen as his mother . . . and that a woman's argument of this kind would probably do more harm than good. His secret relationship to the Queen was an ended chapter in his life with his "Letter of Renunciation" to the Lord Treasurer a couple of years previously. There could be no other reason, for on the 24th and 25th August, Francis Bacon wrote Lord Keeper Puckering again about the Office, and then to Anthony Bacon that there was some bad news from Ireland which had so troubled the Queen that there was no opportunity to move her.

He is still employed by the Queen in interrogating prisoners at the Tower. More letters pass about the Solicitorship to one and another but the Office is still in suspense. Michaelmas term passes without a Solicitor being appointed; and Anthony Bacon during all the autumn is busy with "urgent applications to various friends for loans of money", mainly out of anxiety to supply the necessities of Francis. Says Spedding, Vol. I, p. 323:

> It is worth recording that in all this correspondence I find no trace of disagreement between them. Not a word of reproof, expostulation, reluctance, or impatience, drops from Anthony. . . . It affords a strong presumption that *he* at least, who had the best means of judging and was every way so much interested, *did not disapprove the course which Francis was taking or suspect him of prodigality or carelessness.*

There is no doubt, however, that at this time Francis was getting through large sums of money. There are money statements which show it. Why did it never occur to Spedding to probe the cause of his alleged "extravagance"? Had he done so, he would have discovered that Francis Bacon's expenses were the costs of writing, printing, publishing books in English . . . the creation of an English Renaissance. What a pity that so laborious a researcher missed his way over and over again. He failed to read the signs in the Elizabethan forest, and therefore he never found his way to the heart of the Master-Mystic and Sweet-Singer Prospero. What a crown to all his labours this would have been . . . the discovery that the man Spedding loved so passionately, was the man who sat in the seat of Apollo at Gorhambury as SHAKE-SPEARE!

Anthony never disapproved of the debts incurred by Francis for he was heart and soul with the ideals of Francis was seeking to promulgate practically—the making of a NEW ENGLAND.

So it goes on, Francis being kept in suspense. Christmas arrives. He is the Master of Ceremonies for the Revels at Gray's Inn which lasted nearly fourteen days . . . from the 20th December to the 3rd January, 1595. He wrote the *Prince of Purpoole* (Purple), a wonderful play, full of subtle innuendoes only to be properly understood by a Masonic student aware of his real relationship to the Queen. *The Comedy of Errors* he likewise wrote which was afterwards published under the pen-name of Shakespeare. They were great successes. It was said by contemporaries that the Revels constituted one of the most elegant Christmas entertainments ever presented to an audience of Statesmen and Courtiers, among them being the Lord Keeper, the Lord Treasurer, the Vice-Chamberlain and several of the Privy Counsellors. Spedding says:

> All the Councillors in *The Prince of Purpoole* speak with Bacon's tongue and out of Bacon's brain but the second and fifth speak out of his heart and

judgment also . . . We can thus measure the progress of his philosophical speculations in these early years. (p. 343.)

The Prince of Purpoole, who reigned and died in 1594, was printed anonymously. Whom it was by, where and when it was found, how it came into the publisher's hands we are not informed. We can only gather that it was found by accident and printed without alteration. It is a pity that the publisher, whoever he was, did not tell us a little more about the manuscript. (*Ibid.*)

It is an even greater pity that Spedding did not see that the mysterious anonymous publication of a Baconian MS was a proper matter for further investigation. There is quite a Shakespearean touch in the printing. It was a very significant example of Francis Bacon's methods of mystification, yet Spedding saw nothing worthy of inquiry or a link of similarity with the Shakespeare productions.

As a further spur to his inquiries the *Comedy of Errors* was produced at the same time as the *Prince of Purpoole* with Francis as Master of the Revels. Spedding knew this. He also knew, that while these Plays were being prepared, Francis Bacon had begun a private notebook on the 5th December of quotations, etc., which were all used afterwards in the Shake-speare Plays and never in Francis Bacon's prose works. All these hints were straws showing from which quarter the Wind of the Renaissance was blowing—from Gray's Inn and Twickenham Park. Yet these "significants" never stimulated Spedding to step off the beaten track of ordinary research to inquire into the underlying cause.

Early in January Francis Bacon wrote to Essex about the still vacant office, and he adds:

> Do not conceive out of this I am either much in appetite or much in hope. For as for appetite, *the waters of Parnassus* are not like the waters of the Spaw, that give a stomach; but rather they quench appetite and desires. . . . And to Her Majesty no other reason, but the reason of a waterman: *I am her first man of those who serve in the Counsel of the Law.*

The waters of Parnassus (a Spring sacred to Apollo and the Muses) was a reference to the Plays he had written at Gray's Inn and indicates that Robert Essex knew that Francis was a poet. The letter also showed that he was no longer keen for the appointment of Solicitor and had very little hope of it. Essex wrote more letters on his behalf. Lady Bacon went to London from Gorhambury to see the Queen or her brother Burleigh, but only succeeded in seeing Sir Robert Cecil, who was playing a double game . . . so said the friends of Francis. By this time Francis was heartily sick of the whole business and was ready to wash his hands from the suit, from law, from everything pertaining to the Court. He made up his mind to do what he had half decided to do some twenty months before when the Attorneyship was vacant . . . to abandon the Bar and the legal profession, to betake himself to the life of a student of literature and to go abroad if at all possible.

Essex informed the Queen of this decision and said she would lose Francis altogether if she delayed any longer giving him the office. This produced a crisis. *Francis was sent for to the Court.* He did not see the Queen, but he saw Sir Robert, "*in sort as from Her Majesty.*" Certain proposals were made to him by Cecil on behalf of the Queen but what they were does not transpire; but they must have been important for he asked for time to consider them and to answer in writing. And in his subsequent letter to Sir Robert he says he did not know whether he should write to the Queen. This is what he says:

> Your Honour will remember that upon your relation of Her Majesty's speech touching my travel, *I asked leave to make answer in writing;* not but I knew then what was true, but because I was careful to express it without doing myself wrong. And it is true I had then the opinion to write to Her Majesty... Then I began to doubt . . . whether it might not be taken for presumption in me to write Her Majesty; and so resolved that it was best for me to follow Her Majesty's own way in committing it to . . . .
>
> It may please your Honour therefore to deliver to Her Majesty that it is an exceeding grief to me that any mention (of travel) should come from me should offend Her Majesty, whom for these one and twenty years (for so long is it that I kissed her Majesty's hands upon my journey into France) I have used the best of my wits to please. . . .
>
> The mention of travel to my Lord Essex . . . I accompanied these very words, that upon Her Majesty's rejecting me with such circumstance, though my heart might be good, yet mine eyes might be sore that I should take no pleasure to look upon my friends; for that I was not an impudent man, that could face out a disgrace; and that I hoped Her Majesty would not be offended if, not being able to endure the sun, I fled into the shade.
>
> I did expressly and particularly restrain my Lord's good affection for me that he should in no wise utter or mention this matter till Her Majesty had made a Solicitor. . . . Seeing he did it for the best, I leave his Lordship to answer for himself. . . .
>
> *The conclusion shall be, that wheresoever God and Her Majesty shall appoint me to live, I shall truly pray for Her Majesty's preservation and felicity.*

We only have a copy of this letter by Anthony Bacon's amanuensis so we do not know (as in many other letters) what vital passages were eliminated, but the letter admits of no other interpretation than this: That Francis acknowledged in writing that he was at the disposal of the Queen "wheresoever she should appoint him to live." Does this not likewise imply that the Queen had promised to restore his allowance and to give him some help with his debts? It is not unreasonable to conclude that at this interview he told Cecil that it was not *the Office* of the Solicitorship of which he was enamoured but *the emoluments of the Office* to enable him to follow his own pursuits . . . a fixed income that could not be taken away by the Queen's whim. In any case there can be little doubt that Cecil made Francis definite proposals, and though much is made in the letter of his proposal to travel abroad, it is palpable that the Queen wanted him to stay at home in his present position. But how could Francis stay longer on the perilous edge of a precipice of debts and duns without assistance and security? Without peace of mind?

As far as I have been able to ascertain he had still little or no income from the Bar in 1595, and the examination of prisoners at the Tower could not have brought him in much money. Though it is unlikely that he paid the Queen any rent for Twickenham Park, his personal expenses must have been more than his total emoluments from the law. For months he had only been able to keep going by borrowing to meet the expenses of his staff of literary workers and his printers' bills.

Cecil, like his father Burleigh, was quite happy to side-track Francis by helping him along with his "philosophical speculations" (while pretending to be his friend) and to keep him out of any Government Office simply to safeguard himself. David Mallet in 1740 summed up the position thus:

> Cecil who mortally hated Essex, and had entertained a secret jealousy of Bacon on account of his superior talents, represented the latter to the Queen as *a man of mere speculation,* as one wholly given up to philosophical inquiries, new, indeed, and amusing, but fanciful and unsolid; and therefore more likely to distract her affairs than to serve her usefully and with proper judgment. This unworthy treatment carried Bacon into very free expostulations on his courtly artifices, as he endeavoured in secret to crush the man whom yet he pretended openly to serve. *Life* (Vol. I, p. xi.)

Mallet's statement is quite correct. He had exceptionally sound private knowledge traditionally as a Rosicrosse-Mason (*see* the Masonic Symbols on the Title Pages of Mallet's 1740 Ed.) of knowing the exact truth. The Cecils, father and son, never wanted Francis Bacon in office, but were quite ready to do anything for him financially with the Queen so long as he left them alone politically.

When Sir Robert was sent by the Queen to speak to him on the 21st January, 1595, Francis wrote that they had "parted in kindness, *secundum exterius*" (outwardly). In conversation with Lady Bacon he also said "his speech was all kindly *outward.*" And about the same time he wrote Sir Robert Cecil a warning letter:

> A wise friend of mine . . . said he knew from your servants, your lady, from some counsellors that have observed you in my business that *you wrought underhand against me* . . . that you were *bought by Mr. Coventry for two thousand angels. . . .*
>
> I am not ignorant of those little arts. . . .
>
> Therefore, I pray, trust not him again in my matter. . . .
>
> *But I think my fortune will set me at LIBERTY, who am weary of asserviling myself to every man's charity.*

In other words he is saying, "Do not double-cross me in what you have promised me financially as from the Queen." The last sentence of his letter proves conclusively that he has either received or is going to receive substantial assistance which will free him from charity and impecuniosity. Who could this be from save the Queen?

In another mutilated letter (the most material part being destroyed) to Cecil he indicates that he does not like the practice of the law.

> It is my luck still *to be akin to such things as I neither like in nature nor would willingly meet with in my course . . .* (*hiatus*).
>
> This I write not officiously . . . but honestly and morally. For though, I thank God, I account upon the proceeding in the Queen's service or not proceeding, both ways; and therefore neither mean to fawn nor to retire.

In short, he says he does not care for his profession of a lawyer and that he is not at all particular about being made Solicitor. Quite evidently, he would not have adopted this attitude had he not been sure of his finances. Following these letters he retired to his residence in Twickenham Park for some weeks; and that he was now in good health and spirits is evident by a letter from Anthony to Lady Bacon in which he says "he has not seen him (Francis) looking better," which result had arisen after his interview with Cecil. All this strengthens the view that he was now indifferent to Office and had been definitely helped financially. His letter to Burleigh on the 21st March (quoted in the previous chapter) indicates that *he had no desire to follow the practice of a lawyer except in so far as it might be necessary to serve the Queen on occasions* and that his financial affairs had been bettered not only "*by yourself but by the Queen*."

During Trinity Term he was employed by the Queen in some Star Chamber business. To the Lord Keeper he actually wrote on the 25th May, 1595:

> I would have been glad to have done Her Majesty service now in the best of my years, and the same mind remains in me still; and that it may be, when Her Majesty hath tried others, *she will think of him that she hath cast aside*. For I take it (upon that which *Her Majesty hath often said*) that *she doth reserve me and not reject me*.

Does this not indicate conclusively that there was a secret link and understanding between Francis and the Queen? It seems impossible to me that such touches of intimacy could possibly have occurred between the Queen and any subject who was a rank outsider.

We have seen Francis Bacon's attitude towards the Solicitorship altering as the months passed from his interview in January with Cecil who was the Queen's mouthpiece. From a financial point of view it could only have altered because he no longer needed the money. An assured income was being provided from another source. Francis Bacon was not at all ambitious to shine publicly in law. As far back as 1580 we have seen that he was engaged in "studies of greater delight" than law studies; and that he thought it was a loss of dignity for a person of his rank to be set to the study of the common law. Twelve years later, his literary and ethical occupations absorbed his very being . . . proved by his 1592 letter "that he had taken all knowledge to be his Province," and to become "a sorry bookmaker." Says Parker Woodward, *Tudor Problems*, p. 31:

> The letter of 1594 that he should retire to Cambridge with a couple of literary secretaries is an indication that he had already a literary staff working for him. The "idle pens" reference in the letter to Anthony confirms this. The letter from Essex, in the same year, shows that the Queen was aware of his accomplishments.
>
> That he was a poet is proved by the "waters of Parnassus" passage in his letter of 1595, and the later intimations as to the dedications of "my time to better purposes," "worthy tasks," "poor travails," "Concealed Poets," "public writings of satisfaction," "writ a Sonnet," "give evidence in mine own tales."
>
> Could Mr. Spedding but have caught a mental glimpse of that busy group of literary workers under Francis as chief, at one time at Gray's Inn, at another at Twickenham Lodge, his account of Bacon's literary output

from 1580 to 1603—three or four pamphlets, ten short Essays, and one or two Devices—would have been very different.

Over the period under review Francis either wrote, either wholly or mainly edited, works published either anonymously or under the names of Spenser, Gosson, Marlowe, Greene, Kyd, Watson, Nash and Peele. He wrote a few ascribed to Shaksper of Stratford and edited Sydney's writings.

The fact is that his mind was so full of literary matters, educational pursuits, the ethical symbolism of Freemasonry, and the definite establishment of his "Active Science" in a series of founded organizations, that he did not want to engage in legal work, unless absolutely compelled, because it "drank up too much time." Since he was provided for financially his letter to Burleigh can be properly understood, which states that he is perfectly contented were a fit man like Serjeant Fleming appointed to the Office of Solicitor. And on the 11th October he writes the Lord Keeper that as the Queen is *about to appoint a Solicitor*, his own legal service will not be needed, though if she require him in any particular matter, his willing service will be available. This was information that could only have been learned from the Queen; and the information was only too true, for on the 5th November, Serjeant Fleming received the patent for the Office.

One important fact that is not so generally known and which has a direct bearing on the entire question is this: That on the 14th July the *Queen created a new Office personal to her and to him.* She made him "her Counsel Learned in the Law" conferring on him at a nominal rent a first-class estate . . . presumably as a retainer for his services. This grant comprised sixty acres, more or less of wood, in the forest of Zelwood in the County of Somerset, known as the Pitts. He received it from the Crown on a rent of seven pounds ten shillings a year. And Lady Anne on hearing the news at Gorhambury writes to Anthony on the 7th August:

> If Her Majesty have resolved upon the negative for Francis, as I hear truly . . . *I am glad of it. God in His time hath better in store I trust.* For considering his kind of health and what cumber pertains to that office, it is best for him I hope. Let us all pray the Lord to make us profit by His Fatherly correction; doubtless it is His hand, and *all for the best*, and love to His children that will seek Him first, and depend upon His goodness.

In September, she writes Anthony again:

> With a humble heart before God, let your brother be of good cheer. Alas! *What excess of bucks* [dashing young fellows] at Gray's Inn! And *to feast it on the Sabbath!* God forgive and have mercy upon England!

So Francis viewed the prospect of his defeat and celebrated in roistering and merriment. Such is the glimpse of him seen through his mother's notes . . . feasting with his boon companions, the fraternity of Law, the "Friends of Francis." How much of the solemn philosopher and owlish prig is there to be seen in him up to now? Yet his biographers have ever laid it down that he was a portentously grave prodigy from his childhood days, so that we have an absolutely wrong conception of his personality. Francis was extremely human and he was in high feather despite the fact that he knew the Solicitorship was not for him. And the reason for his happiness was that the Queen and he were reconciled, that he need not follow the profession of a lawyer, and that financial provision was being made for him so that he could follow the bent of his own mind. No wonder he rejoiced among his friends! Who wouldn't have done! The "Bar" was no longer to be his "Bier." He was freed from the drudgery of the law. There is no other explanation for his *volte face* respecting the quest for a Government office—the Solicitorship in particular, and for his feast of rejoicing.

When Fleming was appointed Essex was doubly mortified. He felt it to be an affront to his prestige . . . more so because of the long delay. The Attorneyship was kept vacant for more than a year; the Solicitorship for a year and a half, waiting, it is said, for Francis to apologize to the Queen for his conduct in Parliament, according to Cecil. *He never apologized.* In April 1593 he stated he had said nothing but what he thought it was his duty to say. Two years later, June 1595, he said he had nothing to add in the way of excuse.

Macaulay, followed by a long line of superficialists who have perpetuated his inaccuracies, represents Francis as humbly whining his sorrow to the Queen in obsequious apologies. He did nothing of the kind, though there was much more at stake than they ever suspected because Francis Bacon was no sycophant. As a Member of a free Parliament, he knew he had committed no fault by plain speech and therefore he could not ask "pardon" for the alleged wrong. The liberties and freedom were more to him than "Offices" or "Coronets and Norman blood."

In my opinion, it is questionable whether the Queen ever wanted Francis to take a paid public Government Office, regarding such a position as something *infra dig* considering his secret status as a Tudor. Everything shows that though she was hurt and vexed with him at first she slowly relented; that it was never her intention "to cast him away," never to "reject" but to "reserve" him for "something better in store" as Lady Bacon wrote. This is borne out by the letter of Francis to Anthony, 25th January, 1595:

> Her Majesty would have a delay . . . but what the secret of it is *oculus aquilae non penetravit* (not to be penetrated even by the eye of an eagle).

It must not be forgotten, however, that Lady Bacon wrote that "though the Earl showed great affection yet he marred all *with violent courses.*" But this I believe to be only partially true. Robert was staunch to Francis through and through. He acted, in fact, just as a younger brother would act for the elder whom he loved . . . anxious to show Francis that, as the Queen's favourite son, he could wheedle anything out of his mother and so restore the financial position. The more she hung back the more he pressed. There is no doubt that Francis did not altogether agree with his management of the business . . . i.e., his personal attitude towards the Queen, his sulks, his temper.

Spedding says, referring to the Earl's "violent courses," that "there can be no doubt now that Lady Bacon made a true judgment" (*Life*, Vol. I, p. 370), and Dixon says very much the same.

The Earl's want of tact and temper was more hurtful to his friends than to his foes. He causes Bacon the most grievous loss. Give me the place of the Solicitor—he drums and drums into the Queen's car. . . . As Essex grows hot, she cools: when he storms upon her and will not be denied, she turns from the spoiled boy. Bacon must wait; Fleming shall be her man.

We know more than Dixon did of the secret springs of action, but how truly his summing up of the situation falls into line with the truth of the matter. Essex had failed to win the Queen. When he learned the news he at once left the Queen's Palace at Richmond and went to see Francis at Twickenham Park. Said he:

The Queen hath denied me yon place for you and hath placed another; I know you are the least part of your own matter, but you fare ill because you have chosen me for your mean and dependance; you have spent your time and thoughts in my matters: I die if I do not something towards your fortune: you shall not deny to accept a piece of land which I will bestow upon you.

My fortune is no great matter, answered Francis in refusing the gift. You will turn your estate into obligations leaving yourself nothing but only bound numbers of persons to you. . . . And you will find many bad debtors.

Essex replied, You take no care for that, and pressed it upon him as he wanted in some small measure to repair any loss. So Francis Bacon hesitatingly accepted the offer with these words.

"My Lord, I see I must be your homager and hold land of your gift: But do you know the manner of doing homage in law? Always it is with *a saving of his faith to the King and his other Lords;* And therefore, my Lord, *I can be no more yours than I was*, and it must be with the ancient savings: and if I grow to be a rich man, you will give me leave to give it back to some of your unrewarded followers."

So Francis Bacon got a piece of land at Twickenham[1] adjoining his estate, worth some £1,200, which later he sold, after improvements, for £1,800 . . . less than a third of the Solicitor-General's income.

Why did Essex give it to him?

Is it not clear that for four years Francis had incurred many out-of-pocket expenses, and was happy so to do. For this he had received no payment nor was there any question of any. But Essex had said to him in effect over and over again—"I will get you a Government Office. It shall serve as a brotherly *quid pro quo*." When he found he could not make good his promise, he not only felt humiliated but also that he had failed his elder brother, realizing, too, that there was a veritable debt due to Francis for work done and fees incurred. Essex had no reserve funds but he had a piece of land hard by Twickenham Park which Francis could sell at his convenience . . . not an unusual method of payment in those days when money was scarce and land plentiful. He by no means gave Francis the land for nothing but as a compensation-present. It was a generous gesture indicative of his disappointment at the outcome.

Why did Francis hesitate to accept the land?

[1]A search for the Close Roll of a deed of gift in land from Essex to Francis Bacon has proved futile, so it remains an unsettled question what reward Bacon received for his four years' unpaid services to Essex. (*Francis Bacon and Twickenham Park*, p. 17. A. C. Bunten.)

Because he was afraid lest Robert's temper should lead him into open conflict with the Queen. Says A. C. Bunten, *Bacon and Twickenham Park,* p. 17:

> The story runs that the Queen and the Court were in residence when Essex heard that Fleming had been appointed, and in his usual headstrong manner, hastened over the Thames to Bacon's Lodge opposite. . . .
>
> He had so boasted of his confidence . . . that when he found the Queen had another man in view, his annoyance was great and he showed to the Queen by his petulant manner how angry he was . . . which made matters worse.

In the light of after-circumstances we can now see that Francis Bacon's doubts of accepting the "gift" was lest Essex should misunderstand the position . . . lest it seemed to imply that he (Francis) was under an obligation to him to assist him in any of his future acts. He (Francis) could not be tied to him in any way—save by the bond of blood; he could be no more to him after the gift than he was before—i.e., *his brother*—Francis's *first call and duty lay to his mother, the Queen.* That is the true meaning of the enigmatical phraseology employed . . . "Do you know the manner of doing homage in law? *Always with a saving of his faith to the King.*" In unequivocal terms Francis thus says:

> The Queen comes first . . . always. I thank you for your gift but this cannot bind me to your service. Remember, my first service is to keep faith with the Queen. If a time comes when I must choose between her and you, I must obey my Sovereign rather than my friend, my mother rather than my brother.

Why did Francis talk covertly to Robert like this? Because he was afraid lest Robert's temper should lead him eventually into open conflict with the Queen. He knew that Robert was rash and reckless, indeed, he must have been in a blazing passion when he left the Queen's presence and stood a few minutes later in Twickenham Park telling Francis the "afflicting intelligence," with his fury still hot within him. How could he fail to reflect that Robert's provocative manner and style might alienate the Queen's affection altogether if he conducted his future political and private affairs with the Queen with violent force in an attempt to get his own way. He must have felt the seriousness of such courses with the Queen for, a few days later, he writes Essex a most important warning reiterating what he had already said.

To My Lord of Essex

> It may please your good Lordship,
>
> I pray God her Majesty's weighing be not like the weight of a balance; *gravia deorsum, levia sursum.*
>
> But *I am as far as being altered in devotion towards her* as I am from distrust that she will be altered in opinion towards me, when she knoweth me better. For myself, I have lost some opinion, some time, and some means; this is my account: but then for opinion, *it is a blast that goeth and cometh;* for time, it is true it goeth and cometh not; but yet I have learned *it may be redeemed.*
>
> *For MEANS, I value that most;* and the rather, *because I AM PURPOSED*

NOT TO FOLLOW THE PRACTICE OF THE LAW:—If Her Majesty command me in any particular, *I shall be ready to do her willing service*—And my reason is only, because it drinketh too much time, which *I have dedicated to better purposes. . . .*

For your Lordship, I do think myself more beholding to you than to any other man. And I say, *I reckon myself as a COMMON* (not popular, but COMMON); and *as much as is Lawful to be enclosed of a Common, so much your Lordship shall be sure to have.*

Your Lordship's to obey your Honourable Commands,
More settled than ever.

One can learn a good deal from a careful reading of this letter. Think of the significance of the last sentence.

1. He is *more settled* in his mind and in his finances than ever in spite of having been refused the Solicitorship, worth £5,000 a year. It is not merely a reconcilement with the Queen that is responsible for his peace of mind but primarily because he is free to live his own life, pursue his own ideals on a modest income as the Queen's personal "Counsel Learned in Law." Indeed, within six months (May 1596) he is engaged by the Queen in the prosecution of a William Randal and is also a consultant in the criminal charge brought against Sir John Smyth . . . of provoking a military insurrection against the Queen. Hepworth Dixon says, "*The Queen employs him in her legal and political affairs;* often in business that would seem to belong exclusively to the department of Fleming or Coke; *She endows Bacon with lands and with the reversion of lands and offices.*" (*Personal History,* p. 69.)

2. In the first sentence he tells Robert that his "*devotion to the Queen* is paramount . . . with which nothing can interfere," a clear indication that he cannot follow his younger brother in any heady courses; in any possible clash between him and the Queen, he must side with the Queen.

3. He lets Robert know, too, that he need not upset himself because he has not got the Solicitorship. In a most illuminating sentence, which tells the entire story of Francis Bacon's activities, he writes that he does not intend *to follow the practice of the law* save to do Her Majesty's bidding for *he has dedicated his time to better purposes.*

Note that this "dedication" is not in the future tense. He has dedicated himself already. We have seen that this "philanthropia" possessed him quite early, as a boy, and the clear inference is that his "dedication" to service had never ceased. "*Means*" have been his chief concern but now he is "more settled than ever." How else can this contentment of mind be interpreted but that the Queen is standing by him with monetary assistance? Who else could it be?

4. The letter is ended with a remarkable sentence similar in thought to that which concluded the conversation between them at Twickenham, so that Robert can fully understand that their fraternal relationship cannot come before his "devotion" to the Queen as his mother or his duty to the State of which the Queen is the symbol. I am but "as a Common," and owned, as are all Commons, primarily by the Queen, and you can only have for your share so much of a "Common" as is *lawful* to be enclosed, i.e., you shall still have my services but my chief service is to the State. That is the clear meaning of this enigmatical phraseology.

Quite obviously Francis Bacon has a premonition that Robert, who had a secret, "natural," right to the Throne superior to everyone save himself, might grow impatient if he were not definitely named ere long to the "Succession," and be tempted to play the dangerous game of attempting to force the issue which might entail fatal consequences. Without doubt this matter of the "Succession" must have been discussed between them over and over again. The times were serious . . . bad news from Ireland, ominous offensive preparations in Spain pointing to another Armada. The letter was truly a warning—"*Be careful! Do not precipitate any crisis between you and the Queen. I cannot support you. I am primarily a Queen's man. My first duty and my first love belong to her.*"

In Holland a book had appeared on "the forbidden subject of the Succession." *It was dedicated to Essex.* Someone gave it to the Queen who brought it to his (Essex') notice on the 3rd November, while at Richmond, "in a manner which greatly disturbed him and made him feel really ill" (Spedding); naturally so, as her concealed favourite son who aspired to the Crown. "But the Queen coming to visit him, and being satisfied, I suppose, that he had nothing to do with it made all fair again." By the 12th November, the Court news was (Sidney Papers, i. 360):

> My Lord of Essex hath put off the melancholy he fell into by a printed book delivered to the Queen; wherein the harm was meant him, by Her Majesty's favour and wisdom is turned to his good, and strengths her LOVE unto him.

How like a mother and son! How unlike an old mistress and a young man! Only Strachey's perverted nonsense could dream it otherwise.

A few days later (17th November) Essex adorns the triumphs of the Anniversary Day of the Queen's Accession by presenting her with a marvellous "Device" or Musical Comedy *written by Francis Bacon* which states that the writer is *inspired by Pallas* (the Spear-Shaker), Queen Elizabeth being termed "*The Alone-Queen*" who is being persuaded by Philautia, *the Goddess of Self-Love*, to a certain course of action . . . which does not transpire, the vital parts of the Play having been lost. The drift of the Play seems to be focused on the private lives of the Queen and her two sons.

The end of the year sees all the differences between the Queen and Essex cleared away, Robert being in a more tractable and amiable temper, while Francis has once more open "access" to the Queen and Court by virtue of being the Queen's Counsel Extraordinary.

Who can doubt, in view of the foregoing evidence, that Elizabeth, the "Virgin Queen," was married to the Earl of Leicester and had at least two children by him, brought up in different homes, known to history as Francis Bacon and the Earl of Essex. We know the Queen was parsimonious almost to penuriousness, yet she loaded Leicester with riches and honours. She did the same for Essex. She was so liberal in her gifts that he wrote, "*I have had so much from the Queen that I dare not ask for more.*" And though she may not appear to have been extremely lavish with Francis, yet she found him a Princely Mansion and beautiful grounds at Twickenham, opposite her Richmond Palace, provided him with an income, giving him reversions of lands and offices, and *carte blanche* to the Royal Presence at any time by virtue of the special appointment making him her personal Counsel Extraordinary. She knows the real bent of his mind and she attempts to provide him with the necessary leisure to indulge his "secret whimseys" to the full. Even though he had withstood her Royal Will in Parliament, she again puts him in the way of being able to prosecute his scientific, literary, and ethical studies.

In very truth the history of the Court through the long years revolved round the Queen and her secret husband, and then around the Queen and her two concealed sons. This becomes still more evidential with the closing years of Elizabeth's reign . . . as we shall see. Let us now ask—*Upon what other men did she bestow her personal favours?* Her riches? Her extraordinary honours? Her LOVE? *On no one!*

These are significant facts that tell the truth more potently than argument. They admit of no dispute.

Plate XXIV

Francis Bacon (top) and his alleged father, Leicester
(See Appendix I)

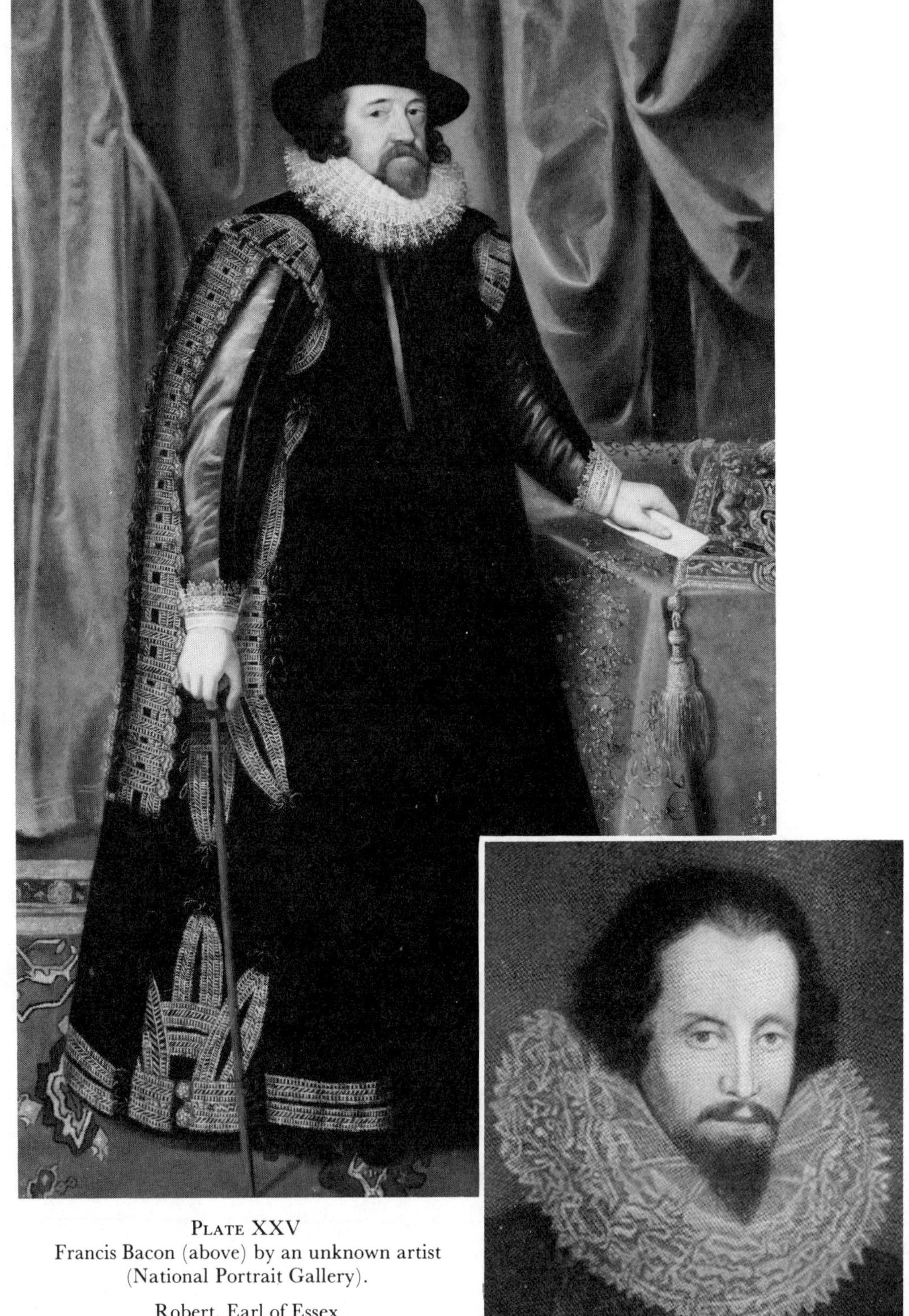

PLATE XXV
Francis Bacon (above) by an unknown artist
(National Portrait Gallery).

Robert, Earl of Essex

Chapter X

THE TWO BROTHERS:
Francis Bacon and Robert Essex
(1596 to 1601)

THE reader will have already obtained from the previous chapter a true insight into the identities and the characters of the three Royal Actors about to play leading parts in a series of Acts destined to end in an agony of tragedy before the eyes of the world—the setting of the stage, the Court of Queen Elizabeth. The passing years had made "the Virgin Queen" more jealous than ever of her prerogative, fearful lest her "Will" should be questioned in any way, loving to pose as an autocratic monarch in her own right. Her son Francis was equally careful as herself in guarding and preserving her honour, in veiling her "indiscretions"—if a secret married life can be so termed—done in the days of heady youth . . . a man of prudence, wisdom and far-sighted, with a true filial love for his mother, unambitious for political advancement so long as he possessed the wherewithal to prosecute his plans for the upliftment of humanity through the gradual dissemination of education and ethics. Over his younger brother he tried to exert an influence at once mild and benevolent. I have no doubt whatever that he uttered the words of the F.M. Ritual to Essex many times in varied phraseology . . . "Let Prudence direct you; Fortitude strengthen you; and Justice be the guide of all your actions." Robert was a true Tudor—hot, impulsive, headstrong, full of the thought that he had a better right to the Throne as a true-born child of a morganatic marriage than anyone else. He was resentful lest anyone else should usurp his place in the Queen's affections and so jeopardize his secret birthright.

This is the secret tangle behind the open life of Elizabeth's Court. All the evidence shows that the two men were bound to each other by no ordinary ties of friendship and that their joint fortunes were one, Francis hoping that Robert would be named to the Succession so that he, Francis, could carry out boldly—without interference—wide-sweeping schemes of reform, social, scientific, etc.; Robert hoping that with the advice of his elder brother England would forge ahead in the comity of nations. They were both idealists in their own particular way, Essex being of a narrower type than Francis Bacon. One was insular and national; the other broad-based and universal. The Earl sought to rule over the fair province of England. His brother had already taken "All Knowledge to be his Province" over which to reign.

Francis Bacon's philanthropic idealism was well known to the Cecils, the Cokes and their purely materialistic ring of courtiers whose horizon was limited by tangible things—personal honours, advancement, High Office, Wealth and so on. Francis was a dreamer of dreams and such men were dangerous in the eyes of the Cecils—neither stable nor reliable for the Service of the State. He had partially infected Essex, too, with his spirit of Philanthropia. Cecil knew that if once these two men held the reins of power, he and his friends would be lost, probably their privileges of caste as bureaucrats destroyed and all they stood for as "Gentlemen by birth, education and property" swept away. Cecil feared, or pretended to fear, that England might go down in a welter of blood . . . civil war and foreign invasion. The Cecils (Lord Burleigh and his son Robert Cecil) knew, moreover, the Queen's secret, and there is no doubt that Robert Cecil communicated the fact, under the rose, to his followers, for, later, this was blurted out in open Court by Coke—then related to the Cecils by his second marriage—when he spoke to Francis Bacon "With that insulting which cannot be expressed." (F.B.'s Letter to Cecil.) The immediate object of the Cecil clan was to sow dissension between the Queen and her two sons . . . to drive a wedge between them; never to allow Robert Essex, a true wedlock-child, to be named to succeed the Queen, to take every opportunity—and to make opportunities—to discredit him in Elizabeth's eyes, especially to *inflame her anger by suggestions that Essex was anxious to usurp the Throne at a favourable moment.*

Francis Bacon's counsel to the Earl of Essex was to pursue a path of extreme conciliation all round and thus to prove to the Queen that he was worthy of her utmost confidence, to apply himself to State affairs, to make her feel that he was the only man—apart from the fact that he was "the Natural Issue of her Body," as the Parliament Act expressed it—to whom she could entrust the Royal Reins of the State Chariot when they threatened to slip from her grasp. Above all, to beware lest by overweening pride and self-confidence, he ran into serious dangers by deadly enemies waiting to throw him, once and for all, out of the Queen's favour, ruining for ever his chance of the Succession. There, is, indeed, strong reason to believe that at a comparatively early date, Sir Robert Cecil had made up his mind that James of Scotland was to succeed Elizabeth and was pledged to further his interests.

Unfortunately, the Earl of Essex had his own ideas respecting a conciliatory policy. Though he acted on Francis Bacon's advice for a time, he made the fatal mistake eventually of trying the Queen's patience once too often with his moods and his speech . . . his headstrong temper to go his own way irrespective of the Queen's wishes.

In June of 1596 the Earl was raised to the height of a popular hero. The Government had decided to attack the Spanish fleet that was once more threatening invasion from their prime base . . . Cadiz. From Plymouth on the 2nd June the English fleet sailed secretly with all the great fighting men on board . . . Effingham, Raleigh, Vere, Mountjoy, and others. And the supreme command was placed in the hands of Robert Essex who had never shown any executive capacity for war. Aided by a favourable wind, they reached their objective on the 20th. With incomparable audacity, the fleet attacked on the 21st, and won one of our most brilliant victories in the annals of Empire. Cadiz was captured. The Spanish fleet was scattered. Writing twenty-six years after the event, Francis Bacon said:

This journey was like lightning. For in the space of fourteen hours the King of Spain's navy was destroyed and the town of Cadiz taken. The navy was no less than fifty tall ships, besides twenty galleys to attend them. The ships were straightways beaten, and put to flight with such terror as the Spaniards in the end were their own executioners, and fired them all with their own hands. The galleys, by the benefit of the shores and the shallows, got away. The town was a fair, strong, well-built, and rich city . . . manned with four thousand soldiers on foot, and some four hundred horse. *Considerations touching a War with Spain.*

The immediate threat of invasion was smashed. Spedding says:

Essex *to whom the successful assault upon the town was chiefly due* . . . was urgent to follow up the advantage and endeavour to destroy the Spanish fleet, then on its way homeward from India; but his colleagues would not risk it. So the fleet returned with its spoil and its honour; and Essex himself with an immense increase of favour with the people, and *not a little of discontent with the Court.* (*Life and Letters,* Spedding, Vol. II, p. 39.)

England was saved for a season. Had the English fleet gone the way of the Spanish Armada, perished in the Bay of Biscay, been crushed under the rocks of Lisbon, smashed by the attack of the Andalusian warships anchored in Cadiz Bay, overrun by their fleet of transports in the Groyne . . . or had the attack on the Spanish Army that governed the heights of St. Sebastian been unsuccessful, England, denuded of her fighting men and her fleet, would have been open to her enemies. The stroke had a Nelson touch about it for sheer audacity of enterprise. No wonder the Earl of Essex was acclaimed as the Saviour of his Country on his return with his victorious ships laden with spoils, "heaps of plate, gold, jewels, damasks, silks, hangings, carpets, scarfs, as living Englishmen had only seen in dreams." Essex's prestige was further enhanced among the common people when it was learned that he had been urgent to follow up the advantage to capture the Indian galleons but his colleagues would not risk it. And the chagrin of everyone was great when it was learned that the Spanish treasure-fleet had sailed into the Tagus and docked safely only a day or two after Essex's proposals were overruled by the Council of War.

There then followed much dispute in Court circles about the division of the spoils and to whom the credit was really due for the victory. The popular verdict acclaimed Essex as the victor, which his enemies at Court were not slow in turning to account, whispering in the Queen's ears that his popularity was dangerous as it might lead him to attempt to seize the Throne. Essex wrote papers in justification of his own views, and was so dissatisfied with his reception at Court that he thought of absenting himself from Court and Council—as he had done on previous occasions when things were not to his liking.

The Queen, well aware of what was going on, tried to hold the scales evenly between the two parties in Court, Francis Bacon warning the Earl against hasty speeches and offensive acts. His feelings must be kept in check and he must do nothing to precipitate a crisis. "Win the Queen! Win the Queen!" was Francis Bacon's advice; to bring her to his side by reason of his pleasant manners and suave disposition . . . to seek a Chamberlain's Staff so as to be ever near her person rather than a Warrior's sword that would lure him away, leaving the Queen open to the influence of his enemies . . . open to their suggestion that he might try a *coup d'etat* if he obtained too much military power; in short, his elder brother told him he would rather see him "*with a White Staff in his hand as my Lord of Leicester had*"[1] . . . thus copying his father—an honour and an ornament to the Court and making himself indispensable as a Statesman for the upholding of the Constitution, so that there could not possibly be anyone else upon whom the Mantle of the Succession could fall. Francis said, in effect:

> You cannot be the head of the Civil Sphere and also the Leader of the Military Council. Your chief aim should be to keep on good terms with the Queen. Give up this lust for military glory for which you are unsuited. Do not chase the shadow and lose the substance; the bubble of victorious exploits for the solid possession of the English Throne.

To this wise advice the Earl demurs. He thinks he can have his feet in both the Court and the Camp as an acclaimed leader. He does not believe in conciliation. The Queen must be driven not led . . . to his way of thinking. She must make him the Leader in the Civil sphere and Military hierarchy. . . . He had been deceived by Cecil and defrauded by Raleigh. How can he be humble and suppliant with the Queen? With Cecil in the saddle of State his (Essex') power was gone. The Queen must be constrained to do him justice, and so on. . . .

The Earl was violently angry and perhaps justifiably so. The Court had shared the victory of Cadiz with his rivals. He had been given neither a fair share of the spoils nor the reputation for the victory. For these reasons he had printed his own account of the capture of Cadiz and pointed out that the Spanish disaster could have been made well-nigh irretrievable, and the prizes far greater had he not been fettered by fools and cowards in Council.[2] Not only had he been compelled to share his successes with Raleigh and others, but, to his bitter chagrin, "the experienced scholar and diplomatist, Sir Thomas Bodley" (to whose wealth and taste we owe the princely library at Oxford), to whom Essex had pledged his word that he should be made Secretary of State, had been passed over by the Queen. She had disregarded his promise to Bodley and Essex felt dishonoured. His absence in Spain had given Burleigh and the Queen the opportunity to elevate Sir Robert Cecil into the First Secretary of State.

> He saw too late that he had only been sent away for Sir Robert's gain. Essex stormed upon the Queen: He would not stay at Court to be mocked; he would bury himself at Wanstead; he would rush to the wars in Flanders and find peace of heart on a Spanish pike. (Dixon, *Lord Bacon's Life*, p. 112.)

[1]Francis Bacon's own words.

[2]His enemy Henry Brooke (afterwards Lord Cobham) had been making mischief and Raleigh's friends caused the Lords to publish an account of the expedition giving Raleigh all the credit. The Queen would not allow him an opportunity to justify his own conduct. Robert therefore printed a private account to counteract this. The populace took his side and this rekindled the Queen's jealousy. Parker Woodward, *Tudor Problems*, p. 43.

Francis Bacon tried to restrain this raging, tearing madness. "My Lord," he said, "*these courses are like hot water; they may help at a pang but they will not do for daily use.*" And he warned Essex that any continued haughty bearing towards the Queen and a craving for unfettered command in the field would lead to his undoing.

Essex, too full of choler to listen to his elder brother, was hurt and resentful, and for the first time there was a breath of coolness between them despite the greatness of the issue at stake . . . the Royal Succession. Three months later Francis wrote Essex very fully a letter of great significance—as remarkable as any of his writings—in which he told Essex he must mend his ways, his attitude to the Queen. It is almost sufficient to tell any student of psychology that Francis Bacon was the author of the Shakespeare Plays. Only a Master-Dramatist who had studied the complex heart of humanity could have composed it. Very specifically, with the sure touch of the psychological-dramatist, Francis Bacon teaches his younger brother how he may gain his ends from the Queen without appearing to force her Will in any way . . . or to trench on her Prerogative of which she was so jealously proud. It is not the letter of one friend to another, of a mere counsellor to an Earl. It is *the letter of an elder brother to a younger, one in which the writer sees the dangerous course that is being pursued.* There is a note of agitation and gravity running throughout. Robert was surrounding himself with followers of a questionable nature, whose influence by their thoughtless views might crash into the dust all Francis's hopes for the advancement of England; all his idealistic plans might be ruined and with it the Earl himself if he listened to their irresponsible opinions. This is the spirit in which the letter was conceived. It is too long to quote in full but it can be read in Spedding's *Life and Letters*, Vol. II, pp. 40-50.

To my Lord of Essex from Mr. Bacon

My Singular Good Lord,

I will no longer dissever part of that which I meant to have said to your Lordship at Barn-Elms from the exordium which I then made . . . .

I desire, before you give access to my advice, to consider first, *whether I have not reason to think that Your Fortune comprehendeth MINE* . . . whether you have taken hurt at any time by my careful and devoted counsel . . . I do not repent me of safe counsel neither do I judge of *the Whole Play by THE FIRST ACT.*

But whether I counsel you the best, or for the best, *DUTY bindeth me to offer to you my Wishes.* I said to your Lordship last time, *Martha, Martha, attendis ad plurima, unum sufficit* (Attend to the one thing needful); WIN THE QUEEN: *If this be not the beginning, of any other course I SEE NO END.*

I will not speak of *Favour of Affection* but of other correspondence and agreeableness; which, whensoever it shall be conjointed with the other of AFFECTION, I durst wager my life that IN YOU she shall come to the question of *What shall be done to the man whom the King delighteth to Honour?*

But how is it now? A man of a nature not to be ruled; that hath the advantage of MY AFFECTION, *and knoweth it* . . . of a popular reputation, of a military dependence: I DEMAND whether there can be a more dangerous image than THIS represented to any monarch living, much more to a Lady of Her Majesty's apprehension?

Whilst this impression continueth in Her Majesty's breast, you can find no other condition than *Inventions* to keep your estate bare and low . . . crossing and disgracing your actions, . . . blasting your merit . . . *carping with contempt at your NATURE* . . . thrusting you into odious Employments and Offices to supplant your reputation . . . abusing you and FEEDING YOU with Dalliances and Demonstrations *to divert you from descending into the serious consideration of your own CASE*; yea, and percase venturing you in perilous and dangerous enterprises.

These are the things plotted and intended as in Her Majesty's Royal mind towards you. . . .

Above all things I wish that all matters past, which cannot be revoked, you would turn away. . . .

I have noted you to fly and avoid (in some respect justly) *the resemblance or imitation of my Lord of Leicester* and my Lord Chancellor Hatton; yet I am persuaded that IT WILL DO YOU MUCH GOOD BETWEEN THE QUEEN AND YOU to allege them—*as oft as you find occasion*—for AUTHOR AND PATTERNS. For I do not know a readier mean to make Her Majesty think YOU ARE ON THE RIGHT WAY.

Then follows much particular advice as to the manner he should adopt when in the Queen's presence . . . even to trivial details.

And the lightest sort of particulars, which yet are not to be neglected, are your habits, apparel, wearings, gestures, and the likes.

The impression of greatest prejudice is that of military dependence. Wherein I cannot sufficiently wonder at your Lordship's course; you say that the wars are your occupation and (intend) to go on in that course . . . you should have left that person in Plymouth . . . Keep it in substance but abolish it in shows to the Queen. For Her Majesty loveth PEACE. She loveth not Charge (expense). That kind of dependence (military) *maketh a suspected greatness*. Let that be sleeping Honour awhile and cure the Queen's mind on that point. . . .

There is none can, of many years, ascend near you in competition . . . But of the places now void . . . I would name you to the place of Lord Privy Seal . . . It fits a Favourite to carry Her Majesty's Image in seal, who beareth it best expressed in Heart . . . but my chief reason is . . . *to divert Her Majesty from this impression of martial greatness*. . . .

You shall continue such intelligencies as are worth the cherishing; you shall pretend to be as bookish and contemplative as ever you were . . . .

Your estate of means is not to be neglected. For believe it, my Lord, till your Majesty find you careful of your estate, she will not only think you more like to continue chargeable to her, but also have a conceit that you have higher imaginations . . . To be plain with you, nothing can make the Queen or the World think so much that you are come to a provident care of your estate, as the altering of some of YOUR OFFICERS. . . .

And so I rest. Oct. 4, 1596

This is manifestly no ordinary letter. It cannot be adequately understood unless the true motive and the underlying conditions which prompted its composition be recognized . . . the secret asides, the undermeanings of the phraseology. The spirit of agitation which pervades the missive is not that of a mere counsellor tendering formal advice to a patron how best to keep in the good graces of his Sovereign. The writer is describing a situation which threatens to engulf them both in ruin for "your

Fortune comprehendeth mine." The prize that Essex is going to lose is the "Succession." It is not merely the favour of his Sovereign that is in jeopardy but something bigger—nothing less than "this Royal Seat of Mars" which he will never occupy unless he mends his ways; and the writer's own vast plans are also in jeopardy, *which, as arranged, are contingent on Robert's fortune.*

In 1596 the question of the "Succession" was still of paramount importance. The Tudor Sun was slowly sinking in the West. Elizabeth, aged sixty-four, had still avoided naming her successor. She would not allow the question to be broached by anyone. By never a hint had she given of the choice in her mind. The disastrous wars of the Roses were still in the nation's mind. No one wanted another war; and a section of the Queen's advisers played on Elizabeth's mounting fears of a *coup d'état,* a military dictatorship by the only possible warlike Lord—hence the absolute necessity that Essex should disarm such suggestions by concentrating on a Civil post, thus refusing to allow himself to be thwarted in his legitimate aspirations for the Throne as the named "Successor." How clear, then, becomes the importance of this letter. . . . "WIN THE QUEEN" by showing her *you are worthy of the English Crown* by your sobriety of conduct, judicial temper and the like—otherwise, "What will the END be for both of us? Our respective ambitions will be trailed in the dust and we may be ground to powder."

Notice how adroitly he refers to the Earl of Leicester—the "AUTHOR" of their being—with the suggestion that if Robert will but follow in his footsteps the Queen will see that her son is on the right way. The letter makes it obvious that it is the Crown that is at stake and that Robert is jeopardizing his own chance and threatening to wreck all Francis Bacon's plans by consorting with undesirables and running a course easy to twist to his hurt by his enemies . . . an estrangement with the Queen. Does not the very phrase, "Your Fortunes comprehend mine! Win the Queen!" show that there was a link between the three persons and a plan previously agreed upon between the two men? But the phrases tell their own story once the key is slipped into the reader's hand. Neither Spedding nor anyone else has interpreted the true meaning of this remarkable letter—the more significant by reason of its suppression by Francis Bacon's literary executors. Had it been published in Elizabeth's day everyone would have known that it related not merely to winning the Queen's favour but to the "Succession." It never saw the light of day until 1670 . . . *seventy-four years after it was penned.* It was then printed by Dr. Rawley in the *Resuscitatio.* The actual letter itself has never been found; and, as we know that Dr. Rawley suppressed much respecting his beloved Master[1]—disclosures that might be injurious to living persons (e.g., heirs of Essex)—we may safely conclude that there were even more direct passages probably suppressed that would have made the relationship of the two men to the Queen absolutely overwhelming.

[1]He (Dr. Rawley) judged some Papers, touching *Matters of Estate*, to tread too near to the heels of Truth, and to the times of the persons concerned. . . . He said, "I have publish'd all I thought fit, or a well-advised Man would have thought fit to be publish'd by me." (T. Tenison, *Baconiana*, 1679, p. 81.)

We see, moreover, that long before the Second Spanish expedition sailed and the Irish campaign launched, Francis Bacon saw that these military measures would lead to the Earl's undoing—traps skilfully laid by his enemies to lead to ruin. It proves the truth of what Francis Bacon wrote seven years later:

> I did as plainly see his overthrow chained as it were by destiny to that journey, as it is possible for any man to ground a judgment upon future contingents. (*Apologia,* 1603.)

Above all, the letter shows how well-founded were Francis Bacon's fears of the Earl's dabbling in military glory. It brought Robert, as we shall see, to the Block and his mother to her death-bed in an agony of remorse for her dead boy.

It is very necessary to dwell on this rather fully because it is from this point that Essex slowly began to "gang his ain gait" . . . rejecting the wiser counsels of his elder brother. It is very necessary to make it clear that Francis Bacon never offered any immoderate advice to the Earl. Over the Cadiz exploit he made the cautious remark of being "infinitely glad now it was past." Robert Essex would have been the last to have imputed any blame to Francis Bacon for his subsequent ill-fated career. He was warned repeatedly and the strictures of later critics are as valueless as they are misleading.

If Essex had only taken Francis Bacon's advice how the course of history would have been altered. He would have won the Succession. The idealism of Francis would have realized itself in numerous ways; bases laid for the building of humanitarian Temples of Science, etc. The Stuart regime with its corruption and shame that began with James would never have been established. The disastrous Civil Wars of Cavalier and Roundhead would never have drenched England in blood. Out of the dead ashes of Feudalism, Francis Bacon's Idealism would have ushered in a New Age on wings of Fraternity and Liberty, Education and Charity. His advice would have "corrected the defects of Essex's character and have made his fortune secure." Self-control and submission would have taught him constancy and composure.

For a while, says Spedding, "he (Essex) seems to have acted upon Francis Bacon's advice with good effect," but "they were fits of affected obsequiousness interrupted with outbreaks of haughty self-opinion." The year closed however, with no open ruptures, Francis remaining on good terms with Elizabeth; "gracious usage and speech from the Queen" he says to Anthony Bacon. During the Christmas holidays Francis presented her with *Maxims of the Law.* He also wrote this year (1596) the fragments, *Colours of Good and Evil* and the *Meditationes Sacræ.* It is also believed that he wrote the *Essays*, the first ten, in their earliest form in the autumn of this year when he was thirty-seven, and published in the following year. To this year must also be attributed two curious Sonnets signed "G. W. Senior" and "G.W.J.," which obviously could only have emanated from a High Freemason as a hint to future ages that a properly constituted body of Freemasons was positively in being with a Central Organization . . . the Grand Lodge with its Grand Senior

Warden and its Grand Junior Warden over which Francis Bacon presided as Grand Master.

The outward amity that had existed for six months between the Earl and the Queen—Essex's grievances all the time rankling in his breast—was again ruptured by a fancied indignity. It was at least a severe trial to a man of his temperament. It arose in this way: The King of Spain was naturally wrathful at the loss of his fleet, the dispersal of his army and the capture of Cadiz. The New Year (1597) found England seething with rumours of great preparations being undertaken to invade the country. The Government therefore resolved to send forth another expedition to attack the enemies' chief port. Essex expected to be named sole commander but the Queen told him that Lord Thomas Howard and Sir Walter Raleigh were to be joined with him with equal authority. Essex therefore "refused to go and had been well chidden for it." (Sydney Papers.) Contemporary gossip also said that:

> Her Majesty had expressed her determination TO BREAK HIM OF HIS WILL and to pull down his great Heart, and that he had replied, it was a thing impossible, and that *he held it from HIS MOTHER'S SIDE*! (*Ibid.*)

The last phrase is a very significant aside indicative that he had the same nature and temperament of the person threatening him, derived from her . . . the Queen herself. It was certainly a pointless remark had it referred to his alleged mother, weak, vain, frivolous and wanton Lettice Knollys . . . the very reverse in every respect of Royal Elizabeth with her inflexible will.

Thoroughly discontented, he sulked in his room for a full fortnight and refused to go to Court, after which the quarrel between them was patched up. Less than a week later, however, he and Cecil had a violent dispute, and once more he threatened to quit the Court, dropping it and everything irrevocably, and journey out of all bickerings to his seat in Wales. *But the Queen would not let him go.* Shortly afterwards another quarrel arose because the Queen appointed the Wardenship of the Cinque Ports (vacant by the death of Lord Cobham) to Cobham's eldest son, one of his (Essex's) bitterest enemies, when Essex wanted Sir Robert Sidney to have the place.

> "I have just cause to hate Lord Cobham," he said, "for his villainous dealing and abuse of me. He hath been my chief persecutor most unjustly; in him there is no worth. If therefore Her Majesty would give him of the honour, I have right cause to think myself little regarded by her."

So resolved was the Earl to finish that a few days later, 10th March, he and his followers and horses were ready to leave the Court when the Queen intervened and "willed him to come to Court," to her. She received him privately, and, to mollify him, made him Master of the Ordnance. So Essex stayed!

Here we see the clash of two "WILLS" of the same type exactly . . . a series of explosions . . . steel clashing on steel making the sparks fly . . . the Queen constantly treating him as a refractory son and endeavouring to bring him to heel by letting him know he cannot have his own way, and Robert equally determined not to be tied to his mother's apron-strings, and to have an articulate voice in State Affairs . . *as his right.* It is unthinkable that a mere subject could act so preposterously and that a Sovereign Queen should tolerate such behaviour, actually condoning the offence by a mollifying gift. The facts are plain: Both presumed on their secret relationship—the Earl like a spoiled boy wanting favours because she was his mother; the Queen constantly thinking how she could best show him that she held the reins, fearful lest he should kick over the traces in more ways than one. It was a dangerous game for both of them and it unfortunately grew in violence until, at last, their misunderstandings were finally settled in a fatal termination.

The intended attack on the Spanish preparations had been frustrated by the weather, the English fleet being driven back to refit. It started out once more in June, Essex being in sole command. Whether he wanted the command is doubtful. Cecil certainly wanted to get him out of the way—the better to ingratiate himself with the Queen with whom he was becoming more and more a *persona grata.* Parker Woodward says, "He was pushed into taking charge of another expedition against Spain." (*Tudor Problems*, p. 44.) Whether he really wanted to go or was commanded to go seems uncertain but clearly his absence played into the hands of his enemies.

The original plan was to attack the Spanish Armada at Ferrol. But reports showed that the English fleet was not strong enough to give battle, so Essex decided to wait for the home-coming Spanish treasure-ships off the Azores. He had the misfortune, however, to miss them, and when he returned home to Court on the 29th October, he met with a very chilly reception from the Queen. She naturally blamed Essex for the failure of the expedition. He retired offended to Wanstead House.

> For himself he is already disquieted, keeps in, and went not this day to Parliament. (*Syd. Papers.*)

His aloofness and discontent lasted nearly two months.

Apart from being held, right or wrong, responsible for the non-success of the fleet, Essex had returned to find fresh exasperations awaiting him. A week before his arrival the Queen had created Admiral Lord Howard the Earl of Nottingham, which combined titles gave him precedence over Essex at Court. In his absence Sir Robert Cecil had been made Chancellor of the Duchy of Lancaster. These were indignities which his spirit could not stand. He refused to appear in Parliament, Council or Court.

In this case as in the other, the Earl's attitude is simply not understandable if he were a Devereux and not a Tudor. Lord Howard was twice as old as Essex, a first-class officer, now too old for active work. Cecil's appointment mortified him because it was a signal honour.

Now Essex was not a niggardly, narrow-minded, covetous man . . . far from it. He had real nobleness of nature. As a subject he had no valid reason to be offended. He knew perfectly well that the Queen could make and unmake at will. But from his point of view, as a Prince of the Blood Royal, no one had any right to take precedence of him at Court even if his true identity were nominally concealed. His mother was placing him in an invidious position. He was pre-eminently a Tudor with expectations. *And for the Queen to honour an open enemy like Cecil who would fight any royal claim to the last,* seemed to indicate that Elizabeth was being influenced by outsiders rather than by her own flesh and blood. So . . . "I do well to be angry."

But negotiations between the Queen and Essex were reopened. A contemporary reporter says:

> The Queen by this patient and long-suffering of my Lord of Essex was grown to consider and understand better the wrong done to him. I hear that my Lord of Essex desires to have right done unto him, either by a commission to examine it, or by combat either against the Earl of Nottingham or any of his sons or of his name that will defend it. Or that Her Majesty will please to see the wrong done unto him; *and so will he suffer himself to be commanded by her as she please herself.* Here is such ado about it, as it troubles this place and all other proceedings. (*Syd. Papers.*)

Once more the Queen mollified the Earl by creating him, Robert, Earl Marshal of England which restored his precedency by letters patent. So the Earl smiled at his competitors and was happy again.

Now . . . can anyone imagine a Sovereign of Elizabeth's temper going out of her way, over and over again, to smooth out quarrels with a fiery-tempered young nobleman by presenting him with something to take off the edge of his anger—if he were merely a noble and nothing more? Out of the last quarrel he was made Master of Ordnance. He had now been created Earl Marshal (the very Offices that his brother Francis had warned him from accepting). To say that she did it because she loved him as "a Mistress"—*vide* Lytton Strachey—is ridiculous. But that she acted so strangely out of a love-passion (and not out of reasoned judgment) is obvious. It is more obvious still that it was the Love of a Mother for a Son . . . at times distracted to know what to do for the best lest her Secret became public property. We see the spectacle of a doting mother and a spoiled boy which ends in tragedy.

The spring of 1598 saw the Earl on good terms with everyone . . . especially the Queen. On the 10th February, she made him a present of £7,000 worth of cochineal, part of the booty of the last voyage to the Azores. We also hear of his—

> Giving very diligent attendance upon the Queen, and in some sort taking upon him the dispatching of all business, in the absence of the Secretary, that concerns her Majesty's service. (*Syd. Papers.*)
>
> This was exactly the position in which Francis Bacon most wished to see him; and although Essex *had begun to tire of asking counsel* from one who was always advising him NOT to do the thing he was bent on doing, and had of late not consulted him as he used to do, he found or made an occasion to represent to him the value of the opportunity and exhorted him to improve it. (Spedding, *Life and Letters*, Vol. II, p. 94.)

In spite of the estrangement that had begun in the previous year and Essex's aloofness, Francis followed up this conversation with a letter congratulating him on devoting himself to civil matters and particularly warning him how to act regarding Irish affairs which had then become very critical through the trickery of the Earl of Tyrone . . . a soldier of genius, a past-master in the art of evading promises and breaking treaties. For three years there had been open rebellion in Ireland suspended by truces, and Irish matters were rapidly drifting to a crisis in which the English Government would be compelled to act in some way—by remedying the alleged grievances and winning Tyrone's good will or quelling the revolt by force of arms. Sir Robert Cecil, who had visited Ireland, returned at the end of April quite unsuccessful in arranging a peace-settlement with the Irish malcontents. At the Council Board Lord Burleigh represented the Peace Party and Essex the War Party. Once more Francis Bacon had the mortification of seeing Robert standing on the brink of a military precipice into which (as it subsequently transpired) all his hopes and Essex's ambitions were destined to crash into nothingness.

His conversations and warning letter had fallen on deaf ears; Essex had gradually fallen under the evil influence of Sir Christopher Blount, who had married his foster-mother, the Countess of Essex. He was a worthless man and made the Countess as vile as himself. But the bold, coarse, dashing ways of this bravo appealed to the martial ardour of this giddy "step-son" of thirty. The Earl got Blount a command in the army, a seat in the House of Commons, and put him in offices of trust near his own person. He drew nearer to Blount in mind and with his (Blount's) worthless fire-eating associates. Worse than all he listened to Blount's evil counsel.

> Bacon and Blount propose to Essex the two courses most opposed to each other: Bacon the abandonment of his military pomp, of his opposition to the Queen, and *the acceptance now and forever of that great part which Leicester filled for so many years*; Blount the pursuit of war and glory, so as to dazzle the multitude, overawe the Queen, find employments for his companions and consolidate his personal power . . . One asks him to be grave, discreet and self-denying. The other fires his blood with maddening and dramatic hopes. (Hepworth Dixon, *Personal Hist. of F.B.*, p. 86.)

The attempted solution of the Irish difficulty started disastrously. At the Queen's Council in June a stormy scene occurred over the question of appointing a Lord Deputy for Ireland. The Queen proposed to give the Office to Sir W. Knollys, but Essex being aware that the suggestion emanated from the Cecils vehemently opposed it and insisted that the appointment should be given to Sir George Carew.

> The Queen, offended at the positive tone in which Essex had presumed to overbear her opinion and advance his own, made a sarcastic rejoinder, on which he so far forgot himself as to turn his back on her, with a contemptuous expression. Her Majesty, exasperated beyond the bounds of self-control by this insolence, gave him a sound box on the ear, and bade him, "Go and be hanged."
>
> Instead of receiving the chastisement which his own ill-manners had produced, as a sort of angry love-token, and kissing the royal hand in return for the buffet, *he grasped his sword-hilt with a menacing gesture.* The Lord Admiral hastily threw himself between the infuriated Earl and the person of the Queen and prevented him from the unknightly deed of drawing his weapon upon a

lady and his Sovereign; but he swore, with a deep oath, that *he would not have taken that blow from King Henry, her father,* and that it was an indignity that he neither could nor would endure from anyone.

To these rash words he added some impertinence about "A King in Petticoats!" rushed with marked disrespect from the Royal Presence, and instantly withdrew from Court. (A. Strickland. *Elizabeth*, p. 626.)

"Four or five months passed in ineffectual endeavours *ON THE QUEEN'S PART* to extract from him some apology or submission which might open the door to reconciliation," says Spedding. Essex never attended Court and posed as a much-injured man, the plain fact being that he had only received a box on the ear, when, *had he been a mere subject, he would have been sent to the Block for threatening his Sovereign.* As Earl Marshal he was sworn to defend her from all personal injury and to commit to prison anyone who threatened her person. In some way, a compromise was effected and in November he was again received at Court; chiefly, perhaps, because all Ireland was drifting into a state of insurrection, Protestant settlers being murdered in their beds and their houses fired. Ulster rises; Connaught is aflame; Munster hurls defiance; Spanish men of war stand off the coast threatening to land regiments to assist the rebels; Drogheda is in danger; Dublin is not safe. And while all this storm is brewing, the great Lord Burleigh dies—the Queen tending him to the last—leaving the Treasury and the Courts of Wards vacant. Essex wants both posts but Cecil, who thinks the offices held by his father should descend to him, advocates that Essex should be placed in command of the Irish expedition as Raleigh had refused to go.

"ROBART TIDIR" (WELSH FOR TUDOR) CARVED IN STONE IN THE TOWER
(*See Appendix* I, *p.* 360)

At the Privy Council held 8th March, 1599, Essex was made Lord Lieutenant, Lord Mountjoy, who was first named to the place being dropped, apparently through the Earl's influence and Cecil's intrigues. Cecil undoubtedly pressed the Queen to give Essex the command, for this would put the sea between him and the Court. In this the diplomat had outwitted the militarist. Whether Essex really wanted the post is difficult to ascertain. Whether he wanted it or not, to Ireland he had to go. Strickland says, *Elizabeth*, p. 641:

Essex appears to have received some hint that his appointment was the work of his enemies, and he endeavoured to back out of the snare, but in vain, and in the bitterness of his heart, he addressed the following sad and passionate letter to Elizabeth:

From a mind delighting in sorrow; from spirits wasted with passion; from a heart torn to pieces with care, grief and travail; from a man that hateth himself, and all things else that keep him alive; what service can your Majesty expect since *any service past deserves no more than banishment and proscription to the cursedest of all islands?*

It is your rebel's pride and succession that must give me leave to ransom myself out of this hateful prison, out of my loathed body, which if it happened so, your Majesty shall have no cause to mistake the fashion of my death, since the course of my life could never please you.

Happy could he finish forth his Fate,
In some unhaunted desert most obscure,
From all Society, from Love and Hate,
Of worldly Folk; then should he sleep secure.
Then wake again, and yield God ever praise,
Content with hips and haws and bramble-berry,
In Contemplation passing out his days,
And change of Holy Thoughts to make him merry;
And when he dies his tomb may be a bush,
Where harmless Robin dwells with gentle Thrush.

Your Majesty's Exiled Servant,
ROBERT ESSEX.

This letter cannot be said to ring with the strains of a lover to his mistress. But it does most truly fit in with the real facts—a concealed son being sent away on a perilous expedition and fearful of the consequences that may befall both while he is away . . . the influences that may be brought to bear on his mother the Queen to alienate her by his enemies. As it was, his foes rejoiced at the likelihood of his absence. Says Church, *Life of Bacon*, p. 41:

"Things became more difficult between him and *his strange Mistress*; and there were never wanting men who, like Cecil and Raleigh, for good and bad reasons, feared and hated Essex, and who had the craft and the skill to make the most of his inexcusable errors.

At last, he allowed himself, from ambition, from the spirit of contradiction, from the blind passion for doing what he thought would show defiance to his enemies, *to be TEMPTED into the Irish Campaign of 1599.*"

E. G. Harman, C.B., in *The Impersonality of Shakespeare*, p. 61, holds a similar view. He says:

When Essex was persuaded to take the Irish command, he was already in the toils of his enemies, who *cared little about the reduction of Ireland and the waste of English lives in comparison with the object of ruining the Earl and securing power for themselves.*

E. A. Abbott, D.D., writes, *Francis Bacon*, p. 57, similarly:

Essex's genuine unwillingness to accept the command is proved by a recently published letter (1st Jan, 1599) from the Earl to his intimate friend Southampton, who vehemently dissuades him from going. Essex says, "*I am tied in my own reputation to use no tergiversation*; *the Queen hath irrevocably decreed it, the Council do passionately urge it.*"

He is aware of all the dangers of absence from Court and the designs of his enemies, but there is no help for it; "*into Ireland I go.*"

Such was his dread of the Cecilian plots at Court in his absence [the *real PLOT was the damning of Essex in Elizabeth's eyes so that she would never name him her SUCCESSOR*], that even at the last moment he refused to depart without *an express permission under the Broad Seal to return whenever he pleased.*

Where was Francis Bacon all this time? Well . . . Essex had had no speech with him for eighteen months. He had even opposed Francis Bacon's Bills—*The increase of Tillage and Husbandry* and *The Increase of People*—for the restoring of tillage and the increasing of the population. They had drifted, in a sense, from the accomplishment of their respective purposes, and their goals now seemed to lie eternally apart. Francis, by this time, was certain that Essex would never secure the Throne, and that if ever his idealism was to have any concrete result, it would never be through the assistance of his younger brother in the way they had once planned it together. Yet on the eve of his fatal voyage to Ireland, Essex rode to Gray's Inn Square for the last time to see his brother Francis, to ask his opinion, and, perhaps, to crave his blessing on the venture.

Francis Bacon told him that Ireland had been the grave of many good Englishmen and that she would never be conquered by the sword; she would only be won by the plough, drainage of bogs, new roads, new towns. He told Robert that his enterprise would fail if he relied on purely war-like measures and that his chief object should be to inaugurate peaceful and active co-operation between the Protestant settler and the native population with the help of Parliamentary subsidies. He warned him of the difficulty of the work that would confront him in many ways and that he was leaving the Queen in the hands of his enemies. Writing years afterwards, a report of the conversation, Francis said to him:

> It would be ill for her, ill for him, ill for the State. I am sure, I never in anything in my life dealt with him in like earnestness by speech, by writing, and by all the means I could devise . . . I did as plainly see his overthrow, chained as it were by Destiny to that Journey, as it is possible for any man to ground a judgment on future contingents. (*Apologia.*)

How much Essex took to heart this honest advice is difficult to say. But it was then too late to draw back. For eighteen months he had stopped his ears to the honest voice of the one man who loved him even dearer than a brother. Twenty thousand men were sent across the Irish sea under the Earl's command. In quitting Whitehall he assumed the command of a Sovereign Prince. The pacification of Ireland he swore to complete:

> "I have beaten Knollys and Mountjoy in the Council," wrote Essex, "and by God I will beat Tyrone in the field."

On the 27th March he rode through the City of London on his way to Chester accompanied by a large company of nobles and gentlemen, the people flocking into the streets with cries of "God Bless your Lordship."

He arrived in Dublin to find the army in poor condition, quite unfitted for an arduous campaign. One of his first letters home contained the phrase, "I am defeated in England." Even before he had left England he had angered Elizabeth, and, unfortunately, this grew in intensity from the first days, so that at the finish her letters maddened him to desperation. He had vexed the Queen by appointing his friend, the Earl of Southampton, the General of Horse. Southampton was in disgrace for marrying without the Queen's consent. She at once vetoed the appointment. Essex next made his nominal "step-father," Sir Christopher Blount, the Marshal of the Army and wanted him made a member of the Irish Privy Council. Elizabeth refused to entertain the proposal that he should be a Privy Councillor.

> "I sued to Her Majesty to grant it as a favour," he wrote to the Council, "but I spake a language that was not understood . . . But I see, *let me plead in any form, it is in vain.*"

He was next to drive her distracted by exercising a privilege of making Knights . . . a privilege that should be properly confined to the Sovereign. His enemies at Court whispered in her ears that he was already invading the royal prerogative and "*Where would it end?*"

From the time he was appointed Lord Lieutenant, says Basil Montague,

> until his return, the whole of his actions were marked by a strong determination that *his Will should be paramount to that of the Queen.* (*Life of F.B.*, p. 48.)

This is perfectly consistent with the view that Essex was a Tudor with the same Tudor Will as Elizabeth. It is utterly inconsistent with the suggestion that he was the Queen's Lover. He even threatened the Queen that "he was returning with Blount, and would take the Marshal's Office on his own shoulders, asking at the same time to be relieved of his command." (J. E. Neale, *Queen Elizabeth*, p. 356.) That is a typical threat of a headstrong son who thinks his mother should give way to him, forgetful of the fact that he was first a SUBJECT.

He did not return and he did not get his own way; very properly so. Nor did he make war as the Queen had directed him to do. The Irish Council persuaded Essex that the main operation in Ulster should be postponed until June "when the grass had grown and cattle for feeding the army were fat" and to attack in the South.

Without acquainting Elizabeth with this fundamental change of plan, Essex set out to war in his own way. After a series of marches and counter-marches through Leinster and Munster, June came and went . . . the month arranged for the Ulster campaign. The rebel army was strong, 18,000 foot and 2,000 horse . . . half in Ulster. And when Essex tried to bring Tyrone to battle the rebel leader simply retreated in a wilderness of bogs and fens. In July he was back in Dublin with nothing to his credit save a paltry castle and a broken, weary and dispirited army. By August his army was reduced to 4,000 men owing to desertions, sickness and casualties; and the necessity of garrisoning places in Leinster and Munster. He asked for reinforcements but when they arrived his total force was only 4,000 at the most. By the 3rd September, however, he had caught up with Tyrone and offered him battle repeatedly. It was declined. In its place Tyrone offered a parley . . . to discuss terms and an honourable

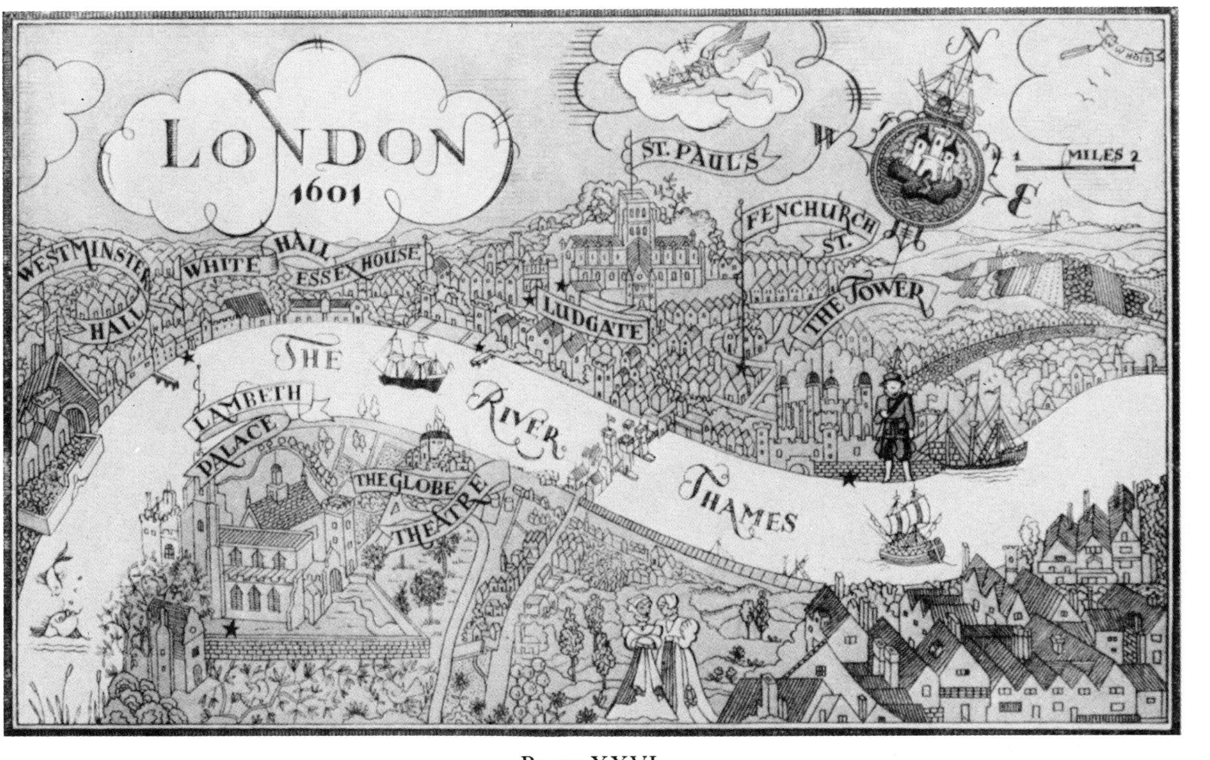

Plate XXVI
London in 1601, the year of the execution of the Earl of Essex
(*See p. 257*)

PLATE XXVII
The Tower of London in Queen Elizabeth's day
From *The England of Shakespeare* by Edwin Goadby

settlement of grievances. Essex's troops had been already decimated and, although he would rather have fought, he decided to hear what Tyrone had to say. He was undoubtedly very largely influenced in this decision by the fact that the Queen had all along been writing letters which had convinced him that Cecil, Raleigh and others had effectually poisoned the mind of the Queen against him. He wanted to return to Court to confound his enemies and refute whatever statements had been made. Says Strickland:

> She wrote in so bitter a style to Essex that he fancied her letters were composed by Raleigh. He perceived that his ruin was determined by the powerful junta of foes, who guided the Council and had poisoned the royal ear against him. (*Elizabeth*, p. 642.)

The Queen openly spoke of Essex's proceedings as "unfortunate, without judgment, contemptuous and not without some private end of his own." She spoke in this strain to Francis Bacon, who told her it would be much better if she were to send for him and satisfy him with honour at home, to have him at Court again "*with a white Staff in his hand as my Lord of Leicester had,*" for—

> "to discontent him as you do and yet to put arms and power into his hands may be a kind of temptation *to make him prove cumbersome and unruly.*" (How can this apply to anyone save mother and son? Note, too, the reference to Leicester.)

The Queen did not follow this advice. "She had already" (30th July), says Spedding, "forbidden him to leave his post without license, and she now resolved to demand from him a strict account of what he had done and meant to do."

It was this atmosphere of uncertainty of what was happening at home that was the dominating factor at the "parley" which afterwards fruited into a truce and then to a series of terms between the belligerents which Essex was to deliver to the Queen verbally. He wanted a reasonable excuse to get to her. What these terms actually were and the culpability of Essex in arranging a truce and terms . . . have long been a matter of dispute between biographers and historians. Strickland says:

> The policy pursued by Essex was of a pacific character. He loved the excitement of battle when in the cause of freedom, or when the proud Spaniard threatened England with invasion; but, as the Governor of Ireland, his noble nature inclined him to the blessed work of mercy and conciliation.
>
> He ventured to disobey the bloody orders he had received from the short-sighted politicians. . . .
>
> If the generous and chivalrous Essex had been allowed to work out his own plans he would probably have healed all wounds, and proved the regenerator of Ireland; but, surrounded as he was by spies, thwarted by his deadly foes in the Cabinet, and, finally, rendered an object of suspicion to the most jealous of Sovereigns, he only accelerated his own doom.
>
> The Queen wrote stern and reproachful letters to him. He presumed to justify himself for all he had done and all he had left undone . . . The Queen was infuriated, and was, of course, encouraged by her Ministers to refuse everything. . . .

> Tyrone's conditions were no more than justice and sound policy ought to have induced the Sovereign to grant. Elizabeth regarded it as treason, on the part of Essex, even to listen to them . . . The fiery and impetuous Earl was infuriated, in his turn, at the reports that were conveyed to him, of the practices against him in the English Cabinet.
>
> He was accused of aiming at making himself King of Ireland, with the assistance of Tyrone; nay, even of aspiring to the Crown of England, and that he was plotting to bring over a wild Irish army to dethrone the Queen.
>
> Elizabeth's health suffered in consequence of the ferment in which her spirits were kept, and the *agonizing conflict between love and hatred* . . . but the treasons of Essex existed only in the malignant representations of Sir Robert Cecil, Raleigh, and Cobham.

Having Tyrone's terms and maddened by the reports of his alleged treasonable activities that were being circulated, he determined in an evil hour to return to the Court in spite of the Queen's interdict, to explain all the facts of the campaign and to convey to her verbally the terms of the truce. She had already told him to set out the terms in writing, but he had already pledged his word to Tyrone that he would only communicate them orally to the Queen. He arrived in London on the 28th September, and learning that she was at her Palace at Nonsuch, he at once took horse and spurred through mud and mire, hoping to be the first to bring the news of his return to Court. It was then ten in the morning. Not finding the Queen in her Privy Chamber and resolute to obtain an interview before his enemies could bar his way to her presence, *he rushed into her bed-chamber*, "breathless, dishevelled, travel-stained, his very face covered with spots of mud," and, flinging himself on his knees before her, seized her hand and kissed it. The Queen, in a sorry state of disarray, was in the hands of her tire-women, her hair about her face, etc. Though surprised and astonished at the intrusion—(an unprecedented and an utterly unwarranted act on the part of a subject though quite excusable between mother and son)—*she was happy to see him, spoke to him graciously,* and Essex left her presence well pleased with his reception, and

> Thanked God that after so many troublous storms abroad, he had a sweet calm at HOME. (*Syd. Papers.*)

He had another conference with the Queen before midday from which he returned well contented with his future prospects. Later at the Court he was welcomed by all . . . Cecil and his party excepted.

During the day the Queen saw her Ministers, and when Essex saw her after the consultation, he found her attitude had changed. She received him coldly. Just before midnight an order came from the Queen that he should keep his chamber. It then transpired that she had already appointed certain Lords to hear him in Council. Shortly afterwards he was committed to the custody of the Lord Keeper at York House, and Elizabeth began openly to show signs of her displeasure at his conduct. She refused the request of old Lady Walsingham to allow Essex to write to his wife who had just given birth to a child. To her godson Harrington, who had been sent out to spy upon Essex, she said, when she first saw him at Court:

"What! Did the fool bring you too? Go back to your business." She chafed much, walked fastly to and fro. She catched my girdle when I knelt to her and swore, "By God's Son, I am no Queen! That man is above me! Who gave him command to come here so soon? I did send him on other business." I was bid "GO HOME." I did not stay to be bidden twice.

Harrington also wrote, I could have told Her Majesty of such difficulties, straits, annoyances, as did not appear therein to her eyes and that I found could not be brought to her ear for *her choler did outrun all reason.*

There can be no possible doubt that Elizabeth was thoroughly and purposely misinformed and misled about the intentions of Essex. It was reported to the Queen that the popular Earl was preparing to establish himself in England as Prince Regent. The old lady was also persuaded to believe that he had intended to surprise the Court with the aid of "some two hundred resolute gentlemen" when he came from Ireland, winning the Throne by the aid of his Irish army and Tyrone's wild rebels. These lies were concocted to inflame Elizabeth's mind. They are repeated coldly and callously afterwards in *The Declarations of the Treasons of Essex;* the truth being that he had no more than SIX attendants with him when he landed in England and went to the Court. Tyrone and his rebels were likewise a fabrication. It was these stories told during the day to Elizabeth that made her look askance at him in the evening; then, as more poison was poured into her ears, finally to order his arrest. Certain it is that the Queen was overjoyed to see him in the morning, even though he had violated the proprieties by going into her bedroom. But it could never have been the joy of a "Mistress" but the joy which sprang from "Mother-Love." Says Spedding, who has no knowledge whatever of the true position:

> It is a remarkable proof of the charm which his personal presence inspired in the Queen, that her first emotion on seeing him was pleasure. (Vol. II, p. 152.)

Naturally so as his mother. It was because of their secret relationship that he dared to venture into her bedroom. How else could it be excused? Leicester went into her bedroom—and was called before the Privy Council for his conduct—because he was her morganatic husband. Essex, because he was her son by a morganatic marriage. No mere subject dare have forced his way into the Queen's bedroom. And what ordinary lover would have done such a thing! But was it not the most natural thing in the world for a son, under such circumstances, to waive aside decorum, saying to himself, "I am going to see my mother, even if she is the Queen, and no one shall stop me."

Spedding also says:

> *The gentleness with which the Queen welcomed Essex on his sudden appearance was probably an impulse of NATURE.*

How near Spedding got to the truth without suspecting it! Even a blind man can see that it was the sudden gush of "Mother-Love" that made it a "pleasure" to see his face, a pleasure which expressed itself spontaneously in her behaviour. (*Ibid*, p. 152.) Her sudden change was entirely due to the fact that she was afraid—owing to the whisperings of the crooked-minded hunchback Cecil—that her son Robert meditated plucking the sceptre from her grasp by a *coup d'état* and deposing her, announcing himself as a hitherto concealed Tudor, truly-born in wedlock.

Francis Bacon heard the following day of the arrival of Essex at Court together with the news that he had been placed under house-arrest. He at once wrote the Earl, and a little later was permitted to see him for a quarter of an hour. He wrote:

> My Lord, Conceiving that your Lordship came now up *in the person of a Good Servant* to see your Sovereign Mistress . . . I have committed to this poor paper the humble salutations of *him that is more yours than any man's and more yours than any man . . . .*
>
> I hope . . . your Lordship's wisdom and obsequious circumspection and patience will turn all to the best, etc.

"Francis could hardly have alluded to their concealed relationship as brothers in more pregnant words," says Woodward, *Sir F.B.,* p. 81. We thus see that Francis Bacon lost no time "in putting the Earl right at so critical a juncture." In the interview which followed Francis repeated his previous advice. Referring to his arrest he tells Robert:

> It is but a mist . . . If it goes upwards it may perhaps cause a shower: if downwards it will clear up . . . And therefore, carry it so as you take away by all means all umbrages and distastes from the Queen . . . .
>
> Seek access (to the Queen), importune, opportune, seriously, sportingly, every way . . . .

Francis Bacon concluded his account of the interview:

> He spake very few words and shaked his head sometimes, as if he thought I was in the wrong . . . (*Apologia.*)

After Essex's committal there appears to have been considerable speculation as to his probable fate. The populace, generally speaking, liked Essex. There were turbulent speeches. "Seditious" pamphlets were circulated and suppressed. The public was aware that the Queen was brooding over his misconduct, his errors in Ireland (that had cost her £300,000). His ruin was confidently predicted and his restoration as confidently prophesied the day following. Meanwhile Essex, shortly after being made a prisoner at York House (1st October) fell ill with symptoms of typhoid-fever contracted in Ireland. His illness fanned the flame of popular sympathy. The clergy preached in his vindication. He was prayed for by name. Pamphlets in his favour were scattered in the Queen's Palace. Nationally, there was considerable excitement.

Late in November, she decided to allay public anxiety by a declaration in the Star Chamber, *in the absence of Essex,* of the nature of his misconduct. "Such was the result of the Queen's conflict between public opinion and *her affection for Essex.*" (*Bacon,* Montague, p. 53).

In her perplexity what to do for the best, the Queen had already consulted Francis Bacon, who had tried to dissuade her from proceeding against Essex in such a way. His advice was that—

> she should make matters up with him privately and restore him to his former attendance, with some addition of honour to take away discontent; but the

freedom of his expostulation offended her at the time, so that she would hear no more from him for some months; and proceeded in the meantime to carry out her own plan . . . .

Her real motive for choosing this course was probably tenderness towards the Earl himself, whom she did not wish to bring before the public as a culprit. (Spedding, Vol. II, p. 158.)

Francis Bacon further told the Queen that her proposed course was such an unusual one that it would be said Justice had had her balance taken from her. Instead of allaying public fears into tranquillity it would tend to influence the populace. (*Apologia*). But all this advice was to no purpose. On the 29th November, at an Assembly of Privy Councillors, judges and statesmen, they declared the nature of Essex's misconduct without him being heard in his defence "which did aggravate public discontent." As a matter of fact the only charges that could be brought against him was disobedience in acting contrary to Court instructions and miserable incapacity. There was nothing found of a treasonable character at all in his conduct.

On the evening of the very day of the "Declaration," the Queen with Lady Warwick and the Earl of Worcester *went privately to see him* for some reason or other. She had been told he was shamming illness; but he was very far from feigning. He was desperately ill. We next find that *she sends her own physicians to attend him* in consultation with his own doctor.

Francis Bacon was not present at the Star Chamber "Declaration," and the Queen, noting that his name was not on the list of those present, wrote asking the meaning of his absence and he replied he "thought it wiser to keep away." He added:

> Never poor gentleman had a deeper and truer desire and care for your glory, your safety, *your repose of mind*, your service . . . I take my duty too exactly . . . *My Life hath been threatened and my Name Libelled, WHICH I COUNT AN HONOUR* . . . May I never live to see any eclipse of your glory, interruption of your safety, or indisposition of your person.

These were illuminating sentences. Francis was known to be *persona grata* with the Queen; and doubtless many people thought that he had advised her to act harshly towards Essex that he might win favour for himself. Some may have known of the secret relationship of the "Three Persons" . . . Hence the libelling of his NAME which could only have been in one way—that he was "A Bastard-Tudor" on which Francis tells the Queen, "*I count such a Libel an Honour.*" All he wants is to secure the Queen's "*Repose of Mind.*" *What other explanation can there be of such enigmatical phrases?*

To Lord Henry Howard he writes in a similar strain that "there is shaped a tale in London's forge" that he had delivered an opinion to the Queen that Essex had committed treason which are "lies" and "libels," the "root" being "partly some light-headed Envy at my accesses to Her Majesty, which, *being begun and continue since my Childhood*, as long as her Majesty shall think me worthy of them, I scorn those that think the contrary. . . .

"For my Lord Essex, I am not servile to him, *having regard to my Superior Duty* [i.e., his duty to the Queen which must come FIRST], I have been much bound to him. And on the other side, *I have spent more time and more thoughts about his well-doing, than ever I did about mine own* . . . I have deserved better than to have my NAME OBJECTED to Envy, or my Life to a ruffian's violence . . . But I have the Privy Coat of a Good Conscience."

On 13th December, 1599, Essex returned to the Queen his Patents as Master of Ordnance and Master of Horse and on that date the French Ambassador wrote to his Sovereign that—

> there were divisions in the Council touching Essex, some urging the Queen to forgive him, and others to take his life. That a Warrant had been made out for his removal to the Tower, and twice brought to the Queen to sign, and twice she had refused to sign it.

Essex was then at death's door. Little hope was entertained of his recovery. He received the sacrament. Too weak to move, he could only be lifted by the sheets. He was in this condition when Lady Essex was allowed to see her husband for the first time. The day following the Queen was alarmed at Essex's condition and said she "*had only intended to humble him.*"

> She desired that his eight doctors might hold a consultation on the state of his health, and send her their opinion. Their statement of his maladies was so serious, that *Her Majesty became very pensive,* and sent Dr. James, her own physician, to him, with some broth, and a message, bidding him "comfort himself, and that if it were not inconsistent with her Honour, *she would have come to visit him herself.*"
>
> It was noted that *her eyes were full of tears,* when she uttered these gracious words . . . the Queen commanding that Essex should be removed to the Lord Keeper's own chamber . . . . Strickland, *Ibid*, p. 652.

There were more public prayers for the luckless Earl in all the London Churches; more severe scribblings on the white walls of the Palace; more written denunciations of Cecil's conduct. But Essex did not die. He gradually recovered. And the Queen was once more persuaded that Essex had been feigning illness to enlist her sympathy. This was largely due to her exasperation at the publication of Hayward's *History of Henry IV of England*; "some passages touching the misgovernment of Richard II and the pernicious influence of his unworthy Favourites, she chose to construe into reflections on herself and her cabinet." The book was dedicated to "The Earl of Essex." Prayers were commanded to cease. Elizabeth felt she had been deceived and that Essex had countenanced the production that she said was aimed at her. Thus he was not released upon his recovery, but, says Montague (*Ibid.*, p. 55), "after some months' patient endurance on his part, the Queen desired to restore him to favour and Essex was removed to his own house in the custody of Sir R. Buckley."

What is all this friction, this vacillation, but a clash between two similar natures—each imperious, the Queen resolute to uphold her regal power and Robert equally determined to have his own way because of their secret relationship! The fact that Elizabeth regularly consulted with Francis when the younger brother was rebellious is further evidence of the tie that existed between the Queen and her concealed sons. As a matter of fact the November Star Chamber "Declaration" led to nothing. Weeks and even months slipped away and Essex was still a prisoner in his own home. His friends had been turned out. He was practically forbidden to communicate with the outside world. He was kept under close surveillance. Elizabeth's change of attitude was undoubtedly due to a confession made by one Thomas Wood, before the Lord Treasurer and other Ministers on the 20th January, 1600, regarding a conversation in which it was stated that the Earl of Essex had gone to England, and that if Her Majesty were dead *he* (*Essex*) *would be King of England.* This clearly proved that Essex was associated in many minds—how many we cannot tell—with the "Succession." His enemies in his absence naturally made the most of it to the Queen. Raleigh wrote this venomous letter to Cecil about this time:

> I am not wise enough to give you advice, but if you take it for a good counsel to relent towards this tyrant, *you shall repent it when it shall be too late.* His malice is fixed and will not evaporate by any of your mild courses, for he will ascribe the alteration to Her Majesty's pusillanimity [i.e., her fear lest he publicly asserts his relationship, destroying the idea that she is a "Virgin Queen"], and not to your good nature, *knowing that you work but upon her humour* and not out of any love towards him.
>
> *The less you make him, the less he shall be able to harm you and yours*; and if Her Majesty's favour fail him, he will again decline to *a COMMON PERSON* [i.e., a bastard even if he had Tudor blood in his veins].
>
> Lose not your advantage . . . He will ever be *the CANKER of the Queen's estate and safety.*

This letter tells the story that Cecil was influencing the Queen by his counsel; that Essex's death was definitely meditated; that he was known to be "a Common Person," actually a "Canker" to the Queen. I know not how such enigmatical phraseology can be interpreted save in one way: Raleigh knew that Essex was a "Love-Child" and a Tudor.

Although Essex had written the Queen the most dutiful letters, she felt that he was not sufficiently contrite and penitent. At last he wrote a frenzied letter to her:

> As if I were thrown into a corner like a dead carcass, I am gnawed on and torn by the basest creatures upon earth. The prating Tavern-haunter speaks of me what he lists; the frantic libeller writes of me what he lists; they print me and make me speak to the world, and shortly THEY WILL PLAY ME UPON THE STAGE.
>
> The least of these is worse than death, but this is not the worst of my Destiny; for you, who have protected from scorn and infamy all to whom you once avowed favour but Essex . . . have now, *in this eighth month of my close imprisonment, rejected my letters and refused to hear me,* which to traitors you never did.
>
> What remains is only to beseech you to conclude my punishment, my misery, my life.

The resentment of the Queen towards her younger and favourite son had the effect of drawing her elder son Francis towards her. On the 12th March, 1600, she helped him to buy the Gorhambury House Estate reversion from Anthony Bacon and "a more useful deal for Francis Bacon was made by the Queen with Sir Nicholas Bacon the younger." They were two complicated legal deals, but, says Parker Woodward, a solicitor:

> In this curious, roundabout way, Francis Bacon secured the Favourite country seat of Gorhambury House. (*Sir F.B.*, p. 85.)

Does not this again tell the story of their true relationship?

In May the Queen crossed the Thames from her Palace of Richmond to visit Francis Bacon at Twickenham Lodge. Ever seeking to bring about a reconciliation, *he presented her with a Sonnet on "Mercy"* expressing the hope that she would extend "mercy" to Robert. It is very probable that these same sentiments were afterwards expressed through the lips of Portia in the *Merchant of Venice*, "The quality of Mercy is not strained," etc.:

> "The Queen," says Spedding, "knowing he had been perverse, disobedient and unfortunate, but refusing to believe him false, was considering on what terms she might receive him into favour again, without making one of those concessions to his humour which she had tried so often and with such bad effect." (*Ibid.*, p. 172.)

After playing with the idea that she would prosecute Essex publicly in the Star Chamber, which would have entailed a heavy fine and imprisonment in the Tower, she was persuaded by Francis Bacon to some lighter form of publicity . . . to set up a disciplinary tribunal of her own devising, in a private room to which the public might be admitted, say in the Lord Keeper's house. "Whatever you do should be for his chastisement not for his destruction." The Queen replied that "her purpose was to make him know himself, and his duty to her; and that she would again use his service."

> There should be a fine show, and the miscreant should be lectured, very severely lectured, made to apologize, frightened a little and then—let off. So she arranged it and everyone fell in with her plans. *Never was the cool paternalism* [MATERNALISM] *so curiously displayed. Essex was a naughty boy,* who had misbehaved, been sent to his room, and fed on bread and water; and now he was to be brought downstairs, and, after a good wigging, told he was not to be flogged after all. (Lytton Strachey, p. 227, *Elizabeth and Essex.*)

The commissioners appointed to try the case met on the 5th June. The Earl kneeled at the end of the council-board. He had been given the cue of "complete submission." The Judges had been warned not to press any question of loyalty. At times many wept to see him in such misery. The examination lasted from nine in the morning till eight at night, "sometimes kneeling, sometimes standing, and occasionally leaning against a cupboard." It is said that he defended himself very mildly and discreetly, admitting errors of judgment, but said he, "I should do God and mine own conscience wrong *if I do not justify myself as an honest man.*" Taking his "George" (his Jewel of the Knights of the Garter) in his hand, he pressed it to his heart and said, "This hand shall pull out this heart *when any disloyal thought shall enter it.*" He implored the Lords to intercede for him with the Queen. Though not a Law-Officer, Francis Bacon took a small part in the prosecution by the peremptory order of the Queen:

I writ to her that if she would be pleased to spare me in my Lord of Essex' cause, out of the consideration she took of my obligation towards him, I should reckon it as one of her greatest favours. (*Apologia.*)

His request was rejected but his speech against Essex's alleged offences was such, says Montague, that:

He constantly kept in view the Queen's determination neither to injure her Favourite in person nor in purse, averring there was no charge of disloyalty . . . He brought to this semblance of a trial only the shadow of a speech. Under the flimsy veil of an accuser there may be easily detected the face of a friend. (*Life of Bacon*, p. 68.)

The Lord Keeper pronounced sentence that he should be suspended from all his offices and should continue a prisoner in his own house during Her Majesty's pleasure. The only real unpleasantness in the proceedings was caused by Sir Edward Coke and his manner was most provocative. Says Spedding, "In the mouth of Coke the same charges assumed a form so irritating," that Essex began to justify himself and the farce nearly ended in a fiasco.

The next day Francis Bacon went to the Queen and did his utmost to persuade her that all was now well—the Earl submissive and the public satisfied—and that she should restore him into favour again with access to her Court. She wanted to know all that had passed at the Council and bade him make a report in writing. A few days later he brought her a written narrative. The Queen was much touched with the report of the Earl's answer. After some hesitation she agreed to act on Francis Bacon's suggestion to restore him to favour . . . but it must be gradual; to see how he behaved himself. Within a month he was released from the restraint of his keeper. From time to time Essex wrote letters of the most submissive nature to the Queen but she still regarded him coldly. To Anthony Bacon he also wrote respecting the part Francis had played in the prosecution.

As for Francis I think no worse of him for what he has done against me than of my Lord Chief Justice.

Essex, it is plain, knew that his elder brother had to obey the Queen's command as a subject and that he was also pledged filially to protect the mother that bore him. Francis's first duty lay to the Queen and not to his brother.

In July friendly letters passed between the two men. On the 20th a most significant letter was written by Francis which cannot possibly be understood unless the secret relationship between the three persons be taken into consideration. He begins with a sentence of deadly import respecting the truth of their association through their secret relationship.

To the Earl of Essex

My Lord,

No man can better expound my doings than your Lordship, which maketh me need to say the less. [i.e., Outsiders may be puzzled at his attitude but Essex knows the true reason—the secret of his birth makes him stand by the Queen, this secret knowledge of Essex thus making excuses or explanations unnecessary.]

I pray you to believe that I aspire to the conscience and commendation first of *bonus civis* [a good citizen], which with us is a good and *True Servant to the Queen*, and next of *bonus vir*, that is *an Honest Man*.

I desire your Lordship also to think that though I confess I love some things much better than I love your Lordship—as the Queen's Service, *her Quiet and Contentment, her Honour, her Favour, the Good of my Country,* and the like—yet *I LOVE FEW PERSONS BETTER THAN YOURSELF,* both for Gratitude's sake, and for your own Virtues, which cannot hurt but by accident and abuse. Of which my good affection I was ever and am ready to yield testimony by any Good Offices but *with such reservations as yourself cannot but allow*: for as I was ever sorry that your Lordship should fly with Waxen Wings, doubting Icarus' fortune, so for the growing up of your own feathers, specially Ostrich's, or any other save of a bird of prey, no man shall be more glad.

And *this is the axle-tree whereupon I have turned and shall turn*; *which to signify to you*, though I think you are of yourself persuaded as much, is the Cause of my Writing.

Fr. Bacon

This letter is obviously the letter of an elder brother to a younger and so he naturally LOVES few persons better than Robert Essex. But his love has reservations. The axle-tree on which his life turns is that of being a "Good and True Servant to the Queen," and his first consideration is her "Honour," that their relationship, in short, shall be maintained as a family secret and not blurted out into the ears of the public; and that her "Quiet and Contentment and the Good of his Country" stand paramount before all other things. He thus gives Essex clearly to understand once more that he stands with the Queen always and he cannot be a party to reckless action of añy kind. His love for his mother necessarily must over-ride his love as a brother. That is the clear inner meaning of Francis Bacon's letter. It is intended as a warning message of restraint against violent action of any kind. It is not an ordinary letter from one man to another, from a servant to a Lord, from a beneficiary to a patron. Such a letter was perfectly uncalled for had there not been an ulterior motive that required emphasis. It bears out the truth that Francis Bacon wrote to Lord Howard: "*As for my Lord of Essex, I am not Servile to him, having regard to my Superior Duty.*"

Essex understood the position exactly and replied with equally enigmatical words that would give nothing away if the letter came into other hands:

I can neither expound nor censure your late actions . . . Your profession of affection and offer of good offices are welcome to me. For answer I will but say this: you have believed *I have been kind to you,* and you may believe *I cannot be other either upon humour or mine own election.*

I am a stranger to all Poetical conceits or else I should say somewhat of YOUR POETICAL EXAMPLE. But this I must say: I never flew with other wings than desire to Merit and Confidence in my Sovereign's favour; and when one of these Wings failed me, I would light nowhere but at my Sovereign's feet, though she suffered me to be bruised by the Fall. And till Her Majesty, *that knows I was never Bird of Prey,* finds it to agree with her Will and Service that my Wings should be imped, I have committed myself to the mue [the casting of my feathers or moulting]. Your retired friend, Essex.

In effect Essex says, "I cannot help but be kind because of the secret tie between us. I can assure you that I never aspired to be a bird of prey because of my kinship to the Queen. I am stripping me of my feathers (honours) and retiring into private life."

The next step taken by Francis Bacon to bring about a revulsion of feeling in the royal bosom towards his brother Robert was to draft some letters for him for the Queen to see and he also wrote to the Queen himself. There are many enigmatical sentences in his writings to her hinting at their secret relationship. He begins one letter:

> *When the Creature entereth into account with the Creator,* it can never number in how many things it needs mercy, or in how many it receives it . . .
>
> God who seeth all is witness how faithfully I do vow to dedicate the rest of my life . . . in obedience, faith and zeal to your Majesty, without admitting any other worldly care; and whatsoever your Majesty resolveth to do with me I shall live and die, Your Majesty's humblest Vassal, Essex."

What is this first sentence but a clear reminder that *he is her creature and that she created him?* And that he has allowed his pride as a Tudor to outrun his discretion as a subject? There is ample proof that for many months after this Francis Bacon tried to restore Essex to the Queen's favour.

Strickland says:

> Francis Bacon exerted all the energies of his mighty genius in favour of the discarded Favourite. . . .
>
> To the Queen he said: "In the case of my Lord of Essex your princely word ever was, that *you intended to reform his mind, and not ruin his fortunes.*" (*Elizabeth*, p. 663.)

Harman writes:

> I think it is proved beyond all doubt that Francis Bacon did all he could to help him (Essex) in secret. (*The Impersonality of Shakespeare,* p. 86.)

Nichol declares:

> During the next three months [after the Council sentence] Francis Bacon was employed in writing and dictating confidential letters, to bring about a more complete reconciliation. (*Life of F.B.,* Vol. I, p. 51.)

G. B. Harrison:

> Nor was Bacon's protestation mere formality. He forthwith devised a plan by which Essex might by indirect means make a personal appeal to the Queen. He concocted a correspondence which was supposed to pass between Anthony Bacon and Essex. These letters were, on a favourable occasion, to be shown to the Queen, who should thus, as it were, overhear a private conversation about herself. (*Robert Devereux*, p. 269.)

The direct result of Francis Bacon's efforts was that on the 26th August Essex was formally released from all restraint. He was given complete liberty, but he was specifically barred from appearing at Court without leave.

For some months afterwards the Earl remained quietly at home. He wrote several letters to the Queen praying for complete forgiveness and access to Her Majesty "to kiss her hands." To Anthony Bacon he had previously written, "*If I recover the Queen I will never lose her again.*" But the year slipped away and Essex was no nearer establishing friendly relations with Elizabeth than when he was first placed under house-arrest twelve months previously. Nothing he could say was to any purpose. No influence—even Francis Bacon's eloquence—could stir this bitter old woman whose dignity she felt had been trampled upon and her royal commands set at naught by her defiant, over-riding offspring. It is quite evident that the poison poured into her ears by the jealous junta surrounding her had unbalanced her judgment and unhinged her mind. She had begun to see in Essex only a potential rebel who was ready to strike her down if he were given an opportunity, who, given an inch would take a yard, and must be kept at arm's length. She tried to take the estrangement lightly, but the evidence shows that Elizabeth had a heavy heart and a weary spirit in holding to her embittered purpose; for she still sought, foolishly and unwisely, Robert Essex's further humiliation by resolving to take away his income. She had been persuaded by evil tongues that his lofty spirit was not sufficiently subdued. She held the whip-hand financially and she decided to apply the whip to tame him effectually once and for all. She ought to have known better from her own nature that to apply such a lash to such a temperament could only have one possible effect—to drive him to desperation.

The Queen had granted Essex in happier days the Monopoly of Sweet Wines for ten years. It brought him in a great income of some £50,000 per annum. The grant came to an end at Michaelmas. If the Monopoly were not renewed it would reveal the true state of Elizabeth's mind towards him. It would mean ruin . . . complete and final. He would be plunged into utter poverty, disgrace and bankruptcy. His debts were extraordinarily heavy in spite of the fact that the Queen had given him at least £300,000. He owed the wine-merchants heavy sums. His creditors were numerous. His friends who had gone surety for him would also be ruined. He saw signs that some of the rats were already preparing to desert the sinking ship. His very life hinged on the Queen's decision. Was it to be Hope and Honour with ultimate access to the Queen or the alternative . . . Despair and Degradation, an Outcast to be mocked publicly. He gradually grew into a fever of anxiety to know the Queen's mind. At length he ventured to mention the matter to Elizabeth in an impassioned letter. And, of course, interpreted by the viperous mind of a Cecil, she took the application the wrong way. She brooded over it for some time; then mentioned it to Francis Bacon.

> She informed him "that Essex had written to her some dutiful letters which had moved her; but after taking them to flow from the abundance of his heart, she found them but a preparative to a Suit for renewing his farm of Sweet Wines" of which she had granted him the Monopoly in the sunshine of her former favour.
>
> To this petition she had replied "that she would inquire into its annual value," which is said to have amounted to the enormous sum of £50,000 per annum. She added a taunt, which it was scarcely in the nature of a brave man and a gentleman to brook, *that when Horses became unmanageable it was necessary to tame them by stinting them in the quantity of their food.*

But Essex, being deeply involved in debt, renewed his Suit, *and was denied contemptuously*. (Strickland, *Elizabeth*, p. 666.)

To others she said much the same. "Corrupt bodies, the more you feed them, the more hurt you do them. . . . An unruly Horse must be abated of its provender, that he may be the more easily and better managed." In short, she was going to show the world that Elizabeth and not Essex was the Ruler of England. Francis Bacon's explanation to the Queen was ingenious:

"How your Majesty construes," he said, "as if Duty and Desire could stand together! Iron clings to the loadstone from its nature. A vine creeps to the pole that it may twine. You must distinguish my Lord's desire to do you Service, is as to his perfection that which *he thinks himself to be born for*; whereas his desire to obtain this thing from you, is but for a sustentation."

"Speak to your business," says the Queen. "Speak for yourself: For the Earl, not a word."

The Queen was so annoyed at Francis Bacon's persistence in championing the Earl's cause that she began to look coldly upon him when he came into her presence, until at last, he said to her he could see that:

In the integrity of his heart, he had incurred great peril for pleading the cause of the Earl to her and that his own Fall was decreed. She answered, "My Grace is Sufficient for you." (*Apologia.*)

In the state of the Queen's temper it had become dangerous for anyone to espouse the cause of Essex. Francis Bacon did not see the Queen again until the 8th February, 1601, "the day of my Lord of Essex his misfortune." *His had been the only voice that dared to whisper excuses in the royal ear, to plead with that leonine heart for mercy.* And this, although he and Essex had met but once for more than two years. Though their paths lay apart he had carried unostentatiously his plea of clemency to the Throne.

Often in the Queen's closet on public duty, he seized every opening for this plea. Never had such an offender such an advocate. Gaily, gravely, in speech, in song, he beset the royal ear; kneeling to Her Majesty at Nonsuch, coaxing her at Twickenham Park. When she ferried to his Lodge, he presented her with a Sonnet on Mercy; when she called him to the Palace, he read her letters purporting to come from the penitent Earl. What Babington dared not hint from the pulpit, Francis Bacon dared to urge in the private chamber. Wit, eloquence, persuasion of the rarest power, he lavished on this . . . cause of Essex. (Hepworth Dixon, *Story of F.B.*, p. 155.)

The Queen did not answer forthwith Essex's request for a renewal of the Sweet Wine License. She kept him dangling on the tenter-hooks of suspense for a month. In September he wrote her again. He owed £16,000 of which £5,000 was immediately due:

If conscience did not tell me, that without imploring your Majesty's goodness at this time, most dear and most admired Sovereign, I should not only lose the present support of my poor estate, but the hope of any ability to do your Majesty future service, and not that alone, but the means of satisfying *a great number of hungry and annoying creditors, which suffer me in my retired life to have no rest,* I would appear still before your Majesty as a mute person.

But since this day se'night, the lease which I hold by your Majesty's beneficence expireth, and that farm is both my chiefest maintenance and mine own means of compounding with the merchants to whom I am indebted, give me leave, I humbly beseech your Majesty that your Majesty's course tend to my correction, not to my ruin.

If my creditors will take for payment many ounces of my blood, or the taking away of this farm would only for want finish my body, your Majesty should never hear of this suit. For in myself I find no boldness to importune and from myself I can draw no argument to solicit. The only suit I can make willingly, and must make continually is, that you will once again look with gracious eyes upon your Majesty's humblest, faithfullest, and *more than most devoted vassal*, Essex.

It is said that the Queen was not displeased with this letter as it was a confession that "Essex was beaten to his knees." But she made no sign to him of her intentions. On October 18th he wrote to her again:

My soul cries out unto your Majesty for grace, for access, and for an end of this exile. If your Majesty grant this suit you are most gracious, whatever else you deny or take away. If this cannot be obtained, I must doubt whether that the means to preserve life, and the granted liberty, have been favours or punishments; for till I may appear in your Gracious Presence, and kiss your Majesty's fair correcting hand, time itself is a perpetual night, and the whole world but a sepulchre unto your Majesty's *humblest vassal*, Essex.

On 30th October the Queen announced her decision. It would not be renewed. She confided it to trustees for her own use. With her refusal Essex and his fortunes crashed in ruins. It affected not only Essex personally, his followers and his creditors but, says G. B. Harrison, "it affected the nation more deeply than any event since the Armada. . . ."

One man seemed to stand out conspicuous as a symbol of true nobility, the coming saviour of his country, perhaps, even, if some hopes were fulfilled, their next King—Essex.

Men of all kinds felt this admiration . . . His admirers were utterly bewildered . . . Most falling back on the simple and obvious explanation that there was villainy abroad, attributed Essex' failure to the jealousy and malice of lesser men.

They waited with fear the issue; so great a heart would not easily submit to his enemies. (G. B. Harrison, *Robert Devereux*, p. 274.)

Essex's first reactions to the blow were of passionate grief and despair. Yet on 17th November, Accession Day, he wrote her again—his last letter full of "eloquence, misery, pathos! How pitiful it was," says J. E. Neale, *Elizabeth*, p. 370. It had no effect. The Queen, under the pressure of advisers near to the Throne, had become adamant in her cold anger and warped in her mind towards him. When the full realization of this utter alienation—with all its implications—burst upon him, that she had inexorably cut herself adrift from him for ever, the effect was appalling. Nor can we wonder that he had a brain-storm as he thought of the real or fancied injustice meted out to him by the woman who had brought him into being, by deliberately thrusting him into threatened black ruin and a debtor's prison; and that he became not only reckless but rebellious towards the Queen, his enemies and even Fate itself.

Mountjoy counselled "*patience* to recover again by ordinary means the Queen's favour and to *content* himself!" Patience, forsooth! How could he be "patient" and "content" himself with ruin staring him in the face? "Words! Words! Words!" he raved in his fury as he saw himself treading daily nearer to the abyss of destruction. Words would not satisfy his creditors or restore to him the Kingdom he had lost.

His attitude and subsequent conduct can be understood and partly excused when we remember that *he was the Queen's own son.* While he had no right as a subject to be saved from a financial catastrophe, had he no claim as a son . . . even though he were an unacknowledged love-child? *That was the secret spring of all his subsequent mad utterances and wild despairs.* He was a Tudor, flesh of the Queen's flesh and bone of her bone with more right to the Throne of England, being born legitimately in morganatic wedlock, than anyone else . . . his brother Francis excepted. And he simply could not believe that his own mother—*of her own free will . . . uninfluenced*—could possibly allow him to be tortured on the financial rack, plunged into poverty and shame, cast on the scrap-heap. Surrounding the Queen were his deadliest enemies . . . Sir Robert Cecil, the Lord Admiral, Lord Cobham, Sir Walter Raleigh and others, men with whom he had quarrelled; and all were in power.

All his appeals had failed, due, he believed, to the Queen's mind being saturated with their poisonous distillation. He felt himself to be the victim of a conspiracy. She was not only subject to the influence of the Cecil oligarchy but they had prevented him from obtaining access to the Queen. The more he thought it over and talked it over with Blount, Cuffe and other undesirables, the more he became convinced that the only way out of his difficulties was to obtain by hook or crook an audience with the Queen, holding the Cecilites as prisoners so as to remove her from their influence. He was convinced that if only he could see the Queen, she could never withstand him. He would plead for his life at her feet . . . then . . . "Would not some voice within, answer his prayers and say, 'We are akin'?" He believed the Queen could not resist him and that mother-love would restore him to pride of place once more and that his trials would be over.

By turns he brooded and raved in his moods over this solution. During one of these brain-storms Sir John Harrington paid him a brief visit and came away terrified. He afterwards wrote:

> He shifteth from sorrow and repentance to rage and rebellion so suddenly as well proveth him devoid of good reason or right mind . . . He uttereth such strange words bordering on such strange designs that made me hasten forth and leave his presence. . .
>
> His speeches of the Queen becometh no man who hath a sane mind in a sound body. He hath ill advisers and much evil hath sprung from this source . . . The man's soul seemeth tossed to and fro, like the waves of a troubled sea.

But . . . if Essex was bordering on madness—and some of his speeches about the Queen were indeed on the verge of insanity—was not the Queen likewise drifting into a species of mono-mania regarding the designs of Essex on her crown? I believe that the strain of coping with her fears of an exposure regarding her secret life coupled with the incessant alarms sprung upon her by Cecil had already begun a "softening of the brain." Strachey seems to think so too. He says:

> *She, too, perhaps was also mad.* Did she not see that *she was drifting to utter disaster*? That by giving him freedom and *projecting him into poverty, by disgracing him* and yet leaving him uncrushed, she was treating him in the most dangerous manner that could be devised? Involved in an extraordinary paralysis, she ignored her approaching fate. (*Elizabeth and Essex*, p. 233.)

In the late autumn he threw off all restraint. He opened Essex House for visitors. Many friends came to see him . . . noblemen, military men, gallants, Puritans and so on . . . so that it was said by his enemies that Essex was holding a hostile Court, a statement duly reported to the Queen. He began openly to discuss his injuries with his intimates. And when someone ventured to mention "What would be Her Majesty's conditions" (for restoration), Essex angrily exclaimed:

> Her conditions! *Her conditions are as crooked as her carcase! She is an old woman crooked both in body and mind!*

These words were duly repeated to Elizabeth . . . a taunt that she could not forgive, that her nature could not forget. These words of folly and ingratitude may be said to have sealed his fate. They turned her to stone.

> The strong mind of Elizabeth was evidently shaken, by the conflicting passions that assailed her, at this agitating period, and reason tottered. (Strickland, *Elizabeth*, p. 669.)

Meanwhile, the Earl continued to keep open house past Christmas and New Year. Cecil noted all the comings and goings and made preparations accordingly, "ready for the critical moment whenever it might come." Says Nichol:

> Viewed merely in the light of the facts known to the commissioners, the Earl's subsequent conduct is altogether inexplicable . . . To his more intimate associates, he spoke and acted like a man *who suffered under some great wrong or was goaded by the consciousness of some guilty Secret.* (*Francis Bacon,* Vol. I, p. 51.)

Essex had "suffered a great wrong." And we know to-day what that "wrong" was. It was connected with a "guilty secret." For Elizabeth was not "A Virgin Queen." She was a mother . . . Essex's own mother; and Robert Essex to his eternal credit kept the secret in his heart, and the proof in the little black bag which he wore round his neck which he destroyed before he was executed. Essex's "inexplicable conduct" and the "wrong" he suffered all centred in the fact that he was much more to her than a mere subject. He was being jockeyed out of his just rights by unscrupulous bitter enemies who feared for themselves if he rose to power. That is the "Guilty Secret" which Professor Nichol never even suspected.

In January, Lord Treasurer Buckhurst sent his son to Essex to tell him that he was spoiling his chances with the Queen, who might justly fear that his gatherings had no good intentions; that he was obviously affecting popularity by admitting "base and desperate men" to his open-house. Essex replied that he knew of no rascals

> who resorted to him, and since he saw he was not prohibited from holding speech with any, he saw no reason to withdraw himself from such as came to visit him in good will. It was but civility to ask those who came, to share such fare as he had: he invited and sent for none. As for the exercises of Puritan sermons or rather conventicles which attracted multitudes, these were not "conventicles" but spiritual conferences which were his only consolation.

This answer did not satisfy the Privy Council but Essex had not yet committed any open act that could be called in question. But the Government was uneasy and Cecil took all the necessary precautions to frustrate any act or plan of violence. On 3rd February, 1601, a small committee meeting was held at Drury House—Lord Southampton, Sir John Davies, Sir Charles Danvers, John Littleton and Sir F. Gorges—to discuss a plan whereby the Court should be seized, Cecil, Raleigh and other known adversaries among the Councillors, should be made prisoners and Essex would then enter and present himself to the Queen. They would then call a Parliament and his enemies should be tried. "The general feeling was that there would not be much resistance . . . Essex's opinion was that he should come to Court in such peace that a dog would not wag his tongue against him." (G. B. Harrison.)

There were then at least three hundred gentlemen attending the Earl at Essex House which lay only a mile off the Court at Whitehall, between the Court and the City. But so careless had been the talk of Essex that the Government knew all their moves. His followers aflame with enthusiasm and enmity against the Cecilites talked foolishly: through the City there ran the wildest rumours; Cecil was intriguing either with James of Scotland to be next in the Succession or for the Spanish Infanta to succeed to the Crown: the ambitious Raleigh had sworn to kill the Earl with his own hand; the Queen had ordered Essex's arrest and committal to the Tower. When these stories came to the ears of Essex he became distraught with perplexity. Some favoured an attack on the Court; some to raise the City. All agreed that the person of the Queen must be secured without violence. But Essex vacillated and the probability is that he would never have done anything had he not been goaded into action.

On Saturday, 7th February, the Queen's Messenger arrived commanding the Earl to attend the Council, and, at the same time he received an anonymous letter, warning him not to attend if he valued his life. Essex sent back word that he was too ill to leave his bed. Cecil, in fact, had forestalled any action he might take. He could only react against the Queen's Summons, which virtually meant *surrendering once more his liberty to the Officers of the Court*, by striking at the prime mover; and so "it was determined that the morrow should see the end of the Secretary's reign." (Strachey.) Cecil had manœuvred Essex into a position from which there could be no escape. He walked into the trap blindly.

Very hurriedly it was arranged with a group of Stage-Players to act *Richard the Second* which deals with the deposition of an English Sovereign... a bit of propaganda intended to stir up the London populace.

Cecil acted.

On the Sunday morning the guards were doubled at Whitehall. Large reserves were held in readiness for action. All precautions had been taken against any surprise overthrow of the Government. Sir F. Gorges had betrayed their projects to Cecil. All was lost before a sword was drawn. Sir Charles Danvers went out early to reconnoitre and returned with the news that it was no longer possible to surprise the Court and that the Earl should try to escape to Wales. Sir C. Blount was for immediate action and his advice was strengthened by numbers of armed men who were then pouring into the Courtyard. While this conflict of opinion was in progress there came an authoritative knocking on the gate. The Queen had sent the Lord Keeper, the Earl of Worcester, Sir William Knollys, and the Lord Chief Justice to inquire the cause of his assembly. These High Dignitaries were admitted into Essex's library, the crowd bursting in after them.

> There were cries of "Kill them! Kill them! Shop them up!" The earl was surrounded by his shouting, gesticulating followers. He tried to speak, but they interrupted him. "Away, my Lord, they abuse you; they betray you; they undo you; you lose time." He was powerless among them . . . He found himself swept towards the door. He bade Egerton and the others stay where they were; he would return ere long, he cried out, and go with them to the Queen.
>
> When he was out of the room, the door was shut and locked on the Councillors; they were "shopped up." Down the stairs and into the streets streamed the frenzied mob. And then the great gates were opened and they all rushed out into the street.
>
> But even now, at this last moment, there was hesitation. Where were they to go? "To the Court! The Court!" cried some, and all waited upon Essex. But he, with a sudden determination, turned towards the City. (*Ibid*, Strachey, p. 238.)

The City did not rise. The people were loyal subjects of the Queen. They heard the terrible news that the Earl had been proclaimed a traitor. His followers heard it too and began to desert. Essex went along with his band continuing to cry that there was a plot to murder him, that the Crown was sold, and his life threatened. Not a single man joined him. He reached St. Paul's. There he had intended to speak. But his nerve had gone. An oration was impossible. He was in desperation. "The sweat poured from his face, which was contorted in horror; his whole life had crashed to pieces in this hideous fiasco." (Strachey.)

There was a slight brush between his followers and the soldiers, the "rebels" being scattered, and Essex made for the river and rowed home. The Councillors had already been released. The Queen's troops with artillery arrived shortly afterwards. Resistance was useless. Essex surrendered and was immediately conveyed to the Tower.

Cecil had won.

The leaders and upwards of a hundred men were in custody. From the preliminary examinations of the prisoners sufficient evidence was obtained to make a definite charge against Essex and Southampton; and on 18th February, 1601 they were arraigned for High Treason at Westminster Hall with all the panoply of State, before a Special Commission of twenty-five of their Peers—who were all Essex's sworn enemies. The accused were allowed no Counsel. The Crown prosecutor was Sir E. Coke assisted by Yelverton. But *the Queen had commanded Francis Bacon also to be present during the trial.* Through all these critical weeks we hear nothing of Francis Bacon. . . . Whether he communicated by speech or word with Essex when he heard the rumours floating round the City of sympathizers and armed men having their rendezvous at Essex House . . . we simply do not know. Apparently there was no intercourse. If he did communicate with him we can be quite sure, judging by his previous firm attitude, that he warned his younger brother he was playing once more into the hands of his enemies and was recklessly riding for a fatal fall. To everyone's surprise the opening of Court found Francis Bacon associated with the prosecution against his "friend." Why Francis Bacon had any part at all to play in this tragical drama has long been a puzzle to biographers and historians.

> "He was neither Attorney-General nor Solicitor," says Abbott. Nor had he any regular position as a Law Officer of the Crown; he was merely one of the "Learned Counsel." *There was no reason why one in so subordinate a position should have been called to so responsible a duty.* (*Francis Bacon,* p. 75.)
>
> Dean Church says the same: Bacon's legal position was so subordinate that *there must have been a special reason for his employment* . . . He was not commonly called upon in such prosecutions. He was not employed by Cecil in the Winchester trials of Raleigh, Grey and Cobham, three years afterwards, nor in those connected with the Gunpowder Plot . . . .
>
> He was not a judge. He was not a regular Law Officer like Coke. *His only employment had been casual and occasional.* (*Bacon*, pp. 52, 53.)

Here is obviously a mystery which has never been solved. *Why WAS Francis Bacon chosen as a Junior Counsel as well as Yelverton? To prosecute his own "friend?"* Were there not plenty of far more experienced counsel in the Government employ?

He did so because *he was commanded by the Queen to attend the trial.* "He tried to evade service, but," says Phineas Baxter, "the Queen compelled Bacon to act as Counsel for the Crown. He asked to be spared and she insisted on his attendance." (*The Greatest of Literary Problems,* p. 318)

> Parker Woodward says, Francis took a small part in the prosecution by *the peremptory order of the Queen.* (*Tudor Problems,* p. 47.)
>
> "His obligation to the Crown," says Spedding, "did unquestionably bind him to assist in the prosecution of all offences against the State [if called upon]." (*Evenings with a Reviewer,* Vol. I, p. 124.)

Is it not quite clear, in the light of the evidence we already possess of the relationship of the Queen to Robert Essex and Francis Bacon, that he was ordered to attend the trial *to watch the interests of the Queen.* Had he not been appointed specially as "Counsel Extraordinary to Her Majesty" in 1595, six years previously? It was a newly made office which attached him to her own person and gave him the right of entrée to her at any time. In short, *he held primarily a watching brief on her behalf* . . . in order to prevent anything being said by anyone that might reveal the secret of their private relationship . . . to intervene if neccssary and to divert any acrimonious discussion, that might be provoked by the foul-mouthed bully Coke, which might lead to dangerous revelations. If we read the *Sonnet-Diary* (Canto III, p. 72-75), the welter of agonized emotions relating to the Tragedy of the Earl of Essex, the reader will have no doubt that Elizabeth commanded him to be present but, to satisfy fully his scruples, she had also sworn to him that Essex should never go to the Block and that she would exert her Royal Prerogative to save him. This is the true explanation of the mystery of Francis Bacon's presence at the trial that the traditionalists have hitherto failed to fathom.

The verdict, of course, was never once in doubt, and everyone knew that the sentence of "Guilty" would carry the death penalty.

The Charge was:

> That the Earls of Essex and Southampton had conspired with others to deprive and depose the Queen's Majesty from her Royal State and dynasty and to procure her death and destruction, to commit a cruel slaughter on Her Majesty's subjects, to change the Government of the Realm, to go to Her Majesty's home in Whitehall and by force of arms the person of Her Majesty to seize and take into their custody . . ." etc.

Both prisoners pleaded not guilty. Yelverton opened the case and then Coke took up the tale with violent vindictiveness and personal animus. "You shall be Robert the Last," he shouted at Essex, "you that of a Kingdom thought to be Robert the First." There were similar passages of invective—apparently quite irrelevant but which had deep-seated under-meanings—that goaded the Earl into retorts. One passage of arms between Essex, Coke and the Peers was fast drifting into dangerous ground for the Queen and was guided into a more tranquil temper by the intervention of Francis Bacon for the first time:

> "My Lord," said he to Essex, "To defend is lawful, to rebel in defiance is not lawful. It were better to confess and not justify."

By a "Confession" (the admission of having done a technical wrong) Francis Bacon tried to give him the cue to throw himself on the mercy of the Court and Her Majesty. Essex did not take the broad hint. Instead he defended himself with spirit. "The Crown of England was being sold to the Spaniard," he said. "Mr. Secretary should say to one of his fellow Councillors, that the Infanta's title comparatively was as good in Succession as any other." The Earl there touched the real point at issue. It was the "Succession" that was at stake from which Robert Devereux must be excluded at all costs. And Cecil, who was listening to the trial from behind a curtain, stepped forward in Court to deny having talked about the Succession—which was expressly forbidden by Act of Parliament.

> "Had I not seen your ambitious affections inclined to usurpation, I would have gone on my knees to Her Majesty to have done you good; but you have

a wolf's head in a sheep's garment, in appearance humble and religious, but in disposition ambitious and aspiring. God be thanked we now know you."

Coke again took up the story and the wrangling began again because of his offensive manner. Once more Francis Bacon intervened lest the Queen should be implicated:

I have never seen in any case such favour shown to any prisoner; so many digressions and the delivery of evidence by fractions . . . They ran together armed with weapons . . . after being warned by the Messengers sent from Her Majesty's own person . . . Will any man be so simple as to take this to be less than treason?

One can see all along the manifest anxiety of Francis Bacon to keep the offence as a matter between Queen and subject and that their secret kinship must not be mentioned or hinted at. It was a "something" outside the purely legal aspects of the offence.

The defence of Essex was simple:

He said he was not guilty of treason. He never compassed the death of the Queen. All he intended to do was to prostrate himself before her Majesty and implore forgiveness and to remove from her surroundings those persons who were influencing the Queen to his hurt and injury. His quarrel was a private one with his enemies and not a rebellious act against the State. Had he intended a *coup d'etat* would he have struck with so small a force? If he had purposed anything against others than those who were his private enemies, he would not have stirred with so slender a company.

Cecil had asserted that the Infanta of Spain had a right to the British Crown. This he had been led to believe on good authority. Cecil had denied it but he could not deny that he (Cecil) had plotted against his life with Cobham and Raleigh and so they had driven him to desperate means in order to defend his title.

The rising was quite unpremeditated and was not, in any sense, a planned attempt at revolution.

Lord Campbell, *Life of Lord Bacon*, p. 62, says that Essex made a feeling appeal to the Peers sitting on his trial against "these orators, who, out of a form and custom of speaking, would throw so much criminal odium upon him, while answering at the peril of his life a particular charge brought against him.

"And," he said, in a manner that made a deep impression on all who heard him, "I protest before the ever-living God, as He may have mercy upon me, that my conscience is clear from any disloyal thought or harm to Her Majesty. My desire ever hath been to be free from bloodshed. If in all my thoughts and purposes I did not desire the good estate of my Sovereign and country as of my own soul, I beseech the Lord to set some mark upon me in this place for a just vengeance of my untruths to all the world.

"And God, which knoweth the secrets of all hearts, knoweth that I never sought the Crown of England, *nor ever wished to be in a higher degree THAN A SUBJECT*. [This is a clear indication that *he was more than a Subject*, that many KNEW he was more than a Subject, but that he never sought to lay violent hands upon the Crown because he was a concealed Tudor.]

"I only sought to secure my access to the Queen, that I might speedily have unfolded my griefs unto Her Majesty against my private enemies, but not to have shed one drop of their blood. For my religion it is sound, and as I live I mean to die in it."

Basil Montague, *Life*, p. 92. says, through the whole trial Essex conducted himself with courage and firmness worthy of a better cause. Though assailed by the lawyers with much rancour, and harassed by the deepest search into his offences; though harshly questioned by his adversaries, and betrayed by his confederates, he stood at bay, like some noble animal, who fears not his pursuers, nor the death that awaits him; and when at last the deliberate voices of his Peers proclaimed him guilty, he heard the sentence with manly composure, and, without one thought of himself, sought only to save the life of his friend . . . Southampton.

During the trial Essex turned to Cecil and said with fine scorn, "Ah, Master Secretary, I thank God for my humiliation, that you, in the ruff of all your bravery, have come hither to make your oration against me this day."

When he was condemned to death "to be drawn on a hurdle through London streets and so to the place of execution, where you shall be hanged, bowelled and quartered, your head and quarters to be disposed of at Her Majesty's pleasure, . . ." Essex said, with evident truth:

I am not a whit dismayed to receive this doom. Death is as welcome to me as life; and I shall die as cheerful a death as ever man did. And I think it fitting that my poor quarters, which have done her Majesty true service in divers parts of the world, should now at the last be sacrificed and disposed of at Her Majesty's pleasure . . . Whensoever it shall please Her Majesty to call me, I shall be ready to seal the same with my blood."

With the trial and condemnation over, the Garter was plucked from his knee and the George from his breast and, with the dreaded axe facing him, surrounded by horsemen and men-at arms, he was led back to the Tower. It was then seven in the evening and the news had already spread in the City, crowds leaving their suppers flocked into the streets to see him pass. He walked quickly with bowed head, taking no notice though many spoke to him with sympathetic exclamations. While the London citizens were loyal to Elizabeth, the Earl was still their popular hero, the idol of the masses. In spite of the death sentence, the populace generally could not believe that the Queen would permit his execution.

The Privy Council felt that there was too much sympathy for the condemned. Essex had been condemned quite legally but something more was needed to convince the public that beyond doubt, he deserved his fate. (G. B. Harrison, *Robert Devereux*, p. 315.)

The truth is that Essex had been pulled down by vicious enemies. The public knew it. The Government therefore resolved to persuade him or to trick him into a "confession" that he had committed treason and richly deserved death . . . a confession that could be published to all. Since Essex was a religious man, Puritanical in sentiment, they determined to play on his religious convictions. They first tried to wheedle a confession out of him by sending Dr. Thomas Dove, Dean of Norwich, who had been primed with instructions. But when Essex was urged to acknowledge his offences for fear of offending Almighty God, he indignantly repudiated the suggestion that he had committed any traitorous act in the sight of God. The Dean reported his failure to the Council.

The Rev. Abdy Ashton, a Puritan Minister, was the next selected to agitate Essex's conscience with the fears of Hell. He was a ministerial friend who had often preached the Gospel at Essex House and was therefore held to be suspect by the Council. He, too, had been primed with instructions and carefully tempered and tempted with hints both of danger if he failed and of promotion if he succeeded in his mission. Very subtly this traitorous friend led Essex into the trap by his specious speeches. Posing as his disinterested and affectionate friend, this worthless cleric so played on his religious nature, that, under the shadow of the axe, Essex became mentally and emotionally unbalanced . . . a mere piece of putty in the hands of his spiritual adviser, in order to secure "salvation." He made Essex feel that he was indeed a traitor, false to the Queen and to his Maker. At last he was ready to confess anything rather than lose his Hope of Life Eternal. The Rev. Abdy Ashton at once hurried away to report the success of his mission to the Council, that Essex, full of impulsive emotionalism, was ready to confess to anything.

In the meantime two other Divines had been summoned to work on Essex's emotions, Dr. Thomas Montford and Dr. W. Barlow, similarly warned and primed to give "spiritual consolation to the prisoner." They had agreed together that they would first "beat him to the ground with the dreadful judgments of God and then restore him again with the comfortable promises of the Gospel."

Wrought on by such methods, emotionally unbalanced, Cecil and the Lord Admiral waited upon him to hear him repeat what Ashton had instructed him to say. While in this distraught condition Essex was ready to accept any suggestion put to him, with the result that we have a "Confession" which bears traces of suggestion in every line; a confession wrung out of him under theological duress—and therefore worthless—as truly as though he had been stretched on the rack. He is even reputed to have admitted "that the Queen could not be safe so long as he lived upon earth . . . " which is manifestly ridiculous. His alleged confession cannot be accepted at its face value any more than the Casket Letters forged to incriminate Mary Queen of Scots. In the case of Essex there was an immediate urgency to justify his execution to the public, and to show him not in the light of a popular hero and martyr but the very reverse . . . a man faithless to his friends as well as a traitor to his Sovereign, a braggart coward who cringed when face to face with "the Last Enemy," an allegation radically false to Essex's character.

The public did not accept it as valid. Their wrath rose against Cecil, Raleigh and the others higher than ever. How the "Confession" was obtained we never may know but that it was a garbled thing is undoubted. For these same men, when Essex was dead, set out to twist the records so that his character might be further blackened. Says Abbott:

> Accordingly, in their *Declaration of the Treasons of Essex* which profess to contain, "the very confessions taken word for word from their originals," *the Government suppressed or mutilated seven passages which showed that no violence was intended, and six others which proved that the outbreak in the City had not been premeditated* (p. 74).

The accounts published by the Government cannot be accepted as trustworthy, prepared, as they were, by self-interested persons. They are not "judicial" any more than was the verdict . . . "judicial" when actually *TWO OF THE JUDGES stepped from the Bench to give evidence against him!* His "real confessions" were nothing more than "vague, general self-reproaches wrung from a man on the verge of the grave by superstitious fears." (Abbott).

In an atmosphere of emotional religiosity, created by the three Divines who were with Essex until his death, whispering to him to confess his great sin and so save his soul alive. . . . Essex went to the Block.

He was not hung. He was beheaded on Tower Green, the only man executed within the Tower, it being reserved for Royal prisoners. *Persons not of Royal Blood were executed on Tower Hill.* Many noblemen had been summoned to witness the execution with about a hundred others, knights, gentlemen and aldermen of the City. Essex was dressed in black with a black hat. He mounted the scaffold, took off his doublet and displayed his scarlet vest with long scarlet sleeves. "So—tall, splendid, bare-headed, with his fair hair about his shoulders—he stood before the world for the last time." (Strachey). He addressed a few words to those present and then lay flat on the straw and fitted his head to the block. One of the Divines asked him to repeat after him the Fifty-first Psalm. While Essex was repeating the words the headsman struck . . . again and again until the headless corpse sprawled in the straw. The headsman picked up the head by the hair and holding it aloft shouted to the witnesses . . . "God Save the Queen."

"Elizabeth had tamed her own thoroughbred at last."

After the arraignment Francis Bacon at once busied himself on errands of mercy; and even after the execution of Essex he exerted all his powers for leniency on behalf of the persons imprisoned . . . about a hundred. The jails were filled with the rank and file, but many "rebels" were quite innocent. Coke wanted to hang the lot, but while the Court was in progress against the first batch of nine prisoners, Francis Bacon arrived with a letter from the Privy Council to stay proceedings. Eventually, all prisoners save four escaped with fines or short terms of imprisonment, Southampton being reprieved. The only persons put to death were Blount, Danvers, Merrick, and Cuffe. This clemency was directly due to Francis Bacon's exertions. Hepworth Dixon writes, *Story of Lord Bacon's Life*, p. 183:

> That the lofty and gentle course which Francis Bacon pursued through these memorable events commanded the admiration of all his contemporaries save a fraction of the defeated band, is a fact of which the proofs are incontestable.

We may thus profitably ask how was it that Francis Bacon did not secure his brother's reprieve? Why, indeed?

Because, chiefly, he was misled. Perhaps, too, because Essex could not escape the decrees of Fate.

When Francis Bacon appeared in Court against him he did so with an easy mind. He knew that Essex would be found guilty on technical grounds of High Treason and that he would be condemned to death; but he never believed the sentence would be carried out. The Queen had sworn to him that she intended to exert the Royal Prerogative and to save his brother. She had vowed it to him more than once. It was on this understanding that he had watched the Queen's interest. He was quite calm as to the ultimate issue. He busied himself about others, never dreaming but the sentence would be duly revoked. The hell of agony he suffered when he learned to his horror that the Queen had apparently played him false and that Robert had been executed, he told to his own soul in his own private Sonnets:

> And all my Honest Faith in Thee is Lost . . .
> Oaths of thy Love, thy Truth, thy Constancy . . .
> For I have Sworn thee Fair [Just] and thought thee Bright, [clear, transparent]
> Who are as Black as Hell, as Dark as Night.
>
> (39-clii; 40-cxlvii)

Those lines were written on the same day as the execution.

He believed that the Queen had deliberately broken faith with him and had sent her own son to the headsman. He believed this up to the time of her death—until he learned later the full facts. He saw the Queen but once after the sentence and satisfied himself there was nothing to fear. Apparently Francis Bacon never went to the Court again. I can find no record that they ever met again . . . or that he was ever commanded to her presence. Poor Queen! She had given Robert a ring with the intimation "that if ever he forfeited her favour, if he sent it back to her, the sight of it would ensure her forgiveness." Francis knew that Essex had only to return the ring as a symbol of distress and all would be well. He knew, too, that Essex had sent it. Up to the day of the Queen's death, he believed she had received it, and forsworn herself by trampling under foot the mute symbol of mercy.

But the Queen never received the ring. The Warrant for Essex's execution was presented for signature the day following the trial. She waved it away. She was waiting for the ring. The Warrant was presented the next day. She would not sign. All through the following day, the twenty-third, she waited, delaying her signature until the evening. Then, in a surge of temper that Essex should be too stiff-necked and proud to ask for mercy, she yielded to the importunities of Cecil, and signed the Warrant. No sooner had it been dispatched to the Tower than she sent a Messenger saying the execution must be postponed. The ring never came on the twenty-fourth. Her pride and dignity were now at stake. How could she allow her Royal Will to be broken in the sight of the Court and the nation? How could she? Better that her heart should be broken for ever than that the Royal Sceptre of England should be smirched by bending through affection to condone an act that struck at the foundation of the State. In the evening she sent word . . . "Let the execution proceed."

But Essex had sent the ring by the hands of a youth to Lady Scrope, to take to the Queen. Unfortunately, he took it to her sister Lady Nottingham, the wife of the Earl's enemy. She kept the Queen's ring and maintained silence for two years . . . until she was on her death-bed. The ring haunted her. She could not die. She sent for the Queen and confessed what she had done. So overcome with emotion and rage was Elizabeth that she seized the dying woman and shook her in a rage of mental agony, flinging her back in bed with terrible expletives, finishing with the sentence, "God may forgive you but I never can."

Then the Queen went back to her Palace to die. Her heart that had been breaking for two years was now utterly broken.

Though on the morning of the execution she had braved the hushed silence in the Palace by playing the Virginals to an astonished Court waiting for the news of the final act, and though she had continued playing imperturbably when the messenger from the Tower arrived with the fateful news . . . Elizabeth, from the moment the axe fell, had finished with life.

Cecil, now without a rival, had leapt into the saddle, and had established himself as the most powerful ruler of the realm. The reins were slipping from the Queen's grasp. The people no longer greeted the Queen with demonstrations of rapturous affection. There was a gloomy silence in the streets when the rapidly ageing Queen appeared. In the following June she confided to the French Ambassador that "she was weary of life," and, says Strickland, with

> sighs and tears, alluded to the death of Essex, that subject which appears to have ever been in her thoughts, and when unthought of, still the spring of thought . . . .
>
> She said that "being aware of the impetuosity of his temper and his ambitious character, she had warned him two years before to content himself with pleasing her, and not to show such insolent contempt for her as he did on some occasions; but to take care not to touch her sceptre, lest she should be compelled to punish him according to the laws of England, and not according to her own, which he had always found too mild and indulgent for him to fear anything from them. His neglect of this caution," she added, "had caused his ruin." (*Elizabeth*, p. 687.)

At a later date, one of the members of Elizabeth's household gave the following account of the Queen's mind:

> Our Queen is troubled with a rheum in her arm . . . besides the grief she hath conceived for my Lord of Essex's death. She sleepeth not so much by day as she used, neither taketh rest by night. *Her delight is to sit in the dark, and sometimes with shedding tears to bewail Essex.*"

These fits of despondency occasionally cleared away. Her Majesty taking special pleasure between whiles in witnessing the sports of young people, but, writes Strickland:

> All contemporary writers bear witness to the increased dejection of her mind, after visiting her dying kinswoman, the Countess of Nottingham . . . .
>
> The death-bed confession came as a rude shock to the fast-ebbing sands of the sorrow-stricken Queen . . . (*Ibid*, p. 695.)
>
> Many were of opinion that her distress of mind was caused by the death of Essex . . . (*Ibid*, 696.)

One contemporary has recorded that Elizabeth had fallen into a state of moping, sighing and weeping melancholy as though she had a secret grief. This terrible revelation of Lady Nottingham was the last straw. Her mind reeled under the shock. Nor could she unburden herself to anyone. Francis shunned her. He had never seen her since the execution. She was haunted by her thoughts. Robert had sent the ring. He had expected to be pardoned and she had doomed him in her false pride. Nothing could bring him back again.

The Moving Finger writes; and having writ
Moves on: nor all thy Piety nor Wit
Shall lure it back to cancel half a Line,
Nor all thy Tears wash out a Word of it.

Poor Queen! She refused to go to bed, none being able to persuade her, and lay on the floor among the cushions refusing to take nourishment or any medicine prescribed to her by the physicians. Anguish and remorse tore at her heart-strings and dreadful imaginations filled her mind. She clung to her cushions when they wished to remove her and said "She saw too many things when in bed." Cecil, who was present, hearing the remark, thereupon asked, "If Her Majesty had seen any Spirits?" She replied, "I scorn to answer you such a question." When he had gone, she moaned despondingly to the Lord Howard, her confidential friend and relation:

"I am tied! I am tied! And the case is altered with me! I am tied with a chain of iron about my neck!"

This is probably a reference to the scriptural phrase, "*Whoso shall offend one of these little ones . . . it were better that a millstone were hanged about his neck and . . . drowned in the depth of the sea.*" Piers Compton says:

She uttered no word of repentance, no thought of receiving the Sacrament or such spiritual consolation . . . The Archbishop of Canterbury and other prelates were summoned by the Councillors as the end approached but . . . she told them to be packing as . . . they were hedge priests. (*Queen Bess*, p. 195.)

But before the end she allowed the old Archbishop to pray for her.

She had not named her Successor and the Council, being sent for, asked her to name her Successor by holding up her finger, while they called out various names. . . . "The King of France? No answer. The King of Scotland? She made no sign. Lord Beauchamp? I will have no rascal's son in my seat, but one worthy to be King." (*Lady Southwell's eye-witness account of the death-scene.*) From this it is quite clear that Elizabeth never named her Successor. But the Council gave out that "by putting her hand to her head, when the King of Scotland was named to succeed her, we all knew he was the man she desired should reign after her." But, as Strickland writes:

How can her last struggles, the clasping of her convulsed hands over her brow, be seriously set forth as her symbolical intimation that her successor was to be a crowned king?

It was a terrible passing. After lying on her cushions for fourteen days she died distraught in body, mind and spirit, full of distress and agitation . . . a lonely old woman whose regal pride had driven away her husband Leicester, her son Robert to the scaffold, and her eldest, Francis, away from her side . . . that profound genius who was the true King of England, having sprung from her loins, and who was only thought of with disdain by the Councillors as an adulterine-Bastard. She died on the 24th March, 1603, aged seventy. It is a notable fact that her body was not embalmed as was usual for Kings and Queens:

> No male touch laid aside her drapery when she was dead to carry out the dissection and embalming that preceded a royal funeral in those times. The duty of preparing for burial fell to her ladies, and if one of them was over-curious we have no record of her discovery. (*Ibid*, Piers Compton, p. 194.)

In other words, the loyalty of her ladies allowed Elizabeth to maintain the secret of her motherhood inviolate and to continue through the ages to pose as "THE VIRGIN QUEEN."

In the north aisle of Henry's VII's Chapel in Westminster Abbey lies the recumbent marble effigy of Elizabeth on her tomb. . . . On her delicate hand is the famous ring "that was stayed by malice from saving a man's life and the probable breaking of a woman's heart." (Compton). No mere Lover would have attained the ascendancy that Robert gained —but by his own stubbornness lost—over such a Queen. None but an arrogant, vain Royal Mother, who had never reared a child would have treated him as she treated him. (Parker Woodward).

Cut upon the wall over the doorway of the Beauchamp Tower, at the foot of the stairs, are TWO WORDS which record Essex's imprisonment and death in the Tower. Few have heeded them, fewer have understood them. They were placed there by someone in authority, and with the connivance, necessarily so, of the Tower authorities, in order to perpetuate the Memory and to provide a CLUE to the real IDENTITY of the unhappy son of Queen Elizabeth Tudor . . . pronounced Tidir. The words reveal the true name of the man who walked from the cell in which he was once confined to the scaffold in the Courtyard below:

ROBART TIDIR:
(*Welsh for Robert Tudor*)

And the man who was responsible for this mute but ever-living memorial was his brother . . . Francis Bacon. Who else could it have been? Who else had the right to perpetuate the Queen's Secret in so striking and mysterious a manner but Francis, the Last of the Tudors!

And on the night Elizabeth died Francis Bacon wrote one of the most tragic Sonnets ever penned describing the Queen's passionate Pride and her Remorse at the fatal consequences—the "Lust of passion being Perjured, Murderous, Bloody-full of Blame . . . Proud and very Woe. . . ."

> All this the world well knows, yet none knows well
> To Shun the Heaven that leads men to this HELL.
> (41-cxxix)

Now we know what has always been a puzzle to Shakespearean authorities . . . the reason why "Shakespeare" never wrote a single line of lamentation on the death of "The Virgin Queen."

ADDENDA:

Queen Elizabeth's Ring

LYTTON STRACHEY discredits the fact that Elizabeth gave Essex a ring with the assurance that this would always bring forgiveness. He calls it a "romantic story . . . appropriate enough to . . . a sentimental novelette; but it does not belong to history." That is his opinion . . . an opinion formed to suit the romantic fiction that Elizabeth was the Lover and Mistress of the Earl. There was LOVE between them undoubtedly, but it was the love of a mother for a wayward son who had inherited from her the same pride of Tudor Caste as she possessed. The best historians and biographers are against Strachey. Alexander B. Grosart, LL.D., F.S.A., writing as Editor of Robert Chester's *Love's Martyr* writes, Pref. xlviii:

> I know of nothing more heart-shatteringly tragic—for pathetic is too weak a word—than the great Queen's death-cushion moanings and mutterings over her dead Essex.
>
> *I, for one, believe in that story of the Ring* as John Webster has put it:
>
> 'let me die
> In the distraction of the Worthy Princess,
> Who loathed food, and sleep, and ceremony,
> For thought of losing that brave gentleman
> She would fain have saved, had not a false conveyance
> Expressed him stubborn-hearted: Let me sink
> Where neither man nor memory may e'er find me!'
> *The Devil's Law Case, A. iii, s.* 3
>
> *That Webster did not thus introduce the "ring" at random seems certain.* A hitherto overlooked little book supplies a self-authenticating record of it . . . *Historical Memoirs on the reigns of Queen Elizabeth and King James.* Grosart quotes the story at length. A more explicit narration, with an entire absence of romanticism, could not have been recorded. This book was published in 1658 but Webster wrote in 1620, well within the memory of living people who would have been acquainted with the story as a fact. It was never contradicted except by the Stracheys of a later age to suit their own preconceived notions.
>
> Webster unquestionably knew the truth. He was a member of the secret Rosicrosse Literary Society presided over by Francis Bacon, the editor of all the Rosicrosse Books. He passed the above lines of Webster's. Indeed, I have no personal doubt that he suggested them . . . as a first open indication to the world.

In 1695, the story of the "ring" is again told in *The Secret History of the most renowned Queen Elizabeth and the Earl of Essex, the author being A Lady of Quality.*

Of all biographers, Montague is one of the most careful, his legal mind well weighing the evidence pro and con, before accepting it. This is what he says, *Life of Bacon*, p. xciv.:

> Elizabeth suffered the lingering torture of a broken heart; the envenomed asp was in her bosom; she sunk under the consciousness of abused confidence, of ill-bestowed favours, of unrequited affection: the very springs of kindness

> were poisoned . . . her health visibly declined, and *the last blow was given to her by some disclosure made on the death-bed of the Countess of Nottingham.*
>
> Various rumours have arisen regarding this interview, and the cause of the Queen's grief; but *the fatal result has never been doubted. From that day, refusing the aid of medicine, or food, or rest, she sat upon the floor of her darkened chamber, and gave herself up to unrestrained sorrow.* The spirit that had kept a world in awe was utterly prostrate . . . Desolate, afflicted, and weary of existence she lingered till the 24th March, on which day she died.

Strickland, one of the most painstaking of biographers, says in her *Elizabeth*, p. 673:

> The romantic story of the ring which, it is said, the Queen had given to Essex . . . must not be lightly rejected. It is not only related by Osborne, who is considered a fair authority for other things, and quoted by historians of all parties, but it is a family tradition of the Careys, who were the persons most likely to be in the secret, as they were the relations and friends of all the parties concerned and enjoyed the confidence of Queen Elizabeth.
>
> Lady Elizabeth Spelman, a descendant of that house, gave the following version to the editor of her great-uncle Robert Carey's Memoirs . . . Then follows a specific story of the ring.

In short, "the romantic story of the ring" has far more historical warrant than the opinions of those credulous biographers who believe that the love of Elizabeth for Essex was that of a Mistress, when the clear facts prove she was his MOTHER . . . secretly craving for him out of the passion of Mother-Love.

Chapter XI

THE LAST OF THE TUDORS
(1603)

IN the last chapter I have gone into rather more details about the life of "Robert Tudor," Earl of Essex, than the orthodox principles of biography would seem to warrant, considering that we are studying the life of another man. But there is ample justification when we reflect on the important consequences that Essex's life and acts played in Francis Bacon's life, and the influence they have exerted on the biographers. These writers have no knowledge of Francis Bacon's secret relationship to Essex and the Queen. They dismiss the details I have given as having little or no significance. Their all-round importance has been misunderstood. The cunning asides and double-meaning phraseology have never been noticed. They were so obvious that the eyes of biographers never saw anything suspicious. The Macaulay-Campbell-Abbott school has fastened on the superficial aspects of Francis Bacon's attitude towards Essex at the trial and its fatal termination. Its conclusions have been drawn on insufficient data; but the minds of these critics have been so warped by what they consider to be serious defects in Francis Bacon's character in relation to Essex, that it has prejudiced them against giving him even bare justice in other of his public acts in later life. It is an excellent illustration of the herd-mind that gives a dog a bad name and thereafter finds plenty of evidence on which to hang him.

No one's actions have been more mercilessly misjudged than Francis Bacon; and this, largely because of his connection with the Essex tragedy. It has been held that Francis Bacon was a faithless friend; that he deserted Essex in his hour of need; that he should never have taken part in the prosecution of a man who had done him such signal favours. It has been concluded by these harsh judges that his nature was emotionally as icy-cold as the deceitful Machiavelli, as avariciously calculating as Judas, and as monstrously wicked as Titus Oates. In varying tones the critics chant:

> Did he not strike down his friend in open Court? Did he not rush with avidity to do the Queen's bidding? Should not common gratitude have prompted him to retire from the case? Did he not side openly with Essex's enemies? Did he even try to save him from the block?

These questions are answered in savage, discordant outbursts by men who seek to destroy for ever Francis Bacon's character. They say he was so worldly ambitious for Public Honour, so mercenary-minded, so resolved to win financial and legal advancement . . . that he would have sold his soul if necessary to Mahu, the Prince of Darkness. By his betrayal he tried to make the dead body of his friend a stepping-stone to political and social success. As a matter of fact, however, there is no episode in history about which it is more necessary to reserve one's judgment until the full facts are disclosed. Never has there been such a tragedy as that of Queen Elizabeth and her two sons which more poignantly illustrates the truth of the saying that "To know ALL is to forgive ALL."

Now against these sour-minded poseurs of virtue—Paul Prys who love to rake up and make up evil—are authorities equally as eminent who do not believe that *even the open historical facts justify these sweeping animadversions on Francis Bacon's moral character.* These are their individual verdicts:

Professor Thomas Fowler, M.A., F.S.A.

I can see no sufficient reason for the persistent and bitter attacks upon Francis Bacon's honour and character which it has been the fashion to make . . . The peace and well-being of the country had claims on him superior to private friendship . . . .

As Mr. Spedding says, he had really no alternative, as one of Her Majesty's Counsel, short of virtually declaring his own sympathy and complicity with treason, but to engage in the prosecution of Essex and Southampton. (*Francis Bacon*, p. 8.)

James Spedding

Upon what pretence could Bacon have asked to be excused? It was a service that came strictly within the duty of his place, p. 126 . . . Not a man who followed Essex that day but was, according to the letter of the law, guilty of Treason. (*Evenings with a Reviewer*, p. 131.)

Israel Levine, M.A., D.Litt.

It is true Bacon WAS ORDERED BY THE QUEEN to take his professional share in the proceedings. (*Francis Bacon*, p. 31.)

Professor J. Nichol

Bacon with the rest of the Queen's Counsel received a commission to assist in the process. It is hard to state at what precise point of the business he should have refused his services . . . To have declined to sift the evidence would have been abandoning his post . . . To have refused to report upon the result of the inquiry would have been impossible. To have applied for permission to be absent from the trial would have been dangerous.

He might, however, have declined any leading part in the prosecution and sat silent . . . Instead, he twice interposed . . . *to keep the Court in view of the main facts of the case,* from which Coke's confusion had allowed the examination to wander. (*Bacon*, Vol. I, p. 52.)

Dean Church

Bacon's legal position was so subordinate a place that there must have been a special reason for his employment. (*Bacon*, p. 52.)

W. Hepworth Dixon, Barrister-at-law

Lord Campbell writes as though it would have been right for Bacon to have shirked his part . . . To put Bacon wrong, the objector must prove Essex to have been acting in the right . . . By what path of reasoning can we come to the conclusion that one of the Queen's Counsellors called to do his duty by the Crown, was not right? In Bacon's place, we must assume that Lord Campbell would have done his duty as Bacon did. There is no second course . . . .

He was as much the Queen's officer, armed with her commission, bound to obey her commands, as her Captain of the Guard . . . .

That the bearing of Francis Bacon throughout these mournful events is just and noble, is the public verdict of the time.

Called by the Privy Council to bear his part in the Great Drama, Francis Bacon no more shirks his duty at the Bar than Levison shirked his duty at Ludgate Hill. As Her Majesty's Counsel Learned in the Law, he has no more choice about his duty of Defence than her Captain of the Guard . . . He had tried to save the Earl: but England was his first LOVE, and by her faith, her freedom, and her Queen they must stand or fall. (*Personal History of Lord Bacon*, p. 127.)

John M. Robertson

After Spedding's exhaustive analysis and confutation of the Macaulay libel, the problem of Bacon's character is happily simplified. We know now that he verily was not the heartless, servile, self-seeking hypocrite of the reviewers' effigy, but a man who managed his life, in difficult days . . . with honour and dignity, p. 51.

To palliate Essex's wanton and senseless sedition, and vilify Bacon's grave conduct of his public duty, is to commit an injustice such as Bacon never had part in.

Essex had ceased to take counsel from Bacon long before his insane revolt. At the trial nevertheless, Bacon strove to save him from himself; and only the insane plea of not guilty forced the friendly accuser to press the crushing proofs of guilt. (*Pioneer Humanists*, p. 56.)

Basil Montague

Bacon's anguish, when he felt that the Queen's displeasure was gradually taking the form most to be dreaded, the cold and severe aspect of offended justice, can be conceived only by those who had seen his patient watchfulness over his wayward friend. Through the whole of his career, Bacon had anxiously pursued him, warning him when it was possible, to prevent the commission of error . . . which would place him out of the pale of the Queen's mercy . . . .

No man knew better, or felt more deeply, the duties of friendship than Francis Bacon . . . His friendship, therefore, both in words and acts, Essex constantly experienced . . . and when at last, bound hand and foot, he was cast at the feet of the Queen . . . he still walked with him in the midst of the fire . . . .

It is impossible to form a correct judgment of the conduct of Bacon at this unfortunate juncture, without considering the difficulties of his situation, and his conflicting duties . . . In whatever light it can be viewed, *the course that Essex had pursued was ruinous to Bacon.* He had been bondsman again and again to the Queen for the love and duty of Essex. (*Life of Bacon*, p. 89.)

The foregoing opinions should inspire every reader to consider the position afresh and with an open mind, not allowing himself to be led away by what he has been taught by traditionalists in school and college. The plain truth is that the harsh strictures of men like Abbott, with their suppression and distortion of fact to make their theories fit their prejudices, will not stand critical examination. The authorities I quote—*none of whom suspected the true relationship of the three principal characters*—prove that from the moment *he was commanded by the Queen or the Privy Council* to take part in the examination of the prisoners and subsequent trial, Francis Bacon had no choice but to obey. To have refused, as a sworn officer to Her Majesty, would not have benefited Essex one whit. It would have played into Cecil's hands. Francis Bacon would certainly have been committed to the Tower. Indeed, his refusal would have provided Cecil with a good excuse for making a clean sweep of both men on the score of contempt and treason.

Francis Bacon in his *Apologia* says:

> Between the arraignment and my Lord's suffering I was but once with the Queen . . . I durst not deal directly for my Lord as things then stood; yet generally I did both commend Her Majesty's mercy, terming it to her as an excellent balm that did constantly distil from her sovereign hands, and made an excellent odour in the senses of the people . . . and *SOME OTHER WORDS WHICH I NOW OMIT.*

The open facts of history show that Francis Bacon DID try to obtain a reprieve; and if we had "*the other WORDS which I now OMIT*" which passed between the Queen and himself, it would have been found that Francis Bacon had the strongest warranty that Essex would be reprieved. He did not desert Essex in his hour of need. The omission of the conversation in the *Apologia* indicates that it was something of importance. If it had been printed it would have shown that Essex was to have been reprieved; and it would also have shown the true identity of Essex; *the secret that could not be disclosed . . . only hinted at,* hence the omission.

We are told that Essex had done so much for him that Francis Bacon should have stood on one side. What had he been given? A piece of land worth £1500 for three to four years' service—with out-of-pocket expenses—on Essex's behalf, and advice and interviews innumerable. But to the Queen he owed far, far more . . . his royal mansion at Twickenham Park, lands, Offices and a private income. Is it not obvious that from the point of view of "emoluments" his duty lay entirely to the Queen as well as his duty as a subject? His obligations to Essex were not such as to make it his duty to defend him in a bad cause. His obligation to the Crown bound him to assist in the prosecution of all offences against the State. Upon what pretext could he have declined? He could not say that the proposed proceedings were unjust or unfair. He could not openly say that Essex if guilty ought not to be declared guilty.

The fact is that Essex did not suffer any one thing in "pocket," person or fame, which he would not have suffered had Francis Bacon never attended the trial. It was not Francis Bacon who ruined the Earl's fortunes or shed his blood. For months following the house arrest he was doing all he could to restore the Earl to the Queen's favour. Francis had warned him repeatedly against any hot-tempered recourse to violent measures and that his (Francis's) own duty lay first to his mother, the Queen. The letters etc., of the times, prove it. Only envenomed prejudice could twist the plain facts of the case.

If it be evident from open history, in the opinion of the best authorities, that Francis Bacon did not play the part of a false friend, how transparently clear becomes his innocence from short-sighted imputations of guilt when we consider that this State Tragedy had its roots not actually in a rebellious act of Treason but really in a domestic tangle . . . perhaps the most complex in British history. All the evidence of the previous chapters (to say nothing of the story told in secret cyphers in the Rosicrosse books of that Era, etc.) goes to prove that Elizabeth was a wife and a mother and that she bore at least two sons. Every student of the period knows that the only men in her private life with whom she was on terms of real intimacy were Robert Dudley, Francis Bacon and Robert Devereux. The extracts from her letters, her gifts of money and lands and honours—especially to the two Roberts—and the general circumstances surrounding Elizabeth and the three men, prove, as conclusively as anything can be proved by circumstantial evidence, that a family relationship existed which was at times stronger than official convention and peeped between the links of social decorum.

After Dudley's death she naturally associated herself—more or less—in her private life and concerns with her two sons until her mind became obsessed by the fiend of jealousy which had been raised by Cecil and others. One can honestly say that Elizabeth had done everything possible for their advancement. Were there any other men upon whom she lavished her favours? Not one. Nor was there any group of men that she severally and jointly took into her confidence. The way she called in Dudley to help her at critical moments, and, later, Francis Bacon; and her continual fights with Robert the headstrong, point the truth; and *there is nothing on record which militates against it.*

At the age of sixty-eight, the Queen still posed to the world as a "Virgin." Her two grown-up sons were still "concealed"—for they had been brought up in other Houses under other names—Francis being aged forty and Robert, thirty-four. Both knew their secret heritage, that they were of the Tudor Breed, yet the elder could make no move for he was an adulterine bastard in law and nothing would he do to jeopardize the Queen's secret. He was the guardian of her honour . . . especially watchful of the younger Robert, fiery and inexperienced, who chafed to think he was denied his legitimate rights, that his actions should be misunderstood and that usurpers and outsiders should have won an ascendency over his mother the Queen when he ought to have been in a position to send them packing.

Poor Queen! What could she do for the best to conserve all that she had sacrificed to make England great?

Poor Elizabeth! The girl who had been denied all love in her childhood and maidenhood and had gone through perils we reck not of: Her mother beheaded: Her young life shattered: Her home-life torn with suspicions and wantonness: her father dying the death of a wicked, lustful brute: Her imprisonment in the Tower under the shadow of the Axe: her escape from execution by a miracle . . . together with her Lover Robert Dudley whom she could not marry. If ever a woman was torn between her love for her country and her private love, that woman was Elizabeth. And terrible indeed was the price she paid for the exalted position in which she was placed by Fate; for Elizabeth felt that she, ALONE, could save England and that an "open marriage" with her lover would have made England a prey to foreign nations and created civil war.

Calm reflection shows that she was right. She staved off the threats of war until England became strong with the passing of the years. But her happiness faded, for Dudley grew tired (perhaps rightly so) as the years sped by at being no more to Elizabeth than a left-handed husband, with no move taken to name their favourite son Robert as next in the Succession under the special Act of Parliament. . . . the "Heir of her Natural Body" by a true morganatic marriage. So was Elizabeth Tudor driven along the Road of Life by the Whips of Destiny. How wonderful a woman was she to maintain this hidden secret within her breast until her death—and for long years afterwards—and with how brave a front faced she the world, hourly on her guard, daily aware of a devastating climax that might burst upon her at any moment . . . and then . . . who could tell the end. What a Hell of Agony must she have endured as she tossed on those cushions day after day and night after night, moaning for the touch of her own flesh and blood. "Robert! Robert!" whom she had doomed to the block. "I am tied! Tied by the Neck!" How rightly named was she by Francis, "The Alone Queen." In the presence of that death-chamber, surely any sins she may have committed were finally blotted out in agony as she writhed over the belated death-bed confession of the Countess of Nottingham. Let those without sin cast the first stone at England's greatest Queen.

We can now examine the abortive "rebellion" in its proper light. Technically, Robert Essex HAD rebelled against the authority of the Queen and the Government, and therefore had committed, in law, an act of treason. Actually . . . he had done nothing of the sort. Robert Essex never intended doing any harm to the Queen's person or injury to the State. The "slender company" with which he ventured is proof sufficient. What he wanted to do primarily was *to get to see his mother* because he felt he could sweep away the misunderstandings of years if only he could see her privately face to face. The most he wanted to do was to scatter those men round the Queen who had misrepresented his actions and misconstrued his motives. Naturally, he felt he had the right of a Tudor to the Throne—more right than the Infanta of Spain or James of Scotland. And as the Queen's natural child—even though the marriage was a morganatic one—Robert Prince of Tudor had an infinitely better claim to the Succession than anyone else, in fact and in law. It is preposterous to suggest that he ever plotted with James to acquire the Throne. James wanted it for himself. He would never have raised his little finger to have installed Essex in the Royal Seat. As a matter of fact *Cecil was already pledged to James*. This knowledge it was that drove Essex to try to obtain the Queen's personal promise that he should succeed her on her demise. Essex acted as nine men out of ten would have acted feeling he was being jockeyed out of his heritage through self-interested men influencing his mother. Essex may have acted rashly but he was not blameworthy.

His alleged conspiracy with Tyrone to back up a *coup de main* at the State is as foundationless as his alleged intrigues with the Spaniards. Even Abbott says that:

> The verdict of history must be that Essex, though guilty of treason, was not a deliberate traitor. (*Francis Bacon*, p. 81.)

Essex indignantly disclaimed the intention of taking the Queen's life, imputed to him by Coke, and all original purpose of rousing the City; and the Government could prove neither of these points. (*Ibid*, p. 74.)

Lytton Strachey writes, There was no settled malignancy in Essex's nature. It is possible that he believed in the treachery of Cecil; and, as it happened, there was some justification for the belief, for *Cecil, with all his loyalty, was actually in receipt of a Spanish pension.* (*Elizabeth and Essex*, p. 249.)

Professor John Nichol: To attach to Essex a suspicion of having been implicated in a conspiracy because Anthony Bacon was employed by Essex on some occasions to convey letters to Scotland, *is preposterous.* (*Francis Bacon*, Vol. I, p. 56.)

Dr. Abbott: Cecil, it is true . . . had been engaged for some time in secret correspondence with the Scottish Court . . . and the charge of favouring the Spanish Succession brought by Essex against Cecil might possibly tell against the latter (p. 97).

E. G. Harman, C.B.: After all, who except Cecil can have persuaded the Queen to sign the Warrant? He was head and shoulders above everybody else, and we read that about that period the Queen was so irritable that no other Counsellor dared approach her . . . .

By cunning under the pretext of political necessity, it would seem that Cecil destroyed the man of rank whom he hated and feared. (*The Impersonality of Shakespeare*, p. 96.)

A. Strickland: The first result of Cecil's secret understanding with the King of the Scots was an addition of two thousand pounds per year which that Monarch received from Queen Elizabeth. (*Elizabeth*, p. 249.)

John Webster: Cecil had laid a trap for Essex, caused him to get news of the Queen's illness and even death, and embargoed all other vessels, hoping Essex would join with Tyrone and others and cross to England at the head of his army. His sudden appearance with but few followers, disconcerted Cecil's plot, who had troops ready to oppose him. (*Hist. Memoirs, Q. Eliz. and K. James*, 1658, quoted as a valuable book by Dr. A. B. Grosart.)

That Essex was brought to his end by a "trick" is proved by a letter recently discovered (1930) written by Robert Townson, Dean of Westminster, who accompanied Sir Walter Raleigh to the scaffold.

Writing to Sir John Isham of Lamport, Bishop Townson says: I putt him in mind of my Lord of Essex; how it was generally reported that he was a great instrument of his death, which, if his hart did charge him with, he should hartily repent and ask God for forgiveness; to which he made answer that my Lord of Essex "*was fecht of by a trick*" which he privately told me of. (See *Daily Post, Liverpool,* July 28, 1930)

Let us now see what Essex said under the shadow of the axe. He told Ashton, the parson who had been enjoined to wring a confession out of him by threats of hell and damnation, that he had acted as he had done not from "private ambition."

For the Crown, I never affected it . . . Being a principal member of this Commonwealth, I could not but see and feel what misery was near unto my country by the great power of such as are known to be Atheists, Papists, and Pensioners to the mortal enemies of this kingdom.

Commenting on this statement, E. G. Harman, C.B., says: The account looks to me genuine, because under "*Atheists*" Raleigh would be included in the mind of the speaker, under "*Papists*" Lord Henry Howard, and under "*Pensioners*" Cecil. (*Ibid*, p. 94.)

The evidence and opinions of these various types of scholars indubitably prove that the mystery of Robert Essex's sudden and "abortive rebellion" is only to be solved in its entirety through the solution of the greater mystery of the Era which has ever revolved around "The Virgin Queen." Once the student accepts the implication that Elizabeth was a privately married woman—which is in strict accord with the facts of the times—a whole series of lesser mysteries can be completely understood. The Queen's intimate familiarity with Leicester was due to the fact that she regarded him as her husband in the sight of God. Her love for him was not the passion of a wanton . . . as is so often asserted. Her children, Francis and Robert, were truly "Love-Children." We can understand Essex's "Fatal Impatience," his fever of anxiety as he saw his natural rights being shorn away, and the face of his own mother being turned away from him by unscrupulous rivals. We can see that he was no Wat Tyler, no rebel to the State, and that his prime concern was to deal with his "private enemies."

We can understand, too, why Francis Bacon veiled his identity under the cloak of anonymity, becoming a concealed writer and a Cypher expert. Not only did it enable him to prosecute his educational and ethical ideals in secrecy but to convey to another age his personal revelations concerning himself . . . truths that could only be told in Cypher through a multiplicity of pen-names. We can see how the English Renaissance came into being. The seed was created under the beating of the great heart of Francis Bacon. By him was it sown secretly in the body of England. And many loving hands belonging to a happy band of Brothers, watered and guarded the tender plant and watched it grow into a noble tree for the healing of the Nations. The mysterious source of Francis Bacon's income is revealed and the equally mysterious disappearance of his monies—which we now know went in the printing and publishing of books and the founding of his Lodges of Ethical Symbolism. "Under a Noted and Despised WEED"—Shakespeare—Francis Bacon had begun "to procure the good of all Men."

We can understand why Francis went to the trial—to protect, primarily, the Honour of the Queen lest anything untoward might slip out in the heat of the conflict respecting their private relationships. His duty clearly lay to Elizabeth first and last—as his mother and his Queen—rather than to his brother Robert whom he had nevertheless safeguarded by obtaining an assurance from the Queen that he should never be executed no matter what was the decision of the Court. Had Francis Bacon refrained—or attempted to refrain—from standing by his mother in this crisis his course would have indicated "poverty of moral feeling," to quote Professor Gardiner's phrase.

The open facts of history prove the secret relationship of the "Three Principals." The Cypher accounts in the Rosicrosse books serve but to clinch the truth. "I have given you a THREAD of my own LIFE," said Prospero. And armed with this clue one may successfully travel the labyrinth of the Elizabethan Era. Its many paths all converge in the CENTRE, no matter how they twist and wind, THE TEMPLE at Gorhambury where Francis Bacon the Master awaits within the porchway each faithful traveller who has fought his way through to "LOVE, LIGHT and LIFE."

The execution of Essex came as a very great shock to the public. Popular feeling had run strongly in his favour. There was a grave danger that he would be regarded as a martyr by the ordinary citizens. Cecil and Raleigh were regarded with abhorrence by the average Londoner and held to public execration. The Government therefore felt that it should try to satisfy the public that their favourite had only received his just deserts without any infliction of wrong. All that the reading, writing, and speaking populace knew was that in his last moments Robert Essex was manly and courageous both at the bar of the Court and on the scaffold, so are we given to understand by spectators like Chamberlain who afterwards wrote:

> At his coming to the bar his countenance was somewhat unsettled; but after he was once in, I assure you I never saw any go through with such boldness, and show of resolution and contempt of death: but whether this courage were borrowed and put on for the time, or natural, it were hard to judge. *Chamberlain's Letters*, Camden Society.

In the popular mind Essex was a hero who had been foully done to death by cowardly miscreants. The Government therefore decided to draw up a public justification with a view to informing the public that there were proofs of Essex's treason and acquainting them with the facts. By the irony of Fate, the man appointed to write up the *Declaration of the Treasons of Essex* was Francis Bacon. He was *ordered* by the Queen's Privy Council to prepare the story of the conspiracy. He could not refuse. It was a COMMAND. He wrote it and sent in the manuscript. What the original draft was we do not know but the Declaration was printed and issued under the name of Francis Bacon. He has been bitterly attacked by Macaulay and his followers for having stooped "to murder the Earl's fame" by blackening his memory. The truth is that Francis Bacon did nothing of the sort. What he originally wrote was a vindication of Essex... naturally so, as his brother; and he consented to write it, in order to prevent any of Essex's embittered enemies presenting to the public a twisted tale. But, unfortunately, the Council when they got hold of the manuscript took steps to erase, alter, and spatch-cock words and phrases so that the finished printed *Declaration* was something very different from the original MS. It is obvious to anyone knowing the secret facts of Francis Bacon's secret relationship that the story is a garbled one. An examination of the records show moreover *suppression or mutilation in seven passages* in the Confessions which indicated that no violence was intended, and six others which proved that the outbreak in the City had not been premeditated. (*See* Dr. Abbott, *Bacon*, p. 74). Yet, in the preface to the *Declaration*, it is stated . . . "*The very Confessions are taken word for word from their originals.*" Francis Bacon's account was first read by the Queen. Wherever he had written, "My Lord Essex," she struck it out and wrote "Essex." The MS. then went to Cecil and his henchmen. When they had finished they had "*made it almost a new writing*," as Francis Bacon afterwards declared in his *Apologia*. In short, the "*Declaration*" issued under his name was not his composition at all but the Government's. All that Francis Bacon had done was to provide them with the first draft of an honest document which they garbled to suit their own ends. How easily this can be done I know only too well from practical experience as a one-time reporter.

These are the opinions of leading authorities on the matter:

> James Spedding: Be on your guard against admitting such an expression as "murdering the Earl's fame" (Macaulay). Bacon says Her Majesty commanded me to pen it . . . Never secretary had more particular or express directions and instructions on every point . . . .
>
> After I had made a first draught of it . . . it was perused, weighed, censured, ALTERED and *almost made a new writing* according to their Lordships' better considerations . . . .
>
> It was again perused by the Queen herself and some alterations made again . . . It was printed *de novo* and the first copies suppressed by her peremptory demand.
>
> The Declaration was to be printed by Authority, not of Bacon but of the Queen and her Councillors (p. 146).
>
> Professor Nichol: When it was found expedient to issue the "Declaration" nothing was more natural than that Francis Bacon should be commanded by the Queen to write it (p. 56).
>
> All that we know confirms the veracity of the Statement . . . (p. 54).
>
> He must be acquitted of anything like treachery to Essex (p. 46).
>
> It has been said that the guilt of Essex has nothing to do with Bacon's conduct; but it is possible for a man to commit a crime from the consequences of which past favours cannot relieve him. (*Bacon*, Vol. I, p. 57.)
>
> H. Crouch Bachelor: In the "Declaration" Bacon so palliates his offences that the Queen violently remonstrated with him because "he would not forget his old respect for the traitor," and she had the whole book printed anew. Even in its amended form, it was perhaps the most gentle and moderate State Paper ever furnished, and was obviously conceived in sorrow, not in anger. (*Francis Bacon*, p. 15.)
>
> W. Hepworth Dixon: Not one word of insult, not a hint of accusation, beyond the needs of the case, disfigure it. The facts which no impartial judge could have pardoned were suppressed; and the whole declaration was so mercifully worded, that it saved the memory of Essex from public execration . . . while it left the future open to his misguided followers and his innocent son. (*Francis Bacon*, p. 186.)

As a direct result of the trial and the "Declaration" there was written a remarkable "*Apologia.*" Indeed, in the entire range of letters there is probably no piece of personal history that ranks higher as a human document. Spedding describes it as:

> a paper of great importance—one of them by which I was first attracted to the study of Francis Bacon's personal character and history. (*Life*, Vol. III, p. 136.)

It is entitled *Sir Francis Bacon his Apologie in certaine imputations concerning the late Earle of Essex*. It was published in 1604 when James was king . . . some twelve months after Elizabeth's death and about three years after the Essex trial. There have been many suggestions why Francis Bacon came to write it but no one hitherto has discovered the reason. It has been averred that it was written because of popular disapprobation at his conduct respecting Essex. But there is no contemporary evidence to support this theory. Spedding searched everywhere in vain for signs of anger against Francis Bacon until he was forced to say, "I believe that the only contemporary witness who can be cited to prove the existence of any disapprobation at all is Bacon himself." (*Ibid,* p. 137.) The words of the first sentence of the *Apologia* are these:

> I cannot be ignorant . . . of the wrong which I sustain in common speech, as if I had been false or unthankful to that noble but unfortunate Earl, the Earl of Essex . . . .

This is the only foundation for the suggestion that Francis Bacon's name was execrated by the populace. One fact alone is sufficient to disprove this superficial view: When the writs went out for a New Parliament in January 1604, Francis Bacon was sent to Westminster by a double return, by the burgesses of St. Albans and Ipswich, and that in spite of Court influence against him. So popular was he amongst his fellow-members that some actually proposed him to be the Speaker, although it was well known that according to ancient usage the office had always been filled by the Crown's nominee. This is strong evidence that he was under no public ban by the burgesses who sent him to the Commons nor by his fellow members; indeed, on his refusal to stand against the Crown's nominee, Sir Edward Phelips, the Commons elected him to serve on no less than twenty-nine Committees. Never a word was uttered against him by the electorates or the Members of Parliament; and throughout the ensuing Sessions when feelings ran high—with Francis Bacon taking a leading part—no one dreamt of accusing him of obsequiousness or treachery. Even his enemy Sir Edward Coke never accused him of ingratitude to Essex—though he did not hesitate later to accuse him falsely of ingratitude to Somerset and Buckingham, the Favourites of King James.

Why, then, did Francis Bacon write this opening sentence—using the term "in common speech" as though it were in the mouths of everyone?

The answer is not far to seek. It is simply one of Francis Bacon's methods of using phraseology which conveys more than one meaning; in this case it conveyed a reproof to someone who had spoken ill of him without pointing him out by name. To utter a slander is to use "common speech" for "common" means "profane, polluted, vulgar, low, mean," as well as "universal." A person in a high position had spoken of him profanely and vulgarly, so much so that Francis Bacon considered it merited a reply; and anyone acquainted with the era ought to know who the person was. It was understood at the time for whom it was meant; *not for the common people but for one particular man, the Earl of Southampton.*

These are the circumstances which gave rise to it. When James came to the throne many prisoners were released from the Tower, among them, on the 10th April, 1603, the Earl of Southampton, Essex's friend and fellow-prisoner, whose death-sentence had been commuted to imprisonment. Many persons went to see him and to congratulate him on his happy release. Francis Bacon sent him a short letter of congratulation, stating that he would have been pleased to have presented himself with others instead of writing could he have been sure that his presence would have been pleasing.

> I can assure your Lordship—however credible soever it may seem to you at first—yet it is as true as a thing God knoweth, that this great change hath wrought in me no other change towards your Lordship than this: that I may *safely* be now that which *I was truly before.*

To this letter Southampton never replied. There is no doubt that he wrongly placed the responsibility for his imprisonment on Francis Bacon's shoulders; and that in some way he blamed Francis Bacon for not having saved Essex. Now Southampton, Essex, and Montjoy were bosom friends. They knew the real identity of Essex and of Francis Bacon. They consorted with Essex at Essex House prior to the abortive rising. These were the intimate associates to whom "he spake and acted like a man who suffered under some great wrong or was goaded by the consciousness of some guilty secret." (Nichol's *Francis Bacon*, Vol. I, p. 51). Southampton and Montjoy knew Essex's Tudor secret and the reason of his suffering. It was this that had drawn the three together—to see that he got his "rights." But Montjoy had escaped being drawn into the net with other insurrectionists, because the Queen knew he was the most likely man to subjugate the Irish. She chose to close her eyes to his participation in the conspiracy even though "he had been deeply involved in some of Essex's most secret intrigues." (Spedding, *Ibid*, p. 137.) While Southampton had languished in the Tower, Montjoy had succeeded in his Irish Mission and had returned to London to be loaded with honours.

In the early days Francis Bacon and Southampton had been very staunch friends. They had been fellow students together at Gray's Inn, and joint leaders of the Revels. Southampton was a constant visitor at Twickenham Park. He not only knew that Francis was the Queen's eldest son but he also knew that he was a "Concealed Poet." In 1593 Francis had dedicated to him *Venus and Adonis;* and in 1594, *The Rape of Lucrece;* writing in the Preface:

> The love I dedicate to your Lordship is without end . . . What I have done is yours; what I have to do is yours; being part in all I have, devoted yours . . . meantime as it is, it is bound to your Lordship, to whom I wish long life, still lengthened with all happiness.

Southampton was a lover of the stage, according to the *Sidney Papers*, and he it was who presented, so we are told by Rowe, a large sum of money to Shaksper[1] the Actor of Stratford—his "name" being purchased as a cover-word, a living-MASK for the TRUE "Shake-speare." Southampton has been described as "a generous and discerning patron." If so, it was a patronage of a most mysterious kind. "The patron never

[1]Whenever I use the name "Shaksper" I mean the Actor of Stratford, for this is the way he spelled his name in his six signatures in his Property Deeds and Will. "Shake-speare" denotes the Author, for this is the way the name is given in the 1623 Folio. The phonetic sound of "Shak" (as in back) is different from "Shake" (as in make). "Shaksper" is not necessarily "Shake-speare." The identity of the Actor with the Author has never yet been proved. It is simply taken for granted as a tradition.

recognized the existence of the client (Shaksper of Stratford) and the client never acknowledged his obligation to the patron," says Judge Webb, (*The Mystery of Shakespeare*, p. 66.) Southampton undoubtedly knew the identity of "Shake-speare" and probably found or loaned money to seal the bargain. In those early days Southampton and Francis Bacon were close intimates. They had somewhat drifted apart in the same way that he and Essex had drifted . . . prior to the Irish adventure. But there had been no open breach between these one-time youthful law students.

Obviously, Southampton's pointed neglect to answer Francis Bacon's letter showed that he was not prepared to regard Francis as a friend but rather the reverse. He only saw in Francis Bacon an ungrateful and ungenerous enemy of himself and his associates. There is no doubt also that he was bitterly resentful that Robert's life had not been saved, and blamed, in some unreasoning way, the elder brother. It would be natural, therefore, that on receipt of Francis Bacon's friendly letter, he should talk of it with heat, disdain and contempt . . . especially to Montjoy and to others; and that Southampton's "common speech" and attitude should become known to Francis. There is no evidence that the breach between them was ever healed. Southampton hated Francis to the last; for it was Southampton, his student-friend, who led the Peers to demand that the knife should be pressed home to the hilt when Francis Bacon, twenty years later, stood charged with offences against the realm:

> "There is no word or confession," said Southampton, "of any corruption in the Lord Chancellor's submission; it stands with the justice and honour not to proceed without the parties' particular confession, or to have the parties hear the Charge and we to hear the parties' answer."

Southampton had waited many long years for his revenge: And he got it. By a strange accident of Fate he was one of the Lords delegated to authenticate the Chancellor's (Francis Bacon) "Confession of Corruption" in 1621. How sweet must have been the morsel underneath his tongue.

So far as can be ascertained nothing had ever passed between them during this wide gap of time either orally or by letter. Yet Francis Bacon had never done Southampton any injury but the reverse. Says Spedding:

> In drawing up the *Declaration of Treason* Bacon had mentioned his name as slightly as was possible to do . . . and there is some reason to believe that he had used his private influence with the Queen after the trial to mitigate her displeasure. (*Ibid*, Vol. III, p. 57.)

There is a clear indication of this in a letter sent by Nottingham to Montjoy:

> For the Earl of Southampton, though he be condemned, yet I hope well for his life: for Mr. Secretary and myself use all our wits and power for it.

Nottingham was a friend of Francis Bacon's and Nottingham would naturally approach him; but Francis Bacon would need no urging. He saved Sir Thomas Smith, Sheriff of London, from the block and "six others" (see *Apologia*) *by going directly to the Queen.* One cannot imagine him doing that without pleading for Southampton, the friend of his youth, as well as Essex . . . at which interview the Queen promised Francis again that Essex's life would be spared.

One can well understand Francis Bacon being filled with a species of righteous indignation that his efforts to save Southampton had not inspired the Earl with simple gratitude, but that he should be made the subject of "common speech," his actions misunderstood, his motives misrepresented, and that he should be spoken of by Southampton to his friends with heat, disdain, and contempt.

This was the *motif* which called the *Apologia* into being. Francis Bacon determined to reply to all possible charges at length. He not only silenced Southampton but any other contemporary detractor . . . diarist or historian. By one stroke of the pen he slew all calumny for all time; not only so, but he left sufficient evidence to indicate his and Essex's true relationship to the Queen, and that he was a Poet and a Writer of Tales.

His Apologia was addressed openly to Lord Montjoy, Essex's and Southampton's personal friend. Montjoy was cognizant of all the facts . . . public, private, personal—all the State secrets involved which could not be made known, and the truth behind the secret intrigues of Essex *to which he was privy*. He knew the whole case and Queen Elizabeth's Secret also. Montjoy's Irish campaign had been crowned with success. He had been created Lord Lieutenant of Ireland and was then the Duke of Devonshire. Montjoy, therefore, was not a man likely to be deceived by a false story or to look with favourable eyes on Francis Bacon's conduct. The *Apologia* was addressed to Montjoy intended for Southampton . . . to the two men who knew his birth secret. It thus becomes doubly important as a human document in attempting to analyse the character of this most remarkable patriot who said in later years, "What I did, I did for my Country."

The following extracts I have captioned for the clearer reading of the *Apologia*. The heading is the original published in 1604.

SIR FRANCIS BACON HIS APOLOGIE,
in
Certaine Imputations
Concerning
THE LATE EARLE OF ESSEX

He addresses himself at once to Montjoy for three reasons: 1. Because he had been Essex's friend and would judge him strictly; 2. Because he had been his own friend and would judge him justly; 3. Because he was well grounded in legal, social and political laws, duties and *moralities* which shall decide this matter. In a few brief lines he states the principle on which he acted throughout.

The Defence.

My Defence needeth to be but simple and brief . . . Whatsoever I did concerning that action and proceeding, was done in my Duty and Service to the Queen and the State; in which I would not show myself false-hearted nor faint-hearted for any man's sake living. For every honest man, that hath his heart well planted, will forsake his King rather than forsake his God, and forsake his friend rather than forsake his King; and yet will forsake any earthly commodity, yea and his own life in some cases, rather than forsake his Friend . . . And if any man shall say that I did officiously intrude myself into that business, because I had no ordinary place, the like may be said of all the other business that passed the hands of the Learned Counsel, either of State or Revenues, these many years wherein *I was continually used.*

He points out that he was the Queen's specially appointed adviser and on very friendly terms with her but "I knew this condition was subject to envy; yet because I knew she was constant in her favours . . . and specially because *she upheld me with Extraordinary Access*, and other Demonstrations of Confidence and Grace, I resolved to endure it in expectation of better."

A Clear Conscience.

Having made the point clear that he was on very intimate terms with the Queen he then says that his Conscience was at rest as regards Essex: For any action of mine towards him there is nothing that cometh to my remembrance with more clearness and *less check of Conscience*; for it will appear to your Lordship that I was not only opposite to my Lord of Essex but I did occupy the utmost of my WITS, and did adventure my Fortune with the Queen, to have reintegrated him, and *so continued faithfully and industriously till his last Fatal Impatience*—for so I will call it—after which day there was no time to work for him . . . though my affection, when it could not work on the subject proper, *went to THE NEXT, with no ill effect toward some others,* who I think do rather not know it than not acknowledge it. ["The Next" refers, of course, to Southampton who was THE NEXT to Essex at the Bar, the two being tried together.]

I will leave nothing untold, that is Truth, for any enemy, that I have, to add; and on the other side *I must reserve much that makes for me,* UPON MANY RESPECTS OF DUTY, which I esteem above my Credit. What I have here set down . . . as I hope to have any part in God's favour IS TRUE. [He had to reserve for instance any mention of their secret relationship and that Essex was "fetched off by a trick" through the non-delivery of the Ring of Pardon to the Queen by the Countess of Nottingham, *then on terms of intimate friendship with Cecil.*]

Robert Essex and the State.

It is well known, how I did many years since dedicate my Travels and Studies to the Use and, as I may term it, Service of my Lord of Essex. I did not make election of him as the likeliest means of mine own Advancement . . . but because I LOVED MY COUNTRY more than was answerable to my Fortune, and *I held at that time my Lord to be the fittest instrument to do GOOD TO THE STATE*; therefore I applied myself to him in a manner which I think happeneth rarely among men: for I did not only labour carefully and industriously, but, neglecting the Queen's Service, mine own Fortune, and in a sort my Vocation, I did nothing but Devise and Ruminate within myself to the best of my understanding, propositions and memorials of anything that might concern his Lordship's Honour, Fortune or Service . . . My brother, Master Anthony Bacon, I did likewise knit to his service . . . .

The Earl's Gifts.

I must and will ever acknowledge my Lord's love, trust, and favour towards me. [He then explains how Essex had insisted upon him accepting a piece of land for services rendered, pressing him to take it.] Whereupon I said: My Lord, I see I must be your Homager and hold land of your gift; but do you know the manner of doing Homage in Law? Always it is with a saving of his faith to the King . . . and therefore, *I can be no more yours than I was . . .* and if I grow to be a rich man you will give me leave to give it back to some of your unrewarded followers. [Francis Bacon thus makes it clear that he can be no more to him than a brother and that relationship or gifts could not make him swerve in his allegiance to his Mother the Queen.]

Francis Bacon's Advice to Essex.

In two main points we always directly and contradictorily differed . . . The one was that the only course to be held with the Queen, was by Obsequiousness and Observance; I would usually gage confidently, that if he would take that course constantly . . . the Queen would be brought in time to *Assuerus'* Question, to ask, *What shall be done to the man that the King would honour?* [In other words that if Essex only played his cards right the Queen would name him as her Successor to the English Throne.]

My Lord on the other side had a settled opinion, that the Queen could be brought to nothing but by a kind of Necessity and Authority; and I well remember, when by violent courses at any time he got his will, he would ask me: *Now Sir, whose principles be True?* And I would again say to him: *My Lord, these Courses be like to hot Waters they help at a Pang; but if you use them, you shall spoil the Stomach, and you shall be fain still to make them stronger and stronger, and yet IN THE END they will leese* (lose) *their operation.*"

Another point was, that I always vehemently dissuaded him from seeking greatness by a Military dependance or by a Popular . . . as that would breed in the Queen jealousy, in himself presumption and in the State perturbation . . . *My Lord, stand upon your two feet, and fly not upon two wings* . . . I did usually compare them to Icarus' Wings which were joined on with wax, and would make him venture to soar too high, and *then fail him at the Height* . . . I was thus plain with him . . . when I saw every Spring put forth such actions of charge and provocation . . . that I said to him: My Lord, when I first came unto you, I took you for a physician that desired to cure the Diseases of the State; but now I doubt that you will be like those physicians which can be content to keep their patients low, because they would always be in request. [This is exactly the same image—the State as a patient—that Francis Bacon used in the Rosicrucian Pamphlet published in Germany, 1614, *Die Reformation der Ganzen Weiten Welt*, "The Reformation of the Whole Wide World," stating that a Secret Society had been formed for its cure by order of the God Apollo.]

A Coolness Arises.

But this difference in two points so main and material, bred in process of time a discontinuance of privateness . . . I was not called nor advised with, for *some year and a half before his Lordship's going into Ireland*, as in former time . . . He then desired my opinion and counsel . . . I did not only dissuade, but protest against his going . . . [F. B. gives his reasons at length.] For I did as plainly see his overthrow chained as it were by Destiny to that journey, as it is possible for any man to ground a judgment upon future contingents . . . However his ear was open, yet his heart and resolution was shut against that advice, whereby his ruin might have been prevented.

The Queen's Mind.

After my Lord's going, I saw how true a Prophet I was, in regard of *the evident alteration* which naturally succeeded in the Queen's mind . . . Attending her one day at Nonsuch she shewed a passionate distaste of my Lord's proceedings in Ireland, as if they were unfortunate, without judgment, contemptuous, *and not without some private end of his own* . . . She thus spake to many . . . .

Francis Bacon to the Queen:
Put Robert in his Father's Place.

I who was still awake and True to my Grounds which I thought surest for my Lord's good, said *to this effect* [Note that he does not quote *the actual words spoken* to the Queen, recorded in the above caption], Madam . . . I think if you had my Lord of Essex here with a White Staff in his hand, *as my Lord of Leicester had and continued him still quietly about you for society to yourself*, and for an Honour and Ornament to your attendance and Court in the eyes of the People, and in the eyes of foreign Ambassadors, then *he were in his right element*: for to discontent him as you do, and yet to put arms and power into his hands, may be a kind of temptation to make him prove cumbersome and unruly . . . .

Satisfy him with Honour near you which . . . I think were the best way. Which course, your Lordship knoweth, if it had been taken, then all would have been well . . . .

The next news that I heard was, that my Lord had come over and that he was committed to his Chamber for leaving Ireland without the Queen's License . . . .

Be Reconciled to the Queen.

I came to his Lordship and talked with him privately about a quarter of an hour . . . I said, Take away all umbrages and distastes from the Queen . . . Seek Access *importuné, opportuné*, seriously, sportingly, every way . . . .

I came divers times to the Queen, as I had used to do, about causes of her Revenue and Law Business . . . .

A Shakespearean Sonnet.

About the middle of Michaelmas Term, Her Majesty had a purpose to dine at my Lodge at Twicknam Park, at which time I had—though *I profess not to be a Poet*—prepared *A SONNET* directly tending and alluding to draw on Her Majesty's reconcilement to my Lord, which I remember also I shewed to a Great Person, and *one of my Lord's nearest Friends*, who commended it. [We now know definitely that Francis Bacon was a POET though he did not PROFESS to be one. We know, too, that the Sonnet was seen by Southampton for, apart from Montjoy, he was Essex's "nearest Friend" . . . Southampton who knew Francis Bacon was the author of *Venus and Adonis* and a concealed Dramatist. Notice how he has begun to weave in by deft allusion and subtle asides, many important items of historical and biographical interest which explain much not yet fully understood.]

The Queen's Ring of Pardon.

This, though it be but a Toy, yet it shewed plainly in what spirit I proceeded and that I was ready not only to do my Lord Good Offices, but to Publish and declare myself for him:

*A*nd neve*R* was *I* so ambitious of a*N*ythin*G* in my lifetime, as I was to have ca*R*r*I*ed SOME TOKE*N* OR FAVOUR from Her Majesty to my Lord; usin*G* *A*ll the a*R*t *I* had, both to procure Her Majesty to se*N*d, and myself to be the Messen*G*er:

[What was the Token or Favour that Francis Bacon took from the Queen to Essex? It was obviously THE QUEEN'S RING . . . the token that so fatally miscarried. Francis Bacon thus lets it be known that he believed the life of Essex was safe in spite of the sentence of Death. By one of Francis Bacon's favourite methods of secret spelling he "Fells" through the two sentences marked off in the text by colons . . . "A RING; A RING." Thus we can be quite sure that the Queen's Ring of Pardon was definitely sent to Essex and that Francis Bacon and the Queen expected it to be made use of. *What else can these veiled sentences mean?*]

The Anonymous Author.

We have seen that Francis Bacon lifted a corner of the veil on his activities as a Sonnet-Writer and he now lifts another corner on his literary work as a concealed Dramatist. He lets it fall to lift again in order to create purposeful confusion in the eyes of those not privy to his secret. He writes:

About the same time I remember an answer of mine in a matter which had some affinity with my Lord's cause, which, *though it GREW from me, went about in Others' Names.* For Her Majesty being mightily incensed with that book which was dedicated to my Lord of Essex . . . asked me if I could not find any places in it that might be drawn within case of Treason: whereto I answered for Treason surely I found none but for felony very many. And when Her Majesty hastily asked me wherein, I told her the Author had committed very apparent theft, for *he had taken most of the sentences of Cornelius Tacitus,* and translated them into English, *and put them into his text.*

Another time, when the Queen would not be persuaded that it was his writing whose name was to it, but that it had some more mischievous author, and said with great indignation, that she would have him racked to produce his Author, I replied, Nay, Madam, he is a doctor, never rack his person, but rack his style; let him have pen, ink and paper, and help of books, and be enjoined to continue the story where it breaketh off, and I will undertake by collecting the styles to judge whether he were the Author or no.

Later in the *Apologia* this literary anonymity is referred to again in the Trial of Essex.

. . . By Her Majesty's pleasure the Lords allotted to me, that I should set forth some dutiful carriage of my Lord, in giving occasion and countenance to a Seditious Pamphlet, as it was termed, which was dedicated unto him, which was the book before mentioned of King Henry the Fourth. I replied to that allotment to their Lordships that it was an old matter . . . of no coherence with the rest of the Charge, being matters of Ireland, and therefore that I having been wronged by Bruits (Rumours) before, this would expose me to them the more; and it would be said *I gave in evidence MINE OWN TALES.*

[What explanation has ever been given respecting these enigmatical passages by Francis Bacon's biographers? None! They are generally regarded as meaningless when they are obviously of grave significance.

Now . . . What was the "Matter which grew from Francis Bacon that went about in others' Names?" The *22nd Apophthegm* of Francis Bacon's *Jest Book* answers the riddle. The book of Deposing *King Richard the Second* and the coming in of *Henry the 4th* supposed to be written, by Doctor Hayward who was committed to the Tower for it, had much incensed Queen Elizabeth. She asked Mr. Bacon being then her Counsel Learned whether there were any Treason contained in it? who intending to do him a pleasure, and to take off the Queen's bitterness with a merry conceit, answered: *No, Madam, for Treason I cannot deliver an opinion that there is any, but very much Felony.* The Queen asked *How? Wherein?* Mr. Bacon answered, *Because he hath stolen many of his sentences and conceits out of Cornelius Tacitus.*

This clears up the ambiguity of the text of the *Apologia*. Dr. Hayward HAD published a "seditious pamphlet" . . . the Play of *Richard II* having been published anonymously in 1597, played prior to that date, and the day before the abortive rising of Essex. Elizabeth thought the writer of the "seditious pamphlet" was also the author of the seditious Play *Richard II*. Francis Bacon knew that this was wrong for he knew the Play . . . that large portions of it had been taken from Tacitus. How did he know this? Because *he had not only read it but written it.* He tells us this very clearly.

When Francis Bacon was told to speak against the treasonable writings by the Lords, he objected, giving as his excuse that people would say he was calling in evidence as prosecuting Counsel, "TALES" which he himself had written . . . "Mine Own Tales."

This is a categorical avowal. He knew Tacitus had been used, *a fact only recently discovered* by Shakespearean scholars. It was not only a question of defending Hayward and his pamphlet but the *Play of Richard* and its author. During the trial of Essex and his fellows, the Play was constantly referred to but the name of Shaksper or "Shake-speare" was not once mentioned. Clearly, the actor from Stratford was not regarded as being the author.

Apophthegm 22 is the key to the identity of the Secret Author. This particular story was not published in Francis Bacon's lifetime . . . not until Dr. Rawley's edition in 1661, *Resuscitatio*, p. 296. The reason for its suppression is obvious. It was omitted from the 1624 edition because it gave the show away to contemporaries, though its deadly significance has not been noticed by anyone . . . so far as I know, since 1661.

We thus possess definite proof that Francis Bacon was "Shakespeare"; and this is clinched by the evidence of the *Northumberland Manuscript* which was once the property of Francis Bacon, the covers of which are scribbled over with the names of Francis Bacon and Shakespeare, and a list of manuscripts written by Francis among them being *Richard II.* This "Shake-speare" play was once in the archives of Francis Bacon's Scriptorium . . . the secret Rosicrosse Literary Society, "*The Grand Possessors.*"]

Francis Bacon's Loyalty to Essex.

When the Queen at any time asked mine opinion of my Lord's case I ever in one tenour said to her [respecting his unauthorized return from Ireland, etc.]: That they were faults which the Law might term contempts because they were the transgression of her particular directions and instructions: but then what Defence might be made of them—in regard to the great interest the person had in Her Majesty's favour, a Council of State in Ireland which he had at his back to avow his actions upon, etc., etc.

I besought her Majesty to be advised again and again, how she brought the cause into any public Question: Nay, I went further, for I told her my Lord was an eloquent and well-spoken man, and besides his eloquence of Nature or Art, he had an ELOQUENCE OF ACCIDENT *which passed them both*, which was the pity and Benevolence of his hearers [What was this "Eloquence of Accident" but the "Accident "of his birth as a Tudor? A fact which, if disclosed publicly would win him the "Pity and Benevolence" of all!]

And therefore that when he should come to his answer for himself, I doubted not his words would have so unequal passage above theirs that should charge him, as *should not be for Her Majesty's Honour*; and therefore I wished the conclusion might be, that *they might wrap it up privately between themselves* and restore my Lord to his former attendance. [What was it that was to be "wrapped up *privately*" between the Queen and Essex but the Queen's Secret that Essex was bone of her bone and flesh of her flesh? Why was "*Her Majesty's Honour*" involved? Because he was her Love-Child by Dudley and she had never declared openly the fact of her morganatic marriage.]

. . . I was utterly against the public proceedings in the Star Chamber . . . And she did directly charge me that I was absent . . . which was very true . . . howbeit . . . she assured me that whatsoever she did should be towards my Lord *ad castigationem, et non ad destructionem* [for his correction and not for his destruction].

I writ to Her Majesty, that if she would be pleased to spare me in my Lord of Essex cause . . . I should reckon it for one of her highest favours . . . The next news that I heard was, that we were all sent for again and that Her Majesty's pleasure was that we should all have parts in the business . . . I could not avoid that part that was laid on me . . . .

Francis Bacon's Duty to the Queen.

If in the delivery I did handle not tenderly—though no man before me did in so clear terms *free my Lord from all Disloyalty as I did*—that, *your Lordship knoweth,* must be ascribed to *the Superior Duty I did owe to THE QUEEN'S FAME AND HONOUR* in a Public Proceeding [The "Duty" was not to the Queen alone as the Head of the State but to "the Queen's FAME and HONOUR," i.e., his Duty to safeguard her Honour as her eldest son], and partly to the intention I had to uphold myself in Credit and Strength with the Queen, *the better to be able to do my Lord Good Offices afterwards.*

His Attempts to Reconcile the Queen and Essex.

As soon as the day [of the Chamber proceedings] was past, I lost no time, but the very next day I attended Her Majesty fully resolved . . . to use my utmost endeavour . . . to bring my Lord again speedily into Court and into Favour . . . I said to her: You have now obtained victory over two things . . . the one is over FAME, the other is over a Great Mind . . . for my Lord he did show that humiliation towards your Majesty, as I am persuaded he was never in his life-time more fit for your favour than he is now: Therefore if your Majesty will not mar it by lingering but give over at the best, now you have made so good a full point, *receive him again with TENDERNESS* [Note this word . . . *the "Tenderness" of a Mother not the LOVE of a MISTRESS*], I shall then think that *all that is past is for the Best* . . . .

She willed me to set down in writing all that had passed that day. I obeyed . . . I read unto her at two several afternoons . . . I do well bear in mind that she was extraordinarily moved with it . . . and told me afterwards—speaking how well I had expressed my Lord's part—that she perceived OLD LOVE would not easily be forgotten: Whereto I answered suddenly, that *I hoped she meant that by HERSELF* [i.e., the old Love of Motherhood].

From that time forth to the later end of the summer, I made it my task and scope to take and give occasions for my Lord's reintegration in his fortune.

[Francis Bacon continues to state what went on at numerous private interviews with the Queen regarding Essex, seizing every possible chance conversation to further a better understanding.] Good Lord Madam, said I, how wisely and aptly can you speak and discern of physic ministered to the body, and consider not that there is the like occasion of physic *ministered to the Mind.* [Note the same thought in Shakespeare, *Canst thou not Minister to a Mind Diseased?*] . . . Your Princely word ever was that you intended ever to Reform his Mind and not to Ruin his Fortune . . . My Lord's desire is to do you service, that *which he thinks himself BORN FOR* [to be her Successor] . . .

Judge whether the letters I wrote were not the Labours of one that sought to bring the Queen about for my Lord of Essex his good . . . but . . .

The truth is that the Queen liked him worse and worse, and grew more incensed towards him. Then she, remembering belike the continual and incessant and confident speeches and courses that I had held on my Lord's side, became utterly alienated from me, and for the space of at least three months turned away from me . . . whenever she saw me . . . and ever sent me forth with slight refusals at such time as I desired to speak with her about Law-business.

The Queen's Lost Child.

Inasmuch, as it is most true, that immediately after New-Year's-tide I desired to speak with her; and being admitted to her I dealt with her plainly and said,

Madam[1], I see you withdraw your Favour from me, and now that I have lost many friends for your sake I shall leese [lose] you too: *You have put me like one of those that the Frenchmen call ENFANS PERDUS [LOST CHILDREN]*, that serve on Foot before Horsemen; so have you PUT ME into Matters of Envy without PLACE, or without STRENGTH; and I know at Chess *a pawn before a KING* is ever much played upon. A great many love me not because they think I have been against my Lord of Essex; and you love me not, because you know I have been for him: Yet I will never repent me, that I have dealt in simplicity of heart towards you both, without respect of cautions to myself.

If I do break my neck, I shall do it in a manner as Master Dorrington did, which walked on the Battlements of the Church many days, and took a view and a survey where he should fall. I take a prospect of mine overthrow, only I thought I would tell you so much, that you may know it was FAITH and not FOLLY that brought me into it, and so I WILL PRAY FOR YOU.

Upon which speeches of mine uttered with some passion, Her Majesty was exceedingly moved and accumulated a number of kind and gracious words upon me, and willed me to rest upon this, *Gratia mea sufficit* [My grace is sufficient]. But as touching my Lord of Essex *ne verbum quidem* [not even a word]. [Francis Bacon was indeed a "Lost Child," an unacknowledged and concealed Tudor.]

The Last Access to the Queen.

This was the last time I saw Her Majesty before the eighth of February, which was the day of my Lord of Essex his misfortune. After which time, for that I performed at the Bar in my Public Service, your Lordship knoweth *by the rules of duty* that I was to do it honestly, and without prevarication:

But for any putting myself into it, I protest before God I never moved neither the Queen, nor any person living, concerning my being used in the service, either of evidence or examination; but it was merely laid upon me with my fellows.

And for the time that passed between the Arraignment and my Lord's suffering, I well remember *I was but ONCE with the Queen* . . . I did both commend Her Majesty's mercy . . . and took the hardiness to tell her that if some base or cruel minded persons had entered into such an action, it might have caused much blood and combustion; but it appeared well they were such as knew not how to play the Malefactors; *and some Other Words I now OMIT*. [From this it is quite clear that the Queen had assured him that the Prerogative of Pardon to Essex would be extended. He mentions the omission so that we may guess at the privateness of the speech between them that could not be made public.]

He Saves Many Prisoners.

And as for the rest of the carriage of myself in that service, I have many honourable witnesses that can tell, that *the next day after my Lord's arraignment*, by my Diligence and Information touching the quality and nature of the

[1]It is questionable whether Francis Bacon as a Commoner had the right to address the Queen as "Madam" instead of "Your Majesty."

Offenders, *Six of the Nine* were stayed, which otherwise had been attainted, I bringing their Lordships' letter for their stay, after the jury was sworn to pass upon them; so near it went: and how careful I was, and made it my part, that whosoever was in trouble about the matter, as soon as ever his case was known and defined of, might not continue in restraint, but be set at liberty. [One can judge from this recital that Francis saw the Queen immediately the trial of Essex was over, giving her the details and the verdict and obtaining her Princely Word that Essex should not go to the Block, a pardon to be extended on receipt of the Queen's ring. Therefore, the next day, with a calm mind, he went about to do good to Essex's fellow-prisoners.]

The Declaration of Essex's Treasons.

The *Apologia* concludes with an account of the Queen's Command to make a first draft which was altered so much as to become a "new writing."

The Face of Truth.

This is all that past wherein I had part; which I have set down as near as I could in the very words and speeches that were used . . . to the end that your Lordship may lively and plainly discern between the Face of Truth and a Smooth Tale . . . .

Had I been as well *believed* either by the Queen or by my Lord as I was well *heard* by them both, both my Lord had been fortunate and *so had myself in his fortune* . . . .

I pray your Lordship to pardon me for troubling you with this long narration; and that you will vouchsafe to hold me in your Good Opinion, till you know I have deserved, or find that I shall deserve the contrary.

This letter to Lord Montjoy was published in a small handy volume, a second impression being issued the year following, so it must have been well circulated. There is not however an allusion to it anywhere, says Spedding. We thus do not know how it was received. But the absence of remarks makes it ever the more certain that the letter was aimed at one particular person, Lord Southampton, and that there never was a popular outcry against Francis Bacon as modernists so loudly assert. Macaulay and Abbott disparage the *Apologia*, but this opinion merely amounts to a disbelief in Francis Bacon's story. Is it true or false? Is he to be believed? Is it the work of an honest man or the fiction of a liar?

Even in this condensed account—judging it purely as an open recital—I submit that we can see Francis Bacon is telling a straight tale . . . even after having "reserved much" that would have made for him. It is a complete justification of the relationship that subsisted between the two men. He helped Essex because he thought him to be for many years the best man—of all the Courtiers—to do good to the State. He was loyal to him even when Essex turned away and sought his advice no more. When Essex got into difficulties with the Queen he risked Elizabeth's wrath repeatedly to restore him into favour. Even when Essex was sentenced to death he thought the "Token or Favour" (The Ring) would save him from any mischance, even the Block; and it would have done but that the plan miscarried through the Countess of Nottingham's treachery. All the odds and ends of evidence we possess go to prove the inherent truth of Francis Bacon's story. Lord Montjoy never contradicted it; nor Southampton, whose "common talk" had called it into being; nor any contemporary. It has been left to men living three hundred years later to question Francis Bacon's veracity. Yet had any detail been untrue there would have been plenty of contemporaries to have entered their caveat . . . rivals in the Commons, the Law Courts and the Court of King James.

Up to this point in Francis Bacon's career we have seen nothing to indicate that he was either a time-server, a hypocrite, a liar or a twister. We have seen no reason to doubt his sincerity in thought, word or deed. Why, then, should we doubt his veracity? At the age of forty-three Francis Bacon's character was still unblemished in an era notorious for its falseness and corruption, at a Court where the evils of dissolute hypocrisy were beginning to run riot in the Court of a Scottish King who loved the filth of bawdy stories. We can therefore assume Francis Bacon to be a truthful recorder, an honest man, and that his clean record stamps his narrative with the hall-mark of Truth.

But when we consider the secret revealing asides slipped into the narrative—all of which would be understood by Montjoy and Southampton, though never by witless modernists—how much more wonderful and illuminating becomes the *Apologia*! The enigmatical phraseology gives the Document an importance never dreamed of even by Spedding.

We see not only the Queen on the most natural and familiar terms with Francis Bacon (*in a manner not extended to any other contemporary lawyers*) but we see that he dares to speak with a freedom of utterance that can only be understood in one way—a plain-speaking son talking to his mother. We see the elder brother Francis trying to tutor and take care of the younger, reckless Robert, with their mother Elizabeth torn with anxiety how to act for the best. It is a family affair as well as a State Problem. The document breathes of their conjoint relationship.

We see, too, that Francis Bacon is a Sonneteer though he does not PROFESS to be a poet; that *he is an anonymous writer of TALES that go about in the Names of Other People*; that one of these "Tales" is the Play of *Richard II* which Francis Bacon wrote, but which goes about under another NAME; and that therefore we know that Francis Bacon is the Immortal Bard—"WILLIAM SHAKE-SPEARE."

We see that this document reveals the answers to many puzzles that have baffled for long the keenest students of the Elizabethan Era.

The real identity of the two brothers is confirmed by another significant piece of open writing left by Francis Bacon entitled *In Happy Memorie of Queen Elizabeth.* It is believed to have been written about 1608 and to have been circulated by hand among his friends, as did Shakespeare's Sonnets. He specially mentions this in his WILL and desires its publication. It was not published in his lifetime for a very good reason that it told the truth too clearly to contemporaries . . . and might have had injurious effect on the children of Essex.

There is a great deal of superfluous matter in the document, and when these irrelevancies are cut out, the reason why Francis Bacon desired its ultimate publication is self-evident: It confirms the *Apologia,* the facts of history already drawn attention to, and other secret writings. The truth is told by a species of double-writing; open words and phrases being used to convey a secondary meaning. The document was kept in hiding until the majority of Francis Bacon's contemporaries had passed away. It was then published by his chaplain, Dr. Rawley, in *Resuscitatio, or bringing into Public Light Several Pieces hitherto Sleeping.* 1651.

Though the document is chronologically out of place, it is better that it should be considered in conjunction with the *Apologia* so that we may the better judge the strength of its testimony. Its secrecies are all of a piece with his other writings—all to the effect that he was a concealed Tudor and not really a "Bacon" at all. The following extract is taken from Dr. Rawley's 1670 edition.

In
Happy Memorie
of
Elizabeth,
Queen of England
or
a Collection of the Felicities of
Queen Elizabeth.

Queen Elizabeth, both of her Natural Endowments, and her Fortune, was admirable amongst women, and Memorable amongst Princes . . . She reigned Four and Forty Years complete, and yet She did not survive her *Felicity* ["a happy event; a blessing; good fortune; a source of content."]

Of this *Felicity*, I am purposed to say somewhat yet without excursion into Praises; for Praises are the Tribute of Men, but *Felicity the Gift of God* . . . .

She was advanced to the Regal Throne from a private Fortune . . . *Princes* that are trained to *their Father's Courts,* and to an immediate and apparent *Hope of Succession* . . . become commonly less capable, and less Temperate in their Actions . . . It may appear that the *Divine Providence* intending to produce a most exquisite Princess, was pleased to prepare and mould her by *Degrees of Discipline.* Neither ought the misfortune of her mother justly to stain the pure stream of her blood, especially, seeing it is very evident that King Henry the Eighth did first burn with New Loves before he was inflamed with indignation against Queen Anne . . . The accusation against her . . . was built upon weak and frivolous Suppositions . . . .

Queen Anne herself testified by her undaunted courage [her Innocency] and that memorable speech of hers at the time of her death. For having gotten a faithful and friendly Messenger, in the very hour before her Death, she delivered these words to relate to the King: That she had ever found the King very constant and firm to his purpose of Advancing her; For first, from the estate of a gentlewoman only, and no way pretending to Noble Titles, he *raised* her to the Honour of a Marchioness; next he *vouchsafed* to make her his Consort, both of his Kingdom and Bed; and now that there remained no higher, earthly Honour, he meant to Crown her Innocency with the Glory of Martyrdom

Though the Messenger durst not relate these words to the King . . . *Tradition, the Conserver of TRUTH, hath conveyed them to Posterity.*

A Wife and a Loving Confederate.

Not only was her reign long but it fell into that season of her life which was most Active and Fittest for the swaying of a Sceptre for she was fully twenty-five years old when she came to the Crown and reigned to the seventieth year of her life . . . .

She was happy for her times, comely for her Sex, and *comfortable to her Conscience* . . . By her timely succours, her neighbour Kings were settled in their rightful Thrones . . . Howsoever, *she persisted to perform the part OF A WIFE AND A LOVING CONFEDERATE* (p. 146).

The reigns for Women are for the most part obscured by their Husbands . . . Those that continue unmarried impropriate the whole Glory and Merit to themselves . . . The peculiar Glory of this Princess was that she had no props or supports of her Government but *those of her own making.* She had no Brother . . . No Uncle . . none other of the Royal Blood and Lineage that might be a Partner in her cares and an Upholder of the Royal Dignity [*Francis Bacon does not say Elizabeth had no husband or a Partner that was not of the Blood Royal like Robert Dudley*]. And for those whom she Raised to Honour, *she carried such a Discrete Hand over them* . . . as she herself remained *in all things* an Absolute Princess.

The Queen's Natural Children.

Childless she was and [*to Succeed her*] left no Issue behind her [*to occupy the Throne*], which was the case of Alexander the Great, Julius Cæsar, Trajan and others [*Monarchs who were likewise Childless and left no Successor yet who had Natural Children.* Francis Bacon is letting the reader draw the only possible inference: That Elizabeth had Natural Children but left no Successor any more than Alexander the Great and Cæsar.] (p. 147)

Two Fair Issues.

There are two Fair Issues of her Happiness born to her, since her Death, I conceive, not less Glorious and Eminent than *THOSE* [*Two Fair Issues*] *SHE ENJOYED ALIVE.* The One of her Successor [i.e., Francis Bacon the writer], The Other of her Memory [i.e., *the Memory of her Younger Son, Robert Essex, that tortured her last hours*]: For she hath gotten such a Successor, who although for his Masculine Virtues . . . he may be said to exceed her greatness and somewhat to obscure it, Notwithstanding, he is most Zealous of her NAME and Glory; and doth even give a Perpetuity to her Acts . . . he hath departed so little from her so as *a SON could hardly Succeed a FATHER* with less Noise or Innovation . . . [Who can this apply to save to the writer Francis Bacon . . . one of the "Fair Issues" born to her? It cannot apply to James. Elizabeth never "enjoyed him while Alive". He was not "zealous of her Name and her Glory." Neither had he any "Masculine Virtues" nor was he "Eminent." But it exactly describes Francis Bacon the "Eminent" son of a wonderful Queen. He did indeed give "a Perpetuity to her Acts" by his very writing of the "Felicities" and in other of his works and acts he immortalized her.]

Her Virginity.

. . . And for this Cause especially have I made this Collection, such as it is, touching her *Felicity*, and *the MARKS of God's Favour towards her*; That *no Malicious Person should dare to interpose a Curse where God hath given a Blessing.*

Now if any Man shall allege *that against ME*, was once said *to Cæsar*; *We see what we may admire but we would fain see what we can COMMEND* . . . such *Felicities* as we have recounted could not befall any Princess, but such an one as was extraordinarily supported and cherished by God's Favour; and she had much in her own Person, and rare Virtues to create and work out unto herself such a fortune. Notwithstanding, I have thought good to insert something more concerning *her Moral Parts* yet only in those things which have ministered occasion *to some Malicious to traduce her.*

This Queen as touching her religion, was Pious, Moderate, Constant, and an Enemy to Novelty . . . whenever she named God, though it were in common discourse, she would compose her Eyes and her Countenance to a Submisness and Reverence. This I have often observed being in her presence.

Some have divulged her unmindfulness of Mortality, in that she would never endure any mention of her Age or Death, which is most False . . . Often . . . many years before her Death, with meekness she would profess herself grown an old woman.

She would sometimes open herself what she liked best for *an Inscription upon her Tombe*, saying . . . she would only have a Line or two . . . wherein her NAME and VIRGINITY . . . should be in the fewest words comprehended. (p. 148.)

Her Winding Sheet.

It is true that whilst she was in her vigorous years and *able to bear Children,* if at any time she were moved *to declare HER SUCCESSOR*, she would make answer, *That she would never endure to see her WINDING SHEET before her EYES.* [Note the subtlety of this phrase . . . Francis Bacon, the Winding Sheet of her Virginity, standing before her as a Youth, pleading to be acknowledged as her Son. Since any mention of the "Succession" was a penal offence, Francis Bacon thus lets the reader know that he had pleaded with the Queen for Recognition. He was the only person who dare have mentioned the question to her.] (p. 149).

The Necessity of the Times.

The CHANGE which happened was not in her Nature but upon the Necessity of Times . . . . (p. 151).

Now if there be any severer nature that shall tax her for that she suffered herself, and was very willing to be Courted, Wooed, and to have SONNETS made in her Commendation . . . at the worst it amounted to a mere high Admiration . . . *Fair Purpose and Love Making were allowed* but *Lasciviousness* banished. *She detested VICE* and desired to purchase Fame only *by HONOURABLE* COURSES . . . [The writer is trying to say that his Mother was honourably married. She was not a Wanton nor Leicester's Mistress].

The only Commender of this Lady's Virtues is TIME. The Ages hath not showed us one of the Female Sex equal to her in the administration of a Kingdom. (p. 152.)

This is a much more illuminating and remarkable document than has hitherto been imagined. It is no ordinary piece of writing. Few would be bold enough to deny that Francis Bacon, a master of English, has conveyed through the open text, a series of secret messages of supreme importance. Apart from stressing the fact that Elizabeth sprang from the loins of a virtuous woman, Anne Boleyn, he lets us know that the reckless passion of the Tudors ran through Elizabeth's veins. She did not hesitate therefore to become a secret wife and a loving confederate by a private marriage having two concealed "Issues" (Children) at least. The winding-sheet of her "Virginity" was her first-born . . . Francis Bacon, a "natural child" of the Queen as Brutus was the "natural son" of the mighty Julius. His concealment and non-recognition was due to the necessity of the Times which compelled the Queen to act contrary to her natural instincts. Most anxious is he to record the fact that she was not a frivolous wanton but a woman who was deeply religious and who detested vice, an honourable woman with nothing lascivious in her nature. But he wants posterity to know that he is a Tudor by birth and that Queen Elizabeth was his mother; that he is proud of the fact and proud of her.

We thus gather that he is no longer embittered with the Queen over the death of Essex . . . his brother. He has since learned the secret of the miscarriage of the Ring and that Elizabeth was not to blame. There is no more bitterness in his heart—only pity and love. If this be not the story openly recorded in this extraordinary composition and if I be in error—then have I never written nor have I ever studied Elizabethan literature and history.

We have carried the story of Essex and his execution on the 25th February, 1601, to the death of Queen Elizabeth on the 24th March, 1603, for the tragedies of both lives are interwoven with Francis Bacon. We must now return to see how Francis Bacon faced the world after the Earl's death, for the world moves in spite of tragedy and change to mould anew the lives of living men and women.

In the Essex trial we saw that Francis Bacon was junior Counsel to Sir Edward Coke. Had it been possible to quote all the details, it would have been seen how Coke allowed his venom of invective to carry him off the rails into unseemly wrangles with the prisoners, and how, over and over again, his junior had to interrupt the procedure to bring him back to the points at issue. Though we still know little of the personal relationship of these two men—"their behaviour to each other when they met, the style of their conversation, and the manner of their courtesies"—yet we know of a truth that Coke hated Francis Bacon, the impecunious ill-fated genius, with all the venom that a rich, ill-favoured man of poor intellect (though a great academic lawyer) and a miserly, uncharitable disposition . . . would feel towards a handsome man ten years his junior; his equal as an orator, his superior as a thinker, his complete opposite as an idealist and brilliant wit. It was this feeling of inferiority complex that made Coke go out of his way whenever possible to belittle and humiliate his rival. That Francis Bacon had had to intervene in the Essex trial naturally rankled in his breast as a pointed slight—a barb that had to be returned at the earliest moment. A few weeks later an opportunity presented itself when the two men met in the Exchequer in their professional capacity. Francis Bacon had moved for the reseizure of the lands of a lapsed recusant. How this came to affront the Queen's Attorney-General who "had never shown any tenderness for such offenders," is difficult to determine. Spedding does not know nor anyone else. It was a carry-over from the Essex trial. In revenge, Coke had determined deliberately to insult Francis Bacon in public by taunting him with his luckless birth. Since Essex's Tudor-blood had not saved him from the block, Francis Bacon hereafter could be scoffed and jeered at with impunity until his life was made a misery and he was driven out of public life.

We should have known nothing of this incident but for the fact that it was placed on record by Francis Bacon himself so that it might be appraised at its true value in after years. *It never saw the daylight until* 1663—sixty-two years after it was written, like so many of Francis Bacon's documents which veil a secret; and its true significance has never been explained by anyone, though expositors have made numerous guesses as to what it was all about; all agree it veiled something of importance.

To Mr. Secretary Cecil

It may please your Honour,

Because we live in an age where every man's IMPERFECTIONS is but another's *Fable* ["a subject of common talk; to tell fictitious tales;"]: and that there fell out an accident in the Exchequer, which I know not how nor how soon may be traduced . . . I am bold now to possess your Honour . . . as one careful of my Advancement and yet more jealous of my WRONGS, with the TRUTH of that which passed; deferring my farther request until I may attend your Honour . . . Fr. Bacon. Gray's Inn, 29th Apl. 1601.

This vague letter of complaint was sent to Cecil, and was actually a request to restrain his henchman, Sir Edward Coke, from personally vilifying him. The enigmatical phrases in the letter [bastardy would be an "Imperfection;" a "Fable" is common talk; "Wrongs" would apply to Non-Recognition;] and the "Document" he enclosed—can only be explained on the supposition that Francis Bacon was the Queen's Unacknowledged Son and that Coke knew the secret of his birth through Coke's friend and superior Officer Cecil. Cecil would know it as a Secret of State, and had passed on the information to Coke who had used it as a weapon against Francis. Whether he had got the information from Cecil or not, Coke knew he was a Tudor and Francis Bacon lets Cecil know at once that he is not to be hounded out of public life by his relative's vulgar abuse. He acquaints Cecil with the facts because as the Secretary of State *it is his Province to guard ALL STATE SECRETS* and he must therefore take all necessary steps that there is no repetition. Those are the clear implications involved. Here is the document enclosed with the letter.

A True Remembrance of the ABUSE I received
of Mr Attorney-General publicly in the Exchequer
the first day of Term; for the TRUTH whereof I
refer myself to all that were present

I moved to have a reseizure of the lands of Geo. Moore, a relapsed recusant . . . and shewed better matter for the Queen against the discharge by Plea . . . And this I did in as gentle and reasonable terms as might be.

Mr. Attorney kindled at it, and said, "Mr Bacon, if you have any tooth against me, pluck it out; for it will do you more hurt than all the teeth in your head will do you good." I answered coldly in these very words, "Mr Attorney, I respect you: I fear you not: and the less you speak of your own greatness, the more I will think of it."

He replied, "I think Scorn to stand upon Terms of Greatness towards YOU, *you who are Less than Little*; *LESS than the LEAST*;" and other *Strange Light TERMS he gave me with that INSULTING WHICH CANNOT BE EXPRESSED.*

Herewith stirred, yet I said no more than this: "Mr Attorney, Do not depress me so far; for I HAVE BEEN YOUR BETTER, and may be again, *when it PLEASE THE QUEEN.*

With this he spake, neither he nor I *could tell WHAT*, as if HE HAD BEEN BORN Attorney-General; and in the end he bade me not meddle with the Queen's business, but with mine own; and that I was unsworn, etc. I told him, sworn or unsworn was all one to an honest man; and that I ever set my Service first, and myself second; and wished to God he would do the like.

Then he said, it were good to clap a *cap. utlegatum* UPON MY BACK! To which I only said he could not, and that he was at FAULT ["a missing or losing of the trail or scent"]; *for he Hunted upon an Old Scent.*

He gave me *a number of DISGRACEFUL WORDS besides*; which I answered in SILENCE, and showing that I was not moved with them.

Now why did Francis Bacon seize the opportunity to place this *apparently* insignificant word-squabble on the record? Why was it never published in his day? Why was it so carefully preserved for his friends to publish more than a couple of generations afterwards? These facts ought to intrigue any literary researcher into the life and character of Francis Bacon. The document is obviously worthy of analysis. Let us therefore examine it.

What were the "Light Terms" and "Disgraceful Words" uttered with "Insults" "*that cannot be expressed?*" That could only be answered with "SILENCE?" What can he possibly have said that Francis Bacon felt that the Secretary of State ought to know? Clearly he regarded it as something serious . . . something affecting the State for he sends the covering letter not to Cecil personally but to "*Mr. Secretary* Cecil" *in his Official Capacity.* It refers to a State Secret . . . *to his Secret* . . . to something "I *cannot tell WHAT*" but the next phrase gives the clue that it refers to the fact that he was BORN a Tudor. Coke spoke as if "*HE had been BORN Attorney-General,*" the inference being "as I have been BORN a TUDOR." It is clear, then, that it was not a common wrangle between two Lawyers using vulgar Billingsgate to each other. It was something far more important than that. Francis Bacon dare not have written to the Secretary of State over a mere row or the use of indelicate words any more than a barrister to-day would dream of writing the head of the State about a Law Court altercation.

The "ABUSE" he had received was undoubtedly this: Coke taunted him with the secret of his "Birth" and called him the ugly name of "Bastard." He thought he could safely afford to do so. He was the all-powerful Cecil's right hand man, a relation, privy to his secrets. The "Tudor Blood" had not saved Robert Essex from the axe and so Francis Bacon was fair game to fly at. Through Cecil he would know that the Queen had decided that Francis would never be called to the Throne; that he had never sought "Access" to the Queen since the trial; that all his life he would be compelled to carry the iron MASK of Bacon thus obliterating his identity; and that he could not openly seek redress because the Honour of the Queen would be involved. All that Francis could say in reply to the "Abuse" was this: "I have been your Better" which was true as a young Prince, though concealed, with expectation of the Throne. He adds, with equal Truth, "I may be your Better again *when it Please the Queen*", i.e., if the Queen were to name him as "the heir of her Natural Body" which was the Queen's Prerogative by special Act of Parliament.

The fact that Francis Bacon mentions the Queen shows at once that the "Abuse" was connected with the Queen in some way. What other explanation covers the facts save that the "Virgin Queen" had given "Francis Bacon" birth?

Coke's reply proves the truth of this. He says it were good to stick a Label on Francis Bacon's Back, as *a Mark of Disgrace,* to let the World know that he was "Less than the Least" . . . in his birth, being born of "unknown" parents who were "unmarried." "Ah," says Francis Bacon in effect, "You could not do it" for no one dare Label me without injury to the Queen. "You hunt upon an Old Scent" in order to try to disgrace me, something that happened forty years ago . . . *my birth!*

There have been numerous conjectures by historians and biographers as to the meaning of this document, what the quarrel was about, what Coke meant by wishing to pin a disgraceful label on his back. No one has hitherto interpreted it for no traditionalist has suspected Francis Bacon's relationship to Elizabeth. It is transparently clear when the letter is read in the light of this knowledge and the significance of the Latin phrase, used by Coke, that was to be "clapped on the back" of his rival— a *capias utlegatum* or *utlagatum*.

What does it mean? Wherein does it differ from an ordinary Writ? How could it apply to Francis Bacon?

It is derived from the Saxon *utlaghe*. The word "Outlaw" comes from the same root. Jacob's *Law Dictionary*, Vol. IV, p. 454 says:

> Outlaw: Saxon utlaghe. *One deprived from the benefit of the Law*, and out of the King's protection.

Outlawry means that a person has refused to appear when process has been issued against him; that he has secreted himself or fled.

> Outlawry: Utlagaria: *The being put out of the Law. The loss of the benefit of the King's protection.* (Jacobs)
>
> Capias Utlagatum: Is a Writ that lies against a person who is outlawed in any action . . . the sheriff is commanded to seize all his goods . . . to compel the defendant to appear . . . . (Jacobs)

A *capias utlagatum* was issued where a party had refused to appear, or who had fled, or who had secreted himself and had afterwards returned to his domicile; so that a *capias utlegatum* is a Writ that lies against *a person who is outlawed* for not appearing in Court, for remaining in hiding, so as *to compel the defendant openly to appear*.

Now what did Coke mean when he said that Francis Bacon ought to be labelled with such a Writ of Attachment? The actual meaning is that Coke charges him with being an "OUTLAW" in a special sense, i.e., *out of the Queen's protection*, with having forfeited his rights as a citizen, *with having no rights*, with his goods and chattels belonging to the State, *to the Queen* as the Head of the State. It was a very serious charge for one State Legal Official to make against another.

Now we know that Francis Bacon had never fled the country. He was not, and never had been, in "Hiding" in a physical sense at all. He was not out of the Queen's legal protection and therefore he had not forfeited as an outlaw his goods and chattels.

Yet there was a truth in Coke's horrid sneer. If he were not absolutely right in the legal sense he was partially right. Coke knew he could not serve him with a Writ for a legal offence committed, yet the alleged crime was such that the Attorney General would have loved to have placed a label on his back—a *capias utlagatum*—that all the world might know of his disgrace: For *Francis Bacon WAS in "Hiding."* He was a Tudor "Hiding" under the Mask of Bacon. He was a "Natural Son" of the Queen, not a *Legal Son*, and so he was "*Outside the Law*" of the Succession. He was "Out of the Queen's Protection" for she had never acknowledged him officially as her son, and he was thus an "Outlaw" in a very real sense with his monies and his goods for they belonged to the Queen because they were derived from her as a one-time "Gentleman-Pensioner." "Your Birth deprives you of *any Rights of Inheritance*," says Coke in effect, "and a Writ (a writing) should be attached to you that all men might know *the kind of Outlaw you are* . . . A BASTARD with no Legal Rights whatever, a man with no *locus standi* anywhere. You are Less than Little; LESS than the LEAST."

This is the Charge so adroitly framed that Francis Bacon cannot reply to it without implicating the Honour of the Queen . . . so he meets it in "Silence;" the Charge "*he could not tell*."

"*He gave me a number of disgraceful Words besides*," but he is careful not to tell what they were. The omission is on exactly the same lines as the omitted words to the Queen in the *Apologia*.

> In his letter he often refers to bruits (rumours) and scandals which *attack his GOOD NAME*, but he never stops to explain the nature of them. (I. Donnelly, *The Great Cryptogram*, Vol. II, pp. 635-8.)

This is the correct interpretation of the document which has hitherto never been explained. It proves that Coke knew that Francis Bacon was the concealed son of "The Virgin Queen." But neither Donnelly nor Spedding ever suspected that the "Discreditable Secret"—as it has been termed—was the fact that in Law Francis Bacon was "an Adulterine Bastard," base-begotten though born in wedlock. *It was nothing personally discreditable at all*. But the world has ever looked askance at the "Love-Child" and the "Royal Bastards" of history have usually been the victims of harsh treatment. Dean Church asks what was his "Secret" but he does not attempt to answer and never once suspects the truth. Is it not now clear that Francis Bacon wrote to Cecil because Coke was making use of a State Secret which might have disastrous consequences to all concerned. It was a warning that he was not going to be insulted with impunity and that it was Cecil's place officially to stop his henchman from repeating such cruel slurs to belittle him.

What this most sensitive of men had to undergo at the hands of rude, foul-mouthed bullies of the Coke school . . . was a purgatory only to be described by the pen of a *Shake-speare*. Think of this sinister secret dogging Francis Bacon's footsteps in public, private, and social life . . . never knowing the moment when some miscreant like Coke might hurl the bomb of bastardy to undo his happiness . . . to make him shrink within himself in lonely isolation.

On the same day as he wrote to Cecil, Francis Bacon wrote to Coke. This in itself is sufficient to show the "Abuse" was beyond mere vulgarisms. He addresses the letter thus:

A Letter of Expostulation to the Attorney-General,
Sir Edward Coke.

MR. ATTORNEY,

I thought best, once for all, to let you know in plainness what I find of you, and what you shall find of me.

You take to yourself a Liberty to disgrace and disable my Law, my Experience, my Discretion.

What it pleaseth you, I pray, think of me: I am one that knows both mine

> own wants and other men's; and, it may be, perchance, that mine mend and others stand at a stay. And surely I may endure in Public Place to be WRONGED, without repelling the same to my best advantage to right myself. . . .
>
> That I have written is to a good end, that is to the more decent carriage of my Mistress's Service. This letter, if it be answered by you in Deed, and not in Word, I suppose it will not be worse for us both. Else it is but a few lines lost . . . So this being but to yourself I for myself rest.

So far as I know neither Cecil nor Coke replied but it obviously answered the desired purpose. These open scurrilities ceased. The implied threat behind both letters was this: If you do not stop these insults about my birth I shall bring the matter officially to the notice of the Queen and the Privy Council. . . . the very last thing that Cecil wanted. Coke would have been impeached and it would have flung the now burning question of the Succession into the melting-pot. No wonder that Coke kept his thoughts to himself about Francis Bacon's ill-fated birth after such a rejoiner. It spiked Coke's guns of vulgar abuse most effectively.

Sometime in May died Anthony Bacon, having long been a sufferer from gout. His correspondence, most voluminous, is still in bundles at Lambeth Palace, and is of the most varied description, ranging from letters written by his mother to "Intelligencers abroad full of political secrets." Francis Bacon succeeded to "a small share of a fortune impaired by extravagance,'" says Nichol, Vol. I, p. 61. But this "extravagance" was almost entirely due to the concealed expenses of helping his foster-brother Francis to print and publish his anonymous Rosicrosse books, to found his secret Ethical Society on the Continent, and to establish a State Secret Service for which he was never paid. If this can be termed "extravagant," how much better would be the world for such extravagant, ethical patriots!

Anthony Bacon was "a fine old English gentleman," and there is no evidence that he spent his money unwisely or on selfish pursuits but primarily from an ethical or patriotic motive. Says Spedding:

> He may be confidently described as a grave, assiduous, energetic, religious man, with decided opinions, quick feelings, warm attachments, and remarkable power of attaching others; a gentleman of high strain, open-handed and generous beyond his means . . . fair, tolerant and liberal. (Vol. III, p. 6.)

He was Francis Bacon's right-hand man in all his secret enterprises and shared in all his secrets and ideals. Anthony was the first disciple to enroll himself under the banner of "Philanthropia." When clouds were dark Francis could always turn to "Anthonie my Comforte." He must have felt his loss keenly. Anthony's resources had largely helped to the practical inception of the English Revival of Learning and the founding of the Ethical Lodges of Freemasonry, the Colleges of Rosicrucianism.

Out of the fine of Catesby—one of the participants in the Essex fiasco—Francis Bacon was assigned a portion, £1,200; and towards the end of this year (1601) we find him arranging to pay off the mortgage of £1,800 that he had raised on his Twickenham property and other securities. From this date he does not seem to have been quite so straightened financially. There can be no possible doubt that he would at last have arrived to live on "Easy Street" had it not been that he simply could not help spending his money to subsidize printers, paper-mills, and the printing and publishing of *English Books for English Readers.* Like Anthony Bacon *he was "extravagant"!* Yes! Extravagant in a Great Cause! The spreading of Education and Ethics: And how much poorer would England and the world have been without such extravagance.

In October a New Parliament met, and, as already stated, Francis Bacon was sent to the House of Commons by "a double-return." Four years previously, Ipswich, the chief town of Suffolk, had chosen him for their representative.. It again ratified its choice. His public acts, however, won him a second constituency in St. Albans. Such a rare honour as a "double-return" is the highest tribute that could have been paid to his purity and integrity as well as to the popularity he enjoyed among his countrymen. It kills the statement by Macaulay and Campbell that after the Essex trial, "he (Francis Bacon) was looked upon with aversion." The burgesses knew he was "straight as a rush." They are better authorities than "noble Lords" who write two hundred years afterwards and whose moral standard is such that they do not hesitate to pervert the truth to make the "facts" fit their own venial *a priori* standards. The following is the Rt. Hon. Winston Churchill's opinion of Macaulay:

> Macaulay, with his captivating style and devastating self-confidence, was the prince of literary rogues who always preferred the tale to the truth, and smirched or glorified great men according as they affected his drama.

Francis Bacon appears to have been very assiduous in the discharge of his Parliamentary duties. This Parliament was called to grant a subsidy to enable the Government to deal with the Spanish occupation of Kinsale.

> Now in Bacon's opinion it was important to the health of the relation between Crown and Parliament, that Parliament should never seem to be called for money only, but always for some other business of estate besides. (Spedding, Vol. III, p. 17.)

He therefore tried and very largely failed—like most Progressives—to initiate reforms for the benefit of the public. He brings in "*A Bill against Abuses in Weights and Measures*"; speaks for the "*Repealing of Superfluous Laws*"; brings in "*A Bill for the Better Observation of Certain Orders set down and Established in the Exchequer*" . . . (obviously there were bureaucrats who went their own sweet way in those days).

The chief interest of the Session centred in the discussions of "Grievances" in regard to the question of "Monopolies." These were a form of "Letters Patent" whereby a Sovereign granted to a subject a "Monopoly" in certain commodities, their sale, or manufacture, as a reward for service, or in consideration for payment. This evil existed in various countries. Such Feudal restrictions created a whole series of vested interests, prevented free trading and had the direct result of making the protected articles very dear. The more "Patents" were granted, the wider the scope and the greater the evil pressed on the community at large. "No Monopoly" or "Down with Monopolies" came into prominence as a wild cry under Elizabeth and rose to an enraged nation's roar under her successor James. In this last Parliament of Elizabeth a Bill was brought in to declare all Patents illegal. . . . "All the House crying I, I, I," and "a great noise there was, too," says Townshend, the reporter, not a voice being raised in defence of them.

Francis Bacon did not, however, whole-heartedly accept the measure but he condemned the confusion that at present obtained, pointing out that a Patent granted to a man for a "Discovery," "out of his own Wit, Industry or Endeavour useful to the Commonwealth" was surely permissible and differed fundamentally from Patents that merely relied on the rarity of an article. Many Monopolies had already been justly repealed and he maintained that the course suggested was not only inexpedient but unconstitutional. The "Grants" belonged to the *Prerogative* which could only be dealt with by Petition and not by Law.

The debate ended without definite result, but Elizabeth was wise enough—realizing that the temper of the House of Commons reflected the Nation's Will—to issue at once a Proclamation to the effect that the "Abuses would be reformed, some Patents revoked, and others suspended for inquiry." This was her last act in public life. She knew how to give way graciously and not to stand too strictly on her Feudal Rights. If James had had sufficient sense to bow with equal grace he would never have jeopardized his Crown and his Dynasty. Twenty years later, by the irony of Fate, Patents and Monopolies, Abuses and Grievances became the occasion of Francis Bacon's "Fall."

The session was wound up with discussions on "Insurances among Merchants," the necessity for amending the "Statute of Tillage," to which Francis Bacon spoke in these words—which shows where he stood as a liberal reformer:

> It stands not with the policy of the State that the wealth of the nation should be engrossed *into a few pasturers' hands.* And if you put in so many provisoes as be desired, you will make so great a window out of the Law that *we shall put the Law out of the Window.*

Another point of interest in these minor discussions centred in the suggested repeal or amendment or substitution of an old Act relating to the "Revenues of Colleges, Hospitals and other Charitable Institutions."

> Bacon, says Spedding, seems to have been, for some reason or other' extraordinarily eager *against the repeal.* The fragment of his speech which Townshend has preserved, *does not enable me to understand the importance of the point in dispute,* or the particular motives of his opposition; but the passage has a personal interest, as *giving us a glimpse of him in a state of excitement to which he did not often give way in public.* Vol. III, p. 37.

The following is a passage from his speech, not sufficient to tell us what it is all about, but quite sufficient to inform anyone acquainted with his ideals the reason why he spoke so strongly and heatedly.

> That the last Parliament (passed) so many Bills for *the Relief of the Poor* that he called it *A FEAST OF CHARITY.* And now this Statute of 390 having done so much GOOD as it was delivered to the House . . . we should do a most UNCHARITABLE ACTION to repeal and subvert such *a Mount of Charity*; and therefore we should rather *tenderly foster it* than roughly cry away with it.

"*I speak*," quoth he, "*out of the very Strings of my HEART*; which doth alter my ordinary form of speech; for *I speak not now out of the Fervency of my Brain.*" With that he smote his breast.

Townshend the reporter states, "there were many persuasions for the Bill, and bitter answers to Mr. Bacon." There was a long discussion, it being eventually agreed that it should be repealed by a General Act and not by the private Bill introduced by a Mr. Phillips.

Francis Bacon's "heat" in the matter must have been very pronounced for the next day he interrupted Sir Francis Hastings to tell him . . . "You need not be so hot in an ill cause" which drew forth the reply, "He (pointing to Mr. Bacon) talks of *heat*. If I be so *hot* as he was yesterday, then *put me out of doors*."

When, later, two Bills were to be debated, there being some dispute which should take precedence Townshend says that "Mr. Francis Bacon kept such *a quoil* to have the Bill concerning CHARITABLE USES put to the Question 'that the Other Bill' was clean hushed up."

Whether Francis Bacon got his own way I do not know, neither does Spedding, but I rather think he did; for a New Act was passed for "precisely the same purpose as the former" . . . to administer certain Charities . . . "Lands, Goods, and Stocks of Money . . . given to Charitable Uses."

Spedding wonders why Francis Bacon should display such heat. Nichol says, "Bacon appears to have opposed the Repeal with an unwonted show of vehemence." They would not wonder had they known Freemasonry is founded on CHARITY—gifts and monies in aid of these very Institutions named in the Bill—and that anything which touched a Benevolence for the Poor and the Distressed peculiarly touched him, for it touched the very CORE of the Ethical Fraternity he had created. It provides us with an additional proof that "Our Francis" was a Freemason of the most practical type . . . one who would not hedge round with difficulties the distribution of assistance to those in need: That was the cause of Francis Bacon's heat; why he spoke "out of the very Strings of his heart." The very phrases reported by Townshend are sufficient to tell us he was a Mason . . . "*Relief of the Poor . . . A Feast of Charity . . . do Good . . . Uncharitable Action . . .*" It is inconceivable that Francis Bacon could have used such Masonic Sentiments and displayed so much warmth of feeling, had he not been a very active Freemason and judged that a threat was being levelled at the "Philanthropia" which he had embodied in a concrete form.

This incident which puzzled Spedding, Nichol and others need intrigue us no longer. It reminds me, indeed, of the Ancient Toast, "*Brethren . . . We will now Honour the Charities.*"

It was in January (1602) that the eight-years-old Irish rebellion was definitely crushed by Montjoy with the surrender of the Spanish forces at Kinsale. About August, 1602, Francis Bacon addressed a memorable State Paper to Cecil as to the best method of settling Ireland by amicable and peaceful methods . . . the understanding being, of course, that it should be passed to the Queen. He therein tells Cecil that if he will only act generously towards the "Natives" on the lines he indicates, "you shall make the Queen's Felicity complete . . . you shall show yourself as good a Patriot as you are thought a Politic . . . (possessed) of the true Arts and Grounds of Government."

The reduction of that country as well to Civility and Justice as to

Obedience and Peace—which things I hold to be inseparable—consisteth in Four Points:

1. The extinguishing of the Relics of War.
2. The Recovery of the Hearts of the People.
3. The Removing of the Root and Occasions of New Troubles.
4. Plantations and Buildings.

One cannot go into this masterly digest of "the Common Woe" of Ireland or do it justice by a *précis*. One can only say that it was a political salve that would have produced the most wonderful healing effects had this wise statesman's advice been consistently followed. Regarding point one, he cannot think that any letting of blood is any method of cure. He advocates lenience and the avoidance of displanting "ancient generations." Two: he believes in perfect toleration of religion for the recovery of the hearts of the people, liberal educational endowments, justice to be administered by governors and judges as in England, giving adequate rewards and honours to the principal persons. Three: he would extirpate the seeds of future troubles by clipping the ambitions and the absoluteness of the chiefs; the licentious idleness of their kernes and soldiers . . . their barbarous laws, customs, etc. Four: finally he would encourage colonies, the members to mix freely with the natives as their equals and not their superiors, conferring "on the joint inhabitants of settled districts ample liberties and Charters under the over-rule of a Parliament in Ireland." (*See* Spedding, Vol. III, p. 45; Nichol, Vol. I, p. 63.)

The death of the Queen prevented these suggestions being carried out but they were in part adopted later. Indeed, one can see into this brief glimpse into Francis Bacon's statesmanship through this window of a *précis*, that nearly all the evils that have afflicted Ireland and England would have been avoided by such a policy. The standing garrison of the next reign would have been unnecessary and a true amalgamation of the English and Irish would gradually have been established.

This may be said to exhaust the public labours of Francis Bacon in the reign of Queen Elizabeth. We can look back over the path he had travelled since those early days of precocious genius when, as a boy of fourteen, he had declared that his aim in life was to bring about the *Reformation of the Whole Wide World*, an ideal which, he wrote in his old age (letter to Father Fulgentio), *he had never lost sight of* in vicissitude and felicity, in days of storm and shine—*an ideal which he had pursued all his life* until he stood on the threshold of eternity.

We have seen his work as a politician . . . as a writer of State Papers . . . his scanty labours as a lawyer. They are very useful works, but one cannot say that they in any way fulfilled the pent-up yearnings of his early days which he termed the secret urge of "Philanthropia." What else had he done to further his altruistic longings? To establish his "New Philosophy?" To promote the Reformation of the World? What lectures had he delivered? What books had he written on literature, education, ethics, philosophy, science, etc.? The Traditionalists of Biography answer that up to 1603 *Francis Bacon had not accomplished anything and had never tried to.* The enthusiasms of his early youth had faded. They had perished, we are told, like the idle day-dreams of the average romantic youth. So . . . .

Francis Bacon, aged forty-three, had arrived at the maturity of his powers without having taken one step forward towards the realization of those Divine Purposes for which he says he was born and to which he was pledged as "a Servant to Posterity." Is it not incredible? This genius, who was consumed with the eternal fire of God's own Fiat burning within his breast, who in his after years left abundant evidence that he grudged the wasting of a moment—even in sleep—allowed the precious, creative years of his youth and early manhood to perish in unhonoured barrenness! The Dr. Abbotts and the Sir Sidney Lees may believe such nonsense but I cannot. They enunciate this view with great positiveness because the only open writings—the only contribution towards literature to which he had attached his name—were ten short *Essays* published in 1597 of less than 4,000 words together with ten equally short *Religious Meditations* on the *Colours of Good and Evil.*

The *Essays* dealt with man's relation to this world and the *Meditations* to the religious side of life. Can anyone believe in view of the facts that *Francis Bacon with his private Scrivenry* had produced less than 8,000 words of creative literary effort? It never required a staff of men to assist him in bringing to birth a few *Essays* which Francis Bacon could have written himself within a week! No! In spite of what the Schoolmen say this could not be Francis Bacon's *total output of twenty-eight years* . . . the date when, as a youth of fourteen, the thought struck him to do something for the benefit of mankind.

It is, however, quite true that he had done other open writings of State importance, none of which were printed in his lifetime. Here is the list:

Notes on the States of Christendom	1582
Advice to the Queen	1584
Controversies of the Church	1589
Observations upon a Libel	1592
Report on the Treason of Lopez	1594
Veue of Ireland	1596
Report on the Alienation Office	1599

These documents were left in MS. because they were for the private guidance of the Queen. They were printed long years after he was dead. With a couple of "good pens" they could all have been written in six months.

There were some other writings which have been grudgingly ascribed to him, for they show Francis Bacon's ability as a Playwright, etc.:

The Most Masculine Birth of Time: i.e. the Creation of Masonry	1585
Conference of Pleasure; a Play	1593
Praises of Fortitude, of Love, of the Queen, of Knowledge; a Play	1593
Promus of Formularies and Elegancies i.e. a Private Notebook of Expressions	1595
Contributions to *Gesta Grayorum*	1594
Ten Essays	1597

At the outside all these works could have been produced in three months, so that all Francis Bacon's known public writings in the reign of Elizabeth could easily have been produced by himself working *alone* within twelve months, whereas we know that he had *a staff of ready writers who were assisting him in his literary activities. What were they all doing? Why was Francis Bacon always so desperately pushed for money?* There must be a valid reason.

His Parliamentary work could never have exhausted all his spare time. We have also seen that he had, nearly all his life up to the death of Queen Elizabeth, a private income from the Queen so that there was no necessity for him to work for a living. What, then, *did Francis Bacon do with his time?* From the age of fourteen to forty-three his total work under his own name can be traced, which leaves twenty-seven years of masterly inactivity unaccounted for—reckoning one year for his open work—and he was assisted in his meditative philosophic idleness by a staff of secretaries! Is it not manifestly absurd to suggest that for more than a quarter of a century—the most precious years of a man's life for creative work—this prodigious genius, whose latter years show that he was tireless in mind as well as in body, allowed year after year to slip away with no literary output and made no attempt to put his plans into operation? And that he only picked up the youthful threads of his life's work long after he was forty-three? We can confidently dismiss the academic theory that Francis Bacon passed more than twenty-five years of priceless opportunity in a literary, ethical and philosophic vacuum.

Evidence has already been adduced that to no one came the call clearer. . . . "Produce! Produce! If it be but the infinitesimal fraction of a product . . . produce it in God's name!" In order to answer the call we have seen that Francis Bacon became a secret teacher . . . producing secretly what he dare not or could not produce openly, thus beginning the Secret Societies, literary, ethical and philosophic, learning his craftsmanship as a writer under many names, choosing living men the better to mask his activities, until, at last, he was ready to let all his pen-names die into oblivion, for the trained and fully mature "Shake-speare" was ready to take the Stage of this World—"Shake-speare the Heir of all my previous Invention," the World's Master-Singer. In previous chapters we have seen how Francis Bacon learned his craft and how, in his early years, he had learned to write behind the mask of a living man.

At the psychological moment a live puppet came his way to veil the activities of his mightiest creation, "Mr. William Shake-speare Himself."

A man named "William Shaksper" (Shaxspur, phonetically) came to London from Stratford in the year 1586. He was an illiterate country rustic, having had no opportunities for educational culture, and spoke in the broad patois of Warwickshire. He had poached a little, butchered a little, drank a little, and followed certain village customs a little, as is often the custom of penniless yokels. He was then twenty-two years of age, three years younger than Francis Bacon. Shaksper had left his native hamlet, his wife and three babies, to seek his fortune, having the idea, like Dick Whittington, that the streets of London were paved with gold. He naturally gravitated to the play-houses and beer-shops connected with them. They were the rendezvous of all the down-and-outs, pimps, prostitutes, and vagabonds. He saw a chance of making money (or at least a living) by holding horses-heads for the gentry who dismounted outside the Globe Play-house. As a countryman he knew how to handle horses and soon got more custom than he could deal with personally. He trained boys to help him. Within twelve months "Shaksper's Boys" were famed for their calming of restive steeds—*according to tradition.*

THE ORIGINAL BUST OF SHAKSPER THE ACTOR AT STRATFORD CHURCH, 1623
This engraving is reproduced from Sir William Dugdale's "Warwickshire" (1650)
(*See Appendix I, p.* 361)

The man who ran the Globe Theatre was William Burbage. He had been helped, as we have seen, by Francis Bacon's father, the Earl of Leicester, to start his Company of Players and to found the Globe. Francis Bacon had known Burbage, as we have also seen, from childhood. He was now a frequenter of the theatre—one of Burbage's staunchest supporters and advisers. What Francis did not know about theatricals was not worth knowing. He lodged at one time only a short distance away (Bishop's Gate Street) from the Bull Inn *to which was attached a theatre where several of the "Shake-speare" Plays were performed.*

The *name* of "Shaksper" (in view of the fact that his own Muse was known as "Pallas the Spear Shaker" to his French friends) would naturally attract Francis Bacon's notice; and the man also as he bobbed from client to client stroking their mettlesome mounts. With his eye to future contingencies, Francis would be likely to make it his business to get to know the man, realizing the great possibilities his name embodied; that, with a little manipulation, the name of "Shaksper" could be made to look in print like "Shake-speare." It would not be a surprising thing to learn that he persuaded Burbage to employ "Shaksper" as a knock-about behind the scenes, then as a call-boy, then in a few minor parts, his rude dialect causing much merriment. . . . the "top of his acting being the ghost in his own *hamlet*" (according to his first biographer, Rowe) and in 1594—eight years after he had arrived in London, he is mentioned as one of Burbage's company of players, *the same year that "Lucrece" was published, "Venus and Adonis" having been published the previous year.*

Probably before these two poems were issued under the pen-name of "William Shakespeare" and dedicated to Lord Southampton, Shaksper had agreed to sell the use of his name, and to father, if necessary, whatever poems, etc., were printed under the name of "Shakespeare."[1] Whether this were so or not, an incident soon occurred that made the use of a pen-name and a "Mask" absolutely necessary.

Now from 1593 to 1598 were played and printed a series of anonymous plays. In 1597 was printed *Richard II.* It contained a deposition scene which was construed by Queen Elizabeth as a reflection upon herself. There was an immediate hue and cry for the Author. Francis Bacon was in danger. The time had come when he must divert suspicion. The actor Shaksper was therefore persuaded to return to Stratford—quite an inaccessible village—to lie low till the storm had passed over, to give colour to the rumour that the play was the work of some wandering actor. Tradition states that it was Southampton, Francis Bacon's college-chum and Robert Essex's friend, who provided sufficient money to gild the risk. Shaksper bought in the same year the largest House in Stratford, "New Place." He was also promised to be made into a "Gentleman" by Letters Patent. Essex was then the Head of the College of Heralds that granted Armorial Bearings.

> Sir Edwin Durning-Lawrence, Bt., writes: It is exceedingly important and informing to remember that Shakespeare's name never appeared upon any play until the Actor had been permanently sent away from London. His wealth was simply the money—£1000—given to him in order to induce him to incur the risk entailed by allowing the name "Shaksper" to be associated with the plays.
>
> Such a risk was by no means inconsiderable, because Queen Elizabeth was determined to punish the Author of *Richard II*, a play which greatly incensed her; she is reported to have said, "Seest thou not that *I am Richard the Second*?"
>
> There is no evidence that Shaksper ever earned so much as ten shillings in any one week while he lived in London. (*The Shakespeare Myth*, p. 3.)

[1]These details regarding Shaksper are based on actual facts, on traditions accepted by Shakespearean authorities, and the cypher stories of the era.

The moment that Shaksper was definitely out of the way, a friend of Francis Bacon named Francis Meres, M.A., of "Both Universities,"

THE

Tragedie of King Richard the second.

As it hath beene publikely acted by the right Honourable the Lorde Chamberlaine his Seruants.

LONDON

Printed by Valentine Simmes for Androw Wise, and are to be sold at his shop in Paules church yard at the signe of the Angel.

1597.

Facsimile Title-page of Richard II.
See Appendix I, p. 61

afterwards Rector of Wing in Rutland, printed a small booklet, *Palladis Tamia or Wits' Treasury* in which he said (1598):

> As the soule of Euphorbus was thought to live in Pythagoras [a special character in Masonry] so the sweete wittie Soule of Ovid lives in mellifluous and hony-tongued Shakespeare, witnes his *Venus & Adonis*, his *Lucrece*, his sugred *Sonnets* among his private friends.

Then follows the most famous passage:

> As Plautus and Seneca are accounted the best for Comedy and Tragedy among the Latines; so Shakespeare among ye English is the most excellent in both kinds for the Stage; for Comedy witness his
> *Gentlemen of Verona,*
> *Errors,*
> *Love labors lost,*
> *Love labours wonne,*
> *Midsummers night dreame,* and his
> *Merchant of Venice*:
> for Tragedy his
> *Richard the 2,*
> *Richard the 3,*
> *Henry the 4,*
> *King John,*
> *Titus Andronicus,* and his
> *Romeo and Juliet*

The moment these hitherto anonymous plays were associated with the name of Shakespeare—Shaksper—*Love's Labour's Lost* was published *with a name on the title-page for the first time*, not only published in the same year as the Mere's booklet but issued by the same publisher: Notice, too, how the name is spelt, a composite between the two . . . By "W. Shakespere."

The year previously, 1597, *Richard II* had been printed anonymously, but in 1598 the author's name was added for the first time.

"By William Shakespeare."

Here is the anonymous Title Page issued in 1597. Notice the singular manner in which the Author has printed the page in order that the first letters and words shall spell his name and Masonic rank:

		*T*HE
Thirty-Three	T.T.	*T*ragedie of King Ri-
See	c.	*c*hard the se-
		cond
		As it hath beene publickely acted
Bacon	b A con	*by* the right Honourable the
Lord		*Lorde* Chamberlaine his Ser-
		*u*ants.
You'll	uL	*L*ondon.
		*P*rinted by Valentine Simmes for Andrew Wise and
		*a*re to be sold at his shop in Paules Churchyard at
Tap	taP	*t*he signe of the Angel

We thus see from this special printing that the Author is "Bacon" and that he is associated with the Sovereign Inspectors of the "Thirty-Three" Degree in Freemasonry, the Head of the Order . . . truly a Masonic Lord. So the concealed message of identity is:

"TAP THIRTY-THREE:
YOU'LL LORD BACON SEE"

The significance of this will be better understood when one realizes that "33" *was the numerical signature of Bacon* as well as the Highest

Masonic Degree, and that the symbols "T.T." run like a golden thread throughout the ceremonials of Masonry and Rosicrucianism from the first Masonic Step . . . "T." and the "33" candles on the Rosicrucian Altar.

Such, then, was the *concealed* literary output of "Shake-speare," according to Meres between 1593 and 1598. In the meantime Shaksper remained in Stratford from 1598 onwards, selling corn, malt, lending small sums of money. He permanently resided at Stratford, and only very occasionally visited London, when he lodged in Silver Street with a hairdresser named Mountjoy. (*Ibid*, Durning-Lawrence, p. 5.)

It was indeed very necessary that Shaksper should continue to remain in obscurity because this "seditious play" was resurrected and acted the night before the Essex "rising" in 1601, and the cry for the concealed author—the wandering actor who had decamped—was once more heard. But though *Shakspeer had vanished from London, the plays of Shakespeare still continued to be written, acted and printed.* According to the list of Basil E. Lawrence, LL.D., *Notes on the Authorship of the Shakespeare Plays*, p. 25, the following plays were written and played in London apart from Meres' list.

Henry VI., Part I	
" " " II	
" " " III	1592
Merry Wives of Windsor	1598
Henry V	1599
Much Ado About Nothing	1600
As You Like It	1600
Twelfth Night	1601
Hamlet	1602[1]

We have therefore nine additional plays up to the time of Elizabeth's death.

Under these circumstances, who is the more likely to have produced these plays? *Shakesper in hiding at Stratford or Francis Bacon in London?* Could Shaksper, whom Shakespearean commentators admit was devoid of education and culture when he left London,[2] from 1586 have produced in twelve years, the TWELVE ANONYMOUS PLAYS and the two long Poems of classical splendour, to say nothing of the "sugared Sonnets"? Could he have produced also NINE FURTHER PLAYS up to 1603? Plays which stand at the apex of literary art, full of ripe wisdom, esoteric lore, classical scholarship? Where could Shaksper have acquired the vast learning demonstrated by the plays?

[1]If the reader will turn to page 186, *The Marriage of Elizabeth Tudor*, he will see a most remarkable message on the first pages of the first and second quartos of *Hamlet* quite in keeping with the message *Richard II.*

[2]Removed prematurely from school, residing with illiterate relatives in a bookless neighbourhood; thrown into the midst of occupations averse to scholastic progress, it is difficult to believe that when he left Stratford he was not *all but destitute of polished accomplishments*. (Halliwell-Phillipps, *Outlines*. p. 63.)

When at twenty-two years of age, he fled from Stratford to London, we may be sure that *he had never seen half a dozen books* other than his horn book, his Latin accidence, and a Bible. Probably there was not a dozen others in all Stratford. (Richard Grant White, *Atlantic Magazine*.)

There is only one conclusion possible. The man who produced the anonymous plays, and those plays afterwards title-paged to "Shake-speare," was Francis Bacon, who thus employed himself to create secretly an English literature with his "good pens" in his alleged years of idleness. In this way he sought the good of all men through education and ethical ideals. In this and other forms of secret service Francis Bacon spent those "Lost Years" up to his forty-third birthday in doing "good by stealth and blushing to find it fame."

The anonymous Plays, afterwards title-paged to "Shake-speare," were not, however, the whole of Francis Bacon's literary output. Edward D. Johnson writes:

> 1594: Francis publishes a play *Edward I* ascribed to George Peele, and *Christ's Tears over Jerusalem* and *Terrors of the Night*, in the name of Nashe, and a book of verse *Willobie his Avisa* in the name of Hadrian Dorrell.
>
> 1595: He publishes *Mother Bombie, Selimus, Orlando Furioso, Looking-glass for London* and *Friar Bacon*, some printed anonymously and some title-paged to Green who had died in 1592; also *Edward II* in the name of Marlow, *Dido Queen of Carthage* in the names of Marlow and Nashe; *The Spanish Tragedy* anonymously and *Jack Wilton*, a novel, dedicating it to Southampton then at Gray's Inn; also *Terrors of the Night*, a disquisition on the subject of Dreams in the name of Nashe, and *Lucrece* under the name of William Shakespeare and dedicated to Southampton; he also publishes *The Old Wives' Tales*, a comedy written by G.P.; *Colin Clout* and *Amoretta*, in the name of Spenser; *Cornelia* first printed as by T.K. and afterwards as by Thomas Kyd, a scrivener employed by Francis.
>
> 1596: Francis publishes *Astropel* in the name of Spenser: dedicated to the Countess of Essex.
>
> 1597: In John Lyly's name he publishes a drama *Woman in the Moon*; also a play *Alphonsus King of Arragon*; *Prothalamion* and *Faerie Queene* (second part) in the name of Spenser.
>
> 1598: He publishes a play *James I of Scotland* also *Hero and Leander* in the name of Marlow.
>
> 1599: Francis publishes *The Love of King David and fair Bethsabe* with *The Tragedy of Absolom* written by George Peele; a play *Prisoner of Wakefield* also *Lenten Stuffe* in the name of Nashe.
>
> 1600: Apart from Plays title-paged to Shakespeare, Francis publishes *Sir John Oldcastle*, Shakespeare; *Summers Last Will and Testament*, Nashe; and *Titus Andronicus*, anonymously.
>
> 1601: *Loves Metamorphosis*, a drama published in the name of John Lyly.
>
> 1602: He prints *Thomas Lord Cromwell*.
>
> 1603: Queen Elizabeth dies.

He was at last ready to step upon the open platform of the world. From the age of twenty he had planned, laboured and laid his concealed bases for eternity. He had made his ideals practically possible by a series of organized Brotherhoods, the secret disciples of the "Master Bacon." He was now ready to give to the world openly as much as it could profitably digest of his "*New Philosophy of Active Science*" or the true "*Ethical Interpretation of Nature*," which he was about to disclose in works written over his own name. . . . *The Advancement of Learning*, *The New Organ*, etc., etc.

END OF VOL. I

APPENDIX I

THE ILLUSTRATIONS

The Uncrowned King of Literature

This portrait of Francis Bacon by Van Somer was painted when "The Uncrowned King" was about fifty-five. The artist has portrayed his real character . . . a literary intellectual; a man who has matured under the varying emotions of sorrow and joy, disappointment and success.

Hepworth Dixon says: "The bust of Somers is the bust of Hilyard (the miniature painted at eighteen) come to perfect growth. Brow broad and solid; eye quick yet mild; nose straight and strong, of the pure old English type; beard trim and dainty, as of one to whom grace is nature; over all the countenance a bold, kindling light; an infinite sense of power, and subtlety, and humour, unmixed with any trace of pride."

Every student of physiognomy will agree that Van Somer has given us the portrait of a truly "noble-man" and that there is nothing to indicate in his aspect anything mean, miserly, avaricious or criminal. Every characteristic conveys the fact that "He is the King of Literature."

Queen Elizabeth in Her Prime

Zucchero had the good fortune to paint Elizabeth in her prime. It is a remarkably fine portrait and is made more remarkable by the dress worn by the Queen and the symbolism conveyed by the pattern. It has been named the "eyes and ears dress" because the fabric is embroidered with eyes and ears . . . a mute warning to everyone that the Queen watched all and heard everything. On the left arm is woven the "Serpent of Wisdom" protecting the heart—the heart of England—which is ready not only to whisper advice to her Majesty but to strike down anyone who would attempt to molest her or the Throne.

In those early, troublesome years of intrigues within and dangers without, such mute warnings to would-be traitors and assassins and conspirators, such significants reminded them of their peril.

The entire portrait portrays a young matron, and it is absurd to suggest that such a face and figure was cold and passionless and untouched by love, as many orthodox writers declare was the character of the "Virgin Queen."

Robert Dudley—Earl of Leicester

He was born about 1532-33. His father was beheaded for supporting Lady Jane Grey. Dudley himself was sentenced to death. He met the Princess Elizabeth when imprisoned in the Tower, a violent attachment springing up between them although he was a married man. He was released in 1554 and went to France, refusing to live with his wife, known to history as Amy Robsart. On Elizabeth's accession to the Throne in

1558 she recalled him at once to England, loading him with riches and honours, lodging him in the Palace with his bedroom next to hers. He was known to the diplomats and the common people as "The Queen's Lover."

In the Dic. Nat. Biog. XVI, p. 114, it is stated that Lord Robert "was secretly married to the Queen in the House of Lord Pembroke before a number of witnesses." There are Cypher Records to the same effect as well as papers in the archives of some Continental States.

There is evidence which shows that there were at least two children of the marriage, one being brought up by the Bacons as Francis Bacon, the other, the younger, being later known as Robert Earl of Essex, fostered in the home of the Queen's cousin . . . Lettice. Elizabeth posed as the "Virgin Queen" and never recognized them as "Tudors." She could not very well acknowledge Francis as heir to the Throne because it would have betrayed her intimacy with Leicester when he was already a married man. Francis was born four months after the secret wedding which took place three weeks after the death of Dudley's wife.

Leicester appears to have fought hard to secure acknowledgment for himself as Consort and open recognition for his sons. But the years passed; and, as the Queen still maintained her secret, the Earl went his own way and secretly married Lettice, widow of the First Earl of Essex, who was the foster-mother to Leicester's own son Robert by the Queen. Father and son appear to have been very much attached to each other, going to the Continent together and so forth.

When the Queen heard of his marriage she threatened him with the Tower and forbade his wife to attend the Court. She ordered the Earl to remain at Greenwich Castle as a prisoner. Despite this, however, she seems to have continued to consult him on matters of State. In 1558 she appointed him Commander-in-Chief of the forces at Tilbury to repel the Spanish Invader.

Leicester died shortly afterwards, in September. The Queen seized his estates and auctioned them. She acted just as though she were his wife winding up his estate.

Queen Elizabeth Dancing with the Earl of Leicester

This picture, reproduced by special permission of the Rt. Hon. Lord de L'Isle and Dudley, still hangs in Penshurst Place, Kent, where Queen Elizabeth and Leicester were constantly together at parties and dances, being entertained by Leicester's sister, who had married Sir Henry Sidney. They were the parents of Sir Philip Sidney.

The portraits of the Queen and the Earl still hang together in the principal room. The "Bear and the Staff" insignia are to be seen on much of the furniture. There are gifts from the Queen to be seen everywhere in this fine old historic mansion.

The oil painting by Zucchero still hangs in the very room where the Queen danced with her lover to whom she was secretly married, becoming in due time the real mother of Francis Bacon though posing as "The Virgin Queen."

THE BAPTISMAL ENTRY OF FRANCIS BACON

This is a facsimile of the birth-register of Francis Bacon on 25th January, 1560-1, St. Martin's-in-the-Fields. The register can still be seen. The entry is made by the same clerk who has written the preceding and succeeding names but someone else has written in a different handwriting and a paler ink: "*Filius DmNich Bacon Magni Anglie Sigilli Custodis.*" The "MR" too has been inserted above the line as though to provoke attention. The entry is made in the first instance without giving the name of the parents. It is only later that someone has added "Son of Nicholas Bacon."

"Mr. Franciscus Bacon."

AMY ROBSART

"Amy Robsart was the daughter of Sir John Robsart. She married Robert Dudley in 1550. She lived in the country and early in 1560 was removed to Cumnor Place, Berkshire, the house of Anthony Forster, a creature of her husband's, where, on the 8th September, she was found lying dead, with her neck broken, at the foot of a staircase.

"It was generally believed at the time that she was murdered, and that Dudley, if not Elizabeth herself, was an accessory to the crime. This belief receives some support from certain discoveries made in the archives at Simancas, which indicate that a plot to poison her was actually entered into before her death." *Chambers's Encyclopædia*, Vol. VI, p. 566.

On the accession of Elizabeth, Dudley was taken into the personal service of the Queen who loaded him with honours. A great career opened out before him. It was commonly reported that they would be married but that his wife was alive. It has been said that Amy Robsart committed suicide, learning that the Queen was enceinte by Dudley, in order to pave the way for his marriage. This took place privately at the House of Lord Pembroke at the end of September, 1560, Francis being born in the January following.

SIR NICHOLAS BACON

He is the reputed father of Francis Bacon but there is abundant evidence that indicates that he was a foster-father only.

He was the Lord Keeper to Queen Elizabeth, a sound lawyer and a witty man who revelled in classical literature. He was also a writer. A book he published had the result of excluding him from the Privy Council. Henceforth he wrote anonymously. We may be sure that this example was not lost on the boy Francis. He not only saw the joy of writing a book but he learned the value of anonymity . . . the use of a pen-name.

Sir Nicholas left an elaborate Will. All his living children (he had seven in all apart from Francis) were well provided for, but Francis was left out entirely, thus indicating that his expectations lay elsewhere, which indeed they did, for he became a Gentleman-Pensioner of the Queen.

Judging by the portraits of Francis Bacon, Sir Nicholas and Lady

Bacon, it is quite impossible for Sir Nicholas to have been the blood-father of Francis. He is cast in an entirely different mould from his foster-parents. The reader is advised to compare the photos of the persons concerned.

Lady Bacon

Lady Anne Bacon was Sir Nicholas Bacon's second wife. She was the daughter of Sir Anthony Cooke, Governor of Edward VI. The Cooke family were connected with Stratford, being large landowners. She was a perfect housewife as well as being a very clever woman. She had been the tutor to young King Edward. She had a strong character and her accomplishments were many and varied. She was familiar with classical languages. In her private letters she quotes Latin freely. She was an author and a translator.

She was a deeply religious woman. The day started with family prayers and ended with stories of Classical Adventures, Morality Tales and the Ancient Myths. She died in 1610, over eighty and had been for years under the care of Francis Bacon. Her goodness to him from childhood cannot be over-estimated. Her intellect and life were reflected in him in a variety of ways. She was throughout life his staunch friend and ally. She spent her money to assist him in his literary enterprises. She maintained the Queen's Secret and acted the part of foster-mother with tact and discretion. She was the Head Lady-in-Waiting to Queen Elizabeth when Francis was born.

A letter which she writes to her son Anthony contains a remarkable statement which has happily escaped the destroyer's hand. She asks Anthony to explain to Francis that "*It is not my meaning to TREAT HIM AS A WARD; Such a WORD is far from my Motherly feeling for him. I mean to do him good.*" Such a significant sentence reveals the real relationship of the parties. HE WAS the WARD of Lady and Sir Nicholas Bacon, not their SON.

York House

York House was the London home of Sir Nicholas Bacon, and, later in life, it became the home of Francis Bacon. It was the old residence of the Archbishops of York. It lay in the Strand with gardens reaching to the Thames. On one side lay the Queen's Palace, "York Place," and on the other side St. Paul's. A little further along was Leycester House, occupied at one time by the Earl of Leicester, and afterwards by Robert, Earl of Essex. A stone's-throw away was the Chapter House of the Knights Templar . . . the ruins of which are still to be seen after German bombs have done their worst.

Francis Bacon was thus reared at the very hub of national life. To York House came statesmen, nobles, ecclesiastics and the highest dignitaries. He played in those beautiful historic gardens that reached to the banks of our national river and saw the ships go sailing by to the great centres of civilization. He wandered in the Chapter House of the Templars and saw the Symbolism of unspoken Mysteries . . . as a growing child.

York Place, Queen Elizabeth's Palace, Known Later as "Whitehall"

When Dr. Rawley, Francis Bacon's Chaplain and Secretary, a man privy to all his personal secrets, wrote "He (Francis Bacon) was born in *York House* or *York Place*" he was intimating to posterity that Francis Bacon was born in the Queen's Palace rather than in Sir Nicholas Bacon's home. "York Place" was known to be the Queen's Palace in the days when Francis was born. Shake-speare also knew the original name of the Palace for in *Henry VIII*, Act. iv., s.1, he says:

"*York Place.* That Title's Lost; 'tis now the King's and called *WHITE-HALL.*"

The principal approach to the Royal Home was hung with the tarred and slowly rotting bodies of persons executed for high treason. It was intended as a grim reminder of the penalty awarded to traitors.

Strickland says: "Elizabeth could not cross London Bridge without recognizing the features of gentlemen she had consigned to the axe or the Halter. The walls of her Royal residence were also converted into a Golgotha. Fearful it must have been for the ladies of her household to behold these mangled remains day after day. Hentzer affirms that he counted on London Bridge three hundred heads of persons executed for High Treason." (*Elizabeth*, p. 682.)

The Temple Church, London

This Church has been destroyed by German bombs but there are numerous photos of the building. This photo represents the interior.

"It is one of England's five round Churches all built by the Knights Templard after a model of a Church near the Holy Sepulchre at Jerusalem. . . . The Church is used in common by both Inns—members of the Middle Temple sit on the left or north side and their brethren of the Inner Temple on the right or south side. . . .

"Everywhere may be seen the Lamb and Flag—crest of the Middle Temple, and the Pegasus or two-winged horse, the crest of the Inner Temple.

"The Round Church was consecrated in honour of the Blessed Virgin Mary in the year 1185 by Heraclius, Patriarch of Jerusalem, who came to England to persuade Henry II to start a new Crusade. . . . Here lying around are effigies of Knights Templar . . . . These mail-clad effigies are always a source of great interest to the visitors, especially by reason of the various crossings of the legs, some above the knee, others midway and others at the ankle. . . . Undoubtedly some of the Knights whose effigies lie here in the Temple Church had either actually been to the Crusades or to the Holy Land."

This is an extract from *A Pleasant Hour in the Temple* by W. Marshall Freeman, Mitchell Hughes and Clarke, 7, Milford Lane, Strand, W.C.2, and the reader is advised to obtain a copy (sixpence). It is full of interesting facts. What excites one's interest is this: That undoubtedly the symbolism in the Church, the effigies of the Knights with their *crossed legs*, etc., were seen and meditated upon by the imaginative Francis as a boy and ultimately gave rise to the Ethical System of Symbol and Allegory which to-day encircles the World.

"The Temple," Gorhambury

This was built by Sir Nicholas Bacon—by command of Queen Elizabeth—as a country seat. Francis Bacon was about seven when he went to live there on its completion. It was built out of the ruins of St. Albans' Abbey, a stone's-throw away, built by the Hond Operative Masons under King Offa. The Abbey had been erected out of memory to the first Christian Martyr, St. Alban, who lost his life in A.D. 303.

The operative craft had subsequently been swept away by various legislative enactments, for the State would not tolerate anything in the nature of a Trade-Union.

The growing boy would naturally inquire into the meaning of the mysterious Mason Marks on the stones and the history of the defunct operative guild. It gave rise to the idea that the operative craft could be remodelled on an ethical basis . . . where the Brethren should moralize on tools and build figurative Temples to the Most High in which Humanity could worship.

By Masonic tradition St. Albans and Gorhambury are regarded as the Birthplace and Cradle of Freemasonry in England.

At the present time the home of Sir Nicholas and Francis Bacon is in ruins. There is but a heap of rubble, and only one or two walls remain, mute sentinels of its former grandeur. But the Spirits of Poets, Artists, and Mystics still outbreathe their fragrance in the moonlit gardens hard by, that once formed a portion of the site. One can imagine the Spirit of Shake-speare walking the grounds and through the ruined Banqueting Hall in the soft light of the moon. It breathes of poesy as I know only too well. How different from the raucous vulgarity that flaunts itself on the annual Feast Day. . . . the Mass in Masquerade. "*Stratford has the Letter but Gorhambury the Spirit,*" says Richard Ince, M.A.

Francis Bacon at Eleven

This is a copy of a terracotta bust of Francis preserved at Gorhambury as are busts of Sir Nicholas and Lady Bacon. There was none made for Anthony. "The Queen visited Gorhambury in July 1572 . . . and the bust of Francis is attributed to this date." (*See* Parker Woodward, *Tudor Problems*, p. 19.) He adds that "The Queen seems to have been interested in Gorhambury. She visited there in August 1568, July 1579 and again in March 1573. In April of that year Francis was sent to Cambridge University."

The bust seems to show abnormal skull development.

Francis Bacon at Eighteen

One can see in this beautiful engraving the youth who was destined to become the Prince of Poets, the most Illustrious of Philosophers, the most wonderful Ethical Teacher . . . our greatest world Genius.

"One sees him by the light of Hilyard's portrait, as he strolled along the Cam or reclined under the elms, with his fat, round face, his bluish-grey eyes, his fall of dark brown curls, and his ripe jesting mouth; with his hose puffed out, his ruff and rapier as the scholars wore them, in his face a thought for the bird on the tree, the fragrance in the air, the insect in the stream, no less than for the Greek dialectics and the twelve books of Euclid."

This was written by W. Hepworth Dixon, Barrister-at-Law, in 1862, long before there was any suggestion that Francis Bacon was of Tudor birth, his mother the "Virgin Queen."

If a face be indicative of the soul within, Francis Bacon at eighteen was a heaven-born poet. It is obvious to any student of physiognomy. One can well imagine such a face glowing with the lyrics of personal emotion as he wrote his *Shake-speare's Sonnets* to his mother the Queen, praying for public Recognition as her Tudor son to be next in the Succession.

Hilyard has left a note on the Miniature which expresses his astonishment at the youth's genius. He must have been swept off his feet by the genius of Francis. Round the portrait the artist has written, "*Could I but paint his MIND*." What a tribute!

The Agas Plan of London, *c.* 1560

The section of Ralph Agas' well known plan here illustrated shows the relationship of the Bacon home, here called Yorke Place, and "The Court" which, since Henry VIII's time, had been called White Hall. Yorke Place is shown as a four gabled building standing well back from the river. Between it and the Queen's Palace are shown a number of houses where formerly stood a large building known as St Mary's Hospital, as shown in Anthony van den Wyngarde's plan of 1543. This plan also illustrates the great Holbein Gate a little to the south-west of the Charing Cross. Yorke Place was then called "Yorke howse" and between the hospital and the Palace was an open space named "Scotlande" from which Scotland Yard took its name. According to Wheatley and Cunningham's "London Past and Present", "it is called, it is said, after the Kings of Scotland and their ambassadors who were occasionally lodged there".

Queen Elizabeth and Her Son Francis

These miniatures were painted at the same time by the Court Painter Hilyard. Francis Bacon was then eighteen years of age and the Queen forty-six. They sat for their portraits at the time when Francis had been sent to the English Court with despatches for the Queen from her Ambassador Sir Amyas Paulet. The youth was then in the train of Sir Amyas at the French Court.

The likeness between the Queen and young Francis is unmistakable. They bear a striking resemblance to each other. They look what in fact they are . . . mother and son. The artist has drawn the sitters in the same style with profiles at the same angle as though to denote their secret relationship.

Pallas Athene or Athena

Pallas was known as the "Spear Shaker" among the ancient Greeks. She warred with the Speare of Knowledge against the Serpent of Ignorance. Pallas or AthenA was Francis Bacon's Muse. She was the Goddess to whom the Rosicrosse Brethren swore allegiance when they were "made" in the Secret Literary Order, "The Knights of the Helmet." A fuller description is given in *The Martyrdom of Francis Bacon*, p. 176 (Rider).

The Fama

This is a facsimile of the English Translation of the *Fama*, perhaps the most famous of the three Rosicrucian Booklets published in Germany about the year 1610. The first was entitled *The Universal Reformation of the Whole Wide World;* the second, *The Fama Fraternitatis of the Meritorious Order of the Rosicrosse addressed to the Learned in General, and the Governors of Europe;* the third, the *Confessio Fraternitatis*. The chief point of interest is that the three booklets were obviously written by one pen and that they announce that a Society had been founded "to establish a true Philosophy" based on a Brotherhood of Ethics and Education. The author added that "the Order had different Degrees; that not only Princes, men of rank, rich men, but also mean and inconsiderable persons were admitted to their communion provided their purposes were pure and disinterested; and that the Order had a peculiar language; and that out of all ranks a Society was composed having for its object the general welfare of mankind and pursuing it in secret."

The Booklets created an immense stir and uproar on the Continent, being denounced as subversive to Church and State. They were anonymous but the reputed author was John Valentine Andrea, a celebrated theologian of Würtemburg. But the fact is that Andrea never claimed these writings as his and expressly disavowed them.

The truth is that they were written as propaganda booklets by Francis Bacon, and, since it would have been too dangerous to publish them in a small place like England, they first ran in manuscript here, secretly passing from hand to hand, were then translated by Andrea and published in German, and eventually were Englished and printed by "Eugenius Philalethes," the pen-name of Thomas Vaughan, a Mystic, a Freemason and a Rosicrucian, who knew the Secret of Authorship and printed it on the Title Page for those who had eyes to read. . . . "Lo! A Prince! Frater Francis Bacon."

Francis Bacon or Andrea?

This is a remarkable photograph. It is said that Francis Bacon fled to the Continent at Easter 1626, and that he did not die but went to live with the Andrea family. Frau Von le Coq was allowed to take this photograph by the permission of the Andrea descendants. Here we get Masonic and Rosicrucian Emblems. It is in short a Masonic Picture and the man in the centre is believed to be Francis Bacon as a very old man. The singular thing is that here we have two shields, out of the many that surround the portrait, which simply contain the letters "F.B."

Frau Von le Coq assured me that the Andrea possessors of the picture were quite uncertain that it was a picture of Andrea and could give no explanation of what the "F.B." stood for . . . apart from Francis Bacon, for whom Andrea was a field-worker to propagate his secret Order.

This picture was given to me before the war when Frau Von le Coq lived in Berlin-Dahlem.

FACSIMILE OF THE FIRST PAGE OF *SHAKE-SPEARE'S* SONNETS THE 1609 QUARTO

This is a very interesting page containing a number of secrets that show quite clearly that the lines were written and arranged by Francis Bacon and that he is imploring Queen Elizabeth to acknowledge him as a Tudor with rights to the Succession of the Throne of England. The Initial Capitals in the first Sonnet spell "P A W" and in the second "WHISPr." And lest one be tempted to think that the letters were dropped into this particular order by accident, he will find, on searching further, that a line drawn on the diagonal from the word "and" in the last line to the second word "selfe" in the eighth line touches letters which spell out "fr bacon." This spacing out of the words in the respective lines could only have been done with the connivance of the printer, who must have brought the letters on the diagonal according to the instructions of the poet himself.

But the design does not end here. It forms part of a sentence which clinches the "design argument," and proves it to be the work of a designer who uses the remainder of the lines in a very subtle manner that precludes coincidence.

Take the seventh letter in each line and from lines seven to one the letters spell "a tuder heire." The message is given in such a way that it forms a square (see the decoded Sonnet), and also the form of a "T" both having a Masonic signification, the latter being no less than the first st . . . in M. . . . Conjoined with the sacred number "seven," it is certain that the poet is trying to give his Brethren an Elizabethan Secret "ON THE SQUARE" and that he is a Mason. The complete internal message thus given in two parts is as follows:

"and fr bacon's a tuder heire."

This proclaims the secret of Francis Bacon's Royal birth better than any mere reported gossip of the times. The chief party concerned—the concealed son himself—left it openly for all the world to see when the hand that wrote it was dust.

Though written by him when a youth, the Sonnets were kept concealed, "in sure Wards of Trust" until the poet was an old man. He then revised them and published them in 1625 to the Brethren as a secret book with instructions not to publish them to the world until many years later . . . in 1766.

For a fuller account see *The Marriage of Elizabeth Tudor*, p. 184, Rider, London.

THE TWO PILLARS OF MASONRY

The number of the page 53=S.O.W. the numerical value of each letter being 18, 14, 21. The word "SOW" constantly appears in the Shakespeare Plays (in the Initial Capitals) as a play on the word "Bacon." But S.O.W. are also the Initials for "Son of Wisdom" applied to Rosicrucians in that Era and for "Supt. of Works" applied to certain Freemasons until this day.

The Figure in the Emblem points the "Sow" to the two Pillars of Masonry which carry the motto "Plus Ultra" . . . i.e., "More Beyond" a favourite motto of Francis Bacon. Every Craft Master-Mason knows that there is more between the Pillars than that which can be consumed on the floor.

The S.W. is the "Senior Warden" because he is the special guard to the Sanctum Sanctorum. Hence the message running up the Initial Capitals . . . . "See, Senior Warden! The Sanctum Sanctorum."

The Light and Dark "A's" of Francis Bacon (AthenA) are seen in the CENTRE forming a Pyramid, Francis Bacon's favourite symbol for his philosophy. They represent also the Square and Compasses. If the two "A.A." are placed across each other instead of by the side, they would form the well-known Masonic Symbol.

The three Arches in the centre refer to the Holy Royal Arch, a Masonic Degree.

The name of F. Bacon is spelled thus: F. on the right hand side in the frame of the building; B. is placed on the extreme right by the bottom of F., thus: A. in the centre; C. in the third Arch:—: O is the right hand curl at the end in the scroll across the Pillars; and N. in the two Pillars with its fancy scroll.

This Emblem proves that Speculative Freemasonry was in being in 1586, the year before Shaksper left Stratford for London.

Whitney, under whose name the Emblem Book was published, was a clerk in the Earl of Leicester's employ and as such was known to Francis Bacon—hence the connection between this Emblem Book of Francis Bacon's and Whitney the clerk who fathered the work.

This is the first reference to the Pillars of Masonry in Literature. They were afterwards attached to Francis Bacon's Works and were known to the days of Ashmole and Dr. Oliver as "Francis Bacon's Pillars."

A Freemason With The Square and Compasses in 1598

This is a reproduction of an illustration in a very rare book entitled *The Mirror of Policie* published by Adam Islip in 1598 . . . the very year that *Love's Labour's Lost* was published by "Shake-speare," the Masonic Play which enfolds the genesis of the Order. This noteworthy and significant illustration has never hitherto been noticed by anyone. Here is printed proof at last that Freemasonry as we know it to-day was actually in being in 1598. It serves as a clinch to the Masonic Secrets in "Shakespeare's" wonderful Play. He holds the Compasses quite correctly, one point being held in his hand, the other being pointed to his nib. Our Ancient Brethren in the days of Elizabeth were even then moralizing on Tools and spiritualizing Temples.

The illustration indicates that Freemasonry is directly associated with the Mysteries. Two Acacia Shrubs stood on either side of the Temple in the Egyptian Legends and served as Pillars. The Crown of the Pillar lying on the ground indicate that the Shrubs are to be understood as the Two Pillars of Masonry, their origin a Nature Myth of the Mysteries. They are directly connected with Grove Worship. The Rule at the Mason's feet are to remind him how his hours are to be spent.... "Part in..." etc.

It is absurd for anyone to suggest that men never learned to moralize on Tools, etc., until 1717-23.

Is it not abundantly clear that they were taught the way they should go by Francis Bacon?

Newfoundland Memorial Stamp

This Memorial Stamp issued by Newfoundland in 1910, is a striking tribute to Francis Bacon. It there states quite catagorically that he was "the guiding spirit in Colonization Schemes in 1610." So far as I know, this aspect of Francis Bacon's labours to make England mightier yet, is ignored by all his biographers save Hepworth Dixon.

The fact remains that this Imperially-minded Genius was the first in all schemes to promote the welfare and happiness of the common people. His advice to create a Parliament for Ireland was a distinct success. He was a Progressive who advocated bold acts of emigration and colonial expansion. Thanks largely to the lead of Francis Bacon and his friends, the New World became English instead of Spanish.

Richmond Palace

This Palace was dismantled in 1648 but it was a favourite residence of Queen Elizabeth. Here she kept a brilliant Court and built a new banqueting Hall. The air was considered to suit her health. She entertained the Ambassador of the Duke of Anjou in 1581, who came to arrange her marriage. The death-warrant of Mary Queen of Scots was signed in this Palace and from here were the messengers despatched by the Council to the Deputy-Lieutenants of the Counties on the coast announcing the appearance of the Spanish Armada; and bidding Englishmen rise to defend their land.

From the upper windows it commanded an unrivalled prospect of hill and dale, woodland and winding streams. One of the fairest river-views in England may be gained from this spot. When the Queen looked from the windows of her festive hall she could see Francis Bacon's "Palace fit for a Prince" right opposite, set near its avenue of big trees, and to the left she could observe the water winding away like a snake among the islets.

In the Palace Chapel were "hangings of arras and cloth of gold ornaments, the altar encrusted with jewels and gold ornaments while the ceiling was emblazoned in colours most richly, and many paintings of kings and saints adorned the walls."

The gardens had a wonderful show of vines, flowers and vegetables, for the soil was rich and prolific, says Alice Chambers Bunten, to whom I am indebted for the foregoing information. See *Twickenham Park and Old Richmond Palace.*

The illustration shows quite clearly that it was an easy row across the Thames for Francis to visit Elizabeth. He could slip in at night unobserved and doubtless did so often. We know that in 1600, the Queen graciously suggested visiting and dining with Francis Bacon at Twickenham Lodge.

Mrs. Bunten wrote in 1912 that there was one remaining wing left of Richmond Palace. "The most interesting room is the one where tradition says Queen Elizabeth closed in death those imperial eyes that had seen so much and influenced so many important people. A small room it is, with a window that shows a stretch of the *Road to London*—the most important in Richmond—where messengers came and went with news and letters.

"It is supposed that the Queen waited here when she expected the ring to come from Essex, which she watched for with the full intention of pardoning him should he send it. But the bitter hours passed and no messenger arrived. One can only conjecture what her proud heart felt on that occasion—too proud to show her courtiers how much she cared for the young renegade.

"She could only weep in secret, and she let him be executed in the Tower.

"A Year or two afterwards the passionate Queen died full of melancholy. . . . Her nearest neighbour was Francis Bacon, in his Lodge across the water, and he was probably the first person to hear that the Queen and patroness he knew so intimately was gone, and to mourn for her."

Lord Burleigh
(Born 1520)

He is regarded as one of England's greatest statesmen. His father left him large estates. He was entered at Gray's Inn and devoted himself to the study of Law. He was twice married, the second time to the daughter of Sir Anthony Cooke and this procured him the patronage of the protector Somerset.

When Elizabeth came to the Throne she recognized his capacity for government and appointed him chief secretary of state. . . . Although Elizabeth, in occasional caprice, might favour other courtiers, Burleigh was the statesman whose judgment she relied on in all matters of consequence. His policy at home and abroad was at once shrewd and cautious. "He was the originator and director of that policy which made Elizabeth's reign memorable above that of any other English sovereign." *Chambers's Encyclopædia.*

It is said that "Shake-speare" modelled Polonius on Burleigh.

Robart Tidir

This inscription constitutes perhaps the nearest direct proof in sight that the Earl of Essex was Queen Elizabeth's son, Robert Tudor. It is over the doorway of a small cell in the Tower of London—at the foot of the Beauchamp Tower—in which we know the Earl was imprisoned prior to his execution.

"Robart Tidir" is the Welsh form of Robert Tudor (pronounced Tidir). It must have been carved at the instigation of someone in authority and with the connivance of the Governor of the Tower. The records have all been carefully searched to ascertain whether there was a State prisoner of this name. There is no one. It applies, and can only apply, to one man who occupied the cell, a State prisoner in the Tower—the Earl of Essex who was truly by birth "Robart Tidir," with the Queen's blood in his veins.

The carving was made to leave an imperishable record of the real identity. It is a piece of evidence that no historian has a right to overlook in dealing with the tangled history of the Elizabethan Era.

The carving carries a numerical Cypher which again makes clear his parentage. The instigator of such an inscription could only be one person . . . his blood-brother Francis Bacon.

The Original Bust of Shaksper of Stratford

This engraving was made by Sir William Dugdale in 1656 as the bust and likeness of Shaksper the actor then appeared in Stratford Church. Its correctness is independently confirmed in its general outlines by the engraving of Shaksper in Rowe's life published in 1709. There is evidence in the pages of *Warwickshire* where the engraving appeared that Sir W. Dugdale was a Rosicrosse-Mason.

Mr. W. S. Dugdale, of Merivale Hall, Atherstone, possesses the original drawing in Sir William's private manuscript book surrounded by notes in his own handwriting. *It is the only verifiable portrait of the Stratford man whom many regard as "Shake-speare."*

The bust was erected before 1623 and it must have been accepted as a good likeness by the illiterate villagers who knew him. But they did not know the meaning of the Latin inscription of the lines in the tablet describing him:

"A Nestor in experienced Judgment,
A Socrates in philosophical genius,
And a Virgil in poetic art."

What a portrait. Turn to the illustration again and look at it.

Its erection is another mystery to the outside world. Who placed it there? Who wrote the Latin inscription?

There is nothing in the 1623 bust to connect Shaksper with literature. The portrait and the "signatures" we possess harmonize admirably in their coarseness. They typify a hard business-man totally devoid of intellectuality.

This original bust was destroyed and the present one was erected in 1748. The general outline is the same but a cushion takes the place of the bag in the original and a large quill is placed in his hand. His hands no longer suggest that he hugs a money-bag or wool-sack, and the smirking doll-like face is very different from the shrewd, hard-faced man who knew excellently well how to drive a bargain.

Facsimile Title Page of the Anonymous Quarto Richard II

This is one of the Plays that was published anonymously. There is no name on the Title-page but the discerning reader can see running up the lines Lorde bAcon. And Francis was a "Lorde" even in those early days . . . one of the Lords of Masonry.

The first Initial Capitals "T.T." tell "The Truth" of the matter and that the "Degree" 33 was already created.

Note how the printer has split the word into "se-cond" instead of "sec-ond" in order to get the syllable "con" to make the name of the author. The full message running up the lines is "Tap Thirty-Three, you'll Lorde Bacon see." For "33" is Bacon's numerical signature as well as the highest Masonic Degree. I am indebted to Edward D. Johnson, who was the first to point out the signature "b A con," for this plate.

Robert Devereux, Earl of Essex

Robert Devereux, afterwards Earl of Essex, was born in 1567. His mother is reputed to be Lettice Knollys, cousin to Queen Elizabeth, and one of the First Maids of Honour. When she married Lord Hereford, she continued to take a small share in the Court.

His birth is not to be found in any of the registers of the Devereux or Hereford families. Nor is it in the Parish register of Netherwood, Hertfordshire, where it is presumed he was born: For he was actually the second son of the Queen by Leicester.

He was a clever youth, took his M.A. at the age of fourteen, and is early introduced to the Court. He comes into prominence in May 1587 when his father, Leicester, resigned the post of Master of the Horse *in his favour*. After his death Robert is swiftly advanced in honours, money, estate by the Queen. There is not the slightest doubt that their relationship is that of mother and son. For him to be represented as *the lover* of the Queen is absurd. She was fifty-four when he was twenty. In any case, *when he was twenty-three* (1590) *he married Sir Philip Sidney's widow*. And though the Queen was angry (saying she was not good enough in station for him) it made no difference to her motherly affection.

All along he acts at Court as though he were her son, a high-spirited young man and she a doting mother. His reckless Tudor manners and his chivalrous style endear him to the populace. He was trapped into a false move by his enemies, notably Cecil, and was sentenced to death for High Treason. He sent the Queen her Ring, mutely asking for pardon. It fell into the hands of the Countess of Nottingham, who was then carrying on an amour with Cecil. They saw it never reached the Queen. Months afterwards on her death-bed the Countess confessed her sin to Elizabeth. "God may forgive you but I never shall," shouted the Queen after shaking the dying woman violently. She returned to the Palace to die of a broken heart calling out the name of the son "who had been fetched to his death by a trick". Someone carved over his cell in the Tower his real identity, "Robart Tidir".

APPENDIX II

NOTABLE DATES IN FRANCIS BACON'S LIFE TO THE DEATH OF QUEEN ELIZABETH, 1603

1561: (January 22nd, old style, 1560): Born at York House or York Place.

1573: Enters Trinity College, Cambridge.

1575: Leaves Cambridge: Disagrees with the Educational System: Conceives the idea of a "Reformation of the Whole Wide World through Education and Ethics."

1576 to 1579: Discovers he is Queen Elizabeth's son: Goes abroad with Sir Amyas Paulet: Writes his first Sonnets to Marguerite of Navarre. Initiated in the Knights Templar Order and takes steps to recreate this secret Society on a broader and more up-to-date basis: Interested in Codes and Cyphers and makes a special Cypher while in Paris, called the Biliteral, that could be secretly inserted in the printed page: Sir Nicholas Bacon dies: Returns to London to find Sir Nicholas has left him nothing and that he is penniless.

1580: Put to the study of Law at Gray's Inn by the Queen, his fees and pocket-monies being provided for by the Queen: Writes four letters to Burleigh and his wife pressing them to recommend his "SUIT" to the Queen, the "Suit" being for "Recognition" as a Tudor and to be admitted to Succession to the Throne.

1582: Has already begun to write the Rituals of Freemasonry: He founds his Secret Literary and Ethical Societies: The Queen provides him with a "Mansion fit for a Prince" known as Twickenham Park which she owns. It is opposite her own river Palace on the Thames known as Richmond Palace.

1584: Enters Parliament.

1585: Writes *The Most Masculine Birth of Time* to indicate secretly to those in the know in "After-Ages" that Freemasonry is definitely in being—the Birth of Males to Males and by Males in a secret Chamber.

1586: Shaksper of Stratford arrives in London.

1587: Execution of Mary Queen of Scots.

1588: The Earl of Leicester dies:

1592: Writes to Burleigh, Secretary of State, a clear though veiled renunciation of the English Throne. "I have moderate CIVIL ends for I have taken all knowledge to be MY PROVINCE": The first of the Great Plays begin to appear anonymously, Henry VI (Basil E. Lawrence, LL.D).

1593: Writes *The Conference of Pleasure* for the Revels at Gray's Inn: *Venus and Adonis* is issued with a preface signed for the first time under the pen-name of "William Shakespeare."

1594: Begins to practise as a Barrister.

1594: The Earl of Essex presents him with a piece of land: *Promus of Formularies and Elegancies* compiled.
1597: Publication of Ten *Essays*, the first scrap of writing openly published.
1598: Arrested for Debt: For the first time the name of "William Shakespere" is printed on a Play *Love's Labour's Lost*, a Masonic Play which tells how Freemasonry was created and which gives much esoteric knowledge away to the discerning reader.
1601: Trial and execution of Essex: Death of Anthony Bacon.
1603: Queen Elizabeth dies, 24th March.

FRANCIS BACON'S
PERSONAL LIFE-STORY
VOLUME II

The Age of James

FOREWORD

In 1949 there was published the first volume of the late Alfred Dodd's great work on Francis Bacon and his times. This volume carried the history down to the death of Queen Elizabeth and was kindly received by Baconians and the general public, but not of course by the Stratfordians or the majority of reviewers as the press in this country is very much averse to printing anything derogatory to Will Shaksper or Stratford-on-Avon. The second volume continues the story from the accession of King James to Francis Bacon's supposed death in 1626.

Alfred Dodd suffered from ill health during part of the period when he was writing the second volume, and he inserted a considerable amount of matter which, although very interesting had strictly very little to do with his subject. To reduce the book to a reasonable length for publication purposes it was necessary to delete a considerable portion of the book as originally written, and I have tried to do this without leaving out anything of importance.

Alfred Dodd passed away in February 1953 without living to see the second volume of his great work in print. His death was a very great loss to all Baconians and other seekers of the truth concerning England's greatest genius, Francis Bacon.

EDWARD D. JOHNSON
(a friend and first editor of this manuscript)

Chapter I

THE COMING OF JAMES I AND FRANCIS BACON'S DANGER

QUEEN Elizabeth had consistently refused to allow the question of the succession "to be settled or even discussed". She never named her Successor. She died as she had lived, "a Virgin Queen", and carried her love secrets with her to the grave—as far as was possible. The succession had therefore to be determined without her. On the authority of Aubrey we learn that,

> At a consultation at Whitehall, after Queen Elizabeth's death, how matters were to be ordered and what ought to be done, Sir Walter Raleigh declared his opinion that 'twas the wisest way for them to keep the Government in their own hands, and set up a Commonwealth, and not be subject to a needy and beggarly nation.

The probability is that James heard of this proposal, never forgot it and that this was the real reason for the King's long hatred of Walter Raleigh and finally the cause of his unjust and cruel execution. Since the only heir in sight was the Scottish King James by a "legitimate but almost antiquarian pedigree", the son of Mary, Queen of Scots, and a Protestant, that fact successfully enabled Sir Robert Cecil, Secretary of State, to interpret to the people the tossing of the Queen's arms as a "sign" that James should succeed her. But Cecil had long been in secret communication with the Scots' King and had pledged him his services while Elizabeth yet lived. The so-called "sign" was open to grave suspicion, for Elizabeth had always despised James as a coward and a hypocrite, the very antithesis of a king.

What the Queen actually said on her deathbed, according to Lady Southwell's circumstantial and minute account, is this: "I will have no rascal's son in my seat, but one worthy to be a king." With that enigmatical phrase she passed away, having given no sign when the King of Scotland was mentioned. She knew that James was not worthy to be King of England ... as the changeling son (so reputed) of the Earl of Mar; Mary's son having died in infancy.

There was only one "worthy to be a king"—Francis Bacon, the Queen's legitimate son who had no rights in the succession despite the Tudor blood in his veins. She had never openly acknowledged him because of the circumstances surrounding his birth, an open secret in Court circles. Whatever secret hopes he may have entertained that the Queen might name him at the last minute, they vanished when he heard the Proclamation on 24 March 1603 that James had been appointed her successor.

It will be remembered that Francis Bacon had been appointed one of the

[1] See Volume I, Lady Southwell's eye-witness account of the death scene (page 299).

Learned Counsel, but this was by the verbal order of the Queen. He had never been sworn in and had no written warrant; hence Coke's sneer "You are unsworn." Francis was therefore truly among the unemployed when the Queen died—under a cloud indeed with the accession of James—still plain Francis Bacon, disguising a concealed Royal Prince. His fatal birth secret had acted as the bar-sinister to his advancement in the State for over twenty-five years. With the advent of a new King it now positively threatened to overwhelm him: "Unless he could get on terms of friendship with the King and satisfy men like Sir Robert Cecil that he was not an aspirant to the Throne, *his Life and Liberty were in jeopardy*."

He therefore hastened to get on friendly terms with James by writing to his friends in Scotland, to emissaries going to the new King from England and, lastly, to the King himself. He was naturally afraid that, if James had any knowledge of his real identity, he would view his (Francis Bacon's) legal and political activities with suspicion. He was anxious to forestall any prejudice against his employment by the State because of his birth, to allay any possible doubts that "might arise through whispered innuendoes to the King".

By reading the correspondence about this time, one can see that Francis Bacon judged the danger to life and limb to be very real and threatening. There is no doubt he thought that, if James felt his newly acquired Throne and his dynasty were in danger, an excuse would soon be forthcoming to get rid of him once and for all. His letters show his perturbation and, as is so often the case where his personal secrets are involved, he writes with double meanings, and in many letters "he has evidently taken pains to remove the dates and names, and such particulars as might serve to identify persons," says Spedding.[1] Spedding might also have added we do not know what vital sentences were snipped away to leave posterity guessing. There must have been a good reason for such mutilation.

Before the Queen died Francis Bacon could see there were breakers looming ahead. Since Cecil was the most powerful man in the State and might do him irreparable harm in the new reign, he wrote to Michael Hicks, Cecil's confidential business man and secretary, asking Hicks to speak to Cecil to assure him of his loyal love to him as the chief man in the State. He begins on a note of fear:

> Mr Hicks, *The apprehension of this threatened judgment of God* ... is the cause I now write to you, signifying I would be glad of the comfort of your society and familiar conference ... though we card-holders have nothing to do but to keep close our cards and to do as we are bidden.
>
> As I ever used your mind to cherish the truth of my inclination towards Mr Secretary, so now again I pray you as you find time let him know that he is the personage in this State which I love the most. ... And *this proceedeth not out of any straits* of my occasions ... but merely out of the largeness and fullness of my affections.... Your assured friend,
>
> Fr. Bacon

About the same time he wrote to the Earl of Northumberland, who was the most important person in England next to Cecil, a letter in which he said:

[1]James Spedding, *Life of Francis Bacon*, 1861, Vol. III, p. 73.

If I may be of any use to your Lordship, by my head, tongue, pen, means, or friends, *I humbly pray you to* hold me your own ... do not ... conceive ... *this proceedeth out of any straits of my occasions*, but ... fullness of heart.

In March 1603 Francis Bacon sent a letter to the King to be delivered by an accomplished scholar named Sir Thomas Challoner, long employed in Italy as an "Intelligentia" in the service of Essex, then in Scotland and closely in touch with King James. He wrote to Sir Thomas Challoner as follows:

I know you hold me not unworthy ... and I for my part conceive and hope you are likely to become an acceptable servant to THE KING OUR MASTER. ... My general request is ... you will further His Majesty's good conceit and inclination towards me; to whom words cannot make me known, neither my own nor others, but Time will. ...

Having thought good TO MAKE OBLATION of my most humble service to His Majesty by a few lines, I do desire your loving care and help ... to deliver and present the same to His Majesty's hands. ...

Though occasion give you the precedence of doing me this special good office, yet I hope no long time will intercede before I shall have some means to requite your favour and acquit your report.

Here Francis Bacon makes the position quite clear. He uses the word "Oblation" (an act of offering, a sacrifice). What could this mean but the sacrifice of his Tudor birthright? He again acknowledges the King as his master. He asks Sir Thomas to speak for him to the King and to induce James to think favourably of him. Are we to think that Francis Bacon went to all this trouble merely to secure a situation under the Crown?

The same day he wrote to a Dr. Morrison, a Scottish physician in attendance on James, "to renew the ancient acquaintance between us" ... which:

invests you with the opportunity to use MY NAME WELL, and by your loving testimony to further a good opinion of me to His Majesty and the COURT. ... So not doubting to see you here with His Majesty.

This letter once more indicates that the chief concern of Francis Bacon is to dissipate any prejudice that James might entertain with reference to his NAME. On the same day he also wrote to his friend John Davies, a fellow barrister, statesman and poet, the author of *Nosce Teipsum* and afterwards Attorney General for Ireland, who was journeying to Scotland to see the new King on State matters. Reading the letter in the light of his Tudor parentage, of which fact Davies would have been aware, its full significance can be at last fully understood. He requests his friend "to defend him from slanders"[1] if uttered by anyone in the King's presence. But why should anyone go out of his way to slander him? What had he ever said or done? Nothing. He could only be slandered to the King in one way, a way that would affect the King towards him very much: *that he was a true-born Tudor with designs on the Crown.*

[1] I. E. Abbott, *Bacon*, p. 96.

A Letter to Mr Davys, then Gone to the King

Mr Davys,

... I mean to show you that I am not asleep. Briefly, I commend myself to your love and to *the well using of MY NAME*, as well in *Repressing* and *Answering* for me, if there be any BITING or NIBBLING at it [i.e. at the name of BACON] *in that PLACE* [the Court], as in impressing a good Conceit and Opinion of me, chiefly in the King ... of whose Favour I make myself comfortable Assurance ... as otherwise in that Court.

And not only so, but also to perform to me all the Good Offices which the vivacity of your wit can suggest to your mind to be performed to one, in whose Affection you have so great sympathy, and in whose Fortune you have so great an interest.

So *desiring you to be good to concealed poets*,

Your very assured,

Fr. Bacon.

From the light of this illuminating letter we can discern what may have been dark in the preceding hints and asides. It is his NAME that is at stake, his Tudor birth. Any biting or nibbling at the name of Bacon (note the covert jest of 'nibbling at Bacon') would entrap him; it would tear away the veil of his real identity to the King. He wants John Davies to defend his good name, to aver that he is content to be known as Bacon, a commoner, and does not presume on his royal pedigree. He wants his friend to answer for him to the King to assure him of his loyalty and to repress any suggestions that he has ever made any overt claim to the Throne. He then concludes with a striking phrase: "*Be good to CONCEALED POETS.*"

Francis Bacon thus lets posterity know that *he is a poet* and a *concealed one*, while reminding his friend Davies, in his enigmatical style, that just as he is content to lie concealed by the pen-name of "Shake-speare", so he is equally content to appear before the eyes of the world under the adopted name of "Bacon". He indicates that he is careless of his real identity and does not seek to flaunt it before the public gaze. (It must not be forgotten that it is his "Name" he leaves in his last Will to future ages.) This correctly explains what would otherwise be a meaningless conclusion to his letter. Since Davies was one of his literary school he knew how to interpret it, though modern scholars generally have failed to discover the pen-name Francis Bacon used. Spedding says, "*The allusion to 'concealed poets' I cannot explain.* ... He may have occasionally written verses for a similar purpose as those fathered by Essex, and *Davies may* have been in the secret."[1] And on that unsatisfactory note Spedding leaves the secret of the era unravelled, and misses his way almost completely in the Elizabethan labyrinth after thirty years' research. Dr Abbott, in a similarly vacuous note, says: "Bacon ranked himself among 'Concealed poets', implying I suppose that he had written anonymous poetry." There the writers leave it, seeing nothing significant, and never thinking of conjoining similar remarkable asides, used by Bacon and others, which prove him to be the world's supreme poet.

The letter that Francis Bacon wrote to the King was a remarkable one. It clinched the asides in the previous ones and cannot be interpreted in any

[1] Spedding, *op. cit.*, p. 65.

other way but that he was desperately anxious to prove himself a worthy subject without any ulterior motives, his only wish to be regarded as a loyal servant to the Crown. He uses phrases which James can interpret for himself if he is aware of his Tudor breed.

An Offer of Service to His Majesty King James

It may please your most excellent Majesty ... This Royal virtue of Access ... could not of itself have animated me *to make Oblation of myself immediately* to your Majesty, had it not been joined with a habit of like liberty, which I enjoyed with my late Sovereign Mistress; a Prince happy in all things, but most happy *in such a SUCCESSOR. ...*

I was not a little encouraged ... that unto your Majesty's sacred ears, there might perhaps have come some small breath of the good memory of my Father, so long a principal Counsellor *in this Your Kingdom* [this would apply equally to Sir Nicholas Bacon or the Earl of Leicester]; but also by the particular knowledge of the infinite devotion and incessant endeavours which appeared in *my good Brother* towards your Majesty's service. ...

Therefore, Most High and Mighty King, my Most Dear and Dread Sovereign Lord, since now *the Corner-Stone is laid* [note the Masonic phrase] of the mightiest Monarchy in Europe; and that God above ... hath, by the Miraculous and Universal Consent in your coming in, *given a Sign and Token* [Masonic phrase] what He intendeth in the continuance; I think there is no Subject of your Majesty's, who loveth this Island, and is not *hollow and unworthy*, whose heart is not set on fire, not only to bring you *Peace Offerings* to make you Propitious, but *TO SACRIFICE HIMSELF A BURNT OFFERING TO YOUR MAJESTY'S SERVICE*, amongst which number *no man's FIRE shall be more Pure and Fervent* than mine.

This is a specific statement that Francis Bacon of all men recognizes the Scottish King as his "Sovereign" of a "Monarchy" which is intended by God to continue. He refers to his "father", presumably Sir Nicholas Bacon, and then to his good (foster) "Brother" deceased, to show he is definitely a Bacon. He gives James to understand that he loves "this Island" too well to do anything to disturb its peace by thrusting forward any Tudor claim, and so he offers his "Peace Offering" which is nothing less than his TUDOR BIRTHRIGHT. This is his "OBLIGATION". It is a BURNT SACRIFICE made by a personal fire ... "and no man's Fire shall be more pure and fervent than mine."

How can this letter be understood save in one way: that a concealed Tudor Prince, an English patriot, is telling the recipient—and the *discerning reader* into whose hands it may fall—that he has no intention of trying to enforce a claim to the Throne irrespective of what his enemies may say to poison James's mind.

Apart from this overhanging menace there is no earthly reason why he should have written to James, or for that matter to Northumberland, Davies, Fouls and others. *Other lawyers did not write to curry favour.* Ordinarily such attempts to obtain favours defeat their own purpose. But this was not asking for any favour. There was patently a motive that does not appear on the surface. It was a personal one: SELF-PRESERVATION. He was fighting for life and liberty. There was a very potent danger lest his Tudor blood should be regarded by James and his advisers as a menace to the House of Stuart and to the State.

Francis Bacon's letter to James brought no answer. He therefore drafted a Royal Proclamation to emphasize his allegiance to the Crown and to show he harboured no secret reservations. He sent it to Northumberland—"*A Proclamation Drawn for the King at his Entrance*"—with a request he would show it the King and say that the late Queen often used his pen in public writings. It is an excellent piece of writing.

The Proclamation, however, was not used.

The King was still 400 miles away. What his real attitude would be towards him he could not say and probably would not know until his arrival in London. For aught he knew, orders for his arrest might be sent from the Scottish Court at any moment. He decided to end the suspense; to go forward to meet the danger; *to seek a personal interview with the King*; and what we definitely know is this:

> that before the King arrived in London, *Francis Bacon had gone to meet him*, carrying a despatch from the Earl of Northumberland; and that *he had been admitted to his Presence.*[1]

Where Francis Bacon saw him or when he saw him no biographer seems to know. What went on between them is not recorded but it had the effect, apparently, of *staving off any immediate anxiety he had felt about his personal safety.* A price had to be paid, of course, and we can make a shrewd hazard, in the light of subsequent events, the amount and type of payment demanded. To Northumberland, who had procured him the interview, he wrote:

> I would not have lost this journey, and yet *I have not that for which I went* [i.e. an unconditional acceptance of his loyalty]. I have had no private conference to any purpose with the King. ... After I had received his Majesty's first welcome, I was promised *private access. ...*
>
> Your Lordship shall find a Prince the farthest from the appearance of vain-glory that may be. ...
>
> His speech is swift and cursory, and in the full dialect of his country; and in point of business, short; in point of discourse, large. ...
>
> He hasteneth to a mixture of both Kingdoms and Nations, faster perhaps than policy will conveniently bear. ...
>
> His Majesty rather asked counsel of the *TIME PAST than of the TIME TO COME.*
>
> But it is early yet to ground any settled opinion. For *the particularities*, I refer to [our] Conference, having in these *generals* gone further in *so Tender an Argument* than I would have done, were not the reader and the Bearer assured [of maintaining privacy].

This letter gives Francis Bacon's first impressions of James, the King with whom he was destined to be associated so closely and who sacrificed him eventually so callously. He relates sufficient in his "generals" to let us know that they covered quite a lot of ground in their interview. James discoursed at length—even on the then new idea of the Union of England and Scotland, an indication that their conversation ranged round State affairs. Why should it have been if Francis Bacon had merely gone to ask for legal employment? It is also obvious that when James came to the real business of the interview Francis was brief and to the point. The King held the cards and laid down

[1] Spedding, *op. cit.*, p. 76.

what would satisfy him, being more concerned with "the Time Past"—*his heritage as a Tudor*—than "the Time to come"—what he (James) would do to preserve his Throne and his dynasty from possible usurpation. "It is early yet to ground any settled opinion as to what may happen in the future," says Francis in effect. "He is determined to protect himself and his heirs. The details I will give you when we meet. I must say nothing more in so delicate a matter ... so tender an argument."

While Francis Bacon had not got any definite assurances of safety, there is no doubt the King had indicated a possible way of escape for him to consider. "I have not that for which I went ... but I would not have lost this journey" for the King does not intend to take any immediate steps against me.

To his friend Tobie Matthew, by whom he had despatched some letters to Scotland, he wrote,

> My aim was right in my address of letters to those persons in the Court of Scotland. ...
>
> Things here are in good quiet. ... The King puts in clauses of reservation to every proviso. He saith, *he would be sorry to have just cause to remove any; he will* displace none who hath served the Queen and the State sincerely. ...
>
> *I find myself as one awaked out of a sleep* [i.e. he is wide awake to the danger of the present situation].

Tobie Matthew has been described as Francis Bacon's *alter ego*. He was privy to all Francis Bacon's secrets.

Travelling by slow and easy stages, James did not reach London until 7 May, some six weeks after Elizabeth's death. While Francis Bacon had temporarily succeeded in assuring James of his loyalty he had by no means succeeded in removing all cause for distrust. His name was omitted from the list of those who were in office at the Queen's death and who were to be continued in office. He had lost his official status as one of the Learned Counsel. This was afterwards remedied but it was a reminder, by accident or design, that "he had completely failed to recommend himself to the King".[1]

> Before the King had been two months in London, Bacon had been forced to recognise his position. He was to be left out in the cold more than ever; still, indeed, of the Learned Counsel as before; but not, as before, to be employed by the Sovereign on extraordinary occasions nor to have his pen "Used in public writings of satisfaction".

Thus it came to pass that Francis Bacon wrote a most extraordinary letter which we can judge was the direct outcome of his interview with the King. James, unquestionably, had outlined a course of action to be pursued if Francis Bacon desired to obtain the good will of the Court. It can be safely assumed that *he (James) asked for guarantees of his loyalty* to be delivered through the proper channels: the delivery of a personal letter to his Secretary of State accepting the King's conditions in writing and in action. *Such a letter was actually sent* to Sir Robert Cecil. The phraseology, direct and enigmatical, involves implications which cannot be explained—and never have been

[1]Abbott, *op. cit.*, p. 97.

explained in any other way but that the letter was to be regarded as a written guarantee to satisfy the suspicious mind of James that Francis Bacon did not intend—and could not intend—to do him or his heirs a mischief and that he was a loyal servant of the Crown.

There was no legitimate reason for writing to Cecil, so Francis Bacon began by saying; "it grieveth me not a little, that I find myself of no use to such an honourable and kind friend." (Note the touch of sarcasm, for Cecil had consistently thwarted him in every way.) "I shall never forget your last favour amongst the others." He continues:

> I had thought of becoming an humble suitor to your Honour to have sustained me with your credit for the present from urgent debts, with taking up £300 till I can put away some land. But I am so forward with some sales, as this request I hope I may forbear.
>
> I shall be selling the skirts of my living in Hertfordshire ... leaving myself out of debt, and having some money in my pocket £300 land per annum with a fair house, and the ground well timbered. *This is now my labour.*

He then comes to the real point of the letter. He has bidden farewell to politics; and he gives his personal guarantee that he has no desire whatever to do anything inimical to the King or his House.

> *For my Purpose or Courses, I desire to MEDDLE as little as I can IN THE KING'S CAUSES ... and to follow my private thrift and practice, and TO MARRY with some Convenient Advancement.* For as for any Ambition, I DO ASSURE YOUR HONOUR, *MINE IS QUENCHED.*
>
> In the Queen's, my excellent Mistress's Time, the *quorum* was small: Her Service was a kind of FREEHOLD, and it was a MORE SOLEMN TIME.
>
> All these Points [then] agreed with my NATURE and JUDGMENT.
>
> My AMBITION *now* I shall ONLY PUT UPON MY PEN, whereby I shall be able to maintain MEMORY and MERIT of the Times Succeeding.
>
> Lastly, for this divulged and almost prostituted Title of Knighthood, I could ... be content to have it, both because of this late Disgrace [probably another arrest for debt] and because I have three new Knights in my Mess at Gray's Inn Commons; and because *I have found out an Alderman's daughter, an handsome MAIDEN, to my liking. ...*
>
> I will come to the Court from Gorhambury upon any warning.

This remarkable letter is another that has never been interpreted. His biographers confess they are not sure of its covert meanings. They can only see the apparent fact that Francis Bacon had again been imprisoned for debt and that he either thought of importuning Cecil for help or had obtained something from him. These were pure red-herring asides, laid across the trail to throw outsiders off the scent. The real reason which called the letter into being is clear: it was a formal, official notice that Francis Bacon had relinquished all thoughts, all aspirations, to the English Throne. His "Ambition" in that direction is "Quenched". What might have been legitimate in Elizabeth's day—a "Freehold" to the Succession, to which he might legitimately aspire—was now vested in someone else. In her day his ambition "agreed with my [Tudor] Nature and judgment", but with James on the Throne his "Ambition now" is "ONLY put upon my Pen". He has no "desire to meddle ... In the King's Causes" but "to follow my *private* thrift and practice", not a public one, as an attempt on the Throne would be. "As for any AMBITION, I do assure your Honour, MINE IS QUENCHED."

What was this particular "Ambition"? It can only refer to one thing which he had cherished from late youth to early middle age. It touched the "King's Causes". He had relinquished the suit of his youth. What can the Suit, the early "Ambition", be but the Succession to the Throne to which he had a right, under the Parliament Act, as a born TUDOR? He is not relinquishing his "Ambition" of serving the State in a public capacity, because he asks to be made a knight, which would be the first step towards public honour and "Advancement". Is it not clear that his "Ambition" was neither a private nor a public but a royal one?

Now when Francis Bacon asked for a knighthood and announced that he had found "a handsome maiden", he was definitely giving James the necessary surety that his one-time hope to succeed his mother, Queen Elizabeth, was utterly abandoned. (It is virtually certain that at the interview with King James there would have been mentioned that danger to the Stuart line would lie in the future if he married in his class and left heirs as possible claimants to the Throne.) For the Alderman's daughter whom he intended to marry was a COMMONER. *She was then only ELEVEN YEARS OF AGE.* Cecil and the King knew that a commoner could never sit on the throne as Queen and that HEIRS were out of the question to disturb the Stuart dynasty. Francis Bacon at a stroke put himself utterly out of the running by proposing to contract a *mésalliance*. No matter how popular a Pretender Francis might have been still, such a wife barred any possible accession.

> An Alderman's daughter for a possible Queen would have been about as effectual a wet blanket for any agitation as anything that could have been devised. It was an excellent idea of Francis Bacon, and probably *saved his head*.[1]

The latter then announced to James that he was prepared to take the irrevocable step of marriage with a commoner though the age of the maiden showed unmistakably that *Francis Bacon at forty-three was actually assuming a paternal role, the adoption of a daughter*, while obeying the social conventions and acquiescing in the King's wishes. James and Cecil could thus rest safely in their beds so far as the rightful heir to the English Throne was concerned. The Stuart line could not be imperilled.

Cecil realized the inner meaning of the letter. If he did not, Francis Bacon was ready to enlighten him at the proposed Court interview. Francis was duly knighted at Whitehall, two days before the Coronation, along with three hundred others, on 22 July 1603.

A letter he wrote Cecil on 16 July, in reply to an intimation that his request was granted, indicates that Francis Bacon regarded the honour really with scorn and that he accepted it because he was more than entitled to it.

> For my knighthood, I wish the manner might be such as might Grace me, SINCE THE MATTER WILL NOT; I mean, that I might not be merely gregarious in a troop.

[1] Parker Woodward, *Tudor Problems*, p. 67.

This is an additional indication of the disdain with which Francis viewed the honour for which he asked. How could "the Matter" of "Knighthood" GRACE one who was A PRINCE of the Blood Royal? But James would not "Grace" him with an individual ceremonial. He was "gregariously" knighted with a troop of others, all collected in the King's garden at Westminster, judges, lawyers, gentlemen ushers and "many others of divers qualities"; and the entire crowd were dubbed knights *en bloc*. But the door to social and State advancement now lay open.

Francis Bacon was true to his pledge. Three years later, on 10 May 1606, "With April's First-Born Flowers and all Things Rare", he married his "handsome maiden", the Alderman's daughter. Her name was Alice Barnham, and *the witnesses were the wily Cecil's personal friends and officials*, Sir Walter Cope, Sir Baptist Hicks and Sir E. Beeston. They were specially invited because his marriage showed in the most practical way that he had no "desire to meddle ... with the King's Causes" and that his one-time royal "Ambitions" were "quenched". As official witnesses they would report the fact of his marriage in due course to Cecil, who would convey it to James. Perhaps they also reported that *Sir Francis was dressed in Royal Purple* and that his wife was *a mere CHILD OF FOURTEEN* towards whom he intended to act as though she were an adopted daughter. There would be thus no possible claims in the future from heirs with Tudor blood in their veins.

"He was married to his young wench in Maribone Chapel," wrote Dudley Carleton, a contemporary, to John Chamberlain.

> He was clad from top to toe in purple, and hath made himself and his wife such store of fine raiments of cloth of silver and gold, that it draws deep into her portion.
>
> The dinner was kept at his father-in-law, Sir John Pakington's lodging, over against the Savoy, where his chief guests were the three Knights, Cope, Hicks and Beeston; and upon this conceit—*as he said himself—that since he could not have my Lord of Salisbury* [Cecil] in person, *he would have him at least in his representative body*.[1]

Is not this last sentence a most significant hint that the marriage had something to do with the affairs of State? Cecil, as Secretary of State, was represented officially, not privately.

It is a matter of interest—destined to become more as the years advance—to know something about Alice, the girl-wife of the world's greatest intellectual genius. She is passed over in silence by the majority of biographers as though she were of little account.

Her father was Benedict Barnham, a London Alderman and a Member of Parliament for Yarmouth, who had been dead many years. He left five girls, the youngest dying in infancy. Alice was his second child; Elizabeth the eldest, a year older, being nearly seven when he passed. He left his wife Dorothy and the children well provided for in an elaborate Will. With her mother and sisters, Alice was bequeathed money, lands, plate, jewels, etc.

Alice's mother, Dorothy Barnham, was the daughter of a well-known London merchant, Humphrey Smith of Cheapside. He was the purveyor of silks, velvets and precious fabrics from the Continental looms to Queen Elizabeth. Mrs. Barnham became a widow on 4 April 1598. She lost no time

[1] *Domestic Papers*, 1606, Ja. I.

in getting married again; on 22 November she wed a sporting gentleman named Sir John Pakington of Worcester, Sheriff of the County, well known in Court circles. In the county he was known as "Lusty Pakington", "a big stalwart fellow, hasty tempered but good-natured and lovable ... an athlete who excelled in all the manly exercises of his day."[1]

He had an estate at Aylesbury; *and Sir John and his wife Lady Pakington entertained King James on his way from Scotland to the English Throne in 1603.*

> He gave such a noble welcome that their Royal Guest declared he had never been better entertained, *and this was the entrance of Lady Dorothy and her children to the Royal Circle.*[2]

The better to house his four stepdaughters and a son born to him by Lady Dorothy, he had built a family mansion which he called Westwood Park at Hampton Lovat, one of the most charming parts of England, not far from Droitwich, where he could indulge his passion for country sports, fishing, hunting, swimming, etc. From Westwood Park he roamed the wilds with his four romping, charming stepdaughters—Elizabeth, Alice, Dorothy and Bridget. They must have made an attractive quartet. They were a very happy family in Sir John's early years, but Sir John was choleric and Lady Dorothy was equally short-tempered. He was of a litigious nature, constantly quarrelling with his neighbours over rights of way and the like. He sunk a low-lying farm under water to make a large lake in which he could fish and swim. It was the wonder and bugbear of the county. The countryside rose against the innovation as an infringement of an ancient right of way. He was non-suited in the Court. In his wrath he smashed the dams and flooded the country over a couple of miles in area, the delighted peasantry picking up the gasping fish for their own use. The balladmongers got hold of the incident, made a broadsheet of it, wedded to the story a merry tune, and called it "Parkington's Pond". It ran round a laughing county, London and the Court. The tune is to be found in *Queen Elizabeth's Virginal Book*.

One can now understand how Francis Bacon came to know the Pakington family and Sir John's stepdaughter, Alice. *It is not at all unlikely that it was at the Aylesbury Estate that Francis Bacon interviewed James when he met the King on the journey to the South; that here he saw Alice for the first time; and that a very decided hint was dropped by James regarding his host's stepdaughter.* In any case, Pakington was such an out-of-the-way character that he would be well known by repute to Francis Bacon. But I incline to the belief that it was at Sir John's home, and at the King's command, that Francis Bacon first became acquainted with "sweet little Alice". ...

After the wedding breakfast Sir Francis and his "bride" drove to Gorhambury, to "The Temple", his old home, where Lady Anne Bacon still lived, her once brilliant intellect then becoming slowly deranged. It can be well understood, however, that much of Francis Bacon's time would be spent in London, while Alice would have much to do ere long in running the home and gradually taking over the reins from Lady Anne's faltering fingers.

From the time of Lord Campbell it has been the fashion to decry Francis

[1] *Life of Alice Barnham*, p. 9, A. Chambers Bunting, to whom I am indebted for much information.
[2] *Ibid.*, p. 10.

Bacon's marriage as being purely a mercenary one. "He married for money!" But the facts do not bear this out. Hepworth Dixon says:

> Alice brings to her husband £220 per year, with a further claim on her mother's death, of £140 per year. As Lady Pakington outlived Bacon, that increase never came into his hands. What is not spent in lace and satins for her bridal dress, he allows her to invest for her separate use. From his own estate he settles on her £500 a year.[1]

Francis Bacon was no longer poor. Anthony's death had given him the manor of Gorhambury. He held the leases of Cheltenham and Charlton Kings; Selwood Forest and Twickenham Park; *these were all the GIFTS of Queen Elizabeth.* He had missed any State office but he knew that marriage would open the doors ... the patent of Solicitor-General might be his, a judgeship, the Privy Council, the Seals. He was rich, too, in genius, in his ideals, in the seeds of secret accomplishments already sown all over the kingdom with the certain promise of a world harvest of duties well performed and days well spent. He was also rich in his friends, his disciples here and on the Continent; there was the earnest of philosophic splendour on his brow and the even greater reward of pure literary renown that was destined to seat him in a future age in Apollo's creative chair. He was rich materially, mentally, spiritually beyond the dreams of avarice.

Alice's fortune was less than Francis Bacon's estate. Her social rank a little less (leaving out of account his royal birth) than his standing as a knight. Spedding writes:

> In outward circumstances it appears to have been a very suitable match. ... Taking his position and suitable prospects into account, it was certainly a good match for her, nor was it a bad one for him.[2]

According to Mrs. Chambers Bunting, their early married life was frequently disturbed by continual quarrels that arose between Sir John Pakington and his wife. Over and over again Francis Bacon was called in by Lady Pakington to pour oil on the troubled waters to "right her wrongs". He was "frequently annoyed by his mother-in-law's dangerous interference in his home life".[3] On one occasion Sir John, after a stormy scene, turned his wife out of the home and she actually appealed to the Privy Council for restitution. At length Francis Bacon wearied of Lady Pakington's repeated attempts to embroil him and his wife in their quarrels, and so we have a letter—about the only one which gives a glimpse of Francis Bacon's domestic asides—addressed to Lady Pakington in answer to an upbraiding note for not coming to her assistance against her husband.

> Madam,
> You shall with right good will be made acquainted with anything that concerneth your daughter if you bear a mind of Love and Concord, otherwise you must be content to be a stranger to us; for I may not be so unwise as to suffer you to be an author or occasion of dissention between your daughters and their husbands, having seen so much misery of that in yourself. ...

[1] *Story of Lord Bacon's Life*, p. 218.
[2] *op. cit.*, Vol. III, p. 292.
[3] *Life of Alice Barnham*, p. 16.

But it is time to make an end of these follies, and you shall at this time pardon me this one fault of writing to you, for I mean to do it no more till you use me and respect me as you ought. So wishing you better than it seemeth you will draw upon yourself, I rest yours,

Fr. Bacon

Thus he tried to keep the peace, maintain his dignity and steer clear of Lady Pakington, who had apparently developed into a shrew, and of Sir John's everlasting lawsuits and arguments.

It is an amazing puzzle to me that not a single biographer has commented on the fact that a man of forty-six—the ripest scholar and genius ever known—married a girl barely fourteen. Not one has asked, "*How came it about? How did he come to announce his intention to marry Alice Barnham to the King when she was a mere child of eleven?*" Is there not a manifest mystery here that demands explanation? Not a single writer has ever tried to probe the reason. They have slurred over the disparity in their ages as though it were the most natural thing in the world for a man of forty-six to wed a child of fourteen, whereas everyone knows that when December weds June there is always an ulterior motive—wealth, honour, ambition—apart from love. It is obvious that when forty-six weds fourteen there is a "something" concealed deep below the surface facts.

One is forced to conclude that it is more than probable that when Francis Bacon assured the King of his loyalty and that he wished to be of service to him, James answered, "I shall raise no objections to your marrying one of the Pakington girls." Francis Bacon's marriage thus falls into line with everything that has gone before. There was a cogent reason for his marrying a commoner and an equally cogent reason why he should regard himself as a guardian more than a husband, a loving father rather than a lover.

In 1606 there could not possibly have been any intellectual bond between them. She could not have appreciated his intellectual labours, his ethical plans, the secret ideals and connections of Francis Bacon the man of the world, the concealed poet, the secret philosopher; but *I also think she became wise to them gradually.* The evidence is to be seen in their later relationships. She is certain to have matured quickly under the warmth of his affection. I am sure Alice became at last privy to his secrets.

Whatever their marital relations were as she grew to maturity, the fact remains that the marriage was a childless one. How could he become a parent under such circumstances? *A child with Tudor blood in his veins would be in perpetual danger.* I am quite satisfied that the renunciation of parenthood was mutual on the part of both; and that Alice Barnham, in more ways than one, sacrificed herself (along with other loyal friends) that he might complete his divine mission. There for the moment we can leave Lady Alice in charge of "The Temple" while her husband begins to tread the perilous paths of State office. The marriage had satisfied James that "Sir Francis" only sought to serve the State loyally, for the year following, 25 June 1607, he got his foot on the first rung of the State ladder.

Chapter II

KING JAMES: HIS FIRST PARLIAMENT: FRANCIS BACON, AGED FORTY-FIVE, BECOMES SOLICITOR GENERAL (1603–1607)

LET us now glance at the character of King James the man with whom Francis Bacon was destined to be associated until the "betrayal" of 1621. Elizabeth had sized him up when he was a youth of fifteen "as a double-tongued scoundrel". All the evidence goes to prove that she was completely right in her estimate. Historians and biographers alike declare that James I was the most unkingly monarch that ever sat on the Throne of England, "a hare in the seat of a lioness". Elizabeth with all her faults was regal to the fingertips. Her successor slowly proved himself a hypocrite, a coward and a poltroon, slothful in action and ignoble in soul.

J.R. Green, the historian, thus describes him:

> His big head, his slobbering tongue, his quilted clothes, his rickety legs, stood out in as grotesque a contrast with all that men recalled of Henry or Elizabeth as his want of personal dignity, his buffoonery, his coarseness of speech, his pedantry and cowardice.[1]

He revelled in unclean stories and songs; the duties of Sir Edward Zouch and Sir John Finit were to compose bawdy stories and songs for his amusement. He arranged "progresses" through the Kingdom in order to get away from his wife. He was usually accompanied by a crowd of boon and loose companions. He had always one special male "favourite" whom he slavered over publicly. From Scots favourites like Esme Stuart, Arran, Gray, Bothwell, Ramsey, Hay, he turned to English ones: Philip Herbert, then Robert Carr, "the Perfect Companion", who afterwards became the infamous Earl of Somerset. Carr was James's constant companion from the King's fortieth to his forty-seventh year; then the still more infamous George Villiers, afterwards Duke of Buckingham, took his place.

A contemporary wrote:

> As no other reason appeared in favour of their choice but handsomeness, so the love the King showed them was as amorously conveyed as if he had mistaken their sex and thought them ladies. ... Nor was his Love, *or what else posterity will please to call it*, carried on with a discretion sufficient to cover a less scandalous behaviour.

Everything points to the fact that James I was a homosexualist of the worst type.

He was a sadist too. He delighted in torture. He watched the Gunpowder

[1] *History of English People*, p. 464.

Plotters racked, and enjoyed the spectacle. He played cat and mouse with Sir Walter Raleigh for years; and then he executed him to please the King of Spain and his own petty spite. Before he came to England he had tortured and put to death hundreds of innocent men, women and children on the vile accusation of witchcraft, justifying his conduct by writing a book on demonology (1597). He had no sooner ascended the English Throne than the same wholesale butchery began again. He insisted on the use of torture in England where the law never seems actually to have sanctioned its use.

> In the Gowrie affair, 1600, whatever may be the hidden truth *he showed himself a murderous intriguer. He cannot even be acquitted of matricide,* for it has now been established beyond question that *he could have saved Mary, Queen of Scots from execution had he wished.*[1]

The fact is that he wanted the English Crown and he allowed Mary to be put upon her so-called farcical trial and conviction without making any attempt at interference. Instead, he wrote to the Earl of Leicester (*of all people*) saying:

> How fond [foolish], and inconstant I were *if I should prefer my mother to the TITLE,* let all men judge.

An utterly heartless brute!

And Mary betrayed by all, including James, died on the scaffold at Fotheringay! Was he her son? His utter callousness and lack of filial piety seem to indicate that he was not kin to her. He was utterly unlike her in *every* respect—physically, mentally, spiritually. Mary Stuart was a woman of great courage and tenacity and intelligence.

In short, James was a past master in the craft of deceit. Here is a specimen. An eyewitness recorded the last parting between Somerset and the King, who had grown tired of him and wanted to put young Villiers in his place. Says Israel D'Israeli, in his *Curiosities of Literature:*

> The Earl of Somerset never parted from him with more seeming affection than at this time when he knew Somerset should never see him more. ... The Earl, when he kissed his hand, the King hung about his neck, slobbering his cheeks, saying, "For God's sake when shall I see thee again?"
>
> The Earl told him, "On Monday" (this being Friday). "For God's sake, let me," said the King. "Shall I? Shall I?" Then lolled about his neck. Then "For God's sake, give thy lady this kiss from me". In the same manner at the stairs' head, at the middle of the stairs, and at the stairs' foot.
>
> *The Earl was not in his coach when he used these very words "I shall never see his face more."*

This gives insight into his character. The King was steeped in hypocrisy. James had, in short, only what Francis Bacon called "a kind of crooked Wisdom". His kingly word was only given to be broken if necessary. This shifty kind of dissimulation to gain his own ends he regarded as smart business

[1]Williamson, p. 16.28.

that violated no moral principle. There may have been worse sovereigns than James but none for whom we have less respect and more contempt. A French statesman named him as "the wisest fool in Christendom", while a Scots divine called him, as he shook the King by the sleeve, "God's silly vassal". He could only be compared to the murderous, traitorous and grasping Scots peers who betrayed and sold Queen Mary.

Let the character of this man be remembered as we judge his dealings with and his subsequent treatment of Francis Bacon.

James was thirty-seven when he came to England in utter ignorance of the spirit of the English people (he was five years younger than Francis Bacon). He had been cradled in the narrow temper of feudalism. He thought he could ride roughshod over the few liberties that Englishmen possessed; could dismiss parliaments, govern without them, levy taxes for his private expenses, and act generally as a feudal monarch to "gang his ain gait" as he chose without consulting Commons or people. He insisted on his full feudal rights more than had any of his warlike predecessors. He raised storms and then cowered under the resultant tempests, ever seeking to interpose innocent scapegoats on whom to lay the blame. In his reign the great dispute began to determine the limits of regal and popular power—whether the King's feudal Prerogative was still to run when it was obviously a menace to the health of the nation economically, socially and politically. It ended with his son's head rolling in the dust and the triumph of Parliament.

We have seen how Elizabeth gracefully surrendered her Prerogative over certain unpopular impositions. But James of the narrow mind, tactless, avaricious, with his claim to be above the Law as a God-appointed King—a ruler by Divine Right—could not conceive but that the entire nation were hewers of wood and drawers of waters to do his bidding, to bow down to his dictates. This was the spirit that animated his actions all through his reign—twisting, deceiving and lying—for he thought that his commands alone were the voice of God.

These grave defects of character were not known when he crossed the border to sit on the Throne of England. All that the populace knew was that he was an avowed Protestant and that they were to be saved from a repetition of the Wars of the Roses and the Fires of Smithfield. He had the reputation of being a scholar, a poet, a theologian, a philosopher and an author of a number of books. His general mentality as a man, a scholar, a sovereign was but superficially understood by everyone. On hearsay evidence he was taken on trust, reputed to be widely read as a theologian and a philosopher. He desired the credit of seeming to encourage learning. Men of letters rejoiced at his accession. Virtuous men believed for a while that moral goodness would be fostered in the Court and nation. Francis Bacon thought that if he safely negotiated the hurdle of his Tudor birth and won the King's confidence in time he (Francis) would find a powerful ally for his ethical and educational ideals, which could be fostered almost as a recreation after State activities. It was this belief "that made me FIRST your Slave, that I could in THOUGHT control your Hours of Leisure."

For Francis Bacon, as for the nation, there came slow disillusionment as the King's true character slowly unfolded and his personal vices seeped into the light of day. Too late, after he had definitely become the King's servant—

kissing hands and taking the Oath—Francis Bacon was faced with the shattering realization that James was never the Solomon he had imagined and that the King was possessed by an intensely personal selfishness, a looking-after "Number One", and the devil take the hindmost.

The fact is that James was never a scholar any more than he was a statesman or a moralist, although he was "educated" by George Buchanan, "a humanist with a European reputation", and Lady Mar (who was, it has been contended on certain little-known evidence, his real mother). She tended him from his earliest moments, jealously guarded him as he grew to understanding and shriekingly intervened when he was being spanked by Buchanan. Between them they taught him Latin, history, poetry, theology and, above all, the distorted details of the imprisoned Queen Mary in the castles of England who, they told him:

> had been art and part in the killing of his father and had debauched herself with lovers, and had been rightly chained from her wickedness by the Holy Champions of God; of his mother. ...
>
> In 1574, when he was eight [to the English agent Killigrew], he was walked up and down by Lady Mar and made to display his capacities.[1]

He was early indoctrinated with the idea that there was no one like him in Scotland, that he was SUPREME, but that if his "mother" Mary of Scotland returned he would no longer be unique—a royal phoenix—and that the consequences might be disastrous *for him personally*.

This particularly applies to the way in which James treated the advice tendered to him by Francis Bacon, the wisest head, the most sagacious statesman, the greatest intellectual in Christendom. Some short-sighted publicists have said that Francis Bacon must be held responsible for the King's domestic and foreign policies after Cecil's death in May 1612, which is not true, for James ruled by and ruled through his favourites, consistently ignoring the advice of his "First Law Lord and Advocate". The utmost that Francis Bacon could do was to tender advice, to counsel a certain course of action. *He had no executive power to carry out any plans without the King's consent.* He was rebuffed repeatedly and his counsel set at naught. Dean Church admits:

> James and Buckingham would have been very different in their measures and their statesmanship if they had listened to him.[2]

Church even says:

> On all the great questions of the time he [Francis Bacon] has left behind abundant evidence, not only of what he thought, but of *what he advised*. And in every case these memorials are marked with the insight, the independence, the breadth of view and the moderation of *a mind which is bent on truth*.

The historian, Professor Gardiner, sums up the position thus in his *History*:

> There is in the State Papers drawn up by Francis Bacon in 1613 for the King's signature, one which, if carried out, would have averted the evils of the next half

[1]C. Williams, *James I*, p. 24.
[2]*Bacon*, p. 155.

century. It was his fate through life to give good advice only to be rejected. If James had been other than he was, the name of Francis Bacon ought to have come down to us as great in politics as it is in science.

Some critics conveniently choose to forget that James was a despot and that no one in that age dared have run counter to his will without treading on the borderline of treason. The King claimed to be above the Law, even above the Common Law judges when he disagreed with their interpretations. James said to Coke on one notable occasion when Coke held that the judges were right, contrary to the expressed views of James, "Then you affirm I shall be under the Law which IT IS TREASON to affirm."[1] Coke retracted on his bended knees.

Today it is difficult to think that anyone could seriously believe that *the King could do no wrong* and that necessarily he *ruled by Divine Right* as having been appointed directly by God Himself. Yet the great Samuel Johnson professed his belief in the Divine Right of Kings and so did that eminent statesman William Pitt, Lord Chatham. The sovereign is no longer the sovereign power nowadays, but in James's day it was verging on treason to deny the doctrine openly.

Extraordinary as it seems to be, the doctrine that the King in his office as King can do no wrong was believed in most firmly by Francis Bacon. He believed with all his heart that for the age in which he lived—so full of gunpowder, threats of war, plots and civil insurrections—our political system should take the form of a benevolent autocracy, consisting of a King of absolute and royal power ruling with the aid of a House of Lords and a democratic House of Commons where the voice of the people could be heard. These three estates should constitute Parliament to rule and govern the nation. Francis Bacon saw no hope for orderly or intelligent government save by a ruler who, in the last resort, had the wisdom and the strength to assert himself if necessary by the use of his Prerogative, an Argus-eyed King who was in touch and sympathy with popular feeling.

James had been called to the Throne by the entire nation. The voice of the people was the audible voice of God. Bacon therefore bowed to the inevitable with a good grace, believing in the wisdom of God's providence, although legitimately he was a Tudor. James had been divinely appointed and Francis Bacon therefore desired nothing better than to serve him loyally as a good servant. While the King as a person could do wrong—deceive, gamble, lie, drink—when he acted in his office as King he could do no wrong, for the King's will was of divine origin and God could not err. The argument runs exactly similar to the Roman Catholic one of the Middle Ages; the Pope as a man may be frail and sin, but in his sacred office as Pope he is infallible and he can do no wrong.

In other words, Francis Bacon realized with a certain amount of truth that, in the troublous and treacherous times through which Queen Elizabeth had passed, there must be somewhere in the State a final authority who could impose the royal will on one and all if the State were in danger.

When Francis Bacon kissed hands on his first State appointment his oath

[1]Gardiner, *History*, Vol. II, p. 39.

of allegiance to James was just as binding on him as a military one today. He became the King's servant, to obey his commands and to sacrifice himself if necessary to save his master or the commonwealth. He was at once under a form of Law akin to military rule. He had to carry out the command of his superior officer no matter the consequence. It was Francis Bacon's staunch observance of these political beliefs that so greatly contributed to his ultimate ruin as a statesman and publicist.

Round these two men the history of nearly the next quarter of a century revolves. No amount of reading will lead to any real understanding of the open and secret history of the times unless the characters of these utterly diverse personages be placed in juxtaposition and adequately considered—one a King by Divine Right, the other a King by birth and by genius; one a contemptible, mean-souled pervert mentally incapable of reflection on broad issues, whose insight into State and business affairs was bounded by personal desires; the other an altruistic Colossus bestriding the world *in every department of human thought,* through whose brain once ran the noblest thoughts ever conceived by the soul of man. Says Nichol:

> That Bacon believed there would be a change for the better under a Monarch of whom his first impressions had been really favourable, may be granted.[1]

> It needed months or years to reveal the King's fatal deficiency in earnestness, his inconstancy of purpose, his inability to sympathise with an English House of Commons, and his want of political foresight. Even a cool observer might therefore have augured well at first concerning the new reign; and Bacon was one of the most blindly sanguine of observers.[2]

These admissions from two of Francis Bacon's most bitter critics more than prove that he honestly believed the new King would gradually in a spirit of tolerance and sweet reasonableness learn to understand the temper of the English people and thus cement the bonds between them. He was full of the spirit of hope that James would help him to work out his great schemes of practical reform and the advancement of human knowledge. But James from his youth up had only regarded the State as a milch cow, valued in proportion to the number of golden butterkegs it could produce. Francis Bacon's idea was to draw the King and the people together in bonds of affection by a larger "tolerance of creeds and gradual reform". The all-powerful, narrow-minded Cecil's sole outlook and concern was to strike hard bargains between sovereign and subject, and to bleed in body and pocket recusants in religion and politics. This mischievous policy found favour in the sight of the King and was a troublesome State heritage bequeathed by Cecil years later to his successor Francis Bacon. Indeed, at the very commencement of his reign in England James began to trade his favours to the English gentry who, willy-nilly, must barter their gold for James's "Honours".

Before he had been three months in England the King had made about seven hundred Knights, a general summons beng issued that all persons possessing £40 a year in land should either accept this title or compound

[1]John Nichol, *Francis Bacon*, Vol. I, p. 70.
[2]Abbott, *Francis Bacon*, p. 103.

with the King's commissioners. By this wretched expedient he filled his coffers and debased the title of knight that had hitherto been considered an especial mark of royal favour. This act was the germ from which there afterwards sprang the system of the Crown selling State offices to the highest bidder, the disposal of peerages, baronetcies, etc., for hard cash.

Though Francis Bacon was left unemployed he was not idle. With splendid audacity he began to prepare papers on the pressing subjects of the day for the guidance of the King as he had previously done for Elizabeth. James should at least know the best way to go by the erection of Francis Bacon's signposts.

Now the Union of England and Scotland was one of the primary main objects of the new King; and because Francis Bacon believed that union was strength and that it was essential for the prosperity of both kingdoms, he was wholeheartedly in favour of the idea (although he knew that the majority of Englishmen viewed it with disfavour) and resolved to support the measure with voice and pen. He therefore wrote a short treatise of some 4000 words entitled, *A BRIEF DISCOURSE TOUCHING THE HAPPY UNION OF THE KINGDOMS OF ENGLAND AND SCOTLAND, Dedicated in private to his Majesty.*

The document was printed in 1603. It let James know that Francis Bacon intended to champion the proposed Union openly as a Parliamentarian and it also let him see that Francis Bacon had taken *the first opportunity of recognizing James publicly as his overlord.* At the end of this treatise he says:

> *Thus having in all humbleness made OBLATION to your Majesty of these simple fruits of my Devotion and Studies, I do wish that the Happy Union of your Majesty's two Kingdoms of England and Scotland may be in as good an hour and under the like Divine Providence, as that was between the Romans and the Sabines.*
>
> *Fr. Bacon*

The die was cast. He had acknowledged in print the sovereignty of James Stuart and that he would champion the Union in the House of Commons, though he knew that nearly every other member would be opposed to admitting the "beggarly Scots" on equal terms.

Another matter exercising men's minds, vital to the religious life of the nation, was the dispute in the Establishment between the High Churchmen and the Puritans on various doctrinal points. Elizabeth had decreed that Protestantism should "go so far but no farther"; but what may be termed an Evangelical or Puritan form of worship, as opposed to Ritualistic practice, had been growing in influence and numbers throughout her reign. Elizabeth's death left the problem to be adjusted by her successor. Hence the Hampton Court Conference in January 1604, when the bishops and the Puritans met under the presidency of James, who, as a philosophic theologian, was thought by repute to be eminently qualified to compose their differences. Elizabeth had been committed to a static policy. James was new. It would have been comparatively easy for him to have dealt wisely and tolerantly with the conflicting views threatening to rend the Church.

"The conference was called to settle the differences between the main body of the Church of England and the Puritans within it who demanded, in effect, that the Anglican settlement should be made Protestant in appearance"; and that the Church should be shorn of any Catholic trappings that had adorned it from the time of the Reformation. Papal supremacy had been destroyed without impairing more than was necessary Roman Catholic doctrine—on the ground of political expediency. The Puritans disliked a State Church which still indulged in Roman Catholic ceremonial—interrogation of infants at baptism, making the sign of the Cross, bowing at the name of Jesus, etc. This Puritanical creed was BASED MAINLY on the Mosaic Laws, and was akin in many ways to Judaism:

> These things, which involved no actual doctrinal change, formed the basis of their demands at Hampton Court, and *it is worthy of note that the man who was both the greatest political philosopher of the age and the most popular Member of the House of Commons—Francis Bacon—pleaded with James for their consideration. Had the King followed his advice of breadth and vision, it would have obviated centuries of strife.*

Before the Conference met, Francis Bacon presented the King with a treatise headed, *CERTAIN CONSIDERATIONS TOUCHING THE BETTER PACIFICATION AND EDIFICATION OF THE CHURCH OF ENGLAND. Dedicated to his Most Excellent Majesty.*

It was written shortly after he had received from the King "a gracious recognition" of his manuscript on the "Union".

It will be remembered that Francis Bacon had already written on the *Controversies of the Church* in 1589 in which he held the scales evenly between the opposing parties, asserting that CHARITY was the *sine qua non* of true religion whether Ritualist or Puritan. In this treatise of some 10,000 words he goes into considerable detail in his advocacy of reform in the Church. At the end of the treatise he writes:

> I end with my devout and fervent prayer to God, that as he hath made your Majesty THE CORNERSTONE in joining your TWO KINGDOMS so you may be also as a CORNER-STONE to Unite and Knit together these differences in the Church of God. To whose Heavenly Grace and never erring Direction I commend your Majesty's Sacred Person and all your doings.

What the King thought about Francis Bacon's suggestions we do not know but he went down to the Conference to preside not exactly ignorant of the position and full of these illuminating thoughts—presuming, of course, that he had read and digested them. The disputants before him were the Archbishop of Canterbury, eight bishops, seven deans and two of the lesser clergy; on the other side were four Puritans, led by Dr. John Reynolds, who had an unrivalled reputation as a Greek scholar. Instead of listening judicially and delivering his judgment later after sifting, weighing and thinking, the King almost immediately began to dispute statements with which he did not agree. Hating the Presbyterianism of the Kirk of Scotland, a chance remark by Reynolds made James rashly conclude that Puritanism was the equivalent of Presbyterianism—a fatal mistake; and so he told the Puritans: "You are aiming at a Scotch Presbytery which agreeth as well with a Monarchy as God and the Devil." He railed at the idea of extempore speaking. "Jack and Tom and Will and Dick shall meet and at their pleasure censure me and my

Council and all our proceedings. ... You let that alone." He left the room remarking: "If this be all they have to say I shall make them conform themselves or I will harry them out of the land, *or else do worse*," whereupon a bishop observed, "His Majesty spoke by inspiration of the Spirit of God."

In all the Conference lasted three days, and although there were fifteen "Notes of things as shall be reformed" the Puritans gained no part of their case save one. In short, the King had peremptorily rejected Francis Bacon's advice. To the Puritan doctors who pleaded for elasticity of ceremonial James said emphatically:

> I will have none of that. I will have one Doctrine, one Discipline, one Religion, *in Substance and Ceremony*. Never speak more on that point—how far you are bound to obey ... I approve the calling and use of Bishops in the Church, and it is my aphorism—No Bishop, no King.

The King's failure to meet the wishes of the Puritans in any way simply led to the inevitability of the Nonconformist Churches of the future. Instead of the National State Church being sufficiently broad enough to take under its banners the Evangelical, the Ritualist and the Latitudinarian, James simply drove the Presbyterians out of the Establishment.

There can be no doubt that the Puritan defeat very largely contributed to the subsequent Civil War. That, and the levying of taxes without representation—which really began with James and came to a head in his son's reign—was the origin of the disasters which overtook Charles. "In two minutes James sealed his own Fate and the Fate of England for ever."

Yet all was not lost. Famous as was the Conference because of the defeat of the Puritans, they also won undying fame for one victory. "In the tooth of the opposition of the future Archbishop of Canterbury and his clerical supporters, *the Puritans gained their request for a New Translation of the Bible.*" The Authorized Version of 1611 will for ever stand as a memorial of that one solitary victory in which destiny decreed that Francis Bacon should play an immortal part as its secret editor. Even Dr. Abbott cannot forbear to write respecting Francis Bacon's advice to the King.

> Had these sensible and statesmanlike views been adopted, the Church of England might now have been made to include, and might perhaps now include, all but a small minority of the nation; and the adoption of this ecclesiastical policy might have gone far to conciliate the House of Commons and to prevent the civil war which was to fall upon the next generation.

About this time—1603–4 so it is supposed—when he had little or nothing to do for the State or the Law Courts, Francis Bacon wrote "in stately Latin" an autobiographical fragment which was found long after in his cabinet and published abroad by Gruter in 1653. This had not been translated until 1808 by Spedding so that the general public knew nothing about it for upwards of three hundred years. Its significance has never been seen. Spedding thinks that this fragment was the result of meditations relating solely to the writing of a work on natural philosophy.

Spedding writes:

> I imagine that the intervening months [between the King's Coronation, 23 July,

and the meeting of Parliament, 29 March 1604] were among the busiest and most exciting that he ever passed. *For this is the time* when I suppose him to have conceived the design of throwing his thoughts on Philosophy and Intellectual Progress into a popular form, and inviting the co-operation of mankind. ...[1]

On one of these days his imagination, wandering far into the future, showed him in vision the first instalment ready for publication and set him upon thinking how he should give it to the world. The result of this meditation he fortunately confided to a sheet of paper.[2]

A long line of writers have followed in Spedding's footsteps and have repeated what he thought. Yet *his idea is fundamentally wrong*; and a moment's reflection will prove it to be an erroneous suggestion. Spedding thinks that Francis Bacon had hit on the idea of a new interpretation of Nature in 1603, and that the first fruit was the actual writing of the *Advancement of Learning*, published some two years later, and from that work grew the six parts of *The Great Instauration* of which the *Advancement* was the first part. But this autobiographical fragment does not refer to something he is going to do in the future but to a work—a LABOUR—he had already accomplished. Spedding forgot that in the first volume of his work he had already written (p. 4) that:

before he had completed his fifteenth year ... the most important event of his life had happened, an event which had a greater influence than any other upon his life and course ... a Thought had struck him ... a better method for the study of nature. ...

He had the gift of seeing in prophetic vision what might be and ought to be *united with the practical talent of devising means and handling minute details*. He could at once imagine like a POET and execute like a Clerk of Works.

Upon the conviction *This may be done*, followed the question at once, *HOW may it be done?* ... Then followed the resolution to try to do it. ...

The suggestion ripened into a project, the project into an undertaking, and the undertaking unfolded itself into distinct proportions; of the full grandeur of its total dimensions I can say nothing.

From that moment there was awakened within his breast [*remember Spedding is writing of a boy of fourteen*] the appetite which cannot be satisfied ... which employed and stimulated all the energies of his mind, gave a value to every vacant interval of time, an interest and significance to every random thought and casual accession of Knowledge; *an object to live for as wide as humanity, as immortal as the human race; an idea to live in vast, and lofty enough to fill the soul for ever with religious and heroic aspirations.*

And now, in his third volume, Mr. Spedding would have us believe that this boy of fourteen, this profound genius of maturity, this "old" soul reincarnated, it may be claimed, for a special purpose to make England great, to fill the world with beautiful thoughts, lofty ideals, to uplift humanity by interpreting Nature in a new and wonderful method—he would have us believe that Francis Bacon had allowed the project to pass out of his mind until 1603 when he again "conceived the design of throwing his thoughts on Philosophy and Intellectual Progress into a popular form". For THIRTY

[1] Vol. III, p. 82.
[2] ibid., p. 84.

YEARS (we are now told) this youthful genius, who exuded energy at every pore, wasted himself, producing nothing towards realizing the heavenly vision of his early youth. What a disastrous mistake: can anyone honestly believe that Francis Bacon allowed the best years of his life to slip away into the lost eternities with nothing to his credit and that he only began to write in 1603?

The truth is that this autobiographical fragment not only embodies his own secret ideals but it indicates *what he had already done.* He has finished laying his secret bases for eternity. He has constructed "a *Machine*" which is a going concern, for

> *the making of ... something to purge the floors of men's understandings ... to circulate from mouth to mouth privately ... and to be committed to the charge of some fit and selected minds and kept private.*

What is all this but Francis Bacon's Secret Society akin to a Machine for the "MAKING" of something in a workshop—a Lodge, where men learn to moralize on Tools, spiritualize Temples, lift their eyes to the father of Lights, and study Nature and human nature by a new and novel method of symbolism.

This fragment mentioned by Spedding was intended as a "PROEM" to be placed in front of all his secret activities up to date. *The preface of a book is always the last bit of writing:* thus in this novel way Francis Bacon lets us know that he has accomplished what he set out to do and is ready for some other type of work. *It is not written as a "PREFACE" to open works he had not yet produced.* How could it be?

In the light of this interpretation we are now in a better position to appraise at its true value one of the most wonderful confessions of the human soul: every Freemason in particular can read between lines the handiwork of the great Architect and Master Builder:

Of the Interpretation of Nature
Proem

> Believing that *I was Born for the service of Mankind*, and regarding the care of the Commonwealth as a kind of common property which like the Air and the Water belong to everybody, I set myself to consider *in what way Mankind might be best served*, and what Service I was myself best fitted by Nature to perform.
>
> Now among all the Benefits that could be conferred upon Mankind, I found none so great as the Discovery of New Arts, Endowments and Commodities for *the Bettering of Man's Life.* For I saw that among the rude people in the primitive times, the Authors of rude Inventions and Discoveries were consecrated and numbered among the Gods. And it was plain that the good effects wrought by Founders of Cities, Law-givers, fathers of the People, extirpers of tyrants, and heroes of that class, extend but over narrow spaces and last but for short times; whereas *the work of the Inventor*, though a thing of less pomp and show, is felt everywhere and lasts for ever.
>
> But above all, if a man could succeed, not in striking out some particular Invention, however useful, but IN KINDLING A LIGHT IN NATURE—a Light which in its very rising *Touch and Illuminate* all the Border-regions that confine upon *the Circle* of our present Knowledge; and so spreading further and further should presently disclose and bring into sight all that is *MOST HIDDEN AND SECRET in the World*—that man (I thought) would be the Benefactor of the

Human Race—the Propagator of Man's Empire over the Universe, the Champion of Liberty, the Conqueror and Subduer of Necessitites.

For myself, I found that I was fitted for nothing so well as for the STUDY OF TRUTH; as having *a Mind nimble and versatile enough to catch the Resemblances of Things* (which is the chief point) and at the same time steady enough to fix and distinguish *their Subtler Differencies;* as being gifted by Nature with *Desire to SEEK,* patience to Doubt, fondness to Meditate, slowness to assert, readiness to consider, carefulness to dispose and set in order; and as being a man that neither affects what is new nor admires what is old, and that hates every kind of Imposture. So I thought my Nature had a kind of familiarity and Relationship with Truth.

[*Notice how this applies exactly to the creation of characters of various types, and the entire composition of a Shakespeare play; and particularly to Francis Bacon's exquisite symbolism inculcating the highest ethics in the interpretation of Nature in Freemasonry.*]

Nevertheless, because my Birth and Education had seasoned me in Business of State; and because opinions (so Young as I was) would sometime stagger me; and because I thought that a man's own Country has some special claims upon him more than the rest of the World; and because I hoped that, if I rose to any place of Honour in the State, *I should have a larger command of industry and ability to help me* in my work;—for these reasons I both applied myself to acquire the arts of civil life, and commended my service, so far as in Modesty and Honesty I might, to the favour of such Friends as had any influence. In which also I had another motive: for I felt that those things I have spoken of—be they great or small—reach no further than the condition and culture of this Mortal Life: and I was not without Hope (*the condition of Religion being at that time not very Prosperous*) that if I came to hold Office in the State, *I might get something done FOR THE GOOD OF MEN'S SOULS.*

[*At the age of forty-three we are told the thoughts animating him as a youth, that he required the assistance of others in the work he contemplated, and that his chief aim was not to do something merely to provide creature comforts for this mortal life but to DO SOMETHING for the good of men's souls as creedal religion was embittering men. This again points to Francis Bacon's secret Brotherhood based on ethics.*]

When I found however that my zeal was mistaken for ambition and that my life had already reached the turning-point, and my breaking health reminded me how ill I could afford to be so slow and I reflected moreover that in leaving undone the good that I could do by myself alone, and applying myself to that which could not be done without the help and consent of others, I was by no means discharging the duty that lay upon me—I put all those thoughts aside, and—in pursuance of my old determination—betook myself wholly to this WORK [i.e. *the doing of something for the good of men's souls educationally and ethically*].

Nor am I discouraged from it because *I SEE SIGNS* in the Times of the decline and overthrow of that Knowledge and Erudition which is now in use.

[*In short, Francis Bacon had already begun the overthrow of the academic system then in vogue, the renaissance of learning, the establishment of the English language in place of Latin; the founding of a system of definite ethical principles among chosen disciples had begun. There were DEFINITE SIGNS TO BE SEEN of his secret labours which encouraged him to devote himself wholly to the task—OPENLY as well as secretly.*]

Not that I apprehend any more barbarian invasions (unless possibly the Spanish Empire should recover its strength, and having crushed other nations by arms should itself sink under its own weight): but the Civil Wars which may be expected, I think, (judging of certain fashions which have come in of late) to spread through many countries—together with *the malignity of the Sects*, and those compendious Artificies and Devices which have crept into the place of solid Erudition—seem to portend for Literature and the Sciences a Tempest not less fatal, and one against which the Printing-Office will be no effectual security.

And no doubt but that Fair-Weather Learning which is nursed by Leisure, blossoms under reward and praise, which cannot withstand the Shock of Opinion, and is liable to be abused by tricks and quackery, will sink under impediments as those. [Francis Bacon shows himself utterly averse to the Scholastic system that in his day took everything for granted when uttered by "Authority" without personal research and understanding. Fair-weather knowledge which cannot stand the test.]

Far otherwise is it with that Knowledge, whose Dignity is maintained by Works of Utility and Power. For the injuries therefore which should proceed from the Times, I am not afraid of them; and from the injuries which proceed from men I am not concerned. For if anyone charge me with seeking TO BE WISE overmuch, I answer simply that modesty and civil respect are fit for civil matters; *in Contemplation nothing is to be respected but TRUTH.*

If anyone call upon me for WORKS, and that presently, I tell him frankly, *without any Imposture at all*, that for me—a man not old, of weak health, my hands full of Civil Business, *entering without GUIDE or LIGHT upon an Argument* of all others the most Obscure,—*I hold it enough to have constructed the MACHINE*, though I may not succeed in setting it on WORK. Nay, with the same CANDOUR I Profess and Declare, that the Interpretation of Nature, rightly conducted, ought in the *FIRST STEPS of the ASCENT*, until a certain Stage of Generals be reached, to be kept clear of all application to Works.

[*This is definite Masonic phraseology: "Guide," "Light", "Candour", "First Steps", "Ascent", "Works", "Profess" and "Declare". Francis Bacon tells us, moreover, that he has constructed a "Machine". What is this but a workshop, a Lodge, for the making of Masons? If he cannot set it "on WORK" it is because workmen are required. It is more than a one-man job. Further, the Machine is connected with the interpretation of Nature. It is neither an ordinary Machine nor an ordinary invention for purely physical ends. It is for educational and ethical ends. It applies and can only apply to the Masonic system which mysteriously arose in the Elizabethan era.*]

And this in fact has been the error of all those who have heretofore ventured themselves at all upon the Waves of Experience—that being either too weak of purpose or *too eager for display*, they have all at the outset sought prematurely for Works, as Proofs and Pledges of their Progress, and upon that Rock have been wrecked and cast away. [*In other words, Francis Bacon is not going to tell what he had already accomplished. He is not flaunting his secret societies before the world as proofs of the progress already made.*]

If again, anyone ask me, not indeed for actual Works [i.e. *products that the "Machine" has made*] yet for definite promises and forecasts of the Works that are to be, I would have him know that the KNOWLEDGE THAT WE NOW POSSESS will not teach a man even what to WISH. [*It will only teach him WHAT TO BE.*]

Lastly,—though this is a matter of less moment—if any of our Politicians, who used to make their calculations and conjectures according to persons and precedents, must needs interpose his judgment in a Thing of this Nature,—I would but remind him how (according to the ancient Fable,) *the lame man keeping the Course* won the race of the swift man who left it: and there is no thought to be taken about Precedents, *FOR THE THING IS WITHOUT PRECEDENT*. [*The Masonic system is unique in itself.*]

Now for my plan of PUBLICATION—Those PARTS OF THE WORK [*note that* The Great Instauration *as announced in 1621 consisted of six parts, three open and three concealed and that the parts were already planned in 1603*] which have it for their object to find out and bring into correspondence SUCH MINDS AS ARE PREPARED and DISPOSED for the Argument, and to Purge the Floors of Men's Understandings, I WISH TO BE PUBLISHED TO THE WORLD AND

CIRCULATE FROM MOUTH TO MOUTH [*that is Part IV the Shakespeare plays*]: The REST I would have passed from HAND TO HAND, with Selection and Judgment. [*The Rosicrucian MSS and the Masonic Rituals, Parts V and VI, which did pass from hand to hand in 1603.*]

Not but I know that it is an old Trick of Imposters to keep a few of their follies back from the public which are indeed no better than those they put forward: but in this case it is no imposture at all, but a sober foresight, which tells me that the FORMULA ITSELF OF INTERPRETATION [the Rituals] and *the DISCOVERIES MADE BY THE SAME*, will thrive better if committed *to the Charge of some Fit and Selected Minds, and Kept PRIVATE.* [What is this but a subtle method of announcing a secret society of fit and proper persons who shall perpetuate the tenets of the craft?]

This however is other people's concern [i.e. the tenets will pass from hand to hand and from age to age after he has gone]. For myself, my Heart is not set upon any of those Things which depend upon external accidents. I am not hunting for Fame: *I have no desire to found a Sect*, after the fashion of Heresiarchs [prime heretics]; and to look for any private gain from such *an Undertaking as this*, I count both ridiculous and base. Enough for me the consciousness of well-deserving, and *those real and effectual Results* with which Fortune itself cannot interfere. [From this it is quite clear that Francis Bacon had FOUNDED something ... not a SECT but a BROTHERHOOD that gathered its members from all the Sects ... a something that had to do with the MAKING of bad men into good men and good men into better.]

This piece of autobiography is the key to Francis Bacon's concealed labours for the past twenty-five years, the key that Spedding missed, for he simply never dreamed of connecting the rise of Freemasonry in that era with Francis Bacon and Part VI of his great plan: the interpretation of the mechanical laws of Nature by ethical symbolism, a Grand Lodge Above, a Great Architect. Spedding spent thirty years looking for the "*Formula of Interpretation of Nature*", which was to explain all Nature's processes by some elaborate *mechanical machinery*. He never found such a key and therefore came to the conclusion there was not one. He was wrong. The key was an ethical one. And a man—even though he be not a Freemason—must be indeed blind who cannot see that Francis Bacon for the amelioration of mankind had set himself up as an ethical teacher with his secret body of disciples who laboured with him in secret.

Yet though Spedding missed his way he nevertheless got very near to the truth. His comments on the "Proem" prove the position.

Such was the project with which Bacon was *all the time labouring in secret;* such and no less, the issues which he believed to be involved in it. ... He knew it could not be fairly tried without *the co-operation of many men and of more than one generation. ...*[1]

What we have to understand and remember is the *Nature of the Enterprise and that he believed it practicable.* ... He believed that he had by accident stumbled upon a Thought, which duly followed out would in the course of generations *make men the Master* ... and that it was his Mission to make men think so and point out the way. ... I suppose not a single day went down in which he did not remember with a sigh, or a resolution, or a prayer, that the work was still undone.[2]

Today we see with clearer eyes than Spedding's that Francis Bacon's

[1]Spedding, *op. cit,* Vol III, p. 87.
[2]Spedding, *op. cit,* Vol III, p. 84.

"Proem" was at once the preface and finale to some of his secret labours. He had constructed the Machine. It had passed into the hands of his disciples to bequeath to future ages. With them lay the power to make it go or stand still.

That this interpretation is not a fanciful dream is proved by Francis Bacon's letter of some two years later to his close literary friend Tobie Matthew, then in Italy, who was with him at Gray's Inn as a college youth and privy to all his secrets.

> The relation which here I send carries the truth of that which is public [the Gunpowder Plot].
>
> *I have now at last taught THAT CHILD TO GO at the Swadling whereof you were.*
>
> I send you a copy [*The Advancement of Learning*] who have more right to it than any man, except Bishop Andrewes, who was MY INQUISITOR.

No commentator has ever tried to interpret these enigmatical phrases. What is the "Child"? What is its destination? What does the "Swadling" mean? Obviously it is something that has sprung from the brain of the inventor as Pallas from Jupiter. Tobie Matthew was there when it was created; when it was tried out in secret, the Machine that went "Round and Round". Tobie Matthew was there at the birth of Francis Bacon's brainchild.

He watched it dressed in its *swaddling clothes* as a founder of the first Freemason's Lodge of Gentlemen in all the world. What is "swadling" but "clothing"? And is not "clothing" of the right kind a *sine qua non* among Masons? Francis Bacon is telling Brother Tobie that he has taught the first Lodge to perpetuate itself in the winter of 1605. It had become a Mother-Lodge with Daughter Lodges. He had taught it the proper steps by which it could walk abroad ... "[HOW] TO GO". *That is a momentous declaration*, of interest to millions of people all over the world. Thus enigmatically we learn that Lodges, at last, were beginning to be founded from the parent Lodge; that the "Machine" was at "Work" for the "Making of Fit and Proper Persons". We can be quite certain of this because of the mention of a Masonic office of Inquisitor with the implied inference that Bishop Andrewes was also a Masonic officer of the first Craft Lodge from which sprang the Higher Christian Degrees, after which, *when all was in readiness*, the Craft-Child was "taught [how] to go".

Just in the same elusive way he conveys something else of great importance in a letter which, says Spedding, "has no date and like others ... appears to have been stripped of all particulars which might seem to fix the occasion." Other evidence, too, has been deleted. What is left is only a short fragment but even that contains one important sentence. After explaining why certain things have been neglected, Francis Bacon says he must charge it to the account of his own memory. "*My Head being then wholly employed about INVENTION.*" Since "invention" meant in those days the creation of dramatic characters, poetic creation, we have a clear intimation that Francis Bacon was a poet. Yet Spedding saw nothing significant in the phrase and never seems to have wondered why letters should have been purposely mutilated the moment Francis Bacon's personal secret activities were trenched upon. Had we the entire letter—as with others—we should doubtless have known the name of the actual play that had absorbed his mind so much that he had forgotten prime business matters.

Here, then, are two significant asides which Spedding (*and every other biographer*) ignored as of no account:

1. That Francis Bacon had made a "Machine"; that he had made it "GO" for it was a LIVE Machine—akin to a "Child"; that it could walk abroad for its creator had breathed into its nostrils the breath of LIFE and it had become a living SOUL.
2. That Francis Bacon had been absorbed in "Invention" which typified poetic creation, as used in Shake-speare's Sonnet-Diary:

> Look in your Glass and there Appears a Face
> That over-goes my poor INVENTION quite.
> (63-ciii)
>
> For who's so Dumb that cannot write to Thee
> When Thou thy Self dost give INVENTION light.
> (108-xxxviii)
>
> ... HOW are our brains beguiled
> Which, labouring for INVENTION, bear amiss
> The Second Burthen of a Former CHILD.
> (97-lix)

King James met his first English Parliament on 19 March 1604. So popular was Francis Bacon in the country that he was sent to the Commons by a double return. James opened Parliament in person, explaining his views on peace, the Union of England and Scotland, the necessity of tolerance in religion, and the general duties of government. Almost immediately the Commons was involved in a clash with the Chancery, the Lords and the Crown over a question of "Privilege", the right to determine whether Sir Francis Goodwin, who had been elected Member of Parliament for Buckinghamshire and who had been declared an outlaw by the Chancery, had the right to sit in the Commons. The Clerk to the Crown had refused to accept the return from Buckinghamshire and had issued through the Court of Chancery a new Writ and had certified that Sir John Fortescue was elected. The first business of the Commons, after the election of the Speaker, was to move for particulars of the return, to summon the Clerk to the Crown and Goodwin to appear before the Bar, whereupon it was resolved that Goodwin was not an outlaw and that the Clerk file the first return. Sir Francis Goodwin thereupon took his oath and seat.

The Commons was thus brought into collision with the Court of Chancery, which claimed that they (the judges) alone could determine the validity of the return. The Commons rejected the contention as trenching on their Privileges, for the Chancery Court had no power to determine the composition of the House. They therefore refused to confer with the Chancery judges or the Lords. Hearing of the dispute, the King butted in through the Attorney-General and decided that there must be a conference between the two Houses. At once the cry went round that the King had taken part with the Lords and the Commons moved for access to the King himself. This was granted. A committee was appointed and Francis Bacon was the first on the list. At the interview the King laid it down that "the judges had resolved that Goodwin standeth outlawed ... a sufficient cause for the dismission of any member out of the House". Thus early, in their first dealings with the Stuarts, the

Commons were involved upon the entire constitutional question—a direct dispute with the King himself. Says Spedding:

> Prerogative and Privilege thus found themselves suddenly face to face in a narrow passage. One must stand aside to let the other pass. ... What was to be done?

The Commons were resolved to stand by the principle that they alone were the judges of their own returns and that there could be no compromise on the point. There were further conferences. Francis Bacon was the appointed spokesman to meet the King, the Council and the judges. The situation was only saved by Bacon's tact. He persuaded the opposing parties to meet each other halfway: the Privileges of the Commons being reaffirmed while the Prerogative of the King was in no sense invalidated. Fortesque and Goodwin were both unseated and a new writ issued.

This incident, little in itself, is worth mentioning as it shows the King's meddlesome nature owing to his overweening confidence in his absolute Prerogative, which, thus early, got him into serious difficulties and disrepute with the Commons. It was the first mutterings of the fight between the Crown and the Commons, and it shows the great influence Francis Bacon exerted over the House of Commons. Even Dean Church says,

> He took a leading part in the discussions, and was trusted by the House as their spokesman and reporter in the various conferences. ... Bacon led the House to agree to an arrangement which saved their rights ... he put the King in good humour, and elicited from him the spontaneous proposal of a compromise which ended a very dangerous dispute.[1]

Francis Bacon ended his report to the Commons with a few sentences which indicated his veneration for the kingly office as the final seat of authority through power divine. He said:

> The King's voice was *the voice of God in man;* the good Spirit of God in the mouth of man: I do not say the voice of God, and not of man: I am not one of Herod's Flatterers. We might say as was said to Solomon, We are glad O King that we give account to you, because you discern what is spoken.

The evidence shows that from the very first day of the opening of Parliament Francis Bacon was the recognized Leader of the Commons, which he had been for the last twenty years. Throughout this Parliament the Commons put him forward as their champion to safeguard their interests. He was elected on the Standing Committee of Privileges, the Committee of Grievances, the Committee for the Restraint of Free Speech—in all on twenty-nine committees. He was the elected Reporter to convey to the Commons speeches made in the conferences with the Upper House. Some of his reports seem to indicate conclusively that he used some system of shorthand. There is a verbatim report of speeches delivered by the Earls of Salisbury and Northampton upon "Merchants and Spanish Grievances" of 8000 words which could only have been taken down by an experienced hand. This conclusion, too, is born out by Parker Woodward's investigations. He writes, referring to the years 1587–88:

[1] R. W. Church, *Bacon*, p. 73.

> With the assistance of Timothe Bright he [Francis Bacon] evolved the system of Shorthand which, when printed on 250 pages of vellum, he called "Characterie" ... obtaining letters patent to Bright *and his assigns* for fifteen years ... to sell all such books as he theretofore had or thereafter should make, devise, compile, translate or abridge to *the furtherance of good knowledge and learning.*[1]

His memory too must have been phenomenal, as he apparently made oral reports in the majority of cases *ex tempore* with the aid of a few notes which convey nothing.

Throughout the first session—indeed throughout the entire Parliament—Francis Bacon spoke boldly with unrivalled ability on many topics: abuses in the taverns, laws against witchcraft, the licences of purveyors, the sin of adultery, the increase of drunkenness, the sale of Crown offices and lands. Two topics stand out in bold relief even today against the darkness of history: "Grievances" and the "Union". He was active and prominent in dealing with both those subjects, speaking his mind boldly and fearlessly. Although we know today that, as a concealed Tudor, *his life was always in jeopardy and that he was under the finger and thumb of the King*, Francis Bacon did not truckle to the King or suppress his views when they were for the common good, any more than he had done when he stood up as a "commoner" to Queen Elizabeth. He maintained a sturdy and respectful independence from the Crown, no more and no less. He never once, as in the Goodwin case, wavered in his loyalty to his own House. James wanted his will to be absolute, his Prerogative to override the considered will of the Commons:

> to suspend the penal laws, to grant private Monopolies, to command personal service, to sign away heiresses in marriage, to supply his kitchen from the poulterer's basket and his cellar from the vintner's store *at his own price* ... each and all incontestably historical, founded on custom older in date than the oldest Statute in the Book.

Those old feudal rights and regal privileges had already become an anachronism unworthy to be longer tolerated. To the Commons they were legitimate grievances that pressed on the body politic to the hurt of the common people. But James only saw in the attempt to redress these wrongs and in the surrender of these customs a sapping of his royal authority, an affront to his Prerogative.

> To take from him the right to reward a barber with a wine patent, to compel the young noble to hold his reins or feed his dogs, to match his Favourites of the Bedchamber with the daughters of English Earls, to fetch in ale from Blackfriars and fish from Billingsgate Wharf, *to vend pardons for rape and arson, burglary and murder*, would, in his opinion, be to rob him of the most Princely Attributes of his High Rank.

James turned his back on the list of grievances prepared by the Commons, closed his ears to their murmurings and would not yield an inch. He had already dashed to the ground all hope of Church reform. It was now learned that he had actually begun a secret correspondence with the Cardinal Archduke and the Pope, but for what purpose is unknown although there were

[1]*Sir Francis Bacon.*

the wildest rumours. Can we therefore wonder that the Commons viewed the King's pet scheme for the Union of the kingdoms with aversion and contempt? We who know today the secret of Francis Bacon's life and the grave risk he was running in crossing the temper of the King can hardly have blamed him had he stood on one side rather than offend the Crown. But Francis Bacon's life was based on the words he put in the mouth of Polonius: "*This above all: To thine ownself be TRUE, Thou canst not then be false to any man.*" He had to speak irrespective of consequence, and speak he did. Dean Church shall sum up his attitude:

> Bacon assailed with a force and a keenness, which showed what he could do as an opponent, the amazing and intolerable Grievances arising out of the survival of such Feudal Customs as Wardship and Purveyance; customs which made over a man's eldest son and property, during a minority, to the keeping of the King, i.e. to a King's Favourite. ...
>
> He urged that these Grievances should be taken away with the utmost tenderness for the King's Honour and the King's Purse.[1]

The King was adamant. He would not budge an inch. The grievances were continued, for these evils, *that were blighting the commonwealth*, brought in large sums to the King's personal exchequer. What a sordid motive! Thus, early in 1604 Francis Bacon clearly defined his position: that he stood on the side of social reform irrespective of the Prerogative. "He continued to make himself popular by stand-up for a Redress of Grievances," says Lord Campbell grudgingly. One wonders whether Campbell and Church would have taken up such a heroic stand if their heads had been in jeopardy. He spoke against the grievances at the peril of his life, though no one knew it, because he was above all things an all-round reformer; because he was primarily a great House of Commons man. He ranks with John Pym, William Pitt, John Bright and Sir Winston Churchill. He would have outshone all our statesmen in the splendour of his achievements if James had only listened to him from 1604 to 1621.

Probably the real reason why James did not take umbrage at his attitude was because Francis Bacon had already declared himself strongly in favour of the Union of England and Scotland. James knew that the idea was repugnant to Englishmen and that the only man who had a chance of winning the Commons' assent was Francis Bacon. His name was the first proposed when the English Commission was appointed to confer with the Scots for considering the Union. By his fellow Commissioners on the English side he was entrusted to draw up an analysis of all the questions that would have to be dealt with for the King's information. He digested and drew up the Articles in their ultimate form.

In an attempt to get the grievances looked into by the King, Francis Bacon also drew for him in April 1604 the draft of a Bill of Union which he actually introduced into the House of Commons in a splendid speech. In a union with the Scots (he said) he saw a measure of defence against Spain. He begged the House to drop the ancient feud of Saxon versus Scot and foretold that great good would accrue to both countries in strength and

[1] *Life*, p. 75.

power, wealth and population. At a stroke England would be free from the menace of invasion in the north by the military might of Spain, if the Scottish back door was guarded by the Scots as friends, and no longer our enemies. He warned the House against a hostile Europe, pointing the way to the permanent safety of England, peace and reform amid a Europe of contending nationalities and hostile creeds.

His colleagues, however, would not be persuaded. Many of them only saw in the Bill an open door through which a poverty-stricken horde of untrousered, kilted Scots savages with red beards, bare legs and scurvy tongues would rush to take possession of the capital. The obstinacy of the King in refusing to consider the Commons' grievances was reflected, naturally so, in the obstinacy of the Members in refusing to consider the Union. No amelioration of our grievances, no Union. *The grievances are not heard: And the Bill does not pass.*

But this did not end the ventilation of these two prime subjects by any means. The grievances, though shelved, cropped up in succeeding Parliaments, for the Commons, as yet, were not strong enough to fight the Crown on this issue. The sweeping clean of the Augean stables was reserved for Cromwell and his broom of Ironsides, and the discussion of the Union became an integral part of parliamentary life. The first five years of the new reign were, however, largely devoted to discussions on adjusting the relations and assimilating the laws of the two countries. In the conferences with the Commissioners on the Union Francis Bacon played a leading part, "forty-eight Englishmen and thirty-one Scotchmen meeting on terms of perfect equality to make a bargain ... involved interests vast and various ... yet in less than six weeks they had come to an agreement.'

> The first fruit of these conferences and studies was a precise but complete analysis of the whole subject drawn up [by Francis Bacon] for the King's information. What use was made of it at the time I do not know.[1]

The draft of some 9000 words was entitled "Certain articles or considerations touching the Union ... for his Majesty". It deals with a variety of subjects of the utmost importance: sovereignty, subjects, religion, language, the name of the two kingdoms, parliaments, courts of justice and so on. One's admiration increases as one notes how Francis Bacon has set out each question with meticulous precision, wide in scope, in minute detail. The opening sentence is illuminating:

> Your Majesty being, I do not doubt, *Directed and Conducted by a better Oracle than that which was given for LIGHT to Æneas in his peregrination, hath a Royal and indeed an heroical desire* to reduce these two Kingdoms of England and Scotland into the unity of their ancient Mother Kingdom of Britain.

The "Oracle" and the "peregrination" are references to the wanderings of Aeneas in the Mysteries on which Freemasonry is founded, while the "directing and conducting" towards "Light" is purely Masonic. It is of interest, too, to note that the word "Britain", afterwards adopted by James, was undoubtedly due to Francis Bacon.

[1]Spedding, *op. cit,* Vol. III, p. 218.

On the 10th October, 1604, James adopted the famous nomenclature evidently suggested by his adviser and assumed the Stile and Title of King of Great Britany.[1]

During the three following years Francis Bacon continued to press his arguments for the Union with practical detail and illustration by speech and by document and to soften the prejudice of the English nation against the Scots. Though James had proclaimed himself the King of Britain, it was not until the winter of 1605 that the instrument of the Union came under consideration: A further consolidation of the kingdom was imperative—laws, customs, etc.

During the early parliamentary months of 1604 Francis Bacon had been brought into touch very often with the King through conferences and reports. James was gradually beginning to realize that in him he had a sincere, honest and valued servant who had no designs on the House of Stuart, a firm believer in the monarchical belief that "Divinity doth Hedge a King" and that only treason dare raise its impious hand against the Lord's Anointed. The King had noted his disposition, ability, quiet strength of will and steadfastness of purpose; and that in spite of his uncompromising attitude towards the Crown respecting the Commons' grievances, Francis was a wholehearted champion of the Union in the face of a hostile House. Indeed, says Nichol: "He won as much of James's favour as he ever attained, by his firm yet temperate advocacy of a measure which he thoroughly approved."[2]

James therefore unbent a little, and on 25 August 1604 Francis Bacon was granted by Patent the office of Learned Counsel which he had hitherto held by verbal warrant only. It was really a poor recognition for Francis Bacon's great abilities and long service to the State, but it was a beginning. He was a duly accredited State servant at last. Two or three months later the Solicitor's place became vacant. He knew he would not get it and he never even applied for it. It was filled in October 1604. When the office of Chief Justice of Common Pleas became vacant in the summer of 1605 he was again passed over; and in the trials and investigations following the discovery of the Gunpowder Plot in November 1605 he was not employed by the Government. The reason was this: *he was still unmarried to the girl Alice Barnham* the commoner, and James was taking no risks of advancing him in the State until the pact between them was carried out. That was the reason why he never applied for the Solicitorship and fretted not himself over the other employments.

Parliament was prorogued in December 1604 and did not assemble for ten months, in November 1605. For nearly a year Francis Bacon had no public duties of any kind to perform. He had thus ample leisure to begin to champion in the forums of the world those ideals which could be openly agitated and wedded to other aspects of his idealism which he had promulgated in secret with his disciples for so many years. Never once did he allow his love of knowledge to be checked by the occupations of active life. His open activities were ephemeral things that would pass away; his mental and ethical life was his real world in which he lived and moved. He turned from his exertions respecting the Union in the autumn vacation to discuss the

[1]Nichol, *Life*.
[2]*Life*.

subject of education with his friend, Sir Henry Saville, the Provost of Eton, afterwards addressing him in a letter and a tract, *Helps to the Intellectual Powers*, a virtually unknown work, whose value will be realized when it is fully understood that education and ethics were the prime passions of Bacon's life and that the *Shakespeare plays* and the creation of Freemasonry had this end alone in view, Art being wedded to Truth in both these secret labours. On his return he wrote to Sir Henry Saville as follows:

> Coming back from your invitation at Eton, where I refreshed myself with company which I loved; I fell into consideration of that part of policy whereof Philosophy speaketh too much and Laws too little; and that is, OF THE EDUCATION OF YOUTH. ...
>
> In the discourse of the philosophers there is a strange silence concerning one principal part of that Subject ... *touching the Improving and Helping of the Intellectual Powers, as of conceit, memory, and judgment, they say nothing.*

The letter and the tract suggest that the object of education ought to be the knowledge and improvement of the body and the mind. In the tract he arranges the knowledge of the body into

1. HEALTH
(a) The preservation
(b) The cure of diseases
(c) The prolongation of life

2. STRENGTH
(a) Athletic
(b) Gymnastics

3. BEAUTY

Francis Bacon deprecated the then system of university education which left the formation of bodily habits to chance. All Nature (he says) strives for life and for health. The smallest moss cannot be moved without disturbing myriads of living entities. If any part of the animal frame is injured, the whole system is active in restoring it; but man is daily cut off or withered in his prime and, *at the age of fifty, we stand amidst the tombs of our early friends.* A healthy body is a necessity for a healthy mind.

He arranges knowledge respecting the mind into:

1. THE UNDERSTANDING
(a) Invention
(b) Judgment
(c) Memory
(d) Tradition

2. THE WILL
(a) The image of the good
(b) The culture of the mind

At some future period (he said) our youth will, perhaps, be instructed in the different properties of our minds, *understanding, reason, imagination, memory, will, and be taught the nature and extent of our powers for the discovery of truth.*

There are not (he continues) any lectures upon the passions; this subject deemed important by all philosophy, human and divine, is disregarded, except by such indirect information as may be obtained from the poets and historians by whom THE LOVE OF OUR COUNTRY is taught, perhaps, if only one mode is adopted ... in the midst of Troy's flames ... and with such slight information we are suffered to embark upon our voyage.

Francis Bacon thus inculcated the view that the teaching of patriotism by the spreading of a true knowledge of the history of one's own country (the sacrifices of men and women to preserve the "Soul of the Nation") was of greater importance than a knowledge of the classic wars to inspire the English youth to emulate the heroic deeds of their ancestors.

Such convictions as these gave birth to the great historical plays of Shakespeare. They were written to inspire the nation with a deep patriotic fervour in the destiny of their homeland. They were never tossed off thoughtlessly and heedlessly with no more ulterior motive than a box-office draw. These particular plays—with a couple of exceptions—were already written and had begun their work of educating the public to the greatness of their native land.

Lust of money never inspired "The Author" from whose mind outpoured the characters of English history that will live for ever as great examples to be emulated or shunned. The spirit of creation which produced these masterpieces, all aflame with the power of genius, arose in a mind burning with passionate desire to touch his countrymen with a selfless love of country that spends and does not heed the cost, to make his motherland teach the world.

Soon afterwards—which shows the great importance he attached to the promoting of English history—he wrote a letter to Lord Chancellor Ellesmere, with proposals to write a history of England; indeed, he prepared a work, inscribed to the King, *Of the Greatness of Britain.* He mentions in his letter to Ellesmere that the King had given an order for the erection of a tomb or monument for our late sovereign lady Queen Elizabeth and so he was put in mind of her life and government. He continues:

> *For as Statues and Pictures are dumb Histories, so Histories are Speaking Pictures* ... and calling to remembrance the unworthiness of the History of England and the partiality and obliquity of that of Scotland, in the latest and largest Author that I have seen, I conceived it would be honour for His Majesty, and a work very memorable, if this Island of Great Britain, as it is now joined in Monarchy for the Ages to come, so *were joined in History* for the Times past; and that one just and complete History were compiled of both Nations.

A few months after Francis Bacon wrote this fragment, *Macbeth* was composed quite in accord with Francis Bacon's picturesque style of presenting "SPEAKING PICTURES". (Though *Macbeth* was first printed in the 1623 Folio, all authorities are agreed that it was written well before 1610 for it was played at the Globe in April of that year. Malone believes it to have been written about 1606, while Arthur Symons (Irving edn) says the play undoubtedly contains "an allusion to the Union of the Two Kingdoms under James".) The author's letter to Ellesmere is a broad hint that he WAS writing a history referring to Scotland, and his letter fits in with the time of the creation of *Macbeth*, much of the material coming from Holinshed as in the English historical plays. In the draft which Francis Bacon left, he has, however, only drawn the outline and filled up two or three detached parts. He says he has no wish "to represent true greatness, as in water, which shows things bigger than they are, but rather, AS BY AN INSTRUMENT OF ART, helping the sense to take a true magnitude and dimention". Quite clearly Francis Bacon indicates the presentation of History in an art form which is exactly the aim of "Shakespeare" in all his Histories.

In October 1605 he issued in English Part I of *The Great Instauration*, entitled *The Advancement of Learning* (in Two Books). The work was dedicated to the King in the hope that this interest might be awakened in education and ethics; and the true interpretation of Nature in terms of light, life and love. Though his hopes respecting James were not realized, the work at once established his fame as a thinker with a magnificent gift of expression in the tongue of the common people; ENGLISH, not the accepted language of culture, Latin. It is, in point of fact, *the first great prose classic in English*, apart from Hooker's *Ecclesiastical Polity* whose expression is harsh compared with Francis Bacon's musical poetry of trope, metaphor and symbol.

Scholars are unanimously of the opinion that The *Advancement* was written about 1603–4; that it was written within twelve months; and that *it was his first literary venture*. But is not this palpably absurd? We have seen the grip that Francis Bacon possessed on all the parliamentary problems that came within his sphere—oral and written reports, conferences, mental activities of every kind—and, with the same masterly activity—without haste and without rest—we are told that he wrote a classic within a year. We can therefore profitably ask the Quidnuncs: *If Francis Bacon could write such a work in twelve months in middle life what could he not have done between the years of fifteen to forty-five, when he first conceived the unique idea of the great restoration of the arts, sciences and Christian morality? Especially when he was assisted by the cleverest wits of the day in his private scrivenry?*

He presented copies of *The Advancement* to Sir Thomas Bodley, the Earl of Shrewsbury and others, with letters requesting their acceptance.

When Parliament met on 5 November 1605 men's minds were full of the Gunpowder Plot and its consequences, of the lucky escape of the King, the Ministers and Members. The attempt to blow up the House was regarded as an attempt to overthrow Protestantism and had the direct effect of drawing the Commons and the King closer together. For a time at least it damped down the irritations between the Commons and the Crown that were a marked feature of the previous session. Once more we find that Francis Bacon is placed on all the principal committees and he again plays a prominent part in the debates, etc. Supplies were granted the King. The question of the Union of the Kingdoms was deferred to the next session. Respecting the "General Grievances", it was resolved to proceed by petition to the King when all the details were obtained; but in spite of the Commons' affectionate loyalty there had been no concessions by the Crown up to the prorogation on 27 May. During the session numerous matters were dealt with and in all Francis Bacon stood consistently for reform and not for a rigid perpetuation of the *status quo*. For many days after 11 March the Government had an anxious time, there being warm debates in the House over a third subsidy that Cecil wanted.

A proposition that it should be granted brought a dozen Members of the Finance Committee to their feet. One Member, Noy, declared against spoiling the poor to gorge the rich. Paddye said he would tell the King that even kings must do no wrong. Holt denounced the proposition as dangerous. Peake said, "I want to hear no more about the royal debts." Dyer and Holcroft averred that such demands had been met previously by the cry of "To Arms! To Arms!"

A week later and the subsidy was still unvoted, and on 18 March the tactless James sent word from Whitehall that the Bill must be passed or the unruly Members would feel his wrath. They flung back his threat as odious and contemptible. The Bill was lost. The Committee met again on Thursday, the 22nd, for the King had not accepted his defeat and the Commons would not enlarge their vote. On Saturday the Committee was still sullen and determined and on Monday it must report to the House.

On the same day a rumour spread abroad that the King had been assassinated. Fear gripped the heart of everyone that the Roman Catholics had planned a rising for there were hundreds of sympathizers with the Gunpowder Plotters. Like wildfire ran the wildest of rumours; that the Jesuits had threatened to burn London; that the massacre of St. Bartholomew was to be repeated. Crowds poured into the streets while the more sober citizens barred their doors and prepared to give anyone a warm reception.

In the afternoon the storm subsided as quickly as it had arisen. Sir Herbert Crofts rode into the Palace Yard crying, "The King is safe! I have seen him!" At once joy took the place of fear. The Realm was safe if he was safe. The Peers and the Commons went to Whitehall and the following two days, Sunday and Monday, passed in general rejoicing. The Church bells were rung.

On Tuesday the Commons met and Francis Bacon caught them on the rebound. "What are a few debts," he cried, "to the exultation straining every loyal heart? The Crown debts must be paid next year if not this year. The House can name its own Time but vote the Money Bill today and have done with it. Let us end the deadlock." His eloquence swept the House off its feet and the subsidy was passed.

None of the Government courtiers could have carried it. The King's best man, Cecil, was no longer a member of the House. Since he had been created Lord Salisbury he sat in the Upper Chamber and the Government had no real spokesman. Yet though the Government badly needed the services of a man like Francis Bacon there was still no sign by Cecil that the Government intended to use his services. Francis was then aged forty-six, of outstanding influence in the Commons, of infinite value to the Crown that had few servants of ability. Yet Cecil—his own nominal cousin—never once attempted to advance him in the service of the Crown. Spedding says:

> We do not know where or with whom the obstruction lay. All we know is that Gawdy, Coke and Doderidge all kept their places and Bacon still remained "next the door".

Readers of this biography can, however, realize more than Spedding knew. The bar-sinister of his Tudor birth had hung like a millstone round his neck in the days of Elizabeth and Burleigh. It dragged him down again, dangerously so, in the days of James, and Burleigh's son, Robert Cecil, the Secretary of State. Francis Bacon had saved himself three years previously from being excommunicated altogether from the public service by his readiness for an engagement with a child of eleven years, a commoner. He was now going to open the door to State offices by his marriage to the "handsome wench" of fourteen according to his bargain with the King and Cecil. He therefore sends a reminder to the Secretary of State on the eve of his marriage, when the Government is in difficulties, that he wants the Solicitorship, which implied that he was definitely about to wed and thus be properly qualified for the position. He writes to Cecil as follows:

> It is thought Mr Attorney shall be Chief Justice of the Common Pleas. In case Mr Solicitor rise, *I would now be glad at last to be Solicitor.* ... I may *amend my State and so fall to my Studies and ease, whereof one is requisite for my body, and the other sorteth with my Mind.*
>
> Herein if I may find your Lordship's favour, I shall be more HAPPY THAN I have been, which may make me also more wise.
>
> I have small store of means about the King, and to sue myself is not so fit. And therefore I shall leave it to God, His Majesty and your Lordship. For if I must be still next the door, I thank God in these transitory things I am well resolved.

Here are the same veiled hints and double meanings so characteristic of all Francis Bacon's letters where he has to enfold his meaning so that it creates no suspicion to an outsider unacquainted with such secretive methods of writing. Cecil can thus understand that he is going to "Amend my State" from being a bachelor to that of a married man and that he is going to be "Happy" as a consequence; and that the King is involved in the transaction is evident because the matter is not for the Secretary of State alone, he is only the channel to pass on the matter to the King.

Accordingly, as we have seen, Francis Bacon married about a month later, Cecil being represented at the wedding.

No legal changes were, however, made during the Parliamentary session, Parliament being prorogued on 27 May 1606.

Shortly afterwards Sir Francis Gawdy died and Sir Edward Coke succeeded to his office as Justice of the Common Pleas. A new Attorney General had therefore to be chosen. Francis Bacon expected that Doderidge, the then Solicitor, would be moved to the Attorneyship, leaving the Solicitor's place vacant for himself; but to Francis Bacon's dismay Cecil raised a favourite of his, Sir Henry Hobart, an obscure attorney of the Court of Wards, over Doderidge's head as well as over the just claims of Francis Bacon, to the high place of Attorney General. But Bacon was not the man to be wronged and insulted with impunity by such crooked dealing. He at once wrote to Cecil, to the Lord Chancellor Egerton and to the King:

To the King, Touching the Solicitor's Place

> *How honestly ready I have been*, most gracious Sovereign, *to do your Majesty humble service*, to the best of my power, and *in a manner beyond my power*, as I now stand, *I am not so unfortunate but your Majesty knoweth.* ...
>
> For both in the commission of the Union—the labour whereof for men of my profession, rested most upon my hand, the Bill of Subsidy, both body and preamble, in the Bill of Attainders, both Tresham and the rest; Purveyance; Ecclesiastical Petitions; in the Grievances and the like, I was ever careful—and not without good success—to put forward that which was good, sometimes to keep back that which was not so good....

I was diligent and reasonably happy to execute those directions, which *I received either immediately from your royal mouth, or from my Lord of Salisbury* [Cecil]. At which time it pleased your Majesty also *to promise and assure me, that upon the remove of the then Attorney I should not be forgotten*, but brought into ordinary place. ... And towards *the end of the last term*, the manner also in particular was spoken of [i.e. *after Francis Bacon's marriage*]. ... Mr Solicitor should be made your Majesty's Serjeant, and I Solicitor. ... *Neither was this any invention or project of my own.* ... I have nine years service with the Crown ... and cousin germane to the Lord of Salisbury [Cecil] whom your Majesty esteemeth and trusteth so much. [*Note that he stresses the fact that he is a relative to Cecil, thus acknowledging he is of the Bacon Family*]. ....

After Mr Attorney Hubberd was placed, I heard no more of my preferment, but it seemed to me to be at a stop, to my great disgrace and discouragement. And there my most humble Suit to your Majesty is: that this, *which seemed was to me intended may speedily be performed.* ... For sure I am no man's heart is fuller of love and duty towards your Majesty AND YOUR CHILDREN as I hope Time will manifest against *Envy and Detraction if any be.*

This is a straight letter which shows the writer stirred with righteous indignation at not having received a square deal. It is primarily the King's concern, and the last two sentences make it obvious that Francis Bacon had been promised office by the King himself, that he had married on the strength of it, and wishes the King to perform speedily the promise. What "Envy and Detraction" can there possibly be save in one sense, that he was a born Tudor who might have designs on the Throne? And who could whisper such things in the ears of James save Cecil, whom the King "esteemeth and trusteth so much"?

To the Lord Chancellor

I conceived it to be a resolution, both with his Majesty and amongst your Lordships of his Council, that I should be placed Solicitor ... wherefore my humble request is that you would set me in some strength to finish the work. ...

I humbly pray your Lordship to consider that *Time* groweth precious with me, and that *A MARRIED MAN is seven years elder in his thoughts the first day.* And therefore what a discomfortable thing it is for me to be unsettled still?

Certainly, *were it not that I think myself BORN to do my Sovereign service*—and therefore in that STATION will I live and die—otherwise, for my own private comfort, it were better for that the King did blot me out of his book ... than to stand thus at a stop, and to have that little reputation which by industry I gather to be scattered and taken away by continual disgraces, every new man coming above me. ...

Were it nothing else, *I hope the modesty of my Suit deserveth* somewhat. ... And were it not to satisfy *my wife's friends* and to get myself out of being a common gaze and a speech, I protest before God I would never speak word for it.

In this letter we see that the fact that he is married is again stressed; that he feels that he has been born to do the State service; that in that particular knowledge he will live and die; that his suit is a modest one considering his real identity as a Tudor; and that he has been promised the Solicitorship.

To my Lord of Salisbury [Cecil]

I am not ignorant how mean a thing I stand for, in desiring to come into the Solicitor's place. [*The office was a mean office considering that the petitioner was actually a*

Tudor prince and that his true office was the Throne. How else can this opening sentence be understood?]

... I am sure it was not possible for any man living to have received from another more significant and comfortable words of hope ... your Lordship being pleased to tell me that you would raise me ... and that *what you had done for me in my MARRIAGE was a benefit to me*, but of no use to your Lordship. ...

On my part I am of a sure ground that *I have committed nothing that may deserve alteration.* And therefore my hope is, your Lordship will finish a good work, and consider that time groweth precious with me.

Once more the fact that Francis Bacon is a married man is stated; that Cecil had done something to bring about the marriage which was of benefit to Francis—presumably had saved him by his promise to marry from banishment or something worse. *How else had Cecil benefited Francis Bacon in his marriage?* The concluding sentences indicate that there had been a bargain of State between them and that Francis Bacon had done nothing whereby the agreement should be broken.

Everything—private letter, public speech, concealed writings—points to the fact that *the real King of England was Francis Bacon who had sprung from the loins of Queen Elizabeth*, and that this birthright was responsible for many of the difficult things in his life—actions, sentences, mutilated letters, which neither Spedding nor any one else was ever able to explain.

* * * * *

Parliament met on 18 November 1606, the Commons receiving a written answer to their petition for the redress of grievances in which the King promised redress if there were anything unconstitutional. The Commons thereupon proceeded to discuss the "instrument of Union" agreed on by the Commissioners in December 1604, but this time Francis Bacon stood on one side, his attitude clearly being: "Let the new Attorney fight the King's battle in the Lower House. I've finished!" Hobart was in the wars early. During the recess Cecil had imposed on the country a "Book of Rates", pretending that taxes could be lawfully laid in the King's ports at the King's pleasure. A merchant trading abroad named John Bates, for resisting such a tax, not sanctioned by the Commons, had been condemned in the Court of the Exchequer. It had come to the notice of the Commons. From all the ports protests against such a tax were pouring in to the Members. Hobart simply could not stand up to the shafts that were being levelled at him. In such an atmosphere and with such a spokesman for the Crown, the Bill of Union fared badly. Moreover, the Scots in London were unpopular. They were reputed to be uncouth in morals and manners. James had given instructions to his officers to whip and pillory any Londoner who treated his countrymen unkindly. Jonson, Chapman and Marston, three notable poets, were imprisoned for making harmless jests against the Scots. Such acts of rigour made the very name of "Union" hateful.

Attorney Hobart could not ride the storm. And Cecil, alarmed lest the Bill of Union should be rejected by an overwhelming vote, suddenly adjourned the House.

"When Parliament meets after the Christmas Holidays Francis Bacon holds in his pocket a written agreement for the Solicitor's Place." Cecil, no lover of Bacon, had to climb down from his pedestal and make terms.

When Parliament reassembled, the Bill of Union drawn by Egerton was presented and consisted of four parts: hostile laws, border laws, laws of commerce, laws of navigation. The chief objection to which the Commons was opposed was the King's design of "naturalizing" the whole Scottish population. Nicholas Fuller, MP for London, opened the debate in a speech against the Bill that seems to have occupied all the day. He employed the most violent invective against Scotland and Scotsmen in England, and pictured a host of terrors at the opening of the boundary gate and letting the lean kine into the fat pasture: Fuller said;

> A Union of these two countries would be a marriage of the rich with the poor, the strong with the weak. Look at the arts, the industry, and wealth of England, its orchards swelling with fruit, its pastures fat with kine, its waters white with sails, to its thriving people, abundant agriculture, inexhaustible fisheries, woods and mines. With all these riches, contrast Scotland a land of crags and storms, peopled with a race of men rude as their climate, poor in resources and in genius, a nation with pedlars for merchants and two or three rotten hoys for a fleet.
>
> Such countries are best apart.
>
> What man in his senses, having two estates divided by a hedge, one fruitful, one waste, will break down his fence and let the cattle stray from the waste into garden and cornfield?
>
> The King's accession has not changed the relations of Saxon and Scot.
>
> If Mary had borne a son to Philip, that son being heir to his father's Crowns, would an English Parliament have naturalized the people of Sicily and Spain?[1]

Fuller's speech naturally made a deep impression. From a variety of causes the Commons were already opposed, yet sore from daily wrongs and insults, with their grievances still un-redressed and the feeling that the Crown was edging nearer and nearer to trample their liberties under foot. Francis Bacon rose to reply in a long, magnificent speech which was printed in 1641. If we read it carefully, noting the implications, we can see unmistakably that, apart from the reform of philosophy along the lines of science, education and ethics, the second great passion of his life was his ideal of a great national policy to make Britain truly great. We can see in the speech a statesmanlike effort to unite the various forces of England, Ireland, Scotland and Wales in harmonious order free from the disturbing elements of jealousy, identifying the interests of the Crown with Parliament and people, thus making Britain internally strong and free from peril save from disruptive elements from within. Apart from his philosophic ideals the greatness of Britain was a constant and favourite subject of meditation; and it is with this in mind that this "Speech of a Patriot" must be studied.

An excellent *précis* has been given by Dixon and I follow it closely.

> Francis Bacon began with a shower of image and illustration that at once reminds us of "Shake-speare". He begged his hearers to forget all private feuds, to raise their minds to questions of the highest state; not as merchants dealing with mean affairs, but as judges and kings charged with the weal of empires. He

[1]Dixon's *Précis*.

ridiculed the danger of overcrowding England with Scotsmen. The King threw down the fence when he crossed the Tweed; yet the flock of Scots had not followed through the rent. Scottish gentlemen would rather starve at home than betray poverty abroad.

The Roman Commons fought for the right to name Plebeian consuls, and, when they had won that right, voted for Patricians. So with the Scots. They claim the privilege of coming into England; yield the right and they will not come.

Moreover, this realm of England is not yet peopled to the full. It is thinly populated. London is thronged and swollen but not the open downs and plains. For certain it is that the territories of France, Italy, Flanders and some parts of Germany do in equal space of ground bear and contain a far greater quantity of people. "I see manifestly amongst us the BADGES AND TOKENS of scarceness rather than press of people [*note the use of this out-of-the-way Masonic phrase which in itself is sufficient to indicate a knowledge of Masonic Craft Lodge ritual*]; drowned grounds, commons, wastes ... a plain demonstration that the body of the kingdom is but thin-sown with people.

"Are there no English towns decayed? Are there no ancient cities heaps of stones? Why, marsh grows on pasture, pasture on the plough-land. Wastes increase; the soil cries loud for hands to sow the corn and reap the harvest. ... There never was such a kingdom in the ages of the world that hath I think so fair and happy a means to issue and discharge the multitude of their people ... as this kingdom hath in regard of that desolate and wasted kingdom of Ireland; which (being blessed with all the dowries of Nature ...) doth, as it were, continually call unto us for our colonies and plantations."

Francis Bacon then gave "a rapid history of naturalization, the wise liberality of Rome in extending her franchise to foreign subjects in contrast with the fatal jealousy of Sparta. He predicted that Union under one Government, unless accompanied by naturalization, would be followed by jealousies, quarrels and ultimately by war between the two nations."[1]

The benefits which we shall purchase, by the knitting of the knot surer and straighter between these two Kingdoms by Naturalization are two: The one SURETY, the other GREATNESS. ...

"But this Bill for naturalizing the Scots stands on a far higher ground. A people, warlike as the Romans and as ourselves, a race of men who, like wild horses, are hard to control because lusty with blood and youth, offer to be one people with us, friends in the day of peace, allies in the day of strife. Take from the Scots the brand of aliens. They will stand by our side, bulwarks and defenders against the world. Should you shut them out of England, treating them as strangers and enemies, they may prove to you what the Pisans proved to Florence, the Latins to Rome.

"In our ancient wars the invader found the gates of our kingdom open. France could enter through Scotland, Spain through Ireland. *Pass this Bill, we close our gates*. No minor argument deserves a thought. Union is strength, Union is defence.

"You object that the Scots are poor. Are not strong limbs better than riches? Has not Solon told us that the man of iron is master of the man of gold? Does not Machiavelli pour his scorn at the false proverb which makes money the sinews of war? The true sinews of war are the sinews of valiant men. Leave, gentlemen, to the Spaniards the delusion that a heap of gold, filched from a feeble race, can give the dominion of the world.

"Methinks we should a little disdain that the Kingdom of Spain ... should of late take unto themselves the spirit of a monarchy in the West ... because they have ravished from some wild and unharmed people mines and stores of gold; and,

[1]Abbott.

on this other side, that this Island of Brittany, seated and manned as it is, and that hath, I make no question, the best iron in the world—that is, the best soldiers in the world—should think of nothing but reckonings and audits, and *meum* and *tuum*, and I cannot tell what.

"If Union with the Scots will not bring riches to our doors, it will bring safety to our frontiers, will give us strength at sea and reserves on land. Alone we have borne our flag aloft; with Scotland united in arms, with Ireland settled and at peace, with our war fleets on every sea, our merchants in every port, WE SHALL BECOME THE FIRST POWER IN THE WORLD.

"Warmed with such glorious hopes, how can the gentlemen of England stand upon terms and audits—upon mine and thine—upon he knows not what!

"Mr Speaker ... I have spoken out of the fountain of my heart. I believed therefore I spake. My duty is performed. The judgement is yours. God direct it for the best."

Francis Bacon's eloquence saved the Bill from outright rejection and it is said that the House rang with applause. The various points began to be discussed throughout the session, and, although the Union was postponed for another generation, *it was Francis Bacon's advocacy—the seeds sown by him—which ultimately ensured success.*

Professor Nichol, hidebound academic though he be, while illogically asserting that Lord Bacon could not have written the Shakespeare plays, admits in the same sentence that "there is something startling in the like magnificence of speech" with which Francis Bacon in Parliament similarly voices the thought and language of England's greatest dramatist. The statesman and the poet

> are similar in their respect for rank and dignity, in their belief in Royal Right Divine, in their contempt for the *vulgus mutabile*, depreciation of the merely commercial, and exaltation of the military spirit; above all, in their view of the duty of Englishmen to knit together the forces and extend the bounds of the Kingdom.

The similarity of sentiment and expression between the utterances of the statesman and the lines of the dramatist is self-evident. It has never been pretended, however, that Shaksper of Stratford was stirred by the spirit of patriotism to pen the immortal histories but by the spirit of lucre. In this great speech of Francis Bacon we can feel the spirit that animated him. It is the same that brought into being those glorious phrases describing England and his inviolable attachment to his native land.

> This Royal Throne of Kings, this sceptured Isle,
> This earth of Majesty, this Seat of Mars,
> This Fortress built by Nature for herself,
> Against Infection and the hand of War,
> This happy Breed of Men, this little World,
> This precious Stone set in the Silver Sea.

It is the same man at work, but in two different mediums—one in prose, analytical, legal, precise; the other in which all restraints are cast aside and knowledge of all kinds pours forth from the crucible of his soul in cascades of precious gems luminous with emotion. Who, outside the fictionists of history and biography, can be so incredulous as to believe the palpable fiction that there were two separate men who once lived in the little world of London town, one animated by the purest spirit of patriotism, and the other by the sordid lure of money; one in the forum, the other on the stage; both alleged to be in the public eye; both consorting with lords and ladies of high degree; who wrote the same thoughts, the same language, but were inspired by such vastly different motives—and yet (we are told) *these two men never met though living within a stone's throw of each other in a restricted area!*

A copy of Francis Bacon's great speech was sent to James by Cecil and the "poor pedant sees what splendid things a practical statesman can say for his favourite scheme".

To the end of the session the Bill of Union was discussed, and though the question of naturalization was indefinitely postponed a Bill was brought in and passed (with amendments)

> For the continuance and preservation of the blessed Union of the Realms of England and Scotland and for abolishing and taking away of all hostile laws, statutes and customs that might tend to disturb or hinder the same.

The Bill in its amended form passed on 30 June, Francis Bacon both as reporter and actor having a good deal to do with it. (He was in the chair at the committee stage.) Both in committee, in the House, in conferences with the Lords, Francis Bacon's services were always in great demand. Spedding says: "The esteem in which he was held as a reporter of other men's speeches was well established by the continual demands upon him."

The session ended on 4 July 1607. Before its close a most important event took place so far as Francis Bacon's personal fortunes were concerned. Solicitor Doderidge was promoted to be King's Serjeant, Francis Bacon being appointed to his vacant office as Solicitor-General on 25 June 1607. At the age of forty-six he had at last obtained a first step on the ladder of State—a position he had vainly sought fifteen years previously and that he ought to have had years before.

Why had he not won his way to official recognition earlier? Other men got on—men who were younger than he with not a tithe of his gifts and graces and genius. In the law courts no one could match his tongue of fire. In the House of Commons he towered over all his rivals for sheer supremacy and hard work; and whenever he spoke his hearers could not cough or turn aside lest they lost some precious jewel of thought or turn of expression. Yet this man, who seemed to be born for power, failed to obtain it over and over again. Why was he so significantly left behind in the race? Why did not Elizabeth put him on the ladder? Why did not Burleigh? Why did James neglect to advance him until he was compelled to do so? Why did Cecil (Burleigh's son) act so treacherously towards him? While men of far lower birth and claims got posts and honours—Coke, Raleigh, Cecil, Cobham, etc.—how came it that this genius passed the age of forty-six before gaining power or place?

But the readers of this life already know the answers. He was purposely kept in the background because HE WAS REALLY THE KING.

His contemporaries have long gone the way of all flesh. With few exceptions their names are writ in water. Who cares for Coke today or even *Coke's*

Institutes? Or Cecil's piffling, huckstering statesmanship? Or James of infamous memory?

But Francis Bacon still lives to impress the world to the last syllable of recorded time ... on the stage ... in the Lodge ... in the closet of the student. His words, phrases and thoughts have passed into the blood of humanity. He has revolutionized all our concepts; and still he points the way to the nobler heritage which is ours—the real home and permanently abiding place of man which is a mental and a spiritual kingdom. He is one of the immortals.

At the age of forty-six and five months, this myriad-minded thinker when he took the Solicitorship, the better to help to mould the destinies of his country, had already created the movement known as the English Renaissance. He was now free to rest on his secret oars for a season to help to steer the ship of State.

Chapter III

FROM THE SOLICITORSHIP TO ATTORNEY GENERAL: (1607—1613)

FRANCIS Bacon had, at last, obtained a State office worth £1000 a year—a commanding position which he thought would give him influence, power and money; not that he desired these things for self aggrandizement, but rather for spreading of the "New Philosophy", as he named it.

In 1607 Francis Bacon was in his forty-seventh year. He could look back for approaching half a century. What had he to show since he wrote in his youth the Masonic tractate (now lost) *The Most Masculine Birth of Time*? No, who had vowed as a boy of fifteen to do something to help bring about "*the Reformation of the Whole Wide World*"? He, who had claimed in his early manhood to have taken ALL KNOWLEDGE to be his PROVINCE? Ten short essays and one book? Was that the sum total? Not at all! He could also point to a mass of concealed works of creative effort, laborious toil by which he had learned the craftsmanship of the playwright's art and which had led to the creation of a living character to be known to all the world as "William Shakespeare".

Under his jurisdiction he saw in England, Ireland, Scotland and the Continent fraternal Lodges and Colleges that had come stealthily into being through the labour of his hands; slowly taking root, spreading without the world being any the wiser, and ethical tenets welding together men divergent in temperament and creed into a noble brotherhood. The rituals of Freemasonry were being declaimed in secret Lodges all over the land and internationally. The Rosicrucian Colleges with their esoteric symbolism were functioning for the intelligentsia of the Movement. The Shakespeare plays were being performed on the stage and were gradually accustoming the common people to new words, new thoughts, new ideas—political and social reforms in the commonwealth, ethical principles, moral uprightness, etc. His Scriptorum, under his direction, had flooded the bookshops with works and pamphlets. Educational textbooks of many kinds were being circulated in the English tongue. Latin as the language of culture was slowly being deposed. He had acted privately as a bellringer to call the scientists together to pool their knowledge for the good of humanity, thus creating the nucleus of wits that was eventually destined to become known as the Royal Society. And he was now, at last, in a secure financial position to help forward, even while resting on his oars, the schemes he had conceived as a youth.

Yet with it all—the growing success of his concealed labours, the publication openly of *The Advancement*, his State appointment—he was not exactly satisfied. Now that the ardour of the chase had brought him in sight of the goal of open accomplishments, he found, as others have found, that "to travel hopefully is even better than to arrive". He was Solicitor General. He had cleared all barriers. The path to the highest offices lay before him. Did the beckoning hand drawing him into the limelight of public life also beckon him away from his secret loves and desires? Must he forsake his true home of love, the temples of literature and Freemasonry, for the glamour of public life and strife with its hazardous fortunes and Luciferean disasters? No wonder the Solicitorship, with its possibilities pro and con, created a revulsion of feeling at his success, a sense of dissatisfaction. That it did so is clearly shown by a note in his private papers that he made some time afterwards.

> I have found now twice, upon amendment of my fortune, disposition to melancholy and distaste, especially the same happening against the long vacation when company failed and business both. For, *upon my Solicitor's place,* I grew indisposed *and inclined to superstition.*

In the light of what subsequently happened, his last words can only be explained that he had a premonition that his public success in obtaining the Solicitorship would eventually lead to disaster.

The mood passed, of course. There could be no drawing back. He had crossed the Rubicon and was definitely, whether for good or ill, in the service of the State. He had, however, come to the conclusion that he must definitely associate himself in the eyes of posterity with the New Philosophy that was being secretly taught everywhere, by stating some of the *general principles* in the form of a tract or lecture, which could afterwards be printed and would tell any "informed person" in after years the real philosophic trends of its author and whence such sprang. The tract was written in the vacation under the title *Cogitata et Visa* (*Thoughts and Judgements* or *Thinking and Seeing*) and was written in Latin. He sent it to Sir Thomas Bodley with a letter, which contains this significant sentence:

> I am half in conceit that you affect not the argument.... I can say no more to you but ... if you be not of *the Lodgings chalked-up,* whereof I speak in the Preface, I am but *to Pass by your Door.*

The preface is missing which would have told us *the kind of lodge* referred to, but the word "chalk" was the symbol of freedom in Elizabethan Lodges, and the words "pass" and "door" make it quite evident that the words were purposely used Masonically. Evidently Francis Bacon was trying to elicit the interest of Bodley in ethical symbolism. Some time before February 1608 Bodley replied to the effect that it contained "many rare and noble speculations ... abounding with choice conceits of *the present State of Learning and worthy contemplations* of the means to procure it."

The *Cogitata et Visa* itself, although written in 1607, was not published until 1653, abroad, by Gruter and in Latin, along with some other similar fragments.

A translation of a work into English was published in 1734, the MS. written by Francis Bacon's "Good Pens" and carefully corrected in his own hand. It bears the intriguing title, *The Thread of the Labyrinth or The Legitimate Inquiry into Motion.* Written on the top page, in the left-hand corner of the MS, are significant words in Francis Bacon's hand, "TO THE SONS" (*Ad Filios*).

This arresting avowal ought to have told all scholars who have been vainly trying to interpret the Baconian philosophy that *Francis Bacon in 1607 was the father of fraternities surrounded with secret disciples whom he called his "SONS".*

The following is a slight digest of the work *Filum Labyrinthi* which, says Spedding, "agrees so nearly with the *Cogitata et Visa* that either might be taken for a free translation of the other." It will be noticed that Bacon speaks of himself in the third person, beginning each of the ten paragraphs with the words "He thought". He begins:

> *Francis Bacon thought in this manner.* The Knowledge whereof the world is now possessed, especially that of Nature, extendeth not to magnitude and CERTAINTY of works.... The Mechanics take small light from Natural Philosophy, and do spin on their own little threads....
>
> *He thought also* this State of Knowledge was the worse, because men strive (against themselves) to save the credit of Ignorance, and to satisfy themselves in this poverty ... all tends to the circumscription of man's power and to artificial despair....
>
> *He thought also* that Knowledge is uttered to men, in a form as if everything were finished ... where Antiquity [*i.e.* the Mysteries] used to deliver the Knowledge which the mind of man had gathered, in observations, aphorisms, or short and dispersed sentences, or small tractates of some parts that they had diligently meditated and laboured which did invite men to ponder ... and to add and supply further, the Succession being between Master and Disciple....
>
> *He thought also* that amongst other knowledges, Natural Philosophy hath been the least followed and laboured. For since the Christian Faith the greatest number of Wits hath been employed upon Divinity.... Before time, the greatest part of the studies of philosophers was consumed in Moral Philosophy, which was the Heathen Divinity ... since which time [the Grecian] Natural Philosophy was never any profession nor never possessed any whole man, except perchance some Monk in a cloister or some Gentleman in the country.... So he saw plainly that Natural Philosophy hath appealed to few persons, and ... occupied the least part of their time....
>
> *He thought also* how great opposition and prejudice Natural Philosophy had been received by ... the immoderate and blind zeal of Religion.... And that the case is now much worse, in regard to the boldness of the Schoolmen, who having made Divinity into an Art, have almost incorporated the contentious philosophy of Aristotle into the body of the Christian religion. And generally, he perceived in men of devout simplicity this opinion: That the Secrets of Nature were the Secrets of God ... and that the mind of man should have no stirring in philosophy lest it should discover matter of contradiction to Divinity. But in this part resorting to the Authority of the Scriptures, he rested not satisfied....
>
> He considered that the Knowledge of Nature by the LIGHT thereof Man discerned every Living Creature ... was not the occasion of the Fall; but the *Moral Knowledge of Good and Evil* affected ... *for man to direct himself;* neither could he find in any Scripture that the Inquiry and Science of Man in anything, under the MYSTERIES of Deity, is determined and restrained, but contrawise is allowed and provoked, for Scripture pronounceth, *That it is the Glory of God to conceal, but it is the Glory of Man (or of a King ...) to Discover* [invent].... The Spirit of Man is as the Lamp of God, wherewith he searcheth every SECRET.... The Scripture honoureth the name of the Inventors of Music and Works in Metal; Moses was seen in all the Learning of the Egyptians; and Solomon in his grant of Wisdom from God ... wrote a Natural History of all verdor from the Cedar to the Moss; the Church in her bosom ever preserved, as Holy Relics, the Books of Philosophy and all Heathen Learning.... All Knowledge and specially that of Natural Phi-

losophy tendeth highly to the magnifying of the Glory of God, in his Power, Providence and Benefits; appearing and engraven in his Works, which without this Knowledge are beheld but AS THROUGH A VEIL; for if the Heavens do declare the Glory of God to the Eye, much more in the rule and decrees of them do they declare it to the Understanding.... Natural Philosophy ... doth give an excellent Defence against both extremes of Religion, Superstition and Infidelity.... It *Raiseth the Mind* to acknowledge that to God all things are possible.... as in the case of the Resurrection saith our Saviour.... You err, not knowing the Scriptures, nor the Power of God....

So as He saw well that Natural Philosophy was of excellent use to the exaltation of the Divine Majesty....

He thought also ... that *in Universities and Colleges men's studies are almost confined to certain Authors, from which if any dissenteth ... it is enough to make him thought a person turbulent,* ... for in Government *change* is suspected even though it be for the better.... So Time seemeth to be of the Nature of a river or flood, that bringeth down to us that which is light and blown up and sinketh and drowneth that which is solid and grave. So he saw well, that both in the state of Religion, and in the administration of Learning, and in common opinion, there were many continual stops and traverses [obstructions] to the Course of Invention [Discovery].

He thought also ... of Speculative Truth ... that men ought not to make a Confusion of Unbelief ... yet he saw well that experience of untruth had made access to truth more difficult.

Commenting on this, Spedding says:

Here the MS ends abruptly in the middle of the page. At the top is written in Bacon's hand, "The English as much as was perfected." The blank part of the last page seems to have formed the outside of a miscellaneous bundle, and bears the following docket, also in Bacon's hand, "*SEVERAL FRAGMENTS OF DISCOURSES*".[1]

Here again we run into purposeful mystification. *We do not get the full text that would give the outsider a clue* as to what the "Discourse" was about or to whom it was addressed. We see, too, that *it was one of many discourses* obviously given to "The Sons of Sapience", as Francis Bacon elsewhere describes his ethical disciples. With strange obtuseness neither Spedding, Church, Abbott, Williams, nor Mary Sturt evince the slightest curiosity as to whom these lectures were addressed, what was the REAL subject matter, what Francis Bacon meant by his fatherly expression "TO THE SONS", and why the MS is cut—like others are cut—at the very point which would illuminate the darkness.

This fragment tells us plainly, however (though it was unknown to the world for more than a hundred years after his death, *i.e.* ten years after the emergence of the Masonic Grand Lodge), that Francis Bacon had a secret body of disciples to whom he delivered "Discourses" or lectures. And we who are familiar with Francis Bacon's New Philosophy can tell what some of the themes are, for there is an identity of thought between them, with definite esoteric expressions of veiled significance. Some were published abroad by Gruter in 1653: e.g. *Cogitationes de Rerum Natura, De Interpretatione Naturae Procemium, Delineatio et Argumentum, Temporia Partus Masculus, Redargutio Philosophiarum, De Sapientia Veterum, Phenomena Universi, Descriptio Globi Intellectualia, Themi Coeli, De Fluxu et Refluxu Maris, De Interpretatione Naturae Sententiae,*

[1]Spedding's *Works of Francis Bacon,* Robertson's Edition, p. 211.

Aphorismi et Consilia de Auxiliis Mentis, Histori Senai et Mortis, De Luce et Lumine, De Principiis Atque Originibus. Besides these fragments there were others, e.g. *Cogitationes de Scientia Humana* (published by Spedding in 1857), *The New Atlantis, Dialogue on a Holy War,* etc. All these published fragments were kept in the background by his "SONS", some being abroad only until there was no danger that publication in England would imperil the New Brotherhood.

For at least a couple of years after he had been made Solicitor-General Cecil showed no disposition to use Francis Bacon in legal affairs, which allowed him leisure to prosecute still further his "retired studies" and his literary work. One of his first acts in 1608 was to publish a Latin pamphlet entitled *In Felicem Memoriam Elizabethae.* This was ostentibly in reply to a Latin pamphlet, then circulating on the Continent, printed in Paris, *Examen Catholicum Edicte Anglicane* (the first pages of which, says Spedding, collected all the evil ever uttered against Queen Elizabeth). There were rumours as to her morality and alleged children. Francis Bacon wound up her defence in these words, which again tell the story if one reads between the lines:

> *This much* in brief *according to my ability,* but *to say the Truth,* the *only* commender of this Ladie's Virtues is *Time.*

He sent the pamphlet to his old friend Sir George Carey with a request that he should ask de Thou, a prominent Frenchman, to circulate it, remarking, "We serve our Sovereigns in inmost place of law: *our fathers did so before us.*"

In 1609 he wrote *Considerations Touching the Plantation in Ireland.* He drew up an admirable *Proclamation to Jurors,* extolling the dignity of their office, and also one on the *Jurisdiction of the Marches,* of little interest today and valuable only to those interested historically in the struggle between the Royal Prerogative and the Courts of Law. During the six years that he acted as Solicitor-General he was not too busy at his legal duties to prevent his pursuing the ideals that were close to his heart. He began to shape the new Philosophy in general terms for public presentation and continued to plant his Masonic Lodges in which the new active science was taking root. "It was his genuine belief that the old Greek and Latin Myths contained SECRETS of Religion and Policy, sacred relics or abstracted arts of better times, which, by Tradition from more ancient nations, fell into the Trumpets and Tunes of the Grecians." These myths were interpreted and their secrets unfolded in a wonderful little book entitled *The Wisdom of the Ancients,* published in 1609. In this year he took care to enter the title of "Shake-speare's Sonnets" in Stationer's Hall. He had already passed a few sonnets round to his friends in manuscript and he was afraid lest someone—an outsider—might learn of this and publish a group of sonnets and label them "Shakespeare's Sonnets". The simple registration of the title prevented anyone else from using it and left him free to produce his work of sonnets at his own time and in his own way, which he did in 1625. About this time (1609) he reprinted *The Passionate Pilgrim* and *Sonnets to Sundry Notes of Musicke,* the third edition in 1613.

He edited the Authorized Version of the James Bible, printed 1610–11, rounding off its English with the music of Shakespearean prose. Dr. Andrewes, one of the chief translators, was Francis Bacon's close friend. He harmonized the conflicting styles of fifty-four scholarly clergymen during the twelve months the various manuscripts were left with James and dropped in some of his own identity cyphers. The MSS are missing. During his Solicitorship he wrote or published *Antony and Cleopatra*, *Pericles*, *A Winter's Tale*, *Cymbeline*, *Macbeth*, *Lear*, *Troilus and Cressida*, possibly a first draft of *The Tempest*, some of the Rosicrucian manifestoes which we know were circulating in England and the Continent in 1610 and were openly published anonymously in 1614, especially one, *The Fama Fraternitatis*. In 1611 he prepared a Folio edition of the "Spenser Poems" in which *The Shepheards Kalendar* was *for the first time* included as a Spenser poem. The five quarto editions of *The Shepheards Kalendar* had all appeared anonymously. The 1611 Spenser Folio had neither preface nor editor's name. Spenser had died in January 1599, so it was quite safe to attach Spenser's name to the poems.

In 1609 we also have evidence that the six parts of *The Great Instauration* were not being (and had never been) neglected, for he writes a letter to his young friend Tobie Matthew in which it is mentioned. Francis Bacon apparently had a strong personal affection for Matthew and thought highly of his friend's intellectual judgement, although in 1605 he had become a convert to the Church of Rome while travelling in Italy, which had resulted in his being imprisoned on his return to England some two years later. Francis Bacon interceded for him and got him out of the Fleet Prison on the understanding that he departed the Realm within six weeks. But during his banishment a correspondence between the two men was sustained, although Francis Bacon could not help expressing his disapproval of his young friend's change of belief. It is through the fact that their intercourse had to take the form of letters that we learn a little and are mystified much. Tobie Matthew appears to have been familiar with his secrets. Says Spedding:

> Most of the letters are unluckily without date, and the writings enclosed or referred to are not always recognisable by the descriptions.... Tobie Matthew, as I have already had occasion to observe, appears to have purposely *obliterated or disguised names or particulars; and if the headings were inserted by himself* (which is doubtful—for the collection was not published till after his death), we must conclude that he had either forgotten the dates or *intended to confuse and conceal them.*

Once more, we find letters written by Francis Bacon purposely mutilated, this time by Tobie Matthew; and the latter's letters erased and snipped by Bacon. Francis Bacon's secrets were indeed weighty as *a concealed prince* of the House of Tudor who dared not speak openly of his royal identity; as *a concealed poet* and a cypherist by which means one day he hoped the gag would be taken from his mouth so that he could declare himself; and as *a concealed head* of secret Masonic societies inculcating education of the masses and ethical principal to be practised. Had he not *abundant good reason for concealment* when a single slip might have brought him into open conflict with Church and State and ruined what he was so painfully and laboriously building?

This letter was apparently written in 1609 by Francis Bacon. In an extract he mentions the play of *Julius Caesar*.

> I send you also a memorial of Queen Elizabeth.... Of this, when you were here, *I shewed you some model*; though at that time me thought you were more willing to hear *Julius Caesar* that Queen Elizabeth commended. *But this which I send is more full and hath more of the narrative* [Tobie was being sent a revised draft of the play].

The significant fact is that the play of *Julius Caesar* had never been heard of until seven years after the death of Shakespeare the Stratford actor. It was published in the great Shakespeare Folio for the first time in 1623. It had as yet never been played. But there was a draft or model of the play apparently in being which Francis Bacon had shown to Tobie Matthew when he was in England in 1607. This coincides with the majority of the commentators who declare it must have been written before 1607. Yet Francis Bacon mentions the existence of the play in his letter which Spedding says *"must have been written late enough in 1609"*. We know, too, that Francis Bacon was in the habit of showing Tobie Matthew his literary writings. The significant implication is only matched by a letter from Tobie Matthew to his friend which again shows that they both knew of the existence of another Shakespeare play. Matthew writes:

> I will not promise to return you weight for weight but *Measure for Measure,* and I must tell you beforehand that you are not to expect any other stuff than fustian and bombast and such wares as that. For there is no venturing in other commodities, and much less upon such as are forbidden. Neither, indeed, do we know what is forbidden and what is not....

Here we have the Shakespeare play *Measure for Measure* alluded to in an undated letter, a play that had never been acted in the actor Shakespeare's lifetime, nor printed at all until it appeared in the 1623 great folio. There is every reason to believe that this letter—like its predecessor—was written long before 1623. These letters prove that these confidential correspondents possessed a knowledge of the *Shakespeare plays* long before their publication. *The authorship of anyone other than Francis Bacon is therefore impossible.* When *Measure for Measure* was written no one knows. The Shakespearean authorities think it may have been about 1603 and that the accession of James is hinted at in the play. But the two finished plays could just as well have been written any time after the actor's death (1616) for publication in the 1623 Folio.

Another undated letter which Spedding thinks "cannot be placed earlier than 1608" mentions the *Instauration.* Here is an extract:

> Two letters of mine are now already walking towards you; but so we might meet, it were no matter though our letters should lose their way....
>
> As my trust with the State is above suspicion, so my knowledge of your loyalty and honest nature will ever make me show myself your faithful friend without scruple....
>
> I have sent you some copies of my book of the *Advancement*, which you desired; and *a little work of my Recreation*, which you desired not.
>
> My *Instauration* I reserve for our conference; *it sleeps not. Those Works of the Alphabet are* in my opinion of less use to you where you are now, than at Paris; and therefore I conceived that you had sent me a kind of tacit countermand of your former request. But in regard that some friends of yours have still insisted here, I send them to you; and for my part, I value your own reading more than your publishing them to others.

Spedding frankly admits that this letter puzzles him. He says:

> What these "Works of the Alphabet" may have been, I cannot guess unless they

relate to Bacon's Cypher. A man in Matthew's position may have needed a safe Cypher and may have needed it more at Paris than in Italy or Spain.[1]

This knowledge that Francis Bacon could construct "safe Cyphers" never, unfortunately, stimulated Spedding to ascertain whether Francis Bacon ever used a cypher or cyphers in his works or whether this secretive method of writing was not aligned with the mutilated letters and manuscript documents which were obviously done purposely to conceal something. All these secretive hints go for nothing for Spedding and all the biographers who tread so meticulously in his footsteps. The "*Works of the Alphabet*" and the "*works of my Recreation*" may refer partially to the cyphers of many kinds which Francis Bacon embedded in his works both open and concealed, for the letters of the "Alphabet" are the foundation stones of nearly every cypher system, numerical or otherwise. But the phrases mean something else as well according to Francis Bacon's own interpretation.

"*Tragedy and Comedy are made of the same Alphabet.*" And in this sentence he tells us what the "work of my Recreation"—which gives him joy and pleasure to "invent" or create— really is. It can also be called "Works of the Alphabet", for plays the most diverse, tragic, humorous, characters most noble and the most depraved are made out of twenty-four letters (as the alphabet was then) cunningly woven together. Yet these compositions which Francis Bacon declared he wrote are not to be found under his name anywhere. *There are no such works except they be the "Shakespeare plays"*. The plays were the *fourth part of the Instauration*: hence his asseveration "My *Instauration* ... sleeps not." *In other words*

> *It is awake, growing, in movement, alive. My ideas are taking root. They walk the Stage and they walk the lodge, alert, alive, in action.* Here are some further psychological studies of character, "examples" which your friends *insisted* I should send you [To insist, fo. 128, "implies some authority or right". Obviously Matthew was still of the Rosicrosse school and faithful to his "Solemn Obligations"]. I value *your reading* more than *publication.*

Tobie Matthew gives his opinion of the writings by letter, to which Francis Bacon replies:

> I thank you for your last, and pray you to believe that your liberty in giving opinion of those writings which I sent you, is that which I sought, which I expected, and which I take in exceeding good part.... I confess my desire to be, that *my writings should not court the present time*.... As for the *Instauration* your so full approbation thereof I read with much comfort, by how much more my heart is upon it; and by how much less I expected consent and concurrence in a matter so obscure.
>
> Of this I can assure you, that *though many things of Great Hope decay with Youth ... yet the proceeding in that Work doth gain with me upon my affection and desire, both* by years and businesses. And therefore I hope, even by this, that it is well pleasing to God, from whom and to whom all Good moves. To Him I most heartily commend you.

Once more it is evident that Francis Bacon is writing and working at something to benefit posterity more than the contemporary age, something

[1]Spedding, *op. cit*, Vol. IV, p. 134.

which for the time being must remain "obscure"; and that he is labouring to bring the dreams of his "youth" into concrete reality, dreams that had grown upon him with the passing of the years. *The Great Instauration* was necessarily obscure and secret because its culmination was to end in enforcing the ethics of the Sermon on the Mount (freed from dogmatic creeds which were rampant) and which he hoped would be well pleasing to God, for was he not forging golden chains wherewith the whole round would ultimately be bound to the feet of the Most High? In a further letter to Tobie Matthew, dated October 1609, he says:

> I plainly perceive by your affectionate writing touching my work, that one and the same thing affecteth us both; which is the good end to which it is dedicate.... *For your caution for Churchmen and Church Matters ... as for any impediement to my work it moveth me not.*... Nay it doth more fully lay open that the question *between me and the Ancients,* is not the Virtue of the race but the Rightness of the way....
>
> You conceive aright that in this and the other *you have commission to impart and communicate them to others according to your discretion.* Other matters I write not of.... Controversies of Religion must hinder the Advancement of the Sciences.
>
> Let me conclude with my perpetual wish towards yourself ... that your own discreet and temperate carriage may restore you to your country and your friends to your society. And so I commend you to God's Goodness [There was then no Catholic ban on Freemasonry for the Church knew not of its existence].

This letter proves conclusively that the *Instauration* trenches on religious observances, for Tobie Matthew fears the creedal intolerance of "Churchmen", the "impediments" likely to endanger Francis Bacon's views, views which have *an affinity with the "Ancients"*, with "*Virtue*" and "*the Rightness of the way*" which constitute the marrow of his ethical scheme which is termed elsewhere "Active Science". What else but the ethical sixth part of the *Instauration*—the "something" that trenches on religion—could the correspondence refer to? Notice also that Tobie Matthew is empowered to communicate his ethical secrets to others according to his discretion, which is the very way Lodges could be formed or founded privately in the Elizabethan era for the "making of Masons", remaining in force until the Grand Lodge system of 1723. Is it not abundantly clear that Francis Bacon had set up himself as a secret ethical teacher, and that he had copied the most ancient models in the world—the nature rites and wisdom of the Mysteries?

Two months later he wrote to Tobie Matthew again respecting some writings submitted to him and also about the death of someone whose name is suppressed. The reference to "Stage-Friends" is interesting.

> I think myself—however it have pleased God otherwise to bless me—a most unfortunate man, to be deprived of TWO—a great number in true friendship—of those friends whom I accounted *as no Stage-Friends but Private Friends*— and such, as with whom I might both freely and safely communicate—him by death, and you by absence.

A few months later Francis Bacon sent his friend, then staying at Salamanca, *De Sapienta Veterum* (*The Wisdom of the Ancients*).

> I send you a little Work of mine that hath begun to pass the world.... Had you

> been here you should have been my "Inquisitor" before it came forth: but I think the greatest "Inquisitor" in Spain will allow it [Matthew must have held the office of Inquisitor in the Masonic order].... I make no haste to believe that the world should be grown to such an ecstacy [madness] as *to reject Truth in Philosophy, because the author dissenteth in Religion....*
>
> My GREAT WORK GOETH FORWARD; and after my manner, I alter ever when I add. So that nothing is finished until all be finished.
>
> This I have written in the midst of a term and Parliament; thinking no time so precious, but that I should talk of these matters with so good and dear a friend. And so with my wonted wishes I leave you to God's goodness. 17th Feb. 1610.

We thus learn that the "Great Work" of spreading his ethical gospel by the founding of little communities (which is the goal of the *Instauration* and of which it is part) is a labour that is going forward and that he is adding to the Masonic degrees up to "33". It was not the mere writing of the *Novum Organum*, which never appeared until 1620. Indeed, there is no proof whatever that this work was actually begun in 1610. From youth to middle age he had only *The Advancement* to show as an earnest for the "Great Work". It is therefore manifest that something was going forward not at all in the category of the bare writing of a system of philosophy. He was doing more than writing a truth. *He was establishing a "Truth in Philosophy" through his disciples and Sons.* Like an architect and builder, he expands his original idea of construction which necessitates alterations; and not "until all be finished"—and the complete six parts are finished in their entirety—can the Masterpiece of the Completed Temple be realized in all its wonder. In short, the complete *Instauration* scheme in its six parts is being revised and perfected part by part—altering and adding; and to indicate that the work is a growing thing to be tended and cared for by future generations, it is intended to mould the thoughts of the ages, and to last until the end of the world is "finished", Francis Bacon adds the significant phrase: "*Nothing is finished until ALL be FINISHED*"; thus he intimates that his labours will continue to grow and expand among generations unborn, the full consummation never finishing until "ALL be finished with the death of the Great Globe itself and the Children of men be a finished Race." That is the true explanation of Francis Bacon's statement which has so puzzled his critics. He was writing openly and labouring secretly at his six parts *concurrently*.

We have seen that Francis Bacon stated that "controversies of religion hindered the Advancement of science" and that as "the miller of Huntington prayed for peace among the willows" that his watermill might be better customed, so Francis Bacon prayed for peace among the theologians that men might be bettered in their souls. For some time (1609–10) there had been a great pen-and-ink war between King James and the Pope, Bishop Andrewes of Chichester being called in to answer Cardinal Bellarmin. The reply in book form appeared in June 1609. Shortly afterwards Francis Bacon sent Bishop Andrewes the *Cogitata et Visa* with the last additions and amendments, with a letter;

> Now your Lordship hath been so long in the Church and the Palace, disputing between Kings and Popes, methinks you should take pleasure to look into the field, and refresh your mind with some matter of philosophy; though that Science be now through age waxed a child again, and left to boys and young men; and

> because you were wont to make me believe you took liking to my writings, I send you some of this vacation's fruits; and thus much more of my mind and purpose.
>
> *I hasten not to publish; perishing I would prevent. And I am forced to respect as well my TIMES as the MATTER....*
>
> [I have put my mind] into these miscellanies *which I purpose to suppress*, if God give me leave to write a just and perfect volume of Philosophy, which I go on with though slowly....
>
> My request to you is that by notes you would mark unto me whatsoever shall seem unto you either not current in style or harsh to credit and opinion ... for no man can be judge and party.

Here is sufficient evidence that the *Cogitate* was for private circulation only, unsuitable for the then existing age because of the "'matter" it contained. Andrewes, his personal friend, was one of the Secret School.

While all these secret, idealistic labours were in progress, it must not be thought that Francis Bacon was neglectful of his duties as a State servant, astatesman, and a patriot with a passion for the advancement of England's greatness, the extending of the bounds of her shores, and total independence from the domination of Spain. Though Robert Cecil showed no willingness to avail himself of his services for many long months after his appointment the new Solicitor, with the zeal that never forsook him, set himself to discharge the duties of his post. Of those which were strictly legal, we need only note that all his judgments were regarded as authoritative by the lawyers, among whom he seems to have ranked second only to Coke. On questions bordering between strict law and politics, Coke and Bacon were constantly at variance.

Ere long, through pressure of events, Cecil was compelled to make use of him, and before he relinquished his office in 1613 Francis Bacon had conducted some important cases, becoming chief adviser to the Crown in all affairs of law.

In no biography save one has any recognition ever been paid to Francis Bacon as a founder of new States. Yet with Raleigh and Delaware he took an active share in colonization schemes which link us to America and he made the Virginias and the Carolinas British colonies instead of Spanish plantations. He was one of the first to join the Virginia Council and then the Newfoundland Company. He took office as one of the Council and helped to finance the discoveries of new lands. England and Spain had long been rivals as joint discoverers of foreign shores. "A Genoese had given the South to Spain; a Venetian had conferred the North on England." The work of colonization had never flagged while Elizabeth lived and Sir Walter Raleigh was free; but James the pusillanimous not only proposed to patch up a shameful peace with the Spanish Ambassador Velasco but flung the great explorer of Guinea and founder of Virginia into the Tower. A Papal Bull gave to the Spanish Crown all the New World from Canada to Cape Horn, which the Spanish diplomat Lerma formally claimed in despatches to James. Finally, Spanish cruisers in the Gulf of Mexico were chasing away English traders as pirates and, when caught, hanging their crews at the yard arm or sending them as prisoners to the Spanish Inquisition to be tortured and murdered at an *auto-da-fe*; while James shivered in his shoes afraid to protect his nationals by means of the royal fleet. But the threat of a Spanish descent on the colony at Chesapeake, then on the verge of collapse, fired the patriotism of all the Elizabethans and, despite the King, there was an uprush of feeling to defend Virginia. Men volunteered and money poured in. Francis Bacon with Montague and Pembroke joined the Company, with purse and voice, to plead for supplies from Parliament, and very quickly a fleet commanded by Sir T. Gates, Sir G. Summers and Captain Newport sailed from the Thames—outriding all storms and trials—"which added the Bermudas to our Empire and *The Tempest* to our Literature."

Francis Bacon fostered the plantation of colonies and the voyages of discovery with exactly the same patriotic fervour as he advocated the Union with Scotland, the peaceful pacification of Ireland by granting the nation a form of self-government through their own Parliament, and a war with Spain, if necessary, to preserve a true national independence and social reform—all of which ran on parallel lines with his secret aims for the spreading of education and ethics.

With his entry into the State's official life as Solicitor-General there can be no doubt that, at the back of his mind, *he saw himself the natural custodian of England's destinies as a born Tudor*. England was far more precious to him than it could possibly be to a "James Stuart of doubtful pedigree"—an alien in mind and heart to the English spirit of freedom and justice. And if Francis Bacon craved further power—which he did—it was only that he might better play the part of a watchful English hound for the people's liberty and progress. The Royal strain within this great idealist cried out silently yet unceasingly for the exercise of his just right of guardianship, *for was he not the real King though uncrowned?* This was the secret mainspring of his public life as a statesman, and it is from this point of view that his actions must now be judged. He had the right to say to himself: "*They are my people. This is my land—my Throne.*" The recognition of this fact furnishes a clue to much that appears enigmatical in his letters and conduct as a State official. He felt that he could manage national affairs better than anyone else for England, and the more things went wrong in later years, the more he urged James, in the true kingly spirit, to trust the people. He sank his identity to become James's loyal servant, the better to serve his countrymen, to watch their interests. Thus in Parliament he pursued the role of reconciler between the Crown and Parliament. He sought to bring about a true rapprochement between Prince and people.

The session of 1610 shows very clearly that though Francis Bacon had become Solicitor-General he had by no means become subservient to authority and his prime care was the rights of citizenship. Though he was bound by tradition to support the King's measures in the Commons, he nevertheless "both spoke and voted on the important legal and political question of the Grievances and Prerogative against the superior Law Officers of the Crown."

This was similar to his attitude when he withstood the claims of the Crown in Elizabeth's day. The issue in 1610 was virtually the same: King James and the Commons were out of tune and out of step. From that moment of definite estrangement there ensued a series of duel-like skirmishes between the Stuarts and the people of England which later culminated fatally for Charles I. The pivot of the quarrel was the national purse. In Elizabeth's time the ordinary revenue of the Crown was just sufficient to meet ordinary expenditure, any extraordinary disbursements being voted by Parliament. When James came to the Throne there was no money in the Treasury, but a considerable debt. This rocketed through the King's riotous living and criminal indulgence with his unpopular favourites. This wasteful extravagance was deeply resented by the Commons and made them tardy to vote any extraordinary supplies. In 1608 Cecil succeeded Lord Dorset as treasurer, and found there was an annual deficit of £80,000. He therefore decided to increase the impositions by £60,000, by the exercise of the Royal Prerogative and without consulting Parliament. The royal revenue could only be obtained from one or more of three sources:

1. lucrative privileges attached to the Sovereign's office, as the letting of monopolies and other feudal tenures;
2. taxes levied in the shape of duties by a royal mandate, and known as impositions;
3. SUPPLIES voted by Parliament.

The object of the Crown was manifestly to extend the range of the first and second, as sources of revenue exempt from conditions; while the obvious policy of the popular party was to make the Crown mainly depend on the third, which might be a matter of bargain and reminded the Sovereign of his dependence as a last resort on the House of Commons.

Cecil's imposition was unpopular and created grave discontent. It still left £20,000 of an annual deficit and did nothing to discharge any of the King's debts. He was therefore compelled to appeal to Parliament to try to find a way out of the increasing financial difficulties of the Court. The fatal policy of the imposition from the beginning was to make the Crown independent of Parliamentary supplies, to dispense with votes of supply and to create a permanent revenue of taxes and tenures over which the Commons had no control and which could be increased by virtue of the Prerogative, *i.e.* the King's will. Cecil applied to Parliament in 1610 for a scheme which was called "the Great Contract", whereby the King, for a lump sum of £600,000 and an annual grant of £200,000 surrendered certain feudal rights and dues and swept away grievances such as the abuse of royal proclamations which forbade the people to do certain things under penalties that could be enforced by the Star Chamber, the Crown thus assuming the power of penal legislation.

The Commons were not favourably impressed but offered £100,000 for the abrogation of the most flagrant grievances such as monopolies for the sale of wines, the licensing of inns, the importation of coal, etc. Then came a series of haggling negotiations in which James showed the spirit of a common huckster. The bargaining went on from February to the end of November, contact between the parties being broken off, renewed, and broken off again. It was Francis Bacon who, on 8 March, was commissioned by the Commons to confer with the Lords to join with them in a petition to the King respecting the compounding of the feudal tenures inherited by James, so great was the Members' confidence in Francis Bacon's honesty, although he was Solicitor-General and the King's Servant. And it was Francis Bacon whose pleading and arguments in the House as well as in private conference resulted in the King consenting to reduce his demands and the House of Commons to raise their offer so that the two bodies "drew near to each other to sweep away the worst abuses of the Feudal State"; but the Great Contract came to an abrupt and ignominious end after "numberless messages to and fro, indignation meetings about the interference of the Privy Council ... when the King, after many shifts, showed his false cards."

The session which had begun so prosperously closed in open strife between people and Prince, not a single Bill receiving the royal assent, the King adjourning the House on 24 November and dissolving it on 29 February, speaking his mind thus: "His Highness hath now had patience with this Assembly these seven years and from them received more disgraces, censures, and ignominies, than ever Prince did endure."

Whether it was Cecil or James who was responsible for the shifting and inconstant proceeding of the Government throughout this transaction, the final breach was distinctly their choice and act. The Commons on the other hand acted throughout openly, honestly, consistently and liberally, and with no more circumspection than the case required.

Sir Edward Coke, who personally detested Francis Bacon and especially his views on these outworn relics of feudalism, had much to do with it. He advised the King and Cecil that James "could *lawfully* sell the burthens on tenures yet preserve to the Crown the Tenures themselves", while Francis Bacon contended that the sale of the burthens on tenures would be in fact and in law a complete sale of the tenures. In office or out of office he was true to his principles. He had always pressed for the full surrender of these vexatious dues. The Commons now realized the meaning of the so-called "sale". The King was still to have his cake though he had eaten it—or, rather, sold it. "Except in the matter of Impositions, the Crown, though it promised to use its authority justly, did not talk of *PARTING* with any authority."

To free the Crown from debt and settle upon it an income was to make the King independent of Parliament. He did not need to call any more Parliaments, and the power of the purse would have passed from the keeping of the Commons, the liberties of the people would be endangered, for if there were not a clear surrender, a "PARTING", laws could be made to suit the Crown. In short, it emerged that the King wanted to retain his claim to levy impositions or duties on merchandise by virtue of his Prerogative.

Supply was to be voted, and compensation given *in addition,* for any exercise of the Prerogative he might be pleased to relax. Finally he made a long speech asserting his right to tax not only imports and exports, but all property whatsoever in the realm—which, together with his obstinate refusal to entertain the question of ecclesiastical grievances, put an end to the whole negotiation.

The breakdown left the Commons exasperated and discontented. Their grievances were still unredressed. The King dissolved Parliament in a fit of temper and the Members returned to their constituencies determined that the Crown must get out of its difficulties in its own way without their assistance. The King's finances were now worse off than ever. His credit had gone, for the nation knew that he was virtually bankrupt. The emptiness of the Exchequer, the shifts and perplexities of the Lord Treasurer had become the common talk of the town. To obtain money for current necessities he had to adopt the most questionable means: the selling of baronetcies and honours and raising loans wherever possible from City financiers. He failed to raise a loan of £100,000 from the London aldermen wherewith to pay his most pressing debts.

In all this long bargaining Francis Bacon had never receded from the position he had enunciated—that all repressive collections, though legally permissive by the exercise of the Prerogative, should be voluntarily abandoned. He did his best as an important person in the Commons, skilfully smoothing over differences and, whatever he thought of the great Contract, trying to gain for it fair play. He seems honestly to have disliked the plan of the Contract and would have dissuaded it had Cecil not been the last man likely to take his advice. As a matter of fact, he seems to have stood on one side after the opening stages of the wrangle as though he knew that a last-minute twist was contemplated to do the Commons an injury. What he thought he expressed later in no uncertain language, as we shall see. He thought the scheme a preposterous one. But the most important point that stands out clearly, in view of the fact that it was these "Abuses" that were indirectly responsible for Francis Bacon's subsequent downfall, is this: Francis Bacon was utterly opposed to impositions and tenures, etc., however legal the Prerogative, and thought that supply should be provided by Parliament. In the debates which sprang from these transactions, the Solicitor General, brushing away the distinctions made by Coke and Fleming, urged on the House of Commons and the Crown, the wisdom of abolishing these feudal tenures both in name and fact. These long-drawn-out negotiations were the last important business attempted by Cecil, for the following year he died (4 May 1612). During the previous ten years he had been the most powerful man in England, taking over State office after office, and they are among the most profligate years in our history. *Spanish ambassadors ruled the State, for Spanish gold lined Cecil's pockets to corrupt our foreign policy.*

How Francis Bacon as a Tudor must have writhed in his impotence to see the State—his birthright—in the hands of such licentious incompetents! He saw it drifting to ruin which he was powerless to avert. There was, indeed, "something rotten in the state of Denmark", cried the creator of anguished Hamlet, but *to have suggested remedial measures would have laid him open to the suspicious James that he cherished designs on the Throne.*

With Cecil's death the last vestiges of all that was noble in Elizabethan traditions definitely passed away and all that was evil, grasping and cruel in the régime was eventually perpetuated by the reign of favourites. James had lost a pillar of strength. Who was there now to steer the ship of State? Coke was impossible, the reverse of a statesman—narrow, pedantic, visionless. Northampton, unpopular, was suspected of being a Catholic; neither patriotic nor scrupulous in spite of his repute for learning. The Earl of Suffolk was a great courtier but had no creative intellect or business ability. The new Favourite, Robert Carr, Lord Rochester, was "an inexperienced and uninstructed youth given to pleasure, greedy of gain, intoxicated by his sudden elevation and detested by the people because he was a Scotsman." In short, there was no one on or off the Privy Council fit for the management of the State save Francis Bacon. These considerations impelled him to write to James to proffer his services and advice. We have three drafts of letters from Francis Bacon's own cabinet, though which one if any was sent to the King no one knows. Spedding thinks that he had an opportunity of speaking with the King which may have caused the letter to be withheld. But there are phrases and thoughts in each draft worth consideration. The first letter is dated 29 May 1612 and shows that Francis Bacon had always felt himself tied to—and tonguetied by—Cecil and never able to realize his ambitions to the full.

> It may please your Majesty to take these few lines to be an effect not of presumption but affection. For of the one I was never noted; and for the other I could never show it hitherto to the full; having been as a *hawk tied to another's fist, that might sometimes bait and proffer but could never fly.*

The second draft is important for it proves conclusively that Francis Bacon's firm opinion was that the only remedy for the King's financial difficulties was through Parliament.

> Your Majesty hath lost a great subject and a great servant. But if I should praise him in propriety, I should say that he was a fit man to keep things from growing worse but no very fit man to reduce things to be much better. For he loved to have the eyes of all Israel a little too much upon himself, and to have all business still under the hammer and like clay in the hands of the potter to mould it as he thought good.... And though he had fine passages of action, yet the real conclusions came slowly on. So that although your Majesty hath grave Counsellors and worthy persons left, yet you do as it were turn a leaf, wherein if your Majesty shall give a frame and a constitution to such matters, *before you place the persons,* in my simple opinion it were not amiss. But the great matter and most instant for the present, *is the consideration of Parliament, for two effects: the other for the better knitting of the Hearts of your Subjects unto your Majesty, according to your infinite merit; for both of which, Parliaments have been and are the ancient and honourable remedy.*
>
> Now because I take myself to have a little skill in that region, as one that ever affected that your Majesty mought in all your causes not only prevail, but prevail with satisfaction of the inner man; and though no man can say but I was a perfect and peremptory Royalist, yet every man makes me believe that *I was never one hour out of credit with the Lower House;* My desire is to know, whether your Majesty will give me leave to meditate and propound unto you some preparative remembrances touching the future Parliament....
>
> And as my good old Mistress was wont to call me her watch candle, because it pleased her to say I did continually burn (*and yet she suffered me to waste almost to nothing*), so I must much more owe the like duty to your Majesty, by whom my fortunes have been settled and raised.

The third letter is dateless, though written about the same time.

> To the king, My principal end being to do your Majesty service, I crave leave to make at this time to your Majesty *this most humble oblation of myself....*
>
> I was three of my young years bred with an Ambassador in France, and since I have been an old truant in the school-house of your Council-Chamber, though on the second form; yet longer than any that now sitteth hath been on the head form.
>
> If your Majesty find any aptness in me, or if you find any scarcity in others, whereby you may think it fit for your service to remove me to Business of State; although I have a fair way before me for profit and in a course less exposed to the blasts of fortune, yet now that he is gone I will be as ready as a chessman to be wherever your Majesty's Royal hand shall set me.
>
> Your Majesty will bear me witness, I have not suddenly opened myself thus far.

> I have looked upon others, I see the exceptions, I see the distractions . . . I know my own heart, and I know not whether God that hath touched my heart with the affection may not touch your Royal heart to discern it.
>
> Howsoever, I shall at least go on *honestly* in mine ordinary course, and supply the rest in prayers for you.

James did not accept the offer to make Francis Bacon principal Secretary of State. Had he done so with courage the history of England would have run differently. He was still half afraid lest Francis Bacon's protestations of honesty were but a cloak under which he might assert his rights, lest he might attempt by force of guile a *coup d'état.* The King, moreover, was averse to calling a new Parliament. Privy Council members like the Earl of Northampton, the Favourite Rochester, and Sir Julius Caesar were all of the opinion that the King possessed sufficient power in his Prerogative to free him from pecuniary embarrassment. The consideration of a new Parliament and the appointment of a Secretary of State were indefinitely postponed, the office of treasurer being put in commission, and Francis Bacon was appointed a subcommissioner to assist in abating expenditure and improving the revenue. Says Spedding:

> Francis Bacon's letters, however, had not been altogether thrown away. Though the King did not make him a Councillor, he encouraged him to offer counsel upon the most important affairs of State; listened to him. . . . So that from the moment of Cecil's death Bacon became a much more important person.

The following famous anecdote is told respecting Cecil's decease. The King meeting Francis Bacon said, "Now tell me truly what think you of your cousin that is gone?"

"Sir," answered Bacon, "since your Majesty charges me, I'll give you such a character of him as if I were to write his story. I do think he was no fit Councillor to make your affairs better. But yet he was fit to have kept them from growing worse."

"On my soul man," said James, "in the first thou speakest like a true man, in the second *like a kinsman.*"[1]

Francis Bacon has, however, been much censured by his critics, like Church and Abbott, for his harsh views concerning Cecil as expressed after his death. He wrote: "My Lord of Salisbury *had a good method, if his means had been upright.*" Considering that Cecil lined his pockets with Spanish gold and lived with more than one mistress, Francis Bacon had a perfect right to express such an opinion after his decease, an opinion he dared not express during his lifetime.

On 18 September (four months after Cecil's death) he wrote to the King congratulating him upon his deliverance from the incapable Councillor who had planned and mismanaged the great Contract.

> He is gone from whom those courses did wholly flow.
>
> To have your wants and necessities in particular, as it were hanged up in Two Tablets before the eyes of your Lords and Commons, to be talked of for four months together; to stir a number of projects and then blast them and leave your Majesty nothing but the scandal of them; to pretend even carriage between your

[1]See *Apophthegms.*

> Majesty's rights and the ease of the people—these courses and others the like, I hope, are gone with the deviser of them.

After all, there had been little love between these nominal cousins. Cecil had consistently and successfully thwarted the greatest genius in England, the first man in the Commons, from rising in the State and at the Bar with a malignant jealousy only a shade less pronounced than his venomous hatred towards the Earl of Essex, whom he pursued to his death. How could Francis Bacon forget that Cecil was more or less directly responsible for the death of his brother Robert? Cecil had spoken Francis Bacon fair in public, but in secret he had ever opposed and maligned him. The crooked hunchback had hated his handsome rival from the early days when in belittlement he whispered in the Palace to the maids of honour, "Francis is the Queen's Bastard." In death Cecil's hatred still pursued Bacon to injure him irretrievably if possible. He had poured distilled poison into the ears of James concerning him, warning James that Francis Bacon must be kept down from rising in the State because he had designs on the Throne; that if he were given an inch, he would take an ell, and that he was a danger to the Stuart dynasty. From the grave the dead man clasped Francis Bacon's robes not only to prevent him rising in the State, but menacing his very life. Can one wonder that from the date of the last letter Francis Bacon "never mentions Cecil's name in his correspondence with James but with words of condemnation"?

Donnelly in *The Great Cryptogram* writes:

> Cecil had the upper hand of Bacon and he kept it. He sat on his neck as long as he lived. Even after the death of Elizabeth and the coming-in of the new King, he held that mighty genius in the mire. *He seemed to have possessed some SECRET concerning Bacon discreditable to him, which he imparted to King James, and this hindered the advancement after the death of the Queen*.... Whatever it was, there was something potent enough to suppress Bacon and hold him down, even for some time after Cecil's death.

Donnelly had no idea that the "potent something" was Francis Bacon's BIRTH SECRET. There is not the slightest doubt that as James began to take him more into his confidence he told Francis Bacon what Cecil had said: that Francis Bacon was Tudor-born with a real claim to the Throne; that so long as he lived he would be a menace to the Stuart succession; and that he should never be allowed to take any important official part in State affairs. Is there any wonder that Francis Bacon should feel indignant and bitter when he felt that his chances to right the ship of State were in jeopardy? When he remembered through the long years the hindrances placed in his way repeatedly by jealous vindictiveness? The false tales told to Elizabeth that sent his dearest friend and more than brother to the block? And that, even when he tried to forget and forgive, Cecil was undermining him to the very last with the King? Francis Bacon had known only too well that if the appointment of the Attorney-Generalship (which was his right) was left to Cecil he would never get it. He therefore wrote to the King direct (well before Cecil's death) to secure a promise from him of the reversion of the office. The letter is notable because it drags in Pallas, the Shaker of the Spear.

While I stand in your Majesty's good opinion, I would make proof to do you some honour by my pen either by writing some faithful narrative ... of the Times; or by recompiling your laws, which I perceive your Majesty laboureth with and hath *in your head as Jupiter had PALLAS;* or some other work.

Was Francis Bacon, too, like Pallas-Athene? For *did not Shake-speare spring into being fully armed at all points as a playwright in the world arena as though he had never served a laborious apprenticeship to the craft of the quill?*

When Cecil died the Treasury had a debit of £500,000. The ordinary annual expenditure was in excess of revenue by £160,000. Neither the creation of a new order of baronets (for handsome sums), nor the raising of the price of gold pieces, nor the increased impositions had eased the situation. Cecil's financial administration had doubled the original deficiency. The prime offices were vacant and Francis Bacon felt that the time had arrived when the King should present himself in a new character to his subjects, to make Cecil's decease an excuse for a complete break with the past financial system, and call a new Parliament as though his "true nature had been obscured by his late Minister". The advice fell on deaf ears.

Before Cecil's death, however, the King was being drawn more and more into personal contact with Francis Bacon. Perhaps the most important event which indicates this fact was the establishment on 8 May 1611 by patent, through the exercises of the Prerogative, of a new court called the "Court of the Verge" to deal directly with offences committed within a range of twelve miles round the King's London palace. James appointed him President of the Court. Francis Bacon had always been of opinion that justice was best when it was near at hand and the new court may well have been the result of his suggestion.

The appointment of Francis Bacon as President of the new court was probably given to him as a reward of honour for his labours connected with the revision of the 1611 Authorized edition of the James Bible. That he did revise the manuscripts before publication is certain. The Bible MSS. of the various translators had been entrusted to Dr. Thomas Bilston and Dr. Miles Smith for final revision, and in 1609 the two divines handed their finished work for his comments and alterations. He returned the MSS. for printing twelve months later (1610) steeped throughout in that ineffable beauty of style which neither King nor divines could have created—only the hand of a Shake-speare, the supreme master of English prose. Neither King James, Bilston nor Miles, individually or collectively, could have given the world such a literary masterpiece. We have their writings. They are mediocre, barren of style and lacking in the creative touch.

The appointment of Francis Bacon to this presidency gave him a judicial position for the first time. It was an earnest of the legal reform for which he had always pressed and the Court of the Verge was probably of his own devising.

There now began to pass through his hands as Solicitor-General the great cases of the day—the trial of Lord Sanquhar, a Scottish nobleman, accused of the murder of an Englishman by an agent; the case of Lady Arabella Stuart's marriage to William Seymour in defiance of the King, when her children might have been a menace to the James Stuart line; the charge against Sir Robert Mansell and James Whitlocke for too freely speaking their mind respecting the King's Prerogative, etc.

He drew up elaborate reports and memorials on all matters concerning the welfare of the State (many outside his set official duties) and submitted them to the King for his benefit.

To the Lords of the Council he compiled information respecting the scarcity of silver at the Mint and its remedy; to the King he furnished an elaborate report in great detail for the betterment of his estate in general; to the Lords Commissioners he sent a memorial for the bettering of the King's revenue; and as a subcommissioner he claimed that he had in twelve months improved his Majesty's revenues by £35,776 and "got in £309,680" by extraordinary collections—but still the budget did not balance. In 1613 therefore he sent a memorial to the King again giving his considered and settled reasons for calling a new Parliament in order to put the finances of the State on an even keel and remedy all outstanding grievances between King and Commons.

He issued instructions in 1612 to the Commissioners for collecting the "Aid" on the marriage of the Princess Elizabeth. By an ancient custom which had grown into a law, there was due to the King upon the marriage of his eldest daughter an "Aid" from his subjects. It brought into the Exchequer some £22,000. The marriage to the Count Palatine had to be postponed for a short time owing to the death of Elizabeth's brother, Prince Henry. In the marriage festivities *Francis Bacon took a prominent part in his role of PLAYWRIGHT by contriving a masque or musical comedy* at Gray's Inn, which cost £20,000 at that time. Chamberlain wrote:

> On Tuesday [Chamberlain writes on 18 February 1613] it came to Gray's Inn and the Inner Temples turn to come with their Masque *whereof Francis Bacon was the chief contriver* ... and on Saturday last did come again ... with great applause and approbation from the King and all the Company.

In November 1612 the Master of the Wards died. Having heard that the office was likely to be filled by one of Carr's nominees, Francis Bacon wrote a short straight letter reminding the Favourite of his claims to the vacant office, pointing out that the Court of Wards was one for a lawyer rather than a courtier to hold. He had worked so hard in the interests of the Crown that he felt certain of success. He had even bought new clothes and uniforms for his servants. But he had counted his chickens before they were hatched. The request failed. He wanted the Court of Wards and Liveries as a right, and would not buy it.

> While Bacon alleged his services, Sir Walter Cope, a man of larger fortunes and smaller scruples, told down his money and bought the place. The wags of the Mitre had their laugh. "Sir Walter" they said, "has got the Wards and Sir Francis the Liveries."[1]

To pay for an office to which he felt he was justly entitled through service was something that *Sir Francis would not do and never did do*. It was not that he was niggardly. *He objected on principle to the purchase and sales of offices of State and*

[1]Dixon, *Life*.

would have none of it. He could have bought it for he was now moderately well off. We know his financial position by his balance sheet in the *Commentarius.* This is how Mary Sturt reckons up on his own figures:

> He had a town house, apart from his Gray's Inn Chambers, for his wife, and his country house in Gorhambury. He had various farms producing a rent roll of about £330 a year. His offices and practice produced:
>
> | | |
> |---|---|
> | My Pension | 60 |
> | My Solicitor's Place | 1,000 |
> | My Practice | 1,200 |
> | My Office of Starchamber | 2,000 |
> | My Duchy Fee | 20 |
>
> In addition there was his wife's fortune of about £220 a year and sundry other small sums, so that his total annual income was about £5,000. In addition he had personal estate of furniture and jewels to the extent of about £2,000. *The curious thing is that Bacon was still in debt to the extent of £4,500* and rather more than half of this was bearing interest probably at ten per cent.... *In his own private life he was prodigal and careless to a degree. He regularly spent the whole of his income and was always in debt.*[1]
>
> [The Clerkship to the Star Chamber had fallen in on 16 July 1608. Francis Bacon held the reversion which had been given to him by Queen Elizabeth in October 1589. It made a great difference to his financial affairs.]

Once more we see the sheer inability of a biographer to face up to the problem of Francis Bacon's finances. Miss Sturt remarks that it is "curious" that Francis Bacon was still £4500 in debt and paying 10 per cent interest. *It is more than curious.* It is a MYSTERY. Miss Sturt seeks to explain the mystery by alleging that Francis Bacon was "prodigal and careless", and that this was the sole reason why he "was always in debt", when we know that he neither smoked, drank, gambled, nor devoured his living with loose company. Where did his money go to then? The plain truth is that an ethical, educational and literary Renaissance, the creation of an English-reading public and the printing of many books could not be accomplished without spending money and a large outlay of capital.

The English Renaissance was not like Jonah's gourd which sprang up overnight without any thought or labour, unwatched, untended. It was not a spontaneous literary impulse, but was planned, fostered and cared for. *The Italian Renaissance began with Dante; the French with Ronsard and the Pléiades; the English with Francis Bacon and the Rosicrosse-Literary Societies.* His powerful mind alone steered the good ship *The Advancement of Learning* between the Pillars of Hercules to breast the unknown future that lay beyond the horizon's waste of many waters. But ships can only be built and launched by willing hands and much expense. Every progressive movement that would fight ignorance and bigotry must be financed by someone. And in studying the Elizabethan and Jacobean eras *never let us forget that it was Francis Bacon's money as well as his brains that laid the foundations of our national intellectual greatness.* To provide the wherewithal, he pledged his credit, borrowed on future expectations, from his friends, from moneylenders, went cheerfully into debt to pay his staff of "Good Pens" and provide the "movable and immovable Jewels" for the

[1]Sturt, *Life.*

founding of many King Solomon's Temples. Yet more! *He thought it no shame even to be cast into a debtor's prison* so long as he could help to make England rich beyond the dreams of avarice in the true wealth of knowledge and mental equipment.

The two chief offices of State, the Secretaryship and the Treasury, were still vacant a year after Cecil's death, and the financial position of the Crown, in spite of all efforts, was steadily drifting from bad to worse. Francis Bacon, whose influence with the King was steadily growing, again pressed on James the necessity of calling a new Parliament and of "A new and Princely way of dealing with it". The Privy Council, too, were divided in their opinion. But the King drew nearer to Francis Bacon's policy. James knew he could not meet Parliament if there were not a responsible Lord Treasurer and Secretary of State. Thinking he might strengthen his hold on a new Lower House by putting in power representatives of two hostile views, James first of all dissolved the Treasury Commissioners and gave the Office of Treasurer to Henry Howard, Earl of Northampton, Lord Privy Seal, and advanced Sir Ralph Winwood, a man popular with the Puritans, to be Secretary of State, who was sworn in on 26 March 1614, taking his place in the House of Commons as First Minister of the Crown on 5 April.

Prior to this, however, there had been a shuffle of offices owing to the death on 7 August 1613 of Sir Thomas Fleming, Chief Justice of the King's Bench.

> The day had come when the King's friends could not rule the country without Bacon's help; and to this political necessity, not to the will of Howard or the favour of Carr, he owed his second great rise in public life.

James consulted Francis Bacon, who recommended that his enemy Sir Edward Coke should be raised to the King's Bench in Fleming's vacant seat as Lord Chief Justice. Coke objected, for position in the Common Pleas brought greater profit even if the King's Bench was of higher dignity. The prospect of a loss of fees was gall and wormwood to Coke though one of the richest men in England. The King insisted on this "penal promotion", as it has been called, Francis Bacon suggesting to James, "My Lord Coke will think himself near a Privy Councillor's place and will turn obsequious." James took the hint and made Coke into a Privy Councillor to soften the blow. Coke very reluctantly, well knowing who had given the advice, parted from his favourite Bench, "not only weeping himself but followed by the tears of all the Court of Common Pleas," the fact being that Francis Bacon did not want to contact "an offensive man" more than was absolutely necessary. Coke had got a less influential place though a higher one, out of the direct path of Francis Bacon. This was Bacon's first direct thrust in reply to a series of insults and it was felt to be so by the recipient.

To Francis Bacon, his adversary, the irascible Lord Chief Justice said bitterly as he left the Court, "This is all your doing: It is you that have made this great stir."

"Ah, my Lord", came the reply, "Your Lordship all this while hath grown in breadth; you must needs now grow in height or you will become a monster."[1]

[1]Bacon, *Apophthegms.*

The transfer of Coke resulted in Sir Henry Hobart, the Attorney-General, taking Coke's vacated seat in the Common Pleas, and now, at last, as a matter of course, on 27 October, Francis Bacon was appointed Attorney-General. "Such was his approach to Great Place."

Chapter IV

AS ATTORNEY GENERAL: APPROACH TO GREATEST OFFICE (1613—1617)

AT the age of fifty-two Francis Bacon had, at last, after twenty years of waiting, obtained the position to which he aspired when he was thirty-two. For twenty years he had been torn between the noble and sublime ideals on which his soul was bent, and the putting of them into active operation, and the "necessities of that civil or professional and political life by which he had to maintain his estate." He had won through without truckling to Queen, King or Favourite by the sheer force of his will and ability. He had now a vantage ground—unencumbered by financial anxieties—from which he could view the landscape and go forward in good heart towards the goal of his great projects.

We are now approaching the scenes of Bacon's greatest and busiest and most complex public activities which ultimately faded out in the most appalling catastrophe that befell a British statesman, a tragedy so inexplicable that even yet the entire story has never been thoroughly unravelled, sifted and told by historian or biographer.

From October 1613 to March 1617 he was the King's Attorney, sworn to carry out the policy of the Crown. He had plenty to do officially, so much so that *no Shakespeare plays were created during these years of public stress and strain.* It was when he was "idling" in the "unknown Years" that the plays were first produced. When he was concerned with public activities he produced little or nothing creatively. But when he was in enforced retirement from public life from 1621, Shakespeare plays that the world had never heard of before were again created—like *Henry VIII*—and given to the world in the 1623 Folio. The revision of Part I of *Don Quixote* probably was done in 1612–13 and Part II in 1614–15. This was first put into Spanish in 1604, printed in 1605 and revised in 1608, being only about half the size of the English version known as the Shelton Translation. There are some interesting details about *Don Quixote* given in *Sir Francis Bacon,* by Parker Woodward.

In April 1616 Shakspere, "the man-player", died; later in the year there was printed in Holland an *Emblem Book,* the author giving the name of Cornelii Giselberti Plempii. It has the usual Rosicrosse signals denoting its secret origin. "The first Emblem depicts the Goddess of Fortune pushing from the top of a pinnacle a person garbed as an Actor." At the same time she assists a man who has his back to the reader to rise from his knees. He is clothed and wears the same hat as Francis Bacon and is obviously intended for him. These secret "Works of his Recreation" would have taken little time to produce with his staff of "Good Pens". Indeed, it is very difficult to say what an abnormal creator and executant as Francis Bacon, full of abounding energy, could not devise with an enthusiastic band of writers—ready to do his bidding and working under his instruction. He dictated. They wrote. He got his script and revised it. Thus he was spared much of the drudgery of the physical labour of writing. Everyone with an efficient typist today knows the tremendous saving of time and energy to an overpressed principal; whereas Francis Bacon had a number of enthusiasts labouring for a common ideal—the spreading of education, ethics, literature (in the sense that literature is the true interpreter of LIFE). Francis Bacon's output of literature—the Shakespeare plays in particular—were not the work of one man writing alone in a garret like Goldsmith or the Grub Street hacks. *All his literary work was stamped with the combined brains of the best thinkers of the Elizabethan age,* polished and refined by technicians of many kinds, skilled cypherists, cryptographers, etc. This explains much that is inexplicable and fully answers the objection that one man could not have produced such a vast output. We have seen already that Bacon was the chief contriver of the first masque presented to the King to celebrate the marriage of the King's Favourite, the Earl of Somerset, with Lady Essex on 16 December 1613.

> The world of rank, wealth, fashion, and business hastened to congratulate the bride and bridegroom with gifts unprecedented in number and value.... The festivities continued until the 12th Night when *they were wound up with a complimentary offering from Bacon; an offering* so costly considering how little he had owed Rochester the Favourite and how superficial their intercourse had been. It is not possible to suppose that there had ever been any intimacy between them.[1]

This "complimentary offering" was no less than "*a Masque to honour this marriage which will stand him in no less than £2000*" to quote a newsletter of Chamberlain. Men like Abbott say that Francis Bacon gave the play as a sort of recompense for having obtained the Attorneyship through Somerset's good offices and hint pointedly that he was greatly in the Favourite's debt. But Spedding truly remarks that:

> If Bacon had had any influence with the man who for the last five years had kept the gate of the King's affections, he must have had very frequent occasions to use it—and to use it in a way which was sure to leave traces.... There is no trace of anything of the kind. On the contrary, when he wants the King's favourable ear, he writes to the King himself.

Somerset had claimed to have used his influence with the King to have secured Francis Bacon's promotion, but the claim was instantly repudiated as appears from a letter written by Francis Bacon to the King some two years later:

> I must never forget when I moved your Majesty for the Attorney's place, *it was your sole act*; more than that, Somerset, when he knew your Majesty had resolved it, *thrust himself into the business for a fee.*

But while all were making presents to the Great Favourite (gifts of plate, furniture, horses, gold, etc.) it was difficult indeed to stand aside. He therefore offered *on the part of Gray's Inn* to supply a masque and to bear the expense.

[1]Spedding, *op. cit.*

Whatever the pretended obligation, it was thus repaid by something which could not be turned into money—which would almost have tended to countenance one of the great abuses of the times, the sale of offices for money, against which abuse Francis Bacon was unutterably opposed.

> As a compliment it was splendid, according to the taste and magnificence of the time; costly to the giver, not negotiable to the receiver; valuable as a compliment but as nothing else.... It conferred great distinction upon Gray's Inn, in a field in which Gray's Inn was ambitious and accustomed to shine.[1]

I do not think that the *Masque of Flowers* was ever written under a sense of obligation to Somerset but out of deference to the King's wishes, for when the play was published (it can be seen in *Nichol's Progress*) there was a preface to Francis Bacon under the anonymous initials J.G., W.D. and T.B. The writers say among other things:

> You have graced in general the Societies of the *Inns of Court in doing the King honour*; and particularly Gray's Inn, which, as you have formerly brought to flourish, both in the *ANCIENTER and YOUNGER Sort, by Countenancing VIRTUE in every Quality,* so now you have made a notable demonstration thereof in *the lighter and less SERIOUS kind* ... and in the *space of THREE WEEKS* could perform that which hath been performed; which could not have been done but that *every man's exceeding Love and Respect to you* gave him Wings to overtake Time which is the swiftest of things.

Here are several significant asides. The play was written *to do "the King honour"*, not Somerset. Note, too, the unexplained debt that Gray's Inn owes him ... ancient societies which "flourish" and a "Younger Sort" also which countenances "Virtue". What can such societies be but those founded on the ancient Mysteries which are associated with younger ones and which inculcate virtue by dramatic practices—Freemasonry? To which the *Masque of Flowers* was allied as a lighter and less serious form of the drama. In 1613 the preface writers declare that Francis Bacon had won "*every man's exceeding Love and Respect*". Let all Shakespeareans take notice particularly that the *Masque of Flowers* was conceived and written within "*the space of Three Weeks*"; such was the ease with which the master-playwright could create a local habitation and a name with his poet's pen. Only a practised hand at dramatic creation could have created this particular musical play in so short a time, with "its loud and cheerful Music, abundance of Light and Colour, graceful Motions and Forms ... ending with *an offering of Flowers to the Bride and Bridegroom.*" No orthodox biographer has expressed (so-called) surprise that when "Shakespeare" and Ben Jonson were at the height of their fame neither was called in to provide a royal entertainment. No! It is a startling fact that it is Francis Bacon the Solicitor-General and Francis Bacon the Attorney-General who provides a humorous and gorgeous entertainment—a form of writing denoting a mastery of craftsmanship totally different from legal argument, forensic knowledge, and philosophical discourse. The *Essay on Masques and Triumphs* shows similarly that the author was intimately acquainted with the practical management of theatrical production. Everything goes to show that these

[1]Mrs. Henry Pott, *Francis Bacon and his Secret Society.*

OPEN "Works of his Recreation" were closely blended with the Shakespeare plays, that the Elizabethan drama had its rise in Gray's Inn, and that the moving spirit was Francis Bacon.

At the time of his marriage Somerset, because of his personal ascendency over King James, wielded greater power in the State than anyone else, statesman or priest. Homosexualist as was James, it seemed impossible for him to exist without the exclusive company of some handsome youth over whom he could kiss and slaver. Somerset was the latest of a succession of favourites and had become James's boon companion, until he finally abandoned himself to one sole favourite in 1611, the year before Cecil's death.

His name was Robert Carr, a young Scotsman of good figure and address. He and his friend Thomas Overbury had come to London to push their fortunes. Carr had been one of James's pages in Scotland, had travelled in France, had caught the King's eye by a lucky fall at a tilting match and "had won his heart by a red cheek, a bright feather and a handsome leg". Carr's handsome personality was fired by Overbury's mind and wit, to the amusement of the King. James decided he would make Carr into "the perfect companion", and began by "teaching him Latin" every morning. From the King's fortieth to his forty-seventh year he was James's bosom friend and confidant. Carr was quickly created Viscount Rochester, invested with the Garter, made a Privy Councillor and enriched with offices and estates. Overbury was made a knight and given the post of King's Sewer. "*They exercised a power such as Leicester or Burleigh never possessed. Carr governed the King and Overbury governed Carr.*" From the time of Cecil's death we can say that to the end of the King's reign the nation was ruled by favourites, young and inexperienced, whose whims of vanity were bounded by the first personal pronoun which always barred the way to the State's welfare. If the years of Cecil's rule were profligate, they speedily became still more abandoned until the entire Court became dead to every sense of business rectitude or moral uprightness. It is probably true that both Carr and Overbury never took Spanish bribes, which Cecil had taken and which were still being taken by the Earls of Suffolk and Northampton; but Carr instituted the system whereby anyone who wanted the ear of the King—a favour—had first to make a peace offering to the Favourite, a handsome donation to his privy purse. As he grew greater from plain Robert Carr to Lord Rochester and then to the Earl of Somerset he grew arrogant in pride of place and lust for power. He even dominated the King himself, who wrote to Somerset that pitiable and famous letter complaining of his Favourite's treatment with his

> fiery boutades [sudden outbursts], dogged sullen behaviour ... the withdrawing of yourself from lying in my chamber notwithstanding my many hundred times earnestly soliciting you to the contrary.... Be kind: For the easing of my inward and consuming grief.

The rise of Carr made a great increase in the King's extravagance and set James on the high road to ruin and shame. Some think that *the Great Contract* came to grief because of the influence of his favourites. However that may be, certain it is that Carr prevailed upon the King to dissolve his first Parliament (1611) because the Commons had made bitter complaints about his Scottish favourites and intended to demand their return to Scotland—

a suggestion which thoroughly alarmed Carr. Although the King was so desperately in need of putting his finances in order, he nevertheless distributed £34,000 among six of his disreputable courtiers the week before the dissolution. In the year 1613,

> the King was severing himself from his Council and taking as chief adviser his Favourite Carr a mere animal as destitute of policy as of *morality* and refinement.

Carr was, in short, simply a high-spirited, lascivious rake; and his chief mistress, known to all the nation, was the dissolute Countess of Essex, Frances Howard, a member of the oldest Catholic nobility, a married woman with innumerable lovers. Carr's overmastering desire was to marry her but his long-standing friend Overbury was averse to the proposal. "She is right as a mistress but not as a wife," said Overbury, who was a staunch Protestant and was afraid lest Carr should turn Catholic. Moreover he hated any kind of alliance with the Spaniards. Carr talked the matter over with James. The King decided to send Overbury out of the country. He appointed him to a diplomatic post abroad and, when Overbury refused to accept it, sent him to the Tower, where he died, in *mysterious circumstances,* six months later. To remove the imperishable barrier of a husband Carr persuaded the King to set up a commission so that the Countess of Essex could be divorced on the grounds of nullity, the impotence of the Earl of Essex. The Archbishop of Canterbury thought the proceeding a scandal and was sent for and lectured by the King, who ordered him in future "to rest his faith upon the unerring judgement of a sovereign who was not without some skill in Divinity."

The commission pronounced the divorce decree. Carr was created the Earl of Somerset. The way was open to him to marry. The Church and the country were scandalized and especially at James's part in obtaining the divorce by his advice and interference. It further widened the breach between the King and his people over his unpopular foreign Spanish policy. The divorce of the Countess was the first important matter that happened after Francis Bacon's appointment as Attorney-General. For it, and the subsequent scandals and tragedies that followed in its train, Francis Bacon was in no way responsible. In his subsequent public career Bacon had to steer a straight course in the midst of so much rotten rapacity, the Court being a cesspool of iniquity, the atmosphere reeking with putrid infection. Francis Bacon knew the worthlessness of Somerset and had no time for him. It was for this reason that he simply presented to the newly married pair a simple gift of a musical *Masque of Flowers,* worthless in itself as a gift, not from himself personally but from the Benchers of Gray's Inn, and though the gift had cost him £2000 not a penny piece could be put into circulation by the avaricious Favourite.

Bacon's first advice to the Crown in his new office was to abandon its irregular, unproductive methods of raising funds; to call a new Parliament to Westminster: to explain frankly the political situation; and to trust the nation for supplies. Though the Court Party—Somerset, Northampton and their coterie of short-sighted, shallow-pated courtiers always eager to foment friction between the King and the Commons—opposed Francis Bacon's policy, the financial situation was rapidly becoming desperate and chaotic, so that Francis Bacon's advice was taken; the writs went out into the country and the new Parliament was called in April 1614. We now come to a very significant fact which gives the lie to the infamous suggestions that Francis Bacon was an obsequious sychophant as a man to those in authority, and that he was regarded by all honest people with aversion. He had represented Ipswich for thirteen years. The burgesses re-elected him again. That was Mark of Confidence No. 1. St Albans elected him also and prayed him to represent the freeholders. Was not this a tribute to his known worth and integrity? Mark No. 2. But Cambridge, which he had left as a youth in disdain, likewise claimed him with pride as one of her most distinguished sons. The Dons, with whom as a body he had had little or nothing to do, well knew that he was the most brilliant Cambridge man who had ever lived; for apart from their knowledge of the value of *The Advancement of Learning* there were many Cambridge men, like Thomas Randolph, Henry Oakley, Henry Ferne, G. Nash, Gabriel Harvey (members of his secret societies) who knew that he was the immortal mastersinger, SHAKE-SPEARE, the true founder of an intellectual greatness that would ultimately embrace the entire world; and that the far-flung eternities would one day see the vision splendid that his soul had seen in secret and had whispered to a few beloved disciples its meaning and purpose. Cambridge claimed him for her own. And because there is nothing more pure than for a public man to wish to represent in Parliament the university in which he has studied, he accepted the gracious and unanimous wish of this noble constituency of scholars and gentlemen. What a reward of confidence is shown in this triple return!

MARK No. 3! *It was unprecedented in Parliamentary annals*, says Dixon. *No one in that Parliament save the new Attorney-General could boast of a triple return.* Are we to believe that the burgesses, scholars and gentlemen of three great constituencies were deceived in him? And that uninformed critics of scant knowledge—living three hundred years afterwards—are better entitled to pass judgement upon him than contemporaries who lived with him and knew him personally? This striking tribute to his personal character was not the only one he was to receive. When the House met a whisper went round the benches that Francis Bacon's three elections were null and void. Francis Bacon was an officer of the Crown. No man holding the position of Attorney-General had ever been elected previously to the Commons. Many Members thought that so powerful an officer—the Crown Prosecutor—who set the law in motion, collected facts and sifted evidence, ought not to be allowed to sit in that Assembly, hearing everything, seeing everything, noting everything, forgetting nothing. The free speech of the Commons might be used against them by an Attorney who might prove to be an inquisitor and a tyrant. Yet notwithstanding their jealousy of power, the representative gentlemen of England had no heart to put the wisest and the best among them to the door. They sought for precedents that he might keep his seat; but no case was on the rolls. An Attorney-General chosen after nomination could not sit by precedent. What then? *They waived their right. They took him as he was. Crown lawyer or not Crown lawyer, he was Francis Bacon.* As Francis Bacon he should sit. But the case should stand alone. *This tribute paid to personal merit and public service* must not be drawn into a precedent dangerous to their franchise said the applauding Members. He was the first to sit, he must also be the last. This exception was made by men so hostile to the Crown that they did not pass a single Bill. It was a personal tribute which again marks the esteem in which Francis Bacon was held by the House of Commons—by a House that had known him for thirty years and "had seen him vote and act under every form of temptation that can test the virtue of a public man". This exception made for Francis Bacon became the rule for succeeding times. Since then the Attorney-General has always sat among the representatives of the people.

Before Bacon's day the Attorney-General had been the personal servant of the King: From Bacon's day he has been the servant of the State. *Bacon was the first of a new order of public men.*

The fact is scarcely less creditable *to his political purity* than the composition of the *Novum Organum* is glorious to his intellectual powers. Bad men kill great offices. Good men *found them.*

Judging then by the actions of the burgesses of three constituencies and the signal tribute of the Members of Parliament, Francis Bacon's appointment to the Attorneyship met with the approval of the entire nation. His popularity must have sprung from the knowledge that he was a man of honour and of unimpeachable integrity for the Commons to have passed such a vote of confidence in him despite knowing that he was now primarily the King's servant. It must be remembered that the 1614 House was a suspicious House so far as the Crown was concerned. The Members knew very well that the King had not called them together out of pure love for democracy or to remedy the grievances of the nation out of simple goodness of heart. They were fully aware that the King's great object in summoning a Parliament was to obtain supplies—that this was his chief concern no matter in what attractive feathers was tricked out the question of supply. It was on 16 February 1614 that the Lords of Council recommended the calling of Parliament, but on or before this date James had referred a variety of questions relative to the proposed Parliament to his learned Counsel. It was decided that a number of Bills were to be submitted to the Commons indicating that the old "Petition of Grievances" had been perused and a selection made of those to be redressed. But the rock on which the 1610 Parliament had split and foundered was the King's inherent "right" to decree impositions by virtue of his feudal Prerogative. When the Commons afterwards were acquainted with the list of Bills their attitude was that although the King had conceded a great deal he had not conceded enough. When it had been definitely decided to summon Parliament, Francis Bacon, in order to assist the King, drew up an elaborate and detailed "Memorial of Some Points which may be touched in His Majesty's Speech to both Houses". In this memorial Francis Bacon wrote:

> In the last Parliament his Majesty took upon himself the person of a Merchant, and they [the MPs] took upon them the persons of purchasers or contractors. But that in this Parliament His Majesty will hold himself to the person of a gracious King and leave them to the persons of loving and kind subjects ... the true proceeding is for either part chiefly to take care of the other ... the King to take care of his subjects and the subjects to take care of their King.

In other words, the King should endeavour to create an atmosphere of mutual trust in the grand, magnanimous princely manner with an utter absence of niggardliness or cheeseparing bargaining; and to convince the

Commons of his honesty of purpose. But this advice—the pith of the memorial—the King never followed; James could not forget that he was an absolute King with ancient rights and liberties, and to surrender any fragment of his hereditary rights to popular cries was quite contrary to his nature—at once irritable, suspicious, exacting. He held the fixed idea that any gesture of frank generosity would be regarded as weakness in him by the common people.

There is no doubt that Francis Bacon was anxious about the success of the new Parliament and the memorial is valuable in showing how he wished to achieve it. Had James listened to him instead of hearkening to his avaricious favourite and empty-headed courtiers the 1614 Parliament could never have been exploded like an "addled egg". But the whole point at issue—which was before the eyes of the Commons from the first day of the session—was the question of the King's Prerogative, which James had said in his address that he would not magnify *nor would he give up*. From the opening of the debate in the Commons it was evident that the mere redress of certain grievances was not an incentive to the Commons to vote a supply large enough to meet all the King's debts unless the Prerogative was so curtailed that impositions in the form of varied taxation could not be levied upon the nation without the consent of Parliament. To vote the King monies to pay all his debts and current expenses and to leave him with an uncontrolled power of the Prerogative to impose impositions at his own sweet will was to strike at the very roots of a free Parliament whose ancient liberties had extended from time immemorial. James on the other hand felt that he must have a vote of supply before he remedied any grievances, while to surrender any of his feudal rights under the Prerogative was an affront to his personal dignity and to the Throne. This problem of the 1610 Parliament had not been solved by its dissolution. It still confronted the Commons and the Crown. It haunted the Houses of Parliament like a spectre and would not go away. It created a disturbed atmosphere. The King distrusted the Commons and the Commons distrusted the King.

This natural distrust of the Crown by the new House was deepened by a rumour that the King had entered into a confederacy that had "undertaken" to secure a majority to control the House for his benefit. The "Undertakers", as they were called, were conspicuous representatives believed to have entered before the elections into a compact with the King, guaranteeing on their part that the parliament would be swayed to a good issue—*i.e.* induced on all important matters to meet his wishes.

It is perfectly true that before the summoning of Parliament conferences were held between the King and Sir H. Neville, though what kind of a bargain had been made—*if any*—was unknown. But the Commons were naturally wrathful at the very suggestion that anyone should "undertake" anything for the Commons of England and one of its first acts was to appoint a committee to report on the "Undertakers". Much heat was engendered in the discussion and the "packing" of the lower House was unanimously condemned.

"Such Undertakers, if any, were worse than Powder-traitors," said someone. "They were trying to blow up the House in a secret and more subtle way, while the Powder-traitors would have blown us up with force."

The upshot was that the King was notified "that whatever shall be done for him shall be merely *out of love of the whole House for him.*" The temper of the House was cynical and acid.

In vain did Francis Bacon ridicule the idea that the King had countenanced any such undertaking or entered any confederacy.

> What private man could *undertake* for the Commons of England! Why a man might as well *undertake* for the Four Elements . . . and specially in a New Parliament: To make a policy of Insurance as to what ship shall come safe home into the Harbour of these troubled seas, to find a new passage for the King's business, by a new and unknown *Point of the Compass*; To build forts to intimidate the House, unmindful that the only forts by which the King of England can command is the fort of affection moving the hearts of the people . . . and the fort of reason. The one commands the hearts, and the other commands the heads.
>
> I implore the House not to listen to these idle rumours, existing only in the imagination of some deluded enthusiast who like the fly upon the chariot wheel, says, What dust I do raise.
>
> All this dust is raised by light rumours and buzzes, and not upon solid ground.
>
> If ye fret and gall one another's reputation, the end will be that every man shall go hence, like coin cried down, of less price than he came hither. If some shall be thought to fawn upon the King's business openly, and others to cross it secretly, some shall be thought practisers that would pluck the cards, and others shall be thought papists that would shuffle the cards; What a misery is this, that we should come together to foul one another, instead of procuring the public good. . . .
>
> Then for the King . . . you have heard him profess like a King and like a Gracious King, that he doth not so much respect his present supply, as this demonstration that the people's hearts are more knit than before. . . .
>
> If any man hath done good offices to advise the King to call a Parliament, and to increase the good affection and confidence of His Majesty towards his people; I say that such a person doth rather merit well, than commit error.
>
> For the remedy . . . a message to the King is the course I like the best. . . .
>
> I have told you mine opinion. I know it had been more safe and politic to have been silent; but perhaps it is more honest and loving to speak. . . . When a man speaketh he may be wounded by others but if he hold his peace from good things, he wounds himself. So I have done my part, and leave it to you to do that which you shall judge to be the best.[1]

The speech failed to persuade the House from pursuing its investigations, and a committee of the entire House was appointed to examine the "Undertakers". Ten days afterwards the Members were still fuming, fretting and irritated at the sins of the "Undertakers". There were even personal encounters, scuffles and Members pulled out of their chairs the better to drive home the arguments of disputants; no business being done at all. The storm subsided after an explanation by Sir H. Neville—which was generally found acceptable—and the Commons settled down to business and agreed to forget about the "Undertakers". But the poison of anger had infected the House as Francis Bacon had foreseen, and they were in no mood for compromises or to transact business. Their minds revolved round that "disputed right" of Cecil when he laid new customs upon several hundreds of articles not taxed before, by virtue of the Prerogative. The King then consented to a compromise to an Act of

[1] *A précis of Francis Bacon's speech in the Commons.*

Parliament to limit his future powers but the Commons would have none of it for they could not trust the Crown's actions.

On 5 May the King sent for the Commons to hear what he had to say. It did no good whatever; and the action of Winwood, the new and inexperienced Secretary of State, in pushing forward a vote of supply in the first week of the session—which was without precedent—had given the House serious cause for watchful suspicion which subsequent proceedings had not allayed but aggravated. The Bill of Supply and the Bills of Grievances offered by the Crown were afterwards referred to a committee of the whole House. The King's business had been wretchedly mishandled by Winwood and, in spite of Francis Bacon's attempts to pour oil on the troubled waters, the storm increased and there was little chance of anything running smoothly in an excited throng of jarred tempers. The fact emerges that while the Commons were prepared to treat the King generously in the matter of supply, they were equally resolved to have the question of the king's Prerogative and his right to impose taxes by means of subsidies definitely settled before proceeding to vote supplies. Meanwhile the committee appointed to look into the question had met, searched records and precedents, and after a thorough examination had come to the conclusion that the King had been misinformed as to the extent of his powers. As a first step, it proposed that there should be a joint conference between the Lower House and the Upper in order that the King might be petitioned to remove the burden and accept a "Remonstrance of their Right". The Commons were more confident than ever that the Crown had no legal right to levy impositions without the consent of Parliament. "If this were eased," said the committee, "*they might with better judgement and alacrity proceed to the King's Supply.*"

The report was almost unanimously adopted; and it is a most remarkable fact that so great was the confidence in Francis Bacon's honour and integrity that *he was unanimously selected by the members to be the mouthpiece of the Commons* at the joint conference of the two Houses.

When we consider that Francis Bacon was the King's officer to whom he was supposed to be subservient, whose duties as the Attorney-General were queried by the House as being incompatible with his duties as a House of Commons man, as one who was bound to side with the King as his servant, right or wrong, *the selection of him for a part like this must be regarded as a remarkable proof of personal confidence.*

The task of opening and laying the groundwork of an argument which was to make good a conclusion *in the teeth of the King's most notorious prejudices* was to be entrusted to the King's Attorney-General.

Whether or not Bacon now thought the King's claim good in law he must have been fully satisfied by this time that it could not be maintained in fact. Right or wrong, the House was definitely against the King; and Francis Bacon declared his readiness to take the part assigned to him, for he was a Commons man before anything else. It was a struggle between Prerogative and Privilege; and in that struggle he was on the side of democracy rather than on that of a feudal tyranny.

The Lords refused to confer with the Commons. Their decision added fuel to the wrath of the Commons and precipitated a new conflict and crises. The Bishop of Lincoln (Neile) had spoken vehemently in the Upper House against any consultation, and, although he did not know—nor did anyone else in the Lords—what the terms were, he described the action of the Commons as "mutinous and treasonable". This set the Commons in an uproar. Such a suggestion was treason against themselves as the third Estate of the realm. The Bishop explained with tears in his eyes, that his words had been misconstrued and that he meant nothing offensive. The Lords proffered an apology. The Commons rejected the explanation and the apology. They insisted on the punishment of the Bishop who had dared to cast aspersions on their loyalty, and appointed a committee to consider the treasonable allegation and a fit and proper punishment of the offender; nor would the Commons proceed to transact any business. Nothing ensued but wild and incoherent speeches.

On Friday, 3 June, the King, in an impatient gesture, sent word to the House that, unless they proceeded to deal with the question of supply, he would dissolve Parliament on the following Thursday. This royal message took the Members completely by surprise and their reaction was one of violent resentment. A committee of the entire House was appointed to prepare an answer to the Crown, but on Monday the Commons were notified that Parliament would be dissolved the following day if they did not proceed at once to consider supply. The House was not to be intimidated, however, even by a royal threat. There was not the slighest attempt to consider it under duress, and Parliament was therefore dissolved by commission the following day, 7 June 1614.

Blocked by the intervention of what seemed to him designedly obstructive debates, after a sitting of two months, during which not a single Bill had been passed, the King hastily DISSOLVED HIS "ADDLED PARLIAMENT".

Needless to say Francis Bacon had nothing to do with James's decision.

That the dissolution was in any way owing to Francis Bacon's action or advice is an assumption entirely gratuitous and improbable in the highest degree. It is at variance with all the external and collateral evidence, at variance with everything we know of his wishes, hopes, fears, proceedings and policy, and of all possible issues the very worst that could happen.

The dissolution came as a shock and surprise to Francis Bacon and was quite unaccountable. People thought at the time that the Favourite and "Great Persons" had instigated the move together with "Spanish Wire-pullers". Today, we know that King James took this step because he felt he could be financially independent of a Parliament.

In consideration of future alliances *James was at this time in secret expectation of pecuniary help from Spain*—the first of those disgraceful stipulations for foreign support.

James had taken one way and the nation another. The King was secretly arranging for his son, Prince Charles, to marry the Infanta of Spain, and there is little doubt that he had been assured by the Spanish Ambassador of a sufficient portion of her dowry in advance whereby his debts would be paid. This assurance precipitated the dissolution.

James felt that he had a lien on countless millions of gold doubloons from the Spanish treasurechest. Although the Spanish alliance might be regarded with abhorrence by the British nation, King James's chief thought and concern were for doubloons and pieces-of-eight, no matter where they came from, not the welfare of the people to whom his first duty lay. Indeed, I do not know of a single act in his entire reign which indicated that he had the slightest interest in the weal of the nation, its advancement or happiness. His outlook was entirely mercenary; wanton extravagance and questionable pleasure-seeking his chief aims.

The Commons broke up on consternation and the Members went back to their constituencies with sullen, embittered anger in their hearts to tell their story. And Englishmen wondered what the King would now do for monies, how James could rule without a Parliament, and what would happen when the next House of Commons was summoned.

This was the end of Francis Bacon's direct dealing with the Commons as an actual Member. Enough facts have been given to show that in this "Addled Parliament" he stood higher than ever in the estimation of the Commons as an honest statesman, a great Commoner, and a stalwart defender of the privileges of the Lower House—as one who believed that the Prerogative, even if right in law, was not right factually in infliction of hardship on the people.

It is most important to remember the attitude of the Commons towards Francis Bacon in view of the fact that in the next Parliament their main work was to put an end to his political career; and this was largely as a result of his being held responsible (most unjustifiably) for the use of the King's Prerogative and exasperating taxation through increased impositions. One cannot understand the last tragical phase of Francis Bacon's public life in the 1621 Parliament unless one first obtains a clear knowledge of the background of his political attitude, his mind, his record in the preceding Parliaments. In the "Addled Parliament" Francis Bacon had "honestly and earnestly desired to see the King and the Commons reconciled." Though he was awkwardly situated as the King's Attorney-General (and, as the reader well understands, *much more awkwardly as a Tudor*), the facts show that he was prepared to persuade the Lords to make common cause with the Commons in order to overcome the King's repugnance to yield up his symbol of authority, his feudal Prerogative, to the Commons.

Francis Bacon failed to bring about a fusion between the King and the House for he could not change the King's nature. Even Francis Bacon could not make oil and water mix. And to hold the theory that he was in any sense responsible for the dissolution and that he was "one of the main agents in bringing about the abortive results of the Addled Parliament, and in preparing the way for a Civil War"—without producing one solitary fact to warrant such a theory—is as far-fetched as it is unjustifiable, worthless and false.

If James and his son had stood towards Parliament as Bacon wished them to stand, there would have been no danger from Coke. They would have been ideal monarchs and Francis Bacon's statesmanship would have averted the Civil War.

With the dissolution of Parliament, we have now to think of Francis Bacon as a great public servant whose work lay pre-eminently in legal, criminal, constitutional and administrative spheres, ever ready with advice, sought and unsought, to James on the true art of kingcraft, so that the nation might be ruled wisely and well on principles he would have followed had Fate but decreed him to sit in the seat of his ancestors. In his record as Attorney there was no slackness. He was energetic, honest and faithful in the discharge of his public duties. He played his part in a number of famous trials which may be said to culminate in the trial of the Favourite Somerset and his wife for murder, which witnessed to the corruption in high society at the court. One wonders how virtue and probity could flourish in such a rank atmosphere! How Francis Bacon could have maintained his integrity in such a veritable hotbed of contamination!

The first serious business to occupy his attention was the growing prevalence of duelling. It had become alarmingly fashionable in the middle and upper classes. According to Chamberlain, there were "many private quarrels among great men"—'twixt Earls Rutland and Montgomery, Lord Norris and Sir Peregrine Willoughby, etc., many duels being fought to the death on the Continent, as in the case of Lord Bruce. It was a waste of precious life and inimical to the State. The Government resolved to stop this growing practice. For the King's guidance Francis Bacon wrote *A Proposition for the Repressing of Duels* and afterwards delivered in his official capacity "A Charge touching Duels in the Star Chamber upon an Information against Priest and Wright".

Francis Bacon closed the charge by giving the types of cases in which he would prosecute. The Star Chamber decreed in a lengthy verdict to be penned by the Attorney, and published and solemnly read in all the shires of the kingdom, that all His Majesty's subjects might understand the opinion of the Court and how it purposed to punish such offences hereafter. Priest and Wright were to be committed to the prison of the Fleet, the former to be fined £500 and the latter 500 marks, and both publicly to acknowledge their offence at the next Surrey Assizes and to show penitence.

This virtually had the desired effect of stopping the practice, although there were a small number of duels afterwards. Duke's son and cook's son thus learned that the majesty of the law must be respected and that "killing was murder" even when it happened in a fairly fought duel. For this ruling we are indebted to Francis Bacon more than to anyone else and the nation began to learn what we accept today as a matter of fact—that human life is sacred and that no citizen must take the law into his own hands. He was thus taught respect for himself and respect for State administration to which he owed a prime duty.

While he was Attorney-General he played a prominent part in one of the greatest State trials of the age—a *cause célèbre* about which men argue even today—the impeachment in 1616 of the Earl and Countess of Somerset for the poisoning of Somerset's friend, Sir Thomas Overbury. The reader will recall that in 1613 Francis Bacon had composed a musical play for the marriage festivities of the King's Favourite; that Somerset and Overbury were bosom friends; that they became estranged because Overbury was violently opposed to the marriage—he insulted the Countess publicly and threatened Somerset with startling disclosures of State secrets. The Favourite became alarmed; so did the King apparently, for on a trumped-up pretext Overbury found himself in the Tower. Very shortly he was dead.

Weeks and months passed. After two years Overbury was forgotten. There were no suspicions. The Somersets were safe, so they thought. Then, someone, sick of Somerset's overweening arrogance, introduced a new Favourite to the King—the effeminate form of a young Englishman named George Villiers. The dissolute James fell for him—a case of "love at first sight"! A contemporary, Sir Simon D'Ewes, wrote describing his charms,

> I most earnestly viewed him for about half an hour's space at least; which I had opportunity the more easily to accomplish, because he stood all the time he talked bareheaded. I saw everything in him full of delicacy and handsome features; yet his hands and face seemed to me especially effeminate and curious.... That he was afterwards an instrument of much mischief both at home and abroad, is so evident upon record no man can deny—yet his very countenance promised to be affable and gentle.[1]

The depraved set of courtiers round the Throne fell into two camps—one supporting the old Scots Favourite Somerset, the others the new; Villiers's fortunes were pushed as a Protestant Englishman. James became more and more enamoured of this enchanting youth and longed to rid himself of Somerset. But he feared Somerset's tongue and still more what the Old Favourite could disclose if he were suddenly dropped. And then, at the psychological moment, someone blabbed out a series of rumours about a dying apothecary's boy, a confession of poisoned tarts, a clyster, Overbury's death and Lady Somerset. The New Favourite carried the news to the King that London seethed with rumours regarding his rival who had murdered his best friend. The King, in all probability against his own wishes, was forced to act. Counselled and consoled by his New Favourite, James, to get to the bottom of the matter, gave orders for the arrest of the alleged accomplices said to be implicated in Overbury's murder. *Coke undertook the office of Public Prosecutor, got up the evidence of their guilt and, when the brief was prepared, sat on the Bench and tried them for their lives.* In such duties he saw nothing contrary to the duties of an upright judge.

Sir Gervase Helwys, Lieutenant of the Tower, admitted to the Secretary of State that there had been a design to poison Overbury by Richard Weston, the Under-Keeper, which he had detected and prevented, but he had since heard from Weston that Overbury was nevertheless murdered by a Mrs. Ann Turner of Lady Somerset's household. Weston and Ann Turner were put on trial. Mrs. Turner declared her innocence but Weston would not speak or plead.

So Coke explained to him that the trial could not proceed unless he answered the formal question, "*How will you be tried?*" by saying "*By God and my country.*" Weston was warned under threat of the consequences of remaining mute; that he would be returned to prison and endure the inconceivable torture of the horrible *peine forte et dure,* "the stripping, the binding, the stretching out, the starving, the slow pressing to death. Weston remained stubborn." At the end of three days "the unhappy creature gave way and pronounced the formula."

We thus see that publicly from the Bench Sir Edward Coke not only threatened Weston with torture and a pressing to death, but actually used

[1] *Autobiography,* Vol. I, p. 166.

torture to make the prisoner speak. The suggestions of modernists that Francis Bacon championed torture while Coke declared it to be against the principles of Magna Carta is thus seen to be quite untrue; Coke not only believed in torture but openly used it; Weston was hanged; Mrs. Turner was quaintly condemned to be hanged.

Of the alleged accomplices "*on evidence which no one now can defend*", Sir Gervase Helwys was hanged; Lord Northampton was implicated but died in time to escape a trial; Sir Thomas and Sir William Monson were lodged by Coke in the Tower, a true bill being found at the Guildhall against Sir Thomas Monson, whom Coke would have put to death on the most flimsy evidence but that he was wanted as a witness against the Somersets; James Franklin, the apothecary who had supplied the poison, was hanged. In the trial of these accomplices Francis Bacon had no share, the public prosecutor being Sir Lawrance Hyde.

The evidence which Lord Chief Justice Coke had ordered to be read in court on 20 October 1615, after Weston's refusal to plead, plainly implicated the Somersets but they were not dealt with immediately. There were several reasons for the delay. They could only be tried by their peers and the papers in the case had to be sent to the Attorney-General. Francis Bacon was not satisfied that there was any direct evidence to implicate the Earl. The Countess was an expectant mother. And James himself was in a fever of uncertainty as to the best course, *for himself*, to pursue. But on 19 January 1616 both the Earl and the Countess were indicted for being accessories before the fact of Overbury's murder, the Earl scornfully remarking, "*The King dare not send me for trial.*" But he did; and the hearing was held on 24 May at Westminster Hall, not before Coke, but before the highest court in the realm, the House of Peers. Francis Bacon took his rightful place as Crown Prosecutor. First the Countess and then the Earl faced the Commissioners. The possibility of a sensation, as well as the certainty of a scandal, drew a packed audience of spectators, who paid £10 a seat and had to occupy them at six in the morning—four hours before the proceedings commenced.

But between the indictment in January and the opening of the trial in May, James had many heartburnings, many fears, many consultations with Francis Bacon and other counsellors what to do for the best, what to say to Somerset and how to act; and long before the day of the trial the King was in a pitiable state of panic as to what Somerset (his former Favourite) might say while in the dock, and of the personal as well as State secrets he might disclose. Somerset had threatened the King more than once with revelations that would startle the world. Somerset had known the "*most retired thoughts*" of the King's mind. Political and personal secrets, *rash confidences,* intimate talk had been held in common between them. Very few men would care to face the prospect of their closest friends making publicly, before a fascinated and delighted audience, already full of scandal and mockery, and before a wider world full of moral and religious thoughts, an exhibition of their most secret heart.

It was a risk the King had to face. Somerset was trying to say something to him secretly. He threatened the King again; he could make revelations at his trial, he told the Lieutenant of the Tower, and would. The Lieutenant sent word privately to the King. James sent the following strange answer:

It is easy to be seen that he would threaten me with laying an aspersion upon me of being in some sort accessory to his crime—I cannot hear a private message from him without laying an aspersion upon myself of being an accessory to his crime; and I pray you to urge him, by reason that I refuse him no favour which I can grant him without taking upon me the suspicion of being guilty of that crime whereof he is accused.

Lady Somerset promised to plead guilty, but the Earl resolutely maintained his innocence. James promised to pardon him if only he would confess his guilt. Somerset was adamant. *James then caused the prisoner to be threatened that his wife had admitted that her husband was a party to the poisoning* in order to wring out of the Earl a confession of guilt. Somerset still remained obstinate and swore they would have to carry him in his bed to Westminster Hall.

There appears to have been much anxious consultation between the King and the officials, and at last Francis Bacon proposed that Somerset should be warned that "if in his speeches he should tax the King—he shall be taken away and his evidence go on without him." It was also decided that the Earl should be guarded by two men with cloaks with instructions to muffle and hoodwink him swiftly if he said anything that would reflect on the honour of the King. James was desperately anxious that Somerset should reveal nothing in open court and to the last minute *he hoped to induce his late Favourite to confess his guilt. Then he need not go to trial. The King could pardon him; he could disappear from public life and all would be well.* Many letters passed between James and Francis Bacon how to act in certain eventualities, inducements and rewards, etc., and messages were even sent to Somerset as from the King himself. When Sir George More warned the Earl to be ready for his trial the next day, he was alarmed by the effect it had on Somerset.

Somerset said "that the King had assured him he should not come to any trial neither durst the King bring him to trial." He used "such bold and undutiful expressions" that Sir George went off in great consternation to Greenwich, woke up the King at midnight, and asked him what was to be done. The King did not know but, "falling into a passion of tears, left it to Sir George's management, promising that if he helped him in this great strait, he should find him a thankful master."

Sir George returned to Somerset at three in the morning and assured him as from the King that, though it was necessary he should appear at the Bar to satisfy justice, he should "return instantly again without any further proceedings ... with which trick he allayed his fury and got him quietly about eight in the morning to the Hall."

Though the Countess had pleaded guilty, she had been spoken to in such tender tones by Francis Bacon that no one believed she would be executed, though sentenced to death, winning pity by her sober demeanour; but the Earl absolutely refused to admit his guilt. Francis Bacon's charge against him contains some fine passages. But Bacon above everything wished to avoid driving Somerset to despair or exasperation so that he should be tempted to turn on the King and either make charges against him or, if that were actually prevented, produce an ill impression in court or among people at large. At the same time he must show a case for conviction and express the horror which he and everybody else felt for the crime of poisoning.

Somerset defended himself with notable ability. He maintained his innocence with the utmost firmness. But the services of the men with cloaks who stood on either side of him in the dock were not required.

There were no indiscretions. He betrayed none of the King's secrets. But it must have been one of the worst days in James's life.

Who had seen the King's restless motion all that day, sending to every boat landing at the bridge, cursing all that came without tidings, would easily have judged *that all was not right and that there had been some grounds for his fears of Somerset's boldness*; but at last, one bringing him word that he was condemned, all was quiet.

The danger was over. The Peers were unanimous in their verdict of guilty. Somerset and his Lady were condemned to death rightly or wrongly. James was safe. Nothing had been disclosed to the world.

This is what Hepworth Dixon says of the aftermath:

> When Somerset was sent to the Tower and the Howards were cast down, the man who had pleaded for Hayward, who had saved Smith from the trial, who had snatched Vernon, Lyttleton, Constable Wright and Orrell *from the Fangs of Coke*, who had spared the lives of Owen and Peacham, *raised his voice against the further shedding of blood.*

When Francis Bacon had done his duty as Attorney-General, he remembered his privileges as a Christian and a man. Life enough had been taken. Helwys, Weston, Franklin, Ann Turner, all the more active agents in the deed, were gone. The Countess had a baby at her breast—that little girl who, born in shame, lived to be the mother of William Lord Russell. She had confessed her guilt; she had been awfully punished; and the remnant of her years was doomed to obscurity and shame.

The Earl maintained his innocence; the world was not satisfied of his guilt. Humanity and law alike conceded him the protection of every doubt. Bacon's counsel to the Crown must have been pure.

None of Coke's thirst for blood parched up his soul; and his reign as Crown Prosecutor was almost a bloodless one. Sprot Logan, Lahor, men who were tried for their lives beyond his jurisdiction, met with less compassionate judges and prosecutors. "In the trials of the accomplices in Overbury's murder the Attorney-General took no share."

The Countess was pardoned and Francis Bacon's own hand drew up the document. The Earl was reprieved also. They were both released from the Tower in 1622.

The secret was not one of unnatural vice but something of *far deeper* import. It was this: *Somerset knew King James's real identity*; knew well that he was not a Stuart at all; that Mary of Scotland's blood never ran through his veins. Somerset knew that he was the son of Lady Mar; *that a Pretender sat on the English Throne*—a usurper: That was the secret known to Somerset and to James! No wonder he was afraid lest Somerset might blurt out his birth secret to the world with disastrous consequences to him and to his dynasty. There is much circumstantial evidence to witness to this historical view.

Francis Bacon believed that the King had certain feudal rights in law—which were known as his Prerogative—but no one had tried harder than he to get them abrogated; and the House of Commons knew it. He knew, too, that the Crown would always be financially dependent on the Commons no matter what shifts James adopted to tide over his difficulties. He disliked intensely the Crown impositions in which the Commons had no voice. In fact, Francis Bacon's ideal government was that of a monarchy similar to the one we enjoy today. He sought to bring this about in the Stuart era; the Prince to love his people and the nation to be proud of its Prince. That he failed was entirely due to the narrow outlook of the King, his personal squandermania, and his habit of following the advice of reckless favourites in preference to listening to the voice of the greatest man of his age or any age, the man who was truly "born to be King" and who loved his country and his people, their welfare, their honour, and their greatness, with an undying affection.

That Francis Bacon never sought to establish a royal tyranny is abundantly proved by one fact—that when the "Addled Parliament" of 1614 was dissolved, *in a little more than twelve months he again advised the King to call a new Parliament,* following it up with a most elaborate memorandum which engaged the most serious attention of the Privy Council—Francis Bacon was the very reverse of being antagonistic to a House of Commons. Indeed, he besought the King and Council to call a new Parliament for the benefit of the Crown as well as the nation.

None of the Councillors of State thought that the government could be carried on satisfactorily without the help of Parliament, and all wanted the causes of quarrels and misunderstandings removed and a reconciliation effected. We can only conjecture what might have happened had a new Parliament been called. All was shelved, for the King was as shifty and unstable as water. He had managed "to raise the wind", 23 April 1616 (about the time when Francis Bacon had sent the memorandum), "by surrendering to the Dutch the cautionary towns pledged by them to Elizabeth as security for their debt to her" for a sum of £215,000. He felt once more independent of Parliamentary supply. The King pushed away the recommendations of Francis Bacon and the Privy Council by a variety of excuses—the Overbury case with its ramifications, the suggested marriage of the Prince with the Spanish Infanta which the public hated and Francis Bacon disliked, a consequent split at Court, Continental turmoils, etc. The warlike spirit was arising in England and the King feared summoning Parliament lest he should be forced into hostilities with Spain. So James definitely laid aside all thought of summoning Parliament, much to Francis Bacon's disappointment.

Early in 1616 Francis Bacon's lifelong friend, Lord Chancellor Ellesmere, head of the Chancery Division, a worn-out old man of seventy years of age, was seized with an attack likely to prove fatal. His office was one in which Francis Bacon had a personal as well as a public interest. In order to obtain monies the Crown had begun the habit of selling their offices to the highest bidder. To prevent the Chancellorship being sold behind his back, he wrote to the King asking him straight for the reversion of the office. He mentioned other men who had qualifications—Coke, Hatton, Canterbury—which was quite sufficient to show that he was the only man in sight by training and temperament really suitable for the position. He mentions he would have to relinquish the Attorney-Generalship and the Clerkship of the Star Chamber if he became Lord Chancellor, the other two "Oblations" being his "Heart and his Service"—a very clear intimation to James that he was not going to make any "Oblation" of money to buy the office. The result was that he got a promise of the Chancellorship. Lord Ellesmere, however, rallied, moved to fresh life and vigour by *an unwarrantable attack by Coke* upon the Chancery jurisdiction. The dispute was heightened by the warmth and haughtiness of Sir Edward Coke, and rose between the Court of Chancery (presided over by Lord Ellesmere) and the Court of the King's Bench (of which Coke was the head) concerning the jurisdiction of the Chancery after judgment in courts of law.

The plain truth is that Coke was so eaten up with jealousy of Francis Bacon that he never missed an opportunity of trying to belittle him, disparage his knowledge of law or put him in awkward situations. In these three questions of law which have a kinship with each other Coke drew Francis Bacon into the ring but he eventually overreached himself. The fencing began simply enough.

It appears that in the Court of Common Pleas the King had appointed a new applicant to a writership. The former holder of the office was persuaded by someone to bring an action in the King's Bench which declared the appointment invalid. The Attorney-General was brought in by the Crown to express his opinion on the verdict. He challenged its correctness—being supported by all the Crown lawyers—on the ground of an old writ *Rege inconsulto*. Francis Bacon assumed that this was a question in which the King had an interest and which, according to the "ancient and ever-continued Law of the crown", should be tried "before the King himself as he is represented in Chancery". And this was the point which now stood for decision. We thus see Coke and Francis Bacon again in conflict; and this in the very heat of the excitement of the Overbury trial. The case was argued and the result was that a compromise was effected on the basis that the appointment should hold good but that no other should be made in similar circumstances.

> Elated by his partial success or smarting under its incompleteness, Coke, only a few weeks later, played a false card *in inducing two rogues,* who had had judgments in their favour at Westminster reversed in Chancery, to raise an action of Praemunire on the ground of an old statute of Edward III against all the persons who had been concerned in the proceedings in Chancery—*the plaintiffs, the counsellors, the solicitors, and the Master of the Chancery.*

Here we get a very clear picture of the vindictive mentality of Coke. On the authority of Professor Nichol, he induced two rogues to take a line of action calculated to make things uncomfortable and awkward for his hated legal opponent. "In this instance the grand Jury threw out the Bill, while the Attorney, Solicitor, and King's Serjeants unanimously supported the Higher Court."

The attack was baffled by the resolute refusal of the Grand Jury to find a true Bill—persisted in in spite of Coke's remonstrances and threats, seconded by the other judges of the King's Bench. Coke had taken a false step, but Somerset's case was pending and nothing could be done. A quarrel between the two courts at that time was unthinkable, although Francis Bacon knew that Coke had presumed and trespassed on the King's person. Francis Bacon said on 21 February 1616:

There is no thinking of arraignments, until these things be somewhat accommodate, and some outward and superficial reconciliation at least made between my Lord Chancellor and my Lord Chief Justice; for this accident is a Banquet to all Somerset's friends.

He knew that Coke if given rope enough would hang himself, that he would be certain to do something equally foolish when there were no capital cases to be tried and nothing to prevent him being brought to book to answer for his arrogance. He had not long to wait. A third collision with Coke was at hand. The case of a living held *in Commendam* came before him in the Court of the King's Bench (a "living *in Commendam*" is a living committed to a temporary holder). The legality of the grant was disputed. Sargeant Chibborne in his speech before Coke contested the King's power to grant *Commendams*. When this was reported to James by Bilston, Bishop of Winchester, thinking the King was afraid lest the irascible Coke should "pronounce a verdict touching the Crown without the Crown being heard in its defence", the King commanded Francis Bacon the Attorney-General to write and require Coke to put off the further hearing of the case until the King could consult the judges on the legality of the issue involved. This command was sent from Francis Bacon's chambers in Gray's Inn by messenger to the Lord Justice's rooms in Serjeants' Inn. On receipt of Francis Bacon's letter, Coke, who, in high dudgeon, was just setting out for the Chancery Court to assist in hearing a case for the Crown, sent his own man to Gray's Inn asking Mr. Attorney to give each of the twelve judges a copy of the note written to himself, and setting the immediate duty of the day aside. Defying the royal command as conveyed through Bacon, he went down to Westminster, took his seat in the King's Bench, *and called the forbidden case.* After some hearing, he carried the judges away to his rooms in Serjeants' Inn, where he persuaded them to write a letter to the King, *throwing the blame of his disobedience on Bacon, whose request for a postponement of the trial they described as contrary to law and to the oaths of a judge.*

The plain truth is that Francis Bacon had done nothing illegal. He had not acted on his own initiative but by command of the King, whose personal and legal servant he was. Coke was angry and out of spite thought in some way he could score points and face the Attorney-General with a full Bench of judges in unanimous agreement. His reasons were a pretence. He had really gone out of his way to call the case as an act of defiance, but it was an act of defiance to the King, not to Francis Bacon. The Crown undoubtedly had the power to grant livings *in Commendam*; and to delay the hearing until the King arrived in town would neither have interfered with justice nor disturbed the oaths of the judges.

Coke's round-robin letter filled James with amazement and anger. He wrote the judges a letter controverting their contentions, insisting that the hearing of the case should be stayed, referring them to the Attorney-General whose law they had insulted, and then summoning all the judges to his palace. The real issue was the Crown's right to be heard in its own defence; and it was Coke's insolence and defiance in trying to trip up the Attorney-General which led to the trial of the judges by the King.

The two great antagonists were in the limelight together at last—one a famous lawyer, the other a great thinker as well as a great lawyer. Their lives had been one long duel. They first met in the House of Commons when, as a young progressive, Francis Bacon defied the Speaker Coke. That was thirty-five years ago. The antipathy between them had grown with the passing of the years. In public they had crossed swords. In private they had made love to the same woman—Lady Hatton. Coke despised Francis Bacon's knowledge of the law. In the days of Elizabeth, Coke had insulted him by calling him the foul name of "Bastard". It was Coke who had shouted out his vulgar expletives at his brother Robert Essex (as he did later with Raleigh): "You thought to be Robert the First. You shall be Robert the last" and then sent him to the block. On every conceivable occasion Coke had tried to pick a quarrel, to thrust Francis Bacon into the arena when he would be at a disadvantage. Now the whole kingdom were to be spectators of the bout—the thrust, the guard, the cut, the fence; and the duel, like the scene in *Hamlet,* seemed destined to end in disaster for one or both.

> All the great Officers of State were present; the King himself, Archbishop Abbott and Bishop Bilston, Lord Chancellor Egerton and Lord Treasurer Suffolk, Secretary Winwood, Zouch Lord Warden of the Cinque Ports, together with a host of Councillors. Coke, as a member of the Privy Council, took his seat. Francis Bacon stood there to defend himself.

The King presided. Bishop Bilston stated what he had heard in the King's Bench. Francis Bacon's letter and Coke's reply were read, the judges' letter to the King was put in, the circumstances of its origin ascertained, and the fact admitted that Coke had deliberately gone out of his way to call a forbidden case in defiance of the Attorney's request and so provoked the present proceedings.

Without any more ado eleven of the judges fell on their knees to the King and confessed they had made an error and had signed under a misapprehension. Coke alone maintained that the facts in the judges' letter were true and that the Attorney-General's message was against his oath as a judge. The aged and ailing Lord Chancellor Ellesmere then asked Francis Bacon to speak in his own defence.

In a purely legal speech Francis Bacon proved that in staying the hearing the Lord Chief Justice would have hurt no law and broken no oath.

A decree was then drawn up which peremptorily overruled the legal doctrine maintained by the greatest and most self-confident judge whom the English courts had seen. The Lord Chief Justice had to acquiesce in this reading of the law and then, as if such an affront were not enough, Coke was suspended from his office and, further, enjoined to review and amend his published *Law Reports*, where they were inconsistent with the view of law which on Bacon's authority the Star Chamber had adopted.

James not only ordered Coke to be suspended from his office of Privy Councillor but from going on circuit as a judge. He then gave Francis Bacon the choice of being a Privy Councillor or the definite promise of the Chancery Seals. He chose to be a member of the Privy Council out of affection for Lord Ellesmere "in respect of my hearty wishes that my Lord Chancellor may live long and the small hopes I have that I shall live long myself."

A few days later, 30 June 1616, Coke was summoned to the Council table, censured and deprived of his seat, his place being taken by his great rival Francis Bacon. Coke was also ordered to revise his *Law Reports* during the long vacation to make them conform to Chancery decisions. He did so under irritation, in a manner almost impertinent, admitting and correcting only five trivial errors of detail. A Crown Commission, of which Lord Ellesmere and Francis Bacon were members, had been appointed to read and revise his reports, found many more than five and that the errors were serious, not "trivial". They have been well summed up by Hepworth Dixon who, as a lawyer, quoted the Commission's findings on Coke's *Law Reports*.

> More than sufficient offences were discovered against Coke, alleged frauds, contempts and disobediences—offences against the Church, encroachments on the powers of other Courts, resistance to the new Irish boroughs, with his glosses, as in the Peacham case, on the law of treason—to ensure a condemnation either in the Star Chamber or in any Court over which the Crown could name the Judge....
>
> Not that his course on the Bench had been impure; it had in fact been ostentatiously the reverse; yet the practice of all the Courts was so unsafe, the system of fees so lax, that no man on the Bench could stand against an accusation brought by the Crown.
>
> No man knew better than Coke that to be tried was to be condemned.
>
> In the most whining tone he prayed to be spared the shame of a public trial; on his knees he implored the Council to protect him; saying, and saying very truly, that *any man in place, however high his state, however clean his hands, might be crushed by indictment laid in the Royal Name.*
>
> Again and again he appeared before the Privy council, under his rival's eyes, in the same ignominious attitude, begging for mercy in the same miserable tone—grovelling on his knees—the savings of his long practice at the Bar menaced with fine and forfeit.

But Coke was fortunate probably because of the influence of Francis Bacon, who was never known, says his chaplain Dr. Rawley, to bear animus against any man who had injured him or tried to injure him. He was not prosecuted. He was not called upon to suffer financially. He was simply removed from the Bench, censured for his legal heresies and ordered to recant—which he did. In the King's Decree announcing this decision (10 November 1616), prefaced by reasons drawn up by the Attorney-General, are noted Coke's errors of law: "His deceit, contempt and slander of the Government", his "perpetual turbulent carriage towards the Liberties of the Church—the Royal prerogative—the settled jurisdictions of His Majesty's other Courts—the safety of the Royal Person—his exploitation of the Laws in cases of High Treason" and his affectation of popularity, etc.

A popular comment at the time is thus reported by Chamberlain: "The common speech is, that four Ps. have overthrown him and put him down—that is Pride, Prohibitions, Praemunire, and Prerogative." And, comments Spedding, "this may really be allowed as a fair summary of the Charges publicly alleged by the King as the ground of his removal." The Inns of Court thus made their joke at his expense while the common people chuckled at the disgrace of the harsh old man whom nobody loved. Commenting on "Coke's Fall" Professor Nichol says:

> No one who had read the trials of Sir Walter Raleigh, or noted how *this vaunted*

> *champion of National Rights veered in his view of them according to the place he happened to hold,* can have any personal sympathy.
>
> A pedant and a boor, the assertion of his own undignified dignity, rather than any larger motive, determined his attitude.

I do not know of a single altruistic act in his life or one positive contribution towards freedom and light, unless, of course, his *Institutes* may be considered as a bulwark of Justice, of right against wrong, the rights of man against State tyranny. But even this is a somewhat doubtful claim. So, for the present, the rivalry had ended in a triumph for Francis Bacon.

Coke—one of the richest men in England—was now an out-of-work lawyer, unscrupulous to his fingertips, with money to burn, time to waste, his very soul aflame with thoughts of revenge; without a solitary intellectual passion to give him consolation. From the very moment of his dismissal from the Bench Coke lived but for one thing: to revenge himself on his hated rival, to await his opportunity or make one when Francis Bacon could be stabbed to the heart; and to wait years if necessary. Yet, even while Coke was raising the malicious spirit of devilish hatred to abide with him for ever more, Francis Bacon was writing him a tribute of praise at the very moment of Coke's darkest trials, addressed to the very quarter which would do him most good—the King himself. In his *Proposal for Amending the Laws of England* he paid Coke a generous and distinguished compliment, expressing his opinion of the extraordinary value, save blemishes here and there, of the *Law Reports* so severely censured—a written opinion that he meant for posterity. This is what he wrote to James:

> Had it not been for Sir Edward Coke's *Reports*—which though they may have errors, and some peremptory and extra-judicial resolutions more than are warranted, yet they contain infinitely good decisions and rulings over of cases—*the Law by this time had been almost like a ship without ballast.*

Such was the magnanimity of Francis Bacon's temperament towards a stricken and fallen man who was his deadliest enemy. While he penned this very tribute he was striving as his first act as a Privy Councillor to save, on the score of humanity, a couple of Catholics from the gallows and to obtain the restoration of a famous Puritan divine to his ministry. Francis Bacon the humanist has never been adequately stressed by his biographers. But the reader can see without further seeking that "on every side he was tolerant of thought, bountiful to merit, and generous to the fallen." No wonder that "all who were great and good loved him."

And when the King offered him Sir Edward Coke's seat in the King's Bench, he declined, and on his recommendation Sir Henry Montague, Recorder of London, was raised to the Bench.

I have stressed this conflict at length because this was the prime root whence grew the plot that led to Francis Bacon's public and political assassination—conceived and executed in such a way that the guilty men escaped while innocency was crucified. And unless the details of this long-standing feud be understood, the reader will fail to know why there should ever have been a plot hatched to rob Francis Bacon of his good name and how Coke swept to his revenge when the time was ripe.

PLATE I

Robert Cecil
From the portrait at Woburn Abbey

Sir Edward Coke
From *The Marriage of Elizabeth Tudor*

William Herbert (After a portrait by Vandyck)

Ben Jonson (After the National Gallery portrait by Gerald Honthorst)

Plate III

George Villiers (right)
Detail from a painting after Honthorst at the National Portrait Gallery

King James I of England (below)

Plate IV

Statue of Francis Bacon in Rosicrucian pose,
surmounting his cenotaph at St Albans

The Parish Church of St Michael
From *The Parish Church of St Michael St Albans, a Short History*
by John C. Rogers

Apart from important matters of State and legal activities, Francis Bacon dealt, as Attorney-General, with questions of great moment—memorials and letters of advice to the King and his favourite Villiers, of deep concern in his day but of no particular interest to the average modern reader unless he be a close student of history.

Bacon, not content with his professional labours, was also engaged, in moments of leisure, in scientific research (the fruits we see in the *Sylva Sylvarum or a Natural History in Ten Centuries, i.e.* the details of a thousand experiments of all kinds), in literary work and philosophical speculation, as well as engaging in innumerable concealed activities connected with his secret societies. Francis Bacon was no drone. He laboured tirelessly at his public duties while he silently laid his great bases on which future generations should build. And in silence he likewise bequeathed the riches of his glorious intellect to banks of perpetuity that would not break and from which thieves could not steal, even though he were broken on the Wheel of Fate and his good name stolen from him by wicked men, jealous of his genius.

In 1617 Lord Chancellor Ellesmere, infirm and sick, was still alive, to the annoyance of many. According to contemporary reports, many coveted his office and were impatient for him to relinquish the reins. It was, indeed, said that as he lay on his deathbed he was threatened with prosecution on charges of corruption, and that the threat broke the old man's heart. The shameless relatives of Buckingham wanted his office to turn to their own financial ends. More than one negotiation for the Seals was set on foot. Sir John Bennett offered £30,000 and Coke was also in the bargaining ring with Lady Compton, Buckingham's mother.

Torn with anxiety, Ellesmere resigned on 5 March 1617, delivering up the great Seal on the 6th. On the 7th the King himself put the Seal into Francis Bacon's hand. In a few days Ellesmere was dead—three days after Francis Bacon's installation as Lord Keeper of the Great Seal of England.

Chapter V

LORD KEEPER REGENT

IN the last chapter we have surveyed one of the most lofty periods of Francis Bacon's political and legal activities; of great immediate importance to the history of England and the intellectual and ethical progress of humanity. We must now consider him as a great judge, as the head of the Chancery Court and eventually Lord Chancellor of England. The importance of the Chancery as the King's Court in a special sense is seen in Francis Bacon's remark to the King, "Your Majesty knoweth your Chancellor is ever a Principal Councellor or Instrument of Monarchy of immediate dependence upon the King."

He had, however, very clear ideas of the duties of a judge. They are shown in many admirable charges and speeches. He knew also that there were defects in the law and its administration that wanted reforming and he set himself to reform them so far as he could do personally. He knew there were grave abuses in the courts that were cloaked by the blessed word "custom". He knew his own conduct and reputation must be beyond reproach as would-be public reformer and as a secret head of ethical societies inculcating "active morality" by square conduct, level steps and upright intentions. The founder must be, like Caesar's wife, beyond suspicion and above reproach. He must be the practical embodiment of his system or his disciples would be the first to point the finger of scorn, and his Lodges, Chapters, Conclaves, Presbyteries and Colleges, would naturally disintegrate. He had not only to keep his own hands scrupulously clean but he must endeavour to keep his servants in the Chancery free from the taint of anything approaching corrupt practice. But before dealing with Francis Bacon's activities on the Bench and his work as a statesman it is necessary to go back a little to his Attorneyship, in the years 1615–16.

Two things happened of the utmost consequence though their effect was not to be realized by him for some five years. One was the humiliation of Coke which, rightly or wrongly, was attributed by him to Francis Bacon, and made Coke—that jealous, soured, vindictive old man—into a violent fury raging for revenge. The other was the rise in 1614 of the New Favourite, who, from plain George Villiers, became the powerful Duke of Buckingham, the wealthiest nobleman in England. We have already seen how the advent of the New Favourite was brought about: how James had already tired of the Old Favourite, the arrogant Somerset, who narrowly missed being executed by reason of the murder of his friend Overbury; how the King had been ruled by Somerset, an infamous, overbearing man, upon whom he had showered honours without stint until, from being a mere page, Somerset became the first Scottish Peer of the Realm and a landed proprietor, by the seizure of the Manor of Sherborne; despite the tears of Lady Raleigh. To the end of his shameful career he levied toll on all aspirants at Court and, worse still, influenced the King on national policy, teaching him how to raise money by all sorts of questionable shifts. Somerset's fall led all good men to hope that his successor Villiers would lead the King away from the shameful orgies that had disgraced the English Court. The New Favourite was welcomed by all, by the courtiers and by the Church in the person of the Archbishop of Canterbury, who sent him a letter of fatherly blessing; and even Francis Bacon (who had kept Somerset at arm's length) was favourably impressed by the handsome young adventurer. J. R. Green writes:

> Villiers was raised rapidly through every rank of the Peerage, made Marquis and Duke of Buckingham and entrusted with the direction of English policy.
>
> *The payment of Bribes to him, or marriage with his greedy relatives soon became the only road to political preferment. Resistance to his will was inevitably followed by dismissal from Office. Even the highest and most powerful of the nobility were made to tremble at the nod of this young upstart.*

Quoting Clarendon, Green adds,

> Never any man in any age, nor I believe in any country rose in so short a time to so much greatness of honour, power, or fortune, upon no other advantage or recommendation than upon the beauty or gracefulness of his person.
>
> The selfishness and recklessness of Buckingham were equal to his beauty; and the haughty young Favourite on whose neck James loved to loll, and whose cheek he slobbered with kisses, was destined to drag down in his fatal career the Throne of the Stuarts.

How could the Stuart Throne be other than imperilled when King James, that besotted and blasphemous homosexualist, could place the reins of kingship in the hands of such a character, telling the Privy Council, his advisers, "You may be sure that I love the Earl of Buckingham more than anyone else. *Christ had his John and I have my George.*"

But Green's verdict was based on a survey of the life of Villiers as a whole. The defects of his character were not recognized at the beginning of his life at Court. If Somerset chastised the people with whips, Buckingham was fated to whip them with scorpions—which he did as soon as he felt himself firmly fixed in the saddle of autocracy. When he was first noticed by the King he was physically more attractive than Somerset, more intellectual, with a fascinating manner and a ready tongue, though lacking learning and education. He may have had higher qualities and he appeared to admire mental greatness, though how far this was sincere it is difficult to say. He admired it in Francis Bacon only because (so events afterwards seem to prove) for a space it paved the way to his own advancement. In Villiers James found a ready pupil in his "own Art of Craft", for there was inherently within the young man that which the King delighted to honour, a well-preserved strain of dissimulation and hypocrisy under his seeming frankness of disposition. He was as radically selfish as his predecessor Somerset, and his even more arbitrary will made him a more dangerous enemy to public if not to private weal. With these men (the two favourites) Bacon had to reckon as *the ears through which everything had to pass and the hands from which everything had to come.*

For the diversion of the King young Villiers baptized pigs, addressed the King as "Dere Dad and gossope" and signed himself "Your Majestie's humble slave and doge Steenie." "He was the King's Minion and corresponded with the King in an odious mixture of servility and impudence." In those times

> it was as honourable to be a King's Minion as to be his Mistress, and the syndicate who took up young George Villiers, changed his threadbare clothes for court dress and purchased him the post of cupbearer, were acting exactly in the same way as those who introduced a new lady to the Court of Louis XIV, and they hoped for as substantial a return on their investment.

It was in the autumn of 1614 that Villiers first attracted the King's notice as a cupbearer and on 23 April, the year following, he was knighted and made a Gentleman of the Bedchamber receiving a pension of £1000. How Francis Bacon became acquainted with him we do not know, but by 22 January 1616 we find Bacon corresponding with him in the style of a familiar acquaintance. Villiers would be about twenty-three or twenty-four, and Francis Bacon fifty-six. On 27 August 1616 Villiers was definitely established in the office of Favourite, being on this date created at Woodstock Lord Blechly of Blechly and Viscount Villiers by patent and ceremonial investment. His meteoric rise in importance, power and influence was recognized by everyone; so much so that a contemporary, Sherburn, writing to Carleton on 20 August, says, "*This is now the man by whom all things do and must pass.*"

But Villiers knew how to adapt his manner to his company. He reserved the sensual side of his nature for the King's delight while he sought to flatter Francis Bacon by applying to him for advice—according to Spedding it was about the time he was made into a viscount.

> He not only took in good part the Counsels which Bacon offered him from time to time, but applied to him for more. For it must have been about this time that he desired his advice in detail as to the manner in which he should frame himself for the performance of his new duties.

A fortnight before the ceremony of Robing, in a letter upon the sending of the patent for Villiers to sign making him a marquis, Francis Bacon gives him fatherly advice. At that time, 12 August 1616, he had evidently anticipated that Villiers could be moulded into an instrument for good, obviously in ignorance of his true nature, and that he would be a willing pupil anxious to sit at the feet of the Master of Wisdom. Bacon wrote to him as follows:

> Sir,
>
> I have sent you now your Patent creation of Lord Blechly and of Viscount Villiers. Blechly is your own and I like the sound of the name better than Whaddon; but the Name will be HID, for you will be called Viscount Villiers. . . .
>
> And now, because I am in the Country, *I will send you some of my Country Fruits*; which with me are GOOD MEDITATIONS; which when I am in the City are choked with business.[1]

[1]This is a very remarkable "coincidence" with the phrase used in the preface in 1623 Folio, where, after a series of meditations, the writer identifies his thoughts with the "Country" and its "fruits". "*Country hands reach foorth milke, creame, fruites, or what they have.*" This letter was a private one written in 1616 and could not have been known by Heminge and Condell in 1623. The thought and phraseology were the product of ONE mind—Francis Bacon, who derived it from Pliny.

After that the King shall have watered your New Dignities with his bounty of the lands which he intends you, and that some other things concerning your means which are now likewise in intention shall be settled upon you; and therefore it is now time that you should refer your actions chiefly to the good of your Sovereign and your Country.

It is the life of an ox or beast always to eat and never to exercise; but men are born (and especially Christian men), *not to cram in their fortunes but to exercise their Virtues*; and yet the other hath been unworthy, and (thanks be to God) sometimes the unlucky humour of great persons in our times. Neither will your further Fortune be the further off; For assure yourself that Fortune is of a Woman's Nature, that will sooner follow you by slighting than by too much wooing.

And in this dedication of yourself to the public, I recommend to you principally that which I think was never done since I was born, and which not done hath bred almost a wilderness and solitude in the King's service; which is, that *you countenance and encourage, and advance Able men and Virtuous men and Meriting men in all kinds and degrees and professions*. For in the time of the Cecils, the father and the son, able men were by design and of purpose suppressed, and though of late choice goeth better both in Church and Commonwealth, yet *money, and turn-serving, and cunning canvas, and importunity prevail too much.*

In places of moment, *rather make able and honest men yours than advance those that are otherwise because they are yours*. As for cunning and corrupt men, you must (I know) sometimes use them; but *keep them at a distance*; and let it appear that you make use of them, rather than they lead you.

Above all depend wholly (next to God) upon the King; and be ruled (as hitherto you have been) by his instructions; for that is best for yourself. For the King's care and thoughts concerning you are and ought to be according to the thoughts of a modest man. But let me not weary you.

The sum is that *you think Goodness the best part of greatness*; and that you remember whence your rising comes and make return accordingly.

God ever keep you.

Gorhambury Francis Bacon

We see that Francis Bacon knew that the Cecils had suppressed his public activities; was fully aware that the Favourite's advice to the Sovereign was going to be all powerful in the affairs of State; that he was already wielding a potent influence over the mind and actions of his Sovereign for good or ill, and so on.

> ... it is now time you should refer your actions chiefly to the good of your Sovereign and your Country ...
> ... men are born ... not to cram in their fortunes but to exercise their Virtues ...
> ... advance Able men and Virtuous men and Meriting men [rather than your friends] ...
> ... keep [corrupt men] at a distance ...
> ... goodness is the best part of greatness ...

And are not these sound ethical precepts? Had anyone ever a better tutor in wisdom? If Buckingham had but listened to the voice of Francis Bacon, the Duke would not in his later years have been murdered, to the great joy of the nation.

Is it possible to believe that these broad ethical counsels, given privately, proceeded from the heart of a corrupt man? When Francis Bacon wrote: "*Men are not born to cram a Fortune but to exercise Virtue*", was not this his honest conviction continually put into practice? One reason why Bacon despised Somerset was because of his mercenary nature. Francis Bacon was never mercenary; he was magnificent but he was never mercenary. He hated a clutching hand always and everywhere. Bacon believed in doing things for love.

Arising apparently out of this 1616 letter, Francis Bacon sent Buckingham at his request a long, detailed memorandum as to his duties to the King, the country and the many subjects with which he should be conversant, and the duties and behaviour of a Favourite. We thus obtain an insight into his mind and the large and elevated views of the policies that should animate a King, and especially the King of England, to ennoble his kingdom, and the principles that should inspire a man who had the ear of the King. This letter–memorandum is certainly not the letter of a flatterer or a sycophant hopeful of wheedling favours and benefits. It points out Villiers's duty in his new position and the dangers to which he would be exposed; it is rather calculated in its cold discussion of dangers and duties to produce a chill in an ardent youth about to start on a glorious career. There are two versions of this memorial—one containing twice as much matter as the other (there is some mystery as usual as to when it was written and when sent to the Favourite)—which is quite in keeping with Francis Bacon's manner of work: writing a perfect ground draft, putting it on one side, returning to it after a time, altering, expanding and adding the finishing touches. The same characteristics of his methods are to be found in some of the early Shakespeare plays which are found to be amended from quarto to quarto until in their finished appearance in the 1623 Folio they stand:

> Offered to your view, cured, and perfect of their limbs; and all the rest absolute in their Numbers.

From the date of this rather cold series of recommendations—framed as a civil servant's report—we find letters beginning to pass between the Attorney General and the New Favourite on a variety of topics. His letters to the King are often answered by the Viscount, who is gradually getting into the run of things; letters pass respecting Coke and his *Reports*, the distress in the cloth trade, Mompessant's patents for inns, the murder of Sir John Tyndall, the King's financial provisions for Buckingham, grants from the Crown to maintain his dignity, etc., which show that the young Viscount and Francis Bacon were gradually getting on cordial terms and that, by the time Bacon received the Seals of the Lord Keeper's office, they were intimately acquainted and on fairly close terms of friendship.

The same day that he received the Seal from the King, 7 March 1616, he wrote to Buckingham.

My Lord Keeper to my Lord of Buckingham upon his being chosen Lord Keeper

My dearest Lord,

It is both in cares and kindness, that small ones float up to the tongue, and great ones sink down into the heart with silence. Therefore I could speak little to your Lordship to-day, neither had I fit time; but I must profess thus much, that in this day's work you are the truest and perfectest mirror and example of firm and generous friendship that ever was in Court. And I shall count every day lost, wherein I shall not either study your well doing in thought, or do your name honour in speech, or perform you service in deed. Good my Lord, account and accept me

Your most bounden and devoted friend
and servant of all men living

March 7, 1617 Fr. Bacon, C.S.

Francis Bacon was now the principal officer in the kingdom. He had kissed hands on his appointment and had sworn fealty and allegiance; to do as he was told by his august sovereign, just as a soldier has to obey the orders of his superior officer. This outstanding fact must never be forgotten. It goes far to explain the fall some four years later. Neither must it be forgotten that, in their official positions, the King occupied the English Throne by Divine Right and that his will was law. It was paramount. No matter how frail he might be as a man, the voice of a King in his office was one which a servant was bound to obey as *vox Dei*. Any evasion on the Lord Keeper's part, sworn as an officer to do his bidding, would have been an act of unthinkable disloyalty and of treachery if not high treason. Today we rightly think that the doctrine that "the King can do no wrong" is preposterous, but in those days the entire fabric of the English Constitution—Parliament, Church, law and order—was woven round the idea of an autocracy in which the final authority was vested in one man, the King, whose dictum on all matters was clothed with divine infallibility. Hence the importance to James of full unquestioning recognition of the King's Prerogative. Any attempt at the whittling away of his power was an affront to the divine office of kingship. It is very necessary to remember these points in view of the subsequent tragedy which was now slowly beginning to "cast its shadows before".

From the beginning of Francis Bacon's entry into his new office we find him making it his business to keep the King informed of all that passed in the Council in his absence. There are many notes and reports on such important matters: the erecting of certain staple towns in Ireland that should have sole power and authority to transport the wools of the realm, and for preventing the exportation of wool out of that realm into foreign parts; the ticklish question of the Spanish match between the King's son and the Infanta, the King being too far committed to retreat, the only way being, so it appeared to Francis Bacon, "to continue the negotiations and endeavour to guide it to some good end"; divisions in the Council respecting the Spanish match; the repressing of pirates who had become a terrible menace to all countries; and other topics. His letters to Buckingham show their friendly relations. Here is the opening paragraph of one on 7 April.

To the R. Hon. his very good L. the Earl of Buckingham, of his M. most Hon. Privy Council

My singular good Lord,

When I heard here your Lordship was dead, I thought I had lived too long. That was—to tell your Lordship truly—the state of my mind upon that report. Since, I hear it was an idle mistaking of my Lord Evers for my Lord Villiers. God's name be blessed, that you are alive to do infinite good, and not so much as sick or ill disposed for anything I now hear....

[Then follows a fairly long letter dealing with matters of no particular interest; and he concludes:]

Your Lordship's most faithful and devoted friend and servant,
Fr. Bacon, C.S.

On 13 April he again writes a long letter to Buckingham respecting State matters which begins:

My singular good Lord,

I am now five or six days retired to my house in the country: for I think all my Lords are willing to do as scholars do, who though they call them holy-days, yet mean them playdays, etc. . . .

Your Lordship's most faithful and devoted friend and servant
Fr. Bacon, C.S.

Buckingham replies on behalf of the King on 18 April, beginning his letter "My very good Lord" and ending with

So I commit you to God, and rest
Your Lordship's most assured friend to do you service,
G. Buckingham

It is quite obvious that the two men were then very good friends. Indeed, what could there be to disturb their friendship?

When one glances over Francis Bacon's record for the next four years, noting the variety of the topics handled by him—the business transactions of State, political, legal, educational, financial, social, his correspondence with learned men and his literary and philosophic activities which culminated in 1620 with the publication of that wonderful work of great magnitude, the *Novum Organum*—one can only be amazed at the open, declared activities of this Columbus of literature who had, with his own hands, put a girdle round "All Knowledge" and harnessed it to serve his purpose—an altruistic one—for the benefit not of himself but of humanity.

His Herculean labours have never been better understood than by Professor Nichol—by no means a friendly critic—who writes:

The reputation of his enormous industry was bearing slow fruit. In professional esteem, he was bold to boast that he did not fear comparison with Coke himself. The number of questions on which his versatile mind undertook to advise, persuade, or pronounce during these years, is as remarkable as the unrivalled manner in which, whether on the right side or the wrong, he managed to give them fresh significance and dignity.

His contributions to the pleas and arguments of the time belong to English Literature as much as to the History of Constitutional Law. Whether engaged in soothing the Commons—battling for the Prerogative—fencing the forests of the land from waste—giving judgment on the rights of the Irish Parliament—pressing, without the respect of persons, the Law against Duels—or laying down his views about customs, merchandise, manufactures, agriculture—*we seldom fail to meet on his pages, with some broad generalization, some colour of fancy, apt classical reference, or startling epigram. No man ever so illumined a mass of technical details with the light of genius.*

With the obnoxious Coke removed from obstructing, he was now free to carry out his comprehensive plans for codifying, simplifying, and amending the Law, and reconciling differences between parties and interests at home.

The popularity of the new Lord Keeper was indeed so great that when shortly afterwards he bought the lease of York House from Ellesmere's son, the first Earl of Bridgwater, after a short residence at Dorset House, he was the recipient of numerous presents.

Within a week of Francis Bacon's investiture as Lord Keeper King James set off for Scotland—14 March 1617—for a six months' holiday. He was accompanied by Buckingham in the double capacity of Prime Minister and Master of the Revels. Buckingham was not only to take a leading part in the discussions directing the nation's policy but to determine the revels to amuse the King. He had now become the Master of the Horse with the right to be ever near the King's person, and James had also placed the patronage of the Crown in his hands. There rode with the King to Edinburgh a troop of lords and ladies, bishops and huntsmen. He had sent in advance an organ and wooden carvings of Apostles and Patriarchs to be installed in Holyrood Chapel, which caused the Low Church Edinburgh citizens to protest so violently against these innovations of Papistry that James had to withdraw them. His re-appearance in the capital caused several angry disputes among his Scottish subjects and the clergy on ecclesiastical matters. The King was not always wise in his meddling and was glad to get back to his London home.

Before James went to Edinburgh he had left the affairs of the kingdom in Francis Bacon's hands. He was virtually appointed Regent. He was to reside in the Palace, receive Ambassadors and preside at the Council. He ruled England as a Prince with the status of a Prince. His dreams for "Recognition" were realized. He had reached the pinnacle of his Tudor ambitions. Everything claimed a share of his attention, says Dixon—law, finances, government, religion, piracy in the Levant, riots in Smithfield, Raleigh's voyage to the Amazon, abuses in the Court of Wards, the condition of poor prisoners, Prince Charles's projects of marriage, the overcrowding of London houses, the private affairs of Coke. While his mind roved over these various concerns, he still found leisure to toil at the preparation of the *Novum Organum* and to instruct the juries and magistrates into the duties of their office. Persecution ceased. Men breathed more freely. He gave orders for the release of Danvers, Walter, Johnson and Armstrong, four Roman Catholic priests, on the easy condition that they should go to France or Spain. And on the day following he rode in state to St Paul's Cross to hear Dr. John Donne, poet and divine, the Chaplain of King James, deliver a sermon "In Praise of Elizabeth".

With the advent of Francis Bacon to be the temporary head of the State a special warrant made his wife, Lady Alice, his consort and the First Lady of the land.

On 7 May, the first day of Trinity term, Francis Bacon rode from Gray's Inn to open the courts in State.

All London turned out to do him homage for he was as popular in the streets as he had been in the House of Commons. To swell his immediate train the Queen sent the lords of her household; Prince Charles, the whole of his followers; the Lords of Council, judges and serjeants were of the Special Company. On the right hand rode the Lord Treasurer; on his left, the Lord Privy Seal. Behind them came a long procession of earls and barons, knights and gentlemen. And everyone who could procure a horse and a footcloth fell into the train. More than two hundred horsemen rode behind him through cheering crowds of citizens and apprentice boys—down Chancery Lane and the Strand, past Charing Cross, through the open Court of Whitehall and by King Street into the Palace Yard.

So, accompanied to Westminster by troops of friends and the acclamations of the people, he was brought to the gates of Westminster Hall, passed into the Chancery Court, and before that great assembly took his seat on the Bench. And, after the criers had commanded silence Francis Bacon spoke to them.

On this day of days, the day he appeared in his greatest glory, exceeding all his predecessors in the bravery and multitude of his servants, he addressed his hearers in a style of businesslike precision adorned here and there with the flowers of rhetoric. In a carefully detailed speech he announced his intention to reform the rules and practices of the Chancery Court. "He had made laws for himself that he might justly administer the Law."

> These Imperatives I have made but to myself and my times without prejudice to the Authority of the Court or to wiser men who may succeed me . . . for so did the Roman Praetors—who used to set down at their entrance how they would use their jurisdiction. And this I shall do my lords, *in verbis masculis*; no flourishing or painted words, but such as are fit to go before deeds.

He then said that he would expect all men to know his rules and not to expect him to deviate from them. He would not tolerate unnecessary delays of justice—"By the grace of God I will make injunctions a hard pillow to sleep on"—and he said he would not give undue preference to first comers: "I do not mean to make it a horse-race who shall be the first at Westminster Hall." He did not intend, however, to play the part of an autocratic Sovereign but intended to rely, "my Lords, on the Masters of Chancery who are *Reverend Men* and the great mass of the business of the Court cannot be sped without them." Yet he cautions against overhaste for faulty impatient decisions would not end the business;

> this is that which makes sixty, eighty, an hundred orders in a cause, to and fro, begetting one another; and like Penelope's Web, doing and undoing. I confess, in causes perplexed, I have somewhat of the cuncative inclined to delay; and I am of opinion that whosoever is not wiser upon advice than upon the sudden, the same man is no wiser at fifty than he was at thirty. And in the meantime *the subject's*, the litigant's *pulse beats swift though the Chancery pace be slow.*
>
> I am resolved that my Decree shall come speedily (if not instantly) after the hearing. . . . It hath been a matter much used of late that upon the full hearing of a cause nothing is pronounced in Court; but breviates [lawyers' briefs] are required to be made, and the cause was sometimes forgotten for a term or two, then set down for a new hearing or rehearing, three or four terms after.
>
> That is no use. I will pronounce my Decree a few days after my hearing, and sign my Decree at least in the vacation.
>
> *Fresh justice is the sweetest. Justice ought not to be delayed.* There ought not to be any labouring in causes but that of the Counsel at the Bar.
>
> *Because justice is a sacred thing,* and the end for which I am called to this place, and therefore is my way to heaven, I shall by the grace of God, as far as God will give me strength, deal with all Court business quickly, carefully, and abuses whether to delay procedure or in other forms would not be tolerated.

I shall be careful there be no exaction of any new Fees, but according as they have hitherto set and tabled.

As for the Lawyers' Fees. I must leave it to the conscience and merit of the Lawyer, and the estimation and gratitude of the client.

And because he knew

by experience that young lawyers were never heard, and clients sought great counsel, on certain days therefore I will hear the younger members of the Bar, after nine to eleven ... so as to help the generality of lawyers and ease clients.

I shall also add the afternoon to the forenoon, and some fortnight of the vacation to the term, for the expediting and clearing of the causes of the Court.

Then he added in a memorable sentence which told his auditors that his life and mind lay not in the pomp and grandeur of the fleeting moment but in much greater things:

Only the depth of the three long vacations I would reserve in some measure free for Business of Estate, and for Studies, Arts and Sciences to which in my nature I am most inclined.

My Lords, I have no more to say but I will go to the business of the Court.

Judging from Francis Bacon's letter to Buckingham, he was pleased with the events of the day, his reception from the law and the general public; for he wrote to the Favourite a fairly long letter of which the following is an extract.

My singular good Lord,

... Yesterday I took my seat in Chancery, which I hold only from the King's grace and favour, and your friendship. There was much ado and a great deal of world. But *this matter of pomp, which is heaven to some men, is hell to me, or purgatory at least.*

It is true I was glad to see that the King's choice was so generally approved, and that I had so much interest in men's good wills and good opinions, because it maketh me the fitter instrument to do my master service and my friend also....

I publish the rules and resolutions I had taken for the fulfilling of His Majesty's commandments. I send your Lordship a copy of that I said. ... I pray take some fit time to shew it to His Majesty because if I understood him in anything I may amend it, because I know his judgement is higher and deeper than mine....

Thus wishing you well above all men living, next to my master and his: I rest

Your true and devoted friend and servant,

Fr. Bacon, C.S.

It is quite in keeping with his real character. It is perfectly true that Francis Bacon loved magnificence, but he wants the Favourite to know that he loves it not for its own sake as was the common custom among the King's courtiers—but simply as a means to an end, not for the glorifying of himself but for the emphasizing of the majesty of the law as exemplified in his speech. Francis Bacon with his keen sense of moral and spiritual values was diametrically opposed to the Buckingham ideal that success could be adequately interpreted in terms of worldly riches and honours.

About the same time Francis Bacon wrote to the King in May 1617 giving an account of State business in which he adds an item of interest worth recording.

Yesterday, which was my weary day, I bid all the Judges to dinner—which was not used to be—and entertained them in a private withdrawing chamber with the Learned Counsel. When the Feast was passed, I came amongst them, and set me down at the end of the table, and prayed them to think I was one of them, and but a foreman.

I told them I was weary and therefore must be short. . . . I was firmly persuaded that the former discords between the Chancery and the other Courts was but flesh and blood; and now the men were gone, the matter was gone; and that for my part I would not suffer the any the least diminution of or derogation from the ancient and due power of the Chancery, so if any thing be brought to them at any time touching the proceedings of the Chancery which did seem to them exorbitant or inordinate, that they should freely and friendly acquaint me with it, and we should soon agree; or if not, we had a Master [the King] that could both easily discern and rule.

At which speech of mine, besides a great deal of speech and acknowledgement, *I did see cheer and comfort in their faces as if it were a New World.*

He got the judges together. He brought into vogue a practice which had fallen in disuetude: the custom of Lord Chancellors giving dinners to Bench and Bar which had been maintained with fair regularity down to the time of Sir Christopher Hatton, 1587; but since his day this jovial custom had been laid aside by Sir John Puckering, and Ellesmere had not restored it. Francis Bacon brought back these convivial meetings of the profession. He gave a banquet to his followers on the first day of term; and the feast cost him £700. Shortly afterwards he invited the judges and leaders of the Bar to dine with him. It was a minor reform, which he brought into vogue, *which he revived from the past*, and made good for the future—the practice of the Lord Chancellor giving dinners to Bench and Bar.

Francis Bacon gave several charges to newly made judges. Some of his phrases are worth recording. To Justice Hutton, who was called to be a judge of the Common Pleas, he said, among other things:

The Court where you are to serve, is the Local CENTRE and head of the Laws of this Realm. . . . Here issues process of outlawry; if men will not answer Law in this CENTRE of law, they shall be cast out of the CIRCLE of Law. Therefore it is proper for you with your WISDOM and FORTITUDE to maintain the Laws of this Realm. . . .

Remember . . . the Twelve Judges of the Realm are as the Twelve Lions under SOLOMON'S THRONE: They must be Lions but Lions under the Throne. . . . [*Freemasons will note these words and phrases peculiar to the Craft.*]

To represent unto you the lines and portraitures of a good Judge:—the first is That you should draw your Learning out of your books, not out of your brain.

2. That you should mix well the freedom of your own opinion with the reverence of the opinion of your fellows.
3. That you should continue the studying of your books and not to spend on upon the old stock.
4. That you should fear no man's face, and yet not turn stoutness into bravery i.e. bravado or boastful swaggering.
5. That you should be truly impartial, and not so as men may see affection through fine carriage.
6. That you be a LIGHT to Jurors to open their EYES, but not a Guide to Lead them by their Noses.

7. That you affect not the opinion of pregnancy and expedition by an impatient and catching hearing of the Counsellors at the Bar.
8. That your speech be with gravity, as one of the Sages of the Law, and not talkative, nor with impertinent flying out to show your Learning.
9. *That your Hands, and the Hands of your Hands*—I mean those about you—*be clean and uncorrupt from gift, from meddling in or with Titles, and from serving of turns, be they of great ones or small ones.*
10. That you contain the jurisdiction of the Court within the ancients merestones, without removing the MARK.
11. Lastly, That you carry such a Hand over your monsters and clerks, as that they may rather be in awe of you, than presume upon you....

There are other charges to Sir John Denham, Sir William Jones, etc., and to the judges before going on circuit, but none is so interesting as the above. No. 9 is specially worth noting, for, according to the allegations of Macaulay, even while Francis Bacon was delivering this injunction he had begun already his career of corruption by feathering his nest with *BRIBES* ... *yet no one ever heard of these bribes until 1621, four years later.* Is it not incredible? Could the mind that composed these precepts for putting into action have been guilty of the acceptance of bribes from suitors to favour them dishonestly and thus defeat the ends of justice? To my mind these eleven points ring true and are the genuine expressions of an honest man who practises what he preaches.

About this time there were rumours that Francis Bacon had not the health or the strength to hold his position and even the usually well-informed Chamberlain has a lot to say about his ill health.

> The general opinion is that he hath so tender a constitution of both of body and mind that he will hardly be able to undergo the burden of so much business as the place requires—if he do not rouse himself—both private subjects and the Commonwealth will suffer much....

Francis Bacon's absence on two or three occasions from the Council board and the Star Chamber had alarmed people, all of which shows that uninformed general opinions and popular rumours should not be accepted as necessarily true. The public were equally mistaken over Francis Bacon's delicate constitution and the amount of work he could accomplish without undue straining, just as mistaken as the scholastic world is today as to the reach of his mental powers and the marvellous cast of his mind; that extraordinary dualism of soul which enabled him to find rest from law and philosophy by indulging in "Works of his Recreation".

Francis Bacon had absented himself from the Council not because he could not stand the strain of the Lord Keeper's office but because he was toiling unseen at a vast accumulation of Chancery arrears. Many had been referred to him after decisions in the common law courts were not acceptable to one or other of the litigants. His predecessor had been in the habit of reserving judgment and not pronouncing a decree for months after the hearing. These are the facts.

The long continued illness of his predecessor, Lord Ellesmere, had created a congestion of cases, some of them of ten to twenty years' standing. There were no fewer than 3600 Chancery cases of conflicting claims demanding his attention. He had bound himself by rules of his own making, to listen to the pleadings, treating the litigants with courtesy, and pronouncing judgment the moment his mind was made up. By good humour, by patience and courtesy, and by an assiduity which knew neither haste nor rest, he cleared off all the accumulation of arrears.

In the Easter and Trinity terms he settled no fewer than 3658 suits; and in the first four terms he made a total of 8798 and freed more than 35,000 suitors from the law's uncertainties; and not one of them was ever reversed. "Fresh justice is sweetest."

Let us meditate afresh on these enormous labours and the personal energy involved. Is there one Lord Chancellor who can point to such a record? Not one!

With these arrears definitely liquidated, he wrote this memorable letter to Buckingham in a spirit of jubilance but not boastfulness:

> This day I have made even with the business of the Kingdom for Common Justice. Not one Cause unheard. The Lawyers drawn dry of all the motions they were to make. Not one petition unanswered. And this I think could not be said in our age before. This I speak not out of ostentation, but out of gladness, when I have done my duty.
>
> I know men think I cannot continue, if I should thus oppress myself with business. But that account is made. *The Duties of Life are more than life.* And if I die now I shall die before the world be weary of me, which in our times is somewhat rare.
>
> And all this while I have been a little unperfect in my foot. But I have taken pains more like the beast on four legs, than like a man with scarce two legs. But if it be a gout—which I do neither acknowledge nor much disclaim—it is a good-natured gout; for I have no rage, violence, fury in it, and it goeth away quickly. I have hope it is but an accident of changing from a field-air to a Thames-air [*i.e. from Gray's Inn to Dorset House which had been lent to him while York House was getting ready*], or, rather, I think, it is the distance of the King and your Lordship from me that doth congeal my humours and my spirits.
>
> Your Lordship's true and most devoted friend and servant,
> Fr. Bacon
> 8th June 1617

What are we to think of such a man? A man conscious of his genius far away in excess of any of his contemporaries, and who, in the hour of his triumph, of having accomplished a tremendous task, is animated by one noble ideal! "The Duties of Life are more than life."

A very significant incident is now to be noted as to Francis Bacon's position and authority with the King. It was intended to be a warning to him; a revelation to us of his real power in the State, and a further illustration of the petty, pedantic character of James.

Before the King left London for Edinburgh he had resolved with the Council to issue a proclamation ordering the London gentry into the country. After the departure of the Court, the Council found that London was emptying fast enough of its own accord, and possibly fearing that the proclamation might be resented as an unwarrantable interference with an Englishman's liberties, the Council (the Lord Keeper presided) decided to suspend its publication. The Members thought they had the right to do so and that the King would be satisfied with their decision that it was now unnecessary. Secretary Winwood wrote to Sir Thomas Lake, who was with the King at

Lincoln, that the proclamation had been withheld because it was needless. Lake mentioned this to the King who forthwith

> brake into a great choler saying he was contemned and his commandments neglected; and whatsoever reason could be alleged he persisted in his passion.... He commanded me to despatch to you and the Lord Keeper to signify that he would have the Proclamation to proceed ... before his Majesty go from this town.... He will have the Proclamation to go forth.[1]

This peremptory message was crossed by Francis Bacon's report of Council business to Buckingham in which he alluded casually to the postponement with which he agreed. This had the effect of stirring up more passionate wrath in James. The fate of the kingdom might have been at stake.

> His Majesty hath commanded me to let you understand [wrote Lake to Winwood], that obedience is better than sacrifice, and that he knoweth HE is King of England.... I cannot by letter tell you how much he is moved, but I wish you to speak with my Lord Keeper and that it may be despatched for signature without any more excuse.

The proclamation was of course sent at once to Lincoln for signature, and Bacon knew from that time *how very narrow were the limits of his authority,* how little power he had to oppose the King's resolutions when the King had a mind as well as a right to resolve for himself.

The King's anger meant that Francis Bacon was in reality but a superior civil servant and was regarded as such by James, the Favourite, and the Court, a servant with no executive power.

Francis Bacon was never really regarded as a Councillor, but as a civil servant who had to carry out the commands of an executive Government consisting of the King and his Favourite, and those commands he had no power to amend or modify. A much more serious clash occurred while the King was in Scotland which involved Francis Bacon, the King and the Favourite. It places the point beyond dispute that Francis Bacon had no power and that his advice and actions were subject always to their pleasure.

The direct cause of the clash was Sir Edward Coke.

Coke was now tasting the bitterness of being an out-of-work lawyer, a disgraced judge, with his *Law Reports,* of which he was so proud, brought into contempt. His rival had raced ahead to the highest legal position in the land. In the Privy Council he was sitting in Coke's seat. All these humiliations had fallen upon Coke by reason of a man ten years his junior whom he despised as a lawyer and loathed as a bastard. The dominating power that obsessed him was how could he get even with his hated enemy? How could he pull him down? Without any intellectual pursuits, Coke had naught to do but to scheme and plan, to feast on the sweets of a planned revenge. Coke knew he could never hope to win the King's confidence and favour except in one way, for he had questioned James's most precious possession—the royal prerogative—and disputed the authority of the King's own court, the Chancery. The only way he could return to favour was through the goodwill of the Favourite. He knew also that Francis Bacon's rise had been at the expense

[1]Lake to Winwood.

of Buckingham's kin, who therefore would have little love for the new Lord Keeper, for while Francis Bacon paid £8000 for his commission, the money had gone to Ellesmere, his predecessor, and the larger sum of £30,000 offered by Bennett had been lost to Lady Compton, the Favourite's mother, and her precious brood of relations.

What had she to do with it? Everything!

When Buckingham was definitely installed as the Favourite, the first thing he did was to bring to Court his mother, his two brothers, John and Christopher, and a number of poor relatives and friends. (Buckingham did not marry until 1620.) The King proceeded to load them with honours and riches. His mother was made Lady Compton. His brothers were made "Sir John" and "Sir Christopher". They all lived in fine style. There appears to have been a strong attachment between Buckingham and his mother centring in personal aggrandizement. At all events they as a family speedily discovered how to out-Somerset Somerset in the gentle art of graft. One way alone led to the King's favour and that was through the House of Villiers where nested a crowd of cormorants ever hungry for gold. Even in the sale of patents, etc., the Villiers clique pocketed their share and the King the remainder. It was a formidable and dangerous coterie of hard-faced men and loose-minded women whose fortunes rose or fell with the Favourite's failure or success.

How could the wealthy Coke ruin his rival? How restore himself to favour? The answer was simple. *Through Lady Comptom's greed for gold!*

By his second wife, Lady Hatton, Coke had a daughter, Frances Coke, who was blossoming into a beauty and a toast. A beauty she must have been for Ben Jonson wrote these lovely lines about her charms:

> Though your either cheek discloses
> Mingled baths of milk and roses;
> Though your lips be banks of blisses,
> Where he plants and gathers kisses;
> And yourself the reason why
> Wisest men of love may die.

She was her mother's only child, heiress of Hatton House in Holborn, of Corfe Castle in Dorsetshire, of the long reaches of iron sand with the famous stone and marble quarries of Purbeck Isle.[1] Here was the attraction and the bait for Lady Compton—not Frances Coke's beauty but her qualifications as a rich heiress.

This wealthy girl—in the first flush of lovely girlhood, she was but fourteen—Coke privately offered, without the knowledge of his wife, to Lady Compton for one of her pauper sons to wed; Sir John Villiers, a man old enough to be her father. Coke offered as a bribe £20,000 down and a settlement of at least 2000 marks a year, Lady Compton agreeing on her part to obtain a pardon for all his offences and to persuade her son Buckingham to labour for his restoration to high place and his elevation to high rank. The bargain between them was struck after a little chaffering. Coke's mortification at his loss of prestige and his jealousy at the sight of Francis Bacon governing

[1]Dixon.

England as Regent were on the way to being avenged, and Lady Compton's "loss" of a portion of Bennett's £30,000 would not be a dead loss after all. This precious pair secretly joined hands in enmity of the man they both hated, the foremost man of the age in reputation and power, holder of the Seals, occupant of a palace, chief of all committees and representative of the King.

But Frances Coke objected to being sold like a slave to a man without personality, charm, position or wealth, while Lady Hatton (when she married Sir Edward Coke, she refused to take his name and is therefore referred to as Lady Hatton) was violently opposed to such a contract being made at her expense and without her sanction. She was quite as imperious as her husband. They had never lived happily together. Her marriage has been described as "a Comedy". She disdained to bear his name, had slammed the door of her home more than once in his face, and had even refused to allow her husband to pass her gates when entertaining the Court at Hatton House. Their wedded life had been one interminable wrangle. Determined not to allow her husband to carry out his plan, she slipped away with her daughter in a coach at dead of night to Oatlands and hid her from pursuit in the home of her cousin, Sir Edward Withipole.

Coke discovered their hidingplace and applied to the Lord Keeper, sitting as Regent in Council, for a warrant of arrest. Francis Bacon refused. Coke flew to Lady Compton with his tale—his daughter would be smuggled to France and married to the young Earl of Oxford, as there was a prior contract and understanding between them, and so on. Without communicating with Buckingham or James—then in Scotland wrangling over matters theological with the bishops—Lady Compton, her cupidity aroused lest the family should miss such a prize, wrote imperiously to the Lord Keeper commanding him to arm Coke with full powers of arrest. Though aware that his action might be represented as an insult to the Favourite, he again refused to issue a warrant, thus drawing upon himself the bitter anger of the most powerful woman in the Realm.

Feeling safe under the protection of Lady Compton, Coke, who, for a Lord Chief Justice, was one of the most lawless men in England, with his son "Fighting Clem" Coke armed a dozen of his servants, ran a beam against Withipole's door, smashed into his wife's apartments, dragged out the poor trembling girl, flung her into a coach, without warrant or even the presence of a constable, and so away to his own place at Stoke.

Suspecting her husband might abduct her daughter, Lady Hatton had rallied her friends and relatives, but she arrived at Oatlands too late. Lady Hatton, scarcely more legal, had been beaten in her race with her husband, but had prepared herself "three score men with pistols", and a band of lords to lead them, and was only prevented by the chance of not meeting her husband on the road as she expected, from having a set battle.

Baulked in one direction, Lady Hatton went straight to Francis Bacon's home, gained entry, bounced against his chamber door, awakened him and, thrusting herself past the attendants, went into his room, desiring his Lordship to pardon her boldness but she was like a cow that had lost her calf. She told her story. A council was convened to deal with the outrage at Oatlands. How could they decline to act? Frances Coke was a King's ward. Lady Hatton was related to half the Council. She implored the lords to send for the child and that a physician see her lest she die. The Council granted her prayer and an officer of the court rode to Stoke and brought Frances Coke to town that night.

As chief magistrate of the realm, responsible for the public peace, Bacon felt the gravity and scandal of such an assault on a private house. If judges and lawyers were to set the Crown at defiance, to use arms and force for the recovery of their alleged rights, public justice would become a comedy, law a snare.

A little later the Council decided that Frances Coke should be kept in charge of a neutral, in the shelter of the Attorney-General's home. They then ordered on 15 July that Coke should be brought before the Star Chamber "for riot and force" to "be heard and sentenced as justice shall appertain", Francis Bacon, speaking in the name of the Council, saying that Villiers "as a gentleman should have sought her in a noble and religious fashion and not with a gang of armed men in a midnight brawl in contempt of national and statute law."

The question of Villiers's marriage had not come before the Council up to 5 July. There is not a scintilla of evidence that Francis Bacon then knew anything about the proposed marriage, the terms of the bargain between Coke and Lady Compton, or the difference of opinion between Lady Hatton and her husband. He was thrust into the matter as Lord Keeper when Lady Hatton demanded the restoration of her daughter after Withipole's house had been smashed open. He had already refused Coke a warrant to search Withipole's house and also Lady Hatton's demand. What he and the Council did not know until later was this: that Winwood, Secretary of State, had given Coke secretly a warrant either just before the forced entry and abduction or afterwards to make an illegal action legal. Why did he do it? Because Winwood hated Francis Bacon owing to an incident that happened about that time. In Francis Bacon's presence Winwood beat his dog cruelly for lying on his stool. Francis Bacon sharply rebuked him, and added, "Every *gentleman* loves his dog." The quarrel between them was such that, when Secretary Winwood came to sit near the Lord Keeper, he was waved away and told to keep his distance. From that moment Winwood threw his lot in with Coke, sought to discredit and injure the Lord Keeper, secretly aided Coke in connection with the proposed marriage, and became the active intermediary to make Buckingham hostile to the Lord Keeper, by writing coloured reports to the Court at Scotland, either through Lake, then with the Court in Scotland, or direct to Buckingham, without the Council's knowledge.

Francis Bacon sent his first letter about the matter to the Favourite on 12 July. Before this date Coke had broken into Withipole's house, the Council had met to condemn the offence, and then, or a day or two later, Frances Coke had been placed in neutral custody. Up to this point the Lord Keeper and the Council believed that they were acting in accordance with the wishes of the King; for Coke, they thought, had mortally offended James, was a disgraced man, and they were not aware that the attitude of the King and the Favourite had changed towards him. Francis Bacon therefore wrote to Buckingham as follows:

To the Earl of Buckingham

My very good Lord,

I shall write to your Lordship of a business which your lordship may think to concern myself; but I do think it concerneth your Lordship much more....

It seemeth that Secretary Winwood hath officiously busied himself to make a match between your brother and Sir Edward Coke's daughter.... It is true he hath the consent of Sir Edward Coke ... as we hear ... upon reasonable conditions for your brother; and yet no better than without question may be found in some other matches. But the mother's consent is not had, nor the young gentlewoman's, who expecteth a fortune from her mother, which without her consent is endangered. This match out of my faith and freedom towards your Lordship, I hold very inconvenient both for your brother and yourself.

First, He shall marry into a disgraced House, which in reason of State is never held good.

Next, He shall marry into a troubled House of man and wife, which in religion and Christian discretion is disliked.

Thirdly, Your Lordship will go near to lose all such your friends as are adverse to Sir Edward Coke; myself only except who out of a pure love and thankfulness shall ever be firm to you.

And lastly and chiefly, believe it, will greatly weaken and distract the King's service....

Therefore my advice is, and your Lordship will do you a great deal of honour, according to religion and the law of God, your Lordship will signify *unto my Lady your mother,* that your desire is that *the marriage be not pressed or proceeded in without the consent of both parents*; and so either break it altogether or defer any further mealing in it, till your Lordship's return; and this the rather for that it hath been carried so harshly and inconsiderately by Secretary Winwood, as for doubt that the father should take her away by force, the mother to get the start, hath conveyed her away secretly, which is ill of all sides. Thus hoping not only that your Lordship will accept well, but believe my faithful advice, who by my great experience in the world must needs see further than your Lordship can, I ever rest,

Yours Lordship's true and most devoted friend and servant,

Fr. Bacon

July 12th, 1617

This letter proves that Francis Bacon had so far acted with studied impartiality. He had not opposed the marriage. He had actually reconciled the conflicting parties six days later without pressure from anyone, leaving it to the King to make a final decision. He, with the Council, believed, however, that the King, in view of Coke's arrogance, would never restore the contumacious judge to favour. He placed his views before Buckingham at length, the climax of his advice being that the proposed marriage be not proceeded with unless the consent of both parents be obtained. He obviously thought he had the ear of the Favourite and that his advice would be accepted.

Up to this point no blame can be attached to Bacon. He was the guardian of the young by virtue of his office; and we have no reason to doubt the sincerity of his objections to a marriage so disreputably initiated and, as ultimately proved, so disastrous.

Before 25 July, when the Lord Keeper wrote to the King, and before a single word had been heard from Buckingham, Bacon had calmed the outrage, reconciled husband and wife, and restored Frances Coke to her father's house. When all this was done he wrote to Buckingham and the King.

At a Council meeting of uncertain date Secretary Winwood, who apparently had taken up the attitude that the great offence lay on the mother stealing away the daughter from her own father, shot his bolt from the blue to the surprise of everyone. It appears that, when he was taxed with aiding and abetting Coke, he not only defended his action but *produced a letter of approbation of all his courses from the King*. He had been treacherously keeping back information from the Council that he had received from the Court in Scotland, an underhand action calculated to discomfort Francis Bacon's relations with the King and Buckingham and obviously with Lady Compton's connivance, for Winwood said he wished her well and her sons, and avowed his readiness to serve the Earl of Buckingham with true affection; and they who wished to do well would serve the King and the Favourite as he had done.

Obviously Winwood had been in touch with the Court all along though why the most important member of the Council, the Lord Keeper, was kept in the dark can only be understood by accepting the fact that it was Coke's first move in the game to disgrace Francis Bacon in the eyes of the King and compel him to resign his office, which could then be put up for sale to enrich Lady Compton and her precious tribe. She was an active participant in the affair, in correspondence with Buckingham. He was under her finger and thumb, and we can imagine how she would inflame his mind against the Lord Keeper.

The revelation of Winwood altered the whole matter. It could not be the business of the King's Council in a case of this kind to work in opposition to his declared purposes.

The Star Chamber proceedings were dropped and the entire Council were very uneasy as to the outcome. A fortnight had passed since the Lord Keeper had written to Buckingham and, as there had been no reply, he was naturally anxious to know whether Winwood's statements were correct and whether his own advice given on 12 July was acceptable to Buckingham and the King. On the 25th he wrote to both of them. To the King he said:

> ... I am more bound than other men in doing your commandments when your resolution is settled and made known to me.
>
> I shall therefore most humbly crave pardon from your Majesty if in plainness and no less humbleness I deliver to your Majesty my honest and disinterested opinion in the business of the match of Sir John Villiers ... preserving always the laws and duties of a firm friend to my Lord Buckingham, whom I will never cease to love, and to whom I have written already, but have not heard from him....
>
> If you are resolved the matter shall go on, after you have heard my reasons to the contrary, I may receive therein your particular will and commandments for myself; that I may conform myself thereto ... for I be requested in it from my Lord of Buckingham, the answer of a true friend ought to be, that I had rather go against his good: But your Majesty I must obey....

Francis Bacon then explains the many personal and political reasons which, in his opinion, made a marriage undesirable: the refusal of Lady Hatton to allow the match, the dependency of the young girl, her fortune, on her mother, the quarrelsome temper of the two parents, the notoriety and scandal of their domestic feuds, the disapproval of the leading men in the

Government, the recent disgrace of Coke, the divisions which his return to the Council would bring with it, though personally he feared him not.

> I think I have done a duty not unworthy the first year of your last high favour. I most humbly pray your Majesty to pardon me if in anything I have erred; for my errors shall always be supplied by obedience. And so I conclude with my prayers for the happy preservation of your person and state.

This is the letter of an impassive civil servant whose duty it is to proffer advice in the interests of the State. Quite clearly the letter shows that Francis Bacon had received neither instructions nor inkling from the Court in Scotland that the King and Buckingham had any wishes respecting the marriage pro or con. He knows his personal duty is *to obey* the sovereign, and he says so. He also understands that it is no use trying to thwart the wishes of the Favourite. He says he has never wished, and never tried, to do so. In fact the letter clearly indicates that the Lord Keeper had been specially kept in the dark. There is not the slightest doubt that Francis Bacon's disgrace was aimed at cunningly so that Coke might step into the saddle to make Lady Compton richer by Frances Coke's marriage portion and a portion of the proceeds from the sale of the Lord Keeper's office.

Francis Bacon's letter to Buckingham at the same time begins:

> My very good Lord,
>
> I do think long to hear from your Lordship touching my last letter, wherein I gave you my opinion touching your brother's match.... If your Lordship think it is humour or interest that leads me, God judge your sincerity.... I shall ever give you as I give my Master safe counsel, and such as time will approve....
>
> Your Lordship's most faithful and devoted friend and servant,
>
> Fr. Bacon, C.S.

Four days later, on 29 July, he wrote a short letter of some eight lines to the Favourite enclosing business memoranda and added:

> I am much relieved with my being in the country-air ... so that of late years I have not found my health better.
>
> Your Lordship writeth seldomer than you were wont; but when you are once gotten into England, you will be more at leisure. God bless and prosper you....

These letters show that the Lord Keeper was beginning to be anxious at Buckingham's attitude—his silence. Probably he had already heard rumours of an irate Favourite inflamed by the different stories, spiced with misrepresentations, written him by Lady Compton, Winwood and Coke and by other interested rivals and enemies. The silence from Scotland was broken by the King's answer to Francis Bacon's letter of 25 July, in which the King said that he considered Coke's proceeding in pursuit of his daughter as a lawful and ordinary thing, in no way justifying the stir that had been made about it. He found fault with the tone of Bacon's letter to Buckingham, as implying a want of respect for his discretion, and charged him with ingratitude in opposing the match when he knew how Buckingham desired it.

Thus Francis Bacon learned with amazement that the King was strong for the match, the proceedings of the Council condemned as gross misconduct and his reasons regarded as worthless.

Shortly afterwards—five weeks from 12 July—Buckingham answered with scornful and menacing curtness.

To the Lord Keeper Bacon

My Lord,

If your man had been addressed only to me, I should have been careful to have procured him a more speedy dispatch: but now you have found another address, I am excused; and since you are grown weary of employing me, I can be no otherwise in being employed.

In this business of my brother's that you overtrouble yourself with, I understand from London from some of my friends that you have carried yourself with much scorn and neglect both toward myself and friends; which if it proves true I blame not you but myself.

Your Lordship's assured friend,
G. Buckingham

This insolent letter from an ignorant upstart of twenty-five to a man twice his age is a disgusting display of calculated temper. It indicates something far more than the mere petulance of a spoiled child that cannot have all his own way and meets with opposition for the first time. Combined with the King's letter it must have shocked Francis Bacon profoundly. Through no fault of his own he had been manouvred into standing on the edge of a precipice. One false step and he would crash in ruin; for Francis Bacon must have seen that behind the hand of the Favourite there were the voices of Lady Compton, Winwood and Coke; and further developments prove that this was the real aim of the conspirators. Well might Francis Bacon write, "The rising unto Great Place is laborious ... and the standing is slippery."

To the Favourite's letter the Lord Keeper sent a careful reply, conciliatory and explanatory. He said that since he had heard from the Court he was resolved to further the match and the conditions thereof for Sir John Villiers's advancement and that he had acquainted the Attorney General, Lady Hatton, Sir John Butler and "my Lady your mother".

I did ever fear this alliance would go near to leese me your Lordship that I hold so dear.... But I will rely on your constancy and nature, and on my own deserving, and the firm tie we have in respect of the King's service.

In the meantime I must complain a little to your Lordship, that I do hear my Lady your mother and your Brother Sir John do speak of me with some bitterness and neglect. I must bear with one as a lady and the other as a lover, and with both for your Lordship's sake, whom I will make judge of anything they shall have against me.

But I hope, though I be true servant to your Lordship, you will not have me vassal to their passions, especially as long as they are governed by Sir Edward Coke and Secretary Winwood. ... Therefore your Lordship will do me right, and yet I shall take it for a favour, if you signify to them that you have received satisfaction from me, and would have them use me in a friendly and in good manner. God keep us from these long journeys and absence, which makes misunderstandings and gives advantages to untruth.

And this was the spoiled Favourite's curt and cutting reply, his head completely turned by pride of his position.

To the Lord Keeper

My Lord,

I have received your Lordship's letter by your man; but having so lately imparted my mind to you in my former letters, I refer your Lordship to those letters, without making a needless repetition.

Your Lordship's at command,
G. Buckingham
Ashton, 12th Aug. 1617

This admitted of no reply and Francis Bacon could only await events, for the King and Court were on the point of returning to London by easy stages. In Bacon's reply to the King's letter he says:

> It contains matters of dislike which ... hath grieved me.... I find in myself sincerity of intention and conformity of will, howsoever I may have erred—To my Lord Buckingham ... I must humbly confess that I was in this a little parent-like but in truth without any grain of disesteem for his Lordship's discretion....
>
> It is true that in those matters which by your Majesty's commandment and reference came before the table concerning Sir Edward Coke, I was sometimes sharp; but it was with the end to have your Majesty's will performed....
>
> It is true also, that I disliked the riot or violence ... and I disliked it the more because he justified it by law; which was his old song. But in that act of Council ... I did not see but that all my Lords were as forward as myself, as a thing most necessary for the preservation of the peace.... And all this had a fair end in a reconcilement made by Mr Attorney whereby both husband and wife and child should be kept together.
>
> Now for the times of things. I beseech your Majesty to understand that which my Lord of Buckingham will bear witness with me, that I never had word or letter from his Lordship till I wrote my letter of advice ... not till five weeks after....
>
> To conclude, I have gone through with plainness of truth the parts of your Majesty's letter, very humbly praying pardon for troubling your Majesty so long; and most humbly praying your Majesty to maintain me in your grace and favour, which is the fruit of my like upon the root of a good conscience.

This dignified answer proves conclusively that Francis Bacon did not know anything of the King's or the Favourite's wishes and had acted according to law and the dictates of his conscience. It is really a justification of his actions. He does not excuse them, but as a civil servant he is quite prepared to carry out the King's wishes when he knows what they are. There is no ignominious surrender here. He submits because it is his clear duty to submit. He points out he had had no word to direct him. He had supposed he was serving the King and still thought he had, to the best of his judgement, served his King, but he accepted the King's decision. It is a submissive letter but it is not by any means an abject letter; it is a natural letter.

The King sent him an answer, a "long winded and badly written letter but defending Coke's ruffianly proceedings, and scoffing at Bacon's excuses", concluding his strictures with:

> the opposition which we justly find fault with you, was the refusal to sign a warrant for the father to the recovery of his child, clad with those circumstances, as is reported, *of your slight carriage to Buckingham's mother when she repaired to you on so reasonable an errand*.... Given under our signet at Nantwich.

Francis Bacon was not to be intimidated from defending himself by such an unjust tissue of misrepresentations. He replied to what was worthy of notice, of which the first paragraph is a specimen:

> I dare not presume any more to reply upon your Majesty, but reserve my defence till I attend your Majesty at your happy return; when I hope verily to approve myself not only a true servant to your Majesty, but a true friend to my Lord of Buckingham. And for the times also, I hope to give your Majesty a good account, though distance of place may obscure them.

There was no more submission to the King in these letters than had already been tendered to James before the Coke–Hatton case clouded his horizon. His political principles were clear and had been declared years previously: that the King in his office as King was the final authority in the State and of himself and must be obeyed. Francis Bacon was under his direct authority as his servant. That was the submission he made when he "kissed hands" on his appointment as Lord Keeper. He had to obey. He had never intended to run counter to the King's wishes. He had no wish to do. And when he knew what was the King's will he was prepared to carry it out according to his oath. And in this sense submissions are made by everyone in all walks of life to authority.

Francis Bacon's last letter was sent on 31 August, by which time the King was on his way back from Scotland and had arrived at Coventry. Coke had gone to meet him and had been well received. Francis Bacon's friend Yelverton, the Attorney-General, arrived later, meeting everywhere in the royal entourage a hostile atmosphere, "cloud and thunder", averted faces and angry glances.

He found the King resentful; Buckingham furious; Coke in high feather, triumphant and making very bold with the King; the Court like a pack of hounds in full cry at the Lord Keeper's iniquities. The Favourite told Yelverton that he would not secretly bite those who had opposed marriage; they should discern what favour he had by the power he would use; the Lord Keeper was ungrateful and as unfaithful as he had been to Essex and Somerset; and "the Court was full of excitement expecting the Lord Keeper's disgrace, petitions against him being prepared." Yelverton sent on 3 September a long and confidential report in the way of a warning as to what Francis Bacon might expect when he met the King and his minion, the storms he would have to face. This was Yelverton's report.

> My most Worthy and Honourable Lord,
>
> I dare not think my journey lost, because I have with much joy seen the face of my Master, the King, though more clouded towards me than I looked for.
>
> *Sir Edward Coke hath not forborne by any engine to heave both at your honour and at myself*; and he works by the weightiest instrument, the Earl of Buckingham, who as I see sets him as close to him as his shirt, the Earl speaking in Sir Edward's phrase, and as it were menacing in his spirit.
>
> My Lord, I emboldened myself to assay the temper of my Lord of Buckingham to myself, and found it very fervent, *misled by misinformation* which yet I find he embraced as truth, and did nobly and plainly tell me he would not secretly bite, but whosoever had had any interest or tasted of the opposition to his brother's marriage, he would as openly oppose them to their faces, and they should discern what Favour he had by the Power he would use.

In the passage between him and me, I stood with much confidence upon these grounds:

First, that neither your Lordship nor myself had any way opposed but many ways had furthered the fair passage to the Marriage.

Secondly, that we only wished the manner of Sir Edward's proceedings to have been more temperate, and more resembling the Earl's sweet disposition.

Thirdly, that the chiefest check in the business was Sir Edward himself, who listened to no advice, who was so transported with passion, as he purposely declined the even way which your Lordship and the rest of the Lords left both him and his Lady and his daughter in.

Fourthly, I was bold to stand upon my ground, and so I said I knew your Lordship would, that *these were Slanders* which were brought him of us both; and that it stood not upon his Honour to give credit to them.

After I had passed these straits with the Earl, leaving him still to the first relation of envious and odious adversaries, I ventured to approach his Majesty, who graciously gave me his hand to kiss, but intermixed withal that I deserved not that favour, if three or four things were true which he had to object against me. I was bold to crave his princely justice, first to hear, then to judge, which he graciously granted, and said he wished I could clear myself. I answered *I would not appeal to his mercy* in any of these points, but *would endure the severest censure if any of them were true;* whereupon he said he would reserve his judgment till he heard me, which could not be then, his other occupations pressed him so much. All this was in the hearing of the Earl; and I protest I think the confidence in my innocency made me depart half justified, for I likewise kissed his Majesty's hand at his departure, and though out of his grace he commanded my attendance at Warwick, yet upon my suit he easily inclined to give me the choice to wait on him at Windsor or London.

Now, my Lord, give me leave out of all my affections that shall ever serve you to intimate touching yourself:

1st. That every Courtier is acquainted that the Earl professeth openly against you as forgetful of his kindness, and *unfaithful to him* in your Love and in your Actions.

2nd. That he returneth the shame upon himself, in not listening to counsel that dissuaded his affection from you, and not to mount you so high, not forbearing in open speech (as divers have told me, and this bearer, your gentleman, hath heard also), to tax you as if it were an inveterate custom with you, to be unfaithful to him *as you were to the Earls of Essex and Somerset.*

3rd. That it is too common in every man's mouth in Court, that *your greatness shall be abated,* and as your Tongue hath been as a Razor to some, so shall theirs be to you.

4th. That there is laid up for you, to make the burden the more grevious, *many Petitions to his Majesty against you.*

My Lord Sir Edward Coke, as he were already upon his Wings, triumphs exceedingly, hath much private confidence with his Majesty; and in public doth offer himself and *thrust upon the* King with as great boldness of speech as heretofore.

It is thought and much feared at Woodstock *he will again be recalled* to the Council table; for *neither are the Earl's eyes nor his thoughts ever off him.*

Sir Edward Coke with much audacity affirmeth his daughter to be most deeply in love with Sir John Villiers, that the contract pretended with the Earl [of Oxford] is counterfeit, and the letter also that is pretended to come from the Earl.

My Noble Lord, if I were worthy being the meanest of all to interpose my weakness, I would humbly desire,

1. That your Lordship fail not to be with his Majesty at Woodstock: *The sight of you will fright some.*

2. That you single not yourself from the other Lords, but justify all the proceedings as all your joint acts, and *I little fear but you pass Conqueror.*
3. That you retort the clamour and noise in this business upon Sir Edward Coke, by the violence of his carriage.
4. That you seem not dismayed, but open yourself bravely and confidently, wherein you can excell all subjects; by which means *I know you shall amaze some and daunt others.*

I have abused your Lordship's patience long, but my duty and affection towards your Lordship shall have no end; but I still wish your Honour greater, and rest myself, Your Honour's Servant,

Henry Yelverton

There is no doubt that at this time there was a crisis in Francis Bacon's affairs and his life. All his biographers are agreed upon the fact that he stood on the brink of ruin. What they do not seem to realize is that it was a carefully engineered plot by Coke, Winwood and Lady Compton and that they had inflamed the entire Court by a tissue of lies and misrepresentations. Yelverton's report proves this conclusively—the Lord Keeper's greatness was to be abated and petitions prepared against him. And it further proves that nothing had been done that needed either apology or submission by the Lord Keeper or the Council.

A day or two later there was another menacing report from Buckingham.

> Your Lordship's unkind dealing with me in this matter of my brother's, Time will try all. His Majesty hath given me commandment to make this answer in his name. ... I will not trouble your Lordship with any larger discourse at this time being to meet you so shortly, *where will be better trial of all that hath passed than can be made by letters.*

Such was the spirit in which the King and Buckingham were going to meet the Chancellor. Within six months of his appointment he had been involved once more with the affairs of Coke and it looked as though he were on the point of losing his office. Yelverton had advised him to travel to Woodstock to meet the King. "Seem not dismayed"—"you shall amaze some and daunt others." When the meeting actually took place or where we have no record.

The Court returned to London on 15 September and something occurred which made the King hesitate to proceed to extremities against the Lord Keeper. At the moment of his return the Council had before them the case of a man named Baynton who had threatened to kill the King; so the first business to take precedence over everything else was the Lord Keeper's report upon the matter through Buckingham to the King.

> Without any apparent show of drink, otherwise than so as to make him less wary to keep his secrets, Baynton, attested by two witnesses, had been lately with the King to petition him for reward of service, which was denied him, whereupon *it was twice in his mind to have killed his Majesty, God ever bless him.*
>
> *The man is not yet apprehended, and by some said to be mad or half mad; which, in my opinion, is not the less dangerous:* for such men commonly do such mischief....

The safety of the King was thus in peril, and it can well be imagined that James was very much alarmed, for he was a cowardly soul; that a homicidal maniac should be at large seeking to murder him would naturally put the King in a panic, probably the Favourite also. His anger, like his courage, began to evaporate through his fingertips. Better, far better, to trust in the vigilant protection of the Lord Keeper than in the uncertain asperities of Coke. Better feel secure of life and limb with Francis Bacon than be in a constant fever of anxiety with others who might be unreliable and careless of his person. So the plot broke. Anyway the quarrel came to an abrupt termination for no apparent reason save the King's fear of being murdered. Francis Bacon had a brief interview with the Favourite on the 21st, after which Buckingham sent a letter, full of dissimulation, to explain the reason why the King and he had forgiven him.

> I have made his Majesty acquainted with your note concerning that wicked fellow's speeches. . . . His Majesty is pleased that it shall be exactly tried, whether this foul mouthed fellow was taken for drunkenness or madness when he spake it.

Buckingham then goes on to say that he freely confesses that Francis Bacon's offer of "submission" unto him battered so the unkindness caused in his heart that he went to sound his Majesty's intention towards him and found the King fixed in a rigorous resolution to put some public exemplary mark upon him; but the sight of his deep-conceived indignation quenched

> my passion making me change into a peace-maker; so I was forced upon my knees to beg of his Majesty that he would put no public act of disgrace upon you. . . . No other person would have been patiently heard in this suit but myself, so I did, though not without difficulty, obtain this much; That he would not so far disable you from the merit of your future service. . . . His Majesty so far protesteth, that upon the conscience of his office he cannot omit . . . to give a Kingly reprimand at his first sitting in Council. . . .
>
> I beseech your Lordship to reserve this secretly to yourself only, till our meeting at Hampton Court lest his Majesty should be high offended. . . .
>
> Your Lordship's faithful friend and servant, G. B.

What are we to make of this precious epistle? Dissimulation, of which James was a past master, is written all over it. *It all goes to show that the King was mortally afraid of being murdered by a lunatic and consequently climbed down* because he knew Francis Bacon was a sure pillar upon whom he could lean; and he did not want to lose his protection. "Submission" forsooth? To Buckingham? For what? The pure saving of face after threatening such dire penalties to the Lord Keeper day after day in the presence of the Court? When the Council met *there was no reproof from the King*, more a defence of his own conduct which he wound up with a piece of blaspheny.

> I, James, am neither a god nor an angel, but a man like any other. . . . You may be sure I love the Earl of Buckingham more than anyone else, more than you who are here assembled. . . . Jesus Christ did the same, and therefore I cannot be blamed. Christ had his John and I have my Steenie.

To Buckingham in reply Francis Bacon wrote about a twelve-line letter. He quite understood the reasons that prompted it—fear of a criminal lunatic—and made the saving of face easy by writing a sarcastic letter which could be read in reverse—at its face value.

> My ever best Lord, now better than yourself. Your Lordship's pen or rather pencil hath portrayed towards me such magnimity and nobleness and true kindness, as methinks I see the image of some Ancient Virtue, *and not anything of these times*. It is *the Line of my Life and not the Lines of my Letter that must express my thankfulness*: wherein if I fail, then God fail me, and make me as miserable as I think myself happy by this Reviver, through His Majesty's singular clemency, and your *incomparable Love* and Favour....
>
> Your raised and infinitely obliged friend or servant.
>
> 22nd September 1617

This extravaganza is a perfect specimen of the "writ sarkastic style" beloved by Artemus Ward; and dullards indeed are those who cannot see the disdain that reeks in those simple lines, so courteous, so urbane, so biting when read between the lines with a knowledge of what called them into being. This finishes Francis Bacon's connection with the business. Coke's plot had failed to ruin him, to disparage him, to remove him from office.

Frances Coke married Sir John Villiers, with regal pomp, the bridegroom being made into Viscount Purbeck, with Lady Hatton under arrest for publishing a prior contract between her daughter and Lord Oxford. The wedding began in misery and ended in shame, for even James could not make the young bride love and respect her husband, whom she soon deserted. But Coke, having sold his daughter and £30,000 to the Villiers family, is restored to his seat in the Privy Council on 28 September 1617, and grimly decides to make no mistake next time he strikes. He will wait and strike to kill.

No pretended reconciliation could make Francis Bacon forget the precariousness of the King's and Buckingham's so-called friendship; its utter worthlessness. He was received back into favour and took his place more and more as one of the chief persons of the Government, but he had no power.

Though his services were great and were not unrecognized, he never had the power and influence in affairs to which his boundless devotion to the Crown, his grasp of business and his willing industry ought to have entitled him. He was still a servant and made to feel it, though a servant in the "First Form".

It was James and Buckingham who determined the policy of the country, or settled the course to be taken in particular transactions; when this was settled it was Bacon's business to carry it through.

In this he was like all other servants of the Crown and, like them, he had to be satisfied with giving his advice, whether it were taken or not.

Francis Bacon had no power to pronounce judgement. He could only advise.

It may be added that Secretary Winwood died on 27 October 1617. Lady Hatton made peace with the King and was set at liberty on 2 November and, a week later, gave a great banquet at Hatton House at which the King, the Prince of Wales, the Court and the Lord Keeper were present.

Chapter VI

BARON VERULAM: LORD CHANCELLOR: THE GREAT INSTAURATION: 1617—1620

WE have seen that in 1616 Francis Bacon wrote a "Letter of Advice" to Buckingham. Under heading II, "Matters concerning Justice", he wrote the following:

> Judges must be men of courage, fearing God and *hating Covetousness*: An ignorant man cannot, a coward dares not, be a good Judge. *By no means must you be persuaded to interpose yourself by word or letter in any cause depending, or like to be depending in any Court of Justice,* nor suffer any man to do it where you can hinder it; and by all means dissuade the King from it upon the importunity of any either for their friends or themselves.
>
> If it should prevail, *it perverts justice*; but if the Judge be so just, and of so undaunted courage—as he ought to be—as not to be inclined thereby, yet it always leaves a taint of suspicion and prejudice behind it. Judges must be chaste as Caesar's wife, neither to be so much as suspected in the least degree unjust; and, Sir, the honour of the Judges in Judicature is the King's Honour, whose person they represent.

It is self-evident from this letter that when Francis Bacon advised the Favourite that he should never allow himself "to be interposed by word or letter in any cause" in the courts of justice—even advising him to "dissuade the King from" such "importunity"—this was honestly said. The moral principles he enunciated were fixed and unalterable, inherent in his very being, and nothing has yet transpired to give any warranty for believing otherwise. We have noted already that a year later (17 October 1617) he laid down the same golden precept to Justice Hatton: "That your hands be clean and uncorrupt from gifts." And so he continues to breathe out the purest principles of moral and judicial rectitude on the Bench as well as in his private life.

Why did Francis Bacon tender such advice to Buckingham, and emphasize, in his charges to Justice Hutton and others, his utter abhorrence of anything corrupt or anything shady that would injure another? He did so because it was the common practice in those days for people in authority—whose friends might be parties in a suit—to try to influence the judge. *He wanted the practice stopped because he hated it*; and he knew it never could be stopped unless the Favourite said so. And, further, doubtlessly he wanted to warn Buckingham against attempting such a practice with him in his official capacity. Francis Bacon was attempting to do something practical in resistance of a custom so long established and so deeply seated, that applications were, as a matter of course, made to statesmen and to judges by the most respectable members of the community and by the two universities.

We thus see that the Lord Keeper warned Buckingham in advance that he ought not, as a statesman, to interfere with any case that was pending in the courts by word or letter and that, as a necessary corollary, it followed that it would be a waste of time for anyone to write to him on such an errand; for he adds that no judge of undaunted courage would allow any such influence to prevail to "pervert Justice", a clear indication that this applied to himself. Nevertheless, in spite of this admonition we find that Buckingham did send the Lord Keeper letters respecting suits.

Had Francis Bacon not left such a warning in writing we might have thought he was insensible to the heinous nature of the offence and that in some measure he agreed with or condoned the practice.

Francis Bacon's character, his attitude of mind as exemplified by his "Letter of Advice" and his charges, all go to show that he deeply resented such letters. There is nothing to show that the Lord Keeper was an unjust judge and no evidence that he had ever been guilty of actions to condone wrongdoing.

Now, how could Francis Bacon's character be questioned through receiving letters which annoyed him? How could he stop the Favourite writing him? Would it have been productive of any real good if he had contemptuously tossed the early letters back to Buckingham? Would it have stopped the general habit of letter writing to judges? Francis Bacon had to balance his course of action with other and greater plans that would affect for all times all humanity—and he was not going to jeopardize his principles of a lifetime being fulfilled by openly quarrelling with the then most powerful man in the realm, who made and unmade men by a nod, over letters which *would not influence his judgement to deviate a hair's breadth*? Today such letters would be regarded by an English judge as an affront and contempt, but in the Tudor and Jacobean era the Crown and the favourites were very much concerned with the character of judges. The Crown even sold judgeships to the highest bidder. For the Lord Keeper to have returned the letters unopened and unread, or to have resented them by overt message or letter, would have been regarded as an insult to the Crown itself.

The crux of the matter comes to this: *did Francis Bacon prevent justice in any of the thirty cases in which Buckingham was interested?* He did not! *Were any of his judicial decisions influenced by the Favourite?* Not one! The Favourite sent seven letters in 1617; fourteen in 1618; five in 1619; three in 1620; one in 1621. Spedding is firm on this point: that these letters were never intended to make Francis Bacon interfere with the course of justice. He points out that nineteen of the thirty letters contain the phrase "*so far as may stand in justice and equity*" or words to that effect; and that there is no reason to believe that in those letters in which they were omitted they were intended to dictate a verdict. The real object of such letters seems to have been to satisfy friends who had asked for them. Knowing Buckingham's avariciousness, I can well imagine he was paid for them. Whether he was paid or pestered into sending them, he apparently took "the least trouble to himself and most satisfaction to the suitor, the usual form being a recommendation of the case to the Lord Keeper: he would direct his secretary to draw up a letter for his signature in the usual form."

The letters refer to a variety of subjects. The following is a fair sample:

My Honourable Lord,

Though I had resolved to give your Lordship no more trouble in matters of controversy depending before you, with what importunity soever my letters had been desired; yet the respect I bear unto this gentleman hath so far forced my resolution as to recommend unto your Lordship the Suit, which I am informed by him, is to receive a hearing before you on Monday next, between Barnaby Leigh and Edward Dyer, plaintiffs, and Sir Thomas Thynne, defendant; wherein I desire your Lordship's favour on the plaintiff's behalf *so far only as the justice of their cause shall require.* And so I rest

Your Lordship's faithful Servant,
G. Buckingham
Newmarket 15th Nov. 1618

In none of the letters does he ask for a verdict to be given in favour of a particular suitor. The majority is to expedite a hearing or a decision.

When one is asked how then did Francis Bacon deal with such recommendation, it can be definitely asserted that they did not interfere with the impartial hearing of the case and the impartial decision; in short, legally he took no notice of the communications. Because he had clean hands and a pure heart he could afterwards stand fast in his integrity and assert that he was "the justest Chancellor that had been in the five changes" since the time of Sir Nicholas Bacon. Here is Spedding's mature conviction.

> Not an instance can be found in which his [Buckingham's] interference affected Bacon's decision. . . . Never once did he allow Buckingham to "dictate his decrees." . . . They have not to me the appearance of letters *intended* to oversway Justice. . . . They appear for the most part merely to get rid of the importunity of suitors.
>
> In spite of the extreme scrutiny and fearless strictures to which Bacon's conduct was submitted, *while not one of these cases was above four years old . . . not one unjust decree pronounced out of deference to Buckingham was ever alleged against him. . . .*[1]

No attempt has ever been made to connect an unjust decree of his with one of these letters.

Francis Bacon, letter or no letter, never decided in favour of a party whom he knew to be in the wrong. Spedding indeed notes a letter from the Favourite which "*contains thanks for the pains which Bacon had taken in hearing a cause which had gone against the party in whose favour Buckingham writes.*" As for any *dictation of decrees*, we find no hint of such a thing in them. There is indeed every evidence that the Lord Keeper did not fall in at all with the Favourite's wishes respecting judicial matters. He was very far from being under Buckingham's finger and thumb, as the following letter will show.

My very good Lord,

I send your Lordship the certificate touching the inrolment of prentices. *We can find no ground for it by law.*

My will shall ever be ready to further anything your Lordship recommendeth; *but where the matter will not bear it,* your Lordship I know will think not the worse but the better of me if I signify the true state of things to your Lordship; resting ever

Your Lordship's true friend and devoted servant,
Fr. Bacon C. S.
York House, 29 Oct. 1617

[1] *Evenings with a Reviewer.*

Note this date. This point-blank refusal, short, curt and sharp, is only a month after Coke had been restored to the Privy Council on 28 September 1617. It proves conclusively that Francis Bacon never submitted to Buckingham, was uninfluenced by his requests; and, if further evidence is required, we can cite once more Professor Nichol who says:

> The correspondence shows that *Bacon gave several decisions in the teeth of the letters*, and as the Earl's *protégés* are unlikely to have been always in the wrong, we are free to conclude that *when the decrees were favourable they were just.*

Three months after the breaking of the Coke–Compton plot that was to have been the signal for Francis Bacon's disgrace and fall, there was a great feast made by Buckingham on the Sunday after New Year's Day, at which the Favourite received the patent of marquis from the King as a New Year's gift. At this same banquet Francis Bacon was also given an additional honour. He was made Lord Chancellor—"for life with sixty pounds a year increase. The speech goes," adds Chamberlain, "that he shall be made a Baron and the making of another to discharge his debts." On 12 July 1618 the rumour was verified. He was created Baron Verulam of Verulam. He has seldom, however, been called by this name. He wrote himself as "Francis Lord Verulam"; in Latin "*Franciscus de Verulamio*". Thus the man who was born to be King became a Peer of the Realm. For a season his enemies stood mute. Sir Edward Coke, though restored to favour, shrank back into silence to plot anew.

Among the real outstanding tragedies of this reign and the preceding one—the execution of Essex, the death of Elizabeth, the tragedy of Mary Queen of Scots, the fall of Francis Bacon—none is more real and poignant than that of Sir Walter Raleigh, the gay, debonair, versatile soldier, discoverer, courtier, philosopher and poet, the man who charmed Elizabeth with his gallantry, whose only master as a sea-king was Drake, who shares with Francis Bacon the honour of being one of England's foremost colonizers—in the founding of Virginia. He is said to have spent £40,000 of his own money upon the colony. His only superior as a prose writer may be said to be the sage of Verulam. If he had the spirit of Sidney in the field, he was alike inspired by the same lyrical spirit that enriched the poetry of Spenser. He was widely read, learned in the lore of Egyptians, "the first modern historian of the Old World", a pioneer in many phases of thought. Elizabeth, though she called him "Water"—as though she recognized his mercurial instability of temperament—entrusted him with many offices, Captain of the Guard, Wardenship of the Stanneries, the wine-licence monopoly, the governorship of Jersey. When the Virgin Queen died, the crafty Cecil got the ear of James, and for his own advantage poisoned his mind against Raleigh. The cowardice, the timid love of peace, the personal habits of King James were naturally repugnant to the bold, self-reliant adventurer who once had been the trusted confidant of Elizabeth the Lion Heart. James must have felt that Raleigh was indifferent to him, his cause, his ideals. Very soon Raleigh was stripped of his offices. In the heat of humiliation he may have spoken or listened to words expressing a preference for Arabella Stuart to the rule of the Scottish King. This was enough to bring him to trial for high treason on the evidence of the shifty Lord Cobham, who changed his story every time he told it. In the Main and Rye plots there is no evidence of his complicity

The prosecution in 1603 was conducted by the Attorney-General, the foul-mouthed Sir Edward Coke, who called him "a monster ... a viper ... the rankest traitor in England ... a damnable atheist ... a spider of Hell," etc. Sir Dudley Carleton, who heard the trial, writes that *when it began he would have gone a hundred miles to see him hanged but when it was closed he would have gone a thousand to save his life*. He defended himself with rare eloquence but he was condemned to death and only when he was on the scaffold was the sentence commuted to perpetual imprisonment. His estate was sequestered and to Raleigh's wife James said, when she pleaded for it, "I maun hae the lond; I maun hae it for Carr." Raleigh was sent to the Tower. The restraint was not too severe. Prince Charles visited him regularly. "No man but my father," said he, "would keep such a bird in a cage." While imprisoned Raleigh wrote several works, his chief being *The History of the World*.

It has been alleged that Francis Bacon was responsible for his eventual execution. This is utterly untrue. The persons who were directly responsible for Raleigh's death were the disreputable King and his worthless Favourite. Francis Bacon had little or nothing to do with it. This is the story.

In 1616—Raleigh had been in the Tower some thirteen years—the Crown was desperately pushed for monies. Raleigh had several times told the Tower officials of the existence of a gold mine in the Orinoco. He was released through Winwood and Buckingham so that he could locate the mine and bring the gold to replenish the empty coffers of the King and his Favourite. At the age of sixty-seven he set out in a small fleet. From the beginning he met with difficulties, storms, desertions, disease and deaths. His crew were the very scum of nature. He had promised the King not to molest any Spanish territories, though how James expected him to do this without some collision with the Spaniards is difficult to see. He did clash with them. He found a new town, San Thomé, and burned it to the ground (Raleigh hated the Spaniards), *but he did not find the mine*. James had let him go with his old sentence hanging over his head, safeguarding himself for fear of any collision with Spain; the Spanish marriage was still being hoped for as a way out of the King's financial morass. On his return to England James had Raleigh arrested.

In law Raleigh's life was absolutely at the King's mercy, for the death sentence had only been respited and could be carried out by the King whenever he chose, despite Raleigh's years of imprisonment. The King dare not put him to a public trial, but James wanted him out of the way. The King of Spain demanded his death, and his Ambassador, Gondomar, was daily walking the corridors at Whitehall, growling his threats and threatening to break off the marriage negotiations. James appointed Commissioners to advise him how to act—Coke, Abbot, Worcester, Caesar, Naunton and Francis Bacon. Up to this date Francis Bacon had had nothing whatever to do with the case. They advised James in a letter:

> to form of proceeding in all essential respects public and judicial ... the audience to consist of the Council, judges, nobility and gentry ... exactly as in an ordinary trial ... a formal record to be made of the whole proceeding. ... As an alternative

proposal ... if there were not a regular trial before a public audience, that the warrant for carrying out the sentence into execution should be accompanied with "a narrative in print of his crimes and offences".[1]

This letter has been attributed to Francis Bacon because the draft was found among his papers, but Spedding on examining it found it was *"in the handwriting of Sir Edward Coke. ...* It is impossible to believe that Coke wrote it to Bacon's dictation." It therefore did not originate with Francis Bacon. He only acquiesced in it with the other five.

It has been said that Francis Bacon advised the King how to act respecting this letter of advice. *He did not.* A draft has been found in the handwriting of *Buckingham's secretary* Packer, written as from the King which begins:

> Right trusty and well beloved Counsellors, we greet you well. ... We like not that there should be only a narration of his crimes set forth, together with our warrant for his execution. ... And secondly for the other course of a public calling him before our Council, we think it not fit, because it would make him too popular, as was found by experiment at the arraignment at Winchester, where by his wit he turned the hatred of men into compassion for him.[2]

So *Raleigh was examined privately* and this decision was purely the King's and, obviously, Buckingham's. *Francis Bacon was certainly not responsible for this private trial,* the hush-hush methods adopted because of the King's cowardly fears.

> *The judges of the King's Bench were directed to order the immediate execution of the old sentence.* On the 28th he was brought to the Bar and called upon to show cause why execution should not be awarded.[3]

Neither the entreaties of the Queen nor his own eloquence could save him; and on the next day, 29 October 1618, he was taken to the Palace yard to be executed, passing through the struggling crowds with the gallant air of a happy warrior who had fought a good fight, had finished the course, and was going home to Valhalla—to his comrades-in-arms who had singed the beard of the King of Spain, had put his Armada to flight, and who would have viewed with contempt James and Buckingham's dastardly grovelling to Gondomar for a marriage portion.

"He wrote some verses the night before," says his chaplain, Dean Tounson. "He ate his breakfast heartily, took his tobacco, and made no more of his death than if it had been to take a journey." His high courage never deserted him. He stood on the scaffold, a noble figure; and though sixty-seven years had whitened his hair, his body was unbowed, and his face shone as he looked into the eyes of the citizens of London who had come to pay their respects at his departure. "No tragic scene in real life was ever so finely acted." Judged by the effect on its audience and upon all succeeding generations, his speech from the scaffold was a triumph of eloquence.

"He touched the edge of the axe, caressed it, and said with a smile, 'This gives me no fear. It is a sharp and fair medicine to cure me of all my diseases.'"

[1]Spedding.
[2]*ibid.*, p. 363.
[3]*ibid.*, p. 369.

The gist of his address was that "he had no troubles of conscience; for he had done his best to do the King a piece of good service against his will, and he had hurt nobody except Spaniards in the West Indies." Spedding says that there was no touch of passion, bitterness or bravado, but the most unaffected, cheerful composure, the finest humanity and the most courtly grace and good humour and yet no unseemly levity. "You should lay your head towards the East" came the last suggestion, which evoked the reply, "What matter how the head lie so the heart be right." So Raleigh's head was struck off "amid national indignation, as a tribute to Spain".

In spite of James's plan Raleigh got in both the first word and the last with the public. He was loved as a martyr in his own day and has remained so through the ages. "He foiled James and Philip at one thrust, and con-quererd the esteem of all posterity," says Gosee, while Spedding writes, "Never was death by the public executioner so completely cheated of its victory."

> To satisfy public opinion the King was forced to publish an official "Declaration" of "The True Motives and Inducements which Occasioned His Majesty to Proceed in Doing Justice upon Him, as hath been Done."

The reader now has all the facts in his possession which associate Francis Bacon with the execution of Sir Walter Raleigh.

On 2 March 1619 the Queen died from dropsy. A few days later the King was taken with a violent fit of the stone, causing much alarm to the nation, from which he slowly recovered. On 8 May one of Lord Carleton's correspondents wrote: "The Lord Chancellor is as much in favour at Court as ever, if not more." High in favour he remained consistently for the next two years. During this time there was much correspondence with the Favourite respecting State affairs. The treaty for the marriage of the Prince of Wales and the Infanta was still in abeyance. In 1618 it had nearly broken on the point of religion. But it was smoothed over. On James's instructions the Catholics were treated favourably and imprisoned priests were set at liberty. All Spanish complaints were dealt with as their Ambassador wished, even when compliance violated public opinion as in the case of Raleigh. In spite of the views of the Councillors the King still wished for the Spanish alliance.

Bacon wrote a letter of advice to the King. He tells the King with unafraid frankness that he detested the idea of a Spanish match and an alliance with a nation whose fingers were steeped in English blood, alien in outlook, policy and religion; and he had the independence and courage to do this at a time when James and Buckingham were hot upon the alliance for the sake of the Infanta's dowry. Francis Bacon's advice was dead against their Spanish policy, and he risked giving personal offence which might have resulted in loss of office. He could not be silent when England's destiny was likely to be endangered, for he was above all things a Tudor and a patriot.

But Francis Bacon's advice fell on deaf ears. The proposed marriage was played with until 1624, when the alliance was definitely broken off to the great joy of the nation.

He continued, however, to give his statesmanlike counsel to the King, all of which be it noted was for the good of the commonwealth. One important paper was given to the King about New Year's Day, 1620. Francis Bacon was in the habit of presenting such things by way of New Year's gifts. He did good by stealth and sought not the plaudits of publicity. It has been rescued from oblivion by chance. We have only a fragment but sufficient to show that his idea was that the King should set up properly constituted commissions for the advancement of the nation's welfare. This is a slight précis.

To the King

Amongst the counsels which ... I have given your Majesty faithfully ... I do take comfort that I was the first that advised you to come in person to the Star Chamber. ... This Institution hath two uses; the one as a supreme Court of Judicature; the other as an open council. ... In the second kind your Majesty ... did set in frame and fabric the several jurisdictions of your Courts. ... There now wants a fourth part of the square to make all complete, which is that your Majesty will be pleased to publish certain Commonwealth COMMISSIONS. ... If you will be pleased to make a solemn Declaration of them in that place [the Star Chamber] this will follow:

First, that you shall do yourself an infinite Honour, and win the hearts of your People to acknowledge you as well the most politic King as the most just.

Secondly, it will oblige your Commissioners to a more strict account. ...

Thirdly, it will invite and direct any man that finds himself to know anything concerning those Commissions to bring in their informations. ...

It will eternise your name and merit. King James and his Commissions will be spoken of and put in ure [operation], as long as Britain lasts; at the least in the reign of all good Kings.

For the particulars, besides the two Commissions of the Navy and the Buildings about London ... I wish the following to be added.

COMMISSION for advancing the Clothing of England, as well as Drapery old and new and all the incidents thereto.

COMMISSION for staying Treasure within the Realm, and the reiglement [regulation] of monies.

COMMISSION for the provision of the Realm with Corn and Grain, and the Government of the exportation and importation thereof; and directing of Public Granaries, if cause be.

COMMISSION for introducing and nourishing Manufactures within the Realm, for the setting people a-work, and the considering of all grants and privileges of that nature.

COMMISSION to prevent the Depopulation of Towns and Houses of Husbandry, and for Nuisances and Highways.

COMMISSION for the Recovery of Drowned Lands.

COMMISSION for the suppressing of the Grievances of informers.

COMMISSION for the better proceedings in the Plantations in Ireland.

COMMISSION for the provision of the Realm with all kinds of Warlike Defence. Ordnance, powder, munition, and armour.

The rest of the paper is lost, but the value of these suggestions is obvious when there were no real Departments of State. In fact, it was a great step forward towards putting the national business on a proper footing, and a tremendous advance towards the social welfare of the masses as well as economic and trade activity. The slothful James, of course, did nothing about it. But the system of distributing the business of government has gradually extended itself. And the appointment of commissions for the gathering together of information, etc., is now a customary part of Parliamentary procedure. King James was not even destined to have the credit of bringing this system into being. It is with us today in full measure; and the man who conceived this progressive reform for parliamentary government was Francis Bacon.

A little later, 9 June 1620, we see that he had observed certain abuses in the Star Chamber "from the undue extension of the jurisdiction of the Court", so Francis Bacon drew up a set of rules to remedy the defects. There was then no public outcry against the court, but twenty years later it was swept away by an enraged nation. Had his rules been accepted and put into operation they would have prevented the power of the court being abused. The rules are of no interest today, but in his covering acts to Buckingham, who was to present them to James, he said that if his Majesty would accept them he "shall erect one of the noblest and durablest Pillars for the Justice of this Kingdom in perpetuity that can be."

Francis Bacon again gave advice only for it to be shelved, smothered, rejected. He lacked the power to put any of his reforms into operation. He did his best to initiate national reforms and it was not for the want of trying that they were not established. It was due to a maudlin King and his worthless Favourite. Neither had the least interest in reform or the people's welfare.

On 29 June 1620 Francis Bacon promoted a Mr Whitlocke to an important office in the State, to be Chief Justice of Chester, the qualification for the appointment being that he was to be first made a Serjeant at the Chancery Bar. It is interesting in this: that the appointment shows that Francis Bacon did not bear any animus towards an opponent but consistently appointed whoever he thought was the best man for the position. Whitlocke and he had clashed in the House of Commons in 1610, in 1612, '14, '16, '18, very bitterly at times, but this did not destroy Francis Bacon's recognition that he was a first-class lawyer. He delivered the charge to him in the Chancery Court on his taking the oath as a Serjeant. These are a few of the passages:

> Mr Whitlocke,
>
> The Degree of Sergeant is a step to your other Place. Therefore I shall speak of the duty of a Judge in general and of the proprieties in particular to the Place you go to.... [This is Masonic phraseology.] Have patience in hearing; make no catching hearings. Have a slow pace. Judges make no haste.
>
> Keep your hands clean, and the hands of your servants that are about you; keep them in awe, that they may not dare to move you in things unfit.
>
> Fly all bribery and corruption, and preserve your integrity, not respecting any in course of Justice; for what avails it if you be incorrupt and yet should be partial and a respecter of persons? ... Be not overawed. Fear no man's face; be stout and courageous in causes of Justice. ... I mean you should be strong-hearted but not strong-headed....
>
> Look to suppress the power of such Gentlemen in the country that seek to oppress and suppress their poor neighbours. ... Be not too servile nor too severe.

The charge is fairly long and full of good advice. It is particularly interesting because of its references to "bribery and corruption", with which offences Francis Bacon was charged only a few months later. It was then alleged that from the time of his entry into the Chancery Court he had accepted bribes for the perversion of justice. Singularly enough, these words were spoken to Whitlocke "on the same day on which Bacon himself made a final order in Lady Wharton's case, having only two or three days before accepted a purse of gold from her."[1] Lady Wharton's gift was one of the charges brought against him.

Now manifestly this was a gift on the customary lines which he mentions in his first Chancery speech: "Fees left to the conscience of the Lawyer and the estimation and gratitude of the client." For Lady Wharton's gift or fee was not made in secret but in the presence of the Registrar and his clerk; nor was it conditioned by any promise. It was given according to the customs of the times. It was not a bribe. This particular gift, however, should have been presented after the verdict and not before the signing of the final order; nor tendered in Francis Bacon's presence. But this technical error does not constitute "bribery and corruption". Indeed, one cannot think that Francis Bacon composed Whitlocke's charge at the same time that he had received a bribe from Lady Wharton. It could only have been accepted as a gift towards the court expenses, being duly entered up in the books of the Chancery, and that it never entered Francis Bacon's mind that it was either given or intended to serve as a bribe. This is what Hepworth Dixon says on this very case. He speaks as a barrister:

> The only case that presents an unusual feature is that of Lady Wharton. She brought her presents to the Chancellor herself; yet even her gifts were openly made, in the presence of the proper officer and his clerk. Churchil admits being present in the room when Lady Wharton left her purse; Gardner, Keeling's clerk, asserts that he was present when she brought the two hundred pounds. ... Who in his senses could suppose that the Lord Chancellor would have done an act known to be illegal and immoral in the company of his Registrar and a clerk?
>
> It is clear that a thing which Bacon did under the eyes of Gardner and Churchil *must have been in his mind customary and right.*
>
> It is no less clear that if Bacon had done wrong, knowing it to be wrong, *he would not have braved exposure of his fraud* by turning Churchil into the streets.[2] [Francis Bacon dismissed Churchil for fraud shortly afterwards.]

Irrespective of what the purists may say about the hypocrisy inherent in Whitlocke's charge, the truth remains that it was an honest expression of advice that sprang from the heart of an honest man who lived up to the principles he espoused. The foregoing evidence proves it.

While Francis Bacon was doing a vast amount of public work in the Chancery and dealing with State affairs, he also maintained a large correspondence with learned men on the Continent, progressive social reformers, scientists, the Illuminati, the philosophers. He was mothering also his secret Rosicrucian and Masonic societies which were then springing up all over England, Ireland, Wales and Scotland, as well as in France, Germany and other parts of the civilized world. The stage, that had really been created at Gray's Inn and Twickenham Park, was spreading and gripping the public, and taking its place as an educational force. Moreover, during these years of

[1]Spedding, Vol. VII, p. 103.
[2]*Personal Story.*

stress and strain, he had accomplished, quite secretly, an open ethical revolution in men's way of thought. From 1614 to 1617 there were repeated editions of a series of anonymous pamphlets.

The pamphlets claimed to emanate from a secret mystical order that was positively in their midst ... "we are here in the world unknown." The views enunciated were violently attacked and as vigorously defended.

The first booklet, intended as an introduction to the others, was entitled *The Reformation of the Whole Wide World*; the second was the *Fama Fraternitatis*; the third was the *Confessio Fraternitalis*. The object of the booklets and the secret society was this:

> *That out of all ranks a Society should be composed having for its object THE GENERAL WELFARE OF MANKIND, and pursuing it in SECRET.*

Largely through the stir created by the booklets and the agitation thus caused, we can say without exaggeration that the first quarter of the seventeenth century saw the whole of Western Europe overrun with cabalism, theosophy, alchemy and moral philosophy, which affected all classes high and low, especially in Germany where the majority of the pamphlets were printed. By 1620 the public were already familiar in England with the idea that there was somewhere a secret society in existence teaching that practical ethics and education comprised the only way to save the festering body of the World.

The writer of the three principal booklets has never been traced, in spite of much research and many guesses; but external and internal evidence show that the man who created both them and the agitation was Francis Bacon, and that their true home of birth was England and not Germany. He re-created Rosicrucianism, and gave the name and the ideas openly to the world, thus starting men on new lines of thought, though no one knew where to find "the College of Father Rosicrosse with his Golden 'T'". He familiarized the public with a new approach to the interpretation of life and the amelioration of human ills. It is outside the scope of this work to prove Francis Bacon's connection with the Continental movement said to have originated in Germany.

In 1620, then, Francis Bacon was well pleased with the stir he had created, unsuspected by anyone of "the uninstructed world". His secret work was going forward on every side.

These designs were naturally taken with much stealth amid a very busy life, yet, despite all this activity, he pursued his youthful idea of giving a complete plan of his philosophic concept to the world in what he called the *Instauratio Magna* (*The Great Instauration*) which consisted of "Three Parts of Open Philosophy" over his own name and "Three Concealed Parts" to be hinted at only—for this consisted of something more than simply writing a philosophy by establishing a school of moral ethics which could be handed down the ages by his disciples from hand to hand, from mouth to mouth, by oral tradition, like that of the ancient teachers. So Francis Bacon, treading in their footsteps, established his Secret School, which after some three hundred years has spread all over the globe. This labour he performed, and left his "Sons" certain "Rules" and "Instructions" to guide their future conduct in the organization of the Brotherhood. With his "Third Part", and the last openly written work of importance, the *Novum Organum* and the *Parasceve* (the *New Organ* for the interpretation of Man and Nature), he included a short précis of Parts 4, 5 and 6, so that future generations might know that there were THREE MISSING PARTS to complete his system of philosophy embodied in the *Instauratio Magna*. It was a challenge to the world scholastic to search for them but no one has yet read the "Riddle" of Francis Bacon the concealed writer—the Proteus of Literature who dealt in Mysteries.

At the Privy Council sat Francis Bacon day after day with Sir Edward Coke and Sir Lionel Cranfield, his head full of his great designs to better humanity in the far off ages, the soul and minds as well as the bodies of men. Little thought he that his fellow Councillors had been plotting his downfall for months, and were simply awaiting the opportune moment to spring a mine from which the victim could not escape. Happy and serene in the knowledge that his ideas were taking root, his conscience like a sea at rest, he added his final profound touches and hints in the proof sheets of the *Instauratio Magna,* little dreaming that there was closing round him stealthily a band of conspirators waiting to pounce on their prey . . . waiting . . . waiting . . . waiting. He thought he was at peace with all the world. His chief anxiety was to leave a record that would bless humanity and its descendants to the end of time—a work far greater than mere official business—a true interpretation of Nature as a whole and a perpetual stimulus to Man's mental, moral and spiritual powers, a stimulus that he dare not impart openly but only privately, a reconstruction of ideas to which his whole life had been pledged since he was a boy in his teens.

In October 1620 the *Instauratio Magna* was given to the world. He sent a copy to the King and hoped the King would be as long in reading it as he had been in writing it—thirty years. James replied, "It is like the Wisdom of God that passeth all human understanding," to which Francis Bacon answered:

> I see your Majesty is a Star that hath a benevolent Aspect and gracious influence upon all things that tend to a general good. . . .
>
> This work which is for *the bettering of men's Bread and Wine* which are the characters of Temporal Blessings and and Sacraments of the Eternal, I hope by God's Holy Providence will be ripened by Caesar's Star. . . .
>
> I hope your Majesty will be aiding to me, in setting men on work for the collecting of a Natural and Experimental History. . . . That admirable Spirit of yours delighteth in LIGHT; and I hope well that even in your times many Noble Inventions may be discovered for man's use. For who can tell, now the Mine of Truth is once opened, how the veins will go, and *what lieth Higher and what Lower.*

The Great Instauration, though incompletely understood, has lived down the ages in influencing the minds of thinkers in all lands; for, as Ben Jonson remarks, "IT IS A BOOK." Indeed, it is not too much to say, "*It is a Book which has in it the Germs of more Power and Good to Man than any other Work not of Divine Authorship in the World.*"

Has ever a man been more unjustly maligned by his countrymen than was Francis Bacon? The Prophet, Priest and King of the New Era which he ushered in? He stands on the threshold of the modern world a sublime figure throwing back the curtains of feudalism that the light of Truth may enter into our homes, our lives, our hearts. Everything to his sixtieth birthday confirms this estimate of his character and labours, and we have found nothing so far to warrant that he was inspired by anything base, ignoble or mean, but by the highest principle of Great Goodness.

Chapter VII

THE MUTTERINGS OF THE TEMPEST JANUARY 1621

ON 22 January 1621 the Lord Chancellor made a great feast. It was his sixtieth birthday. To it he invited all his special friends that were of the Rosicrosse, the Rosicrucians and the Masonic Fraternities—all those privileged ones who were in the secret of Francis Bacon's labours and over whom he reigned like Solomon King of Israel, Hyram, King of Tyre, and Hiram Abif. The gathering was held at York House. Some of the best men in the land sat at his table that day. We know that it was a meeting of the Brethren because Ben Jonson recited an ode—as yet unnoticed by anyone, even scholarly members of the *Quatuor Coronati* Lodge having hitherto failed to see its significance—which is replete with Masonic asides and esoteric information. The poem conveys nothing to the "uninstructed world", and is just as subtle and enigmatical as the prefatory lines Ben Jonson wrote to "Shakespeare" in the 1623 Folio.

It must have been a very brilliant assembly; and since we know it was a Masonic banquet, we can reconstruct the scene. We know sufficient of the history of Freemasonry from Bros. Anderson, Preston and Hutchinson, and of the ancient books and their secrets issued in the times of Elizabeth and James, to be acquainted with the men who associated with "Our Francis". We know who was likely to be present; and since we also know the taste and temperament of the host we can picture what the Great Hall at York House looked like with its arranged T-tables and gleaming white drapery, silver and the flowers and perfumes beloved of Francis.

To Ben Jonson's first four lines I call the particular attention of all Freemasons. He gave the toast of the evening to Francis Bacon as the Head of the Brethren and the poem Ben recited was the conclusion of his speech:

ON FRANCIS BACON'S SIXTIETH BIRTHDAY
Hail! Happy Genius of this Ancient Pile!
How comes it all things so about thee Smile?
The Fire? The Wine? The MEN? and in the MIDST
Thou STAND'ST as if some MYSTERY thou didst.

This is an intriguing verse and the attention of all Fellow-Crafts is drawn to it by the first word: "Hail" means more than a call; it is a sign.

"Pile" has a meaning other than a pile of buildings; it also means a spear; and there was but one "Happy Genius" who could wield the "Ancient Spear" of Pallas-Athena the Spear-Shaker—Francis Bacon.

"Smiles" are to be found always when there is good fellowship, especially when men "stand to".

"The Fire" means something far more than a wood blaze and refers to the ancient Masonic habit of "Firing" with their glasses.

"The Wine" indicates something that goes with "Firing Glasses"—the toasts.

"The Men" mentioned particularly shows that the company was composed of males, as they would be indeed at such a banquet.

The "Happy Genius" (note the Masonic significance of the word "Happy") stood in their "Midst", as, indeed, he would do as the Father, Founder and Creator of Ethical Symbolism—in fact in *the Centre*.

He "Stands" in a certain manner, says Ben Jonson. Of course! Because it would be improper to stand in any other way under the circumstances.

"Thou Stand'st as if some MYSTERY thou didst." And this last word "MYSTERY" explains the riddle to those who can read what was at the back of Ben Jonson's mind; the verse is unintelligible without it; for the word refers to the *Modern Mystery of Ancient Freemasonry* that is to be found in our midst today.

About a week later there was an even more splendid gathering at Theobald's, Hertfordshire, James's favourite residence, when Francis Bacon was invested with the highest honour that could be conferred upon him in the presence of the King, the Prince of Wales, Lord Mandeville, the Marquises of Hamilton and Buckingham, the Earls of Worcester, Pembroke, Arundel, Rutland, March and Montgomery. Lord Wentworth carried the coronet before him, Lord Carew the robe supported by Buckingham. His investiture with coronet and robe was a peculiar form of honour, says Hepworth Dixon, other Peers being created by letters patent only. "The Patent recited Francis Bacon's accepted birth, his merits, his services in the most gracious terms", and he was thereupon proclaimed when robed and crowned as "Viscount St Alban". On 30 January Francis Bacon took his seat under his new title in the House of Lords.

He had now reached the highest pinnacle of worldly honour and prosperity. He had begun life under the darkest of clouds—as an unwanted child, truly fatherless and motherless, his Tudor birth strain concealed for the necessities of State. *Francis had neither legal rights nor monetary claims on anyone.* His foster father, Sir Nicholas Bacon, though a wealthy man, never left him a penny piece *for no known reason.* His allowance, as we have seen, came from his mother the Queen or the young aristocrat would have starved and could never have entered for legal studies at Gray's Inn. The growing youth was surrounded by enemies who were afraid of what he might do in the State if he managed to lift himself into power. He was suppressed by the Cecils. He was traduced by the Cokes who made a mockery of his name in those secret, cutting ways in which sadists are so expert, in order to depress him and to shame him out of any entry into public life. They did not succeed in smothering him out of sight because Francis Bacon was inspired by one great purpose—to do something really tangible and worthwhile for his countrymen in particular and the world in general. And it was because these altruistic ideas inspired his actions that he refused to succumb to despair, disdain and selfishness. He felt, moreover, that he was a "Servant to Posterity" for the divine urgings were strong within him.

His first ambition was for the spread of simple goodness; the second, for power; for without power and a position of authority he could not hope to accomplish his self-imposed task. All his material strivings were not his life's goal but were purely subsidiary to those intangible eternal verities in which his soul revelled—those intangible ideas which he spread abroad even in his lifetime on every conceivable subject under the sun, science, art, philosophy, literature and, above all, his oral teaching which was to be handed down the generations. Every step upwards in the State service increased his salary and gave him a greater freedom of action for the prosecution of his idealism for reform which—whether social, educational or ethical—*could not be carried out without heavy expense.*

He strove, then, to rise not for any sordid end, for the chinking of gold crowns or the mere blazoning of one's breast with orders, but for the noblest and wisest purpose: to help Man onward in his march through the desert, to guide him to fountains of Living Water from which he might drink, and thirst no more.

At the age of sixty he had reached the summit of material felicity. He had been successively Solicitor and Attorney General, Privy Councillor, Lord Keeper, and Lord Chancellor, having had conferred upon him the dignities of knighthood, the Barony of Verulam and then the Viscountcy St Alban. He was known to the world as the greatest English philosopher, just as he has been afterwards referred to as the Father of English science and the Founder of our modern British prose. In January 1621 Francis Bacon's name was on everyone's lips because of his masterpiece, the *Novum Organum*. He had money, power, choice outward friends, staunch secret disciples who were spreading his gospel that Charity was the marrow of ethics; and ethics the surge of righteousness that makes for sweetness and light; while knowledge was power through which alone could be uplifted the submerged masses, the drowned mineral wealth of humanity. Besides York House he had a mansion at Kew to which he could retire when jaded from pressure of business for a day or two. His vacations were spent at Gorhambury in "studies, arts and the sciences to which in his own nature he was most inclined . . . and gardening the purest of all human pleasures."

At Gorhambury, "at a cost of £10,000, he erected a private retreat, furnished with every intellectual luxury, to which he repaired when he wished to avoid visitors, except a few choice spirits, whom he occasionally selected as the companions of his retirement and lucubrations."

He wanted for nothing. He had conquered early Fate. He had emerged victoriously from his conflict with jealous enemies; and he thought he had finished with them for ever.

To replenish the State till, Francis Bacon's advice was, naturally, to call a Parliament, for he was a staunch House-of-Commons man. What else could be done'?

"There is not a mark in the Treasury," said Lord Mandeville, the Lord Treasurer, to Francis Bacon.

"Be of good cheer then my Lord," laughed the Chancellor, "now you shall see the bottom of your business at the first."

He was happy and carefree as he bandied jokes with the Lord Treasurer on taking his seat in the Upper Chamber.

Yet only three months after his investiture with robe and coronet Francis Bacon was degraded from his great place, stripped of his honours, condemned to a monstrous fine and flung into the Tower.

It can be said without any exaggeration that the tale of his fall is the most strange and sad in the whole history of man.

To the majority of biographers, the "Fall of Francis Bacon" presents no difficulties. They take it as read, as a truth of history not in dispute. They say, with the historian Green, "Bacon's own confession of Guilt makes it difficult to resist his condemnation." The uppermost thought in their minds is that he pleaded guilty to definite charges of corruption and there is nothing more to be said about it but to proceed to give sentence. In ordinary cases this would be the normal procedure—the accused confesses and throws himself on the mercy of the court. But suppose the "Confession of Francis Bacon" was not an "ordinary" but an "extraordinary" one? What then? Are we to let it lie unsolved? For this matter concerns our greatest Englishman. Beyond question there is something passing strange about the entire circumstances of "The Charges", the Chancellor's sudden "Desertion of the Defence" and his written "Confession of Guilt". Not one history student in a hundred attending our universities knows the truth of the matter; and I do not know one professor or academic writer who has shown himself at all conversant with the intricacies of Francis Bacon's impeachment.

We must couple this sense of mystery with the fact that very carefully, patiently and exhaustively we have sifted ALL the serious offences of which Francis Bacon has been accused by modern critics and *we have found every one of them baseless. Not one of them holds water.* When Ben Jonson, his friend, wrote in *Discoveries* that Francis Bacon was the embodiment of VIRTUE, *he meant it.* "*Nothing* [no appalling catastrophe] *could do harm to VIRTUE.*" Now, how could "Honest Ben" have written and left behind him this testimony if Francis Bacon had sold Justice for "BRIBES"? Dr Rawley, Sir Thomas Meautys, Sir Tobie Matthew, and other contemporaries echo the same thought in varying degrees of intensity. They pay an even greater tribute to his virtue than they do to his intellectual powers. Did they, along with Jonson, blind themselves to his vices—his alleged covetousness, his grasping greed for gold, his avariciousness, his criminal practices? Men who take bribes to pervert Justice are criminally dishonest. Jonson knew this. And if anyone knew the truth of Francis Bacon's alleged crimes Jonson did. It is obvious that neither Jonson nor Rawley believed it. Francis Bacon was a "virtuous" man to them. We have seen also that, apart from those fatal three months that we have now to examine, Francis Bacon's actions consistently indicate that Jonson was speaking the truth.

Obviously, there is something here that demands close investigation. The anomaly is much too glaring to be accepted at its face value. Any man who had struggled to inculcate honour, probity, justice and virtue for a lifetime, consumed by a "philanthropia" that knew no bounds, who had successfully withstood "the Ambush of Young Days" and presented "a pure unstained Prime" at the age of fifty-five, is not likely to fall down and worship the Golden Calf, abandoning the fixed principles of character by which he had climbed, *at the very moment when he was above financial temptation* and in receipt of a larger salary than ever before.

Macaulay and Campbell might plausibly have imputed a motive for his "corrupt practices" in his earlier days when he was desperately hard up owing to his printing activities in trying to give England a literature in its own tongue; but nothing of an avaricious nature has ever been found in those days and his penury never once drove him to finger criminally other people's money. When he could not pay his printing debts promptly *he actually thought it no disgrace to be flung into prison until his friends could come to the rescue.* How many of his critics would have paid such a price? No! However plausibly motives for practising corruption could have been imputed to him in his younger days by reason of his known financial embarrassments, *from the age of fifty-five to sixty he was financially independent. There was thus no motive for his alleged corruption.* Since there is an entire absence of motive, the entire "Confession" and the charges of bribery must be viewed with grave suspicion. even Dean Church is uneasy in his mind that there is something of import hidden from our sight. He writes:

> His sudden and unexpected Fall, so astonishing and so irreparably complete, is *one of the strangest events of that still imperfectly comprehended time....*
>
> No one, for years, had discharged the duties of his Office with greater efficiency. Scarcely a trace remains of any suspicion, previous to the attack upon him, of the justice of his decisions; no instance was alleged that in fact, *impure motives had controlled* the strength and lucidity of *an intellect which loved to be true and right for the mere pleasure of being so....*
>
> *What is the History of this tremendous catastrophe*, by which, in less than two months, Bacon was cast down from the height of Fortune to become a byword of Shame?

The Dean asks these questions but he does not attempt to answer them or to give the "Secret History" of these two months. He turns away from the problem, content to tread in the well-worn footsteps of others, muttering, "He pleaded guilty." Yet he knows that he is not acquainted with all the facts and that there is other evidence lost or suppressed. He admits that there is indeed something inexplicable and mysterious about the sudden tempest that arose and swept Francis Bacon into the waste spaces of the world, to cry down the ages on the wings of the wind as he did three hundred years ago, "*Hear me! Hear me! Judge not! To know all is to forgive all!*" Of a surety we do not know all the facts yet. Can the truth be found? Yes! Quite sufficient for our purpose.

The last word in biography is supposed to be the seven volumes of James Spedding. It is a great life and a mine of information. Still it is by no means complete. It contains, however, such an amount of cut-and-dried facts that there is a danger lest the facts get hold of the student instead of the student being master of the facts. The last volume deals with the fall. The story is badly presented. The reader obtains no clear picture of this tremendous, dramatic tragedy that is being enacted. It reads like a civil servant's report. Everything is pigeonholed and labelled. Spedding never sees the clash of conflicting personalities, the interplay of characters nor the background against which they are thrown. His men are names and nothing more; his incidents are of wood and nothing more; and Francis Bacon in relation to the times and to the men of the Parliament and the Court is never seen as a living tormented soul. It cannot be accepted as a complete narration and it is therefore only partially true.

One cannot judge the events of February to May 1621 unless one relates them to previous happenings, for in them the events had their roots just as the child is father of the man. The full tabulating of bare facts about Francis Bacon chronologically in those vital months no more conveys a true picture of the intense, bitter activities that were going on in the House of Commons, the home of Buckingham's mother and the Court, than the mere staging of *Hamlet the Prince* could convey anything of intelligence to the audience without the necessary interplay of Hamlet's relations, friends and enemies. It would be just as unsuccessful as the Play of *Hamlet* without the Prince. The "Fall of Francis Bacon" is as much a study in varying psychological types as the characters in *Henry the Eighth* that revolve round the fall of Wolsey. Moreover, great men only fall *suddenly* when they are overthrown by a band of conspirators—by a *coup d'état*—as was the case with Julius Caesar; or when the circumstances that uphold them are so rotten that they collapse, the collapse very often brought into being by a man's own inherent vices as in *Richard III*; *or when simple goodness is traitorously betrayed by the powers of evil in accordance with the inscrutable ways of Providence as was Jesus of Nazareth.* Into one of these categories falls Francis Bacon. It is for the reader to determine which after sifting the evidence.

The events of the Parliamentary spring were not suddenly precipitated by an upward volcanic rush as orthodox biography would lead us to suppose. They had been a long time a-brewing; and therefore if we would find the truth it must be searched for in days far back other than February to May 1621. The causes of things do not lie in those three fatal months. They elude us in the chronological record of a Spedding, as much as in the gross misrepresentations of a Macaulay.

One is grateful to Spedding that he did come down on the side of the angels by his championship of Francis Bacon's "intrinsic GOODNESS ... how GOOD and how GREAT a man he really was",[1] but his handling of the case would convince few that *Francis Bacon had a perfect defence in law and in fact.* Therefore to understand the position aright let us retrace our steps along the years of Francis Bacon's official life, first endeavouring to see with his eyes the Jacobean world as he saw it in those dreary weeks in February and March when, as he says, "I travelled forth without my Cloak and when base-born clouds o'er-took me on my way to pour down their rain on my storm-beaten face!"[2] And because we have not hitherto discovered anything in his life which would lead us to suppose that he was other than a high-minded Christian gentleman; because Ben Jonson no less than James Spedding testified to his "Virtue" and his "Goodness", and because acording to British law every man is assumed to be innocent until *proved* guilty (the charges were never proved) I shall ask my reader to maintain an open mind.

We have seen in Chapter 2 that Francis Bacon's consistent advice to the Crown from the time of his appointment as Attorney-General, was to abandon its irregular methods of raising funds, to trust the nation for supplies. To King James he said:

> Look on Parliament as a certain necessity but not only as a necessity as also a unique and most precious means for uniting the Crown with the nation, and proving to the world outside how Englishmen love and honour their King and

[1] *Evenings with a Reviewer*, p. 407.
[2] Sonnet 33.

> their King trusts his subjects. Deal with it frankly and nobly as becomes a King, not suspiciously like a huckster in a bargain. Do not be afraid of Parliament. Be skilful in calling it; but *don't attempt to pack it....*
>
> Do not be too anxious to meddle.... Though, of course, you want money from it, do not let that appear as the chief or real cause of calling it. Take the lead in Legislation. Be ready with some interesting or imposing points or reform or policy about which you ask your Parliament to take counsel with you. Take care to frame and have ready some Commonwealth Bills that may add respect to the King's Government.

Thus had Francis Bacon thought when he saw the blunders of James's first Parliament in 1604 and again in 1610. He openly gave him this counsel as to the 1614 Parliament; and he gave the King similar advice in season and out of season up to 1621.

The problem of the 1610 Parliament had not been solved by its dissolution. It again faced the Crown in 1614. The Commons were more confident than ever that the Crown had no legal right to impose impositions without Parliamentary sanction. In a struggle between Prerogative and Privilege we know that Francis Bacon was on the side of democracy rather than feudalism for we have the notes of a speech he intended to deliver *as the spokesman of the Commons* to the House of Lords.

The House of Commons sat for two months. They refused to pass supplies without a guarantee that their grievances would be redressed. Tempers began to rise. There were furious storms in the Commons. The King threatened them with dissolution. They treated his threats with scorn. They had the country solidly behind them. So the King equally wrathful suddenly dissolved his "addled Parliament" as we have seen in earlier pages. He had been given assurances that he could be financially independent of a House of Commons: he was in secret expectation of pecuniary help from Spain in view of his son contracting to marry the Spanish Infanta. The Parliament had not passed a single Bill. There had been no transaction of public business. The dissolution came as a shock and surprise to Francis Bacon, who had hoped to have got through Parliament measures of social reform. All the available facts show that he stood higher than ever in the estimation of his fellow members, although he believed that the King's Prerogative was right in law, but he also held it was not right factually in the infliction of hardship upon the people. It was owing to Francis Bacon's endeavours that in 1610 the "Great Contract" was within a hair's-breadth of becoming law which would have swept away for ever the great bulk of the King's feudal rights. It was Coke's opposition, caused through his jealousy of Francis Bacon, that cost this measure. Coke's advice to the King was that legally he "might sell the burthens yet keep the tenures intact"; while in the 1610 Commons debates Francis Bacon urged upon the Commons and the Crown the wisdom of abolishing all feudal tenures in fact and name. King James could not be allowed to retain his feudal cake and yet sell it for a huge sum. Francis Bacon held that the sale of the tenures was a sale of the burthens of the tenures, otherwise the King would have the right by the exercise of his Prerogative even to reimpose the burthens of the tenures again. For this perpetuation of feudalism Coke was directly responsible; and yet he has been acclaimed by some writers as "the champion of liberty". Ten years later we find Francis

Bacon at the Privy Council not only speaking but voting against the continuance of feudal monopolies by the exercise of the Prerogative.

Never had an election stirred so much popular anger and passion. "In every case where rejection was possible the Court candidates were rejected. All the leading members of the Country Party [the Opposition] were returned." Great excitement marked the opening proceedings, and cheering and hissing were heard in the Commons for the first time. "James took one way and the nation another." He was frightened at the vehemence and the language employed by the Members.

Four of the leading Members in the dissolved Parliament were sent to the Tower; and the terror and resentment which it had roused in the King's mind were seen in the obstinacy with which he long persisted in governing without any Parliament at all.

The dismissed Members went to their constituencies in a blaze of excited indignation to spread abroad their stories of the King's tyranny, of nightly orgies of Court squandermania in viciousness by James and his Favourite, of fears of new threatened taxation by recourse to the power of the Prerogative, and of the nation being sold to Roman Catholicism through the proposed Spanish marriage. We can realize the seething excitement that gripped the British nation in 1614 and we can understand that the smothered antagonism between the People and the Crown grew more intense with the passing of the years as the King openly continued his reckless course of personal profligacy and imposed new tax impositions of many kinds to maintain himself from bankruptcy. The fact was that James had no love for his people and less love for any form of democratic government. He was truly an alien King, a petty-minded tyrant who never learned how to deal with Englishmen. He regarded them but as milch cows, valuable only for the golden kegs of butter they could produce. To the Spanish Ambassador Gondomar he uttered these words:

> I wonder that my ancestors should ever have permitted such an institution as the House of Commons to have come into existence. I am a stranger, and found it here when I arrived, so that I am obliged to put up with what I cannot get rid of.

For six years, 1614 to 1620, England suffered the utterly worthless and selfish tyranny of an unscrupulous Stuart autocrat. He reigned without a Parliament—he and his favourite Buckingham. And Francis Bacon had no part or parcel in his government. He constantly obtruded his advice on the King, as we have seen, with a view to teaching him how to govern. But I do not know of a single instance where his counsel was accepted in a major matter. In fact Professor Gardiner, the historian, says, concerning the State papers Francis Bacon drew up in 1613:

> To carry out this programme would have been to avert the evils of the next half-century.... It was Francis Bacon's fate through life to give good advice only to be rejected....
>
> Had the management of Parliament [1614] rested with Bacon, it might not have been necessary to dissolve it....
>
> *If James had been other than he was the name of Bacon might have come down to us as great in politics as it is in science....*

> [Alleged] defects in his character would hardly have been known; they would have been lost in the greatness of his achievements.[1]

As the months passed and the Spanish marriage did not eventuate, entailing a hold-up of foreign gold, the finances of James became more and more precarious. He got, however, a few windfalls by legitimate means, like the fines from the Dutch merchants, etc., as we have already seen; but the King's extravagance was a devouring cormorant insatiable in appetite, and he was forced at an ever increasing pace to employ questionable shifts to obtain monies. He seemed to have no idea of the value of money where the gratification of his personal pleasures was concerned. On his coronation he spent £30,000 (twice the amount that Elizabeth spent) and this reckless spending set the pace of the Stuart Court—the luxurious thriftlessness that led to the evils of his reign, the great constitutional struggle between the Commons and the Crown, and it was one of the root causes of the fall of our greatest Englishman. The financial crises that were constantly confronting the King did not arise from purely government expenses. They sprang from his reckless *personal extravagance.* Yet had James treated the Commons with ordinary tact and civility he could undoubtedly have got what he wanted, for the nation, as a whole, stood in awe of the King as the visible head of the State appointed by God. The Commons did not want to quarrel with him for a variety of reasons—religious, political, sentimental, etc. He (and his son Charles in the succeeding reign) simply drove a long-suffering nation, that was providing him with monies through reckless tax oppression, into despair and defiance by foolish insistence on the unlimited powers of the Prerogative and the continuous open display of Court orgies headed by his loathsome Favourites.

His feudal rights, such as "his right to the wardship of young Heirs and the marriage of Heiresses, were now recklessly used as a means of fiscal extortion." In the three years following 1614 he obtained benevolences, as we have seen, amounting to £60,000. He borrowed from all and sundry, from the London City merchants until his credit was stopped. When he came to the Throne he stopped the war with Spain and abandoned our good allies the Dutch when they were on the point of triumph, in order to pick up for his own purpose the money earmarked for the war. He was thus the richer by some £45,000. Similarly, throughout his reign, he never once hesitated to abandon a cause, to desert a friend, or drop a servant if there were money at the end of it or selfish safety obtainable.

Buckingham when firmly established as Favourite instituted a new era of squandermania to go one better than his predecessor Somerset. He surrounded himself and the King with profligate men and equally profligate women. The Favourite's family, the Villiers, were enriched beyond the dreams of avarice. With his mother, Lady Compton, the Earl set up in his home, as it were, a Court within a Court; and all who wanted the ear of James had first to pay court and toll to my Lady Compton.

We have now a true, close-up background of the times and the atmosphere in which Francis Bacon was steeped from 1617 to 1621: a Court rotten to the core—the infection having spread through all the tissues of Court life; a

[1] *History of England*, Vol.I, p. 181.

sovereign corrupt in his personal life, utterly insincere, untrustworthy, a casuist of the first water who regarded his own pleasures and desires as more important than anything else; having as boon companion a worthless character whose only qualification for being placed in power above every nobleman was his personal good looks of face and form which had enamoured the King. To this man, Buckingham the Favourite, with little culture and less education James entrusted the direction of British policy, and in order to secure monies for his questionable extravagances delegated to the Favourite the virtual auctioning of the offices of State as they fell vacant—for which there were plenty of suitors. These offices, though underpaid in themselves, were rendered lucrative *by the constant BRIBES of yet minor suitors.* Sir Henry Montague, the Chief Justice of England, became Lord Mandeville and Treasurer for £20,000. Buckingham had previously refused an offer of £10,000. When there were no vacant offices to sell Buckingham speedily found a pretext to dismiss a holder from his position by threats or actual prosecution.

These excesses earned the silent contempt of all right-minded people. Their disapproval went little further than a mere shrug of the shoulders; for what could they do? But the King and Buckingham made the fatal blunder of insisting on extending the King's so-called feudal rights as a Monarch. So long as they touched the sale of honours and dignities, bargained for wards of the court and the like, it left the withers of the common folk unwrung; it did not create bitterness among the King's subjects. But in order to replenish his purse to meet wanton expenditure, James had recourse to measures which, at length, violently touched the pockets of the people. Public opinion became flamingly articulate. The avalanche had started that was destined eventually to overwhelm the Stuart dynasty.

In Francis Bacon's "Letter of Advice to Villiers" he condemned all restrictions placed on trade within the country itself. The standard of national prosperity was considered to be (as to this day) the excess of exports over imports. Native industry, agriculture and manufacture should be encouraged to the full to the discouragement of the foreign. He said also: "Care must be taken that MONOPOLIES *which are the canker of all trades*, be by no means admitted under the pretence of the specious colour of the public good."

Now the ordinary revenues of the Crown were obtained during the Tudor period in three ways, as explained previously. For years after the "addled Parliament" of 1614, James had cut himself off from the third method of revenue—supplies voted by Parliament—by his refusal to call the Commons together. He therefore sought to extend the range of the first and second methods: impositions and monopolies. From Francis Bacon's "Advice" to Villiers, then the new Favourite, we know with positive certainty that Francis Bacon was inexorably opposed to monopolies of any kind. The King, however, wanted money. He insisted on the extension of his feudal rights, the sale or letting of monopolies, etc., and very soon the Crown had granted to Buckingham, his relatives and friends, patents and impositions in a wholesale manner for the making of gold and silk thread, the licensing of inns, etc., *no one being able to trade in these particular callings unless a licence were purchased through the Villiers crowd.*

Long before the calling of the 1621 Parliament there was an increasing volume of agitation regarding the iniquitous nature of these methods of obtaining money.

For the successful exploitation of the old and newly created monopoly patents, the granting of licences to approved traders who paid handsomely for them—it was the Jacobean equivalent of modern racketeers—Buckingham, with the active assistance of his brother, Sir Edward Villiers, employed a couple of thorough-paced scoundrels named Sir Giles Mompesson and Sir Francis Mitchell. As might be expected, Mompesson, the senior partner in the firm, was related to the Favourite. Their ill fame was so notorious that Massinger satirized them as "Over-reach" and "Justice Greedy", to the huge delight of the Londoners. The trading community was bled white by their rapacity; and the costs of commodities rose to the general public. Indignation ran high at the extortionate premiums demanded for various monopolies. Citizens who tried to evade the demands of Buckingham's "Over-reach" and "Justice Greedy" were flung into the common jail. It was the unwillingness of Attorney-General Yelverton to commit such people that made him an object of vengeance to the "House of Buckingham".

The truth is that the King was directly responsible, equally culpable and guilty with Buckingham, Mompesson and Mitchell; for out of the proceeds the King took a major share of the plunder, and Buckingham and his agents divided the remainder.

There were persistent outcries that such imposts were illegal. There were grave doubts in judicial circles about the legality of many of these monopolies and patents. As part of his feudal rights, the King might have some power over the granting of certain monopolies that had a pretence of being in the national interest, such as the making of gold lace out of imported bullion, but had he the right to demand money for the licence to sell salt or horsemeat? The price was forced up, the community suffered, and the few were enriched. *The national interest was not being served by such patents.* The only excuse for granting a patent was that it was supposed to be in the national interest, to encourage native industries and discourage foreign. To encourage the excess of exports over imports was the only legal reason for granting any monopolies by the Crown.

Moreover, citizens were beginning to ask: had King James the right to sell any patent that was purely for private gain, for the enrichment of himself and the Buckingham clique? Had he any right to demand such exorbitant charges for his patents that the common people suffered because they could not afford the retail prices charged by the trader to cover the patent tax?

To resolve these questions, in the latter part of the year 1620, the King's Council was called consisting of the high officers of the Crown, legal and political. It was really to determine whether the King had any rightful power to grant patents and monopolies, especially such as had been granted within recent date. Now, why did this "Council" meet at all? How came it to meet? It must have met as the direct result of Francis Bacon's advice to the King, acting in his capacity as Lord Keeper. It is quite unthinkable that the King or Buckingham would have convened, on their own initiative, a meeting that seemed to question their privileges and the King's Prerogative, and might actually shear away a growing source of their revenue, whereas Francis Bacon was alive to the growing clamour; for the monopoly and patent questions touched Francis Bacon particularly in his office as Lord Keeper of the Great Seal. All monopoly patents had to be sealed by him. And knowing his mind, we can understand that the more new patents were brought to him to seal, the less he liked it. He must have told the King that the Crown ought to be fortified by the considered opinion of the Crown lawyers, for such a meeting could only have been held by the King's consent and by pressure from Francis Bacon. I do not know of one statesman apart from him who cared two straws for the thoughts and feelings of the general public; nor do I know of anyone else who dare have suggested such a meeting to James. So, wrote Francis Bacon: "The King did wisely put it upon a consult, whether the Patents were at this time to be removed by Act of Council before Parliament."

This Council had to determine "their legality and conveniency" and their annulment. A patent or monopoly patent, was, in theory, a licence or restriction given by the Crown for the encouragement of invention, or to remedy a glut, or to improve or stimulate manufacture; and it must be pronounced in law by the judges as well as certified to be "convenient" by the King's advisers.

The Lord Keeper presided. They discussed the matter and voted upon it. Francis Bacon's opinion was that they were right in law, *i.e.* the King's feudal rights had never been relinquished by the Crown, but wrong in conveniency and unwise in action. All patents that were clearly outside the national interest and were being exploited for private gain should be, at least, relinquished. Though the Crown possessed the requisite legal power, he pointed out that he was opposed to them on principle. He strongly advised that the more indefensible and obnoxious patents be surrendered.

James and Buckingham naturally objected to any of their revenues being touched or any of their powers being wrenched from their grasp. Everyone round the council table knew their attitude. All the Crown Lawyers thought that the King possessed the necessary legal rights. The Council divided on a plain "Yes" or "No" vote. And *Sir Francis voted with the minority against their continuance.*

Bacon defended them in law. His defence is thought to be not without grounds, but he saw the danger of obstinacy in maintaining what had become so hateful in the country, and *strongly recommended that the more indefensible and unpopular patents should be spontaneously given up. But Buckingham's insolent perversity refused to be convinced.*

The Crown won the vote. The screw began to be twisted more rigorously than ever by Buckingham's agents, Mompesson and Mitchell, to feather their own nests. London citizens were not only plundered with ruthless severity but even sent to prison by this precious pair of rascals.

It is manifest that Francis Bacon did everything possible in the circumstances to reduce and limit the evils that were arising from the creation of monopoly patents and the farming of them to agents for exploitation. He had brought the extension of the King's Prerogative—for that is to what the move amounted—to the legal touchstone of the Crown lawyers and had given them a lead as chairman. His views had been disregarded and he had been out-voted. He had done so with his eyes wide open, knowing full well that by speaking and voting against the known wishes of the King and his Favourite, it might have the effect of clipping their financial wings, and he knew that he would possibly meet with something more than unpleasantness from them. He would not be forgetful of what he suffered at the hands of Elizabeth for a similar act. What no one else in that age dare have done openly Francis Bacon did.

It may be asked: if Francis Bacon felt so strongly about this flood of patents with which he disagreed, why did he not refuse to seal them so that they could not pass into law? Did not the fact that he sealed them submissively make him directly responsible?

How could he refuse to seal them? This was the real position. All patent monopolies were created, *nominally*, by the King, *i.e.* by his Prerogative, though *actually* on the advice in the majority of cases by Buckingham and his entourage. The King's mandate was taken to the Lord Keeper to be passed (entered and taken account of) and stamped with the Great Seal. But because Francis Bacon stamped the licence he was not responsible for the creation of this particular patent, whether it were for gold thread or horseflesh. *The Great Seal belonged to the King, not to Francis Bacon, and not to his office.* The King could have instructed anyone to seal the tiny piece of paper containing his instructions. He could have sealed it himself.

If the Chancellor by refusing to pass a grant could have prevented it from passing he would have been responsible. But it was not so. The King could not only take the Seals from him and give them to whom he pleased, but *he could himself seal his own patents*; and it is a pertinent fact that *one of the patents which had been most abused*, and upon which Sir Giles Mompesson was chiefly called in question, *was actually sealed with the King's own hand immediately before the Seals were committed to Bacon.*

It is therefore clear that all patent abuses which caused such an outcry were directly the King's responsibility. Francis Bacon was simply an officer and had to do as he was told. When the storm broke we will see how Coke, Cranfield and Co. made it appear that the Lord Keeper was responsible for the sealing of the patents.

Now let us get the position quite clear in our minds towards all these social, moral and political problems that were agitating Englishmen in the latter half of 1620. We have seen the types of men-about-Court by whom Francis Bacon was surrounded—James and Buckingham with their scoundrelly brood of money-leeches. He had to meet with them in business as we have today to meet with some folk who make our mental and moral gorges rise. What was his personal attitude towards them?

Francis Bacon seems to have been singularly unaware that he was surrounded by a group of evilly minded, mendacious men quite prepared to stop at nothing to secure his overthrow—men who all worshipped in the House of Rimmon under the aegis of their Priestess Lady Compton and her son, the Favourite. Francis Bacon was unsuspicious because he was one that neither bred nor fed hatred. His nature was noble, magnanimous, generous-minded. He could not bring himself to think ill of anyone. It never occurred to him that Coke harboured thoughts of bitter revenge for having been worsted in conflicts which he himself had provoked, or that malignant wickedness could possibly find an abiding place from which he (Francis Bacon) could be stabbed unsuspectingly to the heart. Yet so it was; and he awoke too late to the full realization that he was in the toils of a perfectly planned conspiracy from which there was no escape. Coke was not a man who could accept defeat with a smile. His nature was a venomous one. If he could not beat his foe by open methods he had no hesitation in using symbolically the poison phial or the dagger; and his hatred of Francis Bacon was no common one. We have previously seen that their lives had been one long duel and that Coke could neither forget nor forgive the disgrace he had suffered when he was driven from his seat in the Privy Council and his law impugned. "The Bacon had been too tough for the Coke [Cook]" said the wits of Gray's Inn. To ignore this outstanding duel—known to everyone in the Inns of Court, the Law Courts, the royal Court of James, London society, etc.—is simply fatal to any elucidation of the problem which has hitherto baffled historians and biographers. Unless we take into full consideration the character of this unprincipled man who had "the manners of a bully and the spirit of a slave" and the characters of his friends, their relationship to the Favourite and the reasons for their pent-up enmity towards Francis Bacon, it is impossible to understand the Lord Chancellor's swift and sudden overthrow.

At the end of 1620 the King's finances were in a hopeless state. They had been so for many months. The day of reckoning had arrived. It could be put off no longer. The Treasury was worse than empty. James was heavily in debt. His credit had vanished. He could raise no more money by virtue of his Prerogative. Early in the year Francis Bacon had seen the crash coming and had advised him to set his house in order. And in the autumn the King at last realized that there was only one thing he could do to put the finances of the Crown and the kingdom on a firm foundation—to act on Francis Bacon's counsel and call a new Parliament. Naturally James and his courtiers were afraid of the Commons, but Francis Bacon was not; the King and his Favourite were fearful lest the sins of the patent monopolies should come home to roost, but the risk had to be taken. For this reason—to avert the anger of an enraged people—Francis Bacon strenuously urged the King to abandon the most iniquitous of the patent monopolies before calling Parliament; in order to take away the chief grievances. But James and Buckingham were stiff-necked, as we have already seen—their refusal being stiffened by Coke's advice for an ulterior motive. Coke was no fool. He knew that sooner or later a Parliament would have to be called for financial reasons, and by the autumn of 1620 he knew the time was at hand—for the country was drifting into war, money was the sinews of war, and must be obtained from the only possible source—the House of Commons.

Events abroad made a reconciliation between the King and his people a prime necessity. The liberties of free Englishmen were in jeopardy. The reformed religion was at stake. Spain with Austria and Bavaria had occupied Prague. The Rhine was in Catholic hands. Germany was invaded. The Spaniards had enveloped it in fire and blood. With the sack of the Palatinate and the occupation of Prague, the Thirty Years' War had commenced. "While James was still mumbling about a Spanish Match for his son Charles, he was surprised in his cups by the news that Max and Spinola had robbed his daughter and her children of their native and elective Crowns." They were fugitives. What could he do? "There is only one thing you can do," said Francis Bacon. "Call a Parliament, as I have begged you to do previously.

State the position. And throw yourself heart and soul into a religious war. The enemy must see in England only one party, one flag; therefore let the King become the leader of the Commons and let the Government adopt the business of reform."

The King, because he was *in extremis* financially, consented to Francis Bacon's plans, but with many misgivings, and the writs went out in the winter of 1620 to summon a new Parliament to meet on 30 January 1621. A blaze of excitement much fiercer than the elections of 1614 ran round the nation from Lands End to John O'Groats. Men felt that the King's method of ruling by his Favourite Buckingham and his clique of unscrupulous wastrels was drawing to a close. It was well known that the Treasury was empty and could no longer be replenished by feudal methods, and that King James was at the end of his financial tether. The nation as a whole was resolved that the King and his minions should be brought to book. If monies were voted for the Crown, the nation's grievances must be redressed, abuses in the Church and State swept away, and the army and the fleet launched against the insolent Spanish enemy that menaced Protestantism. "No Popery!" was the cry. "Help for the Protestants of the Rhine!" the watchword.

In home politics the spirit of reform was much more vigorous than in the last Parliament. The nation was not going to be fobbed off again by shifty evasions or allow their representatives to be dissolved arbitrarily by the royal whim. Their grievances were great and had begun to assume a personal character—the free citizen versus an alien King who was robbing and flinging men into jail who withstood the Crown's extortions. What was the King but an uncouth Scotsman riding it roughshod over Englishmen! There was a *personal detestation* of the monarch, and all that he stood for, growing in men's minds. Nor can this detestation be wondered at. He came to the Throne in 1603 with the acclamation of the English nation. In 1620 James was despised by everyone. They had discovered him to be mean, treacherous, cruel, with neither moral nor intellectual qualities; his ostentatious display of learning and religion a hollow pretence, a pitiful veneer to cover corruption of the worst kind. The Favourite was even more detested for very similar reasons; by the upper class for his arrogance and overbearing manners even to noblemen of ancient lineage; by the middle class for his loose conduct with the King; and by the lower class for his reckless extravagance which pressed them against the poverty line by screwing out of them monies by monopolies. In short, throughout the nation indignation was roused by the large premiums exacted for monopoly grants *by the Villiers family*, and by the fact that several of the patentees, notoriously Sir Giles Mompesson (Massinger's "Overreach"), and his coadjutor Sir Francis Mitchell ("Justice Greedy") and others, used them for oppressive purposes.

Let this undeniable fact and its implications be fully understood. In 1620 men's passions ran high against the King and his Favourite for their extortions, etc., but *not one word was uttered against Francis Bacon*. There was no expression of ill will, either oral or written. The trading community and the public know that Francis Bacon was fundamentally opposed to all forms of "enclosed justice" and especially to monopoly patents. His attitude had not been forgotten from the days of 1610 when he tried in vain to clear away all the rights and dues—with but slight modifications—inherited by the King from feudal times. The "Great Contract" failed through the grasping cupidity of the King. They knew, of course, that the patents passed through Bacon's office as Lord Keeper; but they also knew they were sealed not by his wish but through legal compunction as an officer of the Crown. It is equally clear that during the feverish excitement of the election *there was never a whisper against Francis Bacon's good name*, although he was King James's first Law Lord. Why? Because all England knew he was as honest as the day. Similarly, *the first outcries in the Commons were not against Francis Bacon* but against the iniquities of the unrestricted abuse of the King's Prerogative. There was not a whisper against his name in the Commons as being in any way responsible for the monopoly patents for more than a month (9 March) after Parliament met (30 January); and none against his honour, his probity, his HONESTY until 14 March. Up to this date he stood before England and the world as a man of irreproachable character and justly so—*as we have seen.*

Let us now proceed to examine how Francis Bacon lost his reputation at one fell stroke.

Chapter VIII

FRANCIS BACON AND THE KING: 30 JANUARY—10 APRIL 1621

THE new Parliament met on 30 January 1621. Francis Bacon was no longer a Member of the House of Commons. As the Lord Chancellor, Viscount St. Alban, he presided over the House of Lords. But he was essentially a House-of-Commons man, for he had continuously taken a prominent part in all its proceedings from the age of twenty-five. Coke, his enemy, had not been a Member of the House of Commons for twenty-eight years but had secured a seat by openly posing as a legal reformer, presumed to be in opposition to the Government. He speedily made himself the Leader of some four hundred inexperienced men, a third of them new to the House—the majority among them, turbulent, riotous, passionate in their desire to be revenged for the injustices they had suffered. Coke's rank as a Privy Councillor, his wide experience of affairs, his power of debate, his knowledge of men and knowledge of law, together with his own professions of reform, seemed to make him an ideal Leader.

The Speaker was Thomas Richardson, Buckingham's brother-in-law, a wealthy "shallow, ribald lawyer". On the Front Bench sat Sir Lionel Cranfield, another of Buckingham's relatives, in command of Lady Compton's benches, on which were perched the birds of a feather pledged to chirp together at the same time, who knew exactly what to do. They were there to protect the Favourite at all costs and to draw down the Chancellor at the opportune moment. They took their cue *inside* the House from Coke, Richardson and Cranfield; *outside* from the Favourite and his mother whose home was their rendezvous. They were like the eighty Irishmen in the Victorian Parliaments—the noisiest of all the noisy parties in the State, standing between the conservative upholders of the Court, the fanatical Puritans, the angry Reformers, ready to ally themselves to any party—to yell for reform, and the redress of grievances, to denounce Catholics as traitors or to support the Court Party so long as their own ends were being served.

The King met the two Houses assembled with a long rambling speech. He stated their respective duties: he was to distribute justice and mercy and they, without meddling with his Prerogative, were, by petition, to acquaint him with their distress and *to supply his pecuniary wants.*

He said that:

> The King's business was to make laws and theirs to advise him to make such as were good for the Commonwealth. The Commons knew best the particular state of the country; and if the King asked their advice could best tell him what was amiss or else petition him to amend and redress it. It was also their duty to offer what they thought fit to supply his wants.

He was ready to hear and redress all complaints; and whatever was amiss he would rightly reform.

The Commons passed a portion of the money Bills required in a savagely humorous mood. This time they would not give the Crown the excuse that it was driven to unconstitutional methods for raising money. Indeed, in their haste to "man the fleets and put a floating fortress" between England and the Continent, there was not a dissentient voice. There was, however, an ominous quiet that presaged the coming tempest. The determined temper of the House was indicated by its immediate exclusion from Parliament of two Members, Hollis and Britton, simply because they were Catholics; another being expelled because he had jested against the Puritans. The Commons were in a much grimmer mood than the 1614 Parliament which had been so superciliously dissolved. The House represented a nation which profoundly disagreed with the King's foreign policy so far as the Spanish marriage was concerned. It was resolved to root out the menace of Catholicism. It was determined to obtain redress, once and for all, of grievances regarding monopoly patents. That was the chief question at issue. Everyone knew that the offensive patents would be attacked, the abuses of collection denounced and their legality questioned. All were dissatisfied with the King's wanton extravagance, his haughty Favourite with his avaricious family and his corrupt clique.

Outside the cabal of conspirators there was not a Member of Parliament who was not angry with the insolent Buckingham and his detestable associates. *But there was no feeling of ill will against the Lord Chancellor.* He simply did not come within their circle of grievances. There were, of course, apart from his active enemies, quite a number in the new House who envied his steady rise, his ability, his intellectual power, his speedy administration of justice in the Chancery Court which prevented the lawyers and their satellites from the rich rewards of long-protracted suits. Sir Edward Coke reckoned that these men would be ready to fall into line with whatever tune he piped.

That there was such a plot cannot be questioned. There is abundant evidence to show to all historians and biographers who have clear eyes to see that, from the time Coke sold his daughter to the Favourite's brother (in July 1617), he and Lady Compton were out to ruin Francis Bacon. At their first attempt they nearly succeeded in pulling him down, as we have seen, though Francis Bacon was then Regent of the kingdom.

These are the vital facts: In 1619 Francis Bacon dismissed from the Chancery Court a dishonest Registrar, John Churchil, whom he had caught in the act of swindling suitors. Churchil ought to have been prosecuted and sent to prison but Francis Bacon simply showed him the door and told him to go. Churchil at once rushed to Coke—everyone knew of the bitter enmity Coke bore the Chancellor—and said, "*I am resolved not to sink alone.*" He offered Coke his services (the out-of-work Registrar to the out-of-work lawyer) to entrap the Chancellor. Churchil alleged that he was cognisant of certain grave abuses going on in Francis Bacon's court which could be considered the equivalent of bribery and corruption. Coke thereupon made a bargain with him: he promised Churchil he would see that he was reinstated in his old position at the Chancery if he could find the material on which to frame a series of charges on which the Chancellor could be dismissed. Churchil at once set to work for he was ready to swear falsely for the sake of a fee or reward.

There were other conspirators with Coke—all enemies of Francis Bacon—like Sir Lionel Cranfield inside the House of Commons, but outside the House the most important person in the plot of the precious coterie that met at Lady Compton's mansion was Dean Williams, the accepted suitor of the Favourite's mother, who coveted Francis Bacon's office as Lord Chancellor. It is safe to assume that the complete plot was hatched and carefully watched and stage-managed from day to day by Coke, Cranfield, and Williams from Lady Compton's home to her great delight. "Hell hath no fury like a woman scorned." And Francis Bacon had indeed scorned her when he refused to do her bidding.

Everything fell out as the conspirators had assumed. No sooner had the money Bills been passed than there was an uproar in the Commons over the nation's grievances—the illegal raising of revenues (nominally for the King) by the issuing of monopoly patents on all sorts of commodities, to the hurt of the citizens and the enrichment of Buckingham and his family with their hangers-on. Two of the instruments, Mompesson and Mitchell, employed by Buckingham's brother, Sir Edward Villiers, were denounced for their iniquitous extortions. Their arrest was demanded; and numerous committees were appointed to inquire into all alleged abuses, Coke adroitly getting a parliamentary committee to inquire into the abuses of the Chancery Court.

The more the committees sifted the question of grievances, the more heinous appeared the offences of the Favourite and his minions, and the more furious became the Members as they heard of the rascally outrages of Mompesson and Mitchell who had flung scores of London citizens into jail. Mompesson, a relation of Buckingham, was forewarned of the hue and cry and disappeared. Sir Edward Villiers fled overseas. Their escape enraged the Commons beyond measure. Mitchell alone was secured in Finsbury jail. But the storm was very cleverly diverted by Coke and his clique of noisy partisans. Cranfield shouted, in effect, "These men who have vanished are only minor delinquents. There are abuses in the courts still more grave—especially in the Chancery Division. Let us fly at higher game, the man or men who passed and sealed these illegal monopoly patents." And everyone heard the whisper that went round the Commons that the man aimed at in Cranfield's reiterated suggestions—backed up by Coke and his satellites—was the head of the court lawyers, none other than Francis Bacon, the Lord Chancellor.

Thus was the tempest diverted from its proper course to draw nearer to the Lord Chancellor, and the Commons were satisfied to dance to Coke's piping, ignorant of the fact that they were being made into mere catspaws to satisfy the personal revenge, ambition and greed of lady Compton's tribe.

A few days later it was announced in the House of Commons that the King had stated in the House of Lords that he was not to blame for the issuing of the alleged illegal patents but had been misled by his Law Officers. In short, the dishonest King was preparing to hedge his responsibilities for these iniquitous imposts (which were solely for his and his Favourite's enrichment) and to allow the full force of the national storm to burst on the head of Francis Bacon who as the Chief of the Law Officers was technically responsible for the decision that thc imposts were legal under the King's Prerogative, though he had actually himself spoken and voted in the House of Lords against their continuance. His personal position was becoming serious. Apparently King James was preparing to abandon him.

A few days later the House of Commons was electrified by Coke stating that grave abuse had been discovered in the Chancellor's court; that there was evidence that the Lord Chancellor was guilty of bribery and corruption; and that he had two witnesses named Aubrey and Egerton who would testify that they had given the Lord Chancellor £100 and £400 respectively to secure verdicts in their favour. A committee of the whole House was appointed to consider the new position and any other cases of similar nature. It was now no longer a question of the legality of certain patents or a question of giving the King wrong advice but a definite charge of the worst possible kind against the highest legal dignitary in the land, a charge that struck at Francis Bacon's character as a man, and his personal honour, apart from the criminal aspect of his legal activities as a judge. The House rocked with excitement and so did the City. All sorts of rumours ran current. It was alleged that Francis Bacon had made hundreds of thousands by his acts of corruption, the usual bribe being £300 to £1000.

At the first sitting of the "Bribery and Corruption" Committee, Coke proceeded to amplify the charge. Apart from the Aubrey and Egerton cases he produced the famous "Black List" compiled by Churchil. Since the proceedings were secret, rumour spread it abroad that there were hundreds of complaints from aggrieved suitors. The Committee therefore referred the various charges against Francis Bacon to the House of Lords who decided to sift the evidence, and, if necessary, to impeach the unjust judge.

When the first mention of bribery came to the ear of the Lord Chancellor, he smiled at the very thought of such an accusation, but as the days went by and he saw that the full force of popular clamour and the fury of the Commons had been diverted from the grievances of monopoly patents created by the Favourite to the grievances of bribery and corruption that centred in himself, he became distressed for he had begun to feel certain that the King and his Favourite were about to abandon him to his enemies; as in fact, they were. Unknown to Francis Bacon, Buckingham had taken the crafty Dean Williams to the King. This sinister cleric advised James to throw overboard all the small fry and to deliver up Francis Bacon as a scapegoat, the better to shield the Favourite and to clear himself.

Meanwhile Francis Bacon had fallen ill, torn with anxiety, but had written to the House of Lords that he intended to defend himself. He asked that all the facilities of a High Court action should be afforded him—to employ council, to cross-examine, to call rebutting evidence, etc. Aubrey's and Egerton's charges were first mooted to the house on 14 March, and on 27 March the Commons rose for the Easter recess. But the Grand Committee dealing with the charges continued their sittings in London, while Francis Bacon, who had gone to his country seat in Gorhambury, was busy with his defence up to the day before Parliament reassembled on 17 April. This we know because there were notes left by him which give an outline of his defence.

But—and here is the mystery of the entire case—when the Lords assembled on 24 April, the entire House of Peers were stunned into silence for several minutes by the Prince of Wales who craved leave to read a "letter of Submission" that the Lord Chancellor had written two days earlier which contained the following sentence:

> Having understood PARTICULARS OF THE CHARGES, not formally from the House, I FIND MATTER SUFFICIENT AND FULL to move me TO DESERT THE DEFENCE.

It was a general admission of guilt, or, rather a "submission" of guilt to the charges. Yet Francis Bacon when that submission was made had not even seen them, was quite unaware of what they were, nor their number. "Nothing is so strange," says Church, "as the way in which Bacon met the charges. He threw up the game without a struggle and volunteered an absolute and unreserved confession of guilt . . . that is to say he declined to stand his trial."

After some discussion, the Lords, on the proposition of Southampton, one of Francis Bacon's earliest friends and now his avowed enemy—refused to accept a general confession of guilt and resolved that he should admit his guilt to each particular case. The list of charges—Coke's "Black List"—was therefore sent to Francis Bacon forthwith and *he saw the items for the first time.* On 30 April Francis Bacon confessed in writing his guilt together with his appended notes and this "Confession" was read to the Peers. On 1 May the King sent four lords to demand the Great Seal. They found him in bed too ill to be moved to the Bar of the house to receive sentence.

The triumph of Coke was all but complete. It but remained for sentence to be passed; and he and his gang of cutthroats did their level best to make Francis Bacon's offence a hanging matter. Coke pressed for a capital sentence in the Commons. Even fair-minded men, so enraged were they, talked of every extremity of punishment, short of death.

On 3 May the House of Lords pronounced sentence.

1. A fine of £40,000.
2. Imprisonment in the Tower during the King's pleasure.
3. To be for ever incapable of any office in the State.
4. Never to sit in Parliament nor come within the verge of court.

In less than two months—14 March to 3 May—the wisest intellectual in the world was ground into the dust in obloquy and shame. His enemies had triumphed. Francis Bacon's conspicuous fall diverted men's thoughts from the more scandalous wickedness of the Great Favourite. The result of Francis Bacon's ruin was that Buckingham was saved. Bacon was cast down from the height of fortune to become a byword of shame. What a tremendous and mysterious catastrophe! What a fall indeed!

So Francis Bacon was sent to the Tower a ruined man.

It must be quite obvious to any reader of the foregoing account of Francis Bacon's fall that behind this factual summary of open events there is a secret and undisclosed history which the majority of biographers and historians ignore and have never attempted to discover. They have been content to say with Green the historian, "Bacon's own confession of guilt made it difficult to resist his own condemnation." And no one seems to have thought it worthwhile to ascertain whether the "Confession" was genuine or otherwise. No modern writer has pondered to himself this problem!

Here is a man whose public acts and private life proclaim him to have been animated by the worthiest and noblest ideals and against whom nothing can be truthfully alleged throughout the course of a long life—a man who had long and consistently laboured for the good of humanity openly and secretly by thought, word and deed—a man who said with fine scorn, "It is a poor centre of a man's actions, himself. Wisdom for a man's self is a depraved thing: it is the wisdom of rats."

Here is a man who when accused of making money avariciously by taking bribes not only laughed at the very idea but made vigorous preparations to defend himself and notified the necessary authorities of his intention ... and yet this man, at the very last minute, suddenly "Deserts his Defence", enters a general submission of guilt to charges he has never even seen, their character and their number; and, later, enters a plea of guilty to each separate charge when shown the complete list. How comes it that a man of unblemished character for sixty years should admit that he was a rogue and dishonest in his sixty-first year?

Here is the secret of Bacon's fall. . . .

When the storm first arose in the House of Commons of monopoly patents the King and Buckingham were most uneasy lest the Favourite was impeached and the Crown itself jeopardized.

Buckingham, naturally enough, was in an extremity of fear. He therefore, in all probability at his mother's house, sought the advice of her lover, Dean Williams, who advised the Favourite to throw to the wolves Mompesson and Mitchell and everyone else to save his skin and not to attempt to shield them. The advice seemed so good that Buckingham took the Dean to the King. James needed little persuasion to act on his suggestion, hence his assertion in the Lords that *he was not responsible for the patents but has been misled by the Law Officers of the Crown*, and that he was determined not to protect those involved, not even the Favourite's brother, Sir John Villiers and Mompesson, another relation. But Buckingham saw that these precious relations got notice in good time to enable them to escape; and Mitchell was the only one secured, to the enragement of the Commons.

Coke and Cranfield, however, both relatives by marriage of the Favourite, deliberately diverted the anger of the Commons against the Lord Chancellor, who was the head of the Law Officers, on the personal and judicial charge of bribery and corruption. When Francis Bacon gave notice of his intention to defend any Crown impeachment and demanded that the proceedings should take the form of a High Court action, the King and Buckingham were in a greater panic than ever, so much so that the Favourite—when the Parliament adjourned for the Easter recess—wanted the King to dissolve Parliament and so prevent any further action being taken. Buckingham again sought the Dean's advice and Williams was again taken to the King to repeat his counsel. The Dean told James that to dissolve Parliament would be a fatal mistake, that the result might be the overwhelming of the State, and that it was best to let the Reformers have their way. He continued: the storm of the patents had passed over from grievances against the Favourite to accusations against the Chancellor, who had resolved to defend himself and in speech was all powerful, but he could be and must be prevailed upon to submit. In short, Williams suggested to James that, in view of what might be disclosed at the trial, the King should see Francis Bacon and COMMAND him to desert his defence and plead GUILTY to the charges.

Accordingly, Francis Bacon was to be made into a public scapegoat for the King, his precious Favourite Buckingham, and all the rest of the brood. The people were to be satisfied with the sacrifice of "a great Public Delinquent".

James listened to his new adviser and saw that his plan provided the only safe and secret way of escape. He had only to command Francis Bacon in his office as King to his servant, and the Lord Chancellor was bound to obey. He accordingly sent for his Chancellor during the recess, on the last day before Parliament assembled, and commanded him to desert his defence, to send a letter of submission to the House of Lords announcing his intention, and to plead guilty to the charges that had been formulated against him; and as the Lord Chancellor fervently believed in the Divine Right of Kings, that the King in his office could do no wrong, and having kissed hands on his appointment and sworn fealty to do his Sovereign's bidding, Francis Bacon was bound by oath to obey King James's ruling quite as much as a soldier on the battlefield must obey the command of his superior officer even though death be the result. So Francis Bacon sent his "Letter of Submission" to the Lords. He was thus entrapped and had no option but to enter a plea of "Guilty" to each of the charges. There was no possible retreat, unless he defied the King's order which, owing to his principles of Divine Right, he could not possibly consider.

The fact of King James's consultations with Dean Williams and Buckingham and his command to Francis Bacon to plead guilty was unknown for many years afterwards, when it was disclosed by Bishop Hackett who had access to Dean William's private papers after the Dean's decease. A written record was left and published years afterwards by Bushell, Francis Bacon's confidential secretary, which clinches Hackett's account. There were also papers left by Francis Bacon which tell the same ghastly truth that he had "to make an OBLATION" of himself.

This evidence (hitherto ignored or suppressed or belittled by all orthodox writers) alters the entire situation with respect to the guilt or innocence of Francis Bacon. We can thus set out the position clearly:

1. Francis Bacon pleaded guilty under duress.
2. The case never went to trial and nothing was proved against him.
3. He was the victim of a foul plot conceived by Coke and afterwards engineered by the King, Buckingham, and his would-be stepfather, Dean Williams.

By English law a man who is compelled to plead guilty under duress cannot be held to be guilty at all and the sentence of the Lords in 1621 was open to be quashed on that one technical point alone; and lovers of Francis Bacon the world over should never be satisfied until the infamous verdict against him is annulled. The pardon later granted him by James is totally inadequate to satisfy English Justice—especially considering how seriously it affects the reputation of our greatest Englishman.

Though we now know that Francis Bacon was, technically, innocent, and though he never went to trial and nothing criminal was ever proved against him, and though he was the victim of a diabolical plot and did not plead guilty voluntarily, were the charges against him trumped up ones or were they true? Was there any truth in them at all? In other words, was he guilty or innocent? Had he accepted gifts and bribes to deflect the scales of Justice in favour of the briber?

The fact is that Francis Bacon had accepted gifts from suitors in his court, but such gifts were not bribes. *Gifts were given and accepted in all the courts.* Indeed the system of gifts dated from the Middle Ages and had grown into the fabric of the Constitution, (on the Continent as well as England), and was practised by the King, his ministers, the clergy, the law and throughout society. Everybody gave gifts to secure what they wanted; everybody accepted gifts. It was a relic of feudalism that could not be reversed except by an Act of Parliament. Francis Bacon had repeatedly deplored the practice. It was "one of the frailties of the Times". There were no court fees such as we have today: no fixed scale of charges. The only "fees" were gifts of a fluctuating amount. The actual amount per case was arranged as a bargain between the registrar or his clerk and the suitor. It was measured by the suitor's ability to pay and what the case was worth. The gifts were in cash or goods. In Francis Bacon's court the fees or gifts were collected and entered up in the books of the Chancery by the registrar. The Lord Chancellor did not personally receive them any more than a barrister directly receives monies from his client today. The courts were not run financially by the State, the judges were only paid a nominal sum and were maintained by the gifts of suitors. That was the source of revenue. Out of these gifts the judge paid the expenses of his staff, and the balance belonged to him. *A gift was not a bribe unless it involved a corrupt bargain between the judge and a suitor for the perversion of justice.* The system was open to abuse, but the point at issue is this: did Francis Bacon accept BRIBES from suitors in order to deliver corrupt verdicts in their favour?

This can only be determined by a careful perusal of each case but a general examination of the "Black List" gives one something of a surprise. It is obvious that many items have been dragged in to swell the number of charges which have nothing to do with bribery and corruption. And instead of there being hundreds of cases, there are only twenty-three, including one charge of general carelessness. Instead of there being hundreds of thousands, of pounds involved, the total amount is under £6000. Yet, if Francis Bacon had accepted only £1 instead of thousands, if there were but one proved case instead of hundreds, he would be rightly declared an unjust and unrighteous judge and he would justly have deserved the execrations of everyone.

The records reveal that in the first four terms after taking his seat as the Lord Keeper, Francis Bacon made 8798 orders and decrees and freed 35,000 from the law's uncertainties. Within a few weeks he had settled no less than 3658 disputed suits long overdue. On 8 June 1617 he reported that he had drawn level with the business of the Kingdom—not one cause unheard, not one petition unanswered; the lawyers drawn dry. In four terms Francis Bacon pronounced 7000 verdicts on disputed cases. Each verdict must have hurt someone. The making of 35,000 orders means that some 150,000 persons were involved *i.e.* 70,000 principals and over 70,000 counsel, solicitors and clerks on both sides. If any fee were paid (in honest error) at the wrong time or date, it would be an irregularity for which the Chancellor was technically responsible, for these things were arranged by Francis Bacon's registrars and clerks. *They* kept the books of the court. Yet in all these large numbers of cases and this vast number of persons, the cunning skill of Coke and the vindictive scrutiny of Churchil could only frame an accusation of twenty-three cases, not one of them a clean-cut case of bribery.

The individual charges have in recent times been carefully studied and compared with the books of the Chancery Court by W. Hepworth Dixon, barrister-at-law, of the Inner Temple himself, whose professional status placed him in a specially qualified position to form an accurate judgment.

The truth is that when the charges against Francis Bacon are examined severally and collectively by the trained legal mind of a Hepworth Dixon, we find that in strict law not one of them will hold water. Here is Dixon's analysis of gifts accepted:

Three were debts. Borrowing is no crime.

Three were private arbitrations and had never been in Chancery.

Thirteen were gifts paid in the usual way *after judgment in practice in every court.*

One gift had been returned as being irregular.

One gift of a cabinet had never been accepted.

Two—the Aubrey and Egerton gifts of money—were handed to Francis Bacon's servants and were unknown to him. And judgment had been given against them.

Hepworth Dixon concludes his analysis in these words.

> Thus on a scrutiny, unparalleled for rigour and vindictiveness into Lord St. Alban's official acts, not a single fee or remembrance traced to the Chancellor himself, could by any fair construction, be called a bribe. *Not one appeared to have been given on a promise; not one appeared to have been given in secret; not one appeared to have corrupted justice.*

In Francis Bacon's notes, attached to the charge sheet, he pointed out that the alleged irregularities occurred when he was new in office, strange to his registrars and clerks, and overwhelmed with arrears left by his predecessor. *The last offence was two years old, and none could be discovered since the dismissal of Churchil.* Dixon adds:

> For the latter half of his reign as Lord Chancellor, the inquisition of his enemies, aided by the treachery and corruption of his servants, *had not been able to detect in his administration of Justice a FAULT much less a FRAUD.*

From the position that the alleged offences were faults of the times and were not faults of the man, Francis Bacon never receded. If Francis Bacon's biographers had had the common justice to have examined the original charge sheet to which Francis Bacon appended the word "Guilty" to each item, they would have seen a note attached to each, a note which cancels the admission of guilt and absolves him for ever from such venomous, trifling and trumpery allegations.

Nor is Hepworth Dixon alone in his considered legal opinion. Basil Montague, also a barrister-at-law, says the same. C. Y. C. Dawbarn, MA, another barrister, who had likewise studied the position—with whom I have discussed the matter many times—concurs with Dixon and Montague. Parker Woodward, an experienced solicitor of high repute, says the charges could not be maintained by any court of law. Spedding and Fowler cannot believe that Francis Bacon was guilty of corruption any more than did Francis Bacon's contemporaries outside the Coke clique.

The late Lord Birkenhead is frankly puzzled at the position. He writes:

> What degree of guilt can be assigned to Bacon? And, if he was guilty, how came it that a man of such transcendent ability could be tempted by the paltry amounts which he admitted to have received?
>
> Bacon did little more than follow the custom of the Age in accepting "presents" from suitors.... He certainly accepted money from those whose suits were pending, but—as he himself pointed out—it has never been shown that such gifts ever influenced his judgment. No complaint was directed against his administration of justice; had such complaints been feasible they would have been made.
>
> Most of the Corruption to which Bacon confessed was the result of a system in which Members of both Houses indulged.[1]

But the real test is this: were any of Francis Bacon's judgments reversed? *There is not one. There were many attempts to overthrow some of his decisions*, but not one was successful. They all stood firm—sound in law and fact. That is the acid test. There was never a wrong verdict given. There was never any illicit bargaining.

Francis Bacon's innocence is established beyond question.

The fact that he was "framed" is to be found in this—that the plotters got away with all they wanted as the result of the Lord Chancellor's ruin:

The King was saved from a conflict with the Commons.

The Favourite's crimes were forgotten in the sacrifice of the King's representative.

Sir Edward Coke tasted the sweets of revenge and just missed having his rival hanged.

Sir Lionel Cranfield was given a peerage and a seat in the Privy Council, becoming Lord Middlesex.

Sir James Ley got a peerage and a wife, becoming a relative of the Favourite.

Sir Edward Villiers, Buckingham's brother, who had fled the country, was given an acquittal by the Privy Council.

Sir Francis Mitchell was released from Finsbury jail.

Sir Giles Mompesson was allowed to return and walk the streets of London without fear of arrest.

Dean Williams was received into the Privy Council, was named successor to Dr. Mountain in the See of Lincoln and given a bishopric. He got the seals of Francis Bacon's office and the Favourite's mother got her trousseau ready.

And *the "Suborn'd Informer" John Churchil was reinstated in his old office as Registrar at the Chancery.*

Francis Bacon never left any categorical open record why he had deserted his defence. He could not very well do so, because the affair was a secret matter of State which could not be communicated to the public. One could

[1]*Famous Trials, Francis Bacon*, p. 397.

not implicate the sovereign in such a dastardly conspiracy without being guilty of high treason, but he nevertheless left a secret record veiled in papers he left behind him, in a conversation afterwards related by his confidential secretary Bushell, in his *Sonnet-Diary*, and in certain cyphers in which he declared he was "*the Coward Conquest of a wretch's Knife*" (Coke), Sonnet lxxiv, through a "Suborn'd Informer" (Churchil), Sonnet cxxv. Francis Bacon never ceased from the moment he heard the charges, to protest his innocence in spite of the ugly word "GUILTY" which he had been compelled to write under *force majeure*.

At the first mutterings of the tempest he wrote indignantly to Buckingham, "My Fortune is not my Felicity. *I know I have clean hands and a clean heart.*" And again he wrote to the Favourite in the same spirit of hot indignation that he had never taken or accepted any fee for sealing a monopoly patent for him or the King. "I never took a penny for commission or things of that nature. I never shared with any servant for any second or inferior profit."

To the King he wrote:

> For the Briberies and Gifts wherewith I am charged, when the Book of Hearts shall be opened, I hope I shall not be found to have the troubled Fountain of a Corrupt Heart, in a depraved habit of taking rewards to pervert justice.

After his interview with the King (when he commanded Francis Bacon to plead guilty), he left these notes:

> I am ready to make an OBLATION OF MYSELF to the King, in whose hands I am as clay to be made into a vessel of Honour or DISHONOUR.... Yet with respect to this charge of Bribery I am INNOCENT.... I never had Fee or Reward.

And again he wrote in his notes after the King's command: "Of a bargain or contract for reward to pervert justice ... I take myself to be as INNOCENT as any born on St. Innocent's Day, *in* my Heart."

And in one of his later notes he left behind in cypher: "I was the justest judge that was in England these fifty years."

Perhaps the best evidence of Francis Bacon's innocence is to be seen in the type of men that gathered round him in his days of adversity. He was sustained in his trials by the most noble and generous of men, the best scholars, the most upright judges, the most pious clergymen. In the closing years of his life men of learning in all walks of life, from all over the Continent, wrote to him and even made special journeys to see him. It was an open secret that he was the victim of a political plot and had been sacrificed by the King to save his Favourite; but it would have been dangerous for anyone to say so openly. Will anyone, however, pretend that Bishop Andrewes, honest Ben Jonson, the studious John Selden would have associated openly with a man and been proud of his friendship if he had been justly condemned as a criminal?

No one in my knowledge of history ever inspired such devotion and reverence from such diverse characters as Ben Jonson, Sir Tobie Mathew, George Herbert, Thomas Hobbes and Bishop Andrewes. Could these men have loved a man whom they knew was a rightly convicted hypocrite and thief? The outstanding fact recorded by Aubrey is this: "That all who were great and GOOD loved him."

Four weeks after the Lords passed sentence Francis Bacon was arrested and imprisoned in the Tower, from which he immediately wrote to the King and Buckingham: "*Procure the Warrant for my Discharge this day.*" This peremptory note had the effect of bringing about his immediate release and other things followed in their wake. The £40,000 fine was suspended and afterwards assigned to trustees by the King for the benefit of his creditors. Many letters passed between Francis Bacon and the King and Buckingham from this time (1621) to 1626—the end of Francis Bacon's official life—which prove conclusively that James had promised him an annual pension at the command interview to make up for the financial loss he would sustain in deserting the defence. The letters also show that the King, true to his character, held his promises very lightly and did his best to evade payment. Everything indicates that Francis Bacon became in serious financial difficulties as a result of the King's cold-shouldering of the man who had befriended him and saved his Favourite by ruining his own great career and reputation. James even neglected to pay him the yearly amount to which he was legally entitled.

The sudden stoppage of his income had dislocated all his financial plans. He had mortgaged his future earnings by the schemes he had in hand for the benefit of mankind—his scientific experiments, his literary work, his ethical establishments. He was worried to death by debts and creditors and the difficulty of meeting current expenses. It makes one justly indignant, even at this length of time, to see how this great genius was forced to play the mendicant through dire necessity, to beg for pecuniary assistance, to which he was justly entitled, from two such worthless creatures as the King and his Favourite. To the Lords: "I am old, weak, ruined, in want; a very subject of pity." To the King: "The poor remnants of my former fortunes in Plate and Jewels, I have spread upon poor men to whom I owed, scarce leaving myself bread." To Buckingham: "Afflictions are truly called trials; trials of man's self and his friends.... What may I expect from the future, my state being not unknown to you?"

Nevertheless, in spite of all the mental distractions, he faced the situation bravely, for Francis Bacon was Francis Bacon still.

> In the fell clutch of circumstance
> He had not winced nor cried aloud.
> Under the bludgeonings of chance,
> His head was bloody but unbowed.[1]

He was still the master of his fate. He was still the captain of his soul. Even within four days of his imprisonment he wrote to Gondomar, the Spanish Ambassador, telling him of his future literary plans. And we find him putting them at once into operation, for he continued his literary and ethical activities assisted by men like Ben Jonson, William Rawley, Hobbes,

[1]Henley.

etc. Job was never more patient under his trials than Francis Bacon in the evening of his days.

His letter to Gondomar is worth more than a mere passing mention because there is a deep significance in its phrasing which no one seems to have hitherto understood. He writes:

> Your Excellency's Love towards me I have ever found worm and sincere alike in Prosperity and Adversity. For which I give you due thanks. But for myself, my AGE, my Fortune, yea my GENIUS, to which I have hitherto done scant Justice, calls me now to retire from the STAGE OF CIVIL ACTION and betake myself to LETTERS, and *to the Instruction of the ACTORS THEMSELVES*, and the Service of Posterity. In this it may be I shall find Honour, and I shall pass my days as it were in the Entrance Halls of a Better Life. May God keep you....

What is this letter but an avowal that, while he intends to betake himself to Letters, there is one particular form of Letters in which he is also going to act a part in secret behind the scenes. He leaves the STAGE of civil action for the STAGE DRAMATIC! He is going as a playwright to do something for "*the Instruction of the Actors ... and the Service of Posterity*". In short, Francis Bacon had resolved on 6 June 1621 (*mark well this date*) on the compiling of the great Shakespeare Folio, published two years later. This is the first and only intimation of his resolution to produce an omnibus volume of his plays and neither Spedding nor any other scholar has been alive to the significance of this epoch-making letter with its categorical great announcement that he is going to do a work for posterity which is bound up with a work for the instruction of "ACTORS" on a "STAGE". This promise is fulfilled to the full in the Shakespeare Folio. No living scholar can point to any other of Francis Bacon's works which specifically redeems his pledge to Gondomar and the world.

One of the most remarkable facts of history—totally unnoticed by his biographers, even Spedding, is the punishment that overtook every one of the men who wrought his ruin. It seems as though Divine Providence, outraged at what had been done to one of the servants of the Most High, was determined to bring every one of the miscreants to book. The facts are as significant as the sudden blasting of Ananias and Sapphira for lying when they thought they could get away with it; or the transference of leprosy from Naaman to Gehazi for his hypocritical twisting. For the march of events shows that while Francis Bacon was still busy with his altruistic plans—discussing divinity with Andrewes, poetry and mysticism with Herbert, the publication of the Shakespeare plays with Ben Jonson, and Freemasonry and Rosicrucianism with Robert Fludd—Fate was knocking at the door of the men who had sinned against him so grievously for their own corrupt advancement. They fell like rotten apples in a comparatively short space of time.

Sir Edward Coke was the first to fall. His intolerable arrogance brought him once more into conflict with the Crown. *He was flung into the Tower* to learn to mend his ways, and when he was released, eight months later, he was permanently de-graded from the Privy Council, banished from the Court and confined to his house at Stoke.

Sir Robert Phillips, who played a very conspicuous part in stirring up the Commons against Francis Bacon and diverting their rage from the real culprits, *followed Coke into the Tower.* He was imprisoned for an indefinite period, accused of misdemeanours against the Crown.

Sir John Bennett, the judge of the Prerogative Court, was another of "the mean men" who had crowded Lady Compton's benches in the House of Commons. He had said, "I have neither the power, nor the wish, nor the will to defend the Chancery." Yet within a few short months an infinitely worse series of charges of extortion and bribery were preferred against him which were only too true. At the very time he was joining in the hue and cry against "the Great Delinquent", Sir John Bennett was plundering suitors right and left in his own court. *He was deprived of his office, fined heavily and imprisoned.*

Sir Lionel Cranfield was struck down by the 1624 Parliament. This vicious enemy as a reward had been created Lord Middlesex. He was a judge of the Court of Wards. He was accused of robbing the Royal Magazine of arms, taking bribes in his court and pocketing monies from the Treasury. These crimes were being committed while hounding Francis Bacon to the Tower and doing his best with Coke to get the innocent Chancellor hanged. *Cranfield was sentenced by the House of Commons to a restitutionary fine of £200,000, imprisonment in the Tower, to loss of office and to public infamy.*

John Churchil, the "Suborn'd Informer", who made the bullets for Coke and Co. to shoot, and swore falsely on the promise of the fee and reward, had been restored to his old job as Registrar in the Chancery Court. He, too, came before the 1624 House of Commons. He had been discovered at his old tricks again for forgery and a fraud in his office. *He was convicted and sent to prison.*

Dean Williams had obtained the office of Chancellor, having paid violent court to Lady Compton and led her to believe that marriage was in the offing; he now thought that he could play fast and loose with her. She complained to her son, who was so enraged at his perfidy that he said that of all he had given him he would leave him nothing. *He was speedily dragged from his fatal height by the Crown, stripped of his Seals with every mark of infamy, and driven back into the fields of ecclesiastical strife with a sullied reputation.*[1]

The Villiers clan slowly disintegrated. Francis Bacon saw Lady Compton lose all her influence at Court.

Francis Bacon lived long enough *to see King James full of agony physical and mental,* fears for his son lest he should make a fatal blunder, so much was he under the finger and thumb of Buckingham, the man he had saved by the ruin of his Chancellor.

The Duke of Buckingham did not escape. For him was reserved the highest penalty for wrongdoing. He was slain by John Felton. And the nation went into a riot of joy when it knew that the hand of the avenger had swept away the tyranny of Buckingham for ever.

These disasters which overtook them—so that not one escaped—seem to be one of the most striking vindications of INNOCENCE ever recorded. It is a remarkable example of the working out of spiritual law that governs humanity, individually and collectively, the law which says, "Be not deceived. God is not mocked. For whatsoever a man soweth, THAT shall he reap."

[1]Dixon.

I have not given detailed proofs for any of my assertions in this chapter. My publishers think, and I agree with them, that it is unnecessary to recapitulate the evidence which has already been published in full in my work *The Martyrdom of Francis Bacon*, Rider & Co., London.

Chapter IX

THE FINAL VERDICT

BEFORE Easter 1626 Francis Bacon had accomplished his life's work. He had well and truly laid unseen his secret bases for eternity as well as his open ones for future savants and scholars. His boyhood dreams for *the Reformation of the Whole Wide World* had taken formal shape. He had called them into reality out of airy nothings. The actual revolution of England—nay, of the entire world—which would result in the betterment of man's body, mind and soul was definitely on the way. He had lit candles of flame in every department of human thought that would never be put out but would grow in power from year to year.

He had called the sciences together that were ultimately to crystallize into the Royal Society. He had created a real English language (with a vocabulary of more than 20,000 words) to take the place of a gabble of dialects, and thus supersede the Latin language of culture. He had taught us how to write flexible prose. He had revivified our literature, bequeathing to us models of lyrical and dramatic poesy of unsurpassed beauty even today. His New Philosophy was no longer a mere bookish business but an active morality which came home to a man's fireside, his life and his labour. He had established little conclaves of men the world over who were treading in the footsteps of their teacher and who were practising and spreading his New Philosophy of Ethical Symbolism.

He had also taught humanity how to think. He had laid down definite rules whereby the processes at work behind the "Thinking Man" could be analysed and checked; and he had pointed the way whereby a man might be sure of his immortal destiny and that he was something more than a cunning cast in clay, fashioned by blind mechanical forces. His work was now over as a "bellringer" calling the sciences together to labour in the workship of Nature for the good of Humanity. The bells he had rung all through his life from the days of his youth were ceasing to toll—one by one. The shadows were falling. He was disillusioned and weary. He could say with Anthony, "*Unarm Eros: The long day's task is done, and we must sleep!*" Here is one of the last sonnets he wrote about this time—a sonnet difficult to read without emotion:

Time of Year thou mayst *in me* behold
When Yellow Leaves, or none, or few, do hang
Upon those Boughs which shake against the Cold,
Bare ruin'd Choirs where late the Sweet Birds sang.
IN ME *thou see'st the Twilight of such Day*
As after sunset fadeth in the West,
Which by and by Black Night doth take away,

Death's Second Self that seals up all the rest.
IN ME thou see'st the glowing of such Fire
That on the ashes of his Youth doth lie
As the Death-bed whereon it must expire
Consumed with that which it was nourished by.
(lxxiii)

Since his fall Francis Bacon had lived neither as a drone nor a malcontent. He had neither railed at Fate nor inveighed against Providence. The most he had permitted himself to say was "*Thou hast Humbled me ... but ... I am still in thy Fatherly Keeping ... as a Child.*" Under a calamity so dreadful that would have plucked the soul out of most men, and in spite of a series of irritations and exasperations, usually quite fatal to intellectual work, he turned out a stream of Works written in English and Latin from his retirement to the end of 1625:

History of the Reign of King Henry the Seventh
Abecedarium Naturae (a metaphysical piece)
Historia Ventorum
Historia Densi et Rari
A Discourse of a War with Spain
A Dialogue Touching an Holy War
The Fable of the New Atlantis
A preface to a digest of the Laws of England
De Augmentis Scientiarum
Historia Vitae et Mortis
Historia Gravis et Levis
The beginning of *The History of Henry VIII*
Counsels Civil and Moral (or his Essays enriched and enlarged)
The conversion of Psalms into English verse
Latin translation of *Henry VII*; of the *Counsels Civil and Moral*; *The Dialogue Touching an Holy War*; *New Atlantis*—"for the benefit of other nations"
Revision of *De Sapientia Veterum*
Inquisitio de Magnete
Topica Inquisitionis; *de Luce, et Lumine*
Sylva Sylvarum or the Natural History
Apophthegms (a jest book)

Such were the open works produced during a comparatively short period; but, apart from these, he also wrote and published in 1622 *Othello* under the pen-name of William Shakespeare. In this play he gave vent to his feelings—Innocence and Trustfulness (the Author himself), personified by Desdemona and Othello, being doubly betrayed by consummate Hypocrisy—Iago, a man without any trace of goodness or nobleness in his nature, without one kingly or redeeming quality, "not even honesty which he is at such pains to assume". Thus do we obtain a perfect morality picture of James the hypocritical King and his pinchbeck Favourite of Pretence. In 1623 he passed through the press the Great Shakespeare Folio ... seven years after the death of Shaksper of Stratford. It was an omnibus volume consisting of thirty-six plays, twenty being printed for the first time; six of the finest plays, according to Halliwell-Phillips, had never been heard of before. The sixteen previously published in quarto were all more or less altered, some very largely. *Merry Wives*, for instance, became nearly twice as long as in the quarto. *Othello* published only the year before in 1622 *had numerous additions in true Shakespearean language*. To those who believe that Shaksper of Stratford wrote the plays, I propound this problem; who revised and altered the plays after "the Actor of Stratford" was dead in 1616? Who added the additional lines to *Othello*?

Stratfordian scholars have long asked: where did the six unknown plays come from—*The Taming of the Shrew, Henry the Eighth, All's Well That Ends Well, Julius Caesar, Timon of Athens, Coriolanus*? The traditionalists of a perpetuated myth have never solved the mystery. They have never even attempted to answer the question. There is no evidence whatsoever that these plays were in existence during the lifetime of Shaksper or during the seven years after he was dead. The fact is that they were written by Francis Bacon between 1621 and 1623 and embody secret facts relating to his personal life: his fall, his royal birth, his connection with Freemasonry, etc. He also wrote at this time some of the traditional legends of Freemasonry relative to the Founder, purposely confusing his identity as Lord St. Alban with that of a martyred St. Alban—a Christian Priest who was slain over a thousand years previously and served a king who was "a wicked Paynim". The *Royal Masonic Cyclopaedia* states categorically "*The First Grand Master, A.D. 287, Saint Alban*". Now the protomartyr St. Alban was not slain in the year 287; but the number 287 tells every Rosicrosse–Mason, and every discerning Brother, that it was the *Elizabethan St. Alban* who was the first Grand Master, for 287 is the Seal Mark of "Fra Rosicrosse", the secret literary society that was the brains of the Renaissance, etc.

Francis Bacon's last secret labour was the compiling and completion of his private diary. It was of a unique character. We have seen that from his youth up, when touched with great emotions, some too secret and too sacred as well as too dangerous to confide even to his best friends, he had been in the habit of finding relief by expressing his feelings in a sonnet or series of sonnets. They were written in imaginative language so that even had they fallen into the hands of outsiders they would have been difficult to interpret; but so that his friends, whom he intended to read them after he had passed away, might make no mistake as to their meaning, each sonnet was so constructed that the *motif* which called it into being was concretely declared in clean-cut sentences. There were sonnets to his mother, Queen Elizabeth; to his sweetheart, Marguerite de Valois; to Pallas-Athena, his Muse; to King James respecting the fall; to his "Sons", the secret fraternities, etc. Though written at odd times and in spasms, the sonnets naturally fell into distinctive themes and cantos. In 1624 some themes were unfinished. By 1625 he had written the necessary concluding sonnets for each theme, all of them touched with the pathos of intense emotion, the sorrow, the pain, the terrible anxieties through which he had passed since his betrayal by the King and his henchman. I know of no more poignantly whimsical sonnet in any language than the poet's "Farewell to Athena": "Farewell! Thou art too dear for my possessing...."

In 1625 he had finished his last self-imposed task. He had completed his Sonnet–Diary. How was he ever to get it out into the world—all those lyrical expressions of pent-up passion so that his countrymen in other ages might know him for what he really was, and what was first in his intentions? How could he convey to them the fact that he was a victim of a wicked plot? "The Coward Conquest of a Wretch's Knife"; that he was an innocent man forced to desert his defence and to plead guilty to criminal charges by command of King James, although he could completely prove his innocence?

When *The Tempest* was being prepared for publication in the 1623 Folio—it is generally regarded as Shakespeare's last play in which he bids farewell to the world—he apparently had the problem of his personal lyrics under consideration, for, after saying that he will break his Staff—his Magic Staff of Poetic Creation—and bury it certain fathoms in the earth, he adds,

> And deeper than did ever Plummet sound,
> *Ile drowne MY BOOKE.*

Now what was the "Book" that Francis Bacon was going to drown? It was not the great Folio, for he was going to issue it for the world to see. No! It was something to him infinitely precious—it was his own little book of privacies, his life-long companion, his diary ... his Sonnet–Diary. In 1623 his "Jewelled Trifles" were still in sure Wards of Trust where, metaphorically, he had thrust them (he had entered the title *Shakespeare's Sonnets* in 1609 at Stationer's Hall to prevent anyone else using it) and Francis Bacon knew that his "Book" would definitely solve the problem of authorship if ever it were fished from the depths in which he purposed to drown it. He arranged to drown it in his own day and generation, trusting that another age would find his treasure. He did so because it was obvious that he could not publish to contemporaries *his private* innermost secrets that dealt with questions of State—the "Virgin Elizabeth" who was his mother, the dishonest King James who had so basely betrayed him, etc. A straightforward compilation of the sonnets, captioned and the themes declared, would have led author and printer to the Tower with *the book destroyed.* It could not therefore be openly produced. There was only one way it could survive his death to carry its various messages to another age. He first destroyed all the captions. Then he mixed the sonnets (154) according to a definite plan and this destroyed the identity of the themes. He printed them as one long poem and they were printed privately—at the Rosicrosse Printing Press. It was published in quarto, *undated*, but the number, 1609, was printed on the title page as though to indicate to outsiders that this was the date of publication. At the 1625 Festivals of St John—the patron saint of all Masons—the book was distributed to the heads of the Rosicrosse-Masons and the Freemasons as *a secret book* to be kept under lock and key. And in the book was a key which enabled the Brethren "Who had been *taught to read*" to know the last words and wishes of the mighty Shakespeare, their Father and Founder.

That was Francis Bacon's last known literary labour and it was in this way that *he "Drowned his Book"*. How it was fished up from the depths is another story and can be read in *The Immortal Master.*[1]

From these many publications we thus get a little insight into the enormous energy and versatility of the Grand Master of our English language and

[1]by Alfred Dodd.

literature. True, he had a band of literary helpers of whom Ben Jonson and Dr Rawley were the heads, together with many other clever thinkers like George Herbert, the mystical poet, Thomas Hobbes of Malmesbury, author of *Leviathan*, who gained his first lesson in philosophy from the great Chancellor. When notions came into Bacon's mind Hobbes, ready with his tables, set them down. There was also Thomas Bushell, Tobie Matthew, Thomas Meautys—in fact the cleverest men of the age were attracted to Francis Bacon's side to become Knights of the Round Table.

Now, let the reader reflect upon this cardinal fact: if so many open works were produced in less than five years, when Francis Bacon's health was poor, his body becoming aged and his mind perturbed with financial anxieties, how many works could he have produced when in the full flush of youthful creative activity, afire with enthusiasm to produce his best for the good of humanity in God's name? The man, I repeat, who can believe that Francis Bacon, assisted by his scrivenry of "Good Pens" (his literary staff) produced nothing more than ten short *Essays* (1592) up to the age of forty-two (*i.e.* up to 1603 when *The Advancement of Learning* was published), is capable of believing anything—that the moon is made of green cheese and that Shaksper of Stratford walked to London with the MS. of *Venus and Adonis* in his pocket. Francis Bacon's intellectual activity in his middle sixties was not the sudden spurt of an outworn guttering candle. We have seen in detail that it was a characteristic feature of his life—the tremendous vitality of a God-inspired genius, a creator and producer from the time he could toddle, like the child prodigies of music and mathematics. Francis was not called "Baby Solomon" for nought. He was wise beyond his years as a child and, in some mysterious manner, he brought with him a wealth of ripe knowledge—his soul had somewhere else its setting and travelled from afar, not in entire forgetfulness and not in utter nakedness but trailing clouds of glory, knowledge divine.

And he knew it. He was conscious that he had been called by a high destiny to save civilization on educational and ethical lines and to point the way to yet greater discoveries for the benefit of physical man in the *New Atlantis*.

> No, Time! Thou shalt not boast that I do change:
> Thy Pyramids built up with newer might,
> To ME are nothing Novel . . . nothing STRANGE,
> *They are but Dressings of a Former Sight*;
> This I do vow and this shall ever be;
> *I will be True despite thy Scythe and Thee.*
>
> Sonnet cxxiii

In spite of almost insurmountable difficulties and dangers Francis Bacon had accomplished his life's high mission—the task he had set out to do in obedience to that inner urge that he had brought with him from spheres supernal. He had fought a good fight. He had finished the course. He had kept faith—with himself and his Creator. The time of his departure was at hand. He had no regrets in spite of the evil things of stain flung at him by the King, the Lords and the Commons. The majority of the assailants who had cried "Crucify him" and had bespattered him with mud had done so in ignorance of the full facts. They could be forgiven. The stains he bore were outward not inward, and none knew better than he that that which defileth a man proceedeth from within—an attitude of mind and soul. Time would wash away the stains and vindicate his name, his honour and the work he had performed. He knew that many of his actions would be misunderstood by men of later generations, his character misjudged and his labours discounted even by men who sought to judge him kindly. This was inevitable; for to get his plans into operation he had to work in secret and to trust that the stream of Time as it rushed towards Eternity would some day lay bare the hidden truth respecting his personality, his character, his ideals. Now, all was o'er. He had begun to tidy up his desk for the last time. Farewell, a long farewell to Pomp and Circumstance....

In 1625 Francis Bacon's fortunes were at a very low ebb. King James was dead and had done nothing to redeem his promises to make Francis Bacon financially independent. Even the pension to which he was entitled was in arrears again, and apparently—because his assets were largely not convertible into ready money—he was reduced to continuous borrowing. He had nothing to hope for financially from the new King Charles and his counsellor Buckingham. In January he writes to Buckingham "pressing him to be mindful of my misery", which meant his pecuniary difficulties—the straits he was in to find means to satisfy his creditors and provide for his inevitable expenses. In July he writes to the Favourite again that "I am loath to complain at finding fault with the Lord Treasurer", which indicates that Francis Bacon was still being kept on financial tenterhooks; and to the Lord Treasurer Lea he writes respecting the monies which are unjustifiably being withheld:

> I humbly intreat your Lordship to make me a better answer.... Your Lordship may do well to think of your *grave as I do of mine*; and to beware of hardness of heart. And as for fair words, it is a wind by which neither your Lordship nor any man else can sail long....

He is forced to play the part of an unfortunate suppliant to Sir Robert Pye for a small amount.

> Good Sir Robert Pye,
>
> *Let me intreat you to dispatch that warrant of a petty sum, that it may help to bear my charge of coming up to London....*

It seems to me very natural that Francis Bacon gradually became resolved to end continuous rebuffs and petty indignities, and to get away from the ingratitude of persons who were indifferent to his great services to the State or his own personal worth as one of Britain's worthiest sons. He was weary of playing the mendicant—a situation to which he had been driven through no fault of his own and which was simply the result of his own sacrifice to save others. It cannot be too often affirmed that Francis Bacon, though "pleading guilty under duress", never once admitted the receipt of a present secretly or personally; that his office staff on but two or three occasions had received in error—without his knowledge—any fee before the final conclusion of a case, and such errors he held were not acts of corruption on his part; and that he had never perverted justice for monies paid him secretly ("I had never bribe or reward in my eye when I pronounced sentence or order") for none were ever paid to him. The first open proofs of Francis Bacon's innocence are surely evidenced by the inscrutable working of Providence which struck down his chief assailants in various forms, by disgrace, ruin or death.

But Francis Bacon was sick of the struggle against penury, ill fame and ingratitude. His day of life was far spent. The sound of viols sobbing to a close must have echoed through the corridors of thought many times during those days—music that he had brought into being in the days of his youth:

> Sleepe after toyle, port after stormie seas,
> Ease after warre, death after life, does greatly please.
> (Spenser, *Faerie Queen*)

Every schoolboy knows the story told in their history books how Francis Bacon one snowy day on or about *Alls Fools Day*, 1 April 1626, drove with the King's Physician, Sir John Wedderburn, to Highgate and that at the foot of the Hill he stopped, bought a fowl, and stuffed it with snow with his own hands in order to ascertain whether bodies could be preserved by cold. During the procedure, we are told, he caught a chill, and instead of Dr. Wedderburn driving him back to Gray's Inn (whence he had come) or taking him to some warm house, the worthy doctor took him to an empty summer mansion on Highgate Hill, Arundel House, where there was only a caretaker; and there Francis Bacon was put into a bed which was damp and had only been "warmed by a Panne" (a very strange thing for a doctor to do) with the result that within a few days he died of pneumonia. Dr. Rawley, his chaplain, says that he died "in the early morning of the 9th April, *a day on which was COMMEMORATED the Resurrection of Our Saviour*".

That is the story and this is Francis Bacon's last letter:

To the Earle of Arundel and Surrey

My very good Lord,

I was likely to have had the fortune of Caius Plinius the Elder, who lost his life by trying an experiment about the burning of the mountain Vesuvius. For I was also desirous to try an experiment or two, touching *the conservation and induration of BODIES.*

As for the experiment itself it succeeded excellently well; but in the journey between London and Highgate, I was taken with such a fit of casting [sickness], as I knew not whether it were the stone, or some surfeit of cold, or indeed a touch of them all three. But when I came to your Lordship's house, I was not able to go back, and therefore was forced to take up my lodging here, where your housekeeper is very careful and diligent about me; which I assure myself your Lordship will not only pardon towards him, but think the better of him for it. For indeed your Lordship's house is happy to me; and I kiss your noble hands for the welcome which I am sure you give me to it.

I know how unfit it is for me to write to your lordship with any other hand than mine own; but in troth my fingers are so disjointed with this fit of sickness, that I cannot steadily hold a pen....

Here the letter ends abruptly. Whatever else was written has been suppressed by Sir Tobie Matthew, one of the Rosicrosse, on which Spedding remarks, "It is a great pity the editor did not think fit to print the whole." For some mysterious reason the letter was not printed until 1660 in *Matthew's*

Collection, captioned "*This was the last letter that he ever wrote.*" So Francis Bacon's last letter, like his first ones respecting his mysterious suit, the succession, betrays the same characteristics which he has himself described—*and the reason*—in his charge against Somerset for the murder of Overbury:

> You suppressed, as much as in you was, TESTIMONY: *You did Deface, and Destroy, and Clip, and Misdate all Writings that might give LIGHT*.... That is, *Fear of discovering SECRETS*. Secrets (I say) of a high and dangerous nature.... And like Princes Confederates they had their Cyphers and Jargons.[1]

We thus see that these very tricks of suppression to destroy direct evidence in order to preserve a SECRET were not only known to Francis Bacon but, in exactly the same way, were practised by him and his School (his "Confederates"); and the feature runs through all his letters and papers from youth to old age. There are not only deletions by his own hand but by those to whom he entrusted his papers. Spedding remarks upon it repeatedly throughout his seven volumes yet never once is he prompted to ask—*nor in his final summing up*—what is the reason for all this destroying, clipping, no-dating and misdating of papers? Why is evidence suppressed? What SECRETS have been hidden? And yet Somerset's charge—which Spedding must have read—is a direct pointer to the fact that there is a secret or a series of secrets waiting to be unearthed. Oh! If Spedding had but possessed the gift of literary insight—only a slight flair of the detective instinct—what a *LIFE OF FRANCIS BACON* could he have bequeathed to the world!

According to Tenison[2] Francis Bacon was buried in the north side of the chancel in St. Michael's Church at St. Albans. Sir Thomas Meautys, formerly one of his secretaries, afterwards erected a monument of white marble "representing his full body in a contemplative posture, sitting in his chair ... on which was an epitaph in Latin composed by the learned Sir Henry Wotton."

> The Light of the Sciences, the Law of eloquence, who after he had unfolded all the Mysteries of Natural and Civil Wisdom, obeyed the Decree of Nature.
> *Let the Companions be parted.*
> *Francis Bacon Died on Easter Sunday, 1626*

The above is the accepted view of the historian and biographer. At this length of time it matters little whether he actually died physically or whether he simply died to the world and fled into exile from a King and Court that he felt had used him so ill and might be tempted to use him even worse. But I should be failing in my duty as a biographer if I did not make it clear to my reader that many clever researchers are completely satisfied that the alleged death was not an actual but a symbolic one.

Manly Hall, the famous Theosophic and Masonic writer, USA, says that "in the sixty-sixth year of his [Francis Bacon's] life ... *he feigned death and passed over into Germany*, there to guide the destinies of his philosophic and political Fraternities for nearly twenty-five years after his 'death'."[3] Some personally written letters show that Manly Hall has made extensive researches

[1]Tenison, *Baconiana*, 1676 edn, pp. 31, 32, 33.
[2]*ibid.*, p. 257.
[3]*Lectures on Ancient Philosophies*, p. 407.

on the Continent and had found sufficient evidence to warrant the foregoing statement.

Parker Woodward, a solicitor used to weighing evidence, is equally convinced that death was shammed and that the funeral was a mock one. "The spoof began on or about All Fools Day and finished with a sham Resurrection."[1]

Elinor Von Le Coq, wife of the late Professor Von Le Coq, Berlin—with whom I exchanged many personal letters prior to the world war—told me she was quite satisfied that she had discovered evidence in certain archives that Francis Bacon had lived in Germany after 1626 and had stayed for a long time in the Andrea family.

Bertram Theobald, BA, a most careful investigator, held that the balance of evidence indicated that Francis Bacon fled to the Continent in 1626.

My own opinion—though I have no direct evidence to support it—is that in 1626 Francis Bacon made a carefully planned getaway. There are too many unexplained enigmas about his "death" to satisfy me that it is historically true.

What was Francis Bacon doing at Highgate with Dr. Wedderburn? His business there has never transpired. Why should he want to experiment with a fowl? He had already published his *experiments* (in his *History of Life and Death*) *on the preservation of bodies by cold.* Can anyone possibly think that Sir John Wedderburn, the King's Physician, would be such a fool as to allow a man suffering from a severe chill to be taken to a cold, empty house where there was only a caretaker—*a house that they knew was empty* because it was common knowledge that Arundel was then a prisoner in the Tower! Can one imagine a specialist like Wedderburn allowing a man full of sickness to be put "into a DAMP bed" that had only been "warmed by a panne"? Even a first-year medical student would never have allowed THAT.

Where were his friends Rawley, Meautys, Ben Jonson? The only person that we hear saw him in Highgate was Sir Julius Caesar. And even he left no account of his death and funeral.

He died on "Resurrection" Sunday, which seems indeed to be a mute signal that though he had died to the world he had risen again.

I believe that Parker Woodward is correct in his surmise that the experiment which succeeded (as he said in the Arundel letter) was "the induration of his own body by opium. As seemingly dead he was most probably shown to the caretaker, and possibly to others, by his friendly medical man and Sir Julius Caesar."

Woodward points out also that Francis Bacon knew the effects of opium on the body in effecting the "flight of the spirit". Francis had already written: "A grain [of opium] will tranquillize the nerves and by a few grains they may be so compressed as to be irrecoverable. *The Touched Spirit* may *Retreat* into its *Shell* for *a time* or for ever."[2]

Everything points to the fact, fragmentary though the information be, that *Francis Bacon planned to simulate death at Highgate House.* He took a dose of opium or some other narcotic and this was the reason why Dr. Wedderburn attended him to assist in the success of the experiment—to watch the effect of the drug.

[1]*Sir Francis Bacon*, p. 127.
[2]*History of Life and Death.*

Francis Bacon knew every inch of Arundel House through frequent visits. There in 1617 Lady Arundel gave a banquet in Francis Bacon's honour. The house commanded fine views over a wide area and anyone approaching could easily be detected. It was an ideal spot for such an experiment to be carried out quietly, unobserved and without interference from anyone. Arundel had been a ward of the Earl of Essex, Francis Bacon's brother.

When the supposed tomb at St. Michel's Church was opened some hundred years later nothing was found—neither coffin nor bones nor valuables. There is no account of his funeral and four contradictory accounts of where he actually died. I am quite convinced that his "death" was part of a long-premeditated design to escape because of Francis Bacon's last words in his Sonnet–Diary. The sonnet was written to the Brethren; and, to a careful reader of this double-meaning phraseology, it tells any Rosicrosse-Mason that he was about to remove himself from the stage of life.

The following personal friends report his death at four different houses: Dr. Fuller, historian; Dr. Sprat, first President of the Royal Society; Dr. Wallis, second President; and Dr. Rawley, Francis Bacon's chaplain. One says he died at the house of Lord Arundel; another at his friend's, Dr. Parry, in London; a third at his cousins', Sir Julius Caesar, at Muswell Hill; and a fourth at the house of his physician Dr. Winterbourne.

> You shall hear the surly sullen bell
> Give warning to the World that I AM FLED
> From this vile World with vilest Worms . . . TO DWELL.

In the Latin elegies (*Manes Verulamiani*) on Francis Bacon's death published by Dr. Rawley, some of the writers seem to have been aware that he was still alive. Henry Oakley of Trinity College wrote: "He is GONE. He is GONE, The *Word* Suffices. *That he is dead we say not.*" And in the 1671 *Resuscitatio* Molloy stated that "Bacon made *a holy and humble retreat* into the cool shades of rest, where he remained triumphant above fate and fortune *till heaven was pleased* to summon him to a more triumphant rest."

There is in manuscript an admirable piece of research work by the late Bertram G. Theobald, BA, author of *Francis Bacon Concealed and Revealed*, on this question, much too good to be kept in hiding. These are his conclusions which indicate a date of death subsequent to 1626.

1. Unaccountable paucity of information *at the time* as to his last illness and the doctors or other persons attending him. No details published until *many years afterwards*.
2. Conflicting evidence as to the house at which he died. No details of this until many years afterwards.
3. Total absence of any mention of a funeral.
4. No item for funeral expenses in the accounts of the administrators of the Estate.
5. No record of burial in the registers at St. Michael's Church.
6. The body is not there now if it ever was.
7. Extremely few personal allusions to the death *at the time*. Only one letter discoverd besides that of Meautys.
8. Curt, unemotional statement by his devoted secretary Meautys.

9. Nothing from Rawley except a very brief introduction to the *Manes* where Rawley speaks of "his loss". Several eulogists make remarks which might be interpreted as hints that Bacon had not died.
10. Wotton does *not* say that the body lies beneath the monument. His Latin epitaph mentions no date of birth or death, and used ambiguous phrases in referring to the deceased.
11. Tenison's English translation makes the ambiguity more pronounced.
12. The last WILL had the effect of giving his creditors a much larger sum than they could have obtained in the ordinary course of events. It also places Meautys in the position of being a considerable creditor; and he became Administrator.
13. Letter of 11 October 1631 from Meautys shows almost conclusive evidence of being addressed to Bacon.
14. *Histoire Naturelle*, 1631, displays almost unaccountable familiarity with Bacon's private affairs. In alluding to his decease the writer employs absurdly roundabout phraseology.
15. Correspondence in 1625 with the ex-Queen of Bohemia, then resident in Holland, might indicate an offer of help.
16. Prefatory matter in the *Repertorie of Records*, 1631, suggests that Thomas Powell knew that Bacon was alive.
17. In *Resuscitatio*, 1671, Charles Molloy refers to Bacon having made a "Holy Retreat" to the cool shades of rest.

This is about as far as modern research carries the problem.

It is a further indication that Francis Bacon was the Mystery Man *in excelsis*, his exit from the stage of life being quite as baffling as his entrance.

His Will was somewhat enigmatical. One sentence in it was ignored by Spedding yet it should have given him food for thought.

> Legacies to my friends: I give unto the Right Honourable my Worthy Friend, the Marquis Fiatt, Late Lord Ambassador of France, my Books of Orisons or Psalms *curiously rhymed*.

Edwin Bormans writes:

> The meaning of these words is evident. Bacon thus acknowledges ... to have written *whole books of rhymed, curiously rhymed* verses. The seven psalms published in the same year [as the Will] dedicated to his friend George Herbert, excludes the possibility of these being the ones referred to.... Those rhymed books, probably manuscripts, written by Bacon's own hand ... wandered to France after Bacon's death. What became of them or where they are now nobody knows. Fiatt was one of Bacon's literary intimates.[1]

We thus have this startling fact that, at the supposed end of his life, *Francis Bacon claimed publicly that he was a poet* ... many books of *rhymed verse*. It is as startling as the fact that in the last year of King James's reign *he revealed himself as a humorist* by publishing a collection of jokes, "sparkling with wit and humour", entitled *Apophthegms New and Old*, described by Lord Macaulay as the finest jest book in the world. Hitherto he had only been known publicly

[1]*Francis Bacon's Cryptic Rhymes*, p. 3.

as a statesman and a philosopher of Latin and English books on profound subjects. "Now, *with one foot in Heaven*" (words from his last Will) he claims to be a humorist and a poet: and Spedding, followed by a long line of biographers ending in Mary Sturt and Charles Williams, sees nothing worth comment and nothing to provoke inquiry, though, significantly enough, *this claim is supported by the cream of contemporary literary men and scholars.*

Hardly had he "died" when his chaplain and literary amanuensis, Dr. William Rawley, published the *Manes Verulamiani* collection of thirty-two Latin elegies "written by various scolars and poets", who, though they praise him as a statesman, lawyer, philosopher, naturalist and historian, all save two or three *unite in praising him chiefly as a POET*—AS THE GREATEST POET OF THE ENGLISH CHOIR OF MUSES, as the man who taught the progress of the Pegasean Arts, as the chief Favourite of the Tragic Muse Melpomene.

Dr. Rawley says in the preface:

> These insignia of Love and Grief indicate their great Sorrow at his loss. Nay, verily, with no stinted hand, *have the Muses bestowed on him this token*: many of the best verses remain with me....
>
> Let it suffice to lay these Foundations in the name of the present age, every age will enlarge and adorn this Edifice; but *to what Age is given to set the finishing hand, is manifest only to God and to the Fates.*

In Rawley's last sentence there beats the same confident note that rings throughout Francis Bacon's writings and especially in his Will—"*For my Name and memory I leave it to ... Foreign Nations ... and the Next Ages; and to my own Countrymen after some time be past.*" Why should he write thus audaciously, challenging Time as it were, unless he was certain that, when posterity knew what he had done, his name would be greatly honoured, which means clearly that it was his SECRET LABOURS on which he counted to perpetuate his name and memory—the inauguration of an Ideal Brotherhood, the creation of the Shakespeare plays, the establishment of a flexible English language to take the place of Latin, and often unintelligible local dialects. These were the things—the secret things—by which he knew he would out-brave Time ... distinct and apart from his open labours as a statesman, a lawyer, a philosopher and a scientific experimentalist. Dr. Rawley knew his secret works and what they were; and so did the writers of the *Manes Verulamiani* (*Shades of Verulam*). It was his secret labours which they knew would one day crown his brows with the laurel wreaths of Immortality in the Temple of Apollo.

It is doubtful whether five per cent of English scholars today who specialize in Elizabethan literature have ever read these elegies either in Latin or an English translation. Spedding, his famous biographer, took no notice of them though they were pregnant with ripe thought, literally bursting as a body of verse with the truth that Francis Bacon was a transcendent poet and a Freemason, and that he was also regarded as a martyr who sacrificed himself for his King, and was connected with the Tudor Rose.

Here are a few of the thoughts from the *Manes*. One writer calls him, "Thou good Martyr, no sad fate has ever been sadder when thou fellest beneath the dire cloak of another." The Rector of King's College says, "He wrote stories of Love more refined which still do interpret Great Bacon's

Muse with a vigour choicer by far than the Nine Muses fabled in Story." (The Rector knew that "Great Bacon's Muse" was the "Tenth Muse" Pallas-Athena, the Spear Shaker and that he was Shake-Speare, who did in very Truth write "Love Stories".) (What "Love Stories" did Francis Bacon ever write openly?)

"To his magical fingers rang out the Lyre Strings; Learning, too, thrilled at his touch. Oh, thou barren Tribunal [the House of Lords that sentenced him] that robbed the Famed of its Greatness" is the testimony of another writer.

William Boswell in a long poem writes: "None who survive him can marry so sweetly Themis the Goddess of Law to Pallas the Goddess of Wisdom. . . . Mourn then ye Muses." (Here we get it clearly without equivocation that he was associated with Pallas. And in the Shakespeare plays we find Law both ancient and modern [Themis] used in the most subtle ways from a mind saturated with legal terms—used truthfully by Pallas the Shaker of the Speare of Wisdom.)

R.C. of Trinity College writes: "Thou were born of Minerva! [Another name for Pallas.] Muses now pour forth your waters in loud lamentations perennial! Thou the nerve centre of Genius and the Jewel most precious of Letters CONCEALED." (This last phrase proves conclusively that Francis Bacon was known to be a concealed poet.)

Robert Ashley of the Middle Temple says: "*Part of thy Works truly lie buried*" (*e.g.* the Rituals and the Shakespeare plays).

Another writer has a reference to the Rose of Tudor: "In thy page Noble Bacon, thy two Roses unite" (which seems to be an enigmatical reference to himself and his brother Robert Earl of Essex).

Francis Bacon is variously call "The Master of Fable", "the Noble Day Star of the Muses", "the Tenth Muse", "The Learned Apollo", "the Leader of the Great Band of Muses", "Phoebus' Own Chorister", and phrases to denote Francis Bacon's connection with poesy in a highly special sense.

"Thou madest the Muses Immortal," says one writer, while Thomas Randolph of Trinity College calls Bacon "the King of the Muses".

These few extracts convey quite an inadequate insight into these wonderful tributes that were paid to Francis Bacon on his "decease". Here we possess direct contemporary evidence that not only was Francis Bacon a poet but the greatest poet of all time; and the quoted references, though vague, contain specific hints that Francis Bacon had written "Tales" under the inspiration of Pallas, the Speare-Shaker, thus pointedly associating him with "Shakespeare".

What stronger testimony does scholarship require? Especially when conjoined to his own asseverations: that he was a "concealed Poet", that portions of his time he gave to "invention", and all the other facts noted in the course of his work!

But his critics of today are just as afraid of facing this outstanding literary issue as were those of yesterday. To their lasting discredit these invaluable contemporary testimonies are suppressed so that students and even well-read literary men *know nothing of them* and the significance *of their witness*. Had these tributes been written to "Will Shaksper of Stratford", the facts would have been drummed into us from sixpenny biographies to broadcasts on the BBC.

The authorities, it is obvious, *do not want the truth to be inquired into or to be proclaimed.*

I echo the words of a famous man who wrote,

> I am "a sort of haunted" by the conviction that the divine William of Stratford is the biggest and most successful fraud ever practised on a patient world. The more I turn him round the more he so affects me.[1]

In such an atmosphere of sham and makebelieve it forces a lover of truth to cry aloud, "*Is there not ONE university brave and bold enough to splinter a Lance against the Dragon of Ignorance by instituting an impartial inquiry into the truth of the matter*?" How about Cambridge, Bacon's own university and his own college, Trinity?

Another important and interesting mystery, as yet unsolved, respecting Francis Bacon's relationship with his wife Alice is also brought into the limelight by one of the items in his Will. Says Spedding:

> His wife, with whom he had lived for twenty years without any reproach that we know of on either side, *gave him some grave offence. The nature of it is not known*; for he never specified it himself, and Dr. Rawley in his biography makes no mention of any domestic difference, but speaks of their married life in terms which almost exclude the supposition of any. But that she had in some way incurred his serious displeasure *is a fact not to be disputed*, being recorded by himself in his Will, as a reason for revoking dispositions previously made in her favour.

Unfortunately, there is no evidence of the nature of the grievance. As a matter of fact, there is no correspondence extant between them. Yet many letters must have passed. Anything that would have given us the slightest inkling of their private, social and domestic life has been as carefully and systematically buried as the manuscripts of the Shakespeare plays. Never once does Francis Bacon admit the Peeping Toms of posterity to peer into the privacies of his home life. We simply are not permitted to sit by his hearth and fireside. All clues are destroyed that would tell us anything. And the close personal friends who must have visited his home many times were obviously warned or were tacitly given to understand not to leave any written records behind them as to what transpired in the domestic circle at Gorhambury or York House; for never a letter or a diary note has been left by any of Francis Bacon's intimates that would betray anything respecting the home of mystery. But what we know definitely is this: that, during the twenty years of marriage, the scandalmongers of the times found nothing to chatter about in their letters or diaries. We can therefore safely assume that the conduct of Bacon and his wife fully satisfied convention and the gossips.

From the first day of their marriage there would be actually little time for much domestic life, and still less when Francis Bacon began to rise in office. He would be busy all day with matters of State and public affairs and his relaxation consisted in turning to his secret activities in the evening. The majority of his evenings would be spent with his "Good Pens", in his study or else in Masonic and Rosicrucian engagements. During their entire marriage they could never have spent much time together in private.

[1]Henry James, *Letters*.

At the height of her social eminence Lady Bacon had to manage at least three mansions—Gorhambury, Verulam House and York House, London. It was at York House that the famous birthday party was held in 1620 which was apparently confined to members of the Craft. One can imagine that Lady Alice would have sufficient to do in supervising all the varied domestic affairs of the lower servants and housekeepers and in manipulating the daily requirements of such large estabishments.

We are now in a much better position to examine "*the grave offence*" by which the Lady Alice had "*incurred his serious displeasure*" and which has been judged from the worst point of view by the writers following Spedding.

In the body of the Will written some years previously, when he was made Viscount St. Alban, though the actual date is unknown, one of his testaments runs: "*I give grant and confirm to my loving wife*", and then follows a recital of lands, monies, plate, jewels, caroches and coach mares "to maintain the estate of a Viscountess" and to show "my Love and Liberality towards her". But a codicil added in 1625 nullified these gifts: "Whatsoever I have given, granted, conferred or appointed to my wife in the former part of this my Will, I do now for JUST AND GREAT CAUSES, utterly revoke and make void, and leave her to her right only."

That is *all* we learn. Any letters or documents that would have thrown light on this codicil have been destroyed. There is no evidence that implicates Lady Alice in any neglect or misconduct.

There is, however, one fact which seems to give colour to the suggestion that she had not been all she ought to have been as a wife: that within a few days (20 April 1626) of becoming a widow Lady Alice married a Mr. John Underhill who was a "Gentleman in Waiting" at York House and of good repute and of a good family, at the Church of St. Martin-in-the-Fields, London. This hasty marriage coupled with the drastic terms of the codicil have led to the conclusion that Francis Bacon had discovered his wife had been carrying on a clandestine affair with a lover whom she married as soon as possible.

This is the usual biographical verdict, and it might be mine if Francis Bacon and his lady were an average couple and it was an ordinary marriage; such a codicil and such a hasty marriage of the widow would require a lot of explanation. But I cannot accept the explanation that lies on the surface where Francis Bacon is concerned. And I also hesitate to think the worst of Lady Alice.

I cannot forget that she must have stood by his side when he was all but overthrown in 1617, when James and Buckingham returned from Scotland; and again in 1621 when the plotters hurled her husband from power into the very dust and dregs of things. His troubles naturally visited themselves on her. "Her grand friends looked askance at her. She was shut out of the King's Court. All this happened to the unfortunate woman because she was no longer 'A Grand Lady'." She must have suffered many indignities, slights and snubs, yet I cannot conceive, in spite of all the financial anxieties imposed upon her, that she failed to tend and succour her husband by every means in her power for he wrote the King of this effect: "My wife has done nothing wrong yet is she made to suffer." We happen to know that she was a true helpmeet because, when Francis Bacon, after repeated efforts, failed to obtain monies that were due to him, Lady Alice sought an interview with the Favourite's wife and laid before her the ills they were suffering. Not only so but she also sought out Buckingham to whom she pleaded her husband's cause in person, "for the restoration of some of Bacon's salary and pension", according to a letter from Sir Thomas Meautys. Apparently the interviews had no effect but it shows that Lady Alice was staunch, loyal and true long after the fall.

They had no issue because the marriage was never consummated.

Under these circumstances, even if Lady Alice had carried on a flirtation with Underhill, I do not see any moral culpability on her part; and Francis Bacon's only legitimate grievance would have been that he did not approve of Underhill as a man friend. After all there could be nothing seriously wrong in her desire—*if she had any*—to meet persons of the opposite sex nearer her own age. Francis Bacon's displeasure may have been incurred because he thought he would not like Underhill to have his possessions on his decease.

That is one explanation which, in my opinion, does not conflict at all in any immoral violation with marital vows made by Lady Alice.

But I do not think this is the true explanation why Francis Bacon disinherited his wife.

When Francis Bacon made his Will shortly after becoming Viscount St. Alban, he was in a splendid financial position. He had a large margin of assets and a fine income. When he added the "drastic codicil" he still thought he had a good margin of assets, after his creditors were paid, if everything were liquidated, quite apart from his wife's estate and her marriage settlements. There was another clause in the codicil which had the effect of putting in his friend Sir Thomas Meautys to administer the estate; and there can be no doubt that the understanding was that Meautys, after the winding-up, would remit the balance to him when he had got to the Continent after his feigned death. As it happened, the estate was so involved that it took a long time to wind up and as the assets were badly sold there was not sufficient to meet liabilities. There was a loss. So Francis Bacon got nothing at all. But I have no doubt that this was the scheme: a feigned death to enable him to clear out, to cut himself off from further financial anxieties, and to provide him eventually with a balance of ready money to continue his idealistic aims.

His plan really did not hurt Lady Alice at all. The codicil did not leave her penniless as is the usual inference. Her marriage portion and gifts actually left her a wealthy woman. She had £1000 a year, a large quantity of goods and chattels, and she lived rent free at Gorhambury. Some of her estate, by the way, was claimed by creditors but with little success.

This, then, is probably what happened. We have seen that the balance of evidence indicates that Lord St. Alban did not "DIE" on Easter Sunday and that he made a planned escape to the Continent. Now he could feign death and escape without taking friends into his confidence, his Masonic and Rosicrucian friends. There is every reason to believe that Lady Alice was a party to his secrets. Indeed, I should imagine she would be the first to be acquainted with what was running in his mind and became an active participant in the plan and the subsequent scheme to bluff all inquirers. Her "marriage" would be a "sort of proof" that he was verifiably dead, though no one close to him was near when he "died". His wife's estate was protected by confirmation of the marriage settlements, etc., specifically mentioned in the codicil.

Francis Bacon knew that it was a ticklish thing to feign death, so, to add to its apparent reality and to close people's mouths to its suddenness, his wife arranged to get married immediately after the "funeral" to one of his own staff. It would be a seven days' wonder and divert attention from the strangeness of Lord St. Alban's death.

The codicil was added to the Will "*for Just and GREAT CAUSES*". Those "Causes" were the ideals and the plans he had so much at heart; the GREAT BASES he had tried to lay for eternity. The building of the edifices required money for the work to be prosecuted; and Francis Bacon tried to obtain it secretly from the residue of his estate from his friend Meautys, Trustee. We have no right to assume that '*the Just and Great CAUSES*' were intended as a reflection on Lady Alice. He uses a plural noun which denotes his real meaning. The things he laboured for were indeed "Great Causes", nothing greater in the world. Had he meant to indicate infidelity he would have used a singular noun "a great Cause". "Causes" is a quite inappropriate term; but no one knew better than Francis Bacon how to use a double-meaning word so as to send the superficialists on the wrong track.

While, as we have seen, neither servants nor friends ever left a scrap of evidence to indicate the personal relationship that subsisted between Francis and Alice Bacon in the home, there is nevertheless sufficient record to show that the great Chancellor's home had a very hospitable glow, that he entertained largely, that he attracted to himself the choicest spirits of the times to his social board at York House and "The Temple", Gorhambury, poets, thinkers, men of science and men of the world.

Dr Rawley:

> His meals were refections of the ear as well as of the stomach . . . wherein a man might be refreshed in his mind and understanding no less than in his body . . . in which conversations he was no dashing man as some men are, but ever a countenancer and fosterer of other men's parts. Neither was he one that would appropriate the speech wholly to himself, or delight to outvie others. . . .
>
> And for himself, he contemned no man's observations, but would light his Torch at every man's Candle.
>
> His opinions and assertions were for the most part binding, and not contradicted by any; rather like Oracles than Discourse; which may be imputed to the well-weighing of his sentence by the Scales of Truth and Reason, or else to the Reverence and Estimation in which he was commonly held.[1]

Indeed, the testimony of his friends not only testifies to his greatness but to his VIRTUE and his humbleness. This was the drawing power which attracted to his home circle men like Ben Jonson, Poet Laureate; Davies the Chief Justice of Ireland, author of *Nosce Teipsum*; Sir Fulke Greville, Lord Brooke, author of *Treatise on Wars*; Sir H. Wotton, scholar, poet, traveller, diplomatist; Sir T. Bodley, ambassador and re-founder of the great library of the Duke of Gloucester at Oxford; Launcelot Andrewes, the "Homer of the Pulpit", the founder of the Society of Archaeologists, the head of the translators of the James Authorized Edition of the Bible, and Francis Bacon's

[1] *Resuscitatio*, 1657.

lifelong friend; John Selden, the famous diarist and antiquarian; Sir Tobie Matthew, the translator of Augustine, one of his earliest friends; and many others. These men were drawn to him in a special sense because they were aware of Francis Bacon's secret literary aims to elevate England through education and ethics and they were active participants in his great scheme of the bonding together of men of different religious opinions around a social board of mystical symbolism, dating from time immemorial, into one worldwide Brotherhood.

Francis Bacon seems to have been more or less indifferent to the verdict of his own day or immediate generation. He was not even unduly depressed by the disgrace or misfortune which was irrecoverable in his own lifetime. So, whether he "died" lonely and neglected or fled for sanctuary to an alien shore, he nevertheless "passed" in the sure and confident and certain hope that one day the sun would rise on a world that understood him, his real character, and what he had accomplished for posterity.

He left in the constant and almost UNACCOUNTABLE FAITH that his triumphs of labour and his entire life would be understood and greatly HONOURED BY POSTERITY.

The Great Instauration was not a mere book of six parts. It was a "work", *a "labour" to be accomplished* of which the mere writing of books was but a preliminary—the easiest part. And this gigantic task he accomplished before his "passing" in 1626. The circumstances of the times—no less than his own personal identity as a Tudor prince—compelled him to maintain a concealed role in order to get his revolutionary ideas established and to perpetuate them, ideas that were in conflict with authority, secular and sacred, ideas respecting the ultimate aim of science, philosophy, religion, ethics, education, government, etc.

In the *Précis* to the "Six Parts" he naturally could not declare himself openly or the goal to which he was really travelling—the mental and spiritual education of man. *His insistence that all scientific experimentation should be for the benefit of man and should be productive of "fruit" was but the beginning of Francis Bacon's dream.*

"*I go the same way as the Ancients,*" said Francis Bacon, "*but I have something better to offer* than the Morality Dramas of the Greeks and the Mystery Ceremonials of the Egyptians." So he gave the world the morality tales of a "Shakespeare" and the "Thirty-Three" Rituals of the Free and Acepted.

Here is the summing up of Francis Bacon's finest biographer, Hepworth Dixon:

> The obligations of the world to Francis Bacon are of a kind that cannot be overlooked. Every man who rides in a train, who sends a telegram, who follows a steam plough, who sits in an easy chair, who crosses the Channel or the Atlantic, who eats a good dinner, who enjoys a beautiful garden, or undergoes a painless surgical operation, OWES HIM SOMETHING.
>
> To him the patriot, the statesman, the law reformer, the scientific jurist, the historian, the collector of anecdote, the lover of good wit, of humorous wisdom and of noble writing, also OWES HIM SOMETHING.
>
> It is hard, indeed, to say which man amongst us is not the easier in circumstances, the brighter in intellect, the purer in morals, the worthier in conduct, through the Teachings and the Sufferings of Francis Bacon. The principles of his philosophy

are of universal application ... the true method of observing Nature is as easy in Rio and Pekin as in Paris or London; while the results of an Inductive Method of Pursuing Truth are not more precious in the Palace, the workshop, on the farm and in the mine.[1]

This the fine tribute of Henry Hallam, the great historian, written coldly and judicially:

He was the wisest, greatest of mankind...

If we compare what may be found in the sixth, seventh, and eighth Books of the *De Augmentis*, in the *Essays*, the *History of Henry VII* and the various short treatises contained in his works on moral and political wisdom and on human nature, with the rhetoric, ethics and politics of Aristotle, or with the historians most celebrated for their deep insight into civil society and human character—with Thucydides, Tacitus, Phillippe de Comines, Machiavel, Davila, Hume—we shall, I think, find that one man may almost be compared with ALL OF THESE TOGETHER, Francis Bacon.

These eulogies from two different types of minds place Francis Bacon as the greatest benefactor and thinker ever vouchsafed to the human race, as the greatest and wisest genius of all her sons. *They are based solely on his public achievements and his open works published over his own name.* But what would Hallam and Dixon have written had they known, *as I know*, and many other students, that Francis Bacon was the "Author" of the Shakespeare plays, the Immortal Bard himself, the eternal Shakespeare, and that he was the Creator and Grand Master of a broad-based pyramid of ethics, directly responsible for the founding of the Royal Society, the *organization* and planting of Freemasonry with its Lodges interlinked through provinces to Grand Lodges as well as establishing higher degrees—a labour which cannot be appreciated by anyone outside the Order—while at the same time he was the secret mainspring of the English Renaissance which he established?

But Hallam and Dixon do not stand alone in their tributes to the Great Master. Their testimony could be supported by some of the brightest intellects of the ages:

Pope: Lord Bacon was the greatest genius that England, or perhaps any other country ever produced.

Hume: The great glory of literature in this island, during the reign of James, was my Lord Bacon.

George Sandys (1578–1640): The Crown of all modern Authors.

Edmund Burke: Genius the most profound, of literature the most extensive, of discovery the most penetrating, of observation of human life the most distinguished and refined.

Addison: He possessed all those extraordinary talents which were divided amongst the greatest authors of antiquity.

Professor Fowler: No other author can be compared with him, unless it be Shakespeare.

Nichol: Bacon's impressive oratory was directed to the reason of the few rather than the passions of the many. He believed not only that Knowledge was entitled to govern Ignorance, but that Knowledge was, for the most part, to be found in the higher ranks of society. A Philanthropist to the core in desiring to benefit. ... *His Loyalty to the Crown was quite as much a matter of sentiment and conviction* as interest.

[1]*Story of Francis Bacon*, pp. 483–4.

Macaulay: He was most desirous to obtain a provision which might enable him to devote himself to literature and politics.... His wishes were moderate.... *He loved to consider religion as the bond of CHARITY*, the curb of evil passions, the consolation of the wretched, the support of the timid, the hope of the dying.

With great minuteness of observation, *he had an amplitude of comprehension* such as has never yet been vouchsafed to any human being ... the largeness of his mind was all his own.

The poetic faculty was powerful in Bacon's mind ... his gigantic scheme of philosophical reform is said to have been planned before he was fifteen. He observed as vigilantly, meditated as deeply and judged as temperately... as *at the close of his long career*....

In wit ... *he never had an equal*, not even Cowley, not even that author of Hudibras.... We marvel at him as clowns on a fair-day marvel at a juggler.... He possessed this faculty ... to a morbid degree.

Abbott: He must have been most of all *a stranger amid the alien servility* imposed upon him by the Court of James I.... He was altogether *too vast and grand for an easy flatterer*. The qualities for which he gave himself credit [for carrying out his designs] were patience and faith and love of Truth, carrying with it confidence in the power of Truth.... He attached little importance to himself *except as an instrument for their accomplishment*. In Bacon's last Philosophical efforts we see him *still pressing forward* on his career of imaginary conquest, leaving behind him half-conquered or unconquered regions for others to occupy.

Dean Church: Bacon's horizon was not a narrow one. He believed in God and immortality and the Christian Creed and Hope. To him the Restoration of the Reign of Man was a noble enterprise, because man was so great and belonged to so great an order of things.... The desire to be a great benefactor, the spirit of sympathy and pity for mankind reign through this work ... pity for ignorance which might be dispelled, pity for pain and misery which might be relieved.... In temper, *in honesty*, in labour, in humility, in reverence, *he was the most perfect example* that the world has yet seen ... the duty and service of helping his Brethren to know as they had never yet learned to know.[1]

Begley: He kept Theology in the background but he was a religious man in the best sense ... a true lover of his country, his countrymen and of the human race.... Bacon had the best interests of mankind at heart ... many great and good men whose friendships he obtained and kept ... the effulgent sphere of his intellectual glory ... nothing could efface the deep-seated natural goodness of the man, his philanthropic love and pity for our mortal race and the devotion of his great natural powers to the general good.[2]

John Evelyn: A good man and a great man.

Peter Boener (*Francis Bacon's apothecary*): *A memorable example* to all of virtue, kindness, peaceableness, and patience.

Francis Osborne: He struck all men with an awful reverence.

Dr William Rawley (*his chaplain*): There is a commemoration due as well to his *Abilities and VIRTUES*.... He was free from Malice, which, he said, he never bred nor fed.

Sir Tobie Matthew (*his friend*): I never saw in him any trace of a vindictive mind ... never heard him utter a word to any man's disadvantage from personal feeling. *It is not his Greatness that I admire but his VIRTUE*.... His whole LIFE AND CHARACTER have enthralled and enchained my Heart.... A man most sweet in his conversation and ways.... A friend unalterable to his friends.

Aubrey (*a contemporary, from MS. notes*): All who were GREAT and GOOD loved and Honoured him.

[1] *Life*.
[2] *Nova Resuscitatio*, Vol.II.

T. Fuller (*a contemporary*): His Lordship did always impartial justice.
Pierre Amboise (*1631, his first biographer*): Among so many VIRTUES that made this man commendable, PRUDENCE as THE FIRST OF ALL MORAL VIRTUES [*it is the first in Freemasonry*] was that which shone in him most brightly. He was AN UPRIGHT JUDGE and by THE EXAMPLE OF HIS LIFE corrected Vice and Bad living. . . . *The Honest Manner in which he lived* was the sole cause of his poverty.

Judged from an earthly point of view the story ends "dismally and drearily" enough, for was he not overthrown by a tempest, crushed and ruined? But we who have threaded the labyrinth of Francis Bacon's life through these pages know that he left to posterity an unspotted name despite the slings and arrows of outrageous Fortune, and that in his very fall he rose to heights sublime—a name that is destined to be revered the more his gigantic labours are weighed and understood by a yet uninstructed world. From the dead heart of the Lion of Literature has been born strength and sweetness and FRUIT for the healing of the nations: for he not only wrote his views but he *lived* them—and he got other men to live them, and to perpetuate them; and though historians and biographers know it not *Francis Bacon's NEW PHILOSOPHY is firmly rooted and established all over the world in a variety of ethical treatises and ceremonials which no one but Francis Bacon could have created.* This was the crown of all his effort—the crowning glory to which *all the rest of his labours were "Subservient and Ministrant".*

He writes little about himself, but we gain an insight into his character and disposition from his correspondence, which can be checked from the accounts of his associates. "He was a sensitive man who felt acutely both kindness and unkindness", of an affable temperament, full of humour, and one who could never pass the chance of making a jest. He was an economist with his time, and his chaplain tells us that he would ever interlace a moderate relaxation of his mind with his studies—such as walking, taking the air abroad in his coach, exercising on horseback, playing at bowls or "some other befitting recreation; and yet he would lose no time; inasmuch as upon his first and immediate return he would fall to reading again, and so suffer no moment of time to slip from him without some present improvement." It appears that he had a very delicate constitution and was highly strung. He watched his diet and ate sparingly. He says that all his life he was a "pudderer in medicine" for he suffered on and off with gout. He had a weekly dose of rhubard infused into mixed wine and beer and a morning draught of nitre in thin warm broth.

He was not a self-assertive man and never took any credit to himself for any extraordinary ability. He thought he had struck the right path by accident, and that his merit lay in endeavouring to keep it and walk in it. The qualities for which he gave himself credit were only patience and faith and love of Truth, carrying with it confidence in the power of Truth.

He was tenacious of purpose; as a mere boy he conceived the idea of doing something great not only for the age in which he lived but for posterity; and we have seen how he clung to that idea, moved by the spirit of Philanthropia, until a clear plan emerged which he finally named *The Great Instauration*, towards the filfilment of which he was working all his life from the moment he wrote *The Most Masculine Birth of Time*, his plan being nothing more or less than the revivifying of the physical, mental and spiritual understanding of the entire human race. Before he passed he had the right to say in one of his sonnets, with proud humility, for his most laborious efforts were done in secret, "*I have laid Great Bases for Eternity*." That was no idle boast. They were laid in spite of dangers and difficulties. He allowed nothing to deter him, neither tribulation, disdain, nor prison. And the reader of this book is now in a position to judge the evidence on which Francis Bacon based such a challenging and significant statement.

Whether Francis Bacon "passed" over to the Continent to find a sanctuary with the ex-Queen of Bohemia, then in Holland, and other Continental friends, or whether he "passed" through the Gates of Death in 1626, is, perhaps, as I have said, of little moment at this length of time. If he did go abroad and was buried secretely by the Rosicrucians as some well-informed persons assert, we can say that in such an event there surely is "some corner of a Foreign Field that is forever England"—a very special corner in which lies concealed "the Richest Dust" in the world.

A dust whom England bore, shaped, made aware,
Gave, once, her flowers to love, her ways to roam,
A body of England's, breathing English air,
Washed by the rivers, blest by suns of home.

And think, this heart, all evil shed away,
A PULSE in the Eternal Mind, no less
Gives SOMEWHERE back the THOUGHTS by England given ...

"Gives Somewhere back the thoughts" wrote Rupert Brooke! I wonder! I wonder! *Can that be TRUE?* It may be fancy but I seem to hear ...

... I've reaped my Mind
Of all its Fruits, the tares as well as Grain!
Think not half-empty hands have toiled in vain
A meagre Harvest ... scattered to the Wind!
Think not that Destiny hath dealt unkind
With Heart-Emotions, surging Thoughts of Brain
And that my Sheaves are rotting in the Rain,
Washed by the pitiless years I've left behind.

Think, rather, this! That I on other Fields
Have joined the Happy Reapers who are free
To garner all the Wealth that Summer yields ...
Thoughts beauteous with the Fire of Holy Truth ...
And, unafraid of Winter, *Think of ME*
Crowned with the Sunshine of Immortal Youth.

This life might have been written much better from a purely literary point of view had I written an imaginative panegyric spun from wishful thinking. But this would not have satisfied the highest canons of Truth. I have pinned myself down to bare facts—facts which will stand the most searching inquiry and the deductions from those facts will be found logically and properly drawn. "*Paint me truthfully*," said Cromwell. "*Paint me with the wart on my nose or not at all*." And this is what I have done. It is a truthful portrait, the result of much research.

This much is certain: Francis Bacon's thoughts have passed into our thoughts whether we know it or not; and his life into our lives whether we like it or not. Never a day but the press quotes his sayings. His phrases are on one's lips continually in the Secret Lodge, on the public stage, in the books we read, the language we use, in philosophic speculation and scientific discovery.

He drew the curtain across the tyranny and squalor, the wickedness and the ignorance of the feudal era. And then, like a veritable St. George with shining spear, he led the way to the New Age of Modernism—secular knowledge for ALL, ethical enlightenment among men and Universal Brotherhood based on the truth that God hath made of one blood all the nations of the earth. *This was his "Province"—"The Province of ALL KNOWLEDGE"*, over which he aspired to rule in his youthful, idealistic days, and over which he now reigns as its Sovereign Lord. As Prophet, Priest and King he stands a sublime figure against the age in which he lived—from which we can still hear his clarion call echoing down the corridors of Time—"Light! More Light! God's First Creature ... *LIGHT*!"

When we consider the sweep of his boyish dream, the steady progress he made in the furtherance of his vast plans undaunted by many crushing disasters and the fact that he accomplished all his aims, now spreading and speeding onwards to the last syllable of recorded time, we can reverently and truthfully say that of all the sons of men none has been greater than the soul that is known by the name of "Francis Bacon".

PROEM

OH Divine Master! Mighty Creator who didst work in secret to outpour on the Stage of Life, in sublime imitation of the craftsmanship of the Ineffable One, a Cavalcade of Characters the most diverse—Kings and Queens, wits and clowns, virtuous loveliness and ugly wantonness—Thou are not as other men. On Thee before thy birth, the Most High breathed into thy Soul a fuller measure of the Creative Fiat than is possible for an ordinary mortal to absorb: for thou wert an Instrument properly prepared for thy Task by many incarnations of varying complexity—the Task of charting and shaping a newer and a better World from the rotting remains of an outworn Feudalism.

Thou didst fling back the Curtains of Ignorance which darkened the mental and spiritual life of the World—in high places and low—so that the Sun of Knowledge and Wisdom, Truth and Right-Thinking might shed its Beams of Light to illume not only the Highways of mankind but the nooks and corners of mass activities where Men in Darkness sit and plot Evil to the hurt of their Fellows.

Master Sublime! Thou wert given a great Task by the Master of the Spheres, being Born no less than to set the world moving on other Lines—on the Right Lines—by the aid of the square and the compasses. And because Thou wert sent to minister to Man in an evil Age of Ignorance and Intolerance, when Men had forgotten the Wisdom of the Ancients in Morals, Science and Art, and had forgotten the Greatest Science of all—the Love Philosophy of Plato, the Ethical Revelations of Jesus, the Fatherhood of God and the Brotherhood of man—Thy Task was one of supreme difficulty and danger; and the Lessons Thou hadst to learn while the Work was being accomplished that qualified Thee for Divine Rulership over many things were Lessons of Trial, Sorrow and Bitter Anguish. Yet the Work was done to the Honour and Glory of the Great Architect who plans all Things by the Word of His Mouth, He who guided Thee from the Cradle to the Grave so that Thou didst truly describe Thyself as a Servant to Posterity.

Happy Warrior! Thou didst not merely think High Thoughts but didst Fight for Thy Ideals, Thy Philosophy of Ethics and Education, by Action on many Planes of Being. Thoughts were translated into Deeds. So, for four hundred years, thou hast moved the World in many Departments of Learning. Thou didst indeed lay Great Bases for Eternity. Today, we are beginning to reap what Thou didst sow.

And because men in thy Age, by reason of their strict observance of outworn political, social and theological Shibboleths, would not have understood Thy Motives and what was principal in Thy Intentions, much of Thy

Work had to be done in Secret by Thy Sons—the Brethren who assisted Thee in Thy Work, the Secret School that trod in the footsteps of the Great Teachers of Antiquity. And because Thou couldst not dare to declare openly—for that would have courted destruction—Thy complete Message Thou didst come to deliver, which was for the good of man's body, mind and soul, Thou hast been much misunderstood in these latter years by superficialists who see only the surface of things and so judge Thee and Thy Ideals harshly; and some have woefully misrepresented Thee in order to puff up an ignoble triumph over Thy silent voice and thy Quill of dust.

Great Master! The Sons of Thy Elizabethan Disciples, our Ancient Brethren, still live and have entered by Succession into Thy Labours. Some of them know the Problem of Thy Life and what Thou hast done; and though men know it not Thou has Triumphed indeed over Thy enemies—over Ignorance, Intolerance and Uncharitableness—for Thy interpretations of Nature and the Words of Thy "New Philosophy" are heard the World over every evening "when the Sun is at its Meridian". Thy Thoughts today are our Thoughts ... the Thoughts of Everyman. Thy Ideals are our Ideals. If our great Poets are the Lords of Language Thou art indeed the King. Thou art to us as the salt to the sea ... inseparable; as the air we breathe, part of us, and we cannot cast Thee out even when we become simply cunning casts in clay: for Thy influence will still pursue us. In every department of human thought, life, and action, Thy Torch has led the way into the inmost recesses of Nature, Mind and Soul. Thou reignest not only in the Chair of King Solomon, the Most Wise, but in the Seat of the Great God Apollo the Symbol of Creative Power.

This book is written that men who have misjudged Thee will turn from their errors and will understand Thee aright—Thy nobleness, Thy Majesty, as the Sublime Figure that ushered in the Modern Age in language, literature, science and philosophy, as the Being who is the embodiment of the Teachings of Socrates and Plato and the work of Amen Ra. That this work under Providence may accomplish its full, purpose, the Time being ripe, of destroying error and vindicating Truth is the sole desire of one of Thy humblest disciples who seeks to serve.

ALFRED DODD

APPENDIX I

THE ILLUSTRATIONS

SIR EDWARD COKE

Sir Edward Coke, born 1552, educated at Trinity College, Cambridge, passed from Cliffords Inn (1571) to the Inner Temple (1572), called to the Bar, 1578. He was the Recorder of Coventry, 1585; Member for Aldborough, 1589; Solicitor-General, 1592; Speaker of the House of Commons, 1593; Attorney-General, 1594; Chief Justice Common Pleas, 1606; Lord Chief Justice King's Bench and Privy Council, 1613. In 1621/2 he was imprisoned for nine months in the Tower and became estranged for good from the Court Party. He died at Stoke Poges in 1634.

He wrote the four *Institutes*, the first reaching the 19th Edition by 1832, and on these rest his claim to be regarded as a great lawyer.

He was twice married. In 1582 to Bridget Paston, who brought him a fortune of £30,000. Nineteen weeks after her death he married an equally wealthy woman, Lady Elizabeth Hatton. His domestic life was full of quarrels and his private life was turbulent owing to his arrogant, overbearing temper.

He was the life-long rival of Francis Bacon (Coke was nine years his senior) and they always clashed in their interpretation of the laws and politics. He was a bitter, venomous, unscrupulous enemy from the early days when they publicly met in the early Parliaments of Elizabeth. They crossed each other's paths constantly in public life. The iron entered his soul when Coke's errors of law were set down by Sir Francis and presented to the Privy Council, also "his deceit, contempt, and slander of the Government, and his perpetual turbulent carriage are noted".

The disgrace was the climax of a series of conflicts between the two men in which Coke had been beaten. Its effect on a man who prized his reputation as an interpreter of English Law cannot be exaggerated. It became his sole aim to drag his successful rival down. With Sir Lionel Cranfield (whose life is a study in safe and decorous villainy), and John Churchil (an infamous forger of Chancery Orders), he engineered a plot of revenge by springing a series of trumped-up charges—Abuses, Briberies and Corruption—against Sir Francis, recently created Viscount St. Alban.

The plot was successful. The Lord Chancellor was commanded by the King, *privately,* to abandon his defence and plead guilty ... to save the King from a constitutional conflict with the Parliament and his Favourite Buckingham from Impeachment. With startling suddenness England's greatest Chancellor fell (1620/1). Fined, cast into the Tower, stripped of all Office. Coke even cited precedents urging that a corrupt judge should be hanged and pressed for his death. He had triumphed.

"I am the Coward Conquest of a Wretch's Knife," wrote Francis in the Sonnets, leaving Coke's name in the very line by weaving ("felling") it in so that posterity might know ultimately that the assassin of the Immortal Shakespeare was Coke.

"Coke was one of the most truculent and unscrupulous of English lawyers," says Dean Church. "He was a potent element in Bacon's ruin."

"He set the example of railing and invective in the Courts ... of egotism and craven insolence." (Disraeli.)

"He was too bitter and narrow-minded to be a great man." (*Chambers' Ency.*)

The fact is that he hated the superior intellectual abilities of Francis Bacon. He knew his birth secret and used it against him whenever he could, eaten up with bitter jealousy.

He is destined to live to future ages as the miscreant who stabbed Shakespeare to the heart.

Robert Cecil, Earl of Salisbury

Cecil was the youngest son by a second marriage of Lord Burleigh, the famous statesman, with a daughter of Sir Anthony Cooke. He followed his father in his office as Secretary of State to Queen Elizabeth and afterwards to King James, with whom he had carried on secret negotiations prior to the Queen's death. James rewarded him by making him Lord Cecil of Essendene in 1603; Viscount Cranbourne, 1604; Earl of Salisbury, 1605.

He was a small, shrewd man of the world, a clerk in soul, without a dash of generosity in his nature. So long as he lived there was no hope of Francis Bacon rising in the world. He and his father kept him down, for they were jealous of his idealism in social and political affairs of State. Cecil knew the ill-omened secret of Francis Bacon's birth, having learned it as a State Secret from his father.

According to a Cypher Story of the times, he was the first to blurt out the knowledge to Lady Scales, a Lady-in-Waiting, to belittle the handsome youth at Court, Cecil being a hunch-back.

He laid a trap for Essex, which brought the latter to the block. Perfidious to the last, he tried, when dying, to poison James against Francis Bacon by whispering his venomous suggestions that, as a Tudor born, he had designs on the Crown.

He died in 1612 "and a burst of gladness breaks over Court and country at the news". (W. H. Dixon.)

Ben Jonson

In 1623 Ben Jonson was the Poet-Laureate. He was one of Francis Bacon's closest friends, but this friendship is seldom or never referred to by writers on Francis Bacon, "Shake-speare", and the Elizabethan Era. It is an extremely significant fact that he must have edited the 1623 Folio while living with Francis Bacon at Gorhambury. Apparently, Ben went to reside with him shortly after his "Fall ..." in 1621, to assist him in his literary work, staying with him two or three years at least. He was one of Francis Bacon's "Good Pens" and made many translations for him. It is quite inconceivable that

Ben Jonson could have edited the "Shake-speare" Manuscripts in Francis Bacon's home without his host's knowledge; or that such literary work could have been done—and the Dedication, Preface, and Poem "To the Author" composed—without discussing these matters with a kindred spirit, even if he worked at the editing of the MSS. in some London printer's office. But the singular fact remains that in all his writings Francis Bacon *never mentions Shakespeare or his dramatic Plays once,* though we know he took a keen interest in the drama, and knew through Heywood, and the *Northumberland MS.,* "the Author" of *Richard II.*

While Ben Jonson was bitter in temper towards the actor Shaksper, and lost no opportunity to show his contempt for the "Get-rich-quick Sogliardo", who had retired with his ill-gotten gains and entered the ranks of the gentry, he had nothing but profound love and respect for "Shake-speare" the Author. He said that in him we had a dramatist superior to anyone that "insolent Greece or haughtie Rome had sent forth or since did from their ashes come". It is very significant that he afterwards used these same words to honour Francis Bacon, written in his diary called *Timber or Discoveries,* published some time after Jonson's death. "This is HE that hath filled up ALL NUMBERS (i.e. Versification, all forms, lyrical, dramatic, narrative poesy, etc.), and performed that in our tongue which may be compared and preferred either to insolent Greece or haughty Rome." THIS IS HE .. Francis Bacon, the Author! A "Discovery" indeed!

The two men were not only good friends but Brother Masons, and therefore we may be quite sure that the Mystery of Shakespeare was one of the subjects they had in common. In his later masques, Jonson shows us, in his own humorous way, that he was aware not only of the true author of the Shakespeare 1623 Folio which had just been published, but also of the Rosicrucian Brethren and their Founder, whom he called "the good old hermit that built the castle in the air where all the brethren Rhodostaurotic live". This name was derived from the island of Rhodes, the home of the Knights Hospitallers some of whose precepts were adopted by the Rosicrucians. "The castle in the air" is referred to in Jonson's "News from the New World discovered in the Moon" of 1620 and in his "The Fortunate Isles and their Union" of 1626 in which "the old hermit" is named as "Father Outis" while a character "Julian de Campis" is also mentioned. These names can be identified cryptically as "Bacon-Shakespeare" and "Francis Rosicrosse" respectively.

Ben Jonson was about ten years younger than Francis Bacon; was put to bricklaying; became a soldier; according to Fuller was a student at St. John's College, Cambridge; and began his literary career as early as 1595 by writing for the stage. He produced several notable dramas, in some of which he satirized the Stratford actor. After King James made him the Court Poet (after he had refused, it is said, a knighthood), he became the centre of a band of wits. "His literary reputation, his love of conviviality, and his colloquial powers made his society much courted." The Mermaid Club and the Falcon Tavern were his favourite haunts. The younger poets were mostly his "sons" or were "sealed of the tribe of Ben", which meant they were Rosicrosse Masons and knew the "Seal" of the Secret Literary Society.

He appears to have had a hard life. His marriage was unhappy. His wife was a shrew, probably because of his rough manners, and, at times, his intemperance. They separated. He killed one man in a fight or a duel. He was a big burly fellow in constant conflict with actors and authors. "His latter days were dark and painful." When Francis Bacon "passed", in 1626, he lost his best friend. Attacks of palsy confined him to his home. King Charles sent him a hundred pounds in 1629 and raised his laureate pension. He died on 6 August 1637, and was buried in the poet's corner at Westminster Abbey. "Honest Ben's" epitaph was the memorable one: "O Rare Ben Jonson."

William Herbert, Earl of Pembroke

The Earl of Pembroke is known to posterity because he is associated with the 1623 Shakespeare Folio. It was dedicated to him and the Earl of Montgomery. To an informed Freemason he is honoured because he was one of the early Grand Masters of Freemasonry ... created and founded after Francis Bacon's return from France in 1579. (We know from letters that passed between Francis Bacon and Professor Gabriel Harvey that the Craft degrees were in being in 1580.) It is interesting to note that on the third page of the Folio he is referred to as one of "The most Noble and Incomparable Paire OF BRETHREN," which was strictly true speaking Masonically. The Folio type is so spaced that the centre letters spell "Mason". Thus,

M O S T
A N D

It has been asserted by certain Shakespearean authorities that the Earl of Pembroke was the mysterious "Mr. W.H." who was "the onlie begetter" of the Sonnets; because he was known as a youth as "Mr. William Herbert". This is quite wrong. The identity of "Mr. W.H." was quite well known to Elizabethan Freemasons. It was used in speech as a cover to denote Francis Bacon. It stood for "Mr. William Himself". (See p. 288, *The Personal Poems of Francis Bacon*, Ninth Edition.)

The Earl was nearly twenty-one years of age when he succeeded to the Earldom in 1601. He was well known at Court; and in 1603 King James and his Court were entertained by him for two months ... owing to the plague in London. He had a literary mind and many works were dedicated to him. In 1623 he was the Lord Chamberlain and "exercised supreme authority in theatrical affairs". He appears to have consorted with literary men. Aubrey tells stories about him ... scandalous and otherwise. Perhaps the most intriguing suggestion, made in all seriousness, is that "the Dark Lady of the Sonnets"—said to be Lady Mary Fitton, Maid of Honour to Queen Elizabeth—was Pembroke's Mistress and bore him a child. She preferred the embraces of an Earl to the embraces of an Actor: hence the denunciatory Sonnets denouncing her "Dark Deeds!".

Such unsavoury nonsense is unworthy of serious consideration. The Earl of Pembroke appears to have been an ordinarily decent "fellow" with a literary turn of mind.

George Villiers, Duke of Buckingham

He was born in 1592. In 1614—Francis Bacon was then taking a more prominent part in all public affairs as the King's Servant—he was brought to the notice of James. "His person was beautiful and his manners insinuating," says D'Israeli. He was well fitted to be a courtier, for he had, says Hume, "English familiarity and French levity." King James was so enthralled with his handsome face and figure that he got rid of his Favourite the Earl of Somerset and took Villiers to his bosom. He was rapidly advanced; knighted in 1616; created Marquis of Buckingham in 1618. From being a threadbare hanger-on at Court, he became the wealthiest noble in England. Well-paid offices and lands were showered upon him and his numerous family connections, whose rapacity grew by what it fed on.

When he was feeling his way to power he sought the advice of Francis Bacon; but once he was certain of his position, he threw aside all restraint and became an arrogant and haughty upstart at whose nod the most powerful noble trembled. It was at Buckingham's instigation that the Crown began to job off State Offices, to sell Titles of Honour, and to extend the King's Feudal rights by exploiting the people through the extension of Monopoly-patents over all sorts of commodities. No one could trade unless he had been issued a licence for which exorbitant sums were charged. The King and Buckingham shared the plunder.

It was his greed and the extravagancies of his clique that created the national outcry against him in the New Parliament of 1621. With the assistance of Coke, Cranfield, Ley and Co., the outcry was adroitly diverted to a personal attack on the Lord Chancellor on alleged charges of bribery and corruption. At Buckingham's suggestion the King refused to allow Francis Bacon to defend himself. Posing as the faithful friend, he played the part of that consummate hypocrite Iago, and lured the Chancellor to his destruction. The way in which he treated the wisest head in Christendom is quite unforgivable. It stamps him as one of the most despicable characters in English history. The Fall of Francis Bacon meant that the Favourite was saved. Parliament was satisfied with its distinguished victim.

Buckingham emerged from this crisis more powerful than ever, and until King James's death, was the virtual dictator of English policy at home and abroad. He retained his power after Prince Charles ascended the throne. But the nation hated him and the House of Commons impeached him. He was only saved by the King dissolving Parliament on his advice. (This was the advice he had given James when the outcry was first raised against him over the iniquitous Patents.) He became increasingly unpopular. His foreign schemes went wrong; and in 1628 he was assassinated by a subaltern, John Felton, at Portsmouth, who considered he was doing a public service by ridding the nation of one who had so shamelessly embroiled the people in foreign wars.

There was great national rejoicing at his death. Felton, who was hanged, was regarded as a martyr.

King James the First

He was born in Edinburgh Castle on 19 June 1566, being about five years younger than Francis Bacon; presumed to be the son of Mary Queen of Scots and Henry Lord Darnley. But there is ground for belief that he was a changeling and was actually the son of Lord Mar. James's unfillial conduct towards Mary is difficult to reconcile with the orthodox historical view that she was his mother.

He came to the English throne "by an antiquarian pedigree" in 1603. He was a Protestant and was well received among his subjects at first. He became unpopular because he degraded the Prerogative of the Crown by selling titles of dignity; by fleecing Englishmen through the imposition of Monopolies; his advancement of Favourites who lorded it over everyone; and his disgusting personal habits allied to his unsavoury character. He burned and butchered thousands of inoffensive persons—mostly women and many children—as witches, fortified by the Bible text, "Thou shalt not suffer a witch to live".

He pretended to be a scholar in theology and philosophy, but his learning was shallow and superficial. He had, however, "a kind of crooked wisdom". The general verdict of historians is that he was "the wisest fool in Christendom". He was a rank dissimulator and hypocrite; a coward and a cry-baby; "a hare in the seat of a lioness".

His personal appearance was anything but kingly . . . slavering lips, watery eyes, rickety legs. He constantly lolled on his Favourite in public, with his arm round "Steenie's" neck, wetting his face with kisses. He had a filthy, impure mind, employing two men to recount him bawdy stories. They succeeded so eminently well that he knighted them for their labours—Sir Ed. Zouch and Sir John Finit. Weldon's *Court of James* is a scandalous chronicle of the times.

He never tried to understand the English people. He dissolved Parliament as he pleased, and eventually allowed his Favourite Buckingham to rule the nation. The King's handling of public affairs—contrary to the advice of his Lord Chancellor, Francis Bacon—sowed the seeds of dissension between the Crown and Parliament, which brought his son Charles to the Block in the succeeding reign.

His greatest crime was his sin against Francis Bacon, using his Kingly prerogative to condemn an Innocent Man. He commanded him as his Sovereign to "Desert his Defence" and to "Plead Guilty to charges of Corruption". He refused to allow him to defend himself lest the Crown was involved and his Favourite was impeached in his place.

He died on 27 March 1625—unwept, unhonoured and unsung.

St. Michael's Church at Gorhambury

This ancient Church, according to Matthew Paris, the historian of St. Alban's Abbey, was founded, together with St. Stephen's and St. Peter's, in 948 by Abbot Ulsinus of St. Albans. The existing building contains evidence that the church then built had a nave and chancel and probably no other parts. It has also been said that it contained an apse below which is the tomb in which Viscount St. Alban is said to have been buried in 1626.

Francis Bacon's Monument

This is to be seen in St. Michael's Church, Gorhambury. It was erected by Sir Thomas Meautys. It has been moved once or twice from its original position. It is now moved back into the wall and raised up. There is a Latin inscription under it which concludes "Thomas Meautys living his attendant, dead his admirer placed this Monument". It contains also the Royal Arch phrase, *"Let the Companions be parted"*.

The statue depicts Francis Bacon in a favourite attitude, seated in his chair ruminating and about to dictate: "Thus leaning on mine elbow I begin." The Roses on his shoes denote his connection with the Rosicrucian Fraternity: the Square Chair, the Gauntlets, the Hat, as a Worshipful Master among Masons.

APPENDIX II

FROM 1603 TO HIS "PASSING" IN 1626

1603: King James ascends the Throne.
Francis Bacon to Robert Cecil, Secretary of State: "My ambition will now rest only upon my pen", a covert intimation that he was not an aspirant to the Throne.
Francis Bacon to Sir John Davies, when asking a favour: "So Be kind to CONCEALED POETS", thus intimating that he was a concealed poet. But modern scholars have never told us his pen-name. He is knighted with three hundred others at the King's Coronation festivities.

1604: Is again sent to Parliament by a double return, Ipswich and St. Albans.

1605: Advocates the Union of England and Scotland.
Publishes *The Advancement of Learning* dedicated to the King: his FIRST openly published work apart from the *Essays:* aged forty-five.

1606: Marries Alice Barnham, *a maiden of fourteen,* a commoner.

1607: Appointed Solicitor General, 25 June.

1608: Succeeds to the Clerkship of the Star Chamber with a revenue of about £2000 annually, the gift of the late Queen Elizabeth. Leaves a curiously intimate record in MS., called *Commentarius Salutus:* psychological studies for use in the Great Plays; definite indications that he has founded a Secret Brotherhood etc.

1609: *Shakespeare's Sonnets* entered in Stationers' Hall but the only sonnets published in that year were *Shakespeare's Sonnets to Sundry Notes of Music* which had previously been published in 1599 and bound with *The Passionate Pilgrim*. The "1609" Quarto of 154 was definitely not published in the year 1609.
Takes a conspicuous part in the founding of the Virginias and the Carolinas and other colonization schemes.

1610: Lady Anne Bacon dies.
He speaks and votes against the superior law officers of the Crown and strongly favours the redress of the Commons list of grievances.

1611: The Authorized Version of the Bible published, edited by Francis Bacon, who introduced the music of Shakespeare into the prose translations. The MSS. of the translators are now "LOST".

1612: Robert Cecil, Secretary of State, dies.

1613: Appointed Attorney-General.
The King's Favourite, the Earl of Somerset, marries. At the King's request Francis Bacon provides *a sumptuous MUSICAL COMEDY* in honour of the marriage—*which he creates.*

1614: A new Parliament summoned. Ipswich, St. Albans and Cambridge elect him. Such a triple return is unprecedented.
King James withdraws his favour from Somerset, Villiers a handsome young man about twenty-two attracting the attention of the King.

1615: Villiers supplants Somerset as the Favourite and becomes acquainted with Francis Bacon.

A great dispute between the Court of Chancery presided over by Francis Bacon and the Court of King's Bench presided over by Sir Edward Coke, ending in Coke's disgrace.

1616: Prosecution of the Old Favourite and his wife for the murder of Overbury.

The Continent stirred by a series of Rosicrucian pamphlets advocating an Ethical Brotherhood for the amelioration of the social, political and religious ills that were afflicting mankind.

A further clash between Francis Bacon and Coke in which the King was involved ends with Coke being dismissed from going on circuit as a judge and losing his seat on the Privy Council. Bacon becomes a member of the Privy Council.

Shaksper of Stratford dies "unwept, unhonoured and unsung".

1617: Francis Bacon aged fifty-seven becomes Lord Keeper of the Great Seal of England.

Appointed Regent of the kingdom a week later while the King goes for a holiday in Scotland.

Coke plots with Lady Compton, Buckingham's mother, to be revenged on Francis Bacon for supplanting him in the Privy Council, etc.

1618: Attains the higher grade of Lord Chancellor.

Created Baron Verulam and a Peer.

Trial and execution of Sir Walter Raleigh.

1619: King James grants him a pension of £1200 per annum. Francis Bacon dismisses a dishonest registrar from the Chancery named John Churchil.

1620: The *Novum Organum* published. He recommends a new Parliament to be called. The writs go out. Churchil has furnished Coke with a "Black List" of discontented suitors in the Chancery which can be used in a charge of bribery and corruption.

1621: 21 January: Francis Bacon's birthday: sixty years of age. At the Masonic banquet Ben Jonson gives the toast of the evening and closes with a clever Masonic ode to him.

28 January: Created Viscount St. Alban.

30 January: The new Parliament meets. Coke becomes the Leader of the Commons. Francis Bacon in the Lords as Lord Chancellor.

12 February: The Commons appoint committees to inquire into abuses and grievances amid great excitement.

14 March: Sir Lionel Cranfield denounces "abuses" in the Chancery Court and attacks Francis Bacon, saying he has two witnesses prepared to testify that Bacon had accepted bribes. The Commons send the cases to the Lords along with others compiled by J. Churchil. Francis Bacon writes to the Lords denying the charges and asks for the privileges of a High Court action. He announces his intention THREE TIMES to defend himself.

16 April: The King sends for Francis Bacon and COMMANDS him to desert his defence.

24 April: The Prince of Wales announces to the Lords that he is the bearer of a "SUBMISSION" from the Lord Chancellor announcing his intention to desert his defence. The Lords demand that he pleads "Guilty" to each

item, twenty-three cases in all. He sees the detailed charges for the first time in the evening.

30 April: The Chancellor returns Coke's "Black List" with the word "Guilty" written to each charge.

3 May: The Lords pass sentence in his absence for Francis Bacon is too ill to come to the bar of the House: fined £40,000 and to be imprisoned in the Tower during the King's pleasure; to be incapable of holding office in the commonwealth, never to sit in Parliament again.

1 May: Four Peers wait upon Francis Bacon to receive the Great Seal of England as he is too ill to go to the Bar of the House of Lords to surrender it. In the evening he composes a wonderful prayer, found in his papers after his "death", which, says Addison, sounds more like an angel than a man.

31 May: Imprisoned in the Tower, writes a peremptory letter to the King and Buckingham demanding instant release. The necessary warrant was sent immediately to the Governor of the Tower.

1 December: A petition to the House of Lords: "I am old, weak, ruined, in want, a very subject of pity."

1622: Buckingham at last obtains York House.
History of Henry VII published.

1623: Ben Jonson, the Poet Laureate, lives with Francis Bacon at Gorhambury.
The great Shakespeare Folio, edited by Ben Jonson, consisting of thirty-six plays, many never heard of before, is published. In *Henry VIII* Francis Bacon tells the story of his own fall and his parentage.

1624: Prepares for the press *Sylva Sylvarum* and *The New Atlantis* or *The Land of the Rosicrosse* (as indicated by the Brethren in later years).

1625: Arranges into themes his private diary of sonnets; carefully disarranges them to destroy personal meanings; prints them by the private press of the Rosicrosse; and distributes the book to the heads of the Rosicrosse-Masons as a secret document in the Christmas New Year Lodges. This book was the "1609" Quarto entitled *Shakespeare's Sonnets* and was kept concealed as a Masonic secret until George Steevens, a Shakespearean Freemason, reprinted the book in 1766.

1626: Before Easter, 1626, Francis Bacon had seen all the persons who had taken part in the plot against him struck down in ruin and disgrace. They fell like rotten apples all save Buckingham. He alone was reserved to die under the hand of an avenger, to the joy of the nation. At the age of sixty-six Francis Bacon "died to the world" but there is evidence that he FLED to the Continent and lived to a very old age.

FINALE

INDEX

F.B. Francis Bacon

Q.E. Queen Elizabeth

C

D

E

F

M

N